T0402495

THE CAMBRIDGE HISTORY OF
STRATEGY

*

VOLUME I

From Antiquity to the American War of Independence

Volume I of *The Cambridge History of Strategy* offers a history of the practice of strategy from the beginning of recorded history, to the late eighteenth century, from all parts of the world. Drawing on material evidence covering two and a half millennia, an international team of leading scholars in each subject examines how strategy was formulated and applied and with what tools, from ancient Greece and China to the Ottoman and Mughal Empires and the American Revolutionary War. They explore key themes from decision-makers and strategy-making processes, causes of wars and war aims and tools of strategy in war and peace, to configurations of armed forces and distinctive and shared ways of war across civilisations and periods. A comparative conclusion examines how the linking of political goals with military means took place in different parts of the world over the course of history, asking whether strategic practice has universal features.

ISABELLE DUYVESTEYN is Professor of International Studies/ Global History at the Institute of History at Leiden University. Between 2012 and 2017 she held the Special Chair in Strategic Studies at the Political Science Institute of Leiden University. Between 2008 and 2020 she was a member of the national Advisory Council on International Affairs assigned to advise the Netherlands government on issues of peace and security, and between 2012 and 2021 she was a member of the Scientific Advisory Board of the Netherlands Defence Academy.

BEATRICE HEUSER holds the Chair of International Relations at the University of Glasgow, and is seconded to the General Staff College of the Bundeswehr in Hamburg as Section Chief for Strategy. She has worked at NATO Headquarters as a consultant. She has served on academic advisory boards of the Royal United Services Institute, the French Institute of International Affairs (IFRI) and the French government's strategic studies think tank IRSEM. She has previously taught at universities in the UK, Germany and France.

STRATEGY

The Cambridge History of Strategy presents a global history exploring how leaders of social groups, civilisations, empires and states have practised strategy over the course of the past three millennia. With contributions from leading experts in each subject, these volumes analyse a series of notable case studies to reflect on the formulation and application of strategy rather than on theory. Transcending the traditional Western focus and modern-state-based framework of strategic studies, this Cambridge History offers the inclusion of a wider range of political actors and cases from parts of the world hitherto largely excluded from the literature. This leads to a discussion of whether central claims in the field of strategic studies that the practice of strategy exhibits universal features which apply always hold up against empirical evidence from different centuries and cases beyond the West.

VOLUME I

From Antiquity to the American War of Independence
EDITED BY ISABELLE DUYVESTEYN AND BEATRICE HEUSER

VOLUME II

From the Napoleonic Wars to the Present
EDITED BY ISABELLE DUYVESTEYN AND BEATRICE HEUSER

THE CAMBRIDGE
HISTORY OF
STRATEGY

*

VOLUME I

From Antiquity to the American War of Independence

*

Edited by

ISABELLE DUYVESTEYN
Leiden University

BEATRICE HEUSER
University of Glasgow

 CAMBRIDGE
UNIVERSITY PRESS

Shaftesbury Road, Cambridge CB2 8EA, United Kingdom

One Liberty Plaza, 20th Floor, New York, NY 10006, USA

477 Williamstown Road, Port Melbourne, VIC 3207, Australia

314–321, 3rd Floor, Plot 3, Splendor Forum, Jasola District Centre,
New Delhi – 110025, India

103 Penang Road, #05–06/07, Visioncrest Commercial, Singapore 238467

Cambridge University Press is part of Cambridge University Press & Assessment,
a department of the University of Cambridge.

We share the University's mission to contribute to society through the pursuit of
education, learning and research at the highest international levels of excellence.

www.cambridge.org
Information on this title: www.cambridge.org/9781108479950

DOI: 10.1017/9781108788090

© Cambridge University Press & Assessment 2025

First published 2025

Printed in the United Kingdom by CPI Group Ltd, Croydon CR0 4YY

A catalogue record for this publication is available from the British Library

A Cataloging-in-Publication data record for this book is available from the Library of Congress

Two Volume Set ISBN 978-1-009-41763-1 Hardback
Volume I ISBN 978-1-108-47995-0 Hardback
Volume II ISBN 978-1-108-47992-9 Hardback

This book is dedicated to the past and present victims of war

Contents

List of Maps   page xii
List of Contributors to Volume I   xiii
Preface and Acknowledgements   xix

Introduction to Volume I: The Practice of Strategy   1
ISABELLE DUYVESTEYN AND BEATRICE HEUSER

1 · China to AD 180   21
PETER LORGE

2 · Teispid and Achaemenid Persia (c. 550–330 BC)   40
JOHN O. HYLAND

3 · Ancient Greece: Strategy of the City States (500–300 BC)   53
ROEL KONIJNENDIJK

4 · Philip II, Alexander III and the Macedonian Empire   73
ANDREW FEAR

5 · Ancient Rome: Monarchy and Republic (753–27 BC)   98
LOUIS RAWLINGS

6 · China AD 180–1127   124
DAVID A. GRAFF

7 · Ancient Rome: Principate and Dominate (27 BC–AD 630)   144
MICHAEL WHITBY

8 · The Gupta Empire (AD 400–500)   171
KAUSHIK ROY

Contents

9 · The Sassanian Empire's Strategies   *191*
KATARZYNA MAKSYMIUK

10 · The Rashidun, Umayyad (661–750) and Abbasid (750–1258)
Caliphates   *204*
MEHDI KURGAN KADER

11 · Byzantine Strategy (AD 630–1204)   *226*
GEORGIOS CHATZELIS

12 · Strategies in the Wars of Western Europe, 476–c. 1000   *251*
JOHN FRANCE

13 · Latin Christendom in the Later Middle Ages   *271*
SOPHIE THÉRÈSE AMBLER

14 · Chinggis Khan and the Mongol Empire, AD 1206 to 1368   *292*
TIMOTHY MAY

15 · Hindu and Buddhist Polities of Premodern/Early Modern Mainland
South-East Asia (1100–1800)   *312*
TASSAPA UMAVIJANI

16 · Pre-Columbian and Early Historic Native American Warfare   *334*
PATRICIA M. LAMBERT

17 · Ottoman Expansionism, 1300–1823   *346*
MESUT UYAR

18 · Strategy in the Wars of Pre-colonial Sub-Saharan Africa   *369*
JOHN BURTON KEGEL AND GIACOMO MACOLA

19 · Strategies of the Mughal Empire   *384*
PRATYAY NATH

20 · China, 1368–1911   *403*
KENNETH M. SWOPE

21 · Early Modern Europe: The Habsburgs and Their Enemies, 1519–1659   *424*
DAVID PARROTT

Contents

22 · Naval Strategies   448
ADRI VAN VLIET

23 · The Strategy of Louis XIV   464
JAMEL OSTWALD

24 · Hohenzollern Strategy under Frederick II   488
ADAM L. STORRING

25 · American Warfare in the Eighteenth Century   508
STEPHEN CONWAY

Summary of Volume I   528
BEATRICE HEUSER AND ISABELLE DUYVESTEYN

Further Reading   566
Index   584

Maps

1.1   Chinese strategies to AD 180   *page* 22
2.1   Strategies of the Achaemenid Persian Empire (550–330 BC)   46
3.1   Ancient Greece: strategies of the city states (500–400 BC)   62
4.1   Strategies of Philip II and Alexander III and the Macedonian Empire   86
5.1   Strategies of ancient Rome, Monarchy and Republic (753–27 BC)   99
6.1   Tang operations against the Eastern Türks, AD 629–630   125
7.1   Strategies of ancient Rome: principate and dominate (27 BC—AD 630)   145
8.1   Strategies of the Gupta Empire (AD 400–500)   172
9.1   Strategies of the Sassanian Persian Empire (AD 224–651)   196
10.1   Strategies of the Rashidun, Umayyad (661–750) and Abbasid (750–1258) caliphates   206
11.1   Byzantine strategy (AD 630–1204)   228
12.1   Strategies in the wars of western Europe, 476–*c.* 1000   252
13.1   Strategies in Latin Christendom in the later Middle Ages 1000–1500   280
14.1   Strategies of Chinggis Khan and the Mongol Empire, AD 1206 to 1368   293
15.1   The Burmese marching routes against Ayutthaya in 1765–1767   313
16.1   Pre-Columbian and early historic Native American battles, wars and regional conflict (1000–1860)   335
17.1   Ottoman strategy   358
18.1   Strategy in the wars of pre-colonial sub-Saharan Africa   370
20.1   Strategies of Ming and Qing China   416
21.1   Strategies of the early modern Habsburgs and their enemies, 1519–1659   426
22.1   Dutch naval strategies (1550–1800)   456
23.1   The strategies of Louis XIV   465
24.1   The wars of Frederick II of Prussia   489
25.1   American strategies in the eighteenth century   509

Contributors to Volume I

SOPHIE THÉRÈSE AMBLER is Reader in Medieval History at Lancaster University, where she is also Deputy Director of the Centre for War and Diplomacy. In 2020 she was awarded a Philip Leverhulme Prize for History. Before joining Lancaster, she was a researcher on the Magna Carta Project, funded by the Arts and Humanities Research Council (AHRC), at the University of East Anglia; before this she was a researcher at the University of Glasgow on the AHRCs Breaking of Britain project. She completed her PhD at King's College London, with joint supervision at University College London, and was Thornley Fellow at the Institute of Historical Research.

GEORGIOS CHATZELIS is a Research Fellow at Centre for Advanced Study Sofia and New Europe College, Institute for Advanced Study. He holds a BA in History (Aristotle University of Thessaloniki), an MA in Ancient and Medieval Warfare (Cardiff University) and a PhD in Byzantine History (Royal Holloway, University of London). Previously, he taught Medieval and Byzantine History at Royal Holloway, University of London and Aristotle University of Thessaloniki. He publishes on the Byzantine culture of war, war writing in Byzantine historical narratives and Byzantine education. His latest books include *Byzantine Military Manuals as Literary Works and Practical Handbooks: The Case of the Tenth-Century* Sylloge Tacticorum (2019).

STEPHEN CONWAY is Professor of History at University College London (UCL). He took his first degree at Leeds and did his PhD at UCL. He has been a full-time member of staff in the History Department since 1989, became a Reader in 1994 and a Professor in 2002. He served in a variety of enabling roles, both at UCL and beyond. Between 2012 and 2015, he was Head of the UCL History Department. He is a Fellow of the Royal Historical Society and an editor of *English Historical Review*. He has published extensively on Britain's eighteenth-century wars, especially the War of American Independence.

ISABELLE DUYVESTEYN is Professor of International Studies/Global History at the Institute of History at Leiden University. She completed her PhD at the Department of War Studies at King's College London. Previously she has worked at the Royal Military Academy in the Netherlands, the Netherlands Institute for International Relations and the Department of History of International Relations at Utrecht University. Between 2012 and 2017 she held the Special Chair in Strategic Studies at the Political Science Institute of Leiden University. Between 2008 and 2020 she was a member of the national Advisory

Council on International Affairs assigned to advise the Netherlands government on issues of peace and security, and between 2012 and 2021, she was a member of the Scientific Advisory Board of the Netherlands Defence Academy.

ANDREW FEAR is a Lecturer in Ancient History at the University of Manchester. Educated at Lancaster RGS and New College, Oxford, where he completed his BA and DPhil, he held a Junior Research Fellowship at Jesus College, Oxford, before moving first to Keele and then to Manchester. He has contributed to *The Cambridge History of Greek and Roman Warfare* (2007); Himanshu Prabha Ray and Daniel T. Potts (eds.), *Memory as History: The Legacy of Alexander in Asia* (2007); and Anastasia Bakogianni and Valerie Hope (eds.), *War as Spectacle: Ancient and Modern Perspectives on the Display of Armed Conflict* (2015), and is the joint editor with Jamie Wood of *A Companion to Isidore of Seville* (2015).

JOHN FRANCE is Professor Emeritus in the History Department of Swansea University. His main interests are medieval warfare and crusading, and general military development. Some recent works are *Hattin* (2015); *Perilous Glory: Understanding Western Warfare (BC3000–Gulf Wars)* (2011) and, most recently, *Military History of the French Monarchy 885–1305* (2022).

DAVID A. GRAFF is the Pickett Professor of Military History and Chair of the Department of History at Kansas State University. He received his PhD from Princeton University and his MA from the University of Michigan. A specialist in Chinese military history, especially that of the Tang dynasty, he has been editor-in-chief of the *Journal of Chinese Military History* since its founding in 2012 and organiser of the Chinese Military History Society's annual conferences since 1999. He co-edited *The Cambridge History of War*, Volume II: *War and the Medieval World* (2020) and is a member of several editorial boards.

BEATRICE HEUSER holds the Chair of International Relations at the University of Glasgow, and is seconded to the General Staff College of the Bundeswehr in Hamburg as Section Chief for Strategy. She holds her BA and MA from the University of London (Bedford College and LSE) and her DPhil from Oxford (St Antony's College and St John's College). She also holds a higher doctorate (*Habilitation*) from the University of Marburg. Previously she taught at King's College London at the Department of War Studies and at the University of Reading, and as Visiting Professor at several Parisian universities, the universities of Reims and Potsdam, and at Sciences Po' Paris and Reims. She has worked at NATO Headquarters as a consultant, and in various positions for the Bundeswehr. She has served on academic advisory boards of several museums and research institutes, currently including the Royal United Services Institute, the French Institute of International Affairs (IFRI), and the French government's strategic studies think tank IRSEM.

JOHN O. HYLAND is Professor of History at Christopher Newport University. He completed his PhD in the Committee on the Ancient Mediterranean World at the University of Chicago, and has taught at Christopher Newport University since 2006. He is the author of *Persian Interventions: the Achaemenid Empire, Athens, & Sparta, 450–386 BCE* (2018), and his next book will explore Persia's Greek campaigns in their ancient Near Eastern imperial contexts.

JOHN BURTON KEGEL has taught at the London School of Economics and Political Science and conducted research at London Business School, where he studied the colonial economies of Rwanda, Burundi and the Democratic Republic of Congo. His PhD from the University of Kent, 'The Road to Genocide: A History of the Rwandan Struggle for Liberation', re-evaluates our current understanding of the events leading up to the 1994 genocide by using previously untapped archival material and interviews collected during several stints of fieldwork. The work also combines his long-term interests in African and military history.

ROEL KONIJNENDIJK is an historian of classical Greek warfare. He completed his PhD at University College London in 2015. In the years since, he has held a Past & Present Junior Research Fellowship at the Institute of Historical Research and a Marie Curie Postdoctoral Fellowship at Leiden University. He has taught ancient history at UCL, Birkbeck, Warwick, Oxford and Edinburgh. He is the author of *Classical Greek Tactics: A Cultural History* (2018) and *Between Miltiades and Moltke: Early German Studies in Greek Military History* (2023), as well as being co-editor of Brill's *Companion to Greek Land Warfare beyond the Phalanx* (2021).

MEHDI KURGAN KADER is a strategic theorist and consultant. He served as a counter-terrorism consultant in the aviation security sector, specializing in behavioural detection, red-team activities and critical-infrastructure protection operations. He later served as an independent strategic risk and threat management consultant in the Middle East and North and West Africa, during the early years of the global War on Terror before returning to academia. He completed his BA, MA, MRes and PhD at the Department of War Studies at King's College London. His academic specialisations are in the fields of strategic theory, game theory, counterterrorism and early Islamic warfare. He currently directs a private-sector defence and threat management consultancy.

PATRICIA M. LAMBERT is Distinguished Professor of Anthropology at Utah State University (USU). She completed her MA and PhD in the Department of Anthropology at the University of California at Santa Barbara and held a Postdoctoral Fellowship in Physical Anthropology at the Smithsonian's National Museum of Natural History. From 2012 to 2016 she was Executive Director of the Museum of Anthropology at USU. She is a specialist in the bioarchaeology of violence and warfare in pre-Columbian North America and has published a number of empirical studies and synthetic works on the topic. Her most recent work examines the role of violent conflict in state formation in the Moche valley, Peru.

PETER LORGE is an Associate Professor of Premodern Chinese and Military History at Vanderbilt University. An award-winning teacher, he is also the author or editor of nine books, most recently *The Beginner's Guide to Imperial China* (2021), and *Sun Tzu in the West: The Anglo-American Art of War* (2022). Next in line is *Documents from Early Chinese History*, a sourcebook for premodern Chinese history written with Scott Pearce. He is currently completing an epistolary history of eleventh-century China.

GIACOMO MACOLA is Associate Professor of African History at 'La Sapienza' University of Rome. He holds a PhD from the University of London (SOAS, 2000). Before moving to Rome, he was Reader in African History at the University of Kent at Canterbury. He has held visiting professorships at the University of the Free State (2016) and the University of Cagliari (2017). He is the co-founder and co-editor of Warfare and Militarism in African History, a book series at Ohio University Press, and a member of the editorial committee of the British Academy's Fontes Historiae Africanae. In 2021 he was elected corresponding member of the Belgian Académie royale des sciences d'Outre-mer.

KATARZYNA MAKSYMIUK is Professor of History at Siedlce University, in Poland. She completed her PhD at the Department of Archaeology and Ethnology at Nicolaus Copernicus University in Toruń. She also holds a higher doctorate (*Habilitation*) from the University of Toruń. Her research deals with the history of Iran, with particular attention to the problems of military conflicts. She is the author of *Geography of Roman–Iranian Wars: Military Operations of Rome and Sasanian Iran* (Siedlce, 2015), and co-author of *The Military History of Third-Century Iran* (Siedlce, 2018) and *A Synopsis of Sasanian Military Organization and Combat Units* (Siedlce and Tehran, 2018). She is a member of the Association for the Study of Persianate Societies, the Society of Ancient Military Historians, the Austrian Byzantine Society and the Byzantinist Society of Cyprus. She is editor-in-chief of the scientific journal *Historia i Świat* (History and the World).

TIMOTHY MAY is Professor of Central Eurasian History and Associate Dean of Arts & Letters at the University of North Georgia. He earned his BA at the College of William & Mary, his MA in Central Eurasian Studies at Indiana University, and his PhD at the University of Wisconsin–Madison. He is the author and editor of eleven books, including *The Mongol Art of War* (2007), *The Mongol Conquests in World History* (2012), *The Mongol Empire* (2018), and *Simply Chinggis* (2021). He also serves on the editorial board of several journals. In 2014, he was named the University of North Georgia Alumni Distinguished Professor, and was awarded the UNG Distinguished Teaching Award in 2021.

PRATYAY NATH is Associate Professor of History at Ashoka University, Sonipat, India. His work lies at the crossroads of military history, environmental history and imperial history, with a focus on early modern South Asia. He holds his BA from Presidency College, Calcutta; MA from the University of Calcutta; and MPhil and PhD from Jawaharlal Nehru University, New Delhi. He has previously taught at Miranda House, University of Delhi. He is the author of *Climate of Conquest: War, Environment, and Empire in Mughal North India* (2019) and, with Meena Bhargava, the co-editor of *The Early Modern in South Asia: Querying Modernity, Periodization, and History* (2022). He is one of the editors of the *Medieval History Journal*. He writes in English and Bengali.

JAMEL OSTWALD is Professor of History at Eastern Connecticut State University. He received his PhD in History at the Ohio State University and has published on early modern French and English military history. He is the author of *Vauban under Siege: Engineering Efficiency and Martial Vigor in the War of the Spanish Succession* (2006), and with Anke Fischer-Kattner has edited *The World of the Siege: Representations of Early Modern Positional Warfare* (2019).

DAVID PARROTT is Professor of Early Modern European History at the University of Oxford, where he also received his BA and DPhil. After lecturing at the University of York, he returned to Oxford (New College) in 1992. He teaches European history in the period from 1500 to 1700, with special reference to the history of France and Italy, and European political, military and cultural history. His research interests are in early modern European history, primarily the political, social and military history of seventeenth-century France, but with interests in northern Italy. He has written and published on many aspects of European warfare in this era, with a particular interest in mercenaries and private military organisations. His publications include *Richelieu's Army: War, Government and Society in France, 1624–42* (2001), *The Business of War: Military Enterprise and Military Revolution in Early Modern Europe* (2012) and *1652: The Cardinal, the Prince and the Crisis of the Fronde* (Oxford: Oxford University Press, 2020).

LOUIS RAWLINGS is Senior Lecturer in Ancient History at the School of History, Archaeology and Religion, Cardiff University. Previously he taught at the History Department, University College London, and the Department of War Studies, King's College London. He holds his BA and PhD from University College London. He has published widely on Romano-Italian, Carthaginian, Greek and Gallic warfare. He is the author of *The Ancient Greeks at War* (2007) and co-editor (with J. Hall and G. Lee) of *Unit Cohesion and Warfare in the Ancient World: Military and Social Approaches* (2023).

KAUSHIK ROY is Guru Nanak Professor in the Department of History, Jadavpur University, Kolkata. He was also associated with Peace Research Institute Oslo (PRIO), Norway, as a Global Fellow until 2021. At present, he is a participant in the Warring with Machines project at PRIO. Roy specialises in military history of South Asia. He has published several monographs and his most recent publication is *Military Thought of Asia: From the Bronze Age to the Information Age* (2021).

ADAM L. STORRING is Visiting Research Fellow at the Department of War Studies, King's College London. He completed his BA, MPhil and PhD at St John's College, Cambridge. His doctoral dissertation, supervised by Professor Sir Christopher Clark, was awarded the André Corvisier Prize 2019 for the best dissertation on military history defended at any university anywhere in the world. He was Early Career Fellow at the Lichtenberg-Kolleg, University of Göttingen, and has also held fellowships from the Arts and Humanities Research Council, the Bühler-Bolstorff-Stiftung Berlin, the Deutscher Akademischer Austauschdienst, the Leibniz-Institut für Europäische Geschichte, the Stiftung Preußischer Kulturbesitz and the Stiftung Preußische Schlösser und Gärten. He previously worked in the British civil service, and in international development.

KENNETH M. SWOPE is Professor of History at the University of Southern Mississippi. He is also Senior Fellow of the Dale Center for the Study of War and Society at the University of Southern Mississippi and a Board Member of the Chinese Military History Society. He earned his BA at the College of Wooster (Ohio) and his MA and PhD at the University of Michigan. Prior to teaching at Southern Miss, he taught at Marist College and Ball State University. He was a Visiting Member of the Institute for Advanced Study (2015) and served as the Leo A. Shiffrin Chair in Naval & Military History at the United States Naval

Academy in 2019–20. He is the author of *A Dragon's Head & a Serpent's Tail: Ming China and the First Great East Asian War, 1592–1598* (2009), *The Military Collapse of China's Ming Dynasty* (2014), *On the Trail of the Yellow Tiger: War, Trauma, and Social Dislocation in Southwest China during the Ming–Qing Transition* (2018) and *Struggle for Empire: The Battles of General Zuo Zongtang* (2024), and of numerous chapters in edited volumes and journal articles on late imperial Chinese history. He is currently working on a study of the Three Feudatories Rebellion (1673–1681) in China.

TASSAPA UMAVIJANI is a lecturer in History at Thammasat University in Bangkok, Thailand. He is a PhD Candidate in History at the School of Oriental and African Studies (SOAS). He holds a BA in History from Thammasat University and two MA degrees from King's College London in Ancient History and from the University of Reading in Military History and Strategic Studies. He has special interests in military and strategic development in different cultures. He is now completing his PhD dissertation titled 'The Military Transformation of Nineteenth-Century Siam: Changes and Continuities'.

MESUT UYAR is Visiting Professor of Military History at the University of New South Wales, Canberra. He is a graduate of the Turkish Military Academy, with an MA in Politics and a PhD in International Relations from Istanbul University. As a career officer he served as platoon leader and company and battalion commander, including in several peace support operations; as military observer in the UN mission in Georgia; and as a staff officer in Afghanistan. He was twice wounded in action. Specialising in Ottoman military history, he taught at the Turkish Military Academy and at the University of New South Wales, Canberra, Australia and at the Antalya Bilim University; was the curator of the Military Academy Archive and Museum Division; and spent a year as an instructor and academic adviser at the Peace Support Training Centre in Bosnia and Herzegovina.

ADRI VAN VLIET is Deputy Director of the Netherlands Institute of Military History in The Hague. He received his teacher certificate in 1977 and studied history in The Hague and Leiden. In 1994 he received a PhD from the University of Leiden. Previously he has worked at the National Archive in Noord-Brabant (1989–1999) as head of external services. From 1998 to 1999 he was also part-time Assistant Professor at Leiden University for Maritime History. In 1999 he became Head of the Naval Historical Branch and Director of the Institute for Maritime History of the Royal Netherlands Navy until 2005.

MICHAEL WHITBY is a Professor Emeritus at the University of Birmingham, where from 2010 to 2019 he held the position of Pro-Vice-Chancellor and Head of the College of Arts and Law. He had previously worked at the University of Warwick, where he was Professor of Classics and Ancient History, Chair of Faculty (2002–2003) and Pro-Vice-Chancellor for Education (2003–2010), and at St Andrews University, where he was a member of the Department of Ancient History from 1987 to 1996, latterly as professor. He received his undergraduate education at Corpus Christi, Oxford, after which he worked in the Civil Service for three years at the Scottish Office, before returning to Oxford for doctoral research with James Howard-Johnston, first at Corpus and then at Merton, where he held a Junior Research Fellowship.

Preface and Acknowledgements

Practising strategy is messy, frustrating and often guided by luck rather than anything else. This is the subject of this series. While there are many overviews of the makers and the making of strategy, far fewer focus on practising it. Overviews of great strategic thinkers abound. Appreciations of the drafting of strategy are plentiful. What happens when it is put into action is the subject of these two volumes. More specifically, a comparison of these practices, across time and place, is what the series aims to offer. There is presently no global history of the practice of strategy, with most treatises focusing predominantly on Western experiences or single case studies. Making strategy a focus, even before the invention of the word, brings something new to the field. Moreover, moving the focus beyond the preoccupation with theory and the Western world is not the only ambition. The *longue durée*, as well as the study of other polities than the state and its political instrumentality, is where we hope to offer some food for thought.

The Cambridge Series is a very long-running series with a 100-year history. The current volumes break to some extent with previous traditions of the *Cambridge History of . . .* series. In general, the contributions in the series are not specifically intended to present new research, but rather offer the reader an overview of a particular noteworthy topic or phenomenon. The volumes before you intend to do both. First, they deliberately address a non-specialist readership, as we can assume that none of our readers are familiar with all the Napoleonic Wars, and also with the wars of the Han, Byzantium or the Guptas. This may disappoint some who will find the introduction to their specific period of expertise and interest telling them things they already knew, but even then, while editing the chapters, we had many revelations about periods we ourselves were familiar with, when interrogated systematically from angles previously 'assumed' to be known.

Second, by presenting this case material and the state of the art in their respective historiographies, we offer the opportunity of comparison. Only comparisons uncover assumptions that turn out to be very culture-specific, or else surprisingly widespread when they were thought to be specific to a particular culture. For example, the strategic aims of cementing alliances or of peace confirmation were pursued through the strategic tool of dynastic marriages not only by the Habsburg dynasty, but also by the ancient Chinese, the Macedonians, and the Romans under Principate, Dominate, and then the Eastern Roman/Byzantine dynasties, as well as the Guptas, and all the subsequent European dynasties, albeit not always as spectacularly as by the Habsburgs. Third, based on this comparison, we can aspire to present a global overview of strategic practice that pushes the boundaries of the debate in strategic studies. This case will be made in more detail in the introductory chapter.

This work aims to strike a balance between the particular – the specific cases of this history with all their uniqueness and peculiarities – and the generalisable. Without insisting on the former, we lose the reality of the particular mindsets, culture, world views, and material circumstances that determined them. As Carl von Clausewitz, the Prussian general who wrote the core text in the field of strategic studies almost two centuries ago, rightly put it, 'every age' – and he might have added, every distinct culture within that period –

> had its own kind of war, its own limiting conditions, and its own preconceptions. Each [period], therefore, would have its own theory of war, even if one had been inclined everywhere and at all times to deduce it from philosophical first principles. The events of every age must therefore be judged in the light of its own peculiarities.[1]

Without generalisable aspects, however, we lose the relevance of the past for our own times and our future.

We offer a history of the practice of strategy in two volumes. The first volume is devoted to a diversity of case studies from around 2000 BC until 1800. The second volume looks at case studies from 1800 until today. The exact choices we have made will be detailed and justified in the opening chapters to the two volumes. The richness of this overview could not have been achieved without the contributions of the best and brightest scholars in this field. We are indebted to them for the time and energy they have devoted

---

1 Von Clausewitz, *Vom Kriege*, VIII.3B, 973f.

to producing the chapters. In a review of Jeremy Black's recent book on a global strategy, it was noted that 'Black's invitation to students of war and strategy to acquaint themselves with non-Western perspectives is timely. The challenge is formidable, and the task may well be impossible.'[2] We took up this daunting challenge, but we could not have taken it up alone: we have learned a tremendous amount from our wonderfully knowledgeable, ever-suffering contributors, whom we submitted to endless questions and demands for changes and additions.

The first idea for the series emerged during a dinner party at Leiden University Faculty Club in the spring of 2018. The request for Cambridge University Press was brought into the discussion, as was how such a series could be conceptualised. Isabelle was very inspired but rather daunted by the idea of carrying such a project alone. She approached Beatrice to ask if she would be interested in collaborating on this endeavour. Reluctantly, Beatrice came on board as both agreed that it would be crazy to forgo this exceptional occasion to persuade scholars from all periods and all parts of the world to help us better understand a subject of such passionate interest to both of us. They agreed that it would be unusual to have two women, still hugely underrepresented in the field of strategic studies, editing a contribution to this prestigious series. We are tremendously grateful to Cambridge University Press's Michael Watson, who embraced our idea and encouraged us in its development.

The editors would like to thank the team at Cambridge University Press, Michael Watson, Emily Plater, Lisa Carter and the copy-editors John Gaunt and Linos Edwards.

A special word of thanks goes to Samuel Zilincik, who has acted very diligently as our editorial assistant. Moreover, Carmel Dowling and Vani Dhaka have helped with editing language and references. We have also benefited greatly from the advice of our international advisory board, consisting of Professors Jeremy Black, Martin van Creveld, Isabelle Deflers, Antulio J. Echevarria II, Lawrence Freedman, Kimberley Kagan, Joe Maiolo, Assaf Moghaddam, Michael Rainsborough, Monica Toft, Erwin Schmidl and Matthew Strickland.

---

2 T. G. Otte, 'Military strategy: a global history', *Diplomacy & Statecraft*, 31:3 (2020), 597–9, 598.

Introduction to Volume I

The Practice of Strategy

ISABELLE DUYVESTEYN AND BEATRICE HEUSER

Strategy Making: A Global, Eternal Phenomenon?

With this project, we aim to break new ground: it is our ambition to compile a first truly global history of strategic practice. How did the linking of political goals with military means take place in different parts of the world over the course of history? How have existing ideas and concepts been translated, adopted, enacted, imitated and emulated on and off the many battlefields around the world? There exist individual studies of warfare in the late Middle Ages, or in ancient Greece, or in the China of the Warring Kingdoms, but they are difficult to bring together as they are written by different authors, using different definitions, and many gaps remain. We want to remedy this by bringing together topics over a broad chronological and geographic span, written by the respective experts on the subject, but with strong editorial impositions in order to give the chapters in this series a common framework which alone will enable comparisons to be made.

The study of strategy has a very long pedigree. It could be argued that much of the history of humankind revolves around clashes between groups over resources and interests. A history of the practice of strategy around the globe and throughout recorded history to date, however, does not exist.

There are works that attempt to produce a general history of the 'art of war' – a term that has been used in the past in a way overlapping with 'strategy' as we define it below – but in fact they have tended to be Eurocentric or Western-centric, and often focus only on the very recent past.[1] This is in part a result also of the uneven development of scholarship in different parts of the world. There have been civilisations which quite deliberately turned their backs on their own past, like that of the early

---

[1] E.g. I. G. Bagramjan, S. P. Ivanov et al. (eds), *История войн и военного искусства* (History of War and the Art of War) (Moscow, Воениздат, 1970); L. Freedman, *Strategy* (Oxford: Oxford University Press, 2013).

French Revolution, or of early Communist Russia and Communist China. Most civilisations do take an interest in their own history, but this can take many forms. Some have looked at wars of the past as religious inspirations, others following nationalist agendas, others still for glorification of their armed forces. Even today, even in democracies, a whiff of opprobrium surrounds anybody criticising their own country, their own government, their own military, sometimes even with regard to events that took place centuries back. And in general, visitors from other continents often observe that Europe is (perhaps unhealthily) obsessed with its history, which on the up side may explain the disproportional crop of historical studies – including of military history and the history of strategy – on this small continent. More important than the unequal obsession with history, there is the unequal existence and survival of written historical sources in different parts of the world, and the impossibility for one author to master all the requisite languages to read existing secondary literature on all parts of the globe, let alone engage with sources written in obsolete languages. Arnold Toynbee's ten-volume history of the world is a case in point – it is an unparalleled attempt to encompass all of recorded history, and yet this scholar of Greek and Roman antiquity found it challenging to explain the history of ancient India or China.[2]

Attempts have been made to develop a more inclusive research agenda. Back in 2004 or earlier, Jeremy Black challenged his fellow historians to write a more global military history. He noted that military history up until that point was very much the history of Western exploits, with very little attention to non-Western experiences.[3] His assessment is still correct today. He has written several notable contributions, which have included treatments of other parts of the world, and yet their starting point remains modern history and the spread of empire, most notably the British Empire.[4] A review of Jeremy Black's book of 2004 remarked that 'the traditional canon of Western strategy and military history remains intact, a reflection perhaps of the essential and immutable underlying unity of all strategic calculations'.[5] This is one question we shall set out to ask of our contributors: can we find 'unity of strategic calculations' in all parts of the globe, in all periods of history?

Where extant works on strategy encompass a larger time span, the paucity of sources available to their authors often led to their mixing strategic *thought*

---

2 A. Toynbee, *A Study of History*, 10 vols (London: Oxford University Press, 1934–1961).
3 J. Black, *Rethinking Military History* (London: Routledge 2004).
4 J. Black, *Military Strategy: A Global History* (New Haven: Yale University Press, 2020).
5 T. G. Otte, 'Military strategy: a global history', *Diplomacy & Statecraft*, 31:3 (2020), 597–9, 598.

with less-well-documented strategic *practice*.[6] As writing on strategic thought – mostly preceding the introduction into western European languages of the term 'strategy' – was in fact plentiful in Europe from the sixteenth century,[7] there have been several studies of its evolution.[8] Their focus has been on Europe and later the West, which is fully justifiable as this was to a very large extent a self-contained discourse with very limited interaction with Islamic thought and none with other parts of the world: the work attributed to the Chinese sage Sunzi (Sun Tzu) was first translated into a European language only in the late eighteenth century.[9] While it did have an immediate impact on the strategies of the French Wars,[10] it was then all but ignored for another century and a half, and only became very influential in the West during and after the Vietnam War. There doubtless was much cross-influence in terms of weapons and practices. By contrast, we know of no influence of European writers on Chinese strategic thought before the twentieth century.[11] Even Europe's most immediate neighbour,

---

6 E.g. H. Delbrück, *Geschichte der Kriegskunst*, 4 vols (orig. 1900–1920, repr. Hamburg: Nikol, 2003); M. van Creveld, *A History of Strategy: From Sun Tzu to William S. Lind* (Kouvola: Castalia House, 2015).

7 B. Heuser (ed. and tr.), *The Strategy Makers* (Santa Barbara: ABClio 2010).

8 The notable multi-authored works in this tradition include P. Paret's famous *Makers of Modern Strategy: From Machiavelli to the Nuclear Age* (Princeton: Princeton University Press, 1986); W. Murray, M. Knox and A. Bernstein (eds), *The Making of Strategy: Rulers, States, and War* (Cambridge: Cambridge University Press, 1994); J. Baylis et al. (eds), *Makers of Nuclear Strategy* (London: Pinter, 1991); D. Coetzee and L. Eysturlid (eds), *Philosophers of War* (Santa Barbara: Praeger, 2013); J. Baechler and J.-V. Holeindre (eds), *Penseurs de la stratégie* (Paris: Herman, 2014); T. Jäger and R. Beckmann (eds), *Handbuch Kriegstheorien* (Wiesbaden: Verlag für Sozialwissenschaften, 2011). The more coherent single-authored works are those of M. Handel, *Masters of War: Classical Strategic Thought* (London: Frank Cass, 1992); A. Gat, *A History of Military Thought: From the Enlightenment to the Cold War* (Oxford: Oxford University Press, 2001); B. Heuser, *Evolution of Strategy* (Cambridge: Cambridge University Press, 2010).

9 'Les treize articles sur l'art militaire, ouvrage composé en chinois par Suntse . . .' trans. and ed. by Père J.-M. Amiot and J. de Guignes, *Art militaire des chinois, ou recueil d'anciens traités sur la guerre, composés avant l'ere chrétienne, par différents généraux chinois* (Paris: Didot l'aîné, 1772).

10 S. Kleinman, 'Initiating insurgencies abroad: French plans to "chouannise" Britain and Ireland, 1793–1798', in B. Heuser (ed.), *The Origins of Small Wars: From Special Operations to Ideological Insurgencies*, special issue of *Small Wars and Insurgencies*, 25 / 4 (August 2014), 784–99.

11 T. Andrade, 'An accelerating divergence? The revisionist model of world history and the question of Eurasian military parity: data from East Asia', *Canadian Journal of Sociology/ Cahiers canadiens de sociologie*, 36:2 (2011), 185–208.

the Ottoman Empire, only belatedly took an interest in European writing on warfare, and then only on the most technical aspects.[12]

Where studies of strategy do deal with its *practice*, they are mainly written by military historians, usually with the evolution of a particular campaign centre stage, rather than its causes and strategic aims and context. Scholars with military backgrounds tend to interpret strategy as conducting operations. This again can be explained in part by the paucity of the sources on strategic decision making that have survived prior to the nineteenth or even twentieth centuries. Since 1945, however, the demography of the scholars interested in war has changed. There have been more civilians among them with an interest in strategy as a challenge for decision making, something that they have encountered perhaps in different walks of life.[13]

One recent work has taken a stab at recording and analysing the *practice* of strategy since antiquity and including some other parts of the world, but the selection of cases left many gaps, and the acquaintance of some of the authors with the subjects they discussed shows the lack, again, of the requisite language skills and detailed knowledge of culture and context.[14] Acknowledging that we too cannot go where our language deficiencies cannot take us, we endeavour in these two volumes to make up for our deficiencies by fielding a large team of experts to tackle their respective fields of expertise. The methodology we imposed on them will be discussed below, but it is now high time to explain what we mean by 'strategy' and its practice.

Strategy as a Concept

The word 'strategy' itself derives from the Greek *strategos*, meaning the chief military commander, the general. The word *strategía* in its modern meaning only came into use in the sixth century, in the Eastern Roman (Byzantine) Empire, and was only translated into Western vernacular languages towards the end of the eighteenth century.[15] Coming into use in the West around the

---

12 As can be seen from the very small number of Western works, mainly on fortifications and artillery, translated into Turkish and preserved in the Ottoman imperial library. See E. İhsanoğlu (ed.), *Osmanlı Askerlik Literatürü Tarihi*, 2 vols (İstanbul: İslâm Tarih, Sanat ve Kültür Araştırma Merkezi, 2004).

13 See also L. Milevski, 'Western strategy's two logics: diverging interpretations', *Journal of Strategic Studies*, published online 10 October 2019, available at www.tandfonline.com/doi/full/10.1080/01402390.2019.1672158.

14 For some good examples of this angle, see J. A. Olsen and C. S. Gray (eds), *The Practice of Strategy: From Alexander the Great to the Present* (Oxford: Oxford University Press, 2011). Black, *Military Strategy*.

15 B. Heuser, *The Evolution of Strategy* (Cambridge: Cambridge University Press, 2010).

time of the French Revolution, the meaning of the term has developed greatly since.

Many definitions of strategy have been articulated since. They may be summed up, admittedly clumsily: 'strategy is a comprehensive way to try to pursue political ends, including the threat or actual use of force, in a dialectic of wills'. And as this definition suggests, strategy can avail itself of both military and non-military tools, in ever new mixes, in pursuit of its ends.[16]

The most powerful instrument that can be used in adversarial encounters is the armed forces. Other means – some timeless, some technology- or culture-dependent – exist or have existed: economic leverage in particular. This leverage can take the form of trade or denial of trade, payments (chequebook diplomacy) that can be presented in many forms, ranging from voluntary gifts (such as Germany's payment to the USSR in 1990 to help house Soviet forces repatriated from East Germany) to exaction (such as Danegeld), protection money, tax, the vassals' due to their lord, the tribute to be paid by submitting tribes to their new overlord (which Ottoman Emperor Süleyman I imposed on Emperor Charles V in their five-year truce of 1547, euphemised as a 'gift of honour' by the latter while the Turks cashed it in as a 'tribute'), economic aid, or outright bribes.

Surrendering territory or populations or resources or any combination of these without a fight is surely also an instrument of strategy, designed to protect something more valuable from war and destruction. Other instruments include the conclusion of alliances, either short-term, as in the Greek *symmachia* to defeat a common adversary, or long-term, through kinship (real or perceived), already extant between groups (the Greek *syngeneia*), or created through dynastic marriages or friendship, presumably based on common values (the Greek *philia* sometimes covering this).

Throughout recorded history we encounter propaganda, alongside narratives favourable to one's own side and ambitions, such as passing off battles of uncertain outcome as great triumphs and victories: it is nothing less when we find Assyrian monarchs boasting on stone inscriptions about the towns they have sacked. And such retrospective narratives are the strategic tools of the present and future: rallying support, serving as deterrents and coercive signals towards enemies or third parties, and strengthening the leader's position of power within his (usually, but not always his) own polity.[17] In

---

16 For a comprehensive list, see Heuser, *The Evolution of Strategy*, Chapter 1.
17 A. Altman, 'Tracing the earliest recorded concepts of international law: the early dynastic period in southern Mesopotamia', *Journal of the History of International Law*, 6:2 (2004), 153–72.

short, strategy is generally seen as an instrumental or utilitarian concept and at the same time relational: for something to qualify as 'strategy' rather than an intuitive response, an ends–means link should be present as well as assumptions about an adversary and his plans and aims.

Some scholars claim that strategy did not exist before the word. In this perspective, the idea of strategy only surfaced with the emergence of the 'military Enlightenment'.[18] Napoleon and the practices of war he introduced called for a distinction between war fighting or warfare and the political affairs of state revolving around antagonistic encounters. Many scholars thus assume that it was only with the extension of the battlefield, but also the massive increase of the armed forces in the shape of the *levée en masse*, that strategy emerged. This assumption is made explicitly or implicitly when the works focus only on the time since the French Wars of 1792–1815, which (supposedly) introduced 'warfare as we know it', and is often referred to as 'classical warfare' (which thus does not refer to classical antiquity).[19]

The first problem with this approach is that it excludes millennia of history. If we stick to the letter and claim that strategy only existed once the word 'strategy' was used, we must exclude all of ancient history and all of western European history before the late eighteenth century when Byzantine Emperor Leo VI's work using this term *strategía* was first translated into French and German as *stratégie / Strategie* (and some time later into English, Russian and so on). That would not make sense, as this volume illustrates: complex thinking and planning was devoted to ends and means of warfare well before the eighteenth century. Sometimes we must simply find similar meanings under other labels – what Count Guibert referred to as *tactique* in the mid-eighteenth century is nearly identical with what Napoleon called his *système de guerre* and what Prussians called *das Wehrsystem* in the mid-nineteenth century.

To this day it is debated whether any one Japanese word appropriately reflects the modern meaning of the term 'strategy'.[20] Most of the histories of strategic thought available today emphasise the modern period. The second problem with this approach is that it is vulnerable to the criticism that it is too focused on the 'classical' warfare conducted by states, revolving above all around battles fought between 'regular' armies employed by states. The

18 H. Strachan, 'The lost meaning of strategy', *Survival*, 47:3 (2005), 33–54.
19 D. A. Bell, *The First Total War: Napoleon's Europe and the Birth of Warfare as We Know It* (Boston, MA: Houghton Mifflin Harcourt, 2014).
20 H. Nakatani, 'The development of US extended nuclear deterrence over Japan: a study of invisible deterrence between 1945 and 1970', PhD thesis, University of Reading (2019), Introduction.

recent past, however, especially the decades since the end of the Cold War, has been dominated by violent clashes of other forms, so the charge might be made that Napoleonic warfare and the manifestations of war most often associated with 'major war' since the mid-nineteenth century are no longer 'warfare as we know it' in our own times. (A closer look reveals that these were far from the only ones of that age, as asymmetric wars involving non-state actors at least on one side occurred all along.)

Against the historical background of great variety in the manifestation of war – Clausewitz pointed out that every age, every civilisation, has its own – how can we find evidence for strategy making, in the sense of our definition above? How to prove that some sort of strategic thinking along the lines of these definitions existed prior to the introduction of the term? To cut through this Gordian knot, we shall simply assume that we can find evidence of a 'strategy' when Kimberly Kagan's definition of 'strategy' applies, namely that leaders 'set objectives, establish priorities among them, and allocate resources to them, whether or not they develop or keep to long-range systematic plans'. Strategy is thus 'the setting of a state's [ruler's, oligarchy's ...] objectives and of priorities among those objectives' in order to allocate resources and choose the best means to prosecute a violent engagement.[21] To put it simply, by focusing on the choices that were made about the use of resources to pay for wars and specifically for armed forces, about the creation of means (armed forces, weapons, supplies, fortifications) and their allocation (was the cavalry or the infantry more important? Did they opt for a navy or an army? If a little of both, did they prioritise one over the other? Did they build fortifications or prepare aggressive war? ...), we can infer evidence of strategic decision making. While often direct evidence of such choices is lacking, inferences can be made about them from decisions taken, and from subsequent events.[22]

In order to prove workable, while Kagan's definition speaks of a state, we include under the umbrella of this term any political unit, polity or grouping that has displayed over the course of time the ability to execute this practice of aligning objectives with priorities and resources. In essence we focus on political systems, which can be defined as 'any persistent pattern of human relationships

---

21 K. Kagan, 'Redefining Roman grand strategy', *Journal of Military History*, 70:2 (2006), 333–62, 348.

22 E.g., if the Persians in the 1070s gave the Ottoman Turks '50 000 tents' of Turkmen and Tatars to accompany them on their incursion into the East Roman Empire, we can infer that they had plumped for a war by proxy rather than an undertaking by their own forces. 'Āṣïḳ-Paṣa-zāde, *Vom Hirtenzelt zur Hohen Pforte: Frühzeit und Aufstieg des Osmanenreiches nach der Chronik 'Denkwürdigkeiten und Zeitläufte des Hauses Osman' vom Derwisch Ahmed, genannt 'Aṣik-Paṣa-Sohn*, tr. Richard F. Kreutel (Graz: Styria, 1959), 20f.

that involves, to a significant extent, power, rule and authority'.[23] In our selection of cases detailed below, we have included a diverse set of actors of a diverse nature ranging from terrorist groups and insurgency movements to vast empires. Our concept of agency includes both individual agency, such as the roles of Pericles and Bismarck, and collective processes and procedures of shaping strategy in different empires, states and armed groups. Moreover, strategy is a relational concept as it requires at least one adversary upon whom effects are supposed to be attained. Agency therefore works in at least two ways.

A Strategy for a Conflict, Grand Strategy or Overall Aims in War and Peace?

Further clarification is needed. There is an overlap in the usage of the terms 'strategy' in the sense of 'a strategy for a particular conflict', sometimes rendered as 'plan for an operation', and 'strategy' meaning an overarching, complex plan that might be pursued in war and peace, taking into account multiple factors. Increasingly, we see the term 'grand strategy' employed for the latter. It has been demonstrated that this term was used with multiple meanings,[24] until Basil Henry Liddell Hart wrote that 'the role of grand strategy – higher strategy – is to coordinate and direct all the resources of a nation, or band of nations, towards the attainment of the political object of the war – the goal defined by fundamental policy'.[25] It has since been used in many similar ways to denote a strategy (usually with reference to the USA) that uses multiple tools, including non-violent tools, to pursue a set of overall aims, but no single dominant definition has emerged. This use of multiple tools, including 'political, economic, psychological and military forces as necessary during peace and war', has, at least since the early Cold War, been related to 'strategy' *tout court*, with no need seen to add 'grand' to the mix.[26] We thus see no need to use the term for our purposes here, but emphasise that, throughout our two volumes, when the term 'strategy' is used, we take it to encompass multiple tools.

Moreover, no generally agreed definition of 'grand strategy' has emerged. As the editors of *The Oxford Handbook of Grand Strategy* have noted, 'The more "grand strategy" is associated with war, the more it blurs into military

23 R. Dahl, *Modern Political Analysis* (Englewood Cliffs, NJ: Prentice Hall, 1965), 6.
24 L. Milevski, *The Evolution of Modern Grand Strategic Thought* (Oxford: Oxford University Press, 2016).
25 B. H. Liddell Hart, *The Decisive Wars of History: A Study in Strategy* (London: G. Bell, 1929), 150 f.
26 US Joint Chiefs of Staff, *Dictionary of the U.S. Military Terms for Joint Usage* (1964), quoted in E. Luttwak, *Strategy: The Logic of War and Peace*, 2nd edn (Cambridge, MA: Belknap Press of Harvard University Press, 2001), 239–41.

strategy. Yet the more "grand strategy" is detached from military strategy, the more it expands to encompass seemingly the entire realm of politics.'[27] Given how the term is most frequently used in relation to the USA, with its almost unmatched tools and resources, it is a little embarrassing when attempts are made to attribute 'grand strategies' to small powers, all with the good intention of treating them as equals in international affairs when the distribution of power is clearly at odds with this.[28] For our purposes, it will suffice occasionally to add the word 'overall' to 'strategy' or to speak less grandly about 'overall aims' if there is the need to distinguish between a strategy for a particular war or campaign, and the overall larger aims pursued by the rulers or governments of a polity over longer periods of time.

Studying Strategy

Moving beyond the etymological and conceptual origins of strategy, the field of strategic studies has been subject to a number of biases: occidento-centrism and the heavy focus on recent history discussed above, and the related excessive focus on the here and now.[29] Another is the tendency to see history in linear terms in which the present is a development of the recent past and has less in common with more remote periods of history. Then there is the belief that only we act 'rationally' while decisions based on different beliefs or premises are those of 'irrational actors'. Last but not least, there is the proclivity to focus on material factors such as geography, resources and technology to the exclusion of ideational and cultural factors.

The State-centric Approach

Intimately linked to a preference for contemporary and Western strategic thought is the tendency to look mostly at the state as the standard in strategy rather than other political power brokers and centres of strategic agency.[30] This results in a concentration on aims and means used by the modern state,

---

27 T. Balzacq and R. R. Krebs, 'The enduring appeal of grand strategy', in Balzacq and Krebs (eds), *The Oxford Handbook of Grand Strategy* (Oxford: Oxford University Press, 2021), 1–21, 2.

28 A. Wivel, 'The grand strategies of small states', in Balzacq and Krebs, *The Oxford Handbook of Grand Strategy*, 490–505.

29 I. Duyvesteyn and J. E. Worrall, 'Global strategic studies: a manifesto', *Journal of Strategic Studies*, 40:3, (2016), 347–57. Isabelle Duyvesteyn and Jeffrey H. Michaels, 'Revitalizing strategic studies in an age of perpetual conflict', *Orbis*, 60:1 (2015–2016), 22–35.

30 A notable exception is Freedman, *Strategy*, which includes the 'strategies' of political movements, the rise of industries and business strategies.

which is a product only of Western early modern history. Moreover, politics and resultant strategy as a decision-making process of the modern state hampers the analysis of strategy making in premodern societies, in polities that do not qualify in terms of structure as 'modern states', and of non-state actors of all sorts which have played a part in many wars around the globe, throughout history, as they still do at present. For example, this state-centric approach has obstructed understandings of patrimonial politics in Africa which have provided a distinct political logic to the so-called barbaric 'new wars' on the continent.[31]

Rational and Irrational Actors

Closely linked to the excessive focus on the modern state is the conceptualisation of ends or goals that are pursued in violent engagement. Ideas about what the ends or goals are in warfare have been strictly married to the Western idea of politics and what politics is supposed to entail. Politics as secular, and based on interests, tends to be measured in terms of material objects such as land or resources, or in terms of power for the sake of domination, rather than power to promote some ideal, religion or ideology. When Clausewitz wrote his *opus magnum*, religion as a factor inciting wars had all but disappeared in Europe. As he himself was sceptical of democracy, he trod a difficult path between, on the one hand, grudgingly acknowledging the force of ideology in mobilising the French people, and, on the other, his reluctance to prescribe it for Prussia. His articulation of the relationship between *die Politik* and war as her instrument thus excluded ideology; emotions he relegated to another pole of his wondrous trinity, that which might be associated with the people, but not with policy making.[32] The Clausewitzian tradition in part explains why the mobilising power of political Islam embraced by al-Qaeda and the Islamic State or of Russian neo-imperialist nationalism has been underestimated in the West in recent years.

Contrary to most other significant academic disciplines, strategic studies have made limited headway in exploring alternatives to the narrowly utilitarian, instrumental approaches to strategy. Weighing costs and benefits, and making informed choices guided by what we today would see as a state's (supposedly objective) 'interests', form the dominant lens through which to view the development of strategy. Strategic studies have their roots in two

---

31 I. Duyvesteyn, *Clausewitz and African War: Politics and Strategy in Liberia and Somalia* (London: Frank Cass, 2005).

32 B. Heuser, 'Clausewitz, *die Politik*, and the political purpose of strategy', in Balzacq and Krebs, *The Oxford Handbook of Grand Strategy*, 57–72.

disciplinary domains. One is that of economics, where scholars assume a universal 'objective' reasoning with regard to interests and 'rational aims'.[33] The other is history, both military and diplomatic, and especially the history of the era of the two world wars, written by scholars who lived through this period and who understandably viewed the world as one in which liberty and democracy were constantly assaulted by militaristic authoritarian powers and had to fight back, rather than seek co-operation to survive. As Steven Walt noted in the early 1990s, much of this literature 'overlaps with more general works on international relations, and most of it fits comfortably within the familiar Realist paradigm',[34] 'Realism' being the predominant theory of international relations that largely took great-power relations of the nineteenth century and the first half of the twentieth centuries as an eternal template for all inter-entity relations. Some scholars have even charged the field of strategic studies with being simply 'the specialist military–technical wing of the Realist approach' to international relations.[35] More critical voices have noted that indeed the relationship between Realism and strategic studies can be more accurately described as 'ambiguous'.[36] Other theories of international relations, such as Liberalism and Constructivism, which share the idea that domestic politics and factors are important to understand conflict, have left less of an impact on most writing on strategy. While they share with 'Realism' ideas about the significance of anarchy and uncertainty, as well as a stress on the importance of force in this context, they diverge when it comes to the role of the state and its supposedly objective material conditions when echoing larger structural-versus-agency discussions in the social sciences.

In the 1970s, significant attempts were made to move away from the dominance of the exact-sciences approach and a productive research line into strategic culture emerged. The Soviet military's strategic culture, which had until then been approached as identical to the American culture, came to be seen by the RAND Corporation as a subject worthy of independent study.[37] The British scholar Ken Booth suggested a strong link between

---

33 T. C. Schelling, *Arms and Influence* (New Haven, NJ: Yale University Press, 2008).

34 S. M. Walt, 'The renaissance of security studies', *International Studies Quarterly*, 35:2 (1991), 212.

35 B. Buzan and L. Hansen, *The Evolution of International Security Studies* (Cambridge: Cambridge University Press, 2009), 16.

36 F. Doeser and F. Frantzen, 'The strategic and realist perspectives: an ambiguous relationship', *Journal of Strategic Studies*, published online 2 December 2020, available at www.tandfonline.com/doi/full/10.1080/01402390.2020.1833860.

37 J. Snyder, *The Soviet Strategic Culture: Implications for Limited Nuclear Operations* (Santa Monica: Rand, 1977).

culture and rationality in the context of strategy: 'culture is important because it shapes the end which creates the problem to which rational thinking has to be addressed. If an outsider cannot understand or sympathise with the reasonableness of particular ends, he may not appreciate the rationality of the means'.[38] In his explanation of global strategic practice, Black argues that much variation that can be observed in the conduct of war can best be explained by differences in culture.[39] This builds on a longer line of inquiry in which cultural explanations for war take centre stage.[40]

Indeed, this concerns all sides. What over the last three-quarters of a century mathematicians, economists or systems analysts have deemed to be objective interests has been rooted deeply in prevailing American cultural assumptions. Placing an exceptionally great emphasis on material aspects, these are just as idiosyncratic as any other, and are as much part of a particular world view or beliefs. Again, research has shown that in the Cold War, with a similar geographic distance from Soviet missiles and air-carried bombs, with similar population sizes, industrial bases and GDP, the United Kingdom, France and West Germany developed quite distinct policies and strategic postures with regard to nuclear weapons and nuclear war.[41] The best explanation of this is the influence that historical experiences have had on the collective mentality of each country,[42] and the distinct traditions within subcultures within each. These have led to different assumptions, about the world, inter-state relations, war and peace, and, crucially for our purposes, about what strategy best to pursue to deter further Soviet encroachment on western Europe through both military and non-military means.[43]

While, admittedly, 'Warfare is not always rational and instrumental' when the emotions of the masses are aroused, as Ken Booth noted,[44] and as even Clausewitz acknowledged with his 'Trinity', the inclusion of and indeed emphasis on cultural and ideational factors does not amount to the abandonment of all belief in logic when it comes to strategy making. Logic can build on

---

38 K. Booth, *Strategy and Ethnocentrism* (London: Croom Helm, 1979), 64.
39 Black, *Military Strategy*, in particular the conclusion.
40 J. Keegan, *A History of Warfare* (New York: Knopf, 1993); P. Porter, *Military Orientalism: Eastern War through Western Eyes* (London: Hurst, 2009).
41 B. Heuser, *NATO, Britain, France and the FRG: Nuclear Strategies and Forces for Europe, 1949–2000* (London: Macmillan, 1997).
42 B. Heuser, 'The conceptual heritage of strategic culture and collective mentality', in J. Johnson, K. Kartchner and B. D. Bowen (eds), *The Routledge Handbook of Strategic Culture* (forthcoming).
43 B. Heuser, *Nuclear Mentalities? Strategies and Beliefs in Britain, France and the FRG* (London: Macmillan, 1998).
44 Booth, *Strategy and Ethnocentrism*, 74.

premises we do not share. If some decision makers had or hold different beliefs and operate on the basis of different premises from those of others, they could and still can act on them logically but in ways in which others with other premises/beliefs would not, seeming 'illogical' to them. Whether holding those premises/beliefs was or is rational according to our latest knowledge of the natural sciences is another question.

Most recently, another strand of research has emerged focused on psychological factors such as emotions like fear and revenge in international affairs – a curious rediscovery since Thucydides had already noted them 2,500 years ago.[45] This may be significant for the study of strategy as well. Where appropriate we shall in this volume introduce perspectives on strategy that move beyond the dominant rational-actor paradigm and incorporate cultural, psychological and emotional aspects of strategic practices.[46]

Material Constraints

Another tradition of writing on strategy has put material factors at its centre: to some extent rightly so, as they clearly play a central role. A landlocked polity cannot espouse a naval strategy, deserts and mountain ranges continue to present obstacles to large-scale troop movement even in the era of air power, there were limits to what one could do with navies before the invention of the compass, and a very small nation cannot muster a large army even through conscription. But as with all the excessive preoccupations of writers about the history of warfare and the practice of strategy listed above, it is their neglect of other dimensions – especially those of ideas, culture, ideologies – that limit their usefulness. In his list of preconditions for being a (significant) naval power, Alfred Thayer Mahan included, besides material factors, the need for naval-mindedness: a society with an aptitude for the sea and commercial enterprise, and a government with the influence and inclination to 'dominate' the sea.[47] And yet the geostrategic school, notwithstanding its important contributions to our understanding of strategy, tends to be blind to this dimension. But how else can it be explained that the inhabitants of the British Isles or the Scandinavian peninsula became great seafarers and the Vikings and Britons extended their rule via or over the seas,

45 K. Payne, 'Fighting on: emotion and conflict termination', *Cambridge Review of International Affairs*, 28:3 (2015), 480–97; Y. Ariffin, J.-M. Coicaud and V. Popovski (eds), *Emotions in International Politics: Beyond Mainstream International Relations*. (Cambridge: Cambridge University Press, 2016).

46 Duyvesteyn and Worrall, 'Global strategic studies'.

47 A. T. Mahan, *The Influence of Sea Power upon History, 1660–1783* (Boston, MA: Little, Brown & Co., 1890), 50–3.

while the inhabitants of the Philippines, the Indonesian islands, or the Korean peninsula did no such thing? Even Japan was strikingly uninterested in creating a naval empire – before it was influenced by Euro-American imperialist thinking from the mid-nineteenth century onwards.

The weapons and technology available for the waging of war are another obvious constraint, of course. But ideas drove people to dream about building universal empires long before the entire globe had been discovered by them; the desire to pursue certain overall, often long-term, aims inspired many a technological and administrative innovation, or in a creative mind led to the adaptation of inventions to the pursuit of these purposes. Some cultures would turn to ruses or unusual, perhaps extreme, measures to compensate for the sort of military technology they would have needed to carry out their purposes: think of the use of corpses of plague victims to bombard the enemy at the siege of Caffa in 1346,[48] or of kamikaze bombers by Japan in the Second World War in the absence of missiles. Others, if technological breakthroughs could be imagined, financed research that would lead to them – such innovations usually came in clusters, in response to articulated requirements, as for example the weapons of mass killing that were developed in the early twentieth century, from poison gases and bacteriological weapons to nuclear weapons. Technology is thus not a static condition in which strategy was formulated: strategy could formulate requirements for new technology, and military engineers strive to come up with new technologies to meet the requirements of strategy.

The Universalist Claim in Strategic Studies

In contrast to those who argue that there is little point talking about strategy before the Age of Enlightenment or the French Wars of 1792–1815, another school of strategic studies holds that strategic thinking has been present across time and place and possesses core universal traits. For example, Michael Handel, teacher of generations of US officers, claimed that 'the basic logic of strategy, like that of political behaviour, is universal'.[49] Comparing the works of Sun Tzu (Sunzi) and Carl von Clausewitz, Handel concluded, 'Ultimately, the logic and rational direction of war are universal and there is no such thing as an exclusively "Western" or "Eastern" approach to politics and strategy; there is only an effective or ineffective, rational or non-rational manifestation of politics or strategy.'[50] 'Both Sun Tzu and Clausewitz', he argued, 'view war as an essentially rational activity involving the careful and continuous correlation of ends and

48 M. Wheelis, 'Biological warfare at the 1346 Siege of Caffa', *Historical Review*, 8:9 (September 2002), 971–5.
49 Handel, *Masters of War*, xiii.   50 Handel, *Masters of War*, 3.

means'.[51] Colin Gray made a similarly sweeping claim: 'The practice of strategy, singular, considered as a function, is an eternal, universal, essential, and therefore unavoidable feature of human life. Individually and variably collectively, people perform the strategic function as a competitive necessity for survival.' Moreover, 'Because humans have always had to practice, or try to practice, strategy, it is inescapable to claim that a single, unified general theory must have pertained through all of history – past, present, and future.'[52] Many others in the field have argued along similar lines.[53]

This approach has been criticised for being based on a narrow reading of the history of strategic practices that focuses excessively on Europe and the West. The idea of universalism, it has been argued by Ken Booth, is intimately tied up with the dominance and influence of the Clausewitzean paradigm: 'To imply that the Clauzewitzean paradigm is synonymous with the meaning of war is to exhibit an extreme form of ethnocentrism.'[54] And he went on: 'Strategy itself might be characterized as a universal preoccupation, but that does not mean that it is conceived in universal terms.'[55] As we aim to explore in this work, strategy and its practise may be very much determined by local or specific experience. Strategies might not exhibit universally consistent characteristics, but may be determined by particular cultural views.[56] As Jeremy Black wrote in a review of Colin Gray's *Strategy and Defence Planning*, 'I am not confident that what are presented as the fundamentals of strategy are not in practice culturally located and conditioned, rather than the universals they are suggested to be.' As an example, he raises the possibility that 'uncertainty' in war is culturally and locally determined.[57] Indeed, even in a purely European context, the perception of uncertainty – including fortune, luck and risk – has changed dramatically over time.[58] The same applies to the use of force and understandings of victory and

51 Handel, *Masters of War*, 61.
52 C. S. Gray, 'Conclusion', in Olsen and Gray, *The Practice of Strategy*, 287–300, 287. See also C. S. Gray, 'Strategic thoughts for defence planners', *Survival*, 52:3 (2010), 159–78, 161; and Gray, *The Strategy Bridge: Theory for Practice* (Oxford: Oxford University Press, 2012).
53 E. N. Luttwak, *Strategy: The Logic of War and Peace*, rev. edn (Cambridge, MA: The Belknap Press, 2001), xi; R. Smith, *The Utility of Force: The Art of War in the Modern World* (London: Allen Lane, 2005), 6, 4; J. Angstrom and J. J. Widen, *Contemporary Military Theory: The Dynamics of War* (London: Routledge, 2015), 33.
54 Booth, *Strategy and Ethnocentrism*, 74.   55 Booth, *Strategy and Ethnocentrism*, 20.
56 H. Strachan, 'Strategy and the limitation of war', *Survival*, 50:1 (2008), 31–54; E. Simpson, *War from the Ground Up: Twenty-First-Century Combat as Politics* (London: Hurst, 2012).
57 J. Black and Colin S. Gray, 'Strategy and defence planning: meeting the challenge of uncertainty', *Journal of Strategic Studies*, 39:5–6 (2016), 922–4, 923.
58 B. Heuser, 'Fortuna, chance, risk and opportunity in strategy', *Journal of Strategic Studies* (2022), at www.tandfonline.com/doi/full/10.1080/01402390.2022.2111306.

defeat.[59] A small group of scholars has started to engage with strategy as possessing multiple logics and diverse practices. The British officer-turned-strategist Emile Simpson has taken this argument to a logical endpoint of relativism, seeing strategy as 'a flexible interpretative structure' where winning or losing in war ultimately depends on the perception of the participants.[60]

Applying a conceptual framework based on one set of experiences to another culture can be productive, however. In an attempted to identify a field of 'jihadi strategic studies', Dima Adamsky has used the concepts and theoretical framework from existing strategic studies to question and explain the practices of al-Qaeda and affiliated movements. 'Although divine factors inform the Quranic war fighting doctrine', he argued, 'the Clausewitzeanism in the Islamic way of war is manifested in a strategic–analytical approach toward the opponent and in the regulatory relationship between ideological ends and military means'. And yet he urges caution, for '[a]pplying a Western conceptual framework to explain a foreign operational art, divorcing it from its foreign ideational context and from what the foreigners say to themselves may lead to misperception'.[61]

Our Methodology

The aim of this series is to engage with all these ideas.[62] By presenting a collection of case studies and evidence of practices of a variety of polities from the whole spectrum of civilisations over the past three millennia, this series is devoted to investigating whether this premise is actually reflective of a global reality. We may find, overall, that the practice of strategy displays universal traits. If this is the case, we will seek to gain a deeper understanding of what these are. Or else we might find that the conceptual foundations of strategy are not universal, that alternative understandings are possible and, in fact, have long existed. There might be multiple templates or sets of experiences which echo in specific times and places, but which are subject to change and amendment. We might find that the practice of strategy is unique to time and place, or, as some scholars have

59 J. Akshay, 'Strategic wisdom from the Orient: evaluating the contemporary relevance of Kautilya's *Arthashastra* and Sun Tzu's *Art of War*', *Strategic Analysis*, 43:1 (2019), 54–74, 72; A. Monaghan, 'From victory to defeat: assessing the Russian leadership's war calculus', *Russia Research Network* (2021).
60 Simpson, *War from the Ground Up*, 32.
61 Dmitry Adamsky, 'From Moscow with coercion: Russian deterrence theory and strategic culture', *Journal of Strategic Studies*, 41:1–2 (2018), 33–60, 50.
62 B. Heuser, 'The history of the practice of strategy from antiquity to Napoleon', in John Baylis, James Wirtz, Eliot Cohen and Colin Gray (eds), *Strategy in the Contemporary World* (Oxford: Oxford University Press, 2013), 17–32.

previously argued, that it is more akin to muddling through in uncertain circumstances. For example, Robert Chia and Robin Holt in their study of 'emergent strategies' describe this as 'a practice of strategizing from within the real activity', or, 'relying on a pre-established plan of action or some grand strategic initiative, decisions and action arise from within the habitus of established social practises, occurring *sponte sua* in response to events *in situ*'.[63] These are the central elements the current series aims to further dissect and explore. In sum, we ask, first, whether there is universality in strategic practice. Does it form a consistent social phenomenon across time and place? If there is diversity, then where, how and to what extent? Can we further substantiate or redefine strategy's universality claim?

Second, the objectives. While there have been many suggestions offered over the course of history as to what the objectives of violent actors could be, this study requires a set of parameters as to which factors qualify for inclusion. Strategy revolves around the use of instruments of power to make an adversary comply with your wishes and do as you desire. Conventionally, these objectives and desires have been framed as political will.[64] This is the dominant Clausewitzean discourse of war as 'the continuation of politics with the admixture of other means'.[65] Greed and opportunity have been offered as a lens through which to study objectives in war.[66] Also, as outlined above, we propose that apart from cost–benefit interpretations that say more about our own priorities than about those of the culture and age of each case study, we incorporate their cultural and ideational particularities to help us understand their strategic practice. We propose to open up this perspective to other driving forces, doing justice to the rich debate of recent years.[67]

Third, prioritisation. In any polity a process of calibration will take place as to the connection between the objectives and the routes to attain them within the given context. There are different ways of pursuing objectives involving a host of means and a panoply of methods. If there are objectives but not means, then prioritisation is futile. If there are means but not

---

63 R. Chia and R. Holt, *Strategy without Design: The Silent Efficacy of Indirect Action* (Cambridge: Cambridge University Press, 2009), 134, 143.

64 Von Clausewitz, *Vom Kriege*. 65 Von Clausewitz, *On War*, Book I.

66 Freedman, *Strategy*; M. Berdal and D. Malone, *Greed & Grievance: Economic Agendas in Civil Wars* (Boulder, CO: Lynne Rienner, 2000); D. Keen, *The Economic Functions of Violence in Civil Wars* (Oxford: Oxford University Press, 1998).

67 I. Duyvesteyn and J. Angstrom (eds), *Rethinking the Nature of War* (London: Frank Cass, 2005); H. Strachan and S. Scheipers (eds), *The Changing Character of War* (Oxford: Oxford University Press 2011).

objectives, then there is madness. The most powerful instrument that can be used in adversarial encounters is the instrument of armed force. Others are, for example, coercion, sanction and blockade, but also dialogue and negotiation. How have violent entrepreneurs over the course of time engaged in the process of calibrating the instruments available with the aims they sought to achieve?

In the process of selecting cases, we tried to cast our nets as wide and as broad as possible. The predominant question in the selection of the chapters has been: is there an important story to tell? To help us compare and distinguish between the generalisable and the particular, we have imposed on our authors a rigid framework of interpretation, in which we asked them about the evidence they were using (sources), about who determined strategies in their case study (actors) and through what processes of prioritisation, about who was seen as enemies or adversaries, about the causes of wars (including particularly culture-specific causes), about the objectives for which they were fought, about the means and finally about examples of how planned strategy was applied to practice.

In several of these categories, we encountered great variety. While classicists – students of European antiquity – and medievalists – students of medieval Europe – bemoan the paucity of their sources, we find that most of those that exist have been edited most carefully and gone over by generations of scholars, following widely recognised conventions of referencing, translation and citation. By contrast we see nothing like that for sources from other parts of the world, although some magnificent sources exist, as, for example, the chapters on China illustrate. In other parts still, especially in most of pre-Columbian America and pre-colonial sub-Saharan Africa, we simply do not have indigenous written evidence, and, as is apparent from the contributions on applied strategy in those areas, without such evidence about people's thoughts, very little can be constructed from the scarce remaining material evidence of their actions.

Even where written evidence exists, sources are, of course, very uneven. We thus cannot pronounce authoritatively on the sizes of populations or armies until well into modern times; much of what ancient and medieval European historiographers reported has been assigned to the realm of fantasy by critical scholarship. Even in the twentieth century, we have great problems with firm evidence, and that even in sophisticated states, which in the context of war may well lose some of their faculties. Thus, for example, estimates of Chinese casualties in the Second World War vary by 5 million souls, or what would be a third of the lower and a quarter of the higher overall estimate.

Then, as we have already seen in the debate about the absence of a Western word for 'strategy' before the late eighteenth century, one can equally debate whether decision makers were conscious of aims such as 'deterrence' or 'centre of gravity' before those terms had been invented or applied in literature on war. We believe there is plenty of evidence for this; we see it, for example, in Timothy May's chapter, in what he has called the Mongols' strategy of devastating and then withdrawing from buffer areas, the better then to dominate nearer areas. Nevertheless, in different languages and cultures, something with the net effect of intimidation – exercising extreme brutality towards one city or tribe in order to scare others into submission without fighting – may have had different connotations and implications.

Answers to our question of what aims were pursued is particularly fascinating. Obviously, there were physical limits – geographic, demographic, technological, environmental and climatic. But ideas, and the transfer of ideas, clearly played a role in expansionist agendas, and it does not strengthen modern (wo)man's faith in the beneficence of religions to see just how many prophets, priests and imams told their followers that they had the mission to go, conquer, subject and kill in the process.

Where evidence of strategy formulation is absent or scarce, we have to rely upon evidence for its application or execution, which can greatly distort the strategy itself. What happened in practice may be conditioned more by mismanagement, bungling or ad hoc initiatives than by a coherent strategy. The war crimes committed by Nazi Germany flowed neatly from the Nazi ideology and were an intrinsic part of Hitler's overall strategy aimed at subjecting Europe (especially eastern Europe) to the domination of the 'master race' and exterminating selective parts of its population while enslaving the rest. By contrast, the massacre of My Lai perpetrated by US soldiers in the Vietnam War was the outcome of poor training, poorly enforced discipline and perhaps some latent grass-roots American racism, but not of the overall strategic plan of Washington for the war itself or the larger Cold War context.

By imposing this interpretational grid on our contributors, our ambition has been to produce a work written specifically for non-specialist audiences, keeping in mind the understandable absence of knowledge about European history in other parts of the globe, and of the history of other parts of the globe in Europe, as well as the waning of historical knowledge among younger generations in general. Not understandable but deplorable is the general lack of any knowledge of history prior to the very recent past among scholars of international relations, but it is a fact, and if we want to widen the 'database' on which they test their theories, we must furnish them with accessible literature on the subject.

The resulting chapters – never more than an introduction to each topic – inevitably focus on fewer points and yield less nuance than specialists would wish to find, and would be needed more fully to empathise with each age and culture. But we hope that we have furnished sufficient markers for readers to find out more about each topic on their own. We have thus included references to further introductory reading material at the end of each volume. References to specific secondary literature have been kept to a minimum, indicating sources of quotations and historiographic points made on a particular subject.

An Ecumenical History of the Practice of Strategy

To sum up, all material and ideational obstacles notwithstanding, this *Cambridge History of Strategy* aims to be the first ever global history of the practice of strategy. This global narrative will be based on both a chronological and a thematic analysis of the role of strategy since ancient times, identifying elements of long-term continuity and discontinuity in practices globally. We aim to put together an integrated narrative combining these aspects to shed new and more comprehensive light on strategy, compared to what has been offered before, specifically in the existing large overview studies.

I

China to AD 180

PETER LORGE

Sources

Given the paucity of sources for our subject, the scholarly focus has been mainly on the few sources themselves. These can be roughly divided into the histories and the 'military' books, in Western literature described as the classical treatises on the art of war.

The Histories

The Spring and Autumn period is named after an eponymous chronicle that spans the first part of the Eastern Zhou dynasty. The *Spring and Autumn Annals*, covering the period from 771 to 481 BC, was written in the state or fief of Lu, in modern Shandong province. It is an extremely terse listing of events from the perspective of the Lu court. A later work, the *Zuozhuan*, traditionally understood as a commentary or explanation of the *Spring and Autumn Annals*, provides much greater detail, but is also a more literary or even fictional account of the political and military events of the period. The *Zuozhuan* also became a canonical history, making its narrative of battles and strategy extremely influential.

Like the *Zuozhuan*, the narrative of the *Strategies of the Warring States*, which covers the following period from the end of the fifth to the third centuries BC, but was written after this, is obviously an idealised, literary account of the centuries-long struggle for power leading to Qin's conquest of the other six major states.

The main narrative of the founding of the Qin and Han empires, as well as the construction of the category of 'militarist *bingjia*', which included Sunzi, Wuzi and Sun Bin, comes from Sima Qian's *Records of the Historian (Shiji)*. The military books section of *The History of the Han Dynasty* provides a final gloss on the Han construction of strategy. This approach is relatively concise, though in no way a comprehensive survey of the actual strategies applied

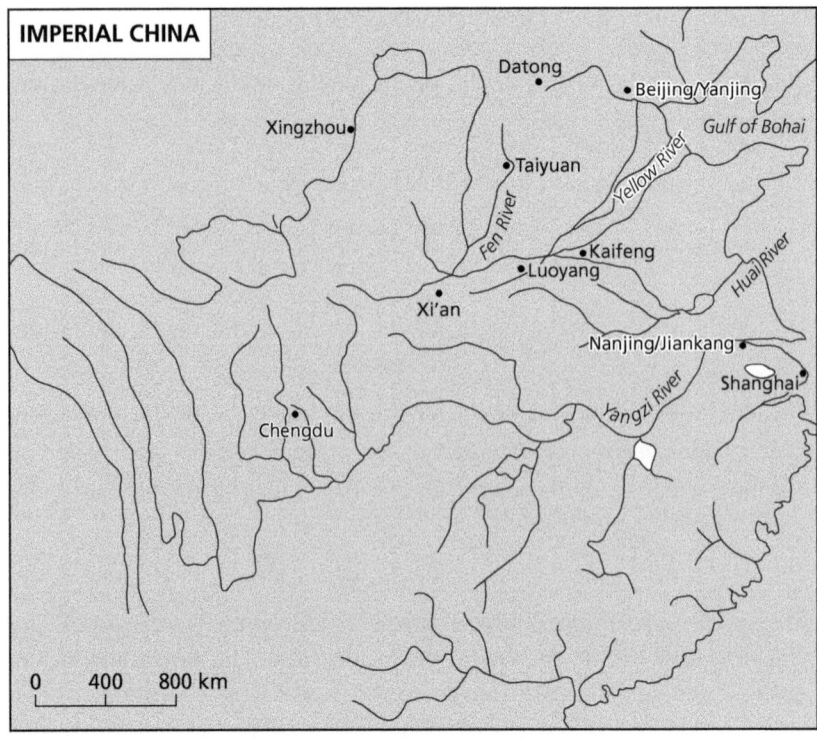

Map 1.1 Chinese strategies to AD 180

over 400 years of Han dynasty history. The *Records of the Historian* was begun by Sima Tan (*c.* 165–110 BC) and finished by his son, Sima Qian (*c.* 145–*c.* 86 BC), to whom the work is usually attributed.

The Classical Treatises on the Art of War

Sima Qian's description of pre-Han history created the category of 'militarist', consisting of Sunzi, Wuzi and Sun Bin. The Warring States period was the golden age of Chinese philosophy, when most of the foundational thinkers lived and taught. It was also when many canonical works, like the *Analects* of Master Kong (Confucius) and the *Art of War* of Master Sun (Sunzi), began to be written down. Master Kong, a Spring and Autumn figure, was mostly concerned to downplay the importance of warfare, a position those Ruists (Confucians) who claimed to follow him also maintained. One of those followers, Master Xun (*c.* 310–*c.* 220 BC), took direct issue with Master Sun and Master Wu (Wu Qi). When the Lord of Linwu and Master Xun were debating military policy in front of the King of Zhao, Linwu first asserted that the key to warfare was, 'Above, utilize the most seasonable times of heaven; below, take advantage of the most profitable aspects of the earth. Observe the movements of your enemy, set out after he does, but get there before him.' Master Xun rejected this, arguing that unifying the people of a state behind a ruler was the most important basis of warfare.[1]

Lord Linwu responded,

> In using arms, one should place the highest value upon advantageous circumstances, and should move by stealth and deception. He who is good at using arms moves suddenly and secretly, and no one knows from whence he comes. Sun Wu and Wu Qi employed this method and there was no one in the world who could stand up against them. Why is it necessary to win the support of the people?[2]

Master Xun's extended rejoinder makes a critical distinction between strategy for an ordinary or even a bad ruler, and strategy for a true king. He back-handedly admits that it is possible for a state like Qin to emphasise warfare and terrorise its people into success in battle, but he insists that stratagems, advantageous circumstances and deception would not be effective against the troops of a benevolent ruler.[3] Rather than arguing against Master Sun and Master Wu, Master Xun might simply have pointed out that both of those military writers did, in fact, advocate for unifying the population behind a moral general or ruler. Sima Qian, for example, would later attribute to Master Wu the saying that strength 'lies in virtue, not in strategic places'.[4] Master Xun chose instead to set them up as straw men in order to urge the king to become a benevolent ruler.

Master Xun also had to respond to his own student, Li Si, who went to work for Qin and ultimately became prime minister to the First Emperor. He argues that the fact that Qin has been winning for four generations is not an indication of sound, long-term strategy, because harsh rule that runs contrary to ritual will fail in the end: 'What proceeds by the way of ritual will advance; what proceeds by any other way will end in failure.'[5] Master Xun's discussion

---

1 B. Watson (trans.), *Hsün Tzu* (New York: Columbia University Press, 1963), 56–78.
2 Setting aside Linwu's eliding the emphasis that Sunzi and Wuzi place on gaining popular support.
3 *Hsün Tzu*, 56–78. Romanization edited for consistency. 'Hsün Tzu' is an earlier Romanization for Xunzi, or Master Xun.
4 '在德不在險'; Sima Qian, *Shiji, juan* 65.   5 *Hsün Tzu*, 56–78.

of military affairs is therefore an early example of the Ruist use of military texts and military matters as a foil for arguments in favour of morality. While the argument for morality and benevolence as the best strategy for a ruler is consistent with the *Zuozhuan* and other Ruist thinkers, it seems (and likely seemed at the time to rulers) unconvincing on a pragmatic level.

Master Xun's arguments in favour of morality and benevolence were particularly difficult to advance while the Qin kingdom had been successfully prosecuting a systematic strategy of conquest for 'four generations'. The Qin government was strongly associated with a school of thought known in the West as 'Legalism'. Legalism focused government policy on instituting and carrying out a strict system of laws that centralised power in the ruler, and rewarded agricultural productivity and success in war. Curiously, two of Master Xun's students, Li Si and Master Han Fei, were later seen as Legalists, rather than as Ruists; Master Sun's *Art of War* and Master Wu's *Art of War*, on the other hand, were consonant with Ruists in several areas (though by no means all). For Master Xun and Ruists, morality and benevolence were the be all and end all of strategy, since they were both idealistically and pragmatically the only way to establish stable political authority.

The *Strategies of the Warring States* presents a considerably less idealistic view of strategy and how to achieve power. A long book with an unknown author (or, more likely, authors), The *Strategies* focuses on diplomacy and political manoeuvring, and is based in the complex history of the continuous struggles in the centuries before the Qin unification of China. The narrative is based upon a compilation of anecdotes describing interactions between rulers, statesmen and aristocrats, few if any of which can be corroborated independently in other sources. (It is currently understood to be a handbook of rhetoric for officials rather than a record of events.) Military events form a backdrop to diplomatic and political manoeuvring, much of which takes place within the courts of the various states. Rulers spend as much of their time trying to decide which minister to trust as they do which policy to pursue, while ministers and generals navigate between multiple courts, rulers, generals and ministers. Slander against one minister or general or another is a constant problem, undermining the loyal and competent, while advancing treacherous power seekers. The individual pursuit of power within a court has critical effects on the fate of states, while family conflicts between the ruling families, as well as among the other elites, continually disrupt diplomacy and policy making.

Given that the audience for the *Strategies* was ministers and officials at imperial, royal or aristocratic courts, it was an extremely pragmatic strategic manual. The *Strategies* provides example after example of the sorts of policy struggle that take place in a highly politicised environment with high stakes. Success led to power, status and wealth, and failure to disgrace, poverty and death.

In the Han period, the question of strategies concerning border problems and their relation to internal concerns is thoroughly debated in the *Discourses on Salt and Iron* (*Yantielun*). A work full of practical strategic discussions, it failed to have any impact on strategic thought or policy making.

The next summation of military books, listed under militarists, came in AD 111 in the bibliographic section of *The History of the Han Dynasty*. The fifty-three writers and 790 chapters of material in the 'Militarist' section of the bibliography are divided into four sections: 'Military Power and Planning' (兵權謀), 'Military Form and Position' (兵形勢), 'Yin Yang' (陰陽) and 'Artful Military Skills' (兵技巧). Some military works were placed in other sections of the bibliography – a *Taigong* in 237 chapters, including eighty-one chapters of plans and eighty-five chapters on war or soldiers, was in the Daoist section, along with a Sunzi in sixteen chapters, though this might be a different Master Sun and not a book on war.

Critically, Ban Gu, the compiler of *The History of the Han Dynasty*, inserts a quote from Master Kong in the description of the military books. This began a very intentional process of bringing abstract works on the military into Ruist ideology. Where Master Xun, as a good Ruist, objected to Sunzi as a false strategist, Ban Gu invoked Master Kong's statement that the people needed to be trained before being used in war. The bibliography section of *The History of the Han Dynasty* does not include a work by Sun Bin (unless it is one of the Master Sun texts, but not specifically indicated as such), but does have Sunzi and Wuzi. The ambiguity of many of the titles, coupled with most of them no longer being extant, makes a clear determination of what was and what was not important in the category of military works impossible. It is apparent, however, that this was a very broad group of books that was *not* defined as 'the art of war' (*bingfa*). The usual category in the Han and subsequent imperial bibliographies was 'military books' (*bingshu*). Presumably, though this must remain speculative, this was because only a few military works or books on strategy had *bingfa* in their titles so the term could not define a category.

Confusing Categories

Some of the narratives of the past came to be seen as 'classics', and some as 'histories', but all of these early works became fundamental parts of an educated man's knowledge. Unlike works of military thought like Sunzi's *Art of War*, these were not considered specialised works, and were not looked down upon because of their association with war. Educated Chinese statesmen were not naive in their aversion to books on war, and they recognised that war and the military were important for their states, but they were more concerned that a ruler would focus on war too much rather than too little. Their problem was not a ruler reluctant to fight, but one who preferred fighting to ruling, or refused to think carefully about when and how to fight. Those concerns were amply reflected in the historical accounts, which repeatedly showed the dangers of careless involvement in war.

Setting aside the very small number of extant military texts, we end up with an account of strategy based on histories and some histories classed as classics. Chinese rulers, statesmen or generals looking for strategic wisdom relied upon histories rather than specialised strategic works. The books most often read and referred to in China with respect to strategy were chosen not only because they offered direct answers to pressing strategic questions, but also because they asserted the primacy of certain cultural norms. Those norms, which grew out of the Ruist political tradition, were in considerable tension with narrowly focused military works like the *Sunzi* during the Warring States period.

The Warring States period's ideology was itself a sharp break from the aristocratic ethos of the Spring and Autumn period, when war was repurposed to serve the state rather than to demonstrate aristocratic status. Earlier texts, or those claiming to be early, were interpreted through Ruist eyes and used to stress the importance of morality over stratagems or even planning. Master Xun argued that the immediate value of strategy was outweighed by the longer-term advantages gained by morality.

Later in the Han dynasty the general category of military books became less suspect in Ruist eyes, or at least in the eyes of some Ruists. The truly operative strategic texts for literate officials remained, however, core histories like the *Zuozhuan*, the *Strategies of the Warring States*, the *Records of the Historian*, and Ruist thinkers like Master Xun. That reliance on military history would later reappear in the post-Han dynasty period when commentators sought to explain passages in Sunzi's *Art of War*.

In this respect, China was no different to anywhere else; to the extent that people learned strategy from books; it was derived from historical narratives of battles and wars, along with the events that preceded and followed them.

The Contenders

The 700 years covered in this chapter saw both wars among Chinese polities and wars with 'foreign' entities. The Warring States period was just that – a period in which Chinese polities fought among themselves, culminating in the success of one, the Qin, defeating and absorbing the other six major states, Qi, Chu, Yan, Han, Zhao and Wei.

In the immediate collapse of the Qin, ambitious men arose within the empire's territory and gathered armies to fight over the ruins. Sima Qian presents the struggle for power culminating in a contest between Xiang Yu (c. 232–202 BC), an aristocrat from the former state of Chu, and Liu Bang (256–195 BC), a commoner who had served as a low-level Qin officer. Liu became the first emperor of the Han dynasty, and was posthumously known as Han Gaozu (r. 202–195 BC). Subsequent Han emperors varied in their foreign policies, in response to foreign threats and their personal inclinations. Han Wudi was the most expansionist emperor, for example, and Han Wendi one of the least.

But then there were also attacks from without on the Chinese-populated lands by the peoples from the steppes. The main threat until the first century AD came from the Xiongnu, though other steppe groups also caused problems.

Causes of War

The Warring States period saw war mainly among seven Chinese principalities with Qin step by step conquering of the other states. The basic question was whether the other six states could unite together to defeat the Qin, fight individually and likely lose, or submit to Qin. Unity required each ruler to overcome their personal feuds with the other rulers, thus putting the interests of their states ahead of their own feelings. Perhaps not surprisingly, and despite the efforts of the great diplomat Su Qin, unity could only be achieved briefly before collapsing.

Without a central court, officials and generals were faced with difficult questions of loyalty versus survival. It was not clear that a man owed loyalty to a ruler who mistreated him, or did not properly value him. Of course, that made it difficult for a ruler to trust the men beneath him, who might decide or be misled into believing that he distrusted them, becoming a self-fulfilling prophecy. Because diplomacy and politicking are stressed, campaign and military strategies usually involve non-military means for achieving power goals. Generals or officials are subverted through clever insinuations, raising sieges, undermining plans and deflecting armies. There are no benevolent rulers or true kings immune to deception, or whose morality insulates them from military action and treachery.

From the point of view of contemporary and later Chinese authors, the success of imposing peace within China, among the Chinese polities, by uniting them into one empire, and thus domestic rule, and policing it well, were thus as important as the skill of using armed force to defeat other armies. Despotic governance could thus become a cause of insurrection or separatism, and thus of war.

Sima Qian's narrative of the Qin founding generally supports Master Xun's perspective on the Qin during the Warring States period: the Qin succeeded by applying harsh Legalist principles to grand strategy, organising society around war and agriculture, and pursuing conquest ruthlessly, but fell after only a few years because of that harsh rule. In this telling, the success and failure of the Qin were due to its particular use of Legalist policies, and that interpretation was largely accepted for the rest of Chinese history. More recent archaeology, however, has shown that Qin was not alone in militarising its state and applying harsh laws to maximise the power of its population.

In practice, the ideological shift required to create an all-encompassing empire was followed by a similarly revolutionary strategic change to maintaining that empire. Inter-state warfare was replaced by domestic rebellions and by defending the northern border from steppe powers. The strategy of an established dynasty aimed to maintain the status quo, but it was unclear whether border threats and rebellions were an acute or chronic problem. If rebellions were caused by misrule, then the strategy for preventing or suppressing them would be very different than if they were caused by occasional episodes of evildoers joining together to make trouble.

In the Han period, the predominant cause of war was incursions into the empire by peoples from the steppes, mainly the Xiongnu. In the *Discourses on Salt and Iron*, we find two sides arguing about the causes of these incursions. The critics of Han government strategy, the 'Worthies and Literati', believed that Han expansion caused a steppe reaction, and that a withdrawal from these forward positions and an end to forays into the steppe would remove this cause of war. Han government ministers, by contrast, believed that Han expansion either had nothing to do with barbarian incursions, or was a necessary response to barbarian incursions. Barbarians, by their nature, would always raid China. There was some truth to both sides, and absolutely no agreement. Both sides offered historical examples to support their policy claims, providing concrete evidence for the effects of war or diplomacy with the steppe barbarians.[6]

Objectives (Ends)

There are two kinds of strategic goal in early Chinese historical accounts: the use of organised violence to achieve cultural aims and the use of organised violence to achieve political aims, functionally the extension or establishment of temporal authority over people and land. While there were occasions when the two areas overlapped, for the most part there was a general shift away from purely cultural aims toward exclusively political aims from the late Spring and Autumn period into the Warring States period. In his classic study of warfare in that time, Mark Edward Lewis argued that sanctioned violence went from being a cultural practice of the aristocracy to a political tool of state.[7] That change was also reflected in the text of the mythical Sunzi (or Sun Tzu), whose *Art of War* asserted that war should be waged for reasons of state rather than the whim of the ruler.

The Warring States period (475–221 BC) was brought to a close by the success of the Qin state's relentless campaigns to create a unified empire. This not only required a new strategic goal, the complete destruction of any subsidiary political authority, but also created a new strategic reality in the form of an empire. Neither Sunzi nor any of the other Warring States strategists had anything to say about these problems. Yet creating a unified empire through conquest marked a sharp ideological break with past practice. Incremental advancements in territory or influence within the existing framework were no longer enough. A ruler would not aim to replace the hostile ruler of another state with a more amenable member of the same lineage; the government of other states had to be completely overthrown. As goals shifted, so too did strategy. The limited-war ideology that underpinned the strategy of pre-imperial works biased tactical and operational practices in a manner that no longer worked. The Qin waged war relentlessly and ruthlessly, a good example being the Battle of Changping in 260 BC, following which the Qin army reportedly slaughtered 450,000 men. Although the number is exaggerated, a mass killing did take place, contrary to any strategist's advice, and ably served the Qin's war aims at that time.

6 Huan Kuan, *Yantielun* 鹽鐵論 (Beijing: Huaxia Chubanshe, 2000).
7 M. E. Lewis, *Sanctioned Violence in Early China* (New York: State University of New York Press, 1989).

The Qin dynasty unified China under its rule and created the first true imperial government in 221 BC. Qin rule proved unstable, however, and barely survived for a few years after the death of the first emperor. In the wake of the Qin fall, there was a fundamental question whether the Qin empire would revert back to the kingdoms of the Warring States period, or the feudal domains of the Spring and Autumn period, or be re-established under another man claiming the new title 'emperor', *huangdi*, created by the Qin ruler. The Han dynasty that emerged from the wars after the Qin fall was initially something of a hybrid. A new emperor was established who theoretically ruled over an empire like that of the Qin, but the first Han emperor had been forced by the expectations of his supporters and family members to bestow fiefs and titles on his generals and imperial clansmen. He and his successors would spend generations fighting to re-create the centralised empire of the Qin.

Han Wudi (157–87 BC, r. 141–87 BC) came to the throne intent on expanding Han territory. To some extent this was an effort to defeat the steppe people who regularly invaded the Han empire. Steppe raiding served both material and political ends, obtaining resources for survival and luxury goods for successful leaders to distribute to their followers. These motives were not always fully understood by Chinese officials, to whom the raids seemed merely to be uncontrollable acts of barbarians.

As we have seen, the domestic critics of the Han government argued that the steppe peoples were reacting to Han expansionism; aiming for peace rather than expansion, the critics advocated for less provocative strategic deployment which would also allow a reduction of indirect taxation domestically (see below). By contrast, Han Wudi and his loyal government ministers put the strategic objective of expansion above peaceful coexistence, arguing that the latter was impossible.[8]

The Available Means

Armies in the Spring and Autumn period were built around chariot-riding aristocrats accompanied by squads of infantrymen drafted from the farmer population. During the Warring States period, most of the aristocrats were replaced by professional officers, and the farmer-soldiers serving as infantry became the main force of the armies. Very little information remains concerning how these armies were raised or deployed in battle.

8 *Yantielun.*

Until the Xiongnu attacks from the steppes, Han armies had relied heavily upon farmers rendering mandatory military service to make up the mass of soldiers. Once the Han dynasty was in place, Liu Bang, who would posthumously be known as Han Gaozu, spent much of his time putting down rebellions and consolidating power. While the problems of internal dissent remained a cause for concern, they gradually gave way in importance to military problems on the northern border. The growing threat of the Xiongnu presented very different strategic problems. It was extremely difficult to defend against fast-moving steppe cavalry when they raided into Han territory, and nearly impossible to attack the Xiongnu in the steppe. The need for a standing army to defend the border required soldiers serving for longer enlistments. Not only Han strategy but also the Han military itself needed to change.

Han Wudi's aim of expanding Han territory was expensive to put into strategic practice. Han farmers had gradually been escaping the control of the central government by placing themselves or being forced to place themselves under the control of powerful lords, officials and families. In order to raise the money that could no longer be extracted from the farmers, Wudi turned to a set of monopolies on salt, iron and liquor. These indirect taxes succeeded in their goal of providing a new source of revenue that enabled Wudi to pursue his policies without confronting the powerholders undermining government authority. Functionally, this was a useful expedient that did not address the larger structural problem of the general loss of government control over land and labour. That loss of control would have serious long-term implications far beyond military strategy.

Han Wudi's adoption of indirect taxes was a sharp break in political ideology, and opened up the possibility of a vast increase in central government power. This change was recognised almost immediately for two reasons. First, it removed economic and manpower restraints on the emperor, since he was no longer solely reliant upon the farming population for men and materials. This was, of course, why the expedients had been adopted in the first place, to get resources formerly available to the throne, but captured by powerful families. Second, an independent source of money increased the power of the emperor with respect to those prominent families contending with the government for control. Emperors could raise and maintain armies without drawing upon the agricultural population. These professional soldiers would be of higher quality and beholden only to the throne. Wudi also employed ministers from merchant backgrounds to carry out these policies, further irritating the existing elites who usually dominated the government bureaucracy.

After Han Wudi's death, during the regency of his successor, Emperor Zhao (94–74 BC, r. 87–74 BC), the salt and iron monopolies and several related policies were criticised by 'Worthies and Literati' who sought to overturn them. It is not clear exactly who they were. They had enough political status to have their objections taken seriously, and to be brought together to debate with several government ministers. They were thus men of some standing, likely from powerful families with a pre-existing relationship with the court. Because the text that later provided an account of these debates, the *Discourses on Salt and Iron*, would be categorised as a Ruist work, and because of the sorts of arguments they made, the Worthies and Literati have usually been seen as Ruists objecting to essentially Legalist policies. Although it is implied in the *Discourses* that the Worthies won the debate, a reader would have to be partisan to their arguments, and hostile to those of the ministers, to come to that conclusion.

The arguments are framed around the connection between taxes, resources, government power, government responsibility and border defence. In other words, the *Discourses* describes a debate over grand strategy. The Worthies argued that the monopolies should be rescinded because they disturbed the people, taking something from the economy that would otherwise belong to the people. The ministers, by contrast, argued that the money was needed for border defence, and that, if uncontrolled, individuals would become rich enough to challenge the state. Which is better, enhanced state power or a limited state within limited borders?

Since it was a debate, there was no move to compromise and develop a policy cognisant of both sides' stronger arguments. In part this was because, as arguments over grand strategy, the fundamental issues of economics, political power and social status far exceeded the specific disagreements over war or government revenue.

The Process of Strategic Prioritisation and the Application of Strategy

Most discussions of Chinese military history and Chinese strategy rely heavily, sometimes exclusively, on Sunzi's *Art of War*, with the occasional inclusion of a few other works of strategy. There is, however, no evidence that Sunzi or any other abstract strategist, mythical or real, influenced the actual course of campaigns or battles.

Rulers made strategic decisions during conflicts, but the historic accounts focus on counsellors' advice and the court debates.

Sunzi's plea to wage war only in the rational pursuit of political or state interests is the very definition of strategy, but it is also an indication that rulers, officials and generals often acted irrationally, or, at least, not in the interests of the state. Even when they acted in the interests of the state, however defined, they did so without consulting abstract works of strategy like the *Art of War*. While literacy was common among government officials, and the contents of works on strategy were available orally or in rare written versions by the fourth century BC at the latest, most strategic decisions were made based upon the limited concrete information available to a given court or council of war. For those historical actors, strategy was not abstract, and the stakes were very high. What was subsequently known about their decisions and the outcomes of their decisions was passed down to later rulers, officials and generals through the lens of a limited number of histories. Those works of history, or perhaps more accurately narratives of the past, informed their readers about strategic decision making at court and on the battlefield.

Whether or not the accounts of battles and wars in the histories are truthful is hard to tell, and beside the point with respect to establishing the normative precepts of strategy. There is a general sense that the descriptions of the political relationships between states and the outcomes of battles are reliable, but that the details of planning, conversations, diplomatic manoeuvring and the courses of battles are, not surprisingly, much more suspect. There is no way to determine whether these accounts are merely cleaned-up versions of reality, or wholly fabricated. Battles are notoriously confusing events whose tactical details are hard to render coherent even when known. It may thus not be a great loss that battles in early Chinese texts are not presented with an unreliable gloss of precision. Much as we might want to know the exact strategic plans of the generals and the events of the battlefield, it is unlikely that most such accounts would be accurate.

The Spring and Autumn Period (771–476 BC)

Very little is known about the course of battles before the Spring and Autumn period, or the strategic deliberations of the participants, so I will begin in the Spring and Autumn period itself, relying on the narrative account of the *Zuozhuan*'s Five Great Battles, before turning to the *Strategies of the Warring States (Zhanguoce)* for the Warring States period.

The *Zuozhuan* tells us about Five Great Battles (the battles of Chengpu, 632 BC; Yao, 627 BC; Bi, 598 BC; An, 589 BC; and Yanling, 575 BC) to which a sixth battle, the Battle of Han, 645 BC, is sometimes added, making the Six Great Battles. These six battles are presented as coherent narratives of the causes leading up to the actual battle, the various debates and discussions of political and military matters, the selection of commanders, a brief description of the battle itself, and a fuller description of the aftermath. The tactical aspects of the battles are neglected in favour of vignettes describing the experiences of noteworthy individuals. The ethos described in the *Zuozhuan* is amoral: once engaged in battle, a general or commander must seize any opportunity that presents itself. The goal of fighting a battle is to win, rather than to have a 'fair' contest that confirms the aristocratic status of both sides regardless of outcome.

In the *Zuozhuan*, and the *Annals*, military operations are never divorced from internal and external political concerns, or larger strategic context. The battlefield is not a separate realm for generals, but one of several different fora in which states struggle for power. That struggle is waged within a cultural matrix that imposes costs on the players who violate its norms. From the histories, we get more insights into the deliberations that were taking place at the rulers' courts than into the military operations or the tactics used on the battlefield. The greatest level of detail in the histories is usually presented for events at the courts of the various rulers, while battles are dealt with cursorily. What happened at those courts would have been better known to the sorts of literate men who might compile a historical account. The literary requirements of historical narratives emphasised dramatic stratagems rather than strategy, morality in general but particularly for a ruler, political manoeuvring, and the success of perceptive predictions.

Military narratives were driven by clashes of personality, and the success of rational strategy over emotionally driven actions. The usual structure for a war or political struggle is for a wise counsellor to admonish his ruler to treat his subjects well, be true to his word, follow correct ritual practice and act in good faith. The ruler who listens to his counsellor eventually succeeds, while the one who doesn't is defeated. Morality is effectively grand strategy in these narratives, a practice for the ruler and his officials and generals that produces military success by establishing a solid foundation for power. Morality generates military power.

Although morality for rulers and elites is important, the *Zuozhuan* is clearly on the side of the newer culture of war that has overtaken earlier aristocratic manners. The cultural practices of the elites that treated war as a gentleman's game wherein he proved his status as an elite are shown to be counterproductive and foolish. Not only have the needs of the state overridden the performative needs of an individual gentleman, but also the culture has moved on. There is no longer anything admirable from the historian's perspective in giving up a military advantage for the sake of manners.

These principles of strategy often appear to be in tension during actual events, and it is the responsibility of the various statesmen and advisers to debate which principles are, in fact, operative. Thus we see in the account of the Battle of Chengpu an instance of Duke Wen of Jin keeping his promise to requite a previous kindness, and give up a military advantage by withdrawing his army a three-day march, instead of attacking the Chu army to rescue the state of Song. His generals object to this on the ground of military expediency, claiming that the Chu army is about to collapse, but an official explains that the withdrawal will, in fact, be the most effective tactic. First of all, the Chu army is not ready to collapse. Second, Duke Wen must keep his earlier promise to pay back Chu if he is to show that he is on the side of correct ritual. Even though the point of the campaign was to protect Song, Duke Wen, given Chu's earlier help when the duke was in exile, could not directly attack Chu to save Chu's enemy, Song. By withdrawing, the duke showed that he was acting with ritual propriety, while still undermining Chu's attack on Song.

Duke Wen was both acting correctly and executing an effective strategy. Indeed, the strategy was more effective, it was argued, because it was morally or ritually correct. The presence of the Jin army nearby, even three days away, forced Chu to raise the siege of Song. The only question was whether Song would simply withdraw, or initiate its own attack on the Jin army. If the Chu army attacked the Jin army after it had withdrawn, then it would be Chu violating ritual, absolving Duke Wen of blame. Good military strategy took into account the larger ritual framework of inter-state relations. By withdrawing a three-day march after meeting the Chu army, Duke Wen manoeuvred Chu into a strategic corner. He immediately seized a superior diplomatic position and presented Chu with the choice of military withdrawal or fighting at a disadvantage.

While the Chu ruler wisely chose military withdrawal, having realised that he had been outmanoeuvred, his commanding general defied his orders and brought on the battle of Chengpu. The defeat of Chu's army at Chengpu is not presented in tactical detail, but it is used to emphasise the critical value for rulers of choosing good generals and listening to advice, and the accuracy of good portent interpretation. The Chu ruler was warned that he had chosen a bad general earlier in the account, and the predictions made by one official are ultimately shown to be accurate. Meanwhile, Duke Wen listened to his wise officials, and had his dreams correctly interpreted, so that he proceeded to victory. The only ambiguity in the account is whether the Chu ruler's decision to take most of his troops with him in retreat when his general defied him and chose to fight was a good or bad choice. He could have lost more troops had he not angrily abandoned the general, or perhaps the general might have won with more men. This was also a refutation of Sunzi's contention that, once in the field, there are commands from the ruler that a good general does not obey. At Chengpu, the general unwisely disobeyed his ruler's better strategic judgement.

Many facets of the Battle of Chengpu are narrative demonstrations of Sunzi's abstract discussion of strategy. A ruler and his general must be moral, or at least publicly moral. Choosing a good general is critical. A bad general can be manipulated into fighting at a disadvantage, and thus defeated. Duke Wen also waited several years before going on campaigns in order to internally unify his state, train his troops and make his subjects prosperous. More generally, Duke Wen had excellent intelligence concerning the state of the opposing army and the Chu leadership. He knew exactly whom he was fighting, and what their capabilities were.

There are also critical differences from Sunzi, which show that the *Art of War* describes a later period of warfare. Both Duke Wen and King Cheng, the Chu ruler, took the field with their armies. Although they used generals to command their armies, and were accompanied by officials who served in both civil and military capacities, rulers during the Spring and Autumn period went on campaign, and either took part in battles or were close by. Perhaps most significantly, the pure *raison d'état* of Sunzi is in some tension with personal and emotional reasons in the *Zuozhuan*. Attacking rulers who offended you is not frowned upon and, indeed, after the Battle of Chengpu, Duke Wen attacks a state that would not allow his army to pass through on the way to Song. Events like the Qin massacre of a reported 450,000 men after the Battle of Changping in 260 BC, which followed a prolonged siege, seems to have run counter to strategic writing, but was tremendously effective.

The *Zuozhuan* described war, politics and strategy as detailed events rather than dwelling on abstract analysis. To the extent that analysis and strategic principles are offered, they take the form of explanations of why specific policies or decisions are strategically correct or to be avoided. A reader is offered stratagems, responses to particular situations, instead of principles. In that sense, the *Zuozhuan* is a store of practical lessons on strategy at actual courts, dealing with rulers, officials and generals.

From the Warring States Period to the Beginning of a Unified Empire (475–206 BC)

The second half of the Eastern Zhou dynasty is usually called the Warring States period. Like the Spring and Autumn period, the Warring States period is named after a history, the *Strategies of the Warring States* (*Zhanguoce*), compiled during the following Han dynasty, and refers to the period from the early fifth to the third centuries BC. Different beginning and ending years are given by various authors, but it roughly encompasses the period from the end of the Spring and Autumn period to the Qin unification of China in 221 BC.

In the historical accounts, the military thinkers and generals Sun Bin and Master Wu are known and mentioned, but in a positive tone. For example, a general holding the town of Liao for the state of Yan against the army of Qi was induced to raise the siege after holding out for over a year by a carefully worded letter. Lu Zhonglian (or Lu Lian) praised the general's accomplishment in holding out:

> Now you have exhausted the people of Liao, and staved off the entire army of Qi for a whole year without relief. This is a feat worthy of Mo Di! You have eaten your soldiers' companions and boiled their bones, yet still they do not mutiny. These are troops fit for Sun Bin or Wu Qi! These acts alone are enough to make you known throughout the length and breadth of the land.[9]

The rest of the very long letter, which was shot into the town, is a tour de force of historical examples explaining why, given the current military situation across China, and the problems at the Yan court, the general would be better off personally, and Yan would be better off militarily, if he marched out and returned to the Yan court with his army intact.

More so than the *Zuozhuan*, the *Strategies* promotes a relentlessly rational approach to affairs. Political and military actors are always calculating what their interests are and how to achieve them, with little regard for real, as opposed to apparent, morality. This may have been because the military and political environment had deteriorated so badly by the fifth century that the earlier sense of aristocratic restraint no longer obtained. Where the struggle

---

9 *Zhanguoce* 燕攻齊取七十餘城; J. I. Crump, *Chan-kuo Ts'e* (Ann Arbor: University of Michigan Press, 1996), 210. King Xiang, book of Qi, fascicle 161. Romanization edited for consistency.

for power in the Spring and Autumn period at least seemed to take place within an established system that adhered to generally agreed values, usually referred to as 'ritual', the remaining seven states in the Warring States period were fighting for survival. There was a new drive not just to achieve dominance in a multi-state environment, but rather to overturn the existing order and directly rule everything. Consequently, war aims went from limited to total.

The Han Dynasty (206 BC–AD 220)

The Han conquest and return to an imperial state also created a new strategic reality. An established unified empire was a very different political and military entity than a state coexisting and competing with other peer or near-peer states. The absolute claim to power that drove the Qin conquest, and the Han conquest that followed it, posited an end to warfare following the establishment of a unified imperial dynasty. Sunzi, in contrast, assumed not only limited warfare, but also a continual state of hostilities. Even in the periods between actual campaigns and battles, the states of the Warring States period were still struggling for power. All that changed when there were no other legitimate states to fight. In theory, at least, the creation of the empire initiated a time of positive peace. One of the main Legalist justifications for investing all power in a single ruler who governed by strict regulation was to create a stable peace.

The *Records of the Historian*, like all the earlier Chinese histories, has very little to say concerning battle tactics and operations of the ambitious aristocrats who fought for predominance after the collapse of the Qin, confining its account to the political manoeuvring in and around battles, with brief mentions of the battles themselves. Battles were clearly important, but the politics dominating strategy were more important. As the contest culminated in the showdown between Xiang Yu from the former kingdom of Chu and the upstart Qin officer Liu Bang, the latter rose to power through competence and determination, but did not win every battle he fought. Xiang Yu, by contrast, who had every advantage of station and mental and physical attributes, won every battle but ultimately lost to Liu Bang.

Much of the narrative of Xiang Yu is an indictment of a supremely talented aristocrat who could not overcome his own ego to pursue an effective strategy for long-term success. Xiang Yu was ambivalent about reconstituting a new empire to succeed the Qin, and chose, instead, to rule as hegemon, enfeoffing Liu Bang as King of the Han in poor Sichuan. It should have been obvious that this was bad strategy since it neither eliminated nor sated the ambitious Liu Bang. Liu Bang soon broke out of his peripheral posting, outmanoeuvred and defeated Xiang Yu at the Battle of Gaixia, and founded the Han dynasty. Sima Qian was at pains to show that Liu Bang, despite many negative aspects of his personality, stuck to his goal of establishing a new empire and becoming emperor.

Sima Qian's portrayal of Liu Bang demonstrates a specific model of leadership for an emperor. Where Xiang Yu was an extraordinary individual who knew he was extraordinary, and relied solely on his own capabilities, Liu Bang was careful to gain the services of capable generals, officials and advisers, and to use them effectively. Liu Bang listened to his advisers even when they disagreed with him, and gave credit to and rewarded his generals when they succeeded. In the simplest terms, Xiang Yu was a hero rather than a ruler, and Liu Bang a ruler rather than a hero. The world could only be settled by someone who subordinated his ego to a larger plan, and made use of talented men in his cause. Although Liu Bang had led armies and fought in combat, it was when he rose above the personal command of armies and fighting that he was able to carry out a larger strategy. For Sima Qian, Liu Bang's actual military experience was not a necessary component to imperial legitimacy, or even desirable. Rulers were not required to be generals, nor was experience of the battlefield required for civilian strategic advisers. Military strategy was something decided at court and carried out by professional generals.

There were no good purely military options. Even if a Xiongnu force was defeated on a raid, much of the defeated force might still escape. Standing on the defensive behind fortifications ceded all the initiative to the Xiongnu, while incurring very high maintenance costs. Han infantry could not proceed very far into the steppe, and their logistic burden also slowed them down. The only solution was to mix diplomacy and war in order to placate some parts of the Xiongnu leadership, raise their costs of raiding and foment factional disputes. This was expensive, forcing the Han to spend money on both military preparations and pay-offs for the Xiongnu. Han princesses were sent as brides to keep the peace. As unpleasant and costly as this mix of practices was, it was somewhat effective. Eventually the combination of Han attacks and, probably more importantly, internal divisions and the rise of other steppe groups in the first century AD ended the Xiongnu as an existential threat to the Han empire.

2

Teispid and Achaemenid Persia
(*c.* 550–330 BC)

JOHN O. HYLAND

In the sixth century BC, Persia expanded from a small kingdom in southern Iran to the largest state yet seen in world history, encompassing most of western Asia and the surrounding regions from the Indus river to Egypt and the Aegean. Two kings of the Teispid family, Cyrus II (r. 559–530 BC) and Cambyses II (r. 530–522), carried out the initial conquests before their cousin Darius I (r. 522–486) seized power and established the Achaemenid dynasty, which ruled the empire for almost two centuries until it fell to the invasion of Alexander III of Macedonia (334–330 BC).

The long-term success of this first major world empire, despite the sources' disproportionate emphasis on selected defeats at the hands of Greek opponents, owed much to the formulation of strategy on a scale commensurate with its unprecedented size. Despite considerable gaps in the surviving source material, we can find indications of deliberation about potential objectives; prioritising between multiple problem regions and adversaries; and the application of military, diplomatic, and economic resources in order to achieve imperial goals.

Sources

An inherent challenge in studying Teispid and Achaemenid strategy is the scarcity of internal narrative sources. While the Persian empire emerged through successful warfare, it did not produce palace annals or chronicles recording its military achievements, in contrast with predecessors such as the Neo-Assyrian Empire. The one significant exception is Darius' Bisotun monument (DB), which celebrated his seizure of power and victory over nine opponents in the resulting civil wars and rebellions (522–521). There is also a Babylonian text, the Nabonidus Chronicle (ABC 7), which covers aspects of Cyrus' initial expansion, and astronomical diaries from fourth-century Babylonia which sometimes refer briefly to warfare, including the final defeat of Darius III by Alexander. Otherwise, most descriptions of Achaemenid campaigns, diplomacy and strategic deliberation appear in the Greek historiographical tradition, especially in Herodotus' *Histories*, Xenophon's *Anabasis* and *Hellenika*, Diodorus' *Library of History*, Plutarch's *Lives*, and the Alexander histories of Curtius and Arrian. Most of the relevant works were composed either decades or centuries after the events in question, and require careful attention to literary agendas and potential distortion or invention; they often treat Persian decision making through stereotypical tropes, and exaggerate the size of the empire's armed forces and the scale and impact of its defeats. It is therefore essential to examine Greek accounts of Persian military activities in the larger context of imperial world views and structures documented by internal Achaemenid sources. The Cyrus Cylinder, composed to legitimise the conquest of Babylon in Babylonian terms, along with Darius' and Xerxes' inscriptions at Bisotun, Naqsh-e Rostam, Persepolis and Susa, provide rich insights into Persian ideology and expectations of kingship, which interacted with systems of administrative, military, and logistical organisation to set the parameters of strategy making. Documentary evidence for the empire's internal mechanics comes above all from the Persepolis Fortification Archive, more than 15,000 administrative tablets from the province of Fars at the heart of the empire (509–493), which illuminate patterns of royal travel, communications and the movement and supply of military and worker contingents; Babylonian private documents and small satrapal archives from Egypt and Bactria also shed light on aspects of military mobilisations and local garrison dynamics.

Actor(s)

Persian kings typically came to power through direct dynastic succession from their fathers, with the exception of the violent rise of Darius I. (This entailed the assassination of a short-lived ruler who claimed to be the last living son of Cyrus, but whom Darius denounced as an impostor, despite the dynastic transition, but Darius emphasised continuity by claiming the Teispid rulers' kinship with his ancestor Achaemenes and marrying Cyrus' daughters.) After Darius' strategic polygamy, most kings had a principal wife who outranked multiple concubines, and designated an heir as early as possible, although this did not prevent the periodic occurrence of succession disputes between princes.

Darius boasts of his intellect as well as his battlefield brawn (DNb §2f–g), and the Persian king was in theory the principal maker of strategy, but major decisions entailed consultation with various advisers. There is no evidence for a formal royal council, and rulers could turn to favoured kinsmen and courtiers to propose or discuss courses of action (see Herodotus 7.5–6, on Mardonios' advocacy for Xerxes' invasion of Greece); court officials with military jurisdiction, such as the commanders of the corps of spear bearers, which escorted the king on campaigns and more common itinerant progresses through the empire's central regions, may have played a frequent role. In some cases, proposals for strategic initiatives originated with a satrap, a royal governor in one of the major provinces, who wrote to the king or visited court to lobby for a certain course of action (see Herodotus 5.30–32; Diodorus Siculus 14.39.1).

The king did not often lead military expeditions in person after the initial conquests; Darius, for example, refrained from taking the field after the first decade of a thirty-six-year reign. Rulers more often delegated authority either to satraps or to generals tasked with specific missions but then expected to return to court rather than retaining permanent military office in the relevant region. While exercising operational command, these subordinates were expected to refer major strategic decisions to the king, who used a fine-tuned system of mounted couriers to communicate with his lieutenants at maximum speed; a message might take two weeks or less to travel between court and the empire's outer frontier zones.[1]

We have more information on the makers of strategy than we do on the underlying premises and processes. There is no evidence for written manuals or theories of strategic practice, and Greek accounts tend to fall back on stereotypical story patterns involving hubristic Persian leaders dismissing cogent warnings (often given by a Greek subordinate) against a proposed course of action.[2] Comparison and competition with earlier kings' activities were significant factors in decision making, and may have influenced Xerxes' choice to march against Greece in person after Darius' generals failed at Marathon (Herodotus 7.8.α–β).

---

1 See H. Colburn, 'Connectivity and communication in the Achaemenid empire', *Journal of the Economic and Social History of the Orient* 56 (2013), 29–52; J. O. Hyland, 'The Achaemenid messenger service and the Ionian Revolt: new evidence from the Persepolis Fortification Archive', *Historia* 68 (2019), 150–69.

2 See J. Rop, *Greek Military Service in the Ancient Near East, 401–330 BCE* (Cambridge: Cambridge University Press, 2019), 11–18.

Adversaries

The initial conquests of Cyrus and Cambyses overthrew and absorbed a number of pre-existing kingdoms, including Media, Lydia, Babylonia and Egypt. In the wake of Persia's early successes, bolstered by Darius' suppression of separatist revolts in 522–521, the empire found itself in a unipolar situation, and arguably lacked peer competitors until the fourth century. Its adversaries were more typically rebels, including Ionian Greeks (499–493), Babylonians (484) and Egyptians (c. 487–485, 463–457 and 405–340).

Persia also faced sporadic resistance and incursions from regional frontier opponents, including the nomadic Saka tribes of the central Asian steppes as well as Greek city states in the Aegean region. Xerxes' famous Greek expedition (480–479) was opposed by Sparta, Athens and a coalition of more than thirty other Greek cities, although numerous Greek communities also contributed troops and ships to the Persian side. Despite Xerxes' burning of Athens, the Persian defeats at Salamis and Plataea led to the loss of control over the empire's Aegean territories, and allowed the Athenians to establish a naval hegemony, sometimes referred to as the 'Athenian Empire', across the region. But the Athenians overreached in attempting to detach Egypt and Cyprus from Persian control, and Artaxerxes I (r. 465–424) restored stability to his Mediterranean frontiers through a compromise peace (c. 449), which recognised Athenian rule over the Ionian Greeks but brought corresponding advantages in taxable trade between Athens and Persia's coastal subjects. Near the end of the fifth century, when Athens' Aegean hegemony crumbled during its Peloponnesian War with Sparta, Persia resumed hostilities against the Athenians, not through direct military action but by financing Sparta's naval campaigns (412–405); the eventual success of this project allowed the empire to reclaim the Ionian Greek cities and establish a condition of patronage over the Aegean's new hegemon. Although Sparta subsequently turned on Persia under the guise of liberating the Ionians, and raided into the empire's western Anatolian provinces, Artaxerxes II (r. 404–358) dispatched naval forces that destroyed the Spartan fleet at Cnidus (394). He temporarily funded Athens and other Greek opponents of Sparta in the Corinthian War (395–387), and finally arbitrated a collective Greek settlement known as the King's Peace (387).

Overall, in dealing with external adversaries and subjects, Achaemenid royal texts indicate a certain ethnocentric pride in the triumph of the 'Persian man' over others (DNa §4), but this was tempered with a pragmatic interest in encouragement of co-operation by non-Persian subject elites;

intermarriage between Persians and non-Persians is attested in Anatolia, Egypt and elsewhere; and the empire attempted to capitalise on the image of subjects' diversity as a hallmark of world rule rather than emphasising a Persian cultural supremacy.

The late fifth and fourth centuries also saw internal challenges by disaffected members of the imperial elite, but most were limited in effect and duration. The most dramatic was a bid for the throne by Prince Cyrus the Younger, who marched from western Anatolia to Babylonia to challenge his brother Artaxerxes II but met defeat and death at the Battle of Cunaxa (401). A more serious threat emerged when the Egyptian revolt metastasised into effective secession from the empire (405–340), producing an independent kingdom that resisted several invasions and threatened Persia's hold on the Levant. Artaxerxes III (r. 358–338) finally reconquered Egypt just before war commenced with the Achaemenids' final adversary, the Macedonian kingdom of Philip II and Alexander III, whose invasion overthrew Darius III (r. 336–330) and brought the Achaemenid empire to an end.

Causes of War(s)

The sources do not present trustworthy evidence on Cyrus' and Cambyses' initial quarrels with the victims of their conquests. The Cyrus Cylinder, asserting a summons from the Babylonian god Marduk to remove Babylon's unsatisfactory monarch and liberate its population from suffering, illustrates the use of propaganda to promote post-conquest stability rather than any genuine humanitarian objectives. It is clear that the conquerors aimed in part at material enrichment through looting of neighbouring kingdoms' wealth, as well as opportunities for the exploitation of subject labour in support of domestic construction and infrastructure projects. Early Persian kings also launched campaigns to fulfil expectations of heroic leadership and prove themselves greater than their predecessors. The inscriptions of Darius I and Xerxes assert prowess in battle as proof of their worthiness to rule. Nevertheless, the Persians did not pursue a general policy of limitless expansion, and royal ideology stressed subjects' benefit from the empire's imposition of stability and peace among peoples (DNa §4, DSe §4, XPh §4a–c).

Although Darius and Xerxes ascribed their victories to support by the Mazdaean creator god Ahuramazda, and claimed to fulfil his will through the creation of universal order, they did not fight 'religious wars' aimed at establishing specific modes or objects of worship among their subjects. (This is not to be ascribed to an anachronistic concept of 'tolerance', but rather to the context of Achaemenid polytheistic worship and the expansive syncretism of ancient religious practice across much of ancient western Asia.) On the other hand, like their predecessors in Assyria and other early empires, the Persians represented rebellion as a crime against divine order, generated by cosmic forces of evil and falsehood (DB Persian §§10–11, 54–5), as opposed to any mismanagement or error on the part of the empire's rulers and agents; the actual causes of revolt, of course, could encompass a wide spectrum of political, economic and social grievances.

In the case of the Greek frontier campaigns, Herodotus emphasises the desire to punish specific affronts, such as the assistance of Athens to Ionian rebels in attacking the satrapal centre of Sardis (5.105), and the Athenians' and Spartans' murder of imperial envoys (7.133–136). He also notes Persian interest in supporting political exiles such as the family of the former tyrants of Athens, but views this as a secondary factor rather than a principal catalyst for military action (6.94.1, 7.6.2–5). Persia's later Aegean policies indicate an unwillingness to engage in prolonged large-scale warfare to retain direct control of a rebellious peripheral region, if diplomatic compromise offered better opportunities for achieving stability and profit. Egypt, on the other hand, represented an essential province that Persia's rulers could not afford to let go, and its prolonged secession in the fourth century engendered a state of war that could not conclude without reconquest. Finally, the Macedonian invasion was one of the Achaemenids' few defensive conflicts, as Philip and Alexander sought war against Persia to consolidate their coercive unification of the mainland Greek city states.

Objectives (Ends)

The objectives of the Teispid conquests included removal of rival monarchs, occupation of royal centres and administrative integration of former kingdoms into the imperial system with maximum stability and profit. In Babylonia, this entailed considerable incorporation of pre-existing bureaucratic structures and elite individuals retained in their posts and rewarded for co-operation with the new regime.

The campaigns of Darius I, after suppressing initial rebellions and stabilising the empire, extended the system of provincial governance and revenue collection into even more distant frontier zones in the Indus valley and Thrace. At the same time, he used armed progresses to the four corners of

Map 2.1 Strategies of the Achaemenid Persian Empire (550–330 BC). Redrawn based on a map in J. Boardman, N. G. L. Hammond, D. M. Lewis and M. Ostwald (eds), *The Cambridge Ancient History*, Volume IV: *Persia, Greece and the Western Mediterranean, c. 525 to 479 BC. 2nd edn. (Cambridge University* Press, 1988), 2–3.

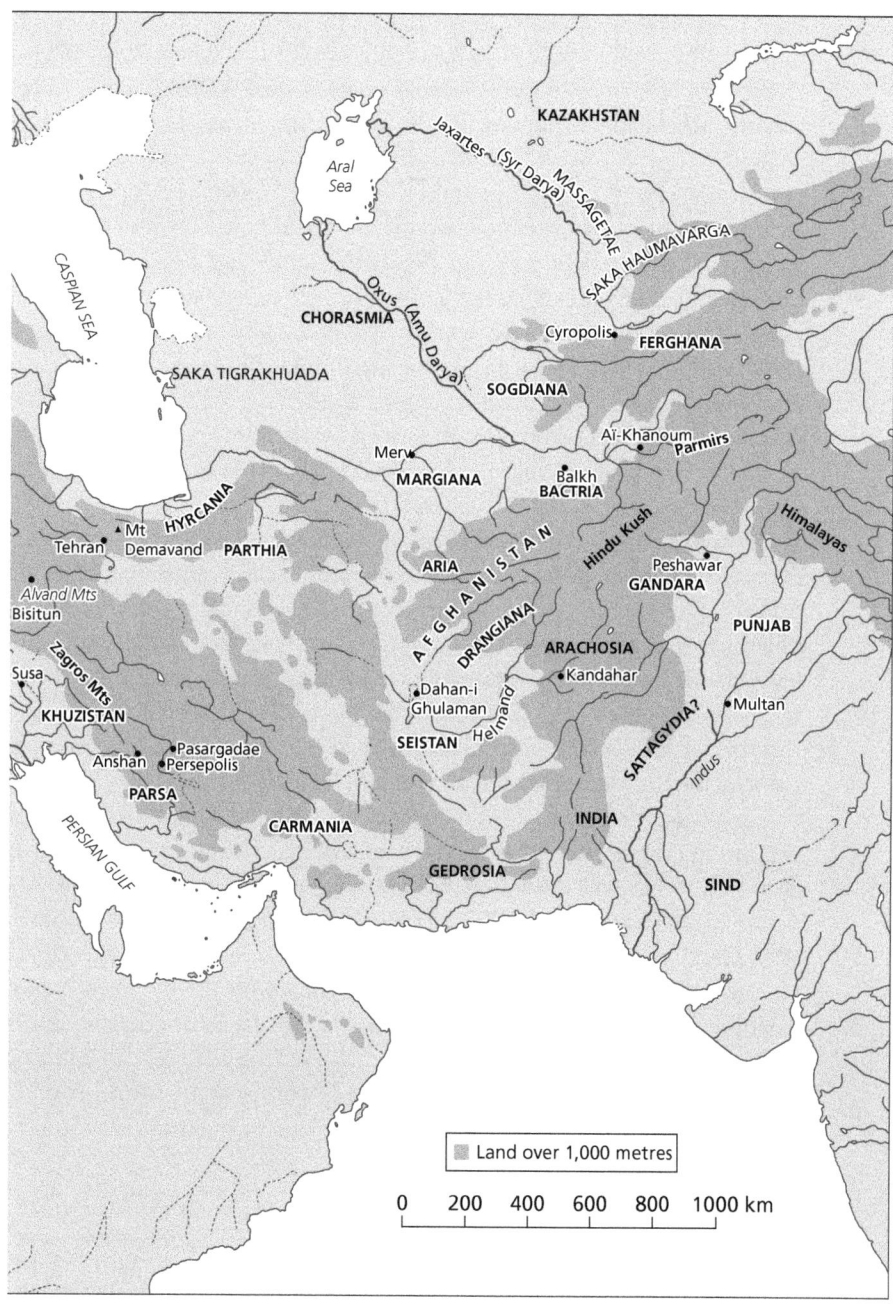

Map 2.1 (cont.)

the empire to act out a claim to world rule, which is further expressed in the most elaborate sequence of Achaemenid royal titles ('great king, king of kings, king of lands, king in this great earth far and wide': DSe §2). While these marches entailed military activity against opponents such as the Saka of central Asia or the Black Sea Scythians, the symbolic performance of geographical spectacle – royal pageantry, parades of imperial troops and construction of monuments on the frontiers – could equal or outweigh more specific political or tactical aims. For both Darius and Xerxes, campaigns beyond bodies of water such as the Aegean were especially attractive due to association with a symbolic world view, going back to the legend of Gilgamesh, that imagined a civilised world bounded by water and associated maritime crossings with heroic journeys to the edge of the earth.[3] On the other hand, the fact that no ruler attempted to repeat a Greek expedition after Xerxes' failure suggests that territorial occupation of the lands beyond the Aegean was not considered an essential objective.

Punitive campaigns and responses to rebellion aimed at the capture and execution of enemy leaders, and exemplary but selective destruction of the urban centre(s) most strongly implicated in resistance; the Ionian city of Miletos is a paradigmatic case, in which a ruthless sack and depopulation intimidated other rebels (Herodotus 6.18–20), but the empire permitted resettlement within less than two decades (cf. Herodotus 9.99, 9.104). A clear goal in the aftermath of revolt was to reintegrate defeated communities into the profitable management of empire.

In managing the frontiers, Persia aimed not only at direct control of subject communities but also at projections of influence over external allies or clients. To this end, Darius II funded the Spartans against Athens, and Artaxerxes II supported the Greek coalition against Sparta in the Corinthian War; Greek theories of a Persian balance-of-power policy probably exaggerate the role of a defensive mentality in dealing with the empire's Aegean neighbours. The imposition of diplomatic patronage, most notably satisfied in the Spartan and Athenian subscription to the King's Peace, can be recognised as an objective of strategic diplomacy complementing the empire's military goals.

---

3 See J. Haubold, 'The Achaemenid Empire and the sea', *Mediterranean Historical Review* 27 (2012), 5–24; R. Rollinger, 'Dareios und Xerxes an den Rändern der Welt und die Inszenierung von Weltherrschaft: Altorientalisches bei Herodot', in B. Dunsch and K. Ruffing (eds), *Herodots Quellen: Die Quellen Herodots* (Wiesbaden: Harrassowitz, 2013), 95–116.

Available Means

The Persian military system included a central, standing palace army, visible in rations to 'spear bearers' in the Persepolis Fortification Archives,[4] as well as in Herodotus' references to elite 'spear bearers' and a larger corps of 'Immortals' (7.40, 41, 83). There were also garrisons in satrapal centres like Sardis and Memphis, but, unlike the Roman Empire, Persia did not permanently station forces capable of major offensive operations in frontier zones; rather, rulers responded to revolts or external threats by mobilising forces in the centre or transferring manpower from various other regions as available.[5] For most campaigns, imperial agents augmented standing forces by assembling larger, temporary forces through various measures, including the hiring of mercenaries and widespread conscription. The latter is best attested in Persian Babylonia in the context of service obligations linked with ownership or rental of certain types of landholding; recruitment was often delegated to entrepreneurial tax farmers, and hiring of substitutes was common practice. Persian authorities might also request contributions of soldiers by autonomous allied communities, as in the recruitment of contingents from the Greek cities of Argos and Thebes for the army that reconquered Egypt.

Campaign forces typically involved infantry-based armies, augmented by cavalry according to context and availability, and capable of co-operation with naval fleets in coastal and overseas warfare. Greek accounts of Persian armies numbering in the many hundreds of thousands or millions are wild exaggerations, but major campaigns could easily assemble many tens of thousands of combat troops on land and trireme rowers at sea, augmented by large forces assigned to support and transport duties, non-combatant camp followers and, in royal expeditions, the personnel of the travelling court. Their operations were supported by sophisticated logistical systems, including storage facilities along the imperial highways, special campaign depots built in advance of the line of march, and requisition from communities in the army's path.

Persia constructed fleets for major Mediterranean campaigns, above all Xerxes' Greek expedition and the assaults on fourth-century Egypt. But trireme warships had a limited service life, typically ten to twenty years,

---

4 See W. Henkelman, 'Exit der Posaunenbläser: on lance-guards and lance-bearers in the Persepolis Fortification Archive', *ARTA* 2002:7(2002), 1–35.

5 See C. Tuplin, 'From Arshama to Alexander: reflections on Persian responses to attack', in S. Gaspa, A. Greco, D. Bonacossi, S. Ponchia and R. Rollinger (eds), *From Source to History: Studies on Ancient Near Eastern Worlds and Beyond. Festschrift for Giovanni B. Lanfranchi* (Münster, Ugarit Verlag, 2014), 668–96.

before requiring replacement, and minimal numbers of ships were maintained outside contexts of active naval operations. In the Peloponnesian War and the early fourth century, the empire achieved its strategic goals in the Aegean by funding Greek allied proxy fleets rather than intervening directly with its own forces.

Diplomatic practice evolved over the course of Achaemenid history, but often involved the reception of foreign embassies at satrapal centres or the royal court. Negotiations were staged to emphasise the superiority of the imperial hosts, and included elaborate gifts to visiting envoys in return for their shows of respect. Outside court visits, there is also evidence for the bestowal of prestige goods such as jewellery and toreutics on external actors such as Thracian and Saka chieftains to reward their friendly attitude and spread imperial influence, but the Achaemenid family did not practise strategic external marriage alliances, although members of the nobility sometimes married women from subject or client elites. By the later fifth century, the empire's vast economic resources facilitated the strategic employment of silver subsidies for the patronage of frontier clients such as Sparta in military contexts. On the other hand, there could be inefficiencies in the transfer of funds between central and regional treasuries and availability for frontier usage, so that Greek sources complain of localised cash flow shortages despite the theoretical availability of overall resources. The anonymous author of the *Hellenica Oxyrhynchia* (22.2), describing a near-mutiny in a Persian fleet, alleged a habit of royal stinginess in funding after the initial stages of a naval campaign, although Artaxerxes II ultimately rose to this occasion by restoring pay to support offensive operations.

Process of Prioritisation

A key element of strategy is the prioritisation of resources between multiple objectives and challenges. This is attested on a number of occasions in Achaemenid history. For example, in the succession wars of 522–521, Darius I led forces against a prominent rebel leader in Media while detaching a separate force to oppose the other contender for the Persian crown in Fars (DB Persian §§31–7, 40–4); this entailed a gamble on the success of the Persia operation, but maintained the larger empire's integrity by regaining control of the east–west communication routes across northern Iran, and re-established strategic co-operation with Darius' father in Parthia, who commanded a separate army and supported Darius' seizure of power.

Several later rulers prioritised between strategic objectives in response to simultaneous challenges in the Aegean region and Egypt. Xerxes' decision to lead an initial Egyptian campaign (Herodotus 7.7), preceding the Greek expedition, may have reflected the greater urgency of suppressing internal revolt, as opposed to punishing Athenian offences that did not constitute an imminent threat to imperial territories. On the other hand, when Artaxerxes II gathered naval forces in Phoenicia for an offensive against Egypt, he decided to divert much of the fleet to respond to Sparta's offensive in western Anatolia and the danger of a Spartan–Egyptian alliance; this proved effective, intercepting an Egyptian convoy of supplies for the Spartans at Rhodes (Diodorus Siculus 14.79.4–8), and winning the battle of Cnidus (Diodorus Siculus 14.83.4–7), but the delay to the subsequent invasion of Egypt (Isocrates 4.140) may have contributed to its failure.

The Execution of Strategy

The early Persian conquests, suppressions of revolt and coercion of Greek powers into clientage illustrate the effectiveness and flexibility of the empire's strategic practice. In purely military terms, the empire showed a consistent mastery of mobilisation, logistics and communications systems, and regularly brought superior armed force to bear against its adversaries. The makers of Persian strategy also showed a capacity to adapt after localised defeats, as illustrated by the transition from Xerxes' Greek invasion to more effective diplomatic measures.

Of course, strategic concentration of force and adaptive diplomacy were insufficient if operational execution fell short. The large and well-supplied forces that invaded fourth-century Egypt were frequently unable to overcome the defensive advantages provided by the fortified delta defences and the Nile floods. The Achaemenid failures against Alexander's invasion were not so much due to strategic error as to poor battlefield performance by Persian armies, ruthlessly exploited by invaders who turned the imperial road system and captured treasuries and depots to their advantage.

Key Historiographic Debates

Scholars continue to debate how best to assess Achaemenid perspectives on the Persian–Greek wars of the early fifth century and the intentions behind trans-Aegean campaigns (province building in Greece or more limited projections of power); one question of particular controversy is whether the Persian kings viewed Athens as an external opponent or a rebellious subject, due to an early diplomatic flirtation in 507 that may or may not have involved a gesture of formal Athenian entry into the empire (Herodotus 5.73). In the area of Persian–Greek diplomacy, a perennial problem is the exact character of the mid-fifth-century Peace of Callias, and whether it entailed a formal treaty or an informal cessation of hostilities.

3

Ancient Greece

Strategy of the City States (500–300 BC)

ROEL KONIJNENDIJK

Introduction

The word 'strategy' (*stratēgia*) is Greek; it was first used by the Greeks of the classical period, between around 500 and 323 BC. But they did not use it in the sense we do today. Derived from the word *stratēgos* ('general'), its original meaning was merely the office of army commander, one of the positions of authority in a state. Those who were appointed or elected to lead armies were said to 'hold a strategy'. By the fourth century BC, the word had also come to mean 'generalship'; that is, the art of being a general (Xenophon, *Cyropaedia* 1.6.12–14, *Memorabilia* 3.1). The elements of this teachable skill ran the gamut from army organisation to battle deployment, supply, campaign planning and the maintenance of morale.

All these aspects of *stratēgia* relate to the practical challenges of service in the field. Long-term military planning, priorities and the allocation of resources to achieve policy aims – in other words, strategy in the modern sense – did not feature in ancient discussions of generalship. Such questions fell outside most Greek generals' remit. Councils and assemblies decided on military plans, then appointed generals and apportioned resources to carry them out.[1] Our notion of strategy had not yet been conceptualised as a distinct aspect of military leadership, and there was little room for it to develop within the institutional framework of classical Greek city states.

Even when we adjust our definitions to fit premodern contexts, then, we should not expect much planning or theory. Only in a few cases can we recognise coherent policies around stated priorities. Most of the relevant material involves either the personal opinion of some author or speaker, or the short-term allocations of resources in pursuit of immediate goals or targets of opportunity. Conditions did change over time, but the rise of rulers

---

1 D. Hamel, *Athenian Generals: Military Authority in the Classical Period* (Leiden: Brill, 1998), 5–31.

and polities with the means to think more seriously about strategy spelled the end of the period of autonomous city states.

Sources

The unexpected positive consequence of the absence of formal strategic planning in classical Greece is that discussion of strategy occurs all over the surviving literature and is particularly evident in historical accounts. Greek states had no permanent military institutions, so communities of citizens had to work out for themselves how to wage war; many a philosopher, poet and politician developed his own thoughts on questions we recognise as strategic. While there is no single treatise that sets out the principles of strategy in the abstract, the military decisions made by particular states in particular circumstances were matters of public interest. They were therefore rehearsed in different contexts and examined from various angles.

We possess a more or less continuous narrative of events from the invasion of Xerxes to the Second Battle of Mantinea (480–362 BC), provided by the historians Herodotus, Thucydides and Xenophon, and extended by Diodorus Siculus. But we also have speeches from Athenian orators (some actually delivered to the council or assembly) that outline strategic priorities and judge military decisions, as well as philosophical treatises like Plato's *Laws* and Aristotle's *Politics* that discuss the defensive policy of an ideal state. The fourth century produced the first military treatises that touch on policy, like Xenophon's *The Cavalry Commander* and Aeneas Tacticus' work on defending cities.

Extant literary evidence focuses overwhelmingly on Athens. But Athens was an anomaly: by far the largest and richest community in mainland Greece, and, for much of the fifth century, in charge of an empire that covered most of the Aegean. Meanwhile, we are almost completely in the dark about the military policies of the hundreds of more typically sized city states that dotted the Mediterranean. Even Athens' most prominent rival, Sparta, is comparatively obscure.

Other forms of evidence are bitty. Inscriptions sometimes preserve entire treaties between cities; some tell us about sources and quantities of funds, the destination of armies, casualty rates and so on. Again the bulk of the evidence is Athenian. Coinage – still a recent introduction at the start of our period – can provide insight into inter-state connections, spheres of influence and strategic interests. Archaeological evidence of the sheer scale of Greek fortifications and defensive outposts is hampered by the fact that isolated small forts and watchtowers are notoriously difficult to date. In short, while material sources of these and other kinds are highly important, we still rely on the rich literary material to draw the general picture.

Actors

The communities of the Greek world were tiny. The largest city states were comparable in size and population to modern micro-states, but the vast majority were far smaller, with total populations between 1,000 and 7,000 on average.[2] The ultimate political authority of most city states rested either in a council of rich men or in an assembly of all male citizens. The former might have a stable composition, but the latter was, in practice, an amorphous collective of those citizens who made it to the assembly on a given day. These bodies of government, and not the commanders of armies, had the agency to make strategy and set military priorities. Even Sparta's kings were not absolute monarchs but hereditary 'generals for life' (Aristotle, *Politics* 1285b.27–8) whose military role was to carry out the directives of the ephors and the assembly (Xenophon, *Constitution of the Spartans* 15.2). There were no standing armies with a professional officer corps, no military academies, no ministries of defence – no institutions that might produce plans or advise on approaches to future military conflicts. Indeed, states had very few public institutions of any kind, and most of the ones they had (including the generalships themselves) were staffed by ordinary citizens with deliberately short tenures in office. This civic model was not merely the result of the states' small size. Whether democracies or oligarchies, Greek states tended to be run on principles of egalitarianism and power sharing within the ruling class. Free citizens distrusted anyone who tried to entrench his power and jealously guarded their right to public office.

This made for a lack of institutional continuity and, consequently, the difficulty of identifying anything we might describe as 'policy'. It was hard to plan ahead unless the whole community agreed on its common goals and held to them regardless of circumstance. Generals elected for one-year terms were unable to make structural preparations; speakers in councils and assemblies had to persuade their changing audience of every new proposal. While long-term strategic decisions were made from time to time, as on the construction of city walls and dockyards, most matters related to warfare

---

2 J. Ober, *The Rise and Fall of Classical Greece* (Princeton: Princeton University Press, 2015), 32–3, 86–7.

were decided only when they arose. Even if particular strategic resources had been prepared in advance, the question of how a war might be fought was typically settled when it was declared, and sometimes when the enemy was already within striking distance. Offensive and defensive capacity was built up in fits and starts, and often allowed to decay until the next crisis. Few individuals or interest groups ever had the ability to steer a state on a consistent strategic course. As we will see, even if they could, the financial and human resources available to most states were so limited that more advanced or sustained forms of warfare could rarely be contemplated.

The makers of strategy, then, were the individual speakers who managed to sway deliberative institutions to their opinion. Mostly they were wealthy male citizens with access to education in rhetoric and a network of elite supporters. Some are only known for their decisive role at a pivotal moment, like Hetoemaridas, the Spartan who persuaded his countrymen not to challenge Athenian naval supremacy after the defeat of Xerxes in 479 BC (Diodorus Siculus, *Library of History* 11.50.5–7), or Sthenelaidas, who finally convinced them to declare war on Athens forty-seven years later (Thucydides, *Histories* 1.86–7). Others had a more lasting presence. Themistocles not only persuaded the Athenians to invest revenue from the silver mines in expanding the fleet to subdue neighbouring Aegina (Herodotus, *Histories* 7.144), but also determined the Athenian strategy against Xerxes, in which the enlarged fleet was the city's key asset. Similarly, Pericles got the Athenians to adhere to his fleet-based imperial strategy until his death in the early years of the Peloponnesian War (Thucydides 2.65.7–9). In Sicily, Hermocrates of Syracuse persuaded the island's Greek cities to make a common peace to avoid being divided and conquered by Athens, but also guided his own city through military reforms to resist the eventual Athenian invasion (Thucydides 4.58–65, 6.72–3). The fourth-century Athenian orators Aeschines and Demosthenes spent decades vying for the assembly's favour with opposing strategies to contain the power of Macedon.

There was little separation between civic and military authority, and the councils and assemblies that approved military policies would often appoint their advocates to go and carry them out. They would also hold those advocates accountable if they failed. When the Spartans dismissed their Athenian allies during the revolt of the helots in the 460s BC, the humiliated Athenians renounced the alliance and exiled all those who had pushed a pro-Spartan policy, including the prominent general Cimon (Plutarch, *Cimon* 17.3, *Pericles* 9.5). The Athenians later found that they could not endure Pericles' passivity in the face of Spartan invasions, so they stripped him of his general-ship and fined him (Thucydides 2.59, 2.65.1–3). After the force they sent to Sicily was annihilated in 413 BC, they turned on those who had persuaded them to vote for the expedition (Thucydides 8.1.1; Xenophon, *Hellenica* 1.4.17). Fines, exile, and even execution were common punishments for Greek generals who were thought to have made bad decisions or given bad advice.

Adversaries

The most common adversaries of Greek states were other Greek states. Communities were often at war with their neighbours. The Thessalians and Phocians were said to hate each other so much that, whichever side the Thessalians chose when Xerxes invaded Greece, the Phocians would choose the other (Herodotus 8.30). The Thebans razed the nearby town of Plataea in 427 BC; when it was eventually rebuilt, the Thebans razed it again in 373 BC. In the course of the fifth century the Athenians first subjected Aegina to tribute, then expelled the Aeginetans from their island, and finally des-troyed the settlement of the surviving Aeginetans in the Peloponnese 'on account of their everlasting enmity' (Thucydides 4.57.4). There are many other examples of such inveterate feuds, and of a particular concern with local enemies. Besides giving general advice about cavalry training and tactics, Xenophon's *The Cavalry Commander* is specifically concerned with the likelihood of an invasion of Athenian territory by the neighbouring Thebans. Many Greeks would fight the same enemy that their fathers and grandfathers had fought.

Of course, with Greek settlements spread around the Mediterranean and the Black Sea, not all the Greeks' neighbours were Greek. In the north, city states perched on the edge of the Thracian and Illyrian world. In Italy and Sicily they interacted with indigenous peoples as well as Carthaginian settlers. Greeks in the western Mediterranean had Celts for their neighbours; those in the Crimea, Scythians; those in Africa, Libyans and Egyptians. In the east lay the Persian Empire, which controlled the Greek and non-Greek communities of Asia Minor for much of the classical period. Most of these 'barbarians' were as coveted as allies and mercenaries as they were feared as enemies. The military methods of communities on the fringes of the Greek world often differed from those in the centre, reflecting the peculiar challenges they faced against their local non-Greek opponents – especially Persia, with its immense wealth and resources.

The adversaries of Greek communities were not always simply their immediate neighbours. The city states were tied together by a complex web of local hierarchies, regional federations, wider hegemonic alliance systems, religious organisations like the Amphictyonic League, and ancestral or situational alliances. These might require a community to march to war against an adversary with whom they had no direct connection or quarrel. A larger state could choose to stay out of a conflict in which they had no stake, like Corinth refusing to join Sparta's campaigns against the Athenian democratic insurgents in 403 BC and against Haliartus in 395 BC (Xenophon, *Hellenica* 2.4.30, 3.5.17). But in the hierarchical networks that marked the period, such refusal might provoke a violent response from the dominant state. Smaller states had little choice, often compelled by treaties to 'share the same friends and enemies' as their hegemon and 'follow wherever they lead, by land and sea' (Xenophon, *Hellenica* 2.2.20, 5.3.26). An alliance like the one between Athens and Sparta in 421 BC implicitly signed up hundreds of subordinate city states to a common foreign policy.[3]

The states that led or served as equal partners in such alliances would usually have the means to pursue more ambitious goals. As the reference to following the hegemon 'by sea' suggests, larger Greek powers might build networks of overseas dependencies, intervene on behalf of distant allies or seek to secure access to trade routes and strategic resources. As a result, their adversaries might include a far wider range of states and communities, whether Greek or non-Greek.

Causes of Wars

The Greeks sometimes portrayed themselves as an impoverished people hacking at each other over 'useless little strips of borderland' (Herodotus 5.49.8). Wars over disputed territory are indeed known from the historical record. But the fact that the contested land was often marginal and remote, and that some conquerors left their prize unoccupied, suggests that it was not a need for land that caused these wars. The conflict between Chalcis and Eretria over the Lelantine plain involved allies from all over the Greek world (Thucydides 1.15.3) who could not expect to benefit materially from taking the plain. Plenty of armed conflicts in Greek history did not feature any

---

3 T. H. Nielsen and A. Schwartz, 'Coalition warfare in the ancient Greek world', in N. B. Poulsen, K. H. Galster and S. Nørby (eds), *Coalition Warfare* (Newcastle upon Tyne: Cambridge Scholars Press, 2013), 29–50, 36–8.

contested farmland at all. What really drove the city states to engage in these wars?

According to Thucydides (1.76.2), the 'all-powerful motives' for states to seek to dominate each other were 'honour, fear, advantage'. It may seem obvious how the third of these motives led to war: armed conflict held the promise of immediate gain from raids, piracy and plunder. The Arcadians joined Sparta's war against Elis around 401 BC specifically because they wanted a share of the spoils (Xenophon, *Hellenica* 3.2.26). But most warfare in this period is unlikely to have made fortunes. Unscrupulous individuals may have expected to gain, but major military campaigns would rarely even recoup their own cost, especially if they required states to deploy fleets or commit to long sieges. The Greeks understood that war emptied state treasuries faster than anything could refill them (Xenophon, *Ways and Means* 5.12). A desire for more structural benefits, in the form of outright conquest, enslavement or subjection to tribute, was a more common cause of conflicts between city states.

Yet Thucydides (1.23.6, 1.88, 1.118.2) believed that the second motive, fear, was the 'truest cause' of the Peloponnesian War: Sparta had become afraid of the growing power of Athens and decided that war was the only remedy. This was not fear of annihilation. Athens did not directly threaten the Spartan sphere of influence and none of the grievances cited against Athens involved the Spartans themselves. Sparta is unlikely to have been concerned about losing territory or autonomy, but rather its status in the eyes of other Greeks – especially its own allies, who looked to Sparta to check Athenian expansion. If the Spartans failed to help their friends, their leadership would lose its legitimacy. If they showed weakness or cowardice in the face of their rivals, their allies would abandon them and their hegemonic system would crumble. In other words, fear seems to have gone together with Thucydides' first motive: honour. This intangible asset must also have been at the centre of wars over marginal lands, in which defeating the enemy was more important than enjoying the spoils.

Honour, then, is the cause most strongly emphasised by modern scholars.[4] In the ultracompetitive culture of ancient Greece, victory was pursued for its

---

4 J. E. Lendon, 'Homeric vengeance and the outbreak of Greek wars', in H. van Wees (ed.), *War and Violence in Ancient Greece* (London: Duckworth/Classical Press of Wales, 2000), 1–30; H. van Wees, *Greek Warfare: Myths and Realities* (London: Duckworth, 2004), 19–26; L. Rawlings, *The Ancient Greeks at War* (Manchester: Manchester University Press, 2007), 14–16; P. Hunt, *War, Peace, and Alliance in Demosthenes' Athens* (Cambridge: Cambridge University Press, 2010), 27–52.

own sake – to assert power, to win glory and to erase shame. Status and honour were hard-earned and jealously defended. Besides, political decisions were often made in the heat of the moment, with emotions riding high. It can be difficult for us to imagine wars starting over slights and grudges, but when the Greeks tell us those were the causes of their wars, we should take them seriously. No ancient author ever offers any reason for the Trojan War other than the violation of the rules of hospitality committed in the abduction of Helen. Herodotus (7.8b.1) believed the Persians attacked Greece largely out of vengeance for Athenian participation in the Ionian Revolt, which he saw as only the last in a series of wars of retribution between Europe and Asia. All historians of the period record regional wars that broke out over matters of disrespect, and the whole string of devastating hegemonic wars between Athens, Sparta, Corinth, Argos and Thebes that defined the classical period can be read as conflicts over relative status and honour more than material gain. In these wars, lesser allies joined to keep their oaths, earning the respect and protection of powerful patron states in turn.

The Spartans liked to claim that they fought to liberate other Greeks – whether from tyrants, the Athenian empire, the Persians or some local hegemonic overlord. This was usually a cynical attempt to gain honour by appearing to stand up for the oppressed; the just cause was little more than a pretext to turn 'liberated' communities into their own dependencies. Other states could use the same rhetoric to justify attacking and overthrowing hostile regimes abroad. The Thebans used it against the Spartans themselves in 370/369 BC, ending centuries of Spartan domination of Messenia and setting up an independent state in the region (Diodorus Siculus 15.66.1).

Finally, all aspects of Greek life were steeped in religion, and the slightest disrespect towards priests, sanctuaries and deities could be cited as a reason to go to war. The member states of the Delphic Amphictyony were sworn to protect the sanctuary of Apollo at Delphi with all their might (Aeschines 2.115), resulting in a succession of 'Sacred Wars'. Attacks on the Persian Empire were always justified with reference to their destruction of Greek temples during the invasion of Xerxes. Lesser conflicts could also erupt over incidents of sacrilege, insufficient sacrifices offered at festivals, infringements on sacred land and so on. Like honour and vengeance, we should treat this as a genuine reason for Greeks to go to war – even if this cause, too, was sometimes just a pretext for aggression (Thucydides 5.53).

Objectives

The aims of Greek warfare can be difficult to determine. They are rarely explicitly defined, and the wars we know of had a great variety of different outcomes. Even for the best-attested wars of the classical period, the goals of both sides can be up for debate. There is still no agreement among historians on Sparta's objectives at the start of the Peloponnesian War: did it pursue a set of minor Athenian concessions to safeguard the status quo, or the destruction of Athens and dissolution of its empire?[5] The disparity of views reveals the range of possibilities – from mere gestures of compliance to the complete annihilation of the enemy.

If we take Herodotus' self-deprecating claim about wars over strips of borderland at face value, we might conclude that the war aims of Greek states were traditionally modest – even symbolic, the point being simply to prove one's superiority over a neighbour by force of arms. But there are many Greek wars that do not fit this pattern. In the early archaic period, Sparta fought its long wars with neighbouring Messenia to gain control over the entire region and its people. Argos similarly captured the territory of nearby Asine and Nauplia, driving the population into exile; in the fifth century it would seize and permanently destroy Mycenae (Diodorus Siculus 11.65). As noted above, the Athenians ended their feud with Aegina by taking the island for themselves; they did the same with other places, from Carystus to Samos, throughout the classical period, casting out the inhabitants and sending their own settlers to occupy the land. In 422 BC the Syracusans forcibly dissolved the town of Leontini (Thucydides 5.4.1); under the tyrant Dionysius I they would later raze the Sicilian cities of Naxos and Catana to the ground (Diodorus Siculus 14.15.2–3). These are just some examples of extreme destruction in Greek warfare.

In wars of conquest, the defeated population were sometimes expelled from their country: the poet Tyrtaeus exhorted the Spartans to fight by reminding them of the sorry plight of refugees who had lost their land (fragment 10, lines 3–14). But it was also common for all adult men to be killed and all women and children to be sold into slavery. Xenophon

---

5 A selection of views: P. A. Brunt, 'Spartan policy and strategy in the Archidamian War', *Phoenix*, 19:4 (1965), 255–80, 255, 258; E. Badian, *From Plataea to Potidaea: Studies in the History and Historiography of the Pentecontaetia* (Baltimore: Johns Hopkins University Press, 1993), 155–6; J. F. Lazenby, *The Peloponnesian War: A Military Study* (London: Routledge, 2004), 31; P. Hunt, 'Thucydides and the first ten years of war (Archidamian War)', in S. Forsdyke, E. Foster and R. Balot (eds), *The Oxford Handbook of Thucydides* (Oxford: Oxford University Press, 2017), 125–44, 140; H. van Wees, 'Peloponnesian War aims and strategies, 432–420: Sparta versus its allies', in S. Gartland and R. Osborne (eds), *Rewriting the Peloponnesian War* (Cambridge: Cambridge University Press, forthcoming).

Map 3.1 Ancient Greece: strategies of the city states (500–400 BC). Redrawn based on a map in Michael A. Flower (ed.), *The Cambridge Companion to Xenophon* (Cambridge: Cambridge University Press, 2017), xviii.

(*Cyropaedia* 7.5.73) calls it 'a law established for all time among all people' that 'when a city is taken in war, the persons and the property of the inhabitants belong to the captors'. This 'law' assumes the extinction of a defeated community through mass enslavement. Over the centuries, a long list of Greek towns suffered this grim fate. Melos (destroyed by Athens in 416 BC) and Thebes (razed by Alexander the Great in 335 BC) are only two of the most famous examples. Conquest, destruction, expulsion, mass killing and enslavement were seen as legitimate forms of inter-state action.

We should therefore not confuse occasionally modest results and measured peace treaties with limited objectives. In principle, the city states aimed

Map 3.1 (Cont.)

to obliterate the armed forces of their enemies, seize their lands and possessions, and end their existence as autonomous communities. But such decisive
results could only be achieved with overwhelming force. In most wars
between Greek states that we know of, the two sides were more evenly
matched. In addition, since war was such a potentially existential threat, it
was often in the interest of both sides to seek terms before it came to a final
confrontation. In practice, then, war aims were usually less ambitious:
settling disputes over status, honours, land use or grazing rights; forcing
independent states into unequal alliance systems; rearranging the laws or
internal politics of hostile states; or generally reducing the power and reputation of rivals. For many of the individual citizens who voted for war, the

principal aims were probably even simpler: making a profit at the enemy's expense while protecting their own possessions. Which objectives could actually be attained would depend largely on the means available and on the power differential between the two sides.

Means

Diplomatically, Greek states furthered their aims by forging alliances and exploiting kinship ties, such as those between mother cities and new foundations. Networks of guest-friendships between local elites also created channels of communication and reciprocal obligations. In dealings with less friendly communities, it was often possible to build ties (openly or in secret) with elements that were either seeking more influence in their existing political system or plotting to overthrow it. Groups of political exiles were particularly useful as keys to foreign states, but even within cities there were often dissatisfied individuals or groups with significant influence. Such elements typically welcomed foreign support and funding; in the fifth century, Athens was seen as a champion of democracies while oligarchies looked to Sparta for support (Thucydides 3.82.1). Rebels would form a fifth column in their territory and city if war broke out. Once established, they would be expected to shape the politics of their state in the interests of their benefactor.

Militarily, the primary means of offensive and defensive warfare in classical Greece was the militia. This consisted of all men between the ages of eighteen and fifty-nine, whether free or enslaved. They received no training, were mustered only when a campaign was called and turned up for war with whatever weapons and armour they could afford. The civic ideal was to fight hand-to-hand as hoplites (heavy spearmen), but many were unable to afford the required equipment and fought as irregular lightly armed missile troops. A small minority of rich citizens formed the cavalry. In the absence of standing armies, some selection of these men – whether hand-picked, raised as volunteers or called up by age group – was responsible for the pursuit of all military objectives. In emergencies, or in response to enemies within a few days' march from home, states could muster *pandēmei* ('all the people') or *panstratiai* ('the whole army'), which meant that every single person eligible for service had to serve.

This approach to warfare allowed the city states to raise enormous armies relative to their size. But these armies had serious strategic limitations. First, the labour of the ordinary men who made up the levy was indispensable. Most people worked on farms; if they lost a harvest due to their absence, their community might starve. Campaigns were therefore necessarily short and seasonal. Only the wealthiest citizens – who used hired or enslaved labour to work their land – were free to serve abroad for more than a few weeks in summer. Second, in both tactics and strategy, the untrained militia was a blunt instrument. The cumbersome mass of heavy infantry and the throng of lightly armed poor were vulnerable to ambush and attacks by more mobile troops. They lacked flexibility and specialist skills; without permanent military institutions, they could only improve by collectively digesting the lessons of experience.

Armies and fleets were typically raised in spring or summer and sent out to do whatever harm they could in the short time they could afford to stay in the field. If particular tactical threats (like strong cavalry) were expected, or if the attacker was planning a siege, specialist troops and equipment might be sent along with the expeditionary force. If allies were mustering in support, the contingents would meet at a predetermined place and discuss their next steps. The main restricting factors were the availability and capability of the troops.

The Greeks did what they could to address these limitations. From the fifth century, they began to offer pay for military service, which allowed forces to stay in the field longer. States like Argos and Thebes funded small standing units of hoplites to provide a reliable and flexible core for their armies. Athens heavily subsidised its cavalry and archer corps as pillars of mobile defence and naval power; in 424 BC the threat of Athenian raids forced the Spartans to raise similar troops (Thucydides 4.55.1–2). States hired mercenaries as operational specialists (notably archers and light infantry, but also sailors and siege engineers) or as a more durable and disposable supplement to their levy. Tyrants, threatened by the citizen militias of the very states they ruled, introduced the concept of large semi-permanent mercenary armies. By the end of the fourth century, Athens had instituted a mandatory two-year military training programme for all male citizens.

The common thread in all these measures is that more sustained and effective warfare came at a price; as Edith Foster summed up the view of Thucydides, 'money is the liberator of military action'.[6] As time went on, Greek wars therefore came to be defined less by raw manpower and more by the financial resources available to each side. Perhaps the ultimate example was the devastating Third Sacred War (356–346 BC), in which the remote village confederation of Phocis held out for a decade against a grand alliance of Boeotians, Thessalians and Macedonians by using the stored wealth of the sanctuary at Delphi to attract tens of thousands of mercenaries.

---

6 E. Foster, *Thucydides, Pericles and Periclean Imperialism* (Cambridge: Cambridge University Press, 2010), 144.

The strain on public finances was increased by two other key strategic assets: fortifications and fleets. The former were considered essential for the autonomy of any state (Aristotle, *Politics* 1330b.33–42); the latter were just as crucial for those with naval interests. Athenian orators directly linked walls and ships with independence and power (Andocides 3.12). As an imperial state, Athens would often render rebel cities defenceless by demolishing their walls and seizing their ships; after defeating Athens in the Peloponnesian War, Sparta repaid it in kind (Lysias 13.14; Xenophon, *Hellenica* 2.2.20). To prevent such humiliation in the future, fourth-century Athens put pressure on its council to order the construction of additional warships every year (Demosthenes 22.8). The instrument of naval power in this period was no longer the privately owned multipurpose pentekonter, but the trireme – a dedicated ship of war with a large specialist crew that had to be stored in purpose-built dry docks to retain its combat effectiveness. Triremes cost so much money to build, maintain and deploy that their adoption prompted a surge of monetisation and expansion of state finances across the Aegean from the late sixth century onward.[7] Similarly, the great fortification projects of the classical period – the 'long walls' connecting Megara, Athens, Argos and Corinth to their respective harbours; the vast new city wall of Syracuse built by Dionysius I; the massive circuits surrounding the fourth-century foundations of Messene and Megalopolis; the network of small forts and watchtowers covering the land borders of Athenian territory – all required a spectacular outlay. The invention of torsion artillery in the early fourth century prompted further spending on building materials and imported technical skills.

The role of money slowly changed the nature and purpose of war.[8] Militia armies were stumped by large fortifications, massed amateurs could not cope with well-trained mercenaries, protection from naval raids and invasions demanded major investment, and diplomatic solutions and inducing betrayal could require copious bribes. To keep up, the city states needed to secure and increase their revenues, which in turn informed their diplomatic and military

---

7 M. Trundle, 'Coinage and the transformation of Greek warfare', in G. Fagan and M. Trundle (eds), *New Perspectives on Ancient Warfare* (Leiden: Brill, 2010), 227–52; H. van Wees, *Ships and Silver, Taxes and Tribute: A Fiscal History of Archaic Athens* (London: I. B. Tauris, 2013), 64–8; B. O'Halloran, *The Political Economy of Classical Athens: A Naval Perspective* (Leiden: Brill, 2019).

8 B. Meißner, 'Politik, Strategie und Kriegführung: Anmerkungen zum klassischen und hellenistischen Griechenland', in B. Meißner, O. Schmitt and M. Sommer (eds), *Krieg, Gesellschaft, Institutionen: Beiträge zu einer vergleichenden Kriegsgeschichte* (Berlin: Akademie Verlag, 2008), 296–302, 311–12.

objectives. States that vied for control of the sea with large trireme fleets found themselves forced to compete for the ultimate strategic asset: the favour of the Great King of Persia, which came with subsidies on a scale that no Greek community could ever hope to match.

Priorities

The strategic priorities of the Greek states are, again, rarely explicit, but they can more easily be guessed. While in some exceptional cases honour ranked higher than survival – the term 'Phocian desperation' was used for those who preferred to take their own lives rather than suffer defeat and subjection – the highest priority for most states was to preserve the lives of their citizens. Since wars could end with the eradication of the losing side, avoiding danger was usually more important than making positive gains. This consideration drove states to adopt cautious strategies, rely on strong walls, seek negotiation early and often, and accept less favourable peace terms. Some communities, like the Athenians during the invasion of Xerxes, even considered voluntarily abandoning their homeland to settle somewhere else rather than stay and run the risk of annihilation (Herodotus 8.62).

The primacy of citizen lives, however, often clashed with the need to protect the community's possessions – especially farmland. Against strong enemies it made sense to seek refuge within the city walls, but this meant leaving the land undefended. Many communities could not risk the resulting disruption and loss of crops. The advantage of the 'long walls' of the classical period was that they allowed certain cities to forfeit the harvest and sustain themselves on imported food; the cornerstone of Pericles' defensive strategy in the Peloponnesian War was for Athens to yield its farmland to the superior Spartan land army and to draw on its naval empire for all its needs (Thucydides 1.143.3–5, 2.65.7). For such communities, trade links and settlements overseas might be more important assets than home territory. But only a few cities could ever afford such a strategy, and even there, the policy to allow the land to be ravaged was controversial.

Greek citizens appear to have felt a strong obligation to stop an invader from ravaging their land, even when they knew they would face steep odds in a direct confrontation. Pride went hand in hand with practical reasoning here: cities were keen to forestall internal divisions that could be exploited by the enemy. Most cities fell by treachery, and Aeneas Tacticus' work on defence devotes more space to the prevention of betrayal than to ways of fighting. Food shortages, unfairly distributed material losses and humiliation might motivate the betrayal of the city. The most reliable countermeasure was to keep the people united behind the cause and to fight the enemy out in the open.

This approach still served the interests of some more than others. Some Greeks believed that landowners were better guides of strategy than city dwellers, since they cared more about protecting the whole territory; others barred residents of borderlands from military decisions, since they could not be expected to judge dispassionately for the common good (Old Oligarch, *Constitution of the Athenians* 2.14; Xenophon, *Oeconomicus* 5.7; Aristotle, *Politics* 1330a.13–32). Debates about defensive strategy often revolved around the basic question whether to march out to confront the enemy or not.[9]

After the security of the population and its possessions, the next priority was a general principle that the Greeks held to as much in their private lives as they did in their military decisions: to help their friends and harm their enemies. States might send aid to friends in order to meet their reciprocal obligations, or to acquire further allies, which could provide manpower, specialist troops, bases or funds. Meanwhile, harming enemies was an open-ended guideline to suit open-ended warfare. Offensive campaigning in the Greek world was a matter of seeking and exploiting opportunities to achieve whatever goals might appear achievable – of doing anything that seemed like it could be done 'cheaply',[10] from small-scale border raids to the seizure of cities. Plans constantly changed in response to circumstance and enemy action. Unless they were singular and obvious, priority targets were rarely spelled out in detail. The Athenian forces sent off to Sicily in 415 BC were told only to support Athens' local allies and 'take all such measures as they judged in the best interest of the Athenians' (Thucydides 6.8.2).

If this brief account of strategic prioritisation makes the Greeks seem largely passive and reactive, the reasons for this are hopefully obvious. Wars between the city states were fought for the highest imaginable stakes, and the main strategic resources were the very men who voted on military decisions and the money they could contribute to the cause. Even in wars of their own choosing, their greatest concern was not to jeopardise what they had. They were not likely to make aggressive moves unless they believed there was a high chance of success, which was itself predicated on the preservation and increase of the state's resources. A rare explicit summary of Athenian strategic concerns in the fourth century confirms this picture

9 R. Konijnendijk, 'Playing dice for the polis: pitched battle in Greek military thought', *TAPA*, 151:1 (2021), 7–10.
10 A. Powell, *Athens and Sparta*, 3rd ed. (Abingdon: Routledge, 2016), 147.

(Demosthenes 18.301–2). In order of appearance, its priorities are to protect the borders from invasion, to secure the grain supply, to protect overseas possessions and to find additional allies. Only after all this consolidation is there any mention of what to do about the enemy, and there Demosthenes offers nothing more concrete than to 'take away their main existing assets'. Stricter guidelines would get in the way of the unbridled opportunism that defined offensive warfare.

The Application of Strategy

The normal form of attack for both land and naval forces was to invade enemy territory and begin ravaging farmland. Armed groups would spread over the countryside, trampling and burning crops, cutting down trees, wrecking mills and olive presses, and stealing anything they could carry. The long-term economic impact of such pillaging is disputed,[11] but lasting damage was probably less important than what Hans van Wees has called 'conspicuous destruction': in wars fought over honour and status as much as material gain, violence inflicted with impunity was an end in itself.[12] Devastation could compel a state to surrender (Thucydides 4.87.2; Xenophon, *Hellenica* 4.6.13–7.1), but, failing that, it was enough to humiliate the defenders by showing that they were at the attacker's mercy. Successive commanders might even take part in competitive ravaging. During his invasion of Argos in 388 BC, the Spartan king Agesipolis worked out how far his rival Agesilaos had advanced the previous year, and then crossed that line, slashing and burning as he went (Xenophon, *Hellenica* 4.7.5). If no enemy forces presented themselves, campaigns of conspicuous destruction could shift their focus to villages, harbours and forts, or culminate in an assault on an enemy city.

Faced with such invasions, the defenders had several options (colourfully reviewed by the tragedian Euripides: *Phoenician Women* 710–50). As noted above, evacuation of the countryside and withdrawal to walled cities and forts was typically safest, if not for the shortages and internal tensions that might result. The quickest and economically cheapest alternative – and the most morally satisfying to citizens steeped in Homeric values – was to muster

11 V. D. Hanson, *Warfare and Agriculture in Classical Greece* (Pisa: Giardini, 1983); L. Foxhall, 'Farming and fighting in early Greece', in J. Rich and G. Shipley (eds), *War and Society in the Greek World* (London: Routledge, 1993), 134–45; J. A. Thorne, 'Warfare and agriculture: the economic impact of devastation in classical Greece', *GRBS*, 42 (2001), 225–53.
12 Van Wees, *Greek Warfare*, 122, 126.

the levy and confront the enemy in open battle. Some states opted to do this repeatedly even if the invader kept winning: Chios fought and lost three battles in a row against an amphibious Athenian force in 412 BC (Thucydides 8.24.3). But their example shows why our sources tend to discourage this approach. The risk of defeat and crippling loss of life to the mobilised men was simply too high. Better options included ambushing the enemy army, staging surprise attacks and using cavalry to harry plunderers and protect the farms. Where possible, another defensive strategy was to block passes and entry points into the territory with either temporary or permanent garrisons. Despite the expense, Thebes and Sparta increasingly relied on this in their fourth-century wars; Athens invested heavily in a network of forts to protect its borders. Plato advocated such fortifications as a more comprehensive defence than city walls (*Laws* 760e–761a, 778e). Indeed, during the invasion of Xerxes in 480 BC, the resisting Greek states had already relied on such a forward defence of geographical choke points. The alliance tried successively to stop the Persians at the passes of Tempe and Thermopylae, the straits of Artemisium and Salamis and the Isthmus of Corinth.

An even more effective way to keep enemies away from the city walls was to build networks of alliances to bolster defences and deflect or absorb aggressors. The sprawling coalitions of the classical period complicate the straightforward picture of invasion and response. In their wars against Sparta and its client states, other city states would try to catch the Spartan levy as early in its campaign as possible, before its clients could join it (Thucydides 5.58.2; Xenophon, *Hellenica* 4.2.11–12). Battles against the whole Spartan alliance tended to go badly for Sparta's enemies. During the Peloponnesian War, the Athenians chose to avoid such engagements entirely. Yet the Spartans knew they could not defeat Athens without challenging its naval power and stripping away its imperial revenues (Thucydides 6.17.8). To risk an assault on or besiege a major city was beyond the means of even the largest of these coalitions, and impracticable if allies might relieve the besieged city. In short, coalition warfare and empire building led to a strategic stalemate in which direct action no longer offered a clear path to victory.

States responded to this stalemate with a variety of indirect approaches. The major wars of the classical period are full of attacks on minor exposed participants, regional campaigns fought for control over additional allies, proxy wars between adherents of either side, and targeted attacks on enemy sources of timber, grain, manpower, and funds. In a process known as *epiteichismos*, invaders established permanent forts in enemy territory to mount constant raids and encourage enslaved people to defect. Often the armies and fleets sent on missions like these were smaller, consisting of selected leisure-class citizens, paid volunteers and mercenaries; they were sometimes expected to remain in the field for years. Their operations were carefully co-ordinated. At the strategic level, states were maximally opportunistic, attacking only when and where they expected their enemies to be preoccupied and vulnerable. At the operational level, they deliberately timed their attacks to coincide with actions elsewhere, dividing their enemies' attentions and ideally drawing enemy troops away from places they were hoping to defend (Thucydides 3.13.3–7, 4.80.1; Xenophon, *Hellenica* 5.4.62). Hegemonic states with the means to support separate expeditionary forces would often be fighting across multiple theatres of war.

In each theatre, however, allied and expeditionary armies and fleets would mostly reduplicate the patterns of wars against single states. Local operations would follow a similar process of ravaging and attacks on targets of opportunity. Even if they contributed to hugely ambitious strategic plans, like Sparta's campaign to support the revolt of the overseas subjects of the Athenian Empire while maintaining a garrison in Athenian territory and pursuing an alliance with Persia, each individual fighting force followed the same general rules: first, to preserve itself, and second, to deal any blows to the enemy's resources and alliances that were most likely to land.

Conclusion

The wars of the city states were intense and devastating, but they can appear oddly clumsy to modern eyes. Tiny communities put their ill-prepared militias into the field at the slightest provocation to do the greatest amount of damage they could with the limited resources they had available. These bursts of violence left little room for what we might call 'strategy'. But the spread of hegemonic alliance systems, the introduction of the trireme, the slow spread of professionalisation and the development of siege techniques gradually changed the nature of warfare. It was no longer possible to overwhelm a serious rival without significant investment and careful planning. Meanwhile, tribute from subject allies and funding from Persia enabled states to embark on forms of military action that had previously been beyond their reach. Their strategy remained focused around the principles of self-preservation and opportunism, but these were now pursued at an unprecedented scale, spread over an unprecedented number of communities, with the final aim of a stable hegemony over all perceived rivals. These changes to warfare made large revenues the greatest military asset. This development, in turn, favoured new powers that could gather such revenues – including Macedon, which eventually outplayed all the city states at the game of hegemony, and ended the age of their military agency.

Due to its apparent simplicity and the limits of the evidence, the strategy of the city states has been explored surprisingly little by modern scholars. No existing study addresses the subject directly and comprehensively. Since the groundbreaking work of Hans Delbrück in the late nineteenth century, debates about Greek strategy have largely revolved around just one question: how exactly did Pericles mean to win the Peloponnesian War? This war, the quintessential conflict between 'the elephant and the whale', has fascinated historians and military theorists; Periclean strategy, as recorded by Thucydides, has sometimes been hailed as the birth of strategy itself. But its nature has divided his modern readers. Pericles urged the Athenians to abandon their farmland, avoid a land battle with the Spartans and look to their fleet to see them through the war. Was this a masterstroke of military thinking, ruined only by the Athenians' failure to stick to it after Pericles' death? Or was it a hopelessly passive and financially ruinous plan that could never have resulted in Athenian victory? The bibliography on this question is considerable, but the matter remains unsettled – partly due to an insufficient appreciation of the general features of Greek strategic behaviour. Meanwhile, strategy in other wars – or in the abstract – has received little attention.

Some recent work has made inroads. Victor Hanson has underlined the novelty of the strategy of Epameinondas of Thebes to dismantle the Spartan hegemony.[13] Adam Schwartz and Thomas Heine Nielsen have stressed the ubiquity and consequences of coalition warfare.[14] Paul Rahe has taken the 'grand strategy' of classical Sparta as the theme of a four-volume series of narrative history, published with Yale University Press (2016–2021). But these works are not intended as a broad study of the strategy of the city states. They also do not fully integrate recent scholarship on Greek warfare into their analysis – especially the new appreciation for the sheer brutality and opportunism of the Greek way of war. Much work remains to be done if we are to understand the unique context, institutions, principles and practice of strategy in classical Greece.

13 V. D. Hanson, 'Epameinondas and the Theban doctrine of preemptive war', in V. D. Hanson (ed.), *Makers of Ancient Strategy: From the Persian Wars to the Fall of Rome* (Princeton: Princeton University Press, 2010), 93–117.
14 Nielsen and Schwartz, 'Coalition warfare in the ancient Greek world'.

4

Philip II, Alexander III
and the Macedonian Empire

ANDREW FEAR

It is difficult to think of a father and son who have had a greater military impact than Philip II of Macedon and his son Alexander the Great. Philip, after inheriting a fringe state on the verge of complete annihilation in 359 BC, turned it into the undisputed hegemon of the Greek peninsula, while the ramifications of his son's conquest of the Persian Empire still shape our politics today.

Sources

No extended contemporary narratives of Philip's or Alexander's reign survive. Sadly, there are no Thracian, Illyrian or Persian accounts of these wars. For Philip, our longest narratives are sections in two world histories both written in the late first century BC during the reign of the Roman emperor Augustus: Diodorus Siculus' *Bibliotheca* and Pompeius Trogus' *Historia Philippica*. Neither work focused specifically on Philip. Moreover, Trogus survives only as a later abridgement made by Justin, whose *floruit* could range anywhere between the second and fourth centuries AD. These works also contain short narratives of Alexander's reign. A series of speeches by Philip's supporters (Isocrates) and detractors (Demosthenes) at Athens provide contemporary information, but reveal more of Athenian politics than of the thinking of the king.

Many of Alexander's marshals wrote memoirs, but none have survived. We have two extended narratives. Arrian's *Anabasis*, written in the second century AD, is normally regarded as the most reliable. Himself a field commander, Arrian explicitly states that he has drawn on the memoirs of Ptolemy, one of Alexander's senior generals, but he rarely acknowledges his source directly. There is also Quintus Curtius' *History of Alexander the Great*. Its first two books have been lost and what survives begins just before the Battle of Issus. There are also lacunae in the rest of the work. Quintus' *floruit* is unclear. It is probably the mid-first century A D, but could be as late as the third century. Quintus, as did Diodorus Siculus, draws on Cleitarchus' (now lost) account of Alexander written in the third century B C. This was a moralising text, very popular, though not regarded as very reliable, in antiquity. In addition, the Greek polymath Plutarch wrote a biography and two short essays on Alexander in the late first century A D. Plutarch regarded Alexander as a Greek culture hero and his biography focuses on Alexander the man rather than Alexander the general.

Actors

Traditionally Macedonian kings had been 'firsts among equals', but the crisis that brought Philip II to power greatly strengthened the hand of the king. Both Philip and his son were very much their own men and their plans were their own. For Philip, Parmenion was the only general that he ever found (Plutarch, *Sayings* 177 c2), and his worth seems to have been in obeying orders rather than formulating plans. Our sources often portray Alexander as overriding his marshals' advice to be more cautious. In Arrian this is particularly true of Parmenion (see especially Arrian, *Anabasis* 2.25; 3.10) whom Alexander eventually executed (on very poor grounds) for treason. It is possible that Arrian contrived these clashes *post eventum* to explain Parmenion's execution. Alexander's close friend Hephaestion appears to have had no influence on Alexander's planning, save that he was promoted beyond his abilities. His mother Olympias wished to influence her son, but was politely ignored. Philip employed Aristotle as a tutor for Alexander in his youth. The philosopher wrote two treatises for his pupil, *On Kingship* and *On Colonies*, which sadly have not survived. He also presented him with a specially annotated copy of the *Iliad* which Alexander treasured. We have no clues as to the nature of the annotations. While the influence of Aristotle on Alexander was stressed in the ancient and medieval periods to make him an ideal 'philosopher-king', modern scholarship has tended to dismiss it. Even ancient sources underline the pupil's independence from his teacher, noting that while Aristotle advised Alexander 'to treat the Greeks as their leader, but all other races as their master', Alexander dismissed this notion in favour of simple meritocracy (Strabo 1.4.9; Plutarch, *De Alex. fort.*, 6).

Opponents

Philip faced three main opponents. The Greek city states to the south, the Illyrians to the north and west, and the Thracians to the north and east. All could be regarded as 'traditional' enemies of Macedon. Low-level and occasionally intensive warfare had occurred with all of them for centuries. Each of these groups had a cultural, but not a political, unity. Historic rivalries between Greek states continued even after their subjugation by Philip. Agis of Sparta failed to gain support from Athens in his uprising against Macedonian domination of Greece in 331 BC. Panhellenism, the doctrine that the Greeks should unite to fight a war of revenge against Persia, was adopted, sincerely or otherwise, by Philip and Alexander, making unity a difficult rallying call for their opponents. Greek armies were based on armoured infantrymen, 'hoplites', whose primary weapon was an eight-foot-long thrusting spear. Apart from Sparta, a spent force by this time, and certain select groups, such as the Theban Sacred Band, these troops were semi-trained militias, not professionals. Neither cavalry nor ranged weapons were of importance. The Thracians and Illyrians were also infantry-based armies, but, particularly the Thracians, more lightly armed and relying more on javelins given the mountainous terrain of their homelands.

Alexander's main opponent was the Persian Empire. This could be regarded as the 'traditional' antagonist of Greece for around 200 years or so. The empire possessed a small imperial standing army and individual provinces (satrapies) also had small armies of their own. The bulk of Persian forces, however, were raw levies. Persian troops were in general more lightly armed than those of Alexander, but also contained substantial numbers of Greek hoplite mercenaries. Overall, the cavalry arm was better than the infantry. While this contained some very heavily armoured elements, the bulk was again lighter than its Macedonian adversaries. Missile weapons do not seem to have played an important role. Archery would have played a larger part in India, but the monsoon season meant that in Alexander's major battle against Porus it was ineffective. Indian elephants, however, posed a significant threat to Alexander and may well have been the reason his army refused to march further into the subcontinent. His battle against Porus at the Hydaspes cost him more casualties than any of those fought against the Persians. Alexander's other main opponents were the Bactrians and Scythians, whose armies were composed of swarms of skirmishing light cavalrymen armed with powerful composite bows. The Bactrians, Scythians and Indians had no history of warfare against Macedon or Greece. They were enemies or subjects that Alexander inherited when he inherited the Persian Empire.

Means

Philip

Philip's means included open bribery (Diodorus Siculus 16.8; Plutarch, *Sayings* 178 b14), diplomacy, polygamous marriages for the purpose of strengthening alliances, and the use and the threat of the use of force. His armies were overwhelmingly composed of volunteers from Macedonia. According to Diodorus Siculus (17.17), Alexander took 12,000 Macedonian phalangites to Asia Minor, leaving a further 12,000 behind. His cavalry included 1,800 Macedonians and he left 1,500 behind. At his death, therefore, Philip's army had a core of 24,000 phalangites and 3,300 cavalry, supplemented by light troops from Upper Macedonia and Thrace.

Philip's stay at Thebes in his teens as a hostage for the good behaviour of his brother, King Alexander II, provided the intellectual stimulus for his reforms. The Theban general Epameinondas had made important innovations to traditional hoplite tactics by deepening the depth of the troops he deployed and 'refusing' parts of his line. These had allowed him to inflict a crushing defeat on the Spartans at Leuctra in 371 BC. Philip will have learnt of the Athenian general Iphicrates' pioneering changes to traditional hoplite equipment, introducing lighter armour and longer spears, even though these had little positive effect on Athenian fortunes. Philip will also have witnessed at first hand the training of the Theban 'Sacred Band', a professional, elite hoplite force (Justinus, *Epit* 7.5.1).

But Philip in turn revolutionised the Greek way of war. Macedon had always been plagued by centrifugal tendencies; the new army was designed to unite the country. He assigned a key role to the cavalry, appropriate to the wide plains of 'horse-loving' Macedon, with its mounted aristocracy. The heavy cavalry was the king's *Companion* cavalry, marking out those who served as men honoured by the king. However, at least part, maybe all, of the infantry phalanx were styled *pezetairoi*, 'foot companions', showing the king's solidarity with his poorer subjects too. One group within the phalanx were designated the *asthetairoi*. Again 'companion' (*etairos*) features in this compound, which may have marked out a group specially selected from Upper Macedon and given a place of honour in the line. This would have helped seal a link between Philip and the more separatist regions of his kingdom. In the same way, the young sons of Macedonian nobles and of regional kings were to serve in the army as the king's 'pages'. This was a mark of honour and no doubt was often received as such, but it also created a useful group of hostages for their fathers' good behaviour.

Prior to Philip's reign, cavalry had played a nugatory role in Greek warfare, simply skirmishing on the fringes of battle and riding down the vanquished when the opportunity arose. Battles were won by hoplites, not horsemen. Under Philip, the cavalry rose to become the queen of battle. Armed with a long lance, the *xyston*, and riding in a wedge-shaped formation, Philip's new cavalry were not skirmishers, but rather the battle-winning element of his army designed to break through the enemy's line and destroy his cohesion. This radical shift in emphasis was something for which Philip's opponents were completely unprepared, and they were equally wrong-footed by the increase in the tempo of warfare that it brought about.

Philip did not, however, merely change the role of his cavalry. An early pioneer of combined-arms warfare, he also made major innovations to his infantry: integrating the two arms to bring about effects that neither could achieve by itself. The close formation of the traditional hoplite phalanx was retained, but given a new depth, perhaps initially ten, but later sixteen, men as opposed to the previously usual eight ranks. Thus weight was added to the phalanx's shock on impact and its ability to intimidate increased. The phalangites were equipped with lighter armour than had been customary: linen rather than bronze. Their helmets were open-faced, not enclosed, and their shields much smaller than previous ones. A new spear, the *sarissa*, became their standard arm. At around eighteen feet in length, it was more than twice the length of the old *dory* of the hoplite. As the tip was counterweighted at the rear, a good two-thirds could be held to the front so that some five ranks of spear points could project outwards from its front line.[1] In this way Philip replaced the notion of defence at the point of combat with an ability to defend oneself at a distance. In old-style hoplite battles the two opposing lines closed with one another; Philip's phalanx was designed to keep its adversaries at a distance. The *sarissa* was not merely for defence; it was a striking weapon, and its blows generally were fatal due to its long, narrow blade and the two-handed, underarm way it was wielded: 'neither shield nor breastplate could resist the force of the *sarissa*' (Plutarch, *Aem.* 20). The

---

1 See A.-H. Jomini, *The Art of War*, tr. G. H. Mendell and W. P. Craighill, (Philadelphia: J. B. Lippincourt & Co, 1862) 44.

phalanx exuded menace and was designed to pin the enemy while the heavy cavalry probed for a fatal weak spot in their adversaries' line or flank.

The main danger in this new system was that the phalanx and cavalry would become separated, leaving a gap between them which could be exploited by an opponent. Philip dealt with this by creating a new, separate type of troops, the 'hypaspists'. The term 'hypaspist' means 'under a shield', more specifically under a large shield like that worn by hoplites (the *aspis*). While some have seen the hypaspists as armed like traditional hoplites, this seems impossible given their role of linking the cavalry and phalanx, which required them to be swift-moving. It is more likely, therefore, that they wore little or no armour and relied on their shields for protection. The army's wider flanks and front were secured by skirmishing light infantry recruited from the mountainous areas of Upper Macedonia.

Philip's command system was improved by the provision of an officer per file, with orders communicated effectively, aided by the open helmets, which maximised the troops' ability to receive both oral and signalled orders. In the words of one Greek general, Charidemus, 'Looking for their commander's nod, they learn to follow their standards and keep their ranks. Everyone hears what is commanded. The troops know as well as their officers how to stand fast, turn a flank, charge forward in a wedge, or change their formation' (Quintus Curtius 3.2.13–14). This was a highly trained, professional army. Professional armies are expensive: thus Philip's keen interest in acquiring the gold and silver mines of Thrace and arguably in the Persian Empire at the end of his reign.

Speed was the hallmark of the new army, which raised the tempo at which battles were fought and manoeuvres enacted. The *sarissa* was formed of two parts and so could be dismantled for ease of carrying.[2] The troops had to carry their own equipment. Philip enforced a ban on carts (Frontinus, *Stratagems* 4.1.6). These were traditionally pulled by oxen and thus travelled more slowly than the troops they accompanied. A ban was also placed on the cloud of camp followers which often accompanied armies and again slowed them down (Athenaeus, *Deipnosophistae* 557b). Philip also explored the potential of engines of war and catapults, recruiting engineers who would build what was necessary at the point of demand rather than carrying siege engines along with the army. The lighter army made longer marches a regular possibility, thus increasing its operational range. The Macedonian army could not merely outmanoeuvre, but also outmarch, its enemies. Philip's, and indeed Alexander's, opponents were in

---

2 It also meant far more timber was available for its manufacture.

the main poorly trained amateur levies who in any circumstances would have found it difficult to match their opponents' evolutions on the battlefield.

Alexander

Unlike his father, Alexander made little use of diplomacy, ostentatiously rejecting peace overtures from Darius in favour of war (Arrian, *Anabasis* 2.14, 2.25). He also in the main rejected marriage as a diplomatic tool. His marriage to the Bactrian princess Roxanne was touted as a love affair in antiquity, but may have been a way of resolving the otherwise seemingly insoluble difficulties of his Afghan campaign (Quintus Curtius 8.4). His marriage to the Persian princesses Stateira and Parysatis at Susa, where he also compelled eighty of his marshals to take Persian brides, does seem to have been an attempt to create a unified ruling class for his new empire (Arrian, *Anabasis* 7.4). Such actions, however, had not been a constant strand of his policy as they had been for his father. Whether they heralded a potential change in attitude for the future cannot be known.

On his expedition Alexander took with him 12,000 Macedonian infantry; some 7,000 Greek 'allies', whom he quickly used as garrison troops; 5,000 Greek mercenaries; and 8,000 light troops from Illyria and Thrace. Apart from his Macedonian cavalry, he took 1,800 Thessalians, 600 other Greeks and 900 light cavalrymen from the north. His expedition thus initially numbered around 38,000 (Diodorus Siculus 17.17). Numbers given for his opponents are entirely impressionistic: our sources had no access to reliable figures. Arrian suggests 40,000 Persians at Granicus, 600,000 at Issus and 1,040,200 (and fifteen elephants) at Gaugamela! The best we can say is that Alexander was heavily outnumbered. On the other hand, it appears that he was only marginally outnumbered when he faced Porus at the Hydaspes in India. As the campaign developed, as well as receiving reinforcements from Macedonia, Alexander was happy to recruit more and more Asians to join his army. Many were trained to fight in Macedonian style, and their inclusion in substantial numbers, as both infantry and cavalry, led to a serious mutiny by his Macedonian troops at Opis towards the end of his reign (Arrian, *Anabasis* 7.8–11).

Causes and Objectives of War

Philip

Before Philip II's reign, Macedonia, which straddled the Greek and Illyrian worlds, had had a chequered history. Although it had made some gains in the fifth and early fourth centuries, these were continually put in jeopardy by a combination of poor military performance and internal political instability. Philip's extraordinary achievement was to resolve and reverse both these problems. On the death of his elder brother Perdiccas III, Philip originally became the regent for Perdiccas' infant son but seized the throne for himself in 359 BC when his country was on the verge of disintegration. Perdiccas' ill-starred attack on Illyria had brought about his own death, the destruction of his army and an Illyrian counterinvasion. Nor were these the only dangers: a pretender backed by Athens, Argaeus, had landed in the south of the country; a further pretender, Pausanias, supported by the Thracians, had invaded from the east; and an attack from the north by the Paeonians seemed inevitable.

Philip took his country from the verge of annihilation to a position of local strength within a year of coming to power. The rest of his reign was to see an expansion of that power so that Macedonia, once regarded as a fringe part of the Greek world, if a member of it at all, became its political centre. Philip's situation was very different to that of his son. Alexander was faced with a single adversary in his wars, while Philip acted in a more complex multi-polar world with many more variables.

Philip's commitment to the ideology of Panhellenism has roused debate since antiquity. For Polybius (3.6.12–13) it was nothing more than a fig leaf to cover aggrandisement; for Cicero, a genuine wish to avenge sacrilege (Cicero, *Rep.* 3.15). Politically, the cause was useful in Greece. Its espousal strengthened Macedon's shaky Greek credentials and cast his opponents in Athens as Medisers, thus weakening any 'Hellenic' reasons why they advanced to oppose Philip. It also embarrassed Thebes, a town of much more concern to him than Athens, as it had Medised in the Persian wars. While not unaware of the power of grand gestures – for example, erecting statues of himself and his family at Olympia, a major Panhellenic site – it seems likely that Philip's interest in Panhellenism was more pragmatic than ideological.

What, for Philip, was the key matter? Many of his opponents saw him as seeking empire and domination from the first. For Trogus, Philip 'looked down from a watchtower [on the Greek World] to lay snares for their freedom' (Justinus, *Epit.*, 8.1.3). All we know of Philip comes from southern Greek sources. Their world, however, was peripheral to Macedon, which had other equally, if not more, important, neighbours. Philip's grand strategy, while not eschewing conquest, was not guided by a wish to conquer for conquest's sake, but rather informed at root by a desire to secure the safety of his homeland. The crisis of 359 made a deep impression on him and formed the resolution that it should never be allowed to recur. Taking due cognisance of this, we can see that throughout his rule Philip acted to protect the integrity of Macedonia. His approach was to expand out from the core of his kingdom on all sides, leaving no avenue to chance. As such his interests lay to the north and east as much as to the south and west, if not more so, and his conquests spread like concentric ripples in a pond, not a tidal wave running in one direction.

Alexander

On Philip's death, in which he may have had a hand, Alexander inherited a situation not unlike that which had confronted his father, as Philip's vassals both north and south began to rebel. Like Philip, Alexander was determined not to fight a war on several fronts. His initial concern was the north, not the south which posed no threat to Macedonia's borders and where Macedonian troops were installed as garrisons.

Greece secured, Alexander left Europe, never to return. We have no explicit statement of his intentions, but his symbolic casting of a spear into Asian soil when landing at Troy (itself a symbolic act) is clear enough. This was to be a campaign of conquest: a war as epic in scope as that once fought at Ilium. It can broadly be divided into five stages: the conquest of Asia Minor, the securing of the rest of the western Middle East and Egypt, the push into Persia proper, the advance into Bactria and actions in northern India. It is possible that the first three of these were motivated by a sincere belief in Panhellenism. His despatch of 300 Persian panoplies to be hung on the walls of the Acropolis at Athens after the victory at the Granicus river (Arrian, *Anabasis* 1.16) and visits to Panhellenic shrines such as that at Didyma, whose exhausted spring was said to flow again after his visit (Strabo 17.1.43), suggest that this was the case. However, it is harder to see Panhellenism as a motive for Alexander's later campaigns. While these have been seen as facets of a grand strategy and, as Plutarch suggests, inspired by a wish to spread Hellenism across the world (Plutarch, *De Alex. fort.*, 4–5), equally they could be the product of a mind that valued conquest itself and *la gloire* above the prizes of conquest.[3] If so, Alexander followed where arms led him, rather than carrying his arms to achieve a predetermined goal. Certainly, on at least two occasions only sickness and mutiny prevented him pushing out further into areas where no immediate objective can be discerned, and there are other actions which also do not seem to fit any greater whole. It also seems

---

3 Among those arguing for an overall strategy is J. F. C. Fuller, *The Generalship of Alexander the Great* (London: Eyre & Spottiswoode, 1958).

clear that at the time of his death Alexander was already planning further campaigns rather than simply consolidating what he held. According to our sources, these included an invasion of Arabia and an advance along the north African coast to the Pillars of Hercules (the Straits of Gibraltar), then looping back through Iberia and Italy to Greece (Arrian, *Anabasis* 7.1; Diodorus Siculus 18.4). The former, for which preparations were under way at Alexander's death, perhaps aimed to unite his eastern possessions via the Arabian Sea and the Persian Gulf, though a wish to be seen to succeed in the desert after the Gedrosian debacle may be the real reason. The latter is more nebulous and perhaps no more than a post-mortem fabrication of our sources or of politicians of the time. Though having a *casus belli* in Carthage's support for Tyre (Alexander was always one to bear a grudge), it speaks of a simple desire to conquer without thought to the strategic consequences. There is also the symmetry of reaching the utmost west, as India had been the utmost east – the mark of a true world conqueror.

The Application of Strategy

While the tactical brilliance in the field of both Philip and Alexander cannot be disputed, as Pompeius Trogus pointed out, the two had very different ways of waging war (*vincendi ratio*). Trogus underlines *sollertia* or 'cunning', a word often applied to Odysseus, the wiliest and most disreputable of Greek heroes, as one of Philip's defining characteristics and one which set him apart from his son: 'He [Philip] rejoiced in tricking his enemies, the other [Alexander] in openly putting them to flight' (Justinus, *Epit.*, 9.8). According to Diodorus Siculus, Philip took more pride in his diplomatic triumphs than in his physical prowess in battle (Diodorus Siculus 16.95). In this, as in many other ways, Philip would have agreed that 'the way of war is a way of deception'.[4]

Philip

Philip handled the crisis that he had inherited with characteristic rapidity. The key to his strategy was to protect the Macedonian heartland while avoiding a war fought on several fronts. Here he relied on bribery and diplomacy as much as on force. While there was little choice in this matter, given that Macedon's army had been left in tatters after the Illyrian debacle, Philip's subsequent combination of diplomacy and force shows an 'Odyssean' modus

---

4 Sunzi, *The Art of War*, Chapter 1, 'Making of plans'.

operandi. When he thought it necessary, Philip threatened to use violence and was ready to make good those threats, but to him force was a tool of last resort. In essence the king was a diplomatist who used force, rather than a soldier who used diplomacy.

As for Sunzi, for Philip a key factor in generalship was to prevent hostile alliances from forming. In the initial crisis, bribery secured the death of Pausanias at the hands of his erstwhile Thracian allies, and a diplomatic marriage, another key tool in Philip's armoury, saw the retreat of the Illyrians to their own land. The Paeonians saw their chances for plunder receding and, after duly receiving 'gifts' from Philip, declined to attack. This left Argaeus and his Athenian supporters as the sole force in the field. The main concern of Athens was not Macedon per se, but Amphipolis, which lay on the vital trade route to the Black Sea. In it Philip saw an opportunity to drive a wedge between the pretender and his backers. He withdrew the garrison established there by his brother, leaving it as a 'free city'. This was enough to weaken Athenian support for Argaeus and their troops remained on the coast at Methone when Argaeus marched inland. Finding no local support, Argaeus was forced to withdraw. Philip ambushed his retreating rival, securing a decisive victory. The Athenians were allowed to retire unmolested (with Philip giving them a pledge that he had no interest in Amphipolis), but he showed no pardon for Argaeus and his Macedonian sympathisers. Here we see two constant aspects of Philip's approach to politics: a desire to avoid unnecessary antagonisms combined with ruthlessness towards those he considered enemies that could be safely annihilated.

Casting aside past promises, Philip then attacked Paeonia in the winter of 359/358 following the death of its king. This opportunist incursion demonstrates Philip's use of speed and surprise (winter campaigns were a great rarity). He effectively annexed Paeonia, securing Macedonia's northern boundaries. Again combining surprise and speed, Philip next crossed into Illyria without resistance and gave battle on ground of his own choosing, the Lyncus Plain. Philip's new heavy cavalry easily drove their Illyrian opponents from the field. The Illyrian infantry formed a protective rectangle to face them down, but it was broken by Philip's infantry and then destroyed by the cavalry.

Philip secured Thessaly by a diplomatic marriage to Philinna of Larissa, Pherae's main rival. He then moved against Amphipolis, again breaking previous promises. A Macedonian Amphipolis would not only safeguard the kingdom's eastern frontiers, but also open the possibility of expansion into valuable mining areas and allow a profitable entrance into the world of trade by sea. Philip moved when his target was least able to resist. Athens was embroiled in the beginning of the 'Social War' with her allies and his attack was timed to ensure that when news reached Athens, the Etesian winds would be blowing and hinder the despatch of any maritime support. Amphipolis's walls, often regarded as impregnable, fell to Philip's siege engines. Technically Philip claimed to have 'liberated' the town, installing puppet rulers. This conquest by proxy was a move designed to assuage the towns of Chalcidice and dissuade them from forming a dangerous alliance with Athens.

Having secured Amphipolis, Philip then turned his attention to Pydna on the Thermaic Gulf. Athens had used nearby Methone as a beachhead into Macedon in 359. The threat of such a repeat attack was clear, especially after Philip's actions at Amphipolis. But by now the Social War was raging and, with the defection of Byzantium, Athens was in danger of losing her route to the Black Sea. Exploiting this concern, Philip promised to restore Amphipolis to Athens, were he given a free hand at Pydna. The Athenians agreed, which, given Philip's past record, seems quite astounding. Trogus notes that Philip was 'eloquent and treacherous', and that his oratory was exceptional, 'full of sharpness and cunning' (Justinus, *Epit.* 9.8). For Athens the temptation, and perhaps her need, was too great. Pydna was abandoned to Philip. It fell by treachery. On its capture, the Macedonian king promptly reneged on his pledge and retained Amphipolis. Once again, Philip took care to divide the Chalcideans from Athens. The following year, after capturing Potidaea, occupied at the time by an Athenian garrison, he handed it over to Olynthus, the leading city of the Chalcidean League. Athens, still embroiled in the Social War, was in no position to help her outpost. His gift both placated the Chalcidean League and soured relations between it and Athens. The Athenian garrison was given free passage home. Its slaughter would have served no purpose and its treatment helped preserve the image of Philip as a 'reasonable' man.

Having secured the west, Philip returned to the east, responding to a call for help from Crenides under attack from Thracian tribes. After driving the Thracians back, Crenides was refounded as Philippi, without any pretence of granting it independence. Even more than Amphipolis, his new town gave Philip access to mineral resources, allowing the funding of Macedonia's professional army to be placed on a secure footing.

Philip now directed his attention once more to the west. Central Greece was embroiled in a 'sacred war' concerning Delphi, in which both Athens and Phocis allied with Macedonia's old rival Pherae, creating a group that could potentially invade the kingdom. In 355 Philip moved to besiege Methone on hearing that its inhabitants had offered it as a 'base for his enemies' – presumably the Athenians (Diodorus Siculus 16.34). Philip had no intention of allowing the town to be an enemy beachhead a second time. His actions were again timed to surprise, but this time Athens did come to her ally's aid. However, another of Philip's traits was persistence in what he thought essential. After a siege of some seven months, Methone surrendered. Philip's use of force, when it came, was characteristically harsh, intended to intimidate others by demonstrating the consequences of non-compliance. Methone's inhabitants were left only with the clothes they stood up in and their city was razed to the ground. Methone's destruction secured Macedon from incursions by sea.

Soon after, Philip was asked to intervene in Thessaly, a welcome invitation that usefully allowed him to pose as a saviour, not an aggressor. His attack secured Pagasae, Thessaly's only useful port. This further reduced Athens's capacity for power projection while increasing Philip's, by both land and sea. Leaving behind a set of bickering states who posed him no threat, Philip left this peripheral part of his world to campaign in Thrace. He was to return in 353 when a Pheran–Phocian alliance threatened to bring the Sacred War to an unwelcome conclusion and leave him with a powerful and hostile southern neighbour. Once more, formally Philip moved at the request of his Thessalian allies. Initial success was followed by disaster when his new opponent, Onomarchus of Phocis, defeated him twice in battle, pushing him out of Thessaly altogether with his army's morale destroyed (Diodorus Siculus 16.35). Philip's defeat was serious enough for Onomarchus to believe it to have been conclusive and to return to fighting against his old enemies further south. This proved a fatal error. By the early spring of 352, to all sides' surprise, Philip was once more in Thessaly. Onomarchus, hurrying from the south, was outmanoeuvred and driven into the sea to die at the Battle of the Crocus Field. His traditional hoplite army proved no match for Philip's phalanx and cavalry. Unlike Onomarchus, Philip was quick to follow up his victory. His prime concern was to dominate Thessaly, thus ensuring a safe south-west land frontier for Macedonia. He obtained for himself for life formal political leadership of Thessaly. In the name of the Thessalian League, not his own, he punished some opponents harshly, but also took careful measures of reconciliation. Philip married Philinna, the niece of Jason of Pherae, making a link to the family who could have proved the most dangerous opponents to the new Thessalian order.

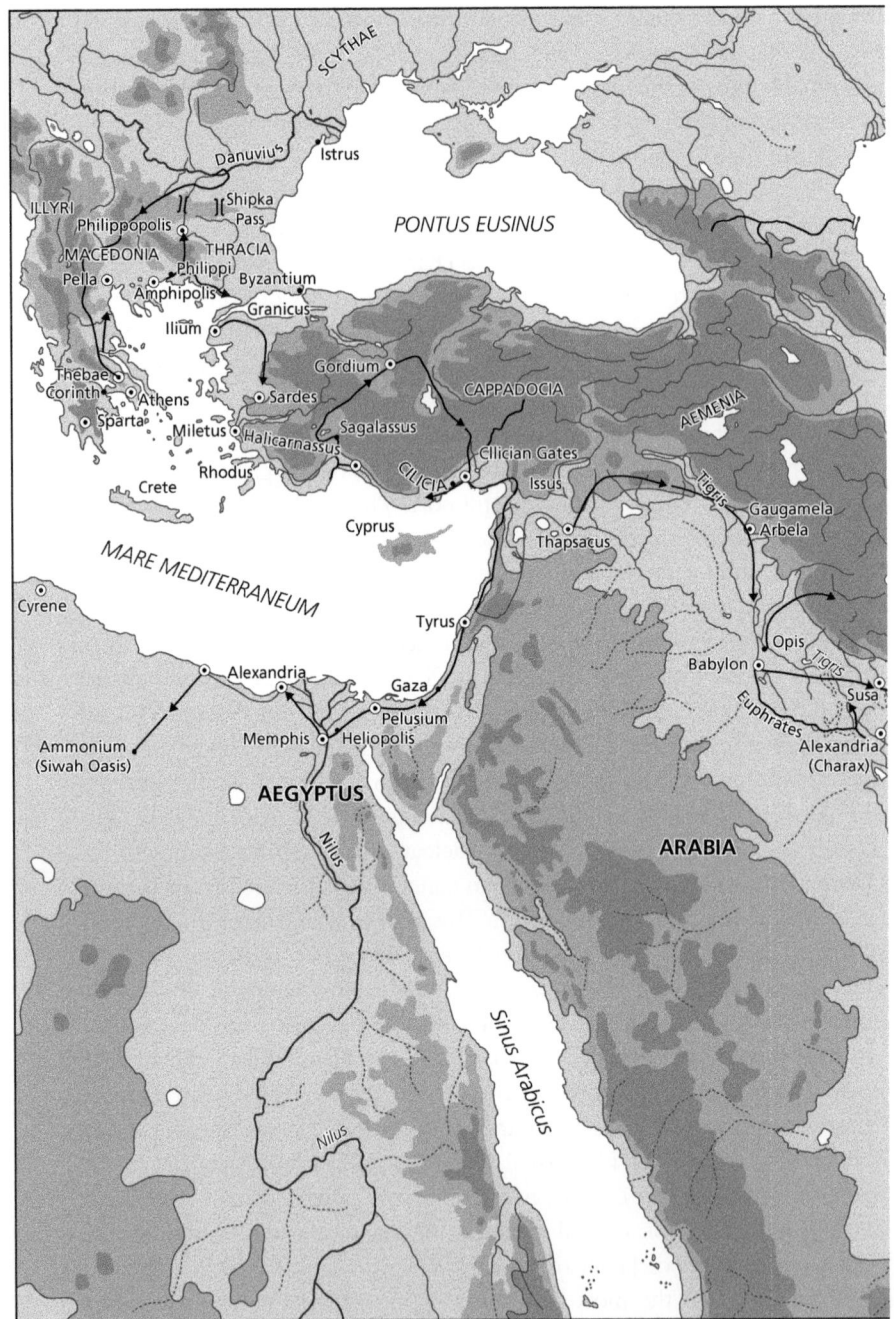

Map 4.1 Strategies of Philip II and Alexander III and the Macedonian Empire. Redrawn based on a map in A. B. Bosworth, *Conquest and Empire: The Reign of Alexander the Great* (Cambridge: Cambridge University Press, 1988), 2.

MARE CASPIUM

ARAL
SEA

MASSAGETAE

Iaxartes

Oxus

Oxus

Alexandria
Eschate
○ Cyropolis
SOGDIANA
● Rock of Chorianes

Rock of
Sogdiana

BACTRIA

Alexandria
in Margiana
(Merv) ○

○ Susia

Bactra/
Zariaspa

Khawak Pass

Massaga

MEDIA

Rhagae ○
Caspian Gates
Ecbatane ○

○ Hecatompylus

Alexandria in Aria
(Herat) ○

Alexandria
in Caucaso

○ Aornus

○ Taxila

Bucephala

Nicaea

Prophthasia ○

Alexandria
in Arachosia
(Kandahar)

Hyphasis

Malli town

Alexandria in India

Persian
Gates ○ Pasargadae
Persepolis ○
PERSIS

Alexandria
in Carmania
CARMANIA

Indus

Kingdom of
Musicanus

Sinus Persicus

GEDROSIA
Alexandria
Rhambacia

Kingdom of
Sambus
Patala

MARE ERYTHRAEUM

—— Route of Alexander (335–323 B.C.)	▓ Land over 1,000 metres
·········· Route of Craterus (325 B.C)	▓ Land over 500–1000 metres
- - - Voyage of Nearchus	░ Land under 500 metres

0   300   600   900 km

Map 4.1 (Cont.)

Philip then marched to Thermopylae on the southern borders of Thessaly, but immediately retired, realising that the time was not right, or perhaps merely wishing to make a warning demonstration in force that he was back and as strong as ever (Diodorus Siculus 16.38). His main attention turned once more to the East. Here he wished to weaken an emerging regional strong-man, Cersobleptes, in eastern Thrace, and also deal with the Greek towns of Chalcidice which had foolishly decided to toy with an alliance with Athens after Philip's previous defeat by Onomarchus. Such a dalliance once again opened up the possibility of an enemy invasion of the Macedonian heartland or an attack on Amphipolis.

Philip had no intention of fighting an open battle against a massed army from Chalcidice. Instead, therefore, of making a direct push into the penin-sula towards its main city, Olynthus, he marched across its head to the east, and there turned south to invade Chalcidice, where its smaller towns were located. Philip began with terror tactics, destroying Stageira entirely. This produced the results the king desired: the other towns of Chalcidice soon surrendered. Olynthus, isolated and alone, held out but fell. Like Stageia and Methone, it too was razed to the ground. Philip characteristically then made alliances with local Chalcideans whom he trusted, killing potential leaders of rebellions. The subjugation of Chalcidice removed the last threat of invasion to the Macedon homeland. The dying embers of Sacred War Thebes and Phocis for control of Delphi (356–346 BC) then gave Philip control of the pass at Thermopylae. Philip could now march south at any time. Athens sought peace; Philip was happy to oblige.

The ensuing Peace of Philocrates and its aftermath again show Philip's Macedo-centric view of the world. The chief formal concession to the king was Amphipolis, and after concluding peace, Philip's interests were once more focused on the north, not the south: first in Illyria and Thessaly and then, and more forcefully, in Thrace. Political unity in Thrace was now his greatest danger. Also, Thrace had much more to offer than southern Greece: it possessed greater mineral resources and better farmland, and gave not only direct access to the Black Sea, but also potential control over the routes to that sea. Moreover, such control would render Athens, with its dependency on Black Sea grain, his de facto vassal.

Philip's initial attacks proved a great success. The power of the Thracian kings was broken, and Philip's armies went on to reach the Black Sea and dominate its coast as far north as Odessus (Varna). Philip both freed Odessus from occupation by the Getae, and also allied himself with them by marrying a Getic princess. Large areas from which Athens had traditionally drawn grain were now under Philip's influence, while his defeat of the Thracians and alliance with the Getae created a shield for his lands in the north and east. Only the Propontis (the Sea of Marmora) was beyond his control.

Athens, however, was now roused and a series of skirmishes on the Thracian Chersonese (the Gallipoli peninsula) led to Philip besieging his erstwhile local ally, Perinthos, which in turn gained support from both Athens and, significantly, Persia. Despite heavy fighting, Philip was unable to take the town. Switching targets, he launched a swift attack on Byzantium, but this too failed, as once more both Athens and Persia moved to aid his adversary. Philip's fleet was now trapped in the Black Sea. Philip withdrew his land armies from the siege of Byzantium and, by carefully spreading false information, succeeded in extracting his fleet without a fight. These setbacks were but a sideshow in Philip's plans; he now launched a major expedition across the Danube delta to defeat the Scythian king Atheas. Thrace and the Black Sea had been the primary aims of his campaign, and there success was total.

The acrimony caused by Philip's expedition made war in the south a near certainty. Philip's opponents were confident of blocking his advance after Thebes captured Nicaea, which commanded the pass at Thermopylae. Philip's riposte was characteristically one of speed and surprise. Instead of attempting to force Thermopylae, he moved his army through the much more difficult Callidromos Pass, a move that might have been impossible for hoplites but was achievable by his lighter phalangites. Even then, Philip's first thoughts were for diplomacy, not open war. However, when this failed, he defeated the combined armies of Athens and Thebes with a display of tactical brilliance at Chaeronea in August 338. The universal judgement of antiquity was that this battle ended the freedom of Greece (see, for example, Orosius 3.13). Philip, however, ruled indirectly, creating a body, normally known as the 'League of Corinth', as his instrument of power. Thus the defeated city states became 'allies' rather than his direct subjects.

Philip's final move was to launch a campaign against Persia in the name of Panhellenism. But in fact Greece may again have been peripheral to the king's main concerns. Persia had become demonstrably hostile to Philip and menaced his gains in Thrace. Philip, as ever, combined diplomacy with force, attempting in 337 to engineer a marriage link with Pixodarus of Caria, an endeavour ruined by his now estranged son Alexander (Plutarch, *Vit. Alex.* 10). The philhellenic Carians could provide a partial buffer and second front with the rest of the Persian Empire, weakening any potential Persian defence of Asia Minor further north. In the same year the Great King Artaxerxes III died, precipitating a political crisis in the empire. Asia Minor was rich and adjacent to Philip's lands in Thrace. Philip saw his opportunity and struck, invading Asia Minor in 336 with an army of 10,000 men under his trusted associate Parmenion. The initial success of the attack was striking, with the army reaching and capturing Ephesus. But the frustrated Pixodarus was now on Persia's side, and a Persian counterattack, with no distractions to delay it, pushed the Macedonians back to the Troad. What Philip would have done next is unknown as he was assassinated in the same year.

While never shy of using force, for Philip war was the continuation of policy by other means. His weapon of choice was always diplomacy, not any 'decisive battle'. A keen observer of the political situation, he oriented his observations to fit Macedonia's circumstances, made his political and military decisions accordingly, and then acted swiftly on those decisions. Correct timing, whether a consideration of the seasons or of the political situation, was his constant concern. Philip was an opportunist, but his opportunism was always informed by his overall aims. This deep engagement with politics in search of furthering his policies led to his opponent Demosthenes coining the word 'Philiping' as an alternative for 'fiddling' (*philopragmosyne*, a pun on *polypragmosyne*: Demosthenes, *Phil*. I, 14). Speed of decision making, 'agility' in Boyd's terms, as much as speed on the field of battle was a vital part of Philip's success, just as the confusion and sense of menace which unpredictable actions and varying speed would cause in the minds of enemies. This was precisely Philip's strength.

Alexander

Alexander was Achilles to Philip's Odysseus. The two were alike, however, in valuing speed. Alexander moved first against the rebel Thracians and then the Getae, thus securing his father's recent gains. A punitive expedition against the Illyrians to the west followed. While in Illyria, news reached him of an uprising among the southern Greeks led by Thebes. Alexander was back in the key border state of Thessaly within a week, circumventing Mount Ossa in a way which would have been impossible for hoplite troops. A week later, he was before the gates of Thebes, having passed through the pass at Thermopylae before the Thebans had prepared its defence. Despite being outmanoeuvred, Thebes still rejected Alexander's terms for surrender. After taking the town, Alexander destroyed it completely, executing its male inhabitants and enslaving the remnant. Like his father, Alexander was determined to show that non-complicity with his wishes carried a high price. He also followed his father's lead by having these acts carried out not in his name, but in that of the League of Corinth.

Alexander's next move was to seize Asia Minor. The initial success of Parmenion's expedition and the previous exploits of Agesilaus of Sparta and Xenophon's 10,000 would have made this seem an eminently possible proposition. The king aimed to ensure a firm line of supply, guard his flanks and liberate the Greek cities of Asia Minor in the name of Panhellenism. He was also eager to engage the Persian army, as, unlike his father, he was a firm believer in 'decisive battles': he would mark the following millennia with this preference, all the way to Napoleon and his interpreters, and the generals of both world wars of the twentieth century. The Persian field army was indeed the strategic centre of gravity of his opponents, though Alexander probably saw matters in more 'heroic' terms: a definitive clash of leaders as found in his favourite reading matter, the *Iliad*. His advance east along the Black Sea coast after crossing the Hellespont ensured him a secure supply line back to Thrace which was out of reach of the Persian navy. His opponents, perhaps buoyed up by Parmenion's failure, ignored advice to use scorched-earth tactics and were eager to engage. Alexander was happy to reciprocate and inflicted a crushing defeat on the Persian army at the Granicus river. Persian ineptitude was in part the reason for the scale of their defeat, but Alexander's speed and mobility were also decisive. Alexander was not to face another Persian field army for over a year. Meanwhile, he advanced down the coast of Asia Minor. The towns he liberated were given a change of local regime and forced to join the League of Corinth. Neutrality, as proposed by Miletus, was not tolerated, as such towns would present a potential threat to Alexander's flank or rear were they to receive a ship-borne Persian force.

This naval threat was Alexander's most serious military problem after Granicus, the Persian navy being both larger and better than his own. His solution was to deny it any chance to engage. After taking Miletus, Alexander burnt his fleet and continued his advance down the coast. The navies of the day needed to come ashore at night; by securing the coast, Alexander thus not only fulfilled his Panhellenic promises of freeing the Greek coastal cities from Persian rule, but also denied a base of operations to the best arm of his adversary. Such a strategy came at the expense of speed. Arguably Alexander could have struck swiftly at the very heart of the Persian Empire by marching directly from Sardis along the Royal Road to Susa: a journey of ninety days' march. Such a strike would, however, have ignored the ostensible Panhellenic goal of the liberation of the Asian Greeks and also exposed him to being cut off from his line of supply. Therefore, sacrificing speed for security, Alexander arrived in Susa only after three years of campaigning.

The southern coast of Asia Minor is devoid of good harbours, so here Alexander turned inland. In the Taurus mountains he met opposition directed more by local rulers than by Persian king Darius. While the phalanx had proved it could fight in such circumstances, it was not ideal, and, as resistance stiffened, Alexander finally compromised by accepting token vassalage in the region. This preserved pride on both sides and allowed the speedy advance to continue without becoming bogged down in costly sieges which would have allowed Darius more time to organise. Thus Alexander found the Cilician Gates (the Gülek Pass), a key defensible point through the mountains, only weakly guarded by the local Persian satrap. Their capture took Alexander down to Tarsus and thus out of Asia Minor and into coastal Cilicia. The Amanus mountains now lay between him and a new Persian field army, this time commanded by the Great King himself.

Darius' position, encamped at Sochoi on the broad plains of Syria, offered the opportunity to envelop Alexander's army, while the narrow coastal strip of Cilicia provided Alexander with a safeguard from precisely such a threat. And yet Alexander advanced directly towards the Belen Pass at the eastern end of the Cilician plain. His intention was to force a battle in the pass itself (a strategy successfully pursued some 300 years later by the Roman general Ventidius Bassus), or perhaps to use his army's superior speed and manoeuvrability to mount a surprise attack on the plains themselves. However, Darius had also moved and managed to descend through the mountains to the coast behind Alexander, cutting his line of communication. Alexander had been strategically outmanoeuvred by Darius' 'indirect approach'.[5] Nevertheless, our sources describe Darius as downhearted (Arrian, *Anabasis* 2.10) and as failing to exploit his advantage. Alexander, showing himself as able to use Col. John Boyd's observe–orientate–decide–act loop at a grand tactical level as his father, successfully reversed his army's direction and defeated the Persians at the river Issus (probably the Pinarus) in 333 BC. Here he drove straight at Darius. The Great King fled and his army disintegrated. After his defeat, Darius wrote offering terms to Alexander. No attempt was made to exploit these; rather they were summarily dismissed. Again, Alexander had no time for the subtleties of diplomacy. However, Darius' escape meant that the decisive battle had eluded Alexander and he here passed up an opportunity to ensnare his adversary, leaving him free to fight again.

Victory at Issus left the Middle East open to Alexander. His two following campaigns are perhaps the most difficult of all to understand. He advanced

---

5 B. H. Liddell Hart, *Strategy*, 2nd ed. (New York: Meridian: 1991), 20.

down the coast to Tyre, whose proposal of neutrality he flatly refused. Tyre was for Alexander what Methone had been for his father. The city had provided a substantial number of ships to the Persian navy and to leave such a major port to its own devices would expose Alexander's rear were he to advance further.[6] Tyre held out and fell only after a siege of seven months. During this time, however, the Persian fleet steadily disintegrated and thus the threat Tyre presented diminished substantially. As such, a diplomatic deal or simply the establishment of a guard post on the mainland would have served Alexander's purposes and saved him much time. Two very different reasons are possible for his persistence. First, Tyre had never been taken and so its capture would have appealed to Alexander's *pothos*, or yearning to show that he was the greatest of men. Second, Alexander's reputation as a victor would have been substantially damaged had he abandoned the siege. While at Tyre, Alexander received another offer of terms from Darius, which again he peremptorily refused, against the advice of his father's friend and general Parmenion (Arrian, *Anabasis* 2.25). Philip would most likely have accepted what was offered, perhaps not to honour it, but to use it to further his own advantage. Alexander, however, who was famously to refuse to 'steal a victory' by subterfuge at Gaugamela (Arrian, *Anabasis* 3.10), would have none of it.

His next move, an advance south to Egypt, is even harder to explain in military terms. With Tyre secured, a move east towards Persia was quite possible. Ever since Droysen's history of Alexander, his excursion south to Egypt has normally been presented as the end of the process of securing the maritime flank of his army.[7] Egypt in fact presents little threat by land to the Middle East (the Sinai desert lies in the way).[8] By now the Persian fleet had completely collapsed and the eastern Mediterranean was a Macedonian lake. Moreover, Egypt, one of the most disaffected parts of the Persian Empire, was a most unlikely place from which a counterattack could be launched. Nor is it easy to see how the political advantages of obtaining Egypt out-weighed the delay the excursus caused. Our sources are very clear, however, that visiting Egypt was an important part of Alexander's plans (Arrian, *Anabasis* 3.1.1). We should see Alexander's excursion as a product of personal desire to consult the oracle of Amon at Siwah, not as part of a strategy to

---

6 It was a decision endorsed by Napoleon. Louis Antoine Fauvelet de Bourrienne, *Memoirs of Napoleon* (ed. R. W. Phipps) (London: Richard Bentley & Son, 1885), 135.

7 J. G. Droysen, *Geschichte Alexanders des Grossen* (Stuttgart: Gotha, 1833), 179.

8 Maximilian Graf Yorck von Wartenburg, *Kurze Übersicht der Feldzüge Alexanders des Grossen* (Berlin: E. S. Mittler, 1897), 31–2. See also the doubts of Liddell Hart, *Strategy,* 21.

conquer the Persian Empire. Overall, his detour shows us that Alexander lacked his father's single-mindedness in the pursuit of a clear goal.

Alexander now had to backtrack to Tyre to press further east. He then delayed further. Perhaps this was to rest his troops and consolidate, or, as suggested by Napoleon, deliberately to allow Darius time to concentrate his forces so that he 'might overthrow at a blow the colossus which he had as yet only shaken'.[9] In other words, Alexander probably wished to precipitate the decisive battle that had evaded him at Issus, and to end the war through the death or capture of the Great King. He therefore now aimed for the heart of the Persian Empire, advancing from the Mediterranean coast to Thapsacus (whose location is lost) and the Euphrates valley. This is the obvious route to Babylon and thence to Persia and had been used in 401 BC by the pretender Cyrus II supported by Xenophon's 10,000 Greek mercenaries. Darius now resorted to scorched-earth tactics, but on reaching the Euphrates, Alexander took an alternative route by continuing north and then turning south down the Tigris valley, a surprise manoeuvre or 'indirect approach', forcing Darius to relocate his army and depriving him of valuable time to train it.[10] When the two sides finally met at Gaugamela, however, Darius had still managed to prepare the ground in advance. Nevertheless, it was Alexander who triumphed. The Persian field army was annihilated, but Darius once more escaped Alexander's grasp. Gaugamela was a tactical tour de force, but not a politically decisive battle, as Alexander realised. He also saw that the Great King, badly damaged by his defeat, now neither posed an immediate threat nor was any longer the locus of authority within the Persian Empire. Alexander thus switched targets from Persia's ruler to its capital, Persepolis. The resistance he encountered in the Zagros mountains during his advance shows that he made the correct decision. His advance into Persia nipped opposition in the bud and its occupation was a military success; henceforth no further organised armed threat from Persia arose.

Politically, there was less success. If Alexander's aim had been to be declared the Great King in Darius' place, this did not happen. He had perhaps underestimated the importance of being part of the Achaemenid clan to make a credible claim to the throne and also misunderstood the nature of the Zoroastrian religion.[11] The subsequent burning of Persepolis is best

---

9 This is a view endorsed by Fuller, *Generalship of Alexander*, 104.

10 Liddell Hart, *Strategy*, 21.

11 Arguably, he had tried to father a child on Darius' wife to become an Achaemenid at one remove. See Plutarch, *Vit. Alex.* 30, Justinus, *Epit.* 11.12. See also the inscriptions of Darius the Great at Behistun and Gandj Nameh.

interpreted as a reversion to the tactics of terror after those of persuasion had failed. It was also a useful Panhellenic gesture to assuage potential troubles in Greece. Nevertheless, the heart of the Persian Empire had been captured; it was time to ensure its security. While now a peripheral figure, Darius, merely by remaining alive, posed a political threat and could potentially become a military one. Alexander thus moved with speed, denying Darius time to organise resistance, but before he could be captured, Darius was assassinated by his own disaffected followers.

With both Darius dead and Persia itself captured, arguably Alexander's task was finished. Nothing remained for the cause of Panhellenism and many of his troops thought this was the end of their journey. Alexander, however, wished to retain his conquests, not simply return home, and saw that the safety of his new realm depended on his being regarded as its undisputed ruler. Darius' assassin, Bessus, had claimed the throne as Artaxerxes III, and his homeland, Bactria, was wealthy and free of Macedonian arms. Alexander therefore continued his rapid pursuit, denying Bessus, as Darius before, time to organise resistance. Though moving at speed, Alexander took care to secure his own line of supply, despatching Parmenion to the Median town of Ecbatana and founding cities, or at least fortified garrisons, along the line of his advance. Bessus was caught out – petrified, according to Quintus Curtius (7.4.1) – by Alexander's rapid advance, in particular his crossing of the Caucasus in midwinter. His failure to cope with this led to the same loss of prestige as Darius had suffered. He was deposed, handed over to Alexander and eventually executed.

But once again Alexander's diplomacy failed him. His new regional allies soon turned against him when it became clear that he intended to impose his rule rather than merely pass through their lands. We can also sense a loss of strategic vision. Alexander had taken his arms not just through Bactria, but also through Sogdiana to the river Jaxartes (Syr Darya) at the edge of the Achaemenid Empire. Not content with this, he crossed the river and fought a successful battle against the Scythians. Only illness and then the uprisings in the region drove him back. There was no strategic reason for this excursion onto the steppe. It is best seen as another product of Alexander's *pothos* – in this case a wish to outdo Cyrus the Great, who had been defeated and killed here. Like many others since, Alexander found it difficult to deal with the tenacious resistance shown in Bactria. His response was twofold. He resettled local populations strategically to deny their support to his enemy and made modifications to the army to address tactical asymmetries.[12] These included additional light missile cavalry armed with bows

---

12 Cf. the Strategic Hamlets programme in Vietnam and the Briggs Plan in Malaya.

and javelins; the shortening of the *sarissa*, unwieldly in this terrain; and reductions in unit size to increase tactical flexibility. These changes bore some results, but, to almost universal surprise, Alexander finally resorted to an old diplomatic ploy of his father's, a strategic marriage to Roxanne, the daughter of a local warlord.

Alexander had now gained the northern boundaries of the Persian Empire and no possible opponents to his rule remained. But he could not resist a call to India. While the Punjab had once been nominally part of the Achaemenid Empire, the boundary between it and Bactria is one which has been honoured through the centuries and it is hard to see his advance as anything other than another expression of *pothos* or yearning for glory. In India, Alexander again sought decisive battle. A grand tactical flanking manoeuvre and river crossing executed by night led to the defeat of King Porus at the river Hydaspes (Jhelum), but at a much higher cost in men than in previous battles. Not content with this, Alexander pressed on still further, marching as he had in Sogdiana, beyond what could ever have been the bounds of the Persian Empire.

Finally, at the river Hyphasis (Beas), seeing no clear end to their adventures, his men had had enough and mutinied, forcing the king to head for home. Alexander chose to retire not the way he had come, but south along the Indus. While it could be argued that this was done to round off the empire's frontiers, and towns such as Alexandria-on-the-Indus (perhaps Uch) were founded en route, it seems more like a face-saving exercise to avoid the direct retracing of his steps. These were bloody campaigns, leaving at least 80,000 Indians dead. Alexander was in no mood to compromise and his attitude would have left a legacy of hatred which would have been difficult to build on. The subsequent decision to journey back to the Middle East on foot across the Gedrosian desert in Baluchistan was a disaster resulting in further heavy losses, and again motivated by *pothos*, not strategic considerations. Alexander died at thirty-two, a bitter and frustrated man in Babylon, his plans for conquest of Arabia and an advance into northern Africa dying with him.

Never beaten in the field, Alexander was a tactical genius. Equipped with his father's revolutionary army, he possessed the ability to see what it could do, the fortitude to carry it out and the mental flexibility to change his plans if necessary. His grasp of strategy, however, seems less sure, and he sacrificed expediency to *pothos* on a number of occasions. In particular, he never possessed, perhaps did not care to possess, his father's ability to manipulate and persuade to achieve his aims. As Trogus puts it, 'the father preferred to be loved, the son to be feared'. Like Achilles, Alexander wished to be a hero and that wish at times took him away from sound planning. In contrast, while there can be no doubts about his personal bravery, Philip was the archetypal unheroic leader, interested in the fruits of victory, not its style. Had Philip lived, he might well have gone on to capture the Persian Empire, but would more likely have ensnared Darius than vanquished him. Trogus perhaps reaches the heart of the matter when he tells us, 'Philip was the more judicious in his plans, Alexander the more splendid in his soul'.

5

Ancient Rome: Monarchy and Republic
(753–27 BC)

LOUIS RAWLINGS

Sources

The early Romans kept a range of official records, including lists of commanders and their theatres of operation, the public celebration of significant victories in the form of triumphs, other military information (such as the number of legions deployed and the enemies killed), treaties made with other states, and records of senatorial debates and decisions, alongside routine civic business. However, very little of that material has survived in its original form and we have no direct records of the strategic planning undertaken by commanders and their staff, in-depth decision making and policy discussion by political authorities, or even public announcements of priorities and objectives.

The surviving historical narratives were created towards the end of our period, in the second and first centuries (and indeed afterwards, under the emperors), when Rome already dominated the Mediterranean. Their presentation of material is heavily filtered by their historical and narrative agendas and tends to be coloured by a hindsight that presents Roman expansion and success in warfare as inevitable. This is the perspective of the fullest surviving narrative, composed by Livy (59 BC – AD 17). At times, we can compare Livy with earlier sources; especially significant is the history of Polybius (c. 200–118 BC), a Greek statesman, whose attempt to understand the importance of Rome in the Mediterranean provides us with a window onto some of the strategic and the structural factors underlying Roman success. Unfortunately, both writer's works have not survived complete, particularly their accounts after 167 BC. Other writers, of the imperial period, such as Plutarch, Appian, Cassius Dio and Justin, provide narratives that cover some of the gaps, but are often less insightful and sometimes of questionable reliability. Ancient writers' accounts of the Monarchic period (traditionally 753–509 BC) are particularly unreliable, being influenced by legends and oral traditions, as

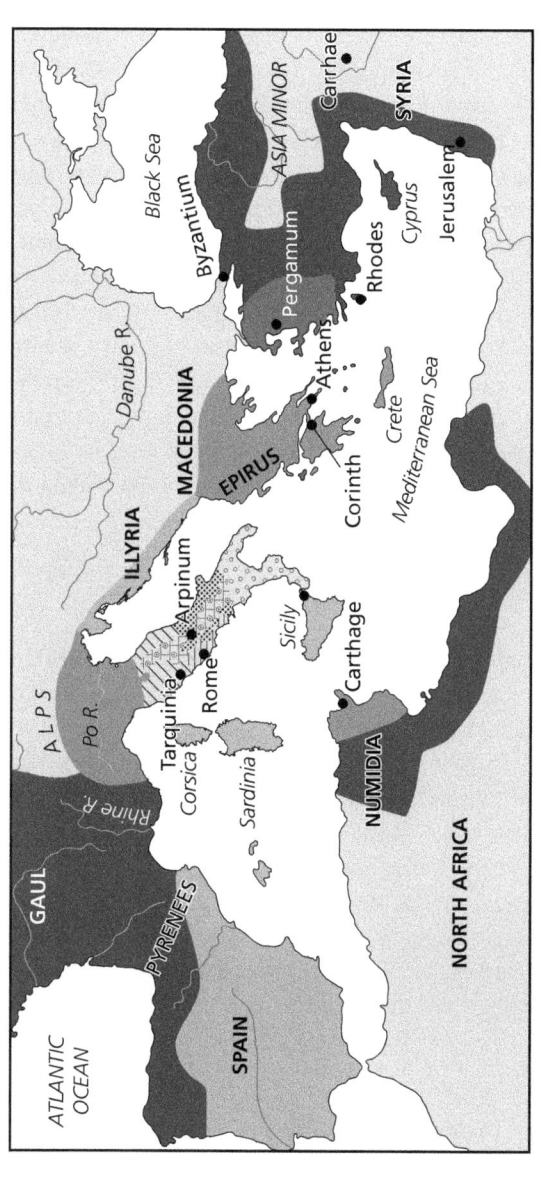

338 After the Latin war

298 Start of 3rd Samnite war

290 End of 3rd Samnite war

272 End of the Pyrrhic war

264 Start of 1st Punic war

241 End of First Punic War

146 End of Third Punic War

133 Territory in Asia Minor given to Rome

44 Death of Julius Caesar

Map 5.1 Strategies of ancient Rome, Monarchy and Republic (753–27 BC)

are the first two centuries of the Republic. It is only towards the end of the fourth century BC that the quality of information on the Roman tradition improves as the historical data become more trustworthy.

Contemporary Roman accounts are extremely rare, but Caesar's commentaries on his campaigns to conquer Gaul (58–50 BC) and during the Civil War (49–45 BC) detail the strategic concerns and constraints on his actions, overlaid by masterful political spin. Speeches and letters by Caesar's contemporary and political rival, Cicero, give a snapshot of issues in the last decades of the Republic. Public inscriptions such as the consular *Fasti* and *Fasti Triumphales* provide official lists of magistrates and their victories, albeit fragmentary, while *elogia* on elite Roman tombstones give a more personal perspective. Public inscriptions from across the Mediterranean provide information on treaties, laws and decrees. Some Greek states, for example, have records inscribed on stone honouring Romans for benefactions or giving information about embassies to Rome. We can also consider the evidence of the infrastructure of Roman conquest, such as roads and colonies. Archaeological evidence can help interpret the nature of colonial settlements, revealing the complex interrelationships of Romans and others as the conquest progressed.

Actors

The Roman state was a complex political organism and its decision-making entities evolved over time. Rome was originally a Monarchy where the king probably made decisions and set strategic objectives, although some evidence suggests that powerful aristocrats and their own followers may have undertaken warfare, with or without community support.[1] Such men may also have been influential in the early Republic, operating even when annually elected magistrates replaced the kings.[2] However, during the early fourth century the state asserted a monopoly over foreign policy and warfare. Polybius considered the Roman Republic to be a mixed constitutional system, with three main centres of power: the Senate, the people and the magistrates, each of whom could impinge on the creation and conduct of strategy (Polybius 6.11–18).

1 L. Rawlings, 'Condottieri and clansmen: early Italian raiding, warfare and the state', in K. Hopwood (ed.), *Organised Crime in Antiquity* (Swansea: Classical Press of Wales, 1999), 97–127; T. J. Cornell, *The Beginnings of Rome: Italy and Rome from the Bronze Age to the Punic Wars (c. 1000–264 BCE)* (London: Routledge, 1995), 143–50, 315–16.
2 J. Armstrong, *War and Society in Early Rome: From Warlords to Generals* (Cambridge: Cambridge University Press, 2016), pp 290–3.

The role of the Senate appears to have developed over time. Originally, it may have been a body that advised the early kings, assembled from friends or the heads of the most prominent households. The establishment of the Republic in 509 BC replaced kings with two annually elected consuls who appear to have had considerable flexibility in selecting their advisers. In such a context, the development of long-term strategic goals may have been almost impossible. The *Lex Ovinia* (*c*. 329–318 BC) appears to have established the Senate as a permanent body, subject to revision by the censors every five years (Festus 290 L).

By the mid-Republic, the Senate had acquired a range of customary powers and responsibilities that gave it considerable oversight of strategic policy. It had a steering hand in diplomacy, receiving foreign ambassadors and sending out delegations. The Senate considered the problems and opportunities presented to the Republic and at the beginning of every year defined each of the *provinciae* (the theatres of military operation), allocating the funds for military operations, thereby providing strategic constraints within which magistrates operated. From 327 BC it sometimes extended military commands (through prorogation of command authority – *imperium*), turning consuls into proconsuls, and providing some continuity in specific campaigns. As ex-magistrates themselves, many senators had experience of exercising command and delivering strategy, and their amassed experience informed debate in the Senate House and influenced policy beyond it. Magistrates were expected to consult with it and a senatorial recommendation, in the form of the *senatus consultum*, was difficult to ignore, given that it reflected the collective wisdom and consensus of the political elite. Nevertheless, policy was ultimately formulated in an internally competitive political system, where ambitious men mobilised supporters: friends and allies among the senate and beyond – their clients, sympathetic voters and interest groups (such as *publicani*, the equestrian class, veterans and even allied communities).[3] Even so, competition for power and influence normally worked within the framework of the current priorities and strategic realities facing the Republic.

Constitutionally speaking, the people were the final arbiters on strategic priorities. The *comitia centuriata*, introduced by King Servius Tullius, voted on war or peace. In the Republic, this citizen assembly also elected the consuls, and so was involved in choosing from the various approaches and courses of action being advocated by individual candidates. Debates in assemblies could range

3 J. Rich, 'Fear, greed and glory: the causes of Roman war-making in the middle Republic', in J. Rich and G. Shipley (eds), *War and Society in the Roman World* (London: Routledge, 1993), 52–60.

from concerns of high principle to specific issues of policy, where the people could be invited to recall past decisions and precedents on relatively detailed matters, such as the treatment of specific communities.[4] This meant that the assemblies were both a sounding board for policy and a real opportunity for popular opinion to influence the direction of strategy, through direct voting. However, although the people were sovereign, resolutions were normally only advanced by presiding magistrates or the tribunes of the plebs, so it is uncertain whether the assemblies would have been able to pursue consistent long-term strategic policies, even if the people were collectively capable of maintaining such a perspective. Furthermore, not every strategic decision reached the people for a vote; the Senate might set a conflict in motion by allocating an army to a *provincia*.[5]

The consuls were the principal military and strategic agents in the Republican system, though at times of extreme crisis a dictator could be appointed with absolute power (for six months). Probably from 366 BC, an additional magistrate, the praetor, could also exercise military command.[6] From 227 BC, two additional praetors were appointed to administer Rome's overseas territories (Sicily and Sardinia) and two more in 197 BC (Spain); the continuous allocation of *provincia* to these territories eventually turned them into provinces and these praetors into governors. As Roman territory continued to expand, governors of other provinces were appointed as either proconsuls or propraetors, exercising their administrative and military authority as they saw fit. In theatre, holders of *imperium* could also create additional strategic flexibility by appointing legates to act on their behalf. P. Cornelius Scipio, consul in 218 BC and proconsul from 217 to 211 BC, delegated his brother Cn. Cornelius Scipio Calvus to command one of the armies in Spain (218–211 BC). Pompey created twenty-four legates to clear the Mediterranean of pirates in 67 BC (Appian: *Mith.* 94), while in his conquest of Gaul (58–50 BC) Caesar appointed as many as fourteen legates to command his legions and provide the strategic flexibility for multiple operations.

Commanders, once allocated to their *provincia* (by lot or by mutual agreement), took the strategic military decisions within theatre, and had the power to deliver the broad objectives as they saw fit. However, since commands were normally limited to a single year in office, generals often

---

4 A.Yakobson, 'Public opinion, foreign policy and "just war" in the Late Republic', in C. Eilers (ed.), *Diplomats and Diplomacy in the Roman World* (Leiden: Brill, 2009), 59–60.

5 Rich, 'Fear, greed and glory', 59–60.

6 F. Drogula, *Commanders and Command in the Roman Republic and Early Empire* (Chapel Hill: University of North Carolina, 2015), 184–5.

acted aggressively to seek a decisive military engagement, aiming to win glory and wealth in order to advance their political standing in Rome.[7] For most consuls it was also their first taste of high command, although they often had a decade or more military experience, as cavalrymen and as one of the six military tribunes within a legion.[8] Commanders were also normally advised by military councils comprising military tribunes, senior centurions and senators present in the army, who provided advice in the planning and execution of objectives. Consequently, although some were incompetent, most Roman commanders proved to be effective military campaigners.

The annual turnover of leaders and military priorities militated against an overall grand strategic policy, but at times of military crisis the people might re-elect experienced commanders as consuls. Thus L. Papirius Cursor and Fabius Rullianus each held office five times during the Samnite Wars, as did Fabius Maximus and Claudius Marcellus in the Second Punic War, while Marius held six consulships, mainly to provide strategic continuity against the threat of the Cimbri and Teutones. At other times, the Senate prorogued commanders to allow them to finish prosecuting campaigns. In the crises of the Second Punic War (218–201 BC) and the Second Macedonian War (200–197 BC), 63 per cent of consuls were prorogued, some, like P. Cornelius Scipio in Spain, over several years.[9]

The assemblies, particularly in the late Republic, also voted long terms to generals, in the contexts of external crises or civil war. These appointments, however, gave opportunities to men such as Sulla, Pompey, Caesar and Octavian to turn commands into power bases that bent the Republic's strategic challenges to their own ambitions. Commanders usually had the freedom to address further threats and opportunities while in theatre, thus after defeating Philip V of Macedon (197 BC), the proconsul Flamininus waged war on Nabis II, King of Sparta (195 BC).[10] Pompey's impressive achievements in the east (67–62 BC) seem to have gone well beyond the original objective of defeating an alliance of Mithridates VI of Pontus and Tigranes of Armenia, and included the provincialisation of the old Seleucid heartland of Syria, a siege of Jerusalem and political settlement in Judaea. Caesar evidently exceeded his original *provincia*

---

7 A. K. Goldsworthy, *The Punic Wars* (London: Cassell, 2000), 52.
8 N. Rosenstein, 'Military command, political power, and the Republican elite', in P. Erdkamp (ed.), *A Companion to the Roman Army* (Oxford: Wiley-Blackwell), 132–47, 139.
9 R. T. Ridley 'The extraordinary commands of the late Republic: a definition', *Historia* 30 (1981), 280–97, 286.
10 Rich, 'Fear, greed and glory', 56–7.

of ensuring the defence of Cisalpine Gaul from Helvetian invasion (58 BC) to wage war against the German king (and Roman ally) Ariovistus (58 BC), undertake the conquest of all of Transalpine Gaul (58–50 BC), campaign across the Rhine (56 BC) and make two forays to Britain (55 and 54 BC).

Commanders, relying on the *imperium* granted them by the Senate and the people, as well as the substantial armies at their disposal, even dealt with monarchs on a seeming equal footing, as can be seen in the negotiations of Flamininus with Philip V (197 BC), of Scipio Asiaticus with the Seleucid king Antiochus III (188 BC), of Sulla with Mithridates VI of Pontus or of Pompey with Phraates III of Parthia (66 BC). Even senatorial commissioners and ambassadors might impose their wills on the international scene, as indicated by the story of former consul Popilius Laenas, who in 168 BC drew a circle in the sand around Antiochus IV and required him to cancel the invasion of Egypt before he stepped beyond it. For the most part, the Senate approved, and the people ratified the initiatives of its officials abroad, and adapted to the longer-term strategic implications of these acts.

Means

In the earliest history of Rome, much warfare probably consisted of low-level raiding conducted by local leaders and their followers, whose acts were akin more to private than state warfare. Where conflict involved the whole community, a levy (*legio*) of the wider population was raised. Most communal armies were seasonal militias and disbanded at the end of the campaign. The temporary nature of legions remained throughout the Republic, but as Rome's commitments became more distant and protracted, some forces were kept in being for years. Such legions were much more experienced and cohesive than Rome's annual levies, but even newly raised legions drew from a pool that contained many men with past campaign experience. In the early Republic, authority was divided between two consuls, and each commanded a legion. Thereafter, expansion in the size of Roman armies accompanied the growth of territory and manpower. By 311 BC, each consular army typically consisted of two legions (each legion of approximately 4,200 infantry and 300 cavalry), and a similar number of allies. From this period, the Republic's heavier military commitments often required proconsuls or praetors to command additional forces. In 295 BC, Rome deployed two consular armies (approximately 40,000 citizens and allies) to the Battle of Sentinum, while a similar number of troops, in three commands, operated in Etruria and Samnium (Livy 10.26–7). By 225 BC, the

Roman state potentially could call on 273,000 citizens (including Campanians) and 497,000 allied *socii* (Polybius 2.24), and indeed it raised 155,000 in that year. Despite huge losses to Hannibal in the early battles of the Second Punic War, Rome deployed twenty-five legions in 212/211 BC, which, with naval commitments of about 200 warships, amounted to around 230,000 combatants.

Rome's huge manpower and command flexibility also allowed it to wage war in multiple theatres. Campaigns in 195 BC in Spain, Cisalpine Gaul and Greece involved 176,000 men. Indeed, every year between 200 and 168 over 90,000 combatants were deployed in various actions across the Mediterranean.[11] From 167 BC, Rome's average annual commitment was 60,000 men (approximately 6.5 legions and allies). After 91 BC, each decade saw years of mobilisation in excess of 90,000, heavier during Rome's civil wars, as Italians were ranged against one another, with peaks of 272,000 in 83–81 BC, and almost 300,000 in 43 BC.[12] By this time, the available manpower of Italy was about 900,000.

Each legion possessed a similar strategic capability for independent action. Mid-Republican legions fought in three lines of heavy infantry preceded by a screen of skirmishers drawn from the young and the poorest elements of Roman society. The heavier infantry were predominantly citizen farmers using body-covering shields, thrown spears and swords. In the late Republic, the legions were reformed to become entirely heavy infantry, supported by foreign auxiliaries. A legion's primary effectiveness was in pitched battle, but it was often used to raid, devastate and besiege. The development of the cohort (approximately 500 men) in the second century, probably in the Spanish theatre, allowed legions to be subdivided for smaller-scale semi-independent operations.[13]

Roman naval power developed during the First Punic War, where it successfully overcame a more experienced Carthaginian navy through a combination of tactical innovation, vast commitment of resources and sheer determination. This is exemplified by the Battle of Ecnomus (256 BC), where it deployed 330 warships (approximately 140,000 men) (Polybius 1.25.7). Thereafter, Rome could always match the navies of its main rivals. After the defeat of the Macedonian and Seleucid kingdoms, its naval power was rarely challenged, although it mobilised large navies to suppress rampant Cilician piracy (67–66 BC), while Caesar briefly operated a fleet in the Atlantic against the Veneti (56 BC) and to invade Britain (55 and 54 BC). The civil wars of the 30s

11 P. A. Brunt, *Italian Manpower, 225 B.C.–A.D. 14* (Oxford: Clarendon, 1971), Table XII, 425.
12 Brunt, *Italian Manpower*, 445, 487.
13 M. J. V. Bell, 'Tactical reform in the Roman republican army', *Historia* 14 (1965), 404–22.

generated huge naval commitments by the protagonists: the Battle of Naulochus (36 BC) involved 600 ships, while at Actium (31 BC) there may have been 900.

Roman legions rarely fought without allies. Early compacts with Latins (493 BC) and Hernici (483 BC) pooled resources for joint operations. In 338 BC Rome replaced these with a network of unilateral alliances, in which it was the senior partner, where each allied community was obliged to contribute troops in proportion to its resources.[14] The allies substantially augmented Roman military power; 50 to 70 per cent of any army might be non-Roman. Consequently, Roman strategy always considered the resources of its allies and the expectation that they would provide men. The fighting approach and armament of the Italian allies (*socii*) gradually came to resemble that of the Romans, so that, after the Social War (91–87 BC), when Roman citizenship was extended to all the *socii*, it was a small step to recruit them into the legions. Thereafter, Italian legionaries fought primarily alongside *auxilia*, drawn from beyond the peninsula. In fact, auxiliaries had featured in Rome's overseas expeditions from the Punic Wars, usually locally recruited natives and allies. At the Battle of Magnesia (190 BC), the troops of King Eumenes II of Pergamum played a major role in breaking the Seleucid left wing. Roman armies increasingly also drew specialist slingers, archers and cavalry from peoples who excelled in these arms, such as the Balearics, Cretans and Numidians.

Rome's wealth supported its warfare. Legionaries received pay, traditionally from 406 BC, at a rate of a denarius every three days. The cost of this stipend was supported by a property tax on citizens (*tributum*) (Livy 4.9), augmented by booty, the sale of war slaves and the indemnities that increasingly flowed into the treasury. The profits from war in Italy were substantial and helped to both sustain and motivate Roman warfare, yet campaigns overseas vastly increased income to the state. Carthage, from 201 BC, was forced to render an annual payment of 1,800,000 denarii over fifty years (Polybius 15.18.8); alone this could have paid for 10,000 legionaries per calendar year.[15] Even more was squeezed from the Seleucids in 188; their annual indemnity was 9,000,000 for twelve years (Polybius 21.43.19). The profits of warfare and, increasingly, taxes raised in the provinces became so great that *tributum* was suspended in 167 BC (reimposed only during the civil wars after 43). While Rome did not tax its Italian allies (although some paid

14 Cornell, *The Beginnings of Rome*, 348–52.
15 F. W. Walbank, *A Historical Commentary on Polybius*, Volume I (Oxford: Oxford University Press, 1957), 722.

war indemnities), they were expected to support their own troops – a cost-effective exploitation of Italian manpower by the Roman state.[16] Rome also recruited *socii navales* for the navy, alongside citizen oarsmen. Fleets were huge consumers of resources, both the materials for their construction and, more substantially, in the recurrent cost of crew pay and supply. The deep pockets of the Republic, however, allowed it to challenge any other naval power.

Adversaries

The Romans inhabited a competitive international environment populated by aggressive rivals. Over seven centuries, as they outgrew the most immediate and earliest threats, they came into conflict with larger polities. Eventually, they challenged the largest powers in the Mediterranean: Carthage and the Hellenistic kingdoms of Macedon, Egypt and the Seleucid Empire (the latter stretched from Syria to Afghanistan). They also encountered many tribal societies in Spain, Gaul (modern France and northern Italy) and Africa, which posed a range of strategic challenges.

The Romans' earliest encounters were with their immediate neighbours: cities of Latins to the south and of Etruscans to the north, as well as upland tribes such as the Aequi, Volsci and Hernici to the east. These communities remained the main adversaries until the middle of the fourth century. Latin and Etruscan cities were independent and competitive, and although they formed into leagues capable of concerted military action, Rome generally had to deal only with individual states or limited coalitions. Indeed, the Etruscan League was also pressured from the north by Gallic tribes who settled in the Po valley during the sixth and fifth centuries. The cities nevertheless each possessed strong military forces, and were walled and strongly sited for defence. Their individual power is indicated by the fact that until 396 BC Rome was still locked in competition with Veii, a city sixteen kilometres distant. The sources claim a sixth-century Roman hegemony over parts of Latium, perhaps confirmed by the first Rome–Carthage treaty (*c.* 508 BC), which asserted Roman control over several coastal Latin cities. Soon after, however, Rome fought the Latin League at Lake Regillus (496 BC), and in 493 BC made a bilateral defensive treaty with 'all of the Latins'. This did not halt sporadic Roman–Latin hostilities, but it allowed for collective resistance to the vigorous depredations of the Aequi, Hernici and Volsci. These tribes,

16 A. Erskine, *Roman Imperialism* (Edinburgh: Edinburgh University Press, 2010), 12–15.

however, were insufficiently unified to overcome the Latin–Roman axis; indeed, the Hernici allied with Rome in 483 BC. The threat from the Aequi and Volsci was much reduced after the Romans, Latins and Hernici defeated them at Mount Algidus (431 BC) (Livy 4.26–9).

In these formative centuries, the scale of warfare and of Roman expansion was relatively limited. The capture of Etruscan Veii in 396 BC enhanced Roman territory and manpower, but Rome remained a regional Italian power. Its vulnerability is evident in the defeat suffered at the river Allia and the subsequent sack of the city by the Gauls (390 or 386 BC). However, this did little to alter the balance of power in the region. By 360 BC, Rome had managed to overcome some of the southern Etruscan cities, though it remained locked into local regional conflicts.

A critical change came in 338 BC, when Rome defeated a coalition of Latins, Volsci and Campanians, and absorbed them into a web of alliances that gave it considerable resources of military manpower. This allowed Rome, over the next fifty years, to confront and subdue the Samnites, a major association of tribes of the south-central Apennines. Their federation could raise formidable armies for aggressive campaigns. In 343 BC, the Samnites threatened the Campanian plain, forcing Capua to call on Roman support and precipitating a first short war (343–341 BC). After provocations from both sides, a more protracted phase of conflict began in 327 BC. The Samnites were a considerable test of Rome's resources; their armies invaded Roman territory (315, 313, 306 BC) and heavily defeated the legions at the Caudine Forks (321 BC) and Lautulae (315 BC). Nevertheless, it was more frequently the Romans who took the offensive, invading the territory of specific Samnite tribes to raid, plunder and reduce their resistance, or to exact vengeance for Samnite depredations. By 292 BC, the tribes had been forced into submission, but they remained a latent threat throughout the third century: some tribes joined Pyrrhus in 280 and Hannibal in 216. Indeed, they formed a core element in the rebellion of allies during the Social War (91–87).

During the fourth and third centuries, Rome had also faced the threat of Gallic armies from Cisalpine Gaul. They captured Rome in 390/386 BC and periodically invaded Roman territory (367, 361–358, 350, 349, 299, 295, 284/283, 225 BC), inflicting damage, trauma and bloodshed. The attacks appear to have been motivated by plunder and glory rather than permanent conquest. Gallic tribes rarely exhibited a consistently aggressive posture to Rome, but they sometimes acted in concert with Rome's other enemies: at Sentinum (295 BC) Rome defeated a Gallo-Samnite army; at Aquilonia (293 BC) and Vadimon

(283 BC) it defeated Gallo-Etruscan forces. The strategic weakness of these collaborations lay in their relatively loose and makeshift organisation, while Rome had from 338 BC established a close-knit alliance system, which only grew stronger as it incorporated its defeated enemies. From 282 to 272 BC, Rome warred in the south against the Greek city of Tarentum, also absorbing the regions of Lucania, Apulia and Bruttium. By 266 BC it had established control in Etruria, Umbria and Picenum, so that it now dominated much of the Italian peninsula.

The Gauls remained relatively quiet until 232 BC, when a provocative policy of Roman settlement on Senonian land (conquered by Rome in 282 BC) triggered a major phase of Gallic conflict. The Boii and Insubres, joined by transalpine warriors, invaded Etruria, but were destroyed at Telamon in 225 BC. This was followed by decades of Roman campaigning to subdue these tribes. Under such pressure, many Gauls allied with Hannibal in 218 BC, providing approximately 20,000 men for his victories at Trasimene (217 BC) and Cannae (216 BC), and they also joined Hasdrubal's advance into Italy (207 BC). However, during much of the Second Punic War, Gallic actions appear directed at the recently established northernmost Latin colonies of Placentia and Cremona. In the post-Hannibalic period, they were forced to act defensively in the face of intense Roman campaigning. At least one consul operated in the area each year between 201 and 190 BC, indicating considerable Roman commitment to the pacification of the region. From 197 BC, the conflict widened to include the Gauls' Ligurian allies, requiring annual Roman campaigning until 172 BC. This fifty-year strategic commitment to the conquest of the northern frontier of Italy was sustained even as Rome campaigned elsewhere in the Mediterranean.

Roman trans-Mediterranean expansion began in 264 BC with a major war in Sicily against Carthage, whose large empire stretched along the coast of Africa, and included Sardinia and western Sicily. This wealthy city operated a powerful navy and employed armies of mercenaries, principally Greeks, Iberians and Gauls, alongside subjects and allies drawn from its Libyan hinterland. Since the late sixth century, it had waged numerous wars with Greek cities in Sicily and it had made several alliances with Rome, with whom it had also co-operated against Pyrrhus. The vast resources of Carthage and its military resilience meant that the First Punic War lasted twenty-three years (264–241 BC). Campaigning took place mostly in Sicily, where Carthage could use fleets to support friendly coastal cities, to raid Italy and defend Sardinia and Africa, though it was unable to prevent a Roman landing near Carthage in 256 BC. The Romans made huge efforts to confront the Carthaginians at sea, requiring the construction of several large fleets throughout the war. Despite defeats on land and sea, Carthage dug deep, repulsing the Romans in Africa (255 BC) and forcing a stalemate in western Sicily. The war exhausted both protagonists, but Roman naval victory at the Aegates islands (241 BC) finally ended the war. Rome occupied Sicily and, soon after, seized Sardinia.

In the interwar period, Carthage conquered a large part of southern Spain, giving it access to substantial silver mines and the manpower of warlike Iberian tribes. It forged a potent veteran army, with which, in 218, Hannibal crossed the Alps into Italy. His strategy appears to have been to defeat the Roman armies in the field and to break up the Roman alliance. His victories at Trebbia (218 BC), Trasimene (217 BC) and Cannae (216 BC) encouraged large numbers of allies to defect, particularly in the south, and sustained his campaign there until 203 BC. The power and extent of the Carthaginian Empire required Rome not only to endure Hannibal in Italy, but also to campaign throughout the western Mediterranean, in Spain, Sardinia, Sicily and Africa. Hannibal's alliance with Philip V of Macedon (215 BC) even drew Roman forces into western Greece. Finally, after victory in Spain (206 BC), a Roman invasion of Africa successfully detached some of Carthage's Numidian allies, and drew Hannibal out of Italy to a final decisive defeat at Zama (202 BC).

Victory over Carthage left Rome with territory in Spain. The region was often restive and saw phases of intense violence (197–175, 154–133, 80–72 BC). While warfare was often low-intensity predation, the tribes did commit warriors to fight pitched battles and conduct sieges, with variable success. The geography of Spain made subjugation of the interior slow and difficult, even though tribes were often concerned with their own local rivals and were unable to offer unified resistance, with few opportunities for charismatic leaders such as Viriathus (147–139 BC) to put together stable coalitions. The developing provinces of Hispania Citerior and Ulterior grew out of the long-term establishment of Roman military presence and government.[17]

Rome's first contact with a Hellenistic Greek power had come during the war against Tarentum (282–272 BC), which had allied with Pyrrhus, the king of Epirus and cousin of Alexander the Great. His heavy defeats of Roman forces at Heraclea (280 BC) and Asculum (279 BC); support from Samnite, Lucanian and Bruttian tribes; and the resilience of Tarentum suggested that

17 J. S. Richardson, *Hispaniae: Spain and the Development of Roman Imperialism, 218–82* B.C. (Cambridge: Cambridge University Press, 1986).

Rome could be vulnerable to other invasions from the Greek east. However, Philip V's alliance with Hannibal (215–205 BC) and Hannibal's alleged attempt to acquire an army from the Seleucid king, Antiochus III, to reinvade Italy (*c.* 192 BC) (Livy 34.60, 36.7), posed only *potential* danger that was never realised. For the most part, wars with the Hellenistic kingdoms were acts of Roman interference, at the behest of lesser states such as Athens or Pergamum, who felt threatened by imperial aggression. The Hellenistic kingdoms of the Macedonians and Seleucids appear as apex predators in an eastern Mediterranean system where, at the regional and local levels, there was almost constant tension and conflict. Although wealthy and aggressive, possessing large and well-disciplined armies, and naval forces of high sophistication, these royal dynasties were never completely secure, and the power of individual kings could be fragile. Their personal reputations were based on military prowess, so that any defeat in battle might undermine their credibility and their grip on their royal territories.

Few Roman wars in the east lasted more than four years, and after defeat in battle these kings could be forced to make peace (such as Philip V after Cynoscephalae in 197 BC and Antiochus III after Magnesia in 190 BC). Even as Rome rose to effective hegemony over the whole Mediterranean, the attention of these kings predominantly focused on traditional dynastic rivalries, and the internal struggles for power and control of their kingdoms. The Seleucids suffered internal decline and were unable to sustain their eastern territories, ceding much to the Parthian kingdom during the years from 165 to 130 BC.[18] With the Roman defeat of Perseus at Pydna (168 BC), which resulted in the break-up of the Macedonian kingdom, none of the remaining states could pose an existential threat to Rome's survival. Even so, fear of a resurgent Carthage caused Rome to destroy the city in a three-year war (149–146 BC). After that, the most serious external threat came from the migration of the Cimbri and Teutones, a confederation of Germanic tribes who plundered Roman-controlled southern Gaul and Iberia, inflicting a massive defeat at Arausio (105 BC), before being crushed at Aquae Sextiae (102 BC) and Vercellae (101 BC).

By the first century BC, Rome was the dominant power in the Mediterranean, although it was challenged (unsuccessfully) by Mithridates VI of Pontus, who had conquered the Black Sea and briefly overran much of Asia Minor (89–85, with further wars in 83–81 and 73–63 BC), but despite two major expeditions in 53 and 37, Rome was unable to conquer the Parthian Empire.

---

18 N. L. Overtoom, 'The power-transition crisis of the 160s–130s BCE and the formation of the Parthian Empire', *Journal of Ancient History*, 7:1 (2019), 111–55.

Nevertheless, Rome enlarged its territories with some major acquisitions, particularly in the 60s BC with Pompey's campaigns in the east that created several new provinces, and in the 50s BC with Caesar's conquest of Gaul (France and Belgium). The major strategic problems of the late Republic were posed by civil wars and internal uprisings. Rome fought a difficult Social War (91–87 BC) in Italy against its own allies (including the Samnites, Marsi and Lucanians), who had demanded more political rights. It also had to put down several slave uprisings (in Sicily in 135–132 and 104–100, and in Italy by Spartacus in 73–71 BC). The Republic struggled to retain control of powerful Roman generals such as Marius, Sulla, Caesar and Octavian, who, at various times, seized control of the state with large armies of loyal veterans. Particularly when ousted from Italy, Roman factions turned to regional allies in Spain, Africa or the eastern Mediterranean, some of which, such as Egypt (30 BC), however, lost their autonomy after backing the losing side.

Causes of Wars

The causes of Rome's earliest wars are suggested by some of its earliest diplomatic procedures. These involved the *rerum repetere*, a demand for the restitution of property and injury from hostile actors, or the surrender of perpetrators.[19] Failure by the offending community to comply created a *casus belli* that could lead to a declaration of 'just war' (*bellum iustum*). This process remained a significant aspect of Roman inter-state relations. In 282 BC the Romans demanded the surrender of Tarentine citizens who had organised attacks on a Roman fleet and a garrison in Thurii, while in 218 BC the Romans demanded that Hannibal be surrendered to them, because he had besieged their Spanish ally, Saguntum (Appian, *Samn.* 7.2–3).

The ideology of just war may also have acted as a brake on some Roman generals, since it made unprovoked attacks on communities morally and politic-ally risky, with possible prosecution on return to Rome (as happened to Aemilius Lepidus for his attack on the Vaccaei in 137/136 BC) (Appian, *Hisp.* 80–83; Orosius 5.5.13).[20] However, even though the Romans were disposed to conduct diplo-macy in a manner that tried to assert a position of moral superiority and invoke just cause, it did not mean that they were incapable of aggressive opportunism and provocation. It was the instigation of M. Aquillus, by forcing Roman allies

---

19 J. Rich, 'The *fetiales* and Roman international relations', in J. H. Richardson and F. Santangelo (eds), *Priests and State in the Roman World* (Stuttgart: Franz Steiner Verlag, 2011), 215–17.

20 Rich, 'Fear, greed and glory', 57–9.

Nicomedes of Bithynia and Ariobazarnes of Armenia, to raid Pontus, which pushed Mithridates VI to war (90/89 BC). Rome also often used diplomacy to persuade, cajole or compel its neighbours and rivals.

Like most states in antiquity, Rome appears to have taken a robust stance in negotiations with its rivals, making demands for compliance that were difficult or humiliating to satisfy, and which might goad them into war.[21] In 149 BC increasingly severe demands by the consul Censorinus finally pushed the Carthaginians over their limit, when, after acquiescing to his orders to deliver hostages and all of their weaponry, he demanded they abandon their city and resettle eighteen kilometres inland.

Furthermore, the Roman state exhibited structural impulses that promoted active bellicosity.[22] The expectations and ethos of both high- and low-status Romans were geared towards making war. Rome was involved in regular military campaigning throughout the Republic. The psychological, political and financial rewards of successful campaigning acted as future encouragement to the Romans to pursue opportunities for war when they arose. First, the Roman elite valued personal military glory and renown. Men such as Valerius Corvus (348 BC), Manlius Torquatus (361 BC), the consul Marcellus (222 BCE, when he was in his forties), and Scipio Aemilianus (151 BC) all enhanced their reputation through single combat.[23] The funeral oration of L. Caecilius Metellus emphasised that he had been the 'foremost warrior, best orator and bravest general' (Caecilius Metellus 221; Pliny, *NH* 7.139–40). In the mid-Republic one-third of consuls earned a triumph, the public celebration for military victory. Second, the competitive political system encouraged members of the elite to enhance their political capital through the pursuit of military achievement. Marius displayed his battle wounds in the assembly to generate popular support (Sallust, *Iug.* 85.29–30; Plutarch, *Mar.* 9.2). In the period from 227 to 79 BC, fifteen of nineteen praetors who won state recognition for military success were later elected consul. Third, in addition to the lustre of a martial reputation, huge wealth could be acquired from warfare. Generals normally kept a proportion of the spoils and distributed the rest to the troops and the state treasury, or used it to build temples and public buildings. Even as the Senate hesitated to become embroiled in its first overseas conflict in Sicily in 264 BC, the consuls appealed to the greed of the electorate,

---

21 A. M. Eckstein, *Mediterranean Anarchy, Interstate War and the Rise of Rome* (Berkeley: University of California Press, 2006), 61–3, 218.

22 W. V. Harris, *War and Imperialism in Republican Rome 327–70 BCE* (Oxford: Clarendon Press, 1979), 9–104.

23 S. P. Oakley, 'Single combat in the Roman Republic', *Classical Quarterly*, 35 (1985), 392–410.

emphasising the booty that war would bring (Polybius 1.10–11). The Roman people thus voted to declare wars because of the expectations of enrichment, just as much as any sense of rightness of cause. Reinforced by tangible benefits of war, many citizens volunteered for the Third Macedonian War 'because they saw that those who had served in earlier wars had become rich' (Livy 42.32).

Finally, in certain periods (338–263, 199–174 BC), there were substantial confiscations of Italian territory from the defeated. Citizens might be settled in colonies on this land, with generous portions that promoted social mobility for the poor. In the aftermath of the Social War (91–87 BC) there was another phase of settlement, on land confiscated from the rebels. Distribution to veterans became a frequent tool in the competition of the late Republican elite, who, playing on the expectations of their soldiers, bought levels of personal support that contributed to the destabilisation of the Republic and to its civil wars.

In addition to internal impulses, the Roman alliance system also provided an underlying pressure to undertake warfare.[24] The Romans taxed their allies not in financial tribute but in manpower, rendered only when called upon in times of war. Furthermore, the defence of allies was a core element of the hegemonic system, since, by claiming to act in their interest, the Romans could perpetuate the alliance system in Italy. From 264, the expedient of the defence of overseas allies could mobilise the Italians for war. An additional mechanism in Roman expansion was the *deditio* – where a minor power sought protection from an aggressor by approaching Rome and submitting to its authority. The Romans, who stood to benefit from an enhancement to their power and reach, usually entertained such approaches favourably, even if it meant becoming embroiled in serious conflict with a third party. Thus, when the Campanians in 343 BC and the Lucanians in 298 BC asked the Republic for protection from the Samnites, the acceptance of their appeals inevitably led to wars between the major protagonists. The appeals of the Mamertines (264 BC) and Saguntines (219 BC) brought Rome into bloody confrontations with Carthage. Conversely, the Roman conflict with Naples (327 BC) brought the Samnites to its defence, and Tarentum called on Pyrrhus (282 BC). Rome's willingness to make allies and render aid meant that by the second century an almost continuous stream of representatives visited it from communities, particularly of the Greek east, seeking favour and arbitration. Rome was now the effective hegemon of the international system in the Mediterranean and was able to choose whether and when to become involved in local conflicts.

24 J. A. North, 'The development of Roman imperialism', *Journal of Roman Studies*, 71 (1981), 1–9.

It is undeniable that Rome was an aggressive state, but its rivals were often equally bellicose.[25] The Republic had been threatened by the invasions of Apennine peoples and of Gallic and Germanic tribes, as well as by the dangerous campaigns of Pyrrhus and Hannibal. Kings such as Philip V, Perseus, Antiochus III and Mithridates VI were powerful, active and ambitious actors. When the Romans were not responding to direct attacks on their territory or that of their allies, they might be tempted to act out of distrust and fear of their neighbours in a pre-emptive manner. Concern about Carthaginian resurgence had caused Rome to provoke the Third Punic War (149–146 BC) and to destroy the city (Polybius 36.9.4).[26] It is arguable that the ruthlessness with which Rome dealt with various Gallic cisalpine tribes in the second century stemmed from a general fear formed during the traumatic invasions of the fourth and third centuries. Such apprehensions combined with the structural impulses that rewarded and promoted military action to provide irresistible motivations for the Romans to go to war.

Strategic Priorities

It is a matter of debate whether the Republic developed long-term strategic objectives or, given the complex interplay between the magistrates, the Senate and the people, whether the political system favoured short-term gains and objectives, predominantly reacting to threats and opportunities as they arose.[27] Although Polybius (3.2.6, 1.3.6) assumed a Roman desire for world domination, and while the censors had asked the gods 'to make the state of the Roman people better and greater' at the end of each census (Valerius Maximus 4.1.10), it is unclear when or whether such aspiration was mapped out in detail.[28] It is unlikely, for example, that the Romans maintained a definite plan for the conquest of Italy, or even that they originally conceived of the peninsula as a coherent whole. It is only as late as the 280s BC that Polybius states that 'they now for the first time attacked the rest of Italy not as if it were a foreign country, but as if it rightfully belonged to them', which suggests that only at this relatively late stage in the conquest had the Romans begun to think in terms of military and ideological control of the whole peninsula (Polybius 1.6.4–6). Polybius notes

---

25 Eckstein, *Mediterranean Anarchy*, 191–216.   26 Rich, 'Fear, greed and glory', 63–4.
27 A. E. Astin, *Politics and Policies in the Roman Republic* (Belfast: Queen's University Press, 1968).
28 Harris, *War and Imperialism in Republican Rome*, 118; Erskine, *Roman Imperialism*, 71–2; see Eckstein, *Mediterranean Anarchy*, 191–3, for objections.

it was their victory over the Gauls at Telamon (225 BC) that 'encouraged the Romans to hope that they would be able entirely to expel the Celts from the plain of the Po' (Polybius 2.31.7). Only once the pacification of Cisalpine Gaul was well advanced, in 183, did the Romans declare the Alps to be the 'impassable frontier' of Italy (Livy 39.54.12), finally taking the concept of *tota Italia* to its logical geographical limit.[29]

It is equally unclear that Rome had a strong strategic vision when it crossed over to Sicily in 264 BC at the outbreak of the First Punic War. Indeed, Carthage may not even have been the original target of the Roman campaign in Sicily, but Syracuse, whose war against the Mamertines had led them to appeal to both Rome and Carthage.[30] Furthermore, Polybius indicates that it was only when considering the aftermath of their victory over the Carthaginians at Agrigentum (262 BC) that the Romans decided they would try to drive them completely from Sicily (Polybius 1.20.1–2). This extension in ambition suggests that Roman strategy was predominantly opportunistic, and we should not think that the original plan matched the conclusion of the war. In order to achieve their new strategic goal of ejecting the Carthaginians from the island, however, the Romans built their first major war fleet (Polybius 1.20.5–9). This was a decision with huge immediate financial and demographic implications for the Roman state (and its coastal Italian allies – the *socii navales*). It was probably less clear at the time that this decision would have a fundamental impact on the balance of power in the Mediterranean and facilitate the Roman projection of overseas might for the following half-millennium.

The system of annual commands and seasonal levies emerged in the warfare and politics of the early Republic, but it remained at the heart of the strategic capabilities of the state, even as its commitments grew longer and more complex. We can see where short-term priorities lay by the annual allocation of consuls or the prorogation of commands and the numbers of legions committed in specific wars or years. Taking a broader temporal perspective, we can assess the overall distribution of wars and their relative frequency.

It is apparent that Roman war making was not of a constant intensity; there were years, even decades, when the Republic either faced less external aggression or chose not to assert itself militarily.[31] Thus Roman

---

29 S. Dyson, *The Creation of the Roman Frontier* (Princeton: Princeton University Press, 1985), 42.

30 B. D. Hoyos, *Mastering the West: Rome and Carthage at War* (Oxford: Oxford University Press, 2015), 30–40.

31 Rich, 'Fear, greed and glory', 46–7.

campaigning in Italy appears relatively limited in the years from 454 to 411, from 264 to 225 and from 172 to 92 BC, though the latter phases reflect its effective subjugation of opposition. Assessments could be made of other regions – for example, in the years from 172 to 154 and 132 to 88 BC Spain saw little significant activity, whereas 218–206, 197–172, 154–133 BC involved substantial conflict. Such regional patterns need to be compared to Rome's broader involvements, since often when violence in one theatre had cooled others became hotter. Overall, the Romans were at war about 93 per cent of the time in the fourth and third centuries. A similar percentage applies to the second and first centuries, but there was almost continuous and heavy warfare from 225 to 168 BC, whilst 167–91 BC was less intense, the latter reflecting Rome's relatively unchallenged hegemonic position in the Mediterranean. Indeed, Polybius explained that the Romans went to war against the Dalmatians (156 BC) because there was a concern that 'the men of Italy would become enervated by long peace, since it had been twelve years since the war against Perseus and their campaigns in Macedonia' (Polybius 32.13.6–7). A similar reason was given for Octavian's attacks on Dalmatia in 35 (Velleius Paterculus 2.78.2). In fact, the first century witnessed considerable military activity, with a complex overlap between external conflicts, rebellions and civil wars – some of which required huge commitments of combatants.

Even though it is difficult to attribute a coherent and long-term grand strategy to the Roman Republic, the evidence does suggest the practical strategic priorities that it faced. Until the mid-fourth century, we can broadly characterise Roman strategy as focused on the security of core territory from neighbours. From 342 BC, Rome increasingly expanded its borders, colonies and alliance system across central Italy, to include much of the peninsula by 264 BC. From 232 to 154 BC it became deeply involved in the pacification of northern Italy, the heaviest activity, from 201 to 172 BC, required the attention of 75 per cent of all the consuls elected in this period.

From 264 BC, Rome also had overseas interests and priorities. These amounted to obtaining ascendancy in its rivalry with Carthage in the western Mediterranean and dealing with the legacy of this conflict in Sicily, Sardinia, Spain and Africa in the following centuries. The eastern Mediterranean, from 200 BC, saw the imposition of Roman hegemony over the international system that had previously been dominated by the Hellenistic kingdoms of the Attalids, Seleucids and Ptolemies. After major victories over the Macedonians (196 and 168 BC) and Seleucids (188 BC), it acted to keep the remaining dynasties weak and divided, often interfering diplomatically in territorial disputes and issues of succession. Thus Polybius noted that in intervening in a dispute between Ptolemy VI Philometor of Egypt and his brother Ptolemy VIII Physcon (*c.* 163 BC), 'many decisions of the Romans are now of this kind: availing themselves of the mistakes of others they effectively increase and build up their own power' (Polybius 31.10.7). By this time, the Romans could choose when and where to fight.

Application/Execution

The Romans' capacity for conquest and victory far exceeded their will to devise exploitative measures.[32] The slow growth in Roman territory in the sixth and fifth centuries suggests that early warfare concerned relatively limited objectives of reprisal and booty, and the predatory motivations of the Romans remained a significant feature throughout the Republic. Many campaigns ended with a profitable Roman withdrawal and often the temporary submission of the enemy. Even when Rome was able and willing to force an enemy to cede territory, it could be a complex process to undertake its exploitation, constrained by the availability of settlers, resources and political energy, and inhibited by the difficulties of securing and defending newly conquered lands.

While colonies were normally walled and acted as effective strongholds to hold down the locals, new settlers might be targeted by the defeated in any renewal of hostilities: the colonies of Placentia (Piacenza) and Cremona were subject to intense military pressure from the Gauls in the first decades after foundation in 218 BC. Placentia was besieged (208 BC) and later sacked (200 BC), and, although it was re-established in 198 BC, extra colonists had to be sent in 190 BC. The difficulties in the assimilation of the conquered and the logistics of settlement by citizens also imposed practical limits on the rate of expansion. So, at Veii, much of the population captured in the siege was enslaved (Livy 5.22, 6.3–5) and the considerable territory was parcelled up for Roman settlers, but it was almost ten years before they were enrolled into four new voting tribes (387 BC). Rome's gradual increase in the number of voting blocks in the tribal assembly (*comitia tributa*) mirrors the piecemeal incorporation of neighbouring populations into the *ager Romanus* (495, 387, 358, 332, 318, 299, 241 BC).[33]

---

32 North, 'The development of Roman imperialism', 2–3.

33 Cornell, *The Beginnings of Rome*, 174; G. J. Bradley, *Early Rome to 290 BCE: The Beginnings of the City and the Rise of the Republic* (Edinburgh: Edinburgh University Press, 2020), 275, 312–15.

The exploitation of overseas territories was slow. Settlement of citizens overseas was extremely limited and provincial mechanisms of control were rudimentary, often overlying and adapting local traditional approaches to governance, and relying on local elites to collude in the control of the territory. Rome gradually and somewhat haphazardly acquired these over-seas provinces. To weaken Carthage, Rome had taken control of Sicily (241 BC), and opportunistically responded to an appeal from a rebellious Carthaginian garrison to seize Sardinia (237 BC). After the Second Punic War, it remained in Spain, committing at least two legions and gradually extending and consolidating its control.

From the 190s to the 150s BC attention was drawn mostly to the subjugation of northern Italy, where large colonial and municipal settlement was under-taken on tribal lands south of the Po, yet this area became a province (known as Gallia Cisalpina) only in 81 BC, even though in 121 BC the conquest of southern France had created Gallia Transalpina (Narbonensis). To deal finally with old enemies, in 148 BC Macedonia and Epirus were made into a province, with a garrison of two legions, and after the destruction of Carthage in 146 BC, its territories became the province of Africa. By contrast, the rulers of Pergamum (133 BC), Cyrenaica (74 BC) and Cyprus (58 BC) peacefully bequeathed these lands to Rome on their deaths. Pompey oversaw a wave of provincial organ-isation: Cyrenaica was joined with Crete (66 BC); he also established Bithynia and Pontus, and the provinces of Cilicia and Syria (64 BC). After Caesar's conquest, Gaul (58–50 BC) became Gallia (subdivided into Lugdunensis, Aquitania and Belgica in 22 BC). Octavian's victories over the foreign supporters of civil-war rivals led to the incorporation of Mauretania and Numidia into Africa (33 BC), and the creation of Egypt (30 BC), Illyricum and Achaea (27 BC).

In addition to these areas of direct rule, Rome cultivated client kingdoms, which were allies, buffers, proxies and forward intelligence sources on the boundaries of the Roman Empire. The patchiness in the process of expansion and the different solutions adopted reinforces the perception of the ad hoc nature of Roman territorial strategy. Military intervention (and usually victory) in some of these areas came decades before administrative provin-cialisation. Usually, the Romans preferred to impose terms or establish client relations with the defeated, before later recourse to annexation, which was often sparked by a later misstep or 'revolt' in the area.

While campaign strategy depended on local contextual factors, there were several principles that the Romans preferred to pursue. Where practicable, the Romans sent their armies to campaign in enemy territory. This facilitated the collection of booty, kept Roman lands safe and applied maximum pressure on the hearts and minds of the opposition. It was the predominant pattern in the Samnite Wars, and in the subsequent pacification of Italy. To deal with the pan-Mediterranean threat posed by the Carthaginian Empire in 218 BC, the initial Roman strategy was offensive and two-pronged: an army was sent to contest the resources of Spain, while another, assembled in Sicily, aimed at an invasion of Africa. Hannibal's arrival in Italy forced the recall of the Sicilian army and put Rome on the defensive. Nevertheless, even in the blackest years of this conflict, with Hannibal in the ascendant in Italy, it maintained the approach of contesting other theatres: Spain, Sardinia, Sicily, Greece and, eventually in 204 BC, Africa. This forward-footedness in the disposition of forces and the course of Roman campaigning is replicated in most of its wars; Caesar, for instance, left his province of Gallia Cisalpina to pursue the migration of the Helvetii deep into Gaul.

In theatre, the main strategic objective was to force the enemy to meet the legions on the battlefield, preferably in tactically suitable open ground, where the legions were most potent. Many campaign accounts reveal a similar pattern, with Roman armies trying to force the enemy to engage them in open battle, principally by targeting vulnerable settlements, devastating farmland or directly threatening principal urban centres with attack or siege. Once they were goaded to risk a general engagement, Roman victory in battle might quickly break the enemy's will to resist or leave their remaining territory and settlements vulnerable. Besides their practical effect on the course of a campaign and the developing strategic environment in theatre, such engagements had symbolic value. They earned glory and enhanced the reputation of the commander, which, as we have seen, could be converted into political capital in Rome. Even when outmatched in the field by Hannibal, the Romans were regularly willing to engage the Carthaginian. The sources record as many as twenty-two battles fought against Hannibal between 218 and 203 BC in Italy, with only a relatively brief 'Fabian' strategy of evasion and scorched earth, after the annihilation of Flaminius' legions at Trasimene in 217 BC, and then with tremendous disaffection and political pressure to reverse the policy.[34]

On campaign, Roman commanders also aimed at fragmenting the cohesion and resolve of the opposition by actively seeking out and rewarding sympathetic individuals and factions who might provide immediate advantage and potentially play a role in any future political settlement. Strikingly,

---

34 L. Rawlings, 'The war in Italy', in B. D. Hoyos (ed.) *A Companion to the Punic Wars* (Oxford: Wiley-Blackwell, 2011), 300–3.

Scipio Africanus made an alliance with Massinissa, even though the Numidian chieftain had played a considerable role in the defeat and deaths of his father and uncle in Spain (Livy 25.34–6).[35] This alliance played a fundamental role in the success of the Roman invasion of Africa and defeat of Hannibal at Zama (202 BC). Massinissa remained a loyal client king until his death in 150 BC, acting as a major constraint on the potential recovery of Carthage.

Clemency and favour granted to those who readily defected were often contrasted with extreme violence directed at resistant communities. Devastation of land, sack of cities and slaughter of populations aimed to break resistance and deter future hostilities. Polybius was particularly struck by the treatment of New Carthage (Cartagena) in 209 BC: 'I think they do this to inspire terror: when towns are taken by the Romans one may not only see the corpses of human beings, but dogs cut in half, and the dismembered limbs of other animals' (Polybius 10.15.5). In 304 BC, after a demand for restitution had been refused, it was claimed that 'thirty-one walled towns ... were sacked and burnt, and the Aequian people were almost exterminated' (Livy 9.45). The treatment of major cities such as Agrigentum (262 BC), Tarentum (209 BC), Carthage and Corinth (146 BC) not only was brutally destructive, but also allowed the Romans to profit from mass enslavement: Agrigentum yielded 25,000 (Diodorus Siculus 23.9.1) and Tarentum 30,000 (Livy 27.16), while Aemilius Paullus collected 150,000 slaves from the towns of Epirus in 167 (Livy 45.34; Polybius 30.15). This was dwarfed by Caesar's campaigns in Gaul, where Plutarch (*Caes.* 15) claimed that he had slain a million in battle and enslaved just as many.

Historiographical Debates

Modern discussion of Roman grand strategy concentrates on the period of the emperors, where the frontier policy evolved over centuries of relative territorial stability. Analysis of the strategies of the Roman Republic occur within a more dynamic context of regular warfare but haphazard expansion, where Rome competed to establish its position in Italy and eventual dominance across the Mediterranean. Scholars have tended to explore Republican strategy by focusing on Roman imperialism and adopting perspectives that are either 'pericentric' (where the strategic and military pressures are argued

---

35 L. Rawlings, 'Warlords, Carthage and the limits of hegemony', in T. Ñaco del Hoyo and F. López-Sánchez (eds), *Multipolarity and Warlordism in the Ancient Mediterranean* (Leiden: Brill, 2018), 151–80, 174–5.

to come from actors at the periphery of the Roman state, such as aggressive enemies or needful allies) or 'metrocentric' (where Rome is the initiator of conflict). Other scholars advocate a 'systemic' approach to Roman expansion (where the international system is shaped by the internal ideologies and practices of each involved community, who are, in turn, forced to react and respond to other actors in the system).[36]

Early twentieth-century scholarship mostly accepted a pericentric view of Roman strategy as predominantly defensive, shaped by the need to resist external threats and provocations, with expansion the consequence of a need to secure frontiers. This model emphasised the concept of *res repetere* and ideology of just war, but it did not sufficiently account for the bellicosity of the Roman state. William Harris attacked the defensive model by revealing the structural and exceptional nature of Roman aggression.[37] His metrocentric analysis has been influential but received important modification. John North emphasised the contribution of the alliance system.[38] John Rich argued for a less relentlessly aggressive state, identifying variations in the intensity and frequency of warfare.[39] He also observed that motives of fear (real or imagined) and concern for developing situations could be as significant as economic or ideological (glory-driven) reasons. Arthur Eckstein reasserted the significance of pericentric factors, emphasising the role of lesser states in their appeals to the major powers, and challenged the view that Rome was an *exceptionally* aggressive state.[40] Using realist international relations theory, he observed that Rome was only one of a number of powerful predators, and that Roman expansion came in the context of a harsh and anarchic inter-state system. Harris's response emphasises the high portion of citizen manpower that Rome employed compared to its rivals, ensuring the continuing vitality of the debate.[41] Other scholars have considered Roman expansion in terms of the development of frontier solutions, some of which have postulated long-term strategic awareness and policy,[42] or focused on the Italian context of colonial development and cultural contact (often identified with the problematic term 'Romanisation'),

---

36 For definitions of 'pericentric', 'metrocentric' and 'systemic' see C. Champion and A. M. Eckstein, 'Introduction: the study of Roman imperialism', in C. Champion (ed.), *Roman Imperialism: Reading and Sources* (Oxford: Wiley-Blackwell, 2003), 6; P. J. Burton, *Roman Imperialism* (Leiden: Brill, 2019), esp. 13–17.
37 Harris, *War and Imperialism in Republican Rome*.
38 North, 'The development of Roman imperialism'. 39 Rich, 'Fear, greed and glory'.
40 Eckstein, *Mediterranean Anarchy*.
41 W. V. Harris, *Roman Power: A Thousand Years of Empire* (Cambridge: Cambridge University Press, 2016), esp. 67.
42 Dyson, *The Creation of the Roman Frontier*.

although Guy Bradley has urged caution in perceiving long-term consequences of security and acculturation in Roman colonisation as deliberate strategising. Instead, he emphasises contextual Roman political motivations, as well as local reasons, for the establishment of colonies or other infrastructure (such as roads) that promulgated Roman control.[43] An important contribution to understanding the culture of imperialism, by John Richardson, examines developments in language and ideology, noting how the concepts of both *provincia* and *imperium* take on territorial aspects in the first century.[44] Paul Burton's systemic approach considers cultural traits that promoted Roman soft power: its use of interpersonal and inter-state friendship (*amicitia*) and its assertion of trustworthiness and reliability (*fides*) that made it popular with its allies and enhanced the rhetoric and impact of its international diplomacy.[45]

43 G. J. Bradley, 'The nature of Roman strategy in mid-Republican colonization and road building', in T. Stek and J. Pelgrom (eds), *Roman Republican Colonization: New Perspectives from Archaeology and Ancient History* (Rome: Palombi, 2014), 60–72.

44 J. S. Richardson, *The Language of Empire: Rome and the Idea of Empire from the Third Century* BCE *to the Second Century* CE (Cambridge: Cambridge University Press, 2008), esp. 109–16.

45 P. J. Burton, *Friendship and Empire: Roman Diplomacy and Imperialism in the Middle Republic (353–146* BCE*)* (Cambridge: Cambridge University Press, 2011).

6

China AD 180–1127

DAVID A. GRAFF

Introduction

This expanse of nearly a millennium, extending from the closing years of the Han dynasty to the fall of Northern Song, saw new departures in religion and philosophy and significant changes in China's social and economic structures. Chinese strategy, however, continued to operate within the framework established during the Warring States and Han. The Warring States period (475–221 BC) not only gave rise to the foundational ideologies of Confucianism and Legalism that together would continue to define the goals and methods of imperial government down to the beginning of the twentieth century, but also produced the most revered texts dealing with military strategy. These included the *Wuzi*, the *Weiliaozi*, the *Liu tao*, and above all the *Sunzi*, better known to English-speaking audiences as 'Sun Tzu's *Art of War*'. One indication of their enduring influence is that the first important strategic writing passed down to us from the period covered by this chapter is the commentary on *Sunzi* penned by the late Han warlord Cao Cao, while one of the last was the *Seven Military Classics*, a Song collection – and in some cases, rearrangement – of military texts dating mostly from pre-Han times, with the *Sunzi* prominent among them. The legacy of the past was found not only in authoritative texts and hegemonic ideas, but also in institutional structures and standard operating procedures. Here it was the Han dynasty – and especially the Western Han, which held sway from 202 BC to AD 9 – that set the precedents and provided the model that later Chinese imperial regimes would aspire to emulate. Although titles and offices changed over time, the basic architecture of centralised imperial government remained remarkably stable. So, too, did the range of potential strategic problems and possible solutions, along with established approaches to problem solving.

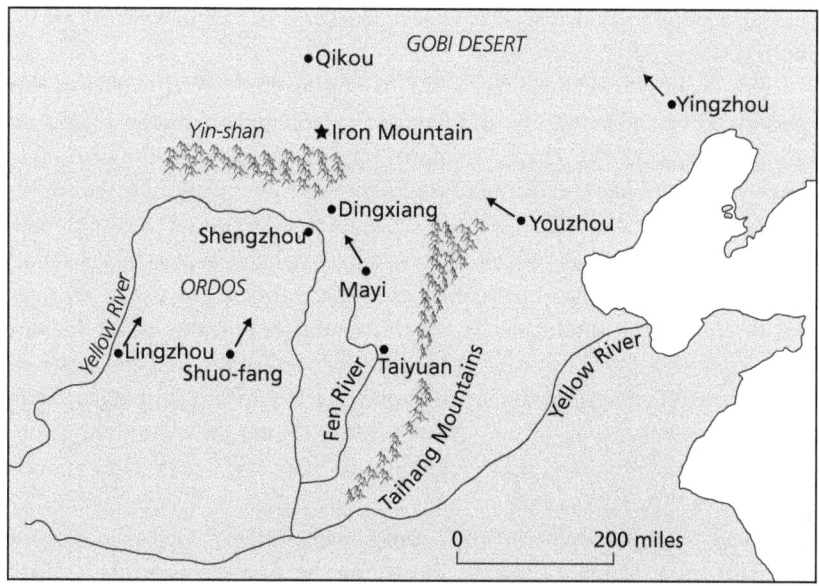

Map 6.1 Tang operations against the Eastern Türks, AD 629–630

Texts and Sources

The major military texts handed down from pre-Han times emphasise a set of key themes and lessons, though not all of these receive equal attention across all of the books. Most fundamentally, war was understood as a means of advancing the state's interests rather than a sort of cultural performance pursued for its own sake, with strategy being seen as a matter of rational calculation that should not be subject to the play of emotion. Calculations and decisions had to be based on accurate information, so there was a strong emphasis on careful observation, intelligence gathering and the judicious employment of spies. By the same token, deception and trickery are presented as essential to success in war, making it possible to achieve the surprise that will lead to victory. Considerable attention was also given to the psychological manipulation of both the enemy and one's own forces, the classic example being Sunzi's recommendation that the general should deliberately put his soldiers in a desperate situation so they will be galvanised to fight with a ferocity born of desperation. Ideally, nothing should be left to chance. The conditions for victory should be prepared in advance, so that when the battle occurs its outcome will be a foregone conclusion. Thanks to the perception and calculations of a sage-like general, eventual victory will be both certain and predictable.

New strategic writings continued to appear throughout the post-Han period. These included essays sometimes attributed to Zhuge Liang, the great strategist of the Three Kingdoms period, and parts of the *Changduan jing* – or *Classic of Advantages and Disadvantages* – a compilation by the eighth-century scholar Zhao Rui. A more substantial contribution was the *Taibai yinjing*, a sort of military encyclopedia said to have been written by a shadowy Tang military administrator named Li Quan. All of these works repeated major concepts and themes already well established in the earlier military literature, although Li Quan's book also included quite a bit on weapons, tactics, provisioning, military ritual and even the standard formats for army paperwork. What was written about strategy during this period, however, sometimes went beyond mere repetition to offer significant elaboration of older ideas. A prime example of this is the *Tang Taizong Li Weigong wendui* (or *Questions and Replies between Tang Taizong and Li, Duke of Wei*), a work cast in the form of a dialogue between the warlike second emperor of the Tang dynasty and one of his top generals, but most likely composed at a much later date.[1] This book is in fact an extended and quite sophisticated disquisition on the interplay of straightforward (*zheng*) and unexpected (*qi*) approaches in warfare, a subject raised in the *Sunzi* but not discussed there at any great length. The *Questions and Replies* is also noteworthy because it has its protagonists discuss various historical instances of the use of *zheng* and *qi*. The use of specific historical examples to illustrate general discussions of strategy was pioneered by the great Tang scholar-official Du You, whose *Tong dian* (*Comprehensive Canons*) dating from circa 800 includes fifteen chapters on military affairs which are organised according to a large number of discrete principles of war, each of which is exemplified in a series of short historical narratives. For example, 'Feign unpreparedness and set an ambush to take them' is illustrated with two historical examples, one from the Northern Wei (386–534) and one from the Northern Zhou (557–581). This approach became a standard feature of later works such as the Northern Song *Wujing zongyao* (*Essentials of the Military Classics*) dating from 1044, which also continues and builds upon the encyclopedic format pioneered by Li Quan's *Taibai yinjing*. Encyclopedic approaches and the use of historical examples

---

1 See, for example, Yang Yongan, *Sui Tang Wudai shi guankui zakao* (Hong Kong: Xianfeng chubanshe, 1987), 85–96.

would continue to characterise much of Chinese military writing beyond the Song and into the Ming (1368–1644) and Qing (1644–1911) dynasties.

As this increased attention to the historical record would suggest, other important sources for the study of imperial Chinese strategy are the dynastic histories, which were usually compiled under the official auspices of the succeeding dynasty from the Tang dynasty onward, as well as private histories and chronologically arranged works, among which the Northern Song scholar-statesman Sima Guang's massive *Zizhi tongjian* (or *Comprehensive Mirror for Aid in Government*), covering the years from 403 BC to AD 959, deserves pride of place. Military events and strategic decisions loom large in these Chinese histories, so much so that works such as the Western Han official Sima Qian's *Shi ji* (*Historical Records*) and the third-century scholar Chen Shou's *San guo zhi* (*Record of the Three Kingdoms*) themselves came to be regarded as important sources for the study of strategy. In the early eighth century, one Tang official even objected to sending the Tibetans copies of Chinese classics, including the *Zuo zhuan*, the canonical narrative covering the Spring and Autumn period (722–481 BC), suggesting that these works contained military wisdom that would be useful to China's enemies.[2] For modern military historians, however, the Chinese histories leave much to be desired. They tend to focus on clever tricks, traps and unusual and sometimes quite elaborate stratagems, while offering little information about weapons and tactics. There is more attention to pre-battle debates and councils of war, and generals are sometimes credited with mastery of the ancient military classics or presented as quoting from specific texts, especially the *Sunzi*. This may, however, be more a literary convention than a matter of historical fact. Not all commanders were well read (or even literate), and the possession of military texts was not always legal. The most compelling reason for doubt, however, is that history was written by scholars who were more likely to be familiar with the textual tradition than military men and had good reasons for emphasising the value of book learning over practical experience of war.

There is also a certain amount of disagreement, sometimes rising to the level of contradiction, between prescriptive military texts and the conduct of war as recorded in the histories. The military classics handed down from the Warring States emphasise that the general's role in battle should be intellectual rather than physical; instead of participating in combat himself,

---

2 Wang Pu (comp.), *Tang huiyao* (Beijing: Zhonghua shuju, 1990), Chapter 36, 667.

he should be the director of others' violent efforts. The point is driven home by a story that the famous Warring States general Wu Qi, putative author of the *Wuzi*, once refused to carry a sword on the ground that bells and drums – the instruments of command – were the only appropriate weapons for the leader of an army. In contrast, Li Shimin, second emperor of the Tang dynasty and one of the most successful military leaders in all of Chinese history, made a point of charging into combat at the head of his black-clad household cavalry and once claimed to have *personally* dispatched more than a thousand opponents in his many battles. Other sorts of advice could also be disregarded. When Li Shimin's generals defeated the *qaghan* of the Eastern Türks in 630, they moved quickly to cut off the *qaghan*'s followers' escape routes – ignoring the many admonitions in the classical military texts that a beaten opponent should not be trapped or backed into a corner (again, so they would not be driven to fight with the courage of desperation).

Magical and cosmological approaches to warfare were largely condemned in the most revered ancient military classics. Yet they found widespread application on medieval Chinese battlefields. During the siege of Yubi in AD 546, the Eastern Wei attackers referred to cosmology to determine the timing and direction of their assaults on the Western Wei fortress, while in 817 the Tang general Li Su took advantage of both a snowstorm and an unlucky day that was considered taboo for military operations to launch a surprise attack against the capital of the rebellious province of Huaixi. Li's action is evidence that not all of China's soldiers were in thrall to such superstitions, but by the same token his very success indicates that others were.

Finally, the military classics devote little or no attention to matters that must have been of paramount importance to medieval Chinese rulers and strategists. Composed at a time when some half-dozen major Chinese states were contending against one another for survival, expansion or dominance, they assume a culturally like-minded opponent and have nothing at all to say about the special problems of fighting against non-Chinese adversaries such as the pastoral nomads of the northern steppes. This is in sharp contrast to other strategic traditions such as the Byzantine, which included systematic discussions of the military styles and techniques of foreign peoples and the best means of countering them. In this regard, the teachings of the military classics failed to serve the needs of Chinese leaders.

Strategic Environment

Looking at the strategic environment in which Chinese rulers had to struggle for survival, we find more complex structures of internal conflict and division in some periods – as during the prolonged age of disunity from the early fourth century to the late sixth century AD – and a more threatening international scene in others. During the nine centuries from the collapse of Eastern Han to the fall of Northern Song, the core agricultural regions of mainland east Asia – sometimes called 'China proper' – assumed a range of different geopolitical configurations. Under the rule of the Western Jin dynasty from AD 280 to 301, the Sui from 589 to 617, the Tang from about 624 to 755 and the Northern Song from 979 to 1126, China was a unified empire facing foreign opponents, of which the most threatening were usually nomadic or semi-nomadic peoples inhabiting the deserts and grasslands to the north, embracing the territories of Manchuria, Mongolia and Xinjiang. But these periods of imperial order and unity were in fact atypical, accounting for less than half of those 900 years.

There were also times when the empire had to deal with internal revolts or rebellions of various sorts, ranging from peasant uprisings to military mutinies and regional or local separatism. Peasant unrest from the early 610s grew into local revolts and eventually a multi-cornered struggle for power between a variety of contenders – including members of the old Sui elite – that was not resolved until the Tang consolidation around 623–624. The Tang rulers themselves were nearly overthrown by a great rebellion of the northern frontier armies led by the Turko-Sogdian general An Lushan in 755; although this revolt was brought to an end in 763 with the Tang ruling house still on the throne, it resulted in a significant diminution of central authority as regional military garrisons seized the opportunity to assert their autonomy. From the outbreak of the An Lushan rebellion to the end of the dynasty in 907, Tang emperors were more concerned about internal disorder and civil conflict than about external threats. On several occasions between AD 200 and 1000, the breakdown of centralised order was so severe that it gave rise to multiple imperial regimes and prolonged periods of multi-state competition lasting for decades or even centuries. In the early third century, the confused, multi-cornered struggle among warlords that attended the collapse of the Eastern Han resolved into the more stable 'Three Kingdoms' configuration of Wei in the north, Wu in the south-east, and Shu in the south-west that endured for roughly half a century. Another half-century on, in the early fourth century, the Western Jin civil war of the 'Eight Princes' created the conditions for a congeries of non-Han groups from both within the empire and beyond its borders to seize power in northern China. The result was a shifting, kaleidoscopic pattern of regional regimes that continued for well over 200 years; the most fundamental geopolitical fault line, between northern and southern China, was not overcome until 589 when the Sui dynasty defeated the Southern Chen dynasty to reimpose a unified political order on the Chinese world. The dynamic of division emerged yet again at the beginning of the tenth century, when the collapsing Tang dynasty splintered into nearly a dozen regional states, a situation that would not be brought to a definitive end until the second Song emperor conquered the last regional holdout (Northern Han, in today's Shanxi) in 979.

Enemies

The Chinese often found themselves facing culturally alien foes such as the Xiongnu, Türks, Tibetans, Uighurs, Kitan, Tanguts, Rouran and Jurchen – to name just a few. In our period, China's periphery saw the rise of strong sedentary states in the Korean peninsula (Koguryŏ, Silla) and Vietnam (Dai Viet), in addition to the continuing presence of nomad polities and steppe confederations to the north, while hybrid peer-level competitors such as Tibet during the Tang period and the Kitan Liao state during Northern Song proved especially troublesome. Although this age of intense geopolitical competition did not give rise to any bold, new departures in Chinese theories of conflict, it did provide the backdrop for some new ways of thinking about strategy – in particular the codification of strategic principles and their illustration by means of historical examples. Having already considered these developments in writing about strategy, we will now turn to look at its practical application.

Among China's foreign adversaries, state rulers and the leaders of tribal confederacies claimed to be calling the shots, but their interests and those of important followers were often at cross purposes. The historical record is filled with examples of destabilising raids carried out by nomadic chieftains at the same time as their overlords were engaged in peace negotiations with the Chinese imperial court. This pattern may be explained with reference to the goals of foreign leaders – and especially steppe rulers – in their relations with China. While some powers such as the Tibetans (in the eighth century) and the Kitan (in the tenth century) took advantage of favourable conditions to annex territories inhabited by sedentary Han Chinese populations, foreign rulers were rarely interested in trying to bring all of China under their control. The Mongol conquest of the thirteenth century was very much the exception rather than the rule. Most often, the goal was to extract resources such as grain, silk and other luxury goods from China through trade, diplomacy and a fair amount of extortion. The past masters of these techniques were the Turkic Uighurs, whose steppe empire dominated the territory of today's Mongolia from the mid-eighth century to the mid-ninth century. Their signature practice was to exchange old, weak and sick horses for far more silk than they were worth, a raw deal that the weakened Tang court felt it had no choice but to accept. Far from seizing the opportunity to attack China, the Uighurs sent strong cavalry forces to sustain the relationship by supporting the Tang court during the desperate days of the An Lushan rebellion. Although the Uighurs were fairly consistent in their strategic behaviour, others found that opportunistic, unauthorised raiding by lesser chiefs could actually strengthen the hand of steppe leaders seeking broad gains through negotiation.

During periods when China was divided, steppe rulers often sought to maintain that division for as long as possible while exploiting it to their own advantage. During the third quarter of the sixth century, the Türks maintained good relations with both of the rival regimes in north China, Northern Zhou and Northern Qi, and sought to play the two off against each other. Later, when the Sui court's authority disintegrated in the early seventh century, the Eastern Türks cultivated a number of local contenders for power, providing them with cavalry mounts, symbols of authority (such as wolf-head standards) and sometimes even direct military support. It was only after the Tang consolidation had proceeded to the point that it was clear this divide-and-rule approach had failed that the *qaghan* of the Eastern Türks began to launch – and lead – large-scale raids deep into Chinese territory.

Allies

Alliances, sometimes intended to be long-term relationships cemented by the bestowal of Chinese 'princesses' as brides for foreign rulers, were another element in the empire's strategic repertoire. Allied contingents of Uighurs, Türks and other steppe peoples provided the tough, mobile cavalry forces that made possible the Tang subjugation of much of inner Asia in the middle decades of the seventh century, and an alliance of convenience with Silla, one of Korea's 'Three Kingdoms' in the same period, facilitated the Tang conquest of the other two kingdoms, Paekche and Koguryŏ. Such arrangements were, however, fraught with danger, as they were often driven by considerations of short-term advantage – on both sides – rather than enduring sentiment. After the Tang annexation of Koguryŏ in 668, Silla, now pursuing its own agenda of territorial aggrandisement directed at the political unification of the Korean peninsula, began to provide support for anti-Chinese resistance forces, and by 677 the Tang garrisons had been withdrawn from the occupied kingdom – with the rising power of Silla as the ultimate beneficiary. A Song alliance with the Jurchen of Manchuria aimed at recovering the Sixteen Prefectures from the Kitan Liao yielded even less satisfactory results. Although the Song armies, with the assistance of their foreign allies, succeeded in recovering this long-lost territory in 1123, the success was only temporary; once the Kitan had been disposed of, the Jurchen turned on their Chinese allies, overran most of northern China, captured the imperial capital at Kaifeng, and took the emperor and many of his relatives as prisoners to Manchuria. For the next century, until the rise of the Mongols, China would be divided between a Jurchen (Jin) state in the north and a remnant Song state in the south.

Actors

The Chinese state was not always a unitary, rational actor capable of recognising and pursuing its own best interest. Strategy was frequently driven by the political or personal needs of individual leaders, not only those at the very top but also figures in the lower echelons. The second Song emperor, for example, launched an ill-advised attack on the Kitan Liao in 979 mainly to burnish his military credentials and legitimacy in the wake of his problematic accession to the throne. In another infamous case, the powerful late Tang general Gao Pian chose not to crush the rebel forces of Huang Chao when he had the chance, on the ground that as long as the rebels were on the loose, he himself would remain indispensable to the imperial court.

The military classics have little to say about strategies and institutional mechanisms to keep the military under control and obedient to the ruler; on the contrary, these texts – and especially the *Sunzi* – devote considerable attention to the importance of allowing generals untrammelled command authority. Yet the decision makers who set strategic goals, established priorities and made strategic choices were usually rulers – or autonomous provincial leaders and would-be rulers – along with the statesmen and generals who counselled them. The range of ability and experience was enormous, running the gamut from capable, experienced and sagacious leaders to feckless neophytes, and from polished, aristocratic courtiers and learned scholars to gruff fighting men risen from the ranks. These strategic actors were usually, but not invariably, male: from about 680 until 712 the Tang court was dominated by women, most notably Wu Zetian, who actually held the title of 'emperor' – not empress – from 690 to 705. Similarly, the Kitan dowager empress Xiao was the top decision maker at the Liao court at the close of the tenth century.

The Ends of Strategy

The ends of strategy varied greatly depending on the geopolitical configuration of the time. During periods of division or civil war, many power holders were concerned primarily with political survival and maintaining control over their own territories. This was almost invariably the case with the autonomous provincial military regimes of late Tang, which were usually eager to retain the façade of harmonious relations with the imperial court even as they withheld tax revenues from the centre and supported large armed forces of their own; it was also true of many tenth-century regional powers such as Southern Tang, Shu and Wuyue. The more powerful contenders, meanwhile, were usually working to expand at the expense of their weaker neighbours with the ultimate goal of reimposing imperial unity on the Chinese world. The Wei-Jin state of the Three Kingdoms period fitted this pattern, as did the sixth-century Northern Zhou regime and its Sui successor state, the Tang founders in the early seventh century, and the Song founders in the second half of the tenth century. Rebels such as An Lushan could also fight with the aim of overturning and supplanting the ruling dynasty, keeping the old structure of government but putting in new leaders at the top.

For a unified empire, the strategic challenge was to keep foreign and domestic opponents at bay and – if possible – assert China's dominance over surrounding states and peoples. Strong dynasties typically began by consolidating their control over the core agricultural regions of China proper, especially the watersheds of the Yellow River and the Yangzi, and then sought to extend their authority to outlying regions inhabited by non-Han peoples. A particular imperative, driven by the need to establish dynastic legitimacy, was to take possession of all the territories that had belonged to strong Chinese empires in the past; this concern helps to explain the determination of the second Sui emperor to conquer the northern Korean kingdom of Koguryŏ (which had once been part of the Han empire) and the Northern Song obsession with the recovery of the Sixteen Prefectures (in the vicinity of today's Beijing), which had been an integral part of the Tang empire.

Strong dynasties that had the wherewithal to do so also sought to extend their control over neighbouring territories to neutralise potential threats and gain access to important resources. The Inner Mongolian grasslands, for example, were a major source of cavalry horses, while the Tarim basin in today's Xinjiang provided access to central Asia and the trade of the Silk Road. By far the most successful Chinese regime of this period was the early Tang, which crushed the Eastern Türks and a variety of other nomadic opponents, received the submission of steppe tribes and trading cities as far west as the borders of Persia, and maintained its hegemony over this vast peripheral zone for nearly half a century.

Weaker empires, such as the Northern Song and the Tang after the An Lushan rebellion, had to content themselves with defending their core territories in China proper. An additional strategic goal of all Chinese regimes, whether weak or strong, imperial court or autonomous province, was to ensure that their own armed forces were not capable of posing a threat to the ruler.

The Means of Strategy

The basic military instruments available to strategists remained largely the same throughout this extensive time span. Taking the very long view of Chinese history, it is clear that continuity rather than change in strategy was the dominant theme of the period from the late second century AD to the early twelfth century. Yet not everything remained the same. In military technology, there were many incremental improvements: the introduction of the stirrup around AD 300, for example, as well as more efficient methods of steel production some two centuries later, more effective polearms during the Sui and Tang dynasties, and continuing advances in both fortification and siegecraft throughout the period. And toward the end of our time frame, during the tenth and eleventh centuries, there was a potentially revolutionary change as gunpowder came to be weaponised, initially in the form of bombs and smoke grenades, followed a little later by rockets and eruptors (flame-throwing devices that were the precursors of gunpowder artillery). There were also advances in administrative tools and techniques, especially the elaboration and refinement of control mechanisms designed to prevent the military from becoming a threat to the ruler – 'coup-proofing', in today's parlance.

Most Chinese rulers relied on armies composed primarily of infantry equipped with edged weapons (swords and spears of various sorts), bows and crossbows.

Although foot soldiers were numerically predominant, cavalry – including both armoured lancers and steppe-style mounted archers – was usually the decisive strike force in battle and was absolutely essential for Chinese armies campaigning in the grasslands of inner Asia.

Given China's ample demographic resources and highly developed bureaucratic tradition dating back to the Warring States period, the armed forces that were raised were often of impressive size. When the Sui founder overwhelmed the Chen dynasty in southern China in 589, he committed more than half a million soldiers along a front hundreds of miles long, from Sichuan to the mouth of the Yangzi river. An even larger force of approximately a million men was reportedly gathered for his successor's attack on the Korean kingdom of Koguryŏ in 612. And when China was divided, even regional powers were capable of supporting armies numbering in the hundreds of thousands. Sustaining such forces in the field was a daunting logistical and administrative challenge that imposed serious constraints on strategists. For the long-range Koguryŏ expedition of 612, more than 2 million men were conscripted to perform logistical support functions, with many of them assigned to haul grain to the front using small carts and wheelbarrows, yet despite this massive effort the Sui army still ran short of provisions. The size of armies often dictated the routes they could follow, tying them to waterborne transport along rivers and canals and discouraging them from bypassing enemy-held fortresses that might interdict their all-important lines of supply.

Chinese rulers also made use of warships and waterborne forces, often in very large numbers, for both riverine and overseas operations. Both the Western Jin attacking the Wu state in 279 and the Sui assailing Chen in 589 built fleets upstream in Sichuan and sent them down the Yangzi in co-ordination with armies advancing overland, while the Later Zhou and Song forces operating against the Southern Tang state from the 950s to the 970s worked in concert with naval flotillas on first the Huai river and later the Yangzi. Expeditions on the open sea were less frequently seen and were directed mainly against the Korean peninsula, with major efforts carried out by Sui in 612 and Tang in 645 and 660 – first against Koguryŏ and then, with greater success, against Koguryŏ's weaker ally Paekche. In one of the rare sea battles of the period, the Tang fleet defeated Japanese forces coming to assist Paekche off the south-west coast of Korea in 663. In contrast to land armies, Chinese fleets were usually not maintained for the long term as forces in being, but were instead purpose-built when the need arose and decommissioned once their usefulness had passed. This happened because Chinese rulers rarely, if ever, faced serious threats coming from the sea. The rule-proving exceptions were regional states such as Wu, Chen and Southern Tang that needed water forces to defend *river* barriers against sustained military pressure from stronger regimes based in northern China.

Static defences such as fortified cities, frontier walls and other obstacles also played a significant role in Chinese imperial strategy. The core areas of China proper, the empire's heartland, were thickly studded with walled cities that dominated the surrounding countryside and served as centres of admin-istration. With walls of pounded earth often tens of feet thick and in some cases faced with brick or stone, these strong points presented major hurdles to would-be conquerors. Though difficult to take by siege or assault, their control was nevertheless essential for securing lines of supply and extending political domination. Capital cities – the locus of ruling elites, storehouses of material resources and symbols of political legitimacy – were the ultimate military objective when rival rulers competed for supremacy in the Chinese heartland and neighbouring sedentary realms (such as those of the Korean peninsula). Static defences were also used to protect Chinese territories against incursions from the grasslands to the north, although the popular image of a single, continuous Great Wall stretching thousands of miles from Shanhaiguan on the sea coast to Jiayuguan in the far west is wide of the mark for this 'middle period' of Chinese history. Some regimes, such as Northern Qi and Sui in the late sixth and early seventh centuries, did build limited sections of wall, but the more usual pattern was a series of discrete, well-garrisoned fortresses to guard strategic points along the frontier. The Six Garrisons of Northern Wei in the early sixth century fit this mould, as did the three 'Fortresses for Receiving Surrender' that the Tang constructed north of the Ordos bend of the Yellow River in the early 700s. Nor did frontier barriers always consist of walls, whatever their size and shape: in the early tenth century, the Northern Song secured one critical, low-lying sector of their frontier with the Kitan Liao by creating an extensive belt of waterways and flooded terrain that historian Peter Lorge has called 'the Great Ditch of China'.[3]

The 'software' of Chinese imperial strategy – military institutions and organisation – was at least as important a factor as the hardware. Later dynasties inherited two basic models of military service from the Warring States, Qin and Han. The first, a product of the intense internecine

---

3 P. Lorge, 'The Great Ditch of China and the Song–Liao border', in D. J. Wyatt (ed.), *Battlefronts Real and Imagined: War, Border, and Identity in the Chinese Middle Period* (New York: Palgrave Macmillan, 2008), 59–74.

competition of the Warring States period, called for mass conscript armies drawn from the general (that is, agricultural) population: all adult males were to be trained for war, and large numbers could be called up for active duty when needed and demobilised to return to their farms once the crisis had passed. This system was well suited for raising the largest possible infantry armies to battle against peer competitors near at hand, and it had the added advantage of being relatively inexpensive (with soldiers responsible for their own upkeep most of the time) while preventing the formation of the sort of long-term relationships between soldiers and their officers that might pose a threat to the central authority. It was not so well suited, however, to fighting nomadic opponents on distant frontiers, so the Western Han period saw the beginning of a shift towards the use of long-service, professional fighting men whose ranks included a much higher proportion of cavalry. Such forces were generally more effective in battle, but they were also relatively costly and potentially dangerous to the state. In the last years of the Eastern Han, following the Yellow Turban uprising of AD 184, military commanders and regional governors were able to privatise their armies, ushering in the rampant warlordism of the Three Kingdoms period. Similar shifts, and problems, would also occur in later periods. The early Tang relied very heavily on the *fubing* system of part-time farmer-soldiers inherited from the Northern Zhou and Sui dynasties, but – for much the same reasons as in Han times – this arrangement gradually gave way to professional frontier armies, loyal to their own commanders, that provided the basis for the An Lushan rebellion of 755–763 and the age of the autonomous provincial warlords following its suppression.

The An Lushan rebellion stands as a warning of what could happen when rulers let down their guard, but army mutinies on such a large scale were unusual. A tremendous range of overlapping institutional and organisational devices were employed by Chinese regimes to keep the military from getting out of hand. Both the Han and Tang dynasties, for example, used tally systems to authenticate military orders: only when the half of the tally sent from the capital was matched with the half held by the local unit could troops be set into motion, and according to Tang law the punishment for an officer who mobilised as few as ten men without permission was a year of penal servitude. Divided command arrangements and systems of checks and balances were the norm. In the early Tang, which built on precedents established in the Sui and Northern Zhou, the safeguards were especially intricate and multi-layered. Part-time soldiers from the provinces were fed into the imperial guard commands in the capital according to a system of rotations that brought together men from many different local units to serve under unfamiliar officers for very short periods of time – and if this was not enough, there was also an entirely separate imperial palace army with its own chain of command to serve as a counterweight. Campaign armies, meanwhile, were assembled from diverse sources and dissolved as soon as they had achieved their objectives, thereby preventing the commanders from forging long-term relationships with their troops. Although many of these systems broke down in the first half of the eighth century, other expedients came into play in the late Tang provincial garrisons and continued into the Song period, most notably the use of picked corps of elite troops – the headquarters guard, the 'Emperor's Army' – to ward off potential threats from less reliable formations and their commanders. Yet another device used by many dynasties to restrain their generals was the appointment of army supervisors, a role that in the late Tang was routinely filled by trusted court eunuchs.

Given the near obsessive attention that Chinese rulers gave to keeping the military establishment on a tight leash, it should not be surprising that they often chose to accomplish the ends of strategy by other than military means. Especially when Chinese states were weak relative to potential opponents, selective concessions and various forms of bribery could be more attractive than the certain costs and uncertain outcome of direct military action. When the second Tang emperor, Li Shimin, newly installed on the throne in 626 after a bloody coup against members of his own family, had to confront a massive incursion by the Eastern Türks that reached almost to the outskirts of his capital, he prudently chose to 'entice them with gold and silk' rather than risk a military engagement.[4] More than a century later, in the wake of the disastrous An Lushan rebellion, his descendants acquiesced to the extortionate exchange of Chinese silk for poor-quality horses in order to secure the forbearance and occasional military support of the Uighurs. And in the early eleventh century the Song emperor Zhenzong secured a lasting peace with the Kitan Liao by conceding control of the coveted Sixteen Prefectures and agreeing to an annual payment of 100,000 taels of silver and 200,000 bolts of silk. Such concessionary tactics could also be used to defuse internal tensions within China. After eight years of fighting, the An Lushan rebellion was finally brought to an end in 763 – not by a decisive Tang victory on the battlefield, but by a series of deals with the remaining rebel commanders that

---

4 Sima Guang, Zizhi tongjian (Beijing: Guji chubanshe, 1956), Chapter 191, 6020. Also see Liu Su, Sui Tang jia hua, Chapter 1, 5, in Zhongguo wenxue cankao ziliao xiao congshu, Volume II (Shanghai: Gudian wenxue chubanshe, 1957); and Li Shutong, Tang shi suoyin (Taipei: Taiwan Commercial Press, 1988), 54–8.

allowed them to retain de facto control of their territories and armies in exchange for nominal acceptance of the authority of the imperial court.

As the heirs to a tradition of strategic thought that emphasised the importance of securing all possible advantages before engaging an enemy in battle, Chinese rulers and commanders not surprisingly made extensive use of propaganda and other methods of psychological warfare. Army strengths were routinely inflated in order to intimidate and demoralise one's adversaries, and leaders were always on the lookout for portents that might provide evidence of divine support to encourage their own supporters while dismaying the enemy. These could be anything from favourable dreams to auspicious cloud formations or stones bearing numinous inscriptions, and when Heaven or nature failed to deliver them, they could be manufactured as needed. When the Western Jin general Li Ju was trying to arouse his troops to launch a surprise attack against the Xiongnu army that was preparing to besiege them in the city of Xingyang in 317, he got a shaman to channel the shade of a revered ancient statesman and announce that 'spirit soldiers' (shen bing) would arrive to assist them in the coming battle.[5] At the most basic level, psychological warfare involved efforts to persuade all who would listen that one's opponent was a monster of depravity. In 588, preparing for his invasion of the Chen state in the south, the Sui emperor drew up a twenty-article indictment against the Chen ruler and had 300,000 copies made for distribution throughout southern China.[6] This approach was grounded in the notion of the Mandate of Heaven, first formulated as early as the eleventh century BC and fully elaborated during the Zhou dynasty, which made political legitimacy dependent on personal virtue – with the caveat that victory in battle was the ultimate proof of Heaven's support for the morally upright.

Strategic Outcomes

In the Sunzi, rulers are advised to approach war with great caution, as something not to be undertaken without careful consideration. The ruler and his counsellors are supposed to perform a series of assessments and calculations in advance to determine which side enjoys the advantage in each

---

5 Fang Xuanling et al., Jin shu (Beijing: Zhonghua shuju, 1974), Chapter 63, 1707. Three centuries later, a beleaguered Sui general would use almost exactly the same ploy; see Wei Zheng et al., Sui shu (Beijing: Zhonghua shuju, 1973) Chapter 70, 1631–2.
6 A. F. Wright, 'Sui Yang-ti: personality and stereotype', in Wright (ed.), The Confucian Persuasion (Stanford: Stanford University Press, 1960), 47–76, 64.

of several categories, and only if the outcome of this exercise is favourable should one proceed towards armed conflict. But if the calculations are favourable and have been performed correctly, one's ultimate victory is entirely predictable.

Throughout the history of imperial China, rulers and generals showed a keen sensitivity to their own capabilities relative to those of their opponents and tailored their strategic behaviour accordingly. Modern students of Chinese strategic culture have pointed to a 'doctrine of absolute flexibility' that enabled decision makers to keep their ends in line with their means, and have distinguished between 'weak-state' and 'strong-state' strategies pursued by Chinese leaders under different circumstances.[7] The Sui dynasty of the late sixth century provides us with an example of a Chinese state proceeding from a position of relative strength and making its strategic decisions accordingly, while the Tang dynasty of the 620s was in a much less advantageous situation and manoeuvred with much greater care and caution to achieve its desired outcomes. Let us consider each of the cases in turn before examining their similarities and differences.

In the late 580s, the Sui was a dynasty on the make. Its ambitious founding emperor, Yang Jian, was the beneficiary of the unification of north China under the Northern Zhou dynasty a decade earlier, and of a series of fortuitous events that had brought to the Zhou throne a child ruler who happened to be his own grandson. Yang Jian replaced the Zhou with his own Sui dynasty in 581 and soon set his sights on the conquest of the southern state of Chen, which ruled most of the remainder of China, roughly from the Yangzi river southward. The balance of power was tilted strongly in Sui's favour, since Chen had a registered population of only about 500,000 house-holds – probably less than one-eighth that of its northern rival.[8] Although protected by the broad expanse of the Yangzi river, Chen was burdened with the defence of a frontier some 900 miles long.

Yang Jian's operational plan involved the assembly of eight large armies totalling more than half a million men along a front from Sichuan in the west to the shores of the East China Sea. The westernmost Sui force would

---

7 A. I. Johnston, *Cultural Realism: Strategic Culture and Grand Strategy in Chinese History* (Princeton: Princeton University Press, 1995); M. D. Swaine and A. J. Tellis, *Interpreting China's Grand Strategy: Past, Present, and Future* (Santa Monica: RAND, 2000).

8 According to Du You, *Tong dian* (Beijing: Zhonghua shuju, 1988), Chapter 7, 146–7, which assigns half a million households to Chen and has Sui inheriting 3,590,000 households from Northern Zhou. Before its attack on Chen, Sui conducted registration drives that added hundreds of thousands more; see Wei Zheng et al., *Sui shu*, Chapter 24, 681.

descend the Yangzi with a huge riverine flotilla to eliminate or at least tie down the Chen armies downriver and prevent them from coming to the relief of the southern capital, Jiankang (today's Nanjing). Several of the eastern armies would then strike directly across the Yangzi at Jiankang.

Despite the enormous numerical advantage enjoyed by the Sui forces, who outnumbered their opponents by roughly five to one, Yang Jian and his generals made every effort to tilt the scales even further in their favour. In addition to the propaganda campaign already mentioned above, they undertook to conceal their preparations while making active efforts to lull their opponents into a false sense of security (for example, Sui troops north of the lower Yangzi regularly carried out large hunts near the riverbank, so that Chen outposts came to view commotion on the other side as nothing out of the ordinary). The attack plan was set in motion at the end of 588 and carried off almost without a hitch, with the Chen capital and emperor falling into Sui hands early in 589. It was only then that things began to go awry. Like other conquerors since then, the Sui commanders had banked mainly on the application of overwhelmingly superior force, while giving little thought to post-conquest stabilisation and the winning of 'hearts and minds'. The result was that the disrespect of newly installed Sui officials for local customs and economic interests provoked a series of uprisings across the former Chen realm that required much additional effort to suppress.

In the mid-620s the founders of the Tang dynasty faced strategic challenges very different from those that Yang Jian had confronted some four decades earlier. Li Yuan and his sons had emerged from a crowded field of armed factions angling to supplant the faltering Sui dynasty; having launched their bid for power in 617, they succeeded in overcoming all of their significant opponents within China by 624. This brought them face to face with the powerful steppe empire of the Eastern Türks, which had taken advantage of the multi-cornered civil war in China to play divide and rule by backing various contenders (including, at one time, the Tang themselves). Seeking to delay or prevent the Tang dynasty's consolidation of power, the Türks launched large-scale raids into northern China every year from 623 to 626.

The initial Tang response was a rather passive, defensive strategy aimed at limiting or containing the nomads' incursions. This approach was dictated by the reality of their situation. Although the Li family were nominal masters of a vast empire with a population and resource base many times greater than that of their steppe opponents, real power across much of China was still in the hands of local strongmen who had only recently offered their submission, making the extraction and employment of human and material resources for an all-out war against the Türks highly problematic. And there was also political uncertainty at the very top of the Tang regime, where Li Yuan's sons were involved in a vicious power struggle that was not resolved until the summer of 626, when the second son, Li Shimin, killed his two brothers and then forced his father to abdicate the throne.

The new emperor continued the cautious policy toward the Türks, while strengthening his own hand by pursuing military reforms and implementing a new training regimen for his troops. A more aggressive approach was not seriously considered until 627, when unusually severe winter weather caused the die-off of much of the nomads' livestock, weakening the Eastern Türks' leader Illig (Xieli) Qaghan and creating the opportunity for many of his subject tribes to rebel. At that time, however, Li Shimin rejected advice that he move immediately to exploit the changed situation by attacking the Türks. Instead, he bided his time for another two years, forming alliances with other steppe peoples opposed to the Türks and even driving a wedge into the enemy's leadership by reaching an agreement with Illig Qaghan's nephew Tuli, an important leader in his own right.

Towards the end of 629, when the Tang ruler finally felt the time was right for a large-scale offensive, he deployed 100,000 men to advance in six columns on a front of 720 miles. The easternmost and westernmost columns aimed simply to pin opposing forces in place, while the larger central columns moved directly against Illig Qaghan's headquarters near the frontier town of Dingxiang. After an initial defeat at Dingxiang, the *qaghan* retreated to Iron Mountain (Tieshan), the gateway to an escape route across the Gobi Desert, and sought to open peace negotiations with the Tang court. The Tang field commander, Li Jing, took advantage of the presence of an imperial envoy in Illig's camp to launch a surprise attack in March of 630. The main force of the Eastern Türks was completely shattered, and over 50,000 of the nomads surrendered when they found that their escape route into the desert had been blocked by a subsidiary Chinese column. This defeat precipitated the complete collapse of the Eastern Türk qaghanate and inaugurated nearly half a century of Chinese dominance over the northern steppes, as the Turkic warriors who had once terrorised the Tang empire became its vassals and played a key role in Tang expansion at the expense of other nomadic peoples to the west and north.

There are obvious similarities between the Sui campaign against Chen in 588–589 and the Tang conflict with the Eastern Türks which culminated in 630 at Iron Mountain. In both cases, we see large forces deployed, manoeuvred and co-ordinated over great distances with a high degree of success, despite the absence of modern communications technologies. We also see a keen determination to gain every possible advantage – especially by means of trickery and deception – in order to ensure that the outcome of the final clash of arms becomes a foregone conclusion.

Yet there are also some significant differences. Li Shimin's military offensive against Illig Qaghan unfolded only after several years of watching and waiting for just the right conditions to emerge, and after extensive efforts had been made to suborn the *qaghan*'s tribal allies and even exploit splits within his own family. There was no such contingent aspect to Yang Jian's conquest of Chen, which proceeded entirely according to Sui's own timetable of fleet building and force mobilisation and involved no serious efforts to create divisions within the southern state or isolate it from potential allies. As victors, the Tang were also more solicitous in seeking to secure the willing co-operation of the defeated. Even after the battle of Iron Mountain, they paid in gold and silk for the redemption of Chinese captives held by the Eastern Türks; many of the Türks' leaders were appointed to high positions in the Tang military establishment, and some were even allowed to marry into the imperial family. In these differences it is possible to discern the bedrock element of Chinese imperial strategy and indeed of all sound strategy: a keen sensitivity to one's own strength and capability relative to those of one's opponent, and a willingness to trim one's ambitions to accord with the prevailing conditions.

7

Ancient Rome

Principate and Dominate (27 BC–AD 630)

MICHAEL WHITBY

Sources

One difficulty in analysing Roman grand strategy is the dearth of evidence.[1] Although military activity was one of the main elements of narrative histories in the classical world, these provide intermittent coverage of the six and a half centuries under consideration: at specific times we are reasonably well informed, as in Tacitus' accounts of the early principate, Josephus on the *Jewish War* (66–73), Ammianus Marcellinus on the mid-fourth century or Procopius on Justinian's wars. For much of the period, however, there is no detailed reliable narrative: thus for the third-century 'crisis' we are largely dependent on a collection of imperial biographies compiled more than a century later, while for the fifth century the histories of Priscus and Malchus survive only in fragments, whose quality underlines the importance of what has been lost.[2] Furthermore, even the best-informed of these historians did not have access to detailed information on the discussions that led to specific decisions at the highest level. As the historian Cassius Dio (53.19) observed, imperial decisions were taken in secret and the information available to the public could not be confirmed. The most detailed description we have for a meeting of imperial advisers is the satirical account by Juvenal (*Satires* 4) of that summoned urgently by Domitian to discuss what should be done with the gift of a giant turbot. Historians might pick up the general gist of a meeting – for example that in 180 the advisers of the recently deceased Marcus Aurelius urged his son Commodus not to abandon the war against the Marcomanni (Cassius Dio

---

1 See K. Kagan, 'Redefining Roman grand strategy', *Journal of Military History* 40 (2006), 350–4; also Fergus Millar, 'Emperors, frontiers and foreign relations, 31 BCE to A.D. 378', *Britannia* 13 (1982), 1–23.
2 For a succinct overview of the sources for Roman warfare, see A. D. Lee, *Warfare in the Roman World* (Cambridge: Cambridge University Press 2020), 20–9.

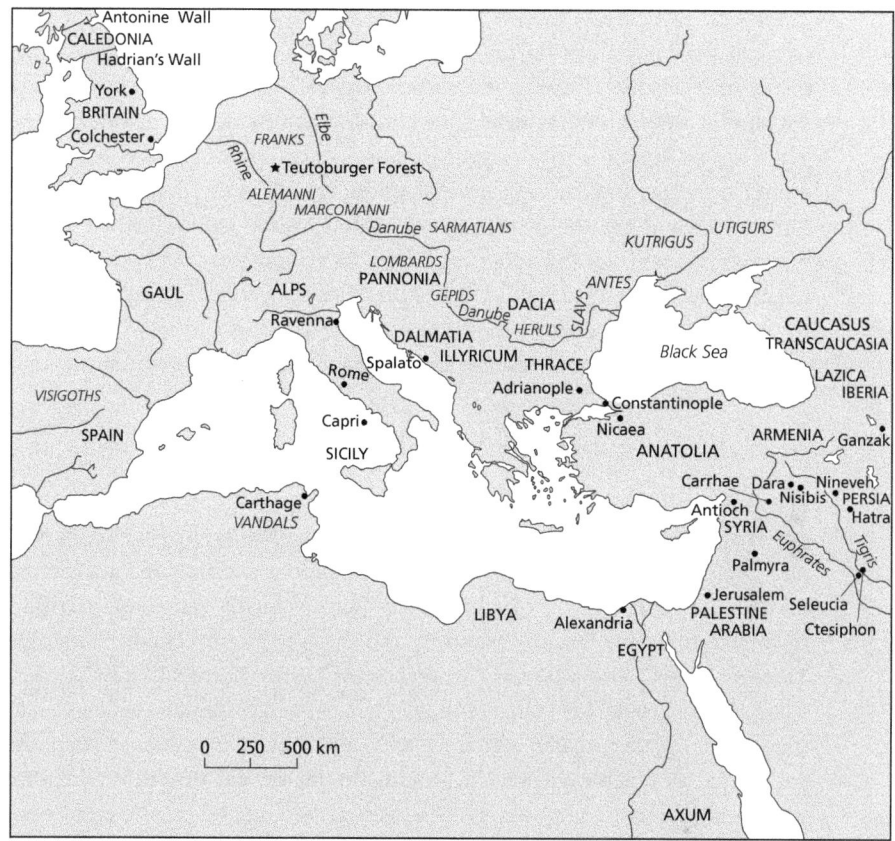

Map 7.1 Strategies of ancient Rome: principate and dominate (27 BC–AD 630)

73.1–2),[3] that in 378 Valens was given conflicting advice about fighting the Goths at Adrianople (Ammianus 31.12.5–7), or that in 590 Maurice overruled his council, including the advice of the Patriarch John Nesteutes, in supporting the exiled Persian king, Khusro II (Pseudo-Sebeos 2; John of Nikiu 96.10–13).[4] In the early empire the Senate retained its traditional role in the reception of foreign embassies, but any record that was made of associated debates does not survive.

3 D. Potter, *The Roman Empire at Bay*, CE 180–395 (London: Routledge, 2004), 86–7, questions the veracity of the story, but even if not entirely true it had to be plausible.
4 A possible exception is Procopius' (*Wars* 3.10.1–24) account of Justinian's decision in 533 to attack the Vandals; he composed a speech opposing the decision for the praetorian prefect, John the Cappadocian, information that he would have obtained from the expedition's commander, Belisarius, who was probably present.

Physical evidence – such as inscriptions carved in stone; records on both papyrus, primarily from Egypt, and wooden tablets recovered at Vindolanda, a fort near Hadrian's Wall; and archaeological remains of Roman military structures – shed no direct light on central decision making or grand strategy. The only exception is the *Notitia Dignitatum*, a comprehensive record of the empire's civilian and military administration, including the deployment of its armed forces across the provinces, probably towards the end of the period between 400 and 425 but reflecting recent developments.[5] As recognised by Kagan, at its best the ancient evidence provides us with some insight into the results of imperial decisions relating to resource allocation, from which we can draw inferences about what factors may have informed the relevant discussions.

Actors

For most of Roman imperial history the key agent in terms of decisions and objectives was, unsurprisingly, the emperor. As *imperator*, or general, he was ultimately in command of all the empire's military forces, after an initial period under Augustus when some provinces with smaller legionary garrisons remained under the Senate's authority. There were rare exceptions. One was Tiberius (14–37), who attempted to reverse Augustus' domination by encouraging senators to debate matters but, when frustrated by their unwillingness to state opinions, eventually withdrew to Capri. But in his absence, senators looked to his praetorian prefect, Sejanus, for decisions.[6] Another exception was during the last eighty years of the western empire, when emperors were overshadowed by a succession of generals, Stilicho, Aetius, Ricimer and finally Odoacer,[7] all of whom controlled crucial decisions and even undermined Majorian's attempt to regain control, until the Scirian Odoacer decided to dispense with the fig leaf of his puppet ruler, Romulus 'Augustulus'.

Emperors never ruled alone, being supported by family members, including women who could exercise considerable influence, senior officials who were often former slaves or members of the non-senatorial equestrian class, select senators and, on occasions, military commanders. Who might be

---

5 The *Notitia* does not provide a single snapshot of military deployment, since its eastern half was updated in the early fifth century, but even in its composite state it provides important evidence for the distribution of imperial resources. For discussion, see A. H. M. Jones, *The Later Roman Empire, 284–602: A Social, Economic and Administrative Survey* (Oxford: Blackwell, 1964), 1419–50.
6 B. Levick, *Tiberius the Politician* (London: Thames & Hudson, 1976).
7 See J. M. O'Flynn, *Generalissimos of the Western Roman Empire* (Edmonton: University of Alberta Press, 1983).

consulted on major issues depended on who had access to the emperor and, particularly when he was on his travels, who was accompanying him, but few of the potential advisers had military experience.[8] A text attached to the tenth-century *De Caerimoniis* claims that before a campaign Constantine the Great would seek expert advice about his intended enemy as well as logistical practicalities; also, to counteract the leakage of sensitive information, he disguised the target by requesting the same about other lands. The text has nothing to do with the fourth-century Constantine,[9] though there are indications that intelligence on the outside world was sought in the sixth century. In the high empire there are a very few examples of fact-finding expeditions,[10] but most information will have been sent in by provincial governors, who made regular reports but whose views might be inaccurate or self-interested. Tacitus (*Agricola* 24) said that his father-in-law Agricola, who hoped to extend his conquests, used to say that he could have subdued Ireland with one legion and some auxiliaries; this view was presumably reported to Domitian (81–96), who did not share his optimism.[11] Normally, emperors appointed, or confirmed the choice of, those who directly controlled the troops in the provinces and led campaigns. Their appointees were expected to carry out instructions, and military initiatives that might bring exceptional fame to their leaders were reined in, as Germanicus found when his German campaign (15–16) was curtailed by Tiberius, or were not authorised, as the Roman general Corbulo experienced in 47, when Claudius ordered an immediate end to operations he had initiated against the Chauci (Tacitus, *Annals* 11.19–20). The speed of communication in the ancient world did usually give governors some leeway in determining actions,[12] and constrained emperors' ability to take decisions.

For the first four centuries of empire, many emperors led major campaigns in person since the bond between ruler and legions was a key element in ensuring the stability of the state, and victory was a crucial aspect of imperial ideology.[13] In the early empire, down to Trajan (98–117), it

---

8 For the imperial entourage, see F. Millar, *The Emperor in the Roman World (31* BCE–CE *337)* (London: Duckworth, 1977), Chapter 3, esp. 69–132, and for decision making, Millar, 'Emperors, frontiers and foreign relations', 4–7.

9 Constantine Porphyrogennitus, *Three Treatises on Imperial Military Expeditions* (ed. and trans. J. F. Haldon) (Vienna: Verlag der Österreichischen Akadamie der Wissenschaften, 1990), Text B; for discussion of date, see 45–53.

10 Millar, 'Emperors, frontiers and foreign relations', 15–16.

11 Even at a tactical level, information might be contradictory: Ammianus 21.13.4.

12 Millar, 'Emperors, frontiers and foreign relations', 9–10.

13 J. B. Campbell, *The Emperor and the Roman Army, 31* BCE–CE *235* (Oxford: Oxford University Press, 1984); Michael McCormick, *Eternal Victory: Triumphal Rulership in*

was, perhaps paradoxically, emperors who lacked a military reputation who were more likely to decide to lead major campaigns, but from the mid-second century it came to be accepted that substantial military forces should be commanded by the emperor or a close relative. No single emperor, however, could be everywhere at once, and from the reign of Marcus Aurelius (161–180) it was common for military necessity to lead to the appointment of co-rulers. This was standardised under Diocletian (284–305): in 286 he first divided the empire with his colleague, Maximian, who controlled the west, and then in 293 further subdivided it by appointing two *caesars*, or junior emperors, to support the senior *augusti*.[14] In 395 with the final division of the empire between Honorius and Arcadius, the two sons of Theodosius I, even emperors with prior military experience almost never took to the field until the crises of the early seventh century forced Heraclius to do so in the 620s.[15]

Means

The main means for emperors to achieve objectives were military force, money and diplomacy, which could be deployed in differing combinations. In the high empire (31 BC–AD 305), force, whether threatened or actual, was the primary agent, although Augustus did use persuasion to secure the return from Parthia of the legionary standards lost at Carrhae, and money was sometimes paid to tribal neighbours in Europe, for example the Dacians by Domitian. At the end of Augustus' reign, following the disaster of the Teutoburger Forest in AD 9 when the provincial governor, Varus, and three whole legions were annihilated, the empire was protected by twenty-five legions, each with a complement of 5,000 to 6,000 citizen soldiers. These were supported by a roughly equal number of auxiliary non-citizen infantry, plus about half as many cavalry. If units were kept near full strength (perhaps an optimistic assumption), the total military establishment would have exceeded 300,000, to which must be added the praetorian guards and sailors in the Mediterranean and river fleets, perhaps a further 50,000 men. Citizen legionaries enjoyed better conditions of service, but

Late Antiquity, Byzantium and the Early Medieval West (Cambridge: Cambridge University Press, 1986).

14 For the emergence of the Tetrarchy, see Potter, *The Roman Empire at Bay*, 280–90.

15 On this change, see M. Whitby, 'War and State in Late Antiquity: Some Economic and Political Connections', in B. Meissner (ed.), *Krieg – Gesellschaft – Institutionen / War – Society – Institutions* (Stuttgart: Franz Steiner Verlag, 2005), 355–85.

auxiliaries did receive citizenship after twenty-five years' service, a considerable benefit. Caracalla's extension of Roman citizenship to most of the empire's free male inhabitants in 212 removed one key distinction between military units.

Augustus lamented the loss of Varus' legions, but did not attempt to replace them, and the mutinies that greeted Tiberius' accession reveal pressure on numbers of citizen soldiers since one grievance was length of service. Recruits to the legions were increasingly drawn from the colonies Augustus had established in the provinces, in Spain and Gaul in particular, to handle the demobilisation of the civil-war armies, and also from veteran settlements that grew up near major legionary bases. Caligula raised two additional legions, Vespasian a further two and Domitian one, to create an army of thirty legions that persisted through the second century until Severus enrolled a further three. In the second century about half the empire's troops were stationed along the Danube, partly reflecting local threats, and partly because they could move rapidly from there to east or west, on occasions taking advantage of the rivers to sail downstream (e.g. Ammianus 21.9.2). Campaigns had largely to be waged with existing resources, by redeploying legions or vexillations to support particular objectives.[16] These moves presumably took some account of the internal stability and external threats in each area, but such assessments were not always correct, as shown by the Jewish revolt that was facilitated by Trajan's removal of troops for his eastern campaigns.

When the shape of military forces can be assessed again after the third-century disruptions, Diocletian is reported to have had an army of 389,704 and a navy of 45,562 (John Lydus, de Mensibus 1.27). The precision may originate in a summation of returns that every military unit regularly provided, but these probably represented paper strengths rather than actual numbers.[17] Although valiant attempts have been made to extract military strengths from the Notitia Dignitatum,[18] the only other overall figure we have is provided by the historian Agathias (Hist. 5.13.7–8), who criticised Justinian for permitting numbers to fall to 150,000 whereas at some

---

16 For a summary of the successive transfers, see Kagan, 'Redefining Roman grand strategy', 354–7.

17 Confidence in the information is somewhat undermined by the fact that John proceeds to assert that Constantine doubled these numbers.

18 Jones, The Later Roman Empire, 1419–50; H. Elton, 'Military forces', in Philip Sabin, Hans van Wees and Michael Whitby (eds), The Cambridge History of Greek and Roman Warfare, Volume II, Rome from the Late Republic to the Late Empire (Cambridge: Cambridge University Press, 2007), 270–309.

unspecified earlier time the empire had been defended by 645,000 troops. Agathias, in pursuit of a rhetorical contrast, probably halved Justinian's establishment by excluding *limitanei*, frontier troops; his initial figure must relate to the whole empire, whereas Justinian's realm did not include the Rhine or British frontiers. At the start of Justinian's reign the empire in theory had five major military commands, two 'in the presence' located near Constantinople and three regional, in Illyricum, Thrace and the east; the large eastern command was subdivided to create a separate command in Armenia, while the recovery of Africa and, ultimately Italy, led to the establishment of armies there. A total official establishment on paper of over 300,000 is plausible, to which should be added the *bucellarii* or 'biscuit men', the retinues, sometimes in their thousands, maintained by senior commanders. The empire's effective operational force is a different matter, however, since, for example, units from the armies 'in the presence' contributed to the expeditions to Africa and Italy and were also stationed in the long term in provinces such as Egypt.

The empire sustained substantial armed forces, far superior to the resources available to any individual enemy, with the exception of Persia and the transient super-federations of Huns and Avars, but a key challenge was to ensure that sufficient troops were available where needed at the right time. Troops were recruited through a levy, *dilectus*, of eligible citizens, with allocations apportioned to all provinces once citizenship had been extended, but often military service was sufficiently attractive to secure volunteers and an obligation evolved that sons of soldiers should enlist.[19] On occasion, and increasingly in the late empire, troops were also recruited externally, or from outsiders who had been permitted to settle within frontiers in return for military service. The balance of forces in Roman armies changed substantially over these centuries. In the early empire infantry comprised about three-quarters of all troops, but from the third century there was a shift towards cavalry, although contrary to some popular perceptions foot soldiers always remained crucial. In response to the Sassanid threat the Romans formed a few units of heavily armoured knights, *clibanarii* or 'boilermen', but a more significant shift occurred in the fifth century when the effectiveness of Hunnic mounted archers led the empire to recruit their own. Training was crucial for all elements, since discipline was an area in which the Romans had an important advantage over most enemies, but was especially important

19 Brief discussion in Lee, *Warfare in the Roman World*, 72–4.

for horse archers who needed excellent equestrian skills and accurate shooting, as well as proficiency with sword and often lance.[20]

The empire was usually far superior to its European neighbours in terms of organisation and technology. The tribal groups on the Rhine and Danube frontiers were not proficient at siegecraft, to the extent that the fourth-century Gothic leader, Fritigern, quipped that he was not going to wage war with stone walls (Ammianus 31.6.4). By contrast Roman cities were provided with increasingly strong sets of defences and their garrisons were equipped with machines for firing bolts and stones. Germanic tribes did occasionally capture a city, usually by surprise. The exceptions were the Huns and Avars, who acquired expertise with siege equipment and were prepared to launch human waves to overwhelm defences; their weakness was the logistical organisation required to sustain a protracted siege beyond the first week or so. In the east, the Persians matched the Romans in their ability to support sieges, in technical skill and in inventiveness.

Roman legionary dispositions were underpinned by a supply system that united the empire in delivering essential resources. Internal provinces generated tax revenues in cash or produce, of which a portion was directed towards supporting the emperor, his court and capital cities, while the majority was funnelled towards the armies to pay wages and donatives and to provide supplies.[21] The richest provinces were located in the east and these supported the troops on the Euphrates and lower Danube; Egypt was a special case, since its bountiful grain harvest supplied the city of Rome until the founding of Constantinople, and it was effectively part of the emperor's private estate. In the west, North Africa, Spain, southern Gaul and southern Britain generated surpluses that provided for the Rhine and north Britain armies. We can do no more than guess at the size of the empire's population or the scale of its economy. For population, a plausible estimate for the peak in the second century, before plague in the 160s and the disruptions of the third century, is 60 million to 80 million.[22] The best that can be said about the economy is that

20 See Elton, 'Military forces'; also M. Whitby, 'Recruitment in Roman armies from Justinian to Heraclius (ca. 565–615)', in A. Cameron (ed.), The Early Byzantine and Islamic Near East, Volume III: States, Resources, Armies (Princeton: Darwin Press, 1995), 61–124; M. Whitby, 'Emperors and armies, 235–395', in S. Swain and M. Edwards (eds), Approaching Late Antiquity: The Transformation from Early to Late Empire (Oxford: Oxford University Press, 2004), 156–86.

21 K. Hopkins, 'Taxes and trade in the Roman Empire (200 B.C.–A.D. 400)', Journal of Roman Studies, 70 (1989), 101–25; Potter, The Roman Empire at Bay, 50–60.

22 W. Scheidel, 'Demography', in W. Scheidel, I. Morris and R. Saller (eds), The Cambridge Economic History of the Greco-Roman World (Cambridge: Cambridge University Press, 2007), 38–86.

there was a fine balance between income and expenditure. It is estimated that tax represented about 5 per cent of the empire's gross domestic product; it was substantially levied on agricultural production, and the rich paid proportionately much less than the poor.[23] The scope to increase revenue in sustainable ways was limited, unless emperors took the politically difficult step of challenging elite privilege,[24] so that the empire was financially squeezed, when military pay and numbers were increased under the Severans; this was exacerbated when invasions disrupted tax revenues and the rapid turnover of emperors entailed lavish donations to troops to purchase loyalty. The only way to stretch the available money was to debase the currency, as happened in the late third century.[25]

Adversaries

The main adversaries on Rome's three major river frontiers, the Rhine, Danube and Euphrates, evolved over the six centuries under consideration. In Europe, in the first two centuries the Romans were confronted by a number of moderately sized tribal groups such as the Chauci, Chatti, Marsi and Tubantes on the Rhine and the Dacians, Marcomanni, Quadi and Sarmatians on the Danube. These tribes fought each other as often as they did the Romans. For them conflict with the Romans was a dangerous enterprise, potentially lucrative but sometimes fatal, whereas coexistence brought economic benefits for those nearest the frontier through control of trade while service in the Roman *auxilia* provided good salaries. If these tribes were to constitute a serious threat, they had to set aside their local differences and create a confederation, such as that led by Arminius under Augustus or the Marcomanni against Marcus Aurelius. On the Euphrates the main enemy for the first 250 years was the Parthian kingdom. Recurrent succession disputes weakened the Parthians and the main source of tension lay in overlapping interests in Armenia and Iberia. In the second century, Trajan, Lucius Verus and Severus all managed to capture the Parthian capital, Seleucia-Ctesiphon, although the Euphrates remained the Roman frontier until the 190s. The Roman Republic had never believed that its authority

---

23 W. Scheidel and J. S. Friesen, 'The size of the economy and the distribution of income in the Roman Empire', *Journal of Roman Studies*, 99 (2009), 61–91.

24 When Honorius tried to tax senatorial wealth in the early fifth century, senators resisted, preferring to protect their assets.

25 Potter, *The Roman Empire at Bay*, 137–9, 273–4; W. Metcalf (ed.), *The Oxford Handbook of Greek and Roman Coinage* (Oxford: Oxford University Press, 2012).

terminated at the boundaries of its formal provinces, since neighbours were expected to heed, or even anticipate, Roman wishes. Under the empire this certainly applied on European frontiers and to client rulers in the east, for example Osrhoene and Armenia.

In the third century, the situation changed dramatically. In the east the Parthian dynasty, its reputation undermined by repeated Roman successes, was overthrown in 224 by the Iranian Ardashir, whose Sassanid dynasty ruled for four centuries. Ardashir, and especially his son Shapur, campaigned energetically to restore Iranian glory, defeating Emperor Gordian (244), sacking Antioch (253) and capturing Emperor Valerian (260). Although there were periods of peace in the east, for example for most of the fifth century, the Romans now had a formidable neighbour who might cause serious trouble, as under Shapur II in the fourth century and Khusro I in the sixth. The emergence of the Sassanid threat coincided with increased tensions in Europe, probably linked to the south-westward move of Gothic tribes, pushing Rome's traditional neighbours towards the empire. By the mid-fourth century, the Goths were established as the main adversary on the lower Danube, while on the upper Danube and the Rhine other tribes had coalesced into larger and more powerful groups referred to as Alamanni and Franks. In turn the Goths were coming under pressure from the westward move of Huns across the Eurasian steppe. This forced them in desperation to appeal for refuge inside the empire and in due course to invade the Balkans, with the catastrophic defeat of Emperor Valens at Adrianople in 378 as the result. Further west this pressure led Franks, Burgundians, Alans, Vandals and others to cross the Rhine in the early fifth century and progressively establish control over former Roman provinces. In the mid-fifth century, Attila, the leader of the Huns, forged a super-federation that briefly threatened the existence of both the eastern and western empires, but this disintegrated at his death, leaving groups of Gepids, Goths, Lombards, Bulgars and Heruls to scrap for territory on both banks of the Danube. In the early sixth century these were joined by Slavs and the related Antes, who had drifted south from near the Baltic, and then in the second half of the century a group of Avars arrived from central Asia to start creating another super-federation.

Causes of Wars

This is a kaleidoscope of external names, but the causes of conflict were often the same. Republican Rome had expanded remorselessly. This drive continued under Augustus, whose generals consolidated control over

Alpine tribes, conducted campaigns in the north-west Balkans that Julius Caesar had once contemplated, and penetrated Germany as far as the Elbe. Even though Augustus' deathbed advice was to maintain current frontiers (Tacitus, *Annals* 1.11), some emperors did initiate wars to secure the glory of annexing new territories to convert into provinces, as Claudius did in Britain. Maintaining frontiers did not entail passive defence, since neighbours had constantly to be reminded of Roman might and the consequences of ignoring its wishes. Territory might be ravaged, reprisals exacted, hostages taken, but the intention was not to annihilate the opponents, in part because the creation of a void beyond the frontier would invite new tribes to occupy the space, and in part because Rome benefited from recruiting established neighbours into its auxiliary units.[26] Demonstrations of power underpinned successful diplomacy, as Tiberius observed when ending Germanicus' German campaigns (Tacitus, *Annals* 2.26).

Wars also arose from the inevitable pressures created by the empire's prosperity, which led its tribal neighbours to exploit chances to conduct raids, as well as by the shifting dynamics of political formations beyond the frontiers, especially when major movements of peoples squeezed other groups. Even the poorest of Roman provinces was wealthy in comparison to conditions outside, and the Rhine and Danube offered tribes some protection against other enemies. Some campaigns were fought to recover lost territories, especially after the empire had surrendered control of certain regions: Justinian regained north Africa and Italy, and in 536 speculated that with divine favour he might even recover all lost Roman territories as far as the Ocean (Justinian, *Novel* 30.11.2), while in 572 Justin II (565–578) chose to exploit a perceived crisis for the Persians, with Christian Armenians in revolt and Turks in central Asia offering to collaborate, in order to recover Nisibis, which Emperor Jovian (363–364) had surrendered.[27]

In the east the Parthian empire appeared to offer scope for territorial expansion, but with the Sassanids the situation was different, since part of their aim, at least down to the long reign of Shapur II (309–379), may have been the recovery of their ancestral Achaemenid empire, a goal that might justify conquering the whole of the Levant, Asia Minor and even parts of

---

26 The cynical assessment that Tacitus put into the mouth of the Scottish leader Calgacus, 'that they create a desert and call it peace' (*Agricola* 30), is obviously an exaggeration of standard Roman practice.

27 M. Whitby, *The Emperor Maurice and His Historian: Theophylact Simocatta on Persian and Balkan Warfare* (Oxford: Oxford University Press, 1988), 250–4.

Thrace.[28] Unlike any European enemy, even the mighty Huns and Avars, Sassanid Persia was an established power with the stability and resources to match Rome.[29] In the sixth century, when acquisition of territory was less realistic, Sassanid rulers still needed the internal prestige of military victory as well as material wealth that could be extracted from Roman cities.[30] As the two lights or eyes of the world with rulers who recognised the status of their neighbour,[31] the empires might co-operate against common threats from the north, but the Romans became increasingly reluctant to contribute to the costs of defending the passes over the Caucasus, since the Sassanids in international dealings liked to present themselves as recipients of tribute from Rome (John of Ephesus, *Ecclesiastical History* 6.23). For the Romans, the normal objective was maintaining the status quo, through possession of key cities and forts along a frontier whose defences were progressively strengthened.[32] One exception was Emperor Julian's Persian campaign of 363, which aimed to demonstrate that adherence to traditional Roman religion brought better results than the Christianity of his predecessor, Constantius II; another was Maurice's expedition to support Khusro II by removing the usurper Vahram.

Premises Underlying Strategic Decisions

The premises that underpinned strategic decisions are rarely known, but Cassius Dio's assessment of Septimius Severus' (193–211) eastern expansion of the empire suggests some: 'Severus ... used to say that he had gained a large additional territory and made it a bulwark for Syria. But the facts themselves show that it is a source of continual wars for us, and of great expenses. For it provides little revenue and involves great expenditure' (Cassius Dio 75.3.2–3). For Severus the security of the provinces, one of the key imperial duties alongside the maintenance of law internally, as well as simple expansion

---

28 M. Whitby, 'Byzantine diplomacy: keeping faith in international relations in late antiquity', in P. de Souza and J. France (eds), *War and Peace in Ancient and Medieval History* (Cambridge: Cambridge University Press, 2008), 120–40, esp. 123.

29 J. Howard-Johnston, 'The two great powers in late antiquity: a comparison', in Cameron, *States, Resources, Armies*, 157–226.

30 M. Whitby, 'The Persian king at war', in Edward Dabrowa (ed.), *The Roman and Byzantine Army in the East* (Krakow: Jagiellonian University Press, 1994), 227–63.

31 M. P. Canepa, *The Two Eyes of the Earth: Art and Ritual of Kingship between Roman and Sasanian Iran* (Berkeley: University of California Press, 2009); Whitby, 'Byzantine diplomacy', 125 ff.

32 J. Howard-Johnston, 'Military infrastructure in the Roman provinces north and south of the Armenian Taurus in late antiquity', in A. Sarantis and N. Christie (eds), *War and Warfare in Late Antiquity: Current Perspectives* (Leiden: Brill, 2013), 853–91.

justified his eastern campaigns, whereas for Cassius Dio as an imperial adviser an assessment of overall benefit was crucial. These factors could be weighed differently: Corbulo had thought that energetic action against the Chauci was the best protection for the frontier, but Claudius at Rome disagreed. It was accepted that personal factors influenced decisions. With regard to Severus' Caledonian campaign, Cassius Dio (77.11.1) commented that the emperor was concerned about his sons' conduct and the effects of inaction on the troops, both of which he hoped to improve by energetic campaigning. Undoubtedly there were other factors, but it is revealing that Cassius Dio expected his audience to accept his cynical assessment of imperial motivation.

A powerful factor was inherited culture: warfare had been a fact of life throughout Roman history, military success usually determined political and social prestige, and public life was surrounded by reminders of past glories. As a result an emperor's personal reputation was a consideration: this was relevant to Claudius' invasion of Britain and to Trajan's campaigns, although personal advantage might be hidden behind other factors, for example the supposed wealth of Britain and the refuge it offered Gallic rebels, or the protection of Syria.

In the Christian empire, shared religion became relevant. In 530/531 Justinian (527–565) appealed to Ella Asbeha, the Christian king of Axum in Ethiopia, to assist him against Persia by breaking the Persian stranglehold of the silk trade (Procopius, *Wars* 1.20.9–12); the Romans had recently ferried the Axumites across the Red Sea to replace a persecuting ruler in south Arabia with a Christian. In 533 the Roman reconquest of Vandal Africa was premised on the belief that the emperor must rescue orthodox Christians, while in 590 Maurice hoped that support for Khusro II might convert him to Christianity.

Last but not least, the Augustan principate had been born from exceptionally bitter civil war, and internal enemies always remained a priority for rulers: external threats might be bought off or stalled, whereas the failure to confront an internal challenge decisively might give greater credibility to a coup. Civil wars were at least as destructive as any external threat, so that actions that enhanced imperial authority and pre-empted challenges might be construed as beneficial to the state. The Year of the Four Emperors (69), which followed the overthrow of Nero, and the Year of the Five Emperors (193), in which the erratic Commodus (180–192) was ultimately replaced by Septimius Severus and Clodius Albinus, were chaotic internally but passed without major external damage. However, the fifty years of crisis in the third century were generated by a downward spiral of frontier failure and internal distractions, while the problems of the early seventh century were exacerbated in 609 when Phocas (602–610) had to face the challenge of Heraclius.[33]

Priorities

For the first 250 years, the empire usually had the luxury of choosing where and whom to fight, so that resources could be marshalled to pursue conquests, such as Britain, or to meet crises, such as the Jewish Revolt of 66.

The early empire did not prioritise the acquisition of allies, although it did claim authority over a number of client states, especially along its eastern borders, the appointment of whose rulers was approved and where activities were monitored until they were gradually subsumed into the provincial system. At the same time, along European frontiers the empire made agreements, *foedera*, under whose terms tribal groups (*foederati*) received recognition, including territory to settle within Roman frontiers, in return for military service. These treaties were granted, and revoked, at Rome's whim and were a mechanism of subjugation rather than alliance. This approach persisted for as long as Rome remained the pre-eminent power; that is, until the fourth century.[34] By the sixth century, however, the balance had shifted and, although some traditional *foederati* remained, such as the Heruls, the eastern empire had to manage a number of relationships that more closely resembled alliances. For example, Justinian established links with the Frankish king Theodebert to dissuade him from intervening in Italy, and had agreements with Gepids, Lombards and Antes, which might include annual payments from Rome, to reduce threats on the Danube.[35] There was, briefly, an alliance with Persia, when Maurice agreed to support the exiled Khusro II on the basis that legitimate monarchs had a duty to help each other.[36]

Rome had always been a combative state, where the total absence of war, symbolised by the closure of the doors to the Temple of Janus, was more unusual than conflict.[37] Legitimacy of conflict was never a problem, since ultimate victory demonstrated that the gods accepted the rectitude of Roman

---

33 On civil wars, see Lee, *Warfare in the Roman World*, 105–11.
34 P. Heather, '*Foedera* and *foederati* of the fourth century', in Walter Pohl (ed.), *Kingdoms of the Empire: The Integration of Barbarians in Late Antiquity* (Leiden: Brill, 1997), 57–74.
35 A. Sarantis, *Justinian's Balkan Wars* (Leeds: ARCA, 2016), 60–5, 251–3, 300–5.
36 Whitby, *The Emperor Maurice and His Historian*, 299–304.
37 Discussion in Lee, *Warfare in the Roman World*, 30–40.

actions. Failure indicated that the gods must be propitiated, as Decius attempted in January 250 by ordering all the empire's inhabitants to sacrifice to the traditional gods, an edict that triggered persecution of Christian recusants. Christianity brought no change, since the Old Testament 'God of Battles' gave victory to his devotees, for example Constantine at the Milvian Bridge outside Rome and Theodosius at the Frigidus. The overall Roman approach to war is encapsulated in the prophecy Aeneas received from his father Anchises in Vergil (*Aeneid* 6.853), *parcere subiectis et debellare superbos*, 'to spare the defeated and overcome the proud'. Emperors were expected to safeguard their territory, preserving the Pax Romana, and the complex dynamics of frontier relations meant that excuses for war in suppressing overmighty neighbours, or anticipating threats, could always be found.

Although we have no direct information about the processes for making strategy, it is possible to identify certain imperial priorities. Internal challenges almost invariably took precedence over external threats, although a ruler might devote some time to ensuring stability on a frontier before removing troops to confront a rival, as Constantius did in the east in 360 before moving to face Julian. The evolution in legionary dispositions shows that by the end of the first century the Rhine frontier was regarded as less dangerous than the Danube, which now had the largest concentration of troops, while the emergence of the Sassanids elevated the importance of eastern frontiers. When under severe pressure emperors were prepared to abandon territories: Aurelian withdrew from trans-Danubian Dacia in the 270s to focus on suppressing the separatist regimes in Palmyra and Gaul, in 363 Jovian sacrificed Nisibis and some territories east of the Tigris in order to extricate the Roman army from Persia (Ammianus 25.9), and in 410 Honorius recalled Roman forces from Britain to confront a usurper. These were lands that could be given up, albeit reluctantly, just as Augustus himself had abandoned the nascent province of Germania after the Varian disaster. At his accession in 117 Hadrian chose not to retain Trajan's conquests in Mesopotamia and Armenia, pulling Roman troops back to the Euphrates frontier.

The clearest evidence for the dynamics of prioritisation comes from the sixth century, especially Justinian's reign. At his accession in 527, he inherited war with the Sassanids, but ratification of the 'Endless Peace' in 532 permitted him to contemplate other projects. Recovery of north Africa from the Arian Vandals was the first opportunity and the surprisingly rapid victory there, coupled with instability in Ostrogothic Italy after Theoderic's death, offered the opportunity to regain more territory, first Sicily and Dalmatia and then Italy. To this end troops were moved from Africa and the east, with unfortunate results: the north African provinces experienced mutinies and Berber incursions, while Khusro found pretexts to break the Endless Peace in 540, just as Justinian's *generalissimo* Belisarius was accepting the Ostrogothic surrender in Ravenna. Therefore troops had to be rapidly shipped back to the east to shore up defences, with the result that in Italy Gothic power dramatically recovered under Totila. Justinian could do little in the west until the eastern frontier had been stabilised in the late 540s with a five-year truce, which enabled troops to be committed to Africa and eventually in 550/551 preparations to be made for a substantial expedition to Italy. All this time the Danube frontier remained Justinian's lowest priority, with its garrison troops dispatched to Italy and successive recruitment drives also removing potential defenders. The supremacy of the east is underlined later in the century, when Tiberius (574–582) and Maurice (582–602) funnelled resources to fight the Persian war that Justin II had initiated in 572. As a result neither emperor could do much in response to desperate requests from Rome for help in opposing the Lombards (Menander fr. 22, 24), while in the Balkans there were few troops to resist the Avars and Slavs until peace with Persia in 591 permitted a substantial shift of units to Europe.

Execution/Application

Augustus as the first emperor gradually developed a comprehensive or grand strategy during his long reign. Quite apart from the chaos of the civil wars, under the Republic there had been no effective central control of military activities or of priorities across all provinces, since individual governors could initiate action with little chance of retribution, as Cato's failed attempt to hold Julius Caesar to account for invading Germany showed. For the first thirty years of his sole reign Augustus essentially attended to unfinished business from the Republic, finishing the conquest of north-western Spain, pacifying the Alpine tribes, securing Italy by asserting control as far as the upper Danube, persuading the Parthians to return captured legionary standards, and extending Caesar's activities in Germany. There was logic to most of this activity, which substantially enhanced security in the provinces, but the driving force was probably cultural expectations of military action that included the assumption that vengeance for Carrhae would be exacted from the Parthians. Vergil's Jupiter promised to grant Rome *imperium sine fine*, empire without end (*Aeneid* 1.279), and Augustus pursued that until his last decade curtailed ambition: a major revolt in Illyricum and Pannonia (AD 6–9) and the Varian disaster (AD 9) terminated expansion into Germany and forced an assessment of how the empire could be run sustainably. After his accession, Tiberius read to the senate a statement on Roman resources that Augustus had prepared, including information on military forces; it finished with advice that the empire be kept within current frontiers (Tacitus, *Annals* 1.11). This comprehensive assessment suggests that Augustus, having, in accepted Roman fashion, pursued unlimited expansion for thirty-five years, had realised the importance of an overall strategic assessment of ways and means, a grand strategy that recognised that frontiers, whether marked by rivers and legionary camps as in Europe or less defined as in the east where client states and deserts separated Rome from Parthia, would require regular military activity in a strategy of aggressive or mobile defence.[38]

The two sides to Augustus' reign define the trajectory of imperial behaviour. Tiberius possessed an excellent military reputation and so was under no cultural pressure to campaign, but the last three members of the Julio-Claudian dynasty lacked his advantage: each was tempted by the pursuit of military glory, Claudius in particular claiming a triumph after arriving in Britain with elephants in time to oversee the capture of Colchester. Caligula and Nero had a reputation for not devoting enough attention to administration, so that grand strategy is unlikely to have contributed to their plans.[39] In the Flavian dynasty, Vespasian (69–79) and Titus (79–81) did not need additional military glory, with the former celebrating peace on his coinage and through a temple in Rome. Vespasian's younger son Domitian was less fortunate, but his military activities fit within the Augustan paradigm of maintaining the empire. A German campaign, although derided by Tacitus (*Agricola* 39) and Suetonius (*Dom.* 6), probably had a more strategic aim than the vanity projects of the later Julio-Claudians: a limited extension to the frontier (Frontinus, *Stratagems* 1.3.10) closed a substantial re-entrant in south-western Germany, thereby improving communications between the upper Rhine and the Danube.[40] Agricola's ambition to subdue all Scotland was halted in 87, since troops were needed to defend the middle Danube against

---

38 J. Thorne, 'Battle, tactics and the emergence of the *limites* in the west', in P. Erdkamp (ed.), *A Companion to the Roman Army* (Chichester: Wiley-Blackwell, 2007), 218–34, esp. 228–32.

39 A. Wallace-Hadrill, *Suetonius* (London: Duckworth, 1983), 120–2.

40 This is clearly shown by the location of forts on the map in T. Cornell and J. Matthews, *Atlas of the Roman World* (London: Phaidon, 1982), 108. Domitian, of course, did not have such visual aids, but itineraries would have revealed the benefits of what he did.

Dacian incursions; Domitian stabilised the situation in the Balkans before trouble on the Rhine distracted him, with the Dacian king Decebalus receiving annual payments to refrain from further attacks.

Dacia remained a clear threat to the frontier, but Domitian's assassination left this task for Trajan (98–117) in two separate campaigns. Decebalus had proved an unreliable client, with the result that in 105 Trajan created the trans-Danubian province of Dacia. Unlike the extensive conquests in Armenia and Mesopotamia, which resulted from Trajan's Parthian campaigns in the second decade of his reign, this extension was retained by Hadrian (117–138). Hadrian, like Augustus, appears to have had a clear sense of what territory could be sustainably controlled, and accepted that a province might have to be created where client arrangements failed, whereas Trajan had been carried away by the dream of emulating Alexander the Great (Cassius Dio 68.29), in contradiction to any sensible grand strategy.

Hadrian's retrenchment was not universally popular, as it flouted the Roman dynamic of continual expansion, but it helped establish an alternative cultural ideal of stable peace:

> In general, possessing by good government the most important parts of land and sea, they prefer to preserve their empire rather than to extend it indefinitely to poor and profitless barbarian peoples ... They surround the empire with a circle of great camps and guard so great an area of land like an estate. (Appian, *Praef.* 2.7, 7.25)

This might sound like an empire-wide strategy, but there were fluctuations on individual frontiers. In Britain, Hadrian's Wall, running from the Tyne to the Solway, separated Roman territory from untamed Caledonia, in its original whitewashed state a stark marker in the landscape. It was not, however, a barrier to movement, since there were numerous crossing points where travellers could be monitored and taxes collected. Antoninus Pius (138–161) advanced the frontier to the Forth–Clyde line where a turf wall was constructed; this was abandoned by Marcus Aurelius, though in 184 a local governor reoccupied the Antonine Wall until a mutiny forced him to withdraw. There was similar movement on the upper Danube. In response to devastating raids Marcus Aurelius campaigned from 166 until his death in 180; he may have planned to establish a province north of the Danube, comparable to Trajan's Dacia, but this project was promptly abandoned by his son, Commodus.[41] If a coherent strategy underpinned all these moves, it would be

---

41 Note, however, the scepticism of Potter, *The Roman Empire at Bay*, 86–7.

that effective frontier defence might entail limited expansion, but equally the changes may have been opportunist initiatives by emperors or local governors.

In the civil wars that brought Severus to sole power between 192 and 197, scant attention can have been paid to external strategic issues, as rivals stripped frontier armies for the sake of personal ambition. Once victorious, Severus spent little time in Rome, whose loyalty he ensured by establishing a new legion only twenty kilometres from the city. Although he defeated the Parthians and captured Ctesiphon, he failed to conquer Hatra, capital of a buffer state between the empires, and his new province in northern Mesopotamia was a vulnerable salient exposed on three sides. He spent his last three years in north Britain, attempting to conquer Caledonia, until his death at York in 211. His final advice to his two sons, 'Get along, enrich the soldiers, and don't give a damn for anyone else' (Cassius Dio 76.15.2), was pragmatic rather than strategic.[42] The elder son, Caracalla (211–217), quickly made peace with the Caledonians, withdrew troops to Hadrian's Wall and murdered his brother, Geta. He was keen on personal military glory, and in 213 responded to pressure from the Alamanni by leading a campaign across the Danube that had to be delayed to ensure his personal involvement; thereafter his attention turned east, where the mirage of Alexander and his father's unfinished business with Parthia attracted him until his assassination.[43]

Cassius Dio (77.11.5) gave a hostile assessment of Caracalla: 'He made many mistakes because of his obstinacy, for he wished not only to know everything but to be the only one who knew anything; and he wished to hold power alone and because of this he used no adviser and hated people who had useful knowledge', in other words, experts. Cassius Dio had a jaundiced view of imperial motivation, belonging as he did to the senatorial elite whose expertise was spurned, but Rome, like modern states at times, had to cope with erratic leaders who paid scant regard to expert advice or strategic reality. In the high empire it survived because there were no serious external threats. The situation changed in the third-century 'crisis', when simultaneous challenges on eastern and European frontiers overwhelmed successive emperors and threatened to split the empire between different units – Palmyra, Gaul, Britain – that looked to their own security.[44] A rapid turnover of rulers meant that individual emperors had to prioritise their own safety, improvising

---

42 Potter, *The Roman Empire at Bay*, 113–24.   43 Potter, *The Roman Empire at Bay*, 133–46.
44 For the period, see Potter, *The Roman Empire at Bay*, Part III.

responses to rapidly evolving challenges, with little time for wider issues until Aurelian (270–275), through energetic campaigning coupled with timely diplomacy, reasserted imperial control within traditional frontiers, abandoning trans-Danubian Dacia in the process.[45]

After a century in which emperors had either little inclination or little time to plan actions on any grand strategic basis, the re-establishment of stability by Diocletian (284–303) and his Tetrarchic colleagues brought the benefits of peace to the provinces, as imperial legislation and panegyrics proclaimed (Prices Edict, *praef.* 6; *Pan, Lat.* 10.14.4). The absence of a strong Sassanid ruler between the death of Shapur I in 270 and Shapur II's adulthood in the 330s was a major boost, since this permitted the Tetrarchs to choose where they focused military resources, stabilising the Rhine frontier while briefly tolerating the independent rule in Britain of Carausius and Allectus until 296. Diocletian appears, like Augustus and Hadrian, to have had the vision and time to consider the totality of the challenges facing the empire and responded progressively.[46] He was praised for restoring fortifications along the Rhine, Danube and Euphrates; he supplemented these with a military road (the Strata Diocletiana between the Euphrates and Palestine); solidified the distinction between more mobile troops which accompanied emperors (*comitatenses*) and local troops with more specific defensive priorities (*limitanei*); began the stabilisation of imperial finances; and intensified central control through the fragmentation of several provinces. Diocletian started the process of improving defences at towns and cities away from the frontiers and along major routes in a strategy that is often referred to as defence in depth, but which also provided a robust platform from which to sustain the traditional aggressive defence of frontiers.[47] His attention extended to the succession, since in 303, after celebrating two decades of rule, he stepped down to retire to Spalato (Split) and made his co-*augustus* Maximian do the same, promoting their Tetrarchic *caesars*, Galerius and Constantius, to succeed as *augusti*.

Diocletian's grand vision for an orderly empire run by collaborative rulers survived less than three years. When Constantius died at York in 306, rather than waiting for the surviving *augustus*, Galerius, to promote the western *caesar*, Severus, his troops acclaimed Constantius' son, Constantine, as *augustus*. This launched a career that took him, as he wrote in a letter to Shapur II,

---

45 A. Watson, *Aurelian and the Third Century* (London: Routledge, 1999).

46 S. Williams, *Diocletian and the Roman Recovery* (London: Batsford, 1985) Part III.

47 A. Sarantis, 'Waging war in late antiquity', in Sarantis and Christie, *War and Warfare in Late Antiquity*, 1–98, esp. 7–25.

from the borders of the British ocean to sole rule of the whole Roman world, thanks to the help of the Christian God (Eusebius, *Vit. Const.* 2.28). Until his final victory in 324 over Licinius (Galerius' successor in the east), Constantine's priority was to expand his realm by overcoming a series of internal rivals and colleagues. When possible, he campaigned to secure frontiers, for example along the Rhine in 308–310, but abandoned this when threatened by Maximian. Civil wars drew external tribes into central Roman affairs, with Licinius and Constantine swapping accusations about their dealings with the Goths and Constantine relying heavily on Franks to defeat Licinius.[48] Religion became a cause of conflict, with Constantine alleging that Licinius had abandoned toleration of Christians, and then at the end of his reign marching against Shapur after claiming the right to protect Christians in Persia and urging the Sassanid to convert.

In addition to his energetic patronage of his new religion, Constantine had continued Diocletian's efforts to re-establish administrative, economic and military stability, and these emperors can jointly claim credit for the resilience of the fourth-century empire, but the reality was that the world was changing. As Potter has observed, in the third and fourth centuries the Roman empire evolved from a hegemonic to a regional power,[49] with the consequence that much greater attention had to be paid to managing external relations since the superiority of Roman arms could no longer be assumed. Emperors and their entourages took time to appreciate the new situation: in 369 Valens had to agree to negotiate with the Gothic leader Athanaric on equal terms in the middle of the Danube, as did Valentinian on the Rhine with Macrianus, and in 375 Valentinian died of apoplexy triggered by the insolent behaviour of Quadi envoys (Ammianus 27.5.9, 30.3.4–5, 30.10). Traditional attitudes persisted: Julian expected to emulate imperial predecessors by capturing Ctesiphon, but could not even lay siege to the city; one reason why Valens at Adrianople in 378 declined to wait for western reinforcements under Gratian was to avoid sharing credit for the expected victory with his western colleague. One change, however, was that religion offered an explanation for both disasters, Julian being an aggressive pagan and Valens an equally fierce opponent of the Trinitarian doctrines of Nicaea that became orthodoxy under Theodosius (379–395).

Theodosius was more realistic: he defused the Gothic problem by granting lands in the Balkans and, though *foederati*, allowing them to retain their tribal leaders, while in the east he partitioned Armenia with the Sassanids, with

---

48 Potter, *The Roman Empire at Bay*, 378–9. 49 Potter, *The Roman Empire at Bay*, 581.

Rome receiving the smaller portion. He also tolerated for several years the rule in the west of the usurpers Magnus Maximus (383–388) and Eugenius (392–394). At Constantinople, his elder son Arcadius (395–408) ushered in a period in which for two centuries emperors rarely left the capital and did not lead armies in person. Consolidation of civilian and military, secular and religious power fostered the growth of administrative traditions, including records housed in the substructures of the Hippodrome, adjacent to the palace. Arcadius and his son Theodosius II (408–451) survived the challenges of Goths and Huns, but the west spiralled into collapse after different tribal groups crossed the frozen Rhine in the winter of 406. Competition between eastern and western empires over the previous decade had not helped, since this had permitted Alaric the Goth to preserve an increasingly powerful military following which captured Rome in 410. Thereafter the desperate struggle to raise revenue, find soldiers and protect territory left scant room for musings over grand strategy, while power was exercised by generals whose priorities were rewarding their troops and eliminating rivals.[50]

In the east there are signs of flexible approaches to external dealings. The relationship with Sassanid Iran evolved from bellicose competition over border areas to co-operation. Between the resolution of the Armenian question in 387 and Kavadh's destructive invasion in 502, there were only two brief periods of hostilities; instead a rhetoric of collaboration evolved that was focused on shared interests in the Caucasus and symbolised by a story that Arcadius had requested that Yazdgard adopt the infant Theodosius as his successor. Constantinople intervened in the west to support Valentinian III (423–455), especially trying to prevent the Vandals from taking over north Africa, and in the Balkans the threat of Attila had to be contained, if possible. Here the Roman objective was to preserve fortified cities, maintain river communications along the Danube and drive invaders back with as little booty as possible. Attila's geopolitical awareness, however, allowed him to make attacks in the east when Eastern Roman forces were engaged in the west, outmanoeuvre Roman diplomacy, consider challenging Persia through the Caucasus, and switch attention between eastern and western empires. His grand strategy was as developed as anything the Romans followed. Attila appreciated the importance of frontier defences for projecting power externally, since he insisted on the creation south of the Danube of an uncultivated no man's land five days' journey in depth (Priscus fr. 11.2.74–8). When possible, emperors re-established authority along

50 O'Flynn, *Generalissimos of the Western Roman Empire*.

the Danube and the importance of the river as a base for active defence is demonstrated by the successful campaigns from there against the Avars during Maurice's final years.[51]

One important response to the empire's new situation was greater attention to information from envoys. From the long account in Priscus (fr. 6) of the embassy to Attila's court in which he participated, through those of the Roman emissaries to Axum, Abraham and his son Nonnosus (Malalas 18.15, 56; Procopius, *Wars* 1.20), to records in Menander (frr. 10, 19) of dealings with the Turks in central Asia, Roman historians believed that audiences would be interested in detailed descriptions of peoples and places that must have originated in official records. Another was to make greater use of Rome's financial strength to achieve what could not be secured by military means. In the late 440s Attila was receiving 2,000 pounds of gold a year, which might seem an enormous sum but was probably cheaper than creating an army capable of resisting him. Traditionalists still hankered after the days when Rome dealt with its neighbours through brute force (Agathias 5.13), but recognition that war could not by itself solve all the empire's problems constituted the basis for a more strategic approach to international dealings.

The new approach is most evident in Justinian's reign. His western conquests, made possible by peace with Persia, were carefully prepared: diversions in Libya and Sardinia preceded the Vandal expedition, while the attack on Ostrogothic Italy followed diplomatic exchanges in which Justinian destabilised the kingdom, came close to persuading King Theodahad to surrender it in exchange for estates in the east, and dissuaded the Franks from open involvement in Italy. The security of the Balkans, such as it was, depended on diplomatic connections that balanced Lombards against Gepids, and Utigurs against Kutrigurs.[52] Religion now made a clear contribution to Rome's international dealings, leading the Christian Laz generally to prefer attachment to Rome, in spite of the injustices of Roman administration, rather than to the Sassanids who promoted observance of Zoroastrian rites.[53] Emperors oversaw the baptism of neighbouring leaders, sometimes successfully, as with the Laz Ztath; sometimes not, as when the baptised Hun Grod was promptly overthrown by his followers (Malalas 17.19, 18.14).

51 Whitby, *The Emperor Maurice and His Historian*, 176–81.
52 Sarantis, *Justinian's Balkan Wars*, 393–7.
53 D. Braund, *Georgia in Antiquity, 550 BCE–CE 562* (Oxford: Oxford University Press, 1994) ch.8.

Justinian was not universally successful, since renewed war with Persia in 540 and the plague in 542 entailed the reallocation of military forces and shrank the empire's resource base. As a result, it is debated whether expansion in the 530s fatally overextended the empire, leaving successors in no position to deal with the Avars (570s–630s) and Arabs (630s), but such criticisms benefit from hindsight. Justinian was a ruler who could be complimented for succeeding 'even if not by war, but then by wisdom' (Menander fr. 5.1.23–4). It is reasonable to talk of the application by Justinian of a grand strategy in a way that is not possible for many previous Roman emperors. Some did consciously take an empire-wide view of options and actions – the elderly Augustus, Tiberius and Hadrian as rulers who eschewed conquest; quite possibly Domitian and Aurelian, and certainly Diocletian's Tetrarchs, as rulers who were more active militarily – but certainly not the likes of Trajan or Severus, who were largely driven by personal reputation and the cultural dynamic of war, or those with limited apparent concern for effective administration, such as Caligula, Nero,[54] Commodus or Caracalla. Some rulers, such as the rapid succession in the third-century 'crisis' or fifth-century rulers in the West, just did not have the time or resources.

A strategy of maintaining frontiers certainly did not entail passive defence, since long-term security often required proactive aggression. Imperial expansion into Britain or Dacia might be presented as a necessary consequence of such activity, but at least in Britain there is no evidence that Roman clients needed a stern reminder of imperial power and the new territory just increased the frontiers that had to be actively managed – as Cassius Dio observed about Severus' eastern acquisitions. The one radical departure from the strategy of prioritising the defence of territory came under Heraclius, when, in 622, faced with the loss of much of the Balkans to Avars and Slavs and of the east to the Persians, the emperor left Constantinople on campaign. Rather than regain territory piecemeal, as Aurelian had done, Heraclius led his army (which in the absence of tax revenues was financed by the appropriation of church treasures) on a daring series of moves through eastern Anatolia, Armenia and Transcaucasia, avoiding encirclement by superior Persian forces as he disrupted their occupation of Roman territory. Even the threat to Constantinople posed by the Avar–Persian attack in 626 did not distract him, since he trusted the strength of the city's defences and the even more powerful protection provided by its divine guardians, especially the Virgin Mary. With the support of the central Asian Turks he gradually wore down the Persians, and in December 627 he

---

54 Wallace-Hadrill, *Suetonius* 120–2.

defeated them in battle at Nineveh, ravaged the hinterland of Ctesiphon in southern Mesopotamia, and then spent the winter at the major Zoroastrian shrine at Takht-I Suleiman near Ganzak. His successes provoked a palace revolution in February 628 that toppled Khusro II, so that the restitution of traditional frontiers could be negotiated with his successors.[55] Heraclius' strategy was, like that of Alexander, to leave his homeland behind and overcome the Persians by directly challenging the prestige of its ruler.

For grand strategy to be a useful tool in assessing the performance of the Roman Empire and its leaders, it must be conceived as something more than a series of knee-jerk responses to external pressures or the identification of means to deliver personal objectives, some of questionable benefit to the empire overall. It was something that not all emperors were able, or even minded, to contemplate. In the high empire the absence of a grand strategy was not of overriding importance, since Rome as the hegemonic power could ultimately cope with all challenges, but as the empire declined to the status of regional power new ways of protecting territory needed to be found. In this situation an emperor such as Justin II (565–578) – who believed that he could turn the clock back, treat neighbours with hegemonic arrogance and reject the compromises of his uncle, Justinian – was a disaster; unsurprisingly, he failed in his bid to 'make Rome great again' and lapsed into insanity in 573 when the war he had provoked with Persia resulted in the loss of the key frontier fortress of Dara.

A salutary warning against attempting to force a coherent grand strategy upon all the centuries of Roman imperial history is Julian's response to advice from his inner circle that he should fight the Goths – he replied that he was looking for better enemies, whereas Galatian slave traders were enough to deal with the Goths (Ammianus 22.7.8). Even for a diligent emperor, the culture that privileged war with Persia trumped the realities that would soon overwhelm the Danube frontier and annihilate a Roman army.

Historiographic Debates

Discussion of the grand strategy of the Roman Empire dates back to the publication in 1976 of Edward Luttwak's *The Grand Strategy of the Roman Empire*.[56] A number of Luttwak's fundamental assumptions, for example relating

---

55 J. Howard-Johnston, *Witnesses to a World Crisis: Historians and Histories of the Middle East in the Seventh Century* (Oxford: Oxford University Press, 2010); J. Howard-Johnston, *The Last Great War of Antiquity* (Oxford: Oxford University Press, 2021).

56 E. Luttwak, *The Grand Strategy of the Roman Empire* (Baltimore: Johns Hopkins University Press, 1976).

to the nature of Roman frontiers, purpose of troop dispositions, or geographical awareness, were open to debate – frontiers were zones of exchange just as much as barriers to movement, an important element in the location of some troops was the need to maintain internal security, ancient conceptions of geography were different to our own, and there were no accurate maps to underpin strategic planning.[57] The outlines of this debate have been conveniently summarised by Kimberley Kagan,[58] who has advanced the topic by proposing a helpful redefinition of grand strategy: crucial elements are the identification of objectives and priorities, consideration of the intentions of decision makers, and the allocation of resources to achieve the state's long-term best interests.[59] With regard to the Roman Empire, for which much relevant information (such as about policy discussions) is lacking, Kagan presents resource allocation, or more specifically the location of military forces, as the key indicator of strategy. Emil Ritterling's study of legionary dispositions helps analyse the pattern of imperial responses to different issues, such as opportunities for conquest or the need to react to challenges. One can conclude that since the empire had a model for allocating resources, imperial decisions were influenced by grand strategy.[60]

The weakness of Kagan's approach is that the movement of legions is a poor proxy for the much richer set of elements that she defined as constituents of grand strategy: it describes consequences rather than illumining decisions that might have been driven by personal considerations rather than grand strategy. There are also two specific problems. The first is chronological since, like Luttwak, Kagan confined her study to the first three and a half centuries of empire, with only a couple of forays into the later fourth century for particular items of evidence. Luttwak had recognised this weakness and set about assembling evidence for a comparable review of

---

57 J. C. Mann, 'The frontiers of the principate', *Aufstieg und Niedergang der römischen Welt*, 2:1 (1974), 508–33, presents frontiers as boundaries of failed expansion; C. R. Whittaker, *Frontiers of the Roman Empire: A Social and Economic Study* (Baltimore: Johns Hopkins University Press, 1994), on frontiers as zones of contact rather than barriers; B. Isaac, *The Limits of Empire: The Roman Army in the East* (Oxford: Oxford University Press, 1990), arguing that internal security was the army's main goal; F. Millar, *The Roman Near East 31 B.C.–A.D. 337* (Cambridge, MA: Harvard University Press, 1993), on the inconsistent treatment of client states; Millar, *The Emperor in the Roman World*, 228–59, 644–51, on emperors as reactive to requests rather than initiators; O. A. W. Dilke, *Greek and Roman Maps* (Ithaca: Cornell University Press, 1985) on cartography.
58 Kagan, 'Redefining Roman grand strategy', 333–62.
59 Kagan, 'Redefining Roman grand strategy', 348–50.
60 E. Ritterling, 'Legio', in Pauly-Wissowa, *Realencyclopädie für Antike und Christentum*, Volume XII (Stuttgart, 1924–5), cols. 1186–1837.

the later Roman Empire and medieval Byzantine, or Eastern Roman, Empire. Its theses chimed more closely with academic views of imperial strategies in the late Roman (c. 284–640) and Byzantine (640–1453) worlds.[61] The second problem of Luttwak's initial analysis is that it ignores a significant element in Roman military activity for which consideration of an externally focused grand strategy might not be a priority, namely the campaigns associated with competition for imperial power. Even Kagan's approach requires some refinement, when attempting to assess the sense of imperial actions and the decisions that perhaps underlay those actions, where both external and internal conflicts were concerned: were changes of direction based on a sensible balancing of risk and advantage that took account of the state's best interests or were they based more on personal whim or cultural conditioning? Given the dearth of sources, both questions can only be answered tentatively, as we have done above.

61 E. N. Luttwak, *The Grand Strategy of the Byzantine Empire* (Cambridge, MA., Harvard University Press, 2009).

8

The Gupta Empire (AD 400–500)

KAUSHIK ROY

Introduction

The Gupta Empire lasted from AD 319 to 544. The Guptas started their career as feudatories of the imperial Kushanas. As the Kushana Empire ebbed in the third century AD, the Guptas became independent and established a petty kingdom in Magadha. The Gupta Empire's history started with Chandragupta I (r. 319–334), the person who transformed the small regional polity into an expanding empire. He neutralised the immediate threat from the regional kingdoms in south Bihar and eastern Uttar Pradesh by matrimonial alliances and launching military expeditions. The son and grandson of two minor kings (raja), Chandragupta then took the title of maharajadhiraja ('great king') and the domain of the Guptas continued to expand under his son Samudragupta, who established an empire.

Between circa AD 400 and circa 500, the empire was at the height of its power. During this time, the Gupta emperors, from their capital, Pataliputra, exercised direct control over north India and indirectly ruled central, west and north-west India through their feudatories and vassal states. However, from the beginning of the sixth century AD Gupta power went into terminal economic slump. Foreign invasions and economic decline accelerated a radical shift in Gupta security policy.

Sources

The principal difficulty in analysing Gupta strategy is lack of adequate reliable sources. Our principal sources are inscriptions, seals, coins and fictional literature. The stone inscriptions are actually *prasastis* (historical eulogies) of the great rulers carved in a poetic style. The Allahabad Stone Pillar Inscription by Harishena throws light on the military achievements of

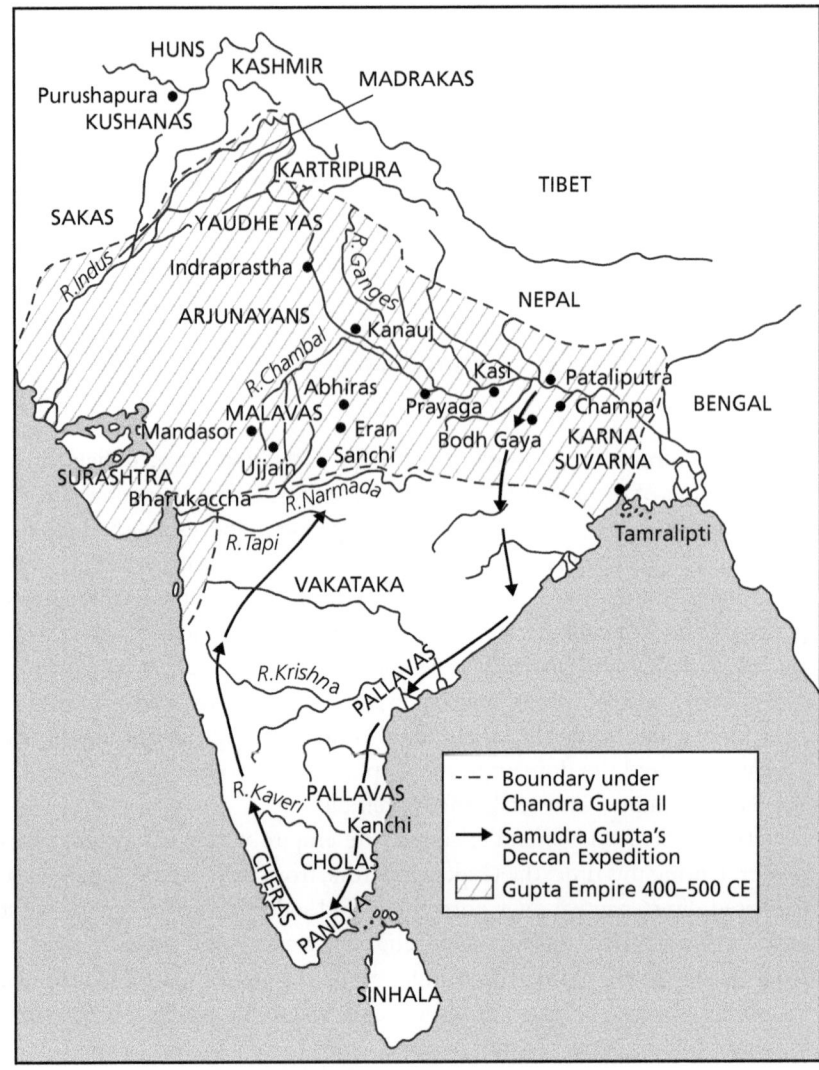

Map 8.1 Strategies of the Gupta Empire (AD 400–500)

Samudragupta in north and south India, and the Mehrauli Iron Pillar Inscription provides details on the reign of Chandragupta II/Vikramaditya, especially his conflicts with the Sakas (Scythians) of west India. The Mathura Pillar Inscription and the Udaygiri Cave Inscription open a window onto the religious policies of the Guptas. The Bhitari Pillar Inscription and the Junagadh Rock Inscription offer details about Skandragupta's wars with the

Pushyamitras and the Huns. And the Mandasore Stone Pillar Inscription provides an account of Yasodharman's political and military achievements. He was a feudatory or subordinate ruler of the Guptas who later became independent. The Rajghat and Eran Stone Pillar Inscriptions throw light on Emperor Buddhagupta when the empire went into a downward spiral. The Kura (Khewra) Inscription of Toramana and the Gwalior Stone Inscription of Mihirakula record the activities of these two Hun leaders, who dealt a death blow to the tottering Gupta Empire.[1]

Next in importance to the inscriptions are the coins (gold and silver) issued by famous rulers to commemorate their accession and victories on the battlefield. For daily economic transactions, copper coins and cowries were used. Kalidasa's historical fictions, Bana's historical autobiography, the Puranas (which are a mixture of historical facts and myths) and certain *niti* texts (written by Kautilya, Kamandaka and Sukra) are of some use in reconstructing the strategic history of the Gupta Empire. Initially these works were transmitted down the generations orally and then in the medieval era were written down in Sanskrit. Kautilya's *Arthashastra* was composed between 300 BC and AD 300 and Kamandaka's *Nitisara* was composed between the sixth and eighth centuries AD. No chronicles or histories as are known from European antiquity exist, or if they did exist they have not survived.

Actors

The rulers themselves were the principal architects of all policy decisions. In the case of 'fighting emperors' like Samudragupta, Chandragupta II and Skandagupta, they also formulated military strategy. These emperors led the army in person. Kumaragupta did not personally lead the army, but towards the end of his reign his son Skandagupta as *yuvaraj* (Crown prince) commanded the Gupta army in the field against the rebellious Pushyamitra tribe in Gujarat. The Crown prince functioned as the deputy of the emperor and often commanded the royal army in person. Skandagupta, later as emperor, commanded the army in various campaigns against the Huns along the river Indus.[2]

However, even a superman cannot rule the empire alone. So, the emperors were always assisted by the *asthapradhan* (a council of eight ministers). The Allahabad Pillar Inscription of Samudragupta tells us about a high-ranking official termed *sandhi vigrahika* who was the minister of peace

---

1 A. Agrawal, *Rise and Fall of the Imperial Guptas* (Delhi: Motilal Banarasidass, 1989), 1–5.
2 R. K. Mookerji, *The Gupta Empire* (1973), reprint (Delhi: Motilal Banarasidass, 1997), 90–3.

and war. Above him was the *sachiva* who was equivalent to the present-day cabinet secretary.[3] While the former was in charge of diplomacy, the latter was in charge of supervising all civilian and military officers. Top military officers included *mahabaladhikrita* (commander-in-chief), *mahadandanayaka* (general), *mahapratihara* (chief of the palace guards in charge of protection of the royal household and the place of royal residence), *mahasenapati* (field marshal), *mahasvapati* (commander of the cavalry branch), *bhatasvapati* (officer in charge of a cavalry contingent) and *mahapilupati* (commander of the elephant establishment), *maha* in each case meaning 'high', 'superior'.[4]

Means

The principal instrument for coercion, control and subjugation of internal and external enemies (both actual and potential) of the Gupta emperors, like most of the rulers of premodern India, was the army. According to one estimate, 50 per cent of central revenues were spent on the military establishment, 8.5 per cent on the civil administration and 17 per cent on welfare activities among the people (which included charity and donations), and there was a reserve fund for emergencies which constituted 16.5 per cent of the budget. The rest of state income was expended on maintaining the royal court.[5]

Ancient Hindu texts noted that a ruler should maintain a *chaturanga bala* (a 'four-limbed army' comprising infantry, cavalry, elephants and chariots) for maintaining internal peace and for defence against external enemies. After the Battle of Hydaspes (May 326 BC), the use of war chariots declined, but elephants and horses continued to be used in the Gupta army. Its infantry were equipped with bows, spears and battleaxes and they wore armour and helmets of iron.[6] The population of India came to about 100 million during the period under review in this chapter.[7] The vast demographic resources of India and the dependence of marginal peasants on military service to tide over years of poor harvests when the monsoon failed, plus the linkage between military

---

3 V. R. R. Dikshitar, *War in Ancient India* (1944), reprint (Delhi: Motilal Banarasidass, 1987), 219.
4 U. N. Ghoshal, 'Political theory and administrative organization', in R. C. Majumdar (general ed.), A. D. Pusalker and A. K. Majumdar (assistant eds), *The History and Culture of the Indian People*, Volume III: *The Classical Age* (1954), reprint (Mumbai: Bharatiya Vidya Bhavan, 2018), 349, 341–69.
5 N. Singh, *The Theory of Force and Organisation of Defence in Indian Constitutional History from Earliest Times to 1947* (Bombay: Asia Publishing House, 1969), 80.
6 H. C. Kar, *Military History of India* (Calcutta: Firma KLM, 1980), 73.
7 S. Guha, *Health and Population in South Asia from Earliest Times to the Present* (2001), reprint (Ranikhet: Permanent Black, 2010), 31.

service and upward mobility, enabled premodern Indian rulers to maintain as large a number of infantry as ancient China. The earlier pan-Indian Maurya Empire (322–185 BC) supposedly maintained 600,000 infantry and the Gupta Empire was two-thirds the size of the former. One could speculate that the Guptas maintained about 300,000 infantry besides elephantry and cavalry; elsewhere we find the figure 200,000 cited for the overall size of the Gupta army, which included 50,000 cavalry. For a particular campaign, the Kushanas could mobilise between 50,000 and 80,000 cavalry. The strength of Harsha of Kanauj's army is given as 50,000 men plus 500 elephants.[8]

Horses were expensive and difficult to procure. The climate and terrain of India did not favour the breeding of warhorses. From ancient times, Indian rulers were dependent on the import of warhorses from central Asia through Afghanistan and Punjab and Arabian horses through Gujarat and Maharashtra. The Maurya Empire had been able to maintain only 30,000 cavalry. The Gupta Empire, which did not control Afghanistan, presumably thus had a much smaller cavalry than its Maurya predecessor. However, unlike Harshavardhana of Kanauj (ruler of north India from AD 612 to 647), the Guptas controlled Punjab and Gujarat. Harsha's army had 10,000 cavalry.[9] We could hazard a guess that the Gupta cavalry was about 20,000 strong.

The Guptas introduced a tactical innovation in their cavalry arm. The Sakas, Parthians and Kushanas, between the first and third centuries AD, introduced mounted archery in India on a large scale. The Guptas fought the Sakas (Scythians) in Saurashtra (Gujarat) and the Kushanas in Punjab and then the Huns, copying them by introducing mounted archery into their army, the only indigenous power in early India to do so. Kalidasa's *Raghuvamsa* says that the Gupta mounted soldiers wore coats of mail down to their knees and were equipped with short composite bows (made of horn and sinew), different from the six-foot-+long simple wooden bows used by the infantry. Coins of Kumaragupta show the emperor on horseback holding such a composite bow. The horses were also covered with armoured plates. In addition, the Guptas' heavy armoured cavalry branch also had lancers. They thus resembled the Eastern Roman *cataphracts* or the originally Persian, later Eastern Roman, *clibanari*, raising questions as to who first invented them. The frescoes of the Ajanta caves show lancers in operation. Heavy cavalry were trained to charge together, in order to break the enemy's battle formation. The use of loop

8 K. Roy, *Warfare in Pre-British India: 1500 BCE–1740 CE* (London and New York: Routledge, 2015), 218.
9 R. C. Majumdar, 'Harsha-Vardhana and his times', in Majumdar, Pusalker and Majumdar, *The Classical Age*, 96–123, 116.

stirrups enabled the riders to use lances without the danger of falling off their mounts, while the latter were at full gallop. Gupta cavalrymen borrowed the custom of wearing long coats, trousers, riding boots and belts of leather and leather straps for holding down the saddle from the Kushanas (who were then ruling in modern Pakistan and Afghanistan).[10]

Like Greek and Arab travellers, the Chinese traveller Xuanzang was also enthralled by war elephants. He noted in his journal, 'The war-elephant is covered with a coat-of-mail and sharp spurs are attached to its tusks.'[11] Elephants had already proved their worth against the Macedonian phalanx at the Battle of Hydaspes. Due to lack of adequate numbers of cavalry, the Indian rulers depended on elephants, which functioned as a battering ram both on the battlefield and in sieges and also functioned as command vehicles. The commander, sitting on a howdah (a wooden square box covered with plates of iron on the outside) on top of the elephant got an elevated view of the battlefield. Elephantry comprised an important branch of the Gupta army.[12]

Already Kautilya, in his *Arthashastra*, had noted the importance of maintaining disciplined infantry who needed to be trained regularly in different tactical manoeuvres. Kautilya also highlighted the requirements of combined-arms training among the various branches of the army to raise the combat effectiveness of the military force. Synergy between the elephants and cavalry in the Gupta army especially during combat achieved a high mark. Overall, we could say that by adapting and adopting certain indigenous and foreign techniques, the Gupta army initiated a revolution in military affairs (RMA). The Huns had unarmoured mounted archers and in close combat Gupta armoured mounted archers had the edge over them. Further, the introduction of armoured lancers was probably influenced by the Sassanian army, which campaigned in Afghanistan, Sind and Punjab against the Sakas, Parthians and Kushanas during the third and fourth centuries AD. And the six-foot bows of the Indian infantry, as Herodotus and Alexander's historians noted, was deadly and could penetrate even the body armour of the Greek phalangites.[13] Added to this were traditional Indian war elephants for launching a massive charge against hostile

10 G. S. Sandhu, *A Military History of Ancient India* (New Delhi: Vision Books, 2000), 380–1.
11 Quoted from D. Devahuti (ed.), *The Unknown Hsuan-Tsang* (2001), reprint (New Delhi: Oxford University Press, 2006), 132.
12 K. Roy, *From Hydaspes to Kargil: A History of Warfare in India from 326 BC to CE 1999* (New Delhi: Manohar, 2004), 10–65.
13 R. C. Majumdar, 'Minor states in north India during the Gupta Empire', in Majumdar, Pusalker and Majumdar, *The Classical Age*, 46–59, 51–2; B. K. Majumdar, *The Military System in Ancient India* (Calcutta: Firma KLM, 1960), 50.

formations. The superior combat effectiveness of the Gupta army was proved by the fact that Chandragupta II was able to smash the Sakas of west India and the Kushanas of Punjab and Skandagupta was able to contain the deadly Huns, who defeated the Sassanian and both the eastern and western Roman armies repeatedly.

Besides the army, the Guptas also utilised diplomacy, matrimonial alliances and religion as part of their statecraft. The Gupta rulers would marry one or at most two queens. Marrying a woman from a powerful family and giving a royal princess to another ruler in marriage constituted important diplomatic moves for the Gupta dynasty. The Guptas accepted wives from stronger powers and gave their daughters to comparatively weaker powers. Chandragupta I married a princess named Kumaradevi from the Lichchavi clan in Nepal, which raised his political status. The alliance with the Lichchavi clan of Nepal also enabled him to deter and then conquer his immediate neighbours.[14] With Lichchavi aid Chandragupta I was able to capture Magadha and made it his base, and then annexed Saketa and Prayag (Allahabad) in eastern Uttar Pradesh.[15]

Chandragupta I was succeeded by his and Kumaradevi's son Samudragupta, who expanded the Gupta realm to cover the whole of the Gangetic valley. He was succeeded by his son Chandragupta II. In AD 395, the Vakataka ruler Rudrasena II married the daughter of Chandragupta II named Prabhavatigupta. Rudrasena II rejected his father's religion, Saivaism, and converted to Vaishnavism, the religion of his father-in-law and wife. The Saivas are worshippers of Shiva and the Vaishnavas worship Vishnu, respectively two gods of the main Hindu trinity or triumvirate of gods. The Gupta emperors portrayed themselves on their coins as avatars of Vishnu (reincarnations of the god Vishnu on earth). Friendship with the neighbouring Vakatakas, the premier power in central and west India, was important for safeguarding the southern flank of the Gupta dominion. It was also important for the security of the Gupta line of communications between Magadha (homeland of the Guptas) and the principal Gupta field army in Malwa which was readying under Chandragupta II to advance against the Sakas of Gujarat. Rudrasena died early and Prabhavatigupta became the queen regent and shaped Vakataka foreign policy in tune with Gupta interests. Prabhavatigupta's influence in the Vakataka royal court enabled the Guptas

14 R. S. Sharma, *India's Ancient Past* (2005), reprint (New Delhi: Oxford University Press, 2012), 232.
15 D. N. Jha, *Early India: A Concise History* (New Delhi: Manohar, 2004), 157.

to secure their southern border even during the early part of the reign of Kumaragupta (the son of Chandragupta II).[16]

In addition, the Guptas used the Sanskrit language as an instrument for expressing and legitimising their imperialism. Sheldon Pollock writes that from the beginning of the Common Era, Sanskrit, hitherto confined to being the sacred language of Hindu religious practice, was rebooted as a code for universal political expression. And all aspiring imperial powers used Sanskrit, the language of gods and universal rulers, to establish and consolidate their rule. Pollock terms this the Sanskrit cosmopolis, which extended from Punjab in the west to Cambodia in the east. In north India, Sanskrit started replacing Prakrit and other regional languages during the Kushana Empire. Under Gupta rule, this process accelerated. The literary works (*kavya*) of Gupta court poets like Kalidasa and the royal *prasastis* were composed in Sanskrit. *Kavya* and *rajya* (kingdom) were interrelated in Sanskrit works like the double helix of DNA. Upinder Singh says that the *mahakavya*, like Kalidasa's *Raghuvamsa*, deals with issues like war and empire, which were integral to kingship. The *digvijaya* (universal domination) of Raghu (the hero of the poem) is somewhat similar to the *digvijaya* of Samudragupta as portrayed in the Allahabad *prasasti*. The audience for such poems was the urban educated elite with a common background in Sanskrit. Such works raised political consciousness and political legitimacy by focusing on the interrelationship between statecraft, royal genealogy and divinity. Most of the Hindu empire builders encouraged the production of royal *prasasti* which represented a permanent expression of royal will in the public domain. All the Sanskrit texts and inscriptions reiterate trans-regionality, which fitted well with the Gupta aspiration to 'universal rule', the ultimate aim of the Kautilyan *charavartin*. Further, not only did Sanskrit become the proper vehicle for expressing imperial will, but also to be learned in Sanskrit was an important aspect of kingliness. Hence the courtly epics and *prasastis* depict the Gupta emperors like Samudragupta and Chandragupta II Vikramaditya as patrons of Sanskrit arts and literature and themselves as being learned persons.[17]

---

16 G. Jouveau-Dubreuil, *Ancient History of the Deccan* (trans. from the French by V. S. S. Dikshitar) (1920), reprint (New Delhi: Asian Educational Services, 1991), 75; D. C. Sircar, 'Deccan in the Gupta age', in Majumdar, Pusalker and Majumdar, *The Classical Age*, 177–223, 179–82.

17 S. Pollock, *The Language of the Gods in the World of Men: Sanskrit, Culture, and Power in Premodern India* (2006), reprint (Ranikhet: Permanent Black, 2018), 1–36, 249–58; U. Singh, 'The power of a poet: kingship, empire, and war in Kalidasa's *Raghuvamsa*', in K. Chakrabarti and K. Sinha (eds), *State, Power and Legitimacy: The Gupta Kingdom* (Delhi: Primus Books, 2019), 731–59.

Adversaries

The political context and distribution of power on the Indian subcontinent and beyond facilitated the rise of Gupta power. When the Gupta rulers, in the fourth century AD, started transforming their local kingdom into an empire, there was no paramount power in the Indian subcontinent. The Indian landscape comprised three systems: the Indo-Gangetic system comprising north India (Aryavarta), the Oxus–Indus system comprising central Asia and west India and finally Dakshinapatha, which was the region south of the river Narmada and Vindhya mountain range. The north of the Indo-Gangetic system is bounded by the Himalayas, which separate the subcontinent from Tibet, and at the south of Dakshinapatha is the Indian Ocean. The east of Dakshinapatha is rounded by the Bay of Bengal and to the west lies the Arabian Sea. The east of Aryavarta is bounded by the impassable malarial tropical jungles of East Bengal, which separates the Indian subcontinent from Burma. South-west of the Indus system is the Makran Desert of Baluchistan and at the north-west of the Indus are the mountain ranges of Afghanistan.

During the late third century, the Kushana Empire, which encompassed north and central India along with parts of Afghanistan and Bactria, was breaking up. A Kushana chieftain became independent and established a kingdom in Punjab in the early fourth century. The Kushanas of Punjab constituted a local power. During the time of the imperial Kushanas, the Sakas functioned as *kshatrapa*s (provincial governors) of Sind, Baluchistan and Gujarat. After the collapse of the imperial Kushanas, the *kshatrapa*s proclaimed themselves *mahakshatrapa*s and declared their independence. They fought the Satavahana Empire of western Deccan. At the beginning of the fourth century AD, the Sakas controlled only Gujarat and were balanced by the Vakataka Empire which had replaced the Satavahanas. Both the Sakas and the Kushanas were being threatened by the Sassanian Empire of Iran on their western borders. Further, the Kushanas were also pushed southwards by the Huns at Tokharistan on their northern borders. And north India was divided among many rival potentates.[18]

This scenario allowed the Guptas to establish their far-flung dominion from their base at Magadha, which was centrally located in the Indo-Gangetic system. It was at the centre of inland and riverine trade routes connecting west with east India. Moreover, the elephant forests of Magadha and its iron mines gave an added advantage to the ruler of this principality. In addition,

---

18 R. C. Majumdar, 'The rise of the Guptas', in Majumdar, Pusalker and Majumdar, *The Classical Age*, 1–6, 1.

the ruler of Magadha could use the navigable Gangu–Jamuna (Yamuna) rivers for power projection along the eastern and western sides of the Indo-Gangetic valley.

The adversaries of the Gupta Empire changed with time. Their immediate adversaries were the powers ruling north India. Some of these were king-doms and others were tribal republics. After conquering north India, the Guptas clashed with the Vakatakas. Samudragupta defeated Rudrasena Vakataka at the First Battle of Eran (AD 348/349?).[19] Vakataka power was extinguished in central India, which came under Gupta hegemony, but the former was allowed to continue as a subordinate ally of the Gupta Empire in Maharashtra.

The Gupta Empire followed an offensive strategy under Samudragupta and Chandragupta II. Kumaragupta, who did not lead any wars to expand the empire, followed a strategy of consolidation. However, towards the end of Kumaragupta's reign, the empire was seriously threatened by a combination of internal and external threats. Then the empire's control over Gujarat was challenged by the Pushyamitra tribe who operated along the bank of the Narmada river. The old and ailing emperor Kumaragupta was unable to take the field in person. So his son Skandagupta reigned on his behalf. After defeating the Pushyamitras, in AD 455–456 Skanda marched to Punjab to battle the Huns, who threatened to enter India from Afghanistan.[20] Skanda strictly followed a defensive strategy against the Huns, who constituted the principal threat to the empire.

The Huns, a tribe from north of China, were the main external threat to the Indian subcontinent. From AD 130, they gradually migrated westwards, and after reaching central Asia divided themselves into two groups. One group, termed the Black Huns, moved into south Russia and their march further into Europe would spread tremors in Constantinople and Ravenna. A branch which moved down into Balkh were known as White Huns or Hunas among Sanskrit scholars. Between AD 200 and 350, they defeated the Parthians, Sakas and Kushanas and established their dominion between the Oxus and Kabul rivers. Then they attacked both India and Iran. After being defeated by Skandagupta in 456–457, the Huns turned their attention towards Iran and killed King Firuz in 484. Towards the end of the fifth century, Hunnic rule was secure in central Asia and western Iran. Then they

---

19 V. R. R. Dikshitar, *The Gupta Polity* (1952), reprint (Delhi: Motilal Banarasidass, 1993), 74–5.

20 R. S. Tripathi, *History of Kanauj to the Moslem Conquest* (1964), reprint (Delhi: Motilal Banarasidass, 1989), 20–1.

concentrated on India. So for the Gupta monarchs at that time the Huns posed an existential threat. The Huna chief Toramana (d. AD 515) established his base in Punjab and then launched attacks into Malwa in central India. His son Mihirakula (r. AD 515–530), from his capital, Sialkot, captured Gwalior and Kashmir.[21]

Causes of Wars

The idea that Hinduism is a peace-loving religion and that the Hindus are passive is an early twentieth-century product. M. K. Gandhi propounded the idea that Hinduism is pacific in nature and the British from the late nineteenth century propounded a dubious theory that while the Hindus were cowardly and peace-loving, the Muslims were martial. In fact, ancient Hinduism was quite militaristic and the trends of militarism are evident not only in the Hindu texts but also in the history of early India.

The Guptas were originally Vaishyas (third rank in the *varna*/caste structure) and later, after achieving politico-military power, they fashioned a Brahmin-cum-Kshatriya identity (highest rank in the fourfold *varna* structure). The *varna*-centred social structure included Brahmins at the top, then Kshatriyas, followed by the Vaishyas and then the Shudras at the bottom; far inferior were the untouchables who remained outside the *varna* system. In ancient India, acquisition of political, military and economic power enabled a community to raise itself on the *varna* scale.

Inherited culture especially among the second-highest caste of the Kshatriyas who wielded political power and became rulers was one of the principal factors behind war. The status of the Kshatriyas depended on their martial values. The ancient *niti* treatises also highlighted the importance of fighting and dying in wars as part of gaining social prestige and *moksa* (salvation). The two Hindu epics *Ramayana* and *Mahabharata* treated death in war as a sort of religious sacrifice, where even the meanest person when killed in battle earns salvation. Manu and Yajnavalkya lay down that dying in war is an act of the highest merit.[22] In accordance with the *Mahabharata*, one who cannot fight is a *napuksak* (unmanly – half woman and half man), the

---

21 D. K. Chakrabarti, *The Geopolitical Orbits of Ancient India: The Geopolitical Frames of the Ancient Indian Dynasties* (New Delhi: Oxford University Press, 2010), 67; V. C. Bhutani, 'Historical geography of Kashmir from the earliest times to c. 1935', *Indian Historical Review*, 23 (2000), 4–11.

22 S. K. Bhakari, *Indian Warfare* (New Delhi: Munshiram Manoharlal, 1981), 15.

lowest possible derogatory status in ancient India. Manliness depends on displays of bravery, loyalty and courage on the battlefield.

There were two models of kingship in early India. The Hindu model of kingship propounded that a successful king has to initiate *digvijaya* (conquest of the earth, meaning the Indian subcontinent) and carry his arms to the four corners of the world in order to become *ekarat* or *samrat* (sole ruler of India/emperor). In contrast, the Buddhist model of kingship emphasised that a truly great ruler should follow *dhammaghosa* (rule by justice) rather than *bherighosa* (rule by force). Among the kings of early India, only Ashoka followed this policy. However, Ashoka followed *dhammaghosa* only after establishing his rule over India and he maintained a huge army to ensure the internal security and external defence of the empire. The Buddhist canon did not proclaim that rulers should disband their armies, but laid down that a just king only conducts defensive wars.[23]

A successful hegemonic ruler had to perform *asvamedha*, the Vedic ritual of paramountcy. It meant that a special horse was allowed to roam outside the borders of the hegemon's kingdom accompanied by the army of the hegemon (*vijigisu*). If any ruler dared to stop the horse then his kingdom was liable to be attacked by the army of the would-be hegemon. If a ruler allowed the horse to wander in his kingdom then, theoretically, he became the vassal of the hegemon. Both Samudragupta and Kumaragupta I performed the *asvamedha* ritual.[24]

At times economic factors also accelerated the decision to wage war over particular territories. Samudragupta annexed Vanga (Bengal) and then marched along the eastern coast of India through Kalinga (Orissa) down to Tamil Nadu in order to control the profitable coastal trade which occurred along the Coromandel coast and also the overseas commerce between Vanga and south-east Asia and China. The port of Tamralipti in South Bengal was the maritime gateway of east India. The important ports of Kalinga were Palura, Ganjam, Kalinganagar and Charitra, where both overseas maritime commercial activities and internal riverine trade were carried out.[25] The Saka Kingdom in Gujarat did not pose any threat to the Gupta Empire under Chandragupta II which controlled north India. However, Chandragupta II

23 K. Roy, *Military Thought of Asia: From the Bronze Age to the Information Age* (London and New York: Routledge, 2021), 37–45.
24 K. Sinha, 'Revisiting the Gupta kingdom: state, power and legitimacy', in Chakrabarti and Sinha, *State, Power and Legitimacy*, 1–40, 5.
25 A. N. Mishra, *Glimpses of Maritime History of Ancient Odisha* (New Delhi: Kunal Book Publishers & Distributors, 2010), 11; K. N. Dikshit, 'Archaeological remains of the Gupta period', in Chakrabarti and Sinha, *State, Power and Legitimacy*, 89–104, 90.

decided to annex Gujarat to his ever-expanding realm. One of his objectives was to tap the revenues flowing from the lucrative overseas commerce between Mediterranean Europe, west Asia and west India. Roman and Iranian ships regularly visited the port of Borach/Bargyza on the Gujarat coast.[26] We can speculate that land revenue, which was the principal source of income for the Gupta Empire, was supplemented by taxation of overseas and internal commerce.

Samudragupta attacked Kalinga and central India because of the elephant forests there which bred excellent war elephants. The elephants were so effective in battles and sieges that even the Huns in the early sixth century raided central India in order to acquire these beasts.

Premises Underlying Strategic Decisions

The ancient Hindu term for grand strategy is *dandaniti* (literal meaning 'policy of the rod'). It is an amalgam of *rajniti* (politics), *arthaniti* (economics), *kutniti* (diplomacy) and *samarniti* (military strategy). While Kautilya's *Arthashastra* stresses that for a successful ruler wars of external conquest are most important, *Manusmriti/Manusamhita* (composed around the beginning of the Common Era) asserts that the primary task of the ruler is not conquest of foreign territories but maintenance of domestic peace, stability and prosperity by crushing all his domestic enemies and promoting trade and commerce.[27] In this connection, it may be mentioned that Sukracharya in *Sukranitisara* argues that a ruler who fails to maintain internal peace is liable to be replaced by domestic stakeholders.[28]

Kamandaka's *Nitisara* rejected the *Mahabharata*'s depiction of war as sacrifice and the *Ramayana*'s portrayal of it as a heroic act. Nor should war be waged for the glory and prestige of the ruler, as Kautilya had argued. Rather, Kamandaka laid down that before going to war, the ruler should assess the material cost and chances of success. Kamandaka cautioned the ruler that the prospect of economic gain rather than anger, ambition or misplaced concepts of revenge and honour should be the principal premise for declaring war.[29]

---

26 T. Roy, *India in the World Economy: From Antiquity to the Present* (2012), reprint (Cambridge: Cambridge University Press, 2013), 32.

27 G. P. Singh, *Political Thought in Ancient India* (1993), reprint (New Delhi: D. K. Printworld Ltd, 2005), 113.

28 N. K. Acharya, *The Polity in Sukranitisara* (Bikaner: Vagdevi Prakashan, 1987), 203.

29 U. Singh, *Political Violence in Ancient India* (Cambridge, MA: Harvard University Press, 2017), 322–5.

From theory now let us move to historical reality. Overall, there was an understanding among the rulers of India not to ransack the countryside unnecessarily. A scorched-earth policy was not followed. The objective was to defeat the hostile army in a battle and then to capture and enjoy the material resources of the enemy and not to damage the economic base of the enemy state during the course of war. Xuanzang, the Chinese monk who discussed the affairs of India during the seventh century AD, pointed out that the rulers of India engaged in incessant wars among themselves, but the countryside was little injured by their actions.[30] And after capturing a piece of territory, the rulers focused on agricultural developments by building irrigational facilities. In the Gupta Empire, it was the duty of the provincial governors and district officials to construct and repair dams, wells and water tanks. This was because agriculture constituted the principal item of taxation.[31]

Priorities

The Gupta rulers assured their dynastic succession with the strategic tools of warfare and marriage. The Guptas never fully applied the rule of primogeniture. So civil wars after the death of an emperor were common. After the death of Chandragupta I, a war of succession broke out between Kacha/ Kaca, the eldest son of the ruler (who by the principle of primogeniture would have succeeded his father), and Samudragupta, a younger brother. From this war Samudragupta emerged victorious and became the ruler. To strengthen his position, he went for *digvijaya* – expansionist war. Through a series of brilliant campaigns, he destroyed nine kings of Aryavarta (north India) and annexed the whole Gangetic valley to his fledgling empire. Then he led an expedition to Dakshinapatha (South of the River Narmada) and descended upon Tamil Nadu. However, instead of annexing this region, he released the defeated kings after capturing them. The defeated rulers agreed to become his vassals and paid tribute.[32] Probably the long distance from Magadha and the necessity of maintaining a large occupation force, which would prove costly, prevented Samudragupta from directly annexing

30 P. C. Chakravarti, *The Art of War in Ancient India* (1941), reprint (Delhi: Low Price Publications, 1989), 188.
31 U. N. Ghoshal, 'Economic conditions', in Majumdar, Pusalker and Majumdar, *The Classical Age*, 590–607, 590–1.
32 R. Thapar, *The Penguin History of Early India from the Origins to* CE *1300* (2002), reprint (New Delhi: Penguin, 2003), 283.

Dakshinapatha to his empire. Nevertheless, Samudragupta was exceptionally successful in establishing the Gupta Empire as the paramount power in India: external war served to strengthen a monarch's hold on his throne.

Similarly, Chandragupta II came to the throne after murdering his elder brother, Emperor Ramagupta, and marrying his widow, Dhruvadevi, contrary to Hindu custom. To legitimise these two heinous acts and gain public acclaim, Chandragupta II declared war against the accursed heathens: the Sakas of Gujarat.

But, the problem in the late fifth century AD was that civil wars were occurring when an external threat in the shape of the Huns had arrived. Even when the empire was threatened seriously by a combination of internal and external enemies, assuring one's rights to the throne, even at the cost of civil war, remained the principal priority for members of the royal family. Failure to ascend the throne either resulted in political anonymity or death at the hands of royal competitors. Therefore members of the royal family needed to fight usurpers to claim the throne. For instance, Skandagupta was the son of a junior queen of Kumaragupta. So, even when the empire was attacked by the Pushyamitra tribes in central and west India and by the Huns in northwest India, Skandagupta concentrated on the war of succession with his half-brother Purugupta.[33] It was only after defeating Purugupta and establishing his hold over the power structure that Skanda marched against the Pushyamitras and the Huns.

After the death in AD 467 of the last great Gupta emperor, Skandagupta, who by following a mobile defensive strategy was able to hold the Huns along Indus, the empire was rocked by a series of convulsions. Kumaragupta II and Buddhagupta, the two claimants to the Gupta throne, fought among themselves when the Huns were moving into Punjab.[34]

The later Gupta emperors faced a tough choice. They required the support of their feudatories to check the Huns, but the very process of their dependence made these feudatories powerful. Caught between the devil and the deep blue sea, the Gupta emperors chose the feudatories because they at least accepted the nominal sovereignty of the Gupta emperors while the Huns aimed at the complete extinction of the empire.

From AD 500 onwards, the disruption of overland trade routes as a result of Hun attacks and decline of Indo-Roman trade resulted in a serious shortage of metallic currency and a decline of the urban centres. The Gupta Empire,

33 R. C. Majumdar, *Ancient India* (1952), reprint (Delhi: Motilal Banarsidass, 1994), 237.
34 R. C. Majumdar, 'The imperial crisis', in Majumdar, Pusalker and Majumdar, *The Classical Age*, 29–32, 29.

facing the Hun threat, was forced to pay its feudatories with land grants. In return, the feudatories provided military contingents to the Gupta rulers. However, possession of land grants with administrative jurisdictions over them tended to become hereditary and enabled the feudatories to establish their own autonomous bases of power. And the feudatories challenged the authority of the Gupta emperors and established their own local polities.[35] One such example was Yasodharman (r. 530–540) who fought the Huns and later established his own dominion in central India resulting in the eclipse of Gupta power along the Narmada valley and Berar. In fact, Yasodharman became so powerful that he also overshadowed the Gupta monarch in north India and attacked Bengal, which was under his Gupta overlord.

Execution of Strategy

Just after ascending the throne in AD 325, Samudragupta in person led an army for the conquest of the 'known world'. His immediate threats were the existing powers in north India. He defeated nine rulers of Aryavarta and annexed their kingdoms. These nine kings were Rudradeva, Matila (ruler of Bulandshahr), Nagadatta (a Naga ruler), Ganapatinaga (another Naga chieftain and ruler of Gwalior), Nagasena and Nandin (two Naga chiefs), Chandravarman, Acyuta (ruler of north Bihar) and Balavarman. The point to be noted is that several Naga chiefs who were allied with Chandragupta I were threatened by the rising power of their erstwhile Gupta ally and fought his son Samudragupta to maintain their independence. Next, Samudragupta turned his attention to the forest chieftains of central India. The conquest of this region was necessary for further expansion to the south: Dakshinapatha and towards west India. After subduing the forest chieftains, Samudragupta led his army on a long forced march reminiscent of Caesar's exploits, along the east coast of India through South Bengal and Orissa all the way to Kanchi. The twelve defeated rulers of Dakshinapatha who became vassals were Mahendra of Kosala (ruler of Raipur and Sambhalpur), Vyaghraraja of Gondwana, Mantaraja (ruler of the region around the Mahanadi river), Mahendra (ruler of Godavari district), Svamidatta (ruler of Ganjam), Damana, Vishnugopa of Kanchi, Nilaraja, Hastivarman of Vengi (Ellore), Kubera (ruler of Viazagapatnam), Ugrasena of Nellore and Dhananjaya of North Arcot.[36]

35 R. S. Sharma, *Early Medieval Indian Society: A Study in Feudalisation* (2001), reprint (Hyderabad: Orient Blackswan, 2013), 13–15.
36 R. S. Tripathi, *History of Ancient India* (1942), reprint (New Delhi: Motilal Banarasidass, 1999), 241–3.

Samudragupta's strategy was to establish direct rule over the core (north India), which in turn was surrounded by a string of feudatory states and vassal kingdoms. Along the western and north-western parts of India, the feudatories were the Arjunayanas (in Jaipur), Yaudheyas (settled along both banks of the river Sutlej in Punjab) and the Malavas in eastern Rajasthan (settled in Mewar, Tonk and Kotah).[37]

After the death of Samudragupta in AD 370, his eldest son, Ramagupta, became the emperor. Ramagupta moved with his army to Malwa, the most sensitive border of the Gupta Empire at that juncture. The Vakatakas of Maharashtra and Hyderabad and the Sakas of Gujarat were two potential threats and if they joined forces then the Guptas would be in serious trouble. Ramagupta moved his army and his court to Malwa, probably to deter these two powers and also to legitimise his own accession to the throne. The Sakas trapped the Gupta army while it was passing along the Vindhya mountains. The Sakas occupied the mountaintops and then, by rolling down boulders, blocked the narrow passes. Their archers shot at the trapped Gupta army below. The Sakas were able to cut off all communications and supplies of food and water to the Gupta camp. The Saka monarch demanded the surrender of Ramagupta's Queen Dhruvadevi or else threatened the annihilation of the Gupta army and a massacre of the members of the royal court. The Saka monarch's aim was to prevent any future Gupta incursion into Malwa, which the former considered his own sphere of interest, by destroying Ramagupta's prestige. A hapless Ramagupta had to agree to such humiliating terms.

This set the scene for Chandragupta II, the most daredevil among the Gupta emperors, then the heir designate and deputy of his elder brother, Emperor Ramagupta. The emperor sent news to the Saka king that Queen Dhruvadevi would come to the Saka camp accompanied by her 500 female servants. Chandragupta decided to turn this into a commando attack on the enemy camp: he prepared a special force of 500 men and dressed them in female garb. They moved to the Saka camp, where the Scythian ruler was already feasting in expectation of the arrival of Queen Dhruvadevi. Taking advantage of the surprise, Chandragupta and his team suddenly attacked the unsuspecting Sakas, killing the king and inflicting turmoil on the Saka camp, while Chandragupta and his men escaped to the main Gupta camp. Taking advantage of Chandragupta's commando raid and the demoralisation of the

---

37 R. C. Majumdar, 'The foundation of the Gupta Empire', in Majumdar, Pusalker and Majumdar, *The Classical Age*, 7–16, 8–9.

Saka soldiers due to the unexpected murder of their king, the Gupta army broke through the Saka blockade and reached the plains of north India. Chandragupta presented himself as a hero, while Ramagupta was derided as a *napuksak*. Soon Ramagupta was murdered by Chandragupta II, who ascended the Gupta throne in AD 375 and took the title Vikramaditya.[38]

By the beginning of the sixth century AD, the Gupta Empire had started to totter due to defeat in battle at the hands of the Huns, rebellion of the feudatories and intense dissension in the royal family. The collapse of the central government at Pataliputra resulted in the division of the Gupta Empire. Vainyagupta became independent in Bengal in around AD 507, Bhanugupta established a separate principality in Madhya Pradesh in AD 510 and Narasimhagupta was left with the rump Gupta state in north India. The three Gupta emperors, ruling simultaneously over different parts of the erstwhile empire, did not co-operate with each other. When the Huns under Toramana invaded Madhya Pradesh, the other two Gupta rulers refused to aid the Gupta ruler Bhanugupta. The latter, with his loyal feudatory Goparaja, advanced to give battle to the Huns. The army of the united Gupta Empire could have checked them. However, defeat was inevitable when the Gupta royal army was fragmented into three parts. In the Second Battle of Eran, Bhanugupta was defeated and Goparaja killed, and Malwa passed under Hunnic domination.[39]

Next, the Huns turned their attention towards Narasimhagupta and forced him to pay tribute. Narasimhagupta gathered all the feudatories and made a last-ditch effort against the Huns. Between AD 526 and 535, the Huns in central Asia were coming under pressure from a Turkic Confederation in the Eurasian steppe. Moreover, the hot and humid climate of India and the landscape, dotted with paddy fields and lacking grasslands, did not suit the Hunnic steppe cavalry equipped with composite bows. So the Huns had to retreat. However, it brought no respite to Narasimhagupta, who had taken the title Baladitya. The feudatories who had aided the Gupta monarch in fighting the Huns declared their independence and only theoretically acknowledged the superiority of the shadowy Gupta ruler. India north of the Narmada river was divided into a series of regional polities, only some of

38 H. C. Raychaudhuri, *Political History of Ancient India from the Accession of Parikshit to the Extinction of the Gupta Dynasty* (Calcutta: University of Calcutta, 1972), 488–9; R. C. Majumdar, 'The expansion and consolidation of the empire', in Majumdar, Pusalker and Majumdar, *The Classical Age*, 17–28, 17.
39 R. C. Majumdar, 'The disintegration of the empire', in Majumdar, Pusalker and Majumdar, *The Classical Age*, 33–41, 33–4.

whom acknowledged the political suzerainty of the Guptas. But under the following Gupta rulers, regional princes ceased to see themselves as their feudatories, and the grip of the Guptas slackened, with the Gupta Empire passing into history at the end of the sixth century.[40]

Historiographic Debates

There are several debates about different issues in Gupta history, like the origins of the Guptas, the identity of Kaca, the authenticity of the Ramagupta tradition, equating King Chandra with Chandragupta II and the Vikramaditya tradition, and so on. However, I have tried to reconstruct a linear homogeneous story by balancing the different contradictory sources.

Vincent Smith, the colonial historian, first propounded the idea that the Gupta Empire represented a 'Golden Age' in India. He opined that Hindu art, architecture, literature and science reached their height under the Guptas. After the Gupta collapse feudalism set in, followed by Islamic invasions which resulted in the beginning of the 'Dark Age' of Indian history that ended with the establishment of British paramountcy in the subcontinent during the early nineteenth century. The British division of Indian history into Hindu, Muslim and British periods was continued by the nationalist historians who also accepted the concept of a Hindu Golden Age under the Guptas and the beginning of the Dark Age with the onset of Muslim conquest from the eleventh century.[41] However, the concept of a Golden Age is challenged by several Indian Marxist scholars. One of them, D. N. Jha, asserts that feudalism was set in motion by the 'mighty Guptas' themselves. For instance, Harishena who composed the Allahabad *prasasti* (actually a panegyric) for Samudragupta, occupied several posts simultaneously and the civil and military posts tended to become hereditary.[42] This practice gave rise to feudatories who brought down the empire in conjunction with external enemies.

A group of scholars argue that all the precolonial polities of India did not quite qualify as states, as they had no fully developed bureaucracies, standing armies or defined borders. The armed forces maintained by them are

---

40 R. C. Majumdar, 'The fall of the Gupta Empire', in Majumdar, Pusalker and Majumdar, *The Classical Age*, 42–5, 42–3.

41 V. A. Smith, *Early History of India: From 600 BC to the Muhammadan Conquest* (Oxford: Clarendon Press, 1906); G. V. Devasthali, 'Literature', in Majumdar, Pusalker and Majumdar, *The Classical Age*, 291–326.

42 D. N. Jha, *Ancient India in Historical Outline*, revised and enlarged ed. (1977), reprint (New Delhi: Manohar, 2003), 153.

portrayed as undisciplined rabbles recruited ad hoc during emergencies, capable of fighting only in an unorganised manner, raiding, skirmishing and plundering. They claim that decisive battles and sieges were absent in precolonial India.[43] One senses here the influence of historians like John Keegan, Victor Davis Hanson and Geoffrey Parker. Stephen Peter Rosen argues that the Indian armies reflected the caste divisions which were prevalent in Indian society. And the caste-ridden premodern Indian armies, so the argument runs, were incapable of co-ordinating their movement on the battlefield; other than for raiding, they were just for show. Only the British in the eighteenth century were able to create a disciplined army separated from society.[44]

A growing body of scholarship which could be categorised as nationalist–Marxist counterargues that the ancient Indian empires were as strong and every bit as powerful as the larger Graeco-Roman entities. The ancient and early medieval Indian polities had centralised bureaucracies that could afford to maintain disciplined standing armies organised in complex tactical formations that were capable of conducting decisive sieges and battles.[45] The achievements of the Guptas lend weight to the second school of thought.

43 B. Stein, *A History of India* (1998), reprint (New Delhi: Oxford University Press, 2004); P. Barua, *The State at War in South Asia* (Lincoln: University of Nebraska Press, 2005).
44 S. P. Rosen, *Societies and Military Power: India and Its Armies* (New Delhi: Oxford University Press, 1996).
45 U. P. Thapliyal, *Warfare in Ancient India: Organizational and Operational Dimensions* (New Delhi: Manohar, 2010).

9

The Sassanian Empire's Strategies

KATARZYNA MAKSYMIUK

Sources

Chief among the Sassanian sources is the inscription of ŠKZ Šābuhr (Shapur) I (242–272) at Kaʾbe-ye Zartošt in Naqš-e Rostam, referred to in the literature by the Latin name *Res gestae divi Saporis* (The Things Accomplished by the Divine Shapur). The trilingual (Middle Persian, Parthian and Greek) inscription describes in detail the three victorious wars with Rome fought by Iran in the third century. Albeit rather short, other Sassanian sources, written towards the end of the dynasty (sixth–seventh centuries AD) can be used both in the analysis of Sassanian strategic objectives, such as the *Kār-nāmag ī Ardašīr ī Pābagān* (The Book of the Deeds of Ardaxšīr, Son of Pāpag), and, more importantly, in the strategy of warfare, such as the *Abar Wizārišn ī Čatrang ud Nihišn ī Nēw-Ardaxšīr* (On the Explanation of Chess and Backgammon). The latter text describes how the game of chess was introduced to Persia from India and how Persian sages invented the game of backgammon. According to them, chess is a kind of battle game and the chessboard is like a battlefield. The chess pieces described in this 'manual' correspond to the command system of an army; for example, the chess piece (which we call the queen) appears as the *artēštārān sālār*, or chief of the warriors, and the *aswārān sālār* (horse or knight at present) as the chief of the horsemen. Further inferences can be made from a series of monumental triumphal royal reliefs (at Dārābgerd, Naqš-e Rostam and Bišābuhr) depicting the defeated Roman emperors: Gordian (238–244) lying under the hooves of the horse of Šābuhr I, the captured Valerian (253–260) and Philip (244–249) on his knees begging the *šāhān šāh* for peace. To what extent the lost *Xwadāy-Nāmag* (Book of Lords/Kings) was the foundation for later texts remains debated.

Beyond this, we must rely heavily on foreign sources, mainly Roman, which relate mainly to the western politics of Iran. While evidence for the third century is patchy (Cassius Dio's and Herodian's histories end at the beginning of the century, and the *Scriptores Historiae Augustae* lack a description of the events of 244–259), there is abundant material for the later period. Exceptional works are the *Res Gestae* of a Roman soldier and historian, Ammianus Marcellinus, who personally participated in Roman campaigns in the Middle East in the fourth century AD, and the *History of the Wars* of Procopius, who accompanied the general Belisarius in Emperor Justinian's wars in the sixth century AD. Of particular importance is the *Strategikon*, a manual of war, generally attributed to the Emperor Maurice (582–602). While the author primarily presents the tactics and formation of the Byzantine army, it seems that these tactics were modelled on the actions of the heavy Persian cavalry, which was the primary strike force of the Sassanian *Spāh* ('army'). Further evidence can be gleaned from the works of the classical Arabic historians (ninth and tenth centuries AD) Ṭabarī or Dīnawarī and, above all, the epic of the *Šāh-nāma* (Book of Kings) written by the Persian poet Ferdowsī.

Actors

The ultimate power in Iran was held by the *šāhān šāh*, whose authority was, to some extent, limited by the hierarchical internal structure of the state (the *Nāma-ye Tansar*, trans. M. Boyce, 1968, pp. 38–9). It seems that the strategy of the empire was determined not only by the king, but also by the first three hereditary categories of the nobility: the *šahrdārān* (local kings), the *wāspuhragān* (members of Sassanian family), and the *wuzurgān* (the most important noble families, first of all of Parthian descent), who together with the higher Zoroastrian clergy constituted a supreme council of the state. Decisions were made by vote (Ammianus Marcellinus 18.5.6). The importance of the council is demonstrated by the fact that it chose the new monarch from among the Sassanian family (Ṭabarī 836; Procopius 1.20.20–2, 1.21.17–19).

For major military campaigns the king had to use contingents of the aristocratic houses. The sources illustrate the influential presence of the Parthian dynastic families within authority structures of the Sassanian Empire (ŠKZ 29/24/57, 31/25/62, 32/26/62). The representatives of the Parthian aristocracy commanded the Sassanian armies. The members of the Parthian clans of Sūrēn (Ammianus Marcellinus 24.3.1, 24.4.7) and Mehrān (Ammianus Marcellinus 25.1.11, 25.3.13) commanded the army of Šābuhr II (309–379). This peculiar 'alliance' of the Sassanian kings with part of the *wuzurgān* remained unchanged even after the introduction of the quadripartition of military power in the sixth century AD, when Khusro/ Husraw I (531–579) replaced the single army commander with four *spāhbeds* responsible directly to the king (Ṭabarī 894). Military authority in three of the four quarters was exercised by members of the Parthian aristocracy.

It should be emphasised that the existence of a strong aristocracy in Iran did not equate to a weak ruler. The successes of the king were at the same time the successes of the secular and religious elites of the state.

Adversaries

The Sassanians seized power in Iran under favourable geopolitical circumstances. To the east, the Kushan Empire, which held central Asia and part of India at the beginning of the third century, was already in decline. The new dynasty subjugated the local rulers without much difficulty (ŠKZ 3/2/4).

The only strong opponent of Iran was the Roman Empire in the west. The Sassanians 'inherited' this enemy from the Parthian dynasty of Arsacids, whom they had overthrown. The Emperor Septimius Severus (193–211) not only humiliated Iran by capturing the capital in Ctesiphon (Cassius Dio 75.9.1–12.5; Herodian 3.9.1–12), but more importantly created the Roman provinces of Mesopotamia and Osroena, in an area considered, until then, an integral part of the Iranian state. Military competition for influence in northern Mesopotamia, Armenia and the Caucasus region dominated Iranian–Roman relations, orienting the strategic activities of the early Sassanids to the western fringes of the empire.

The breakthrough came in the mid-fourth century, with the emergence of the Kidara Huns in the east. Iran faced a 'strategic dilemma'; it was crucial to avoid wars on multiple fronts. Šābuhr II assessed the invasion of the nomadic tribes as a greater threat than the Roman army in the west, as evidenced by the immediate suspension of military operations in northern Mesopotamia and the redeployment of the entire Iranian army and the personal presence of the *šāhān šāh* in north-eastern Iran (Ammianus Marcellinus 16.9.4). The Hephthalites or White Huns became the most important enemy of the Sassanians until the end of the following century; the adoption of such a strategic paradigm enforced the maintenance of peace with the Roman Empire in the west. Iran's focus on the east is evidenced by the fact that the *šāhān šāh* Pērōz (459–484) perished in battle against that nomadic power in 484 (Ṭabarī 873; Procopius 1.4.1–14). A turning point in Iranian strategy was the assistance given by the Hephthalites to Kawād I (488–496, 498–531) in reclaiming the throne of the *šāhān šāh* (Procopius 1.6.1–10). The Sassanian ruler, having secured the eastern territories, was able to move against Iran's age-old enemy, Rome, this way beginning a period of wars in the west that, with few interruptions, lasted almost until the collapse of the Persian state. Although Khusro I in around 558 defeated the Hephtalites in alliance with the Gök Türks, leading to the partition of their territories (Dīnavarī 69; Ṭabarī 895), it soon became clear that from the strategic point of view Khusro's actions in the east proved to be a blunder. Not only had a recent ally invaded Iranian territory (Dīnavarī 70; Ṭabarī 895–896), but diplomatic talks on an alliance between Byzantium and the Gök Türks had taken place (Theophylact Simocatta 3.9.3–10; Menander frg. 10. 1–3, frg. 13. 5) which forced Iran to fight on two fronts.

Causes of Wars

It would seem that Iran's wars with Rome, from the fourth century onwards, when Emperor Constantine the Great (306–337) considered himself the 'protector' of the Persian Christians (Eusebius, *Vita Constantini* 4.8), were primarily religious in nature, pitting Zoroastrian Iran and Christian Rome against each other. However, the assumption that the expansion of Iran towards the west was determined by the desire to spread Zoroastrianism is incorrect. Excepting for the reign of Šābuhr II, the idea of a planned and massive persecution of Christians by the Sassanids is unattested. Moreover, Persian rulers showed tolerance towards Christians, as seen in the flourishing of the Nestorian church in Iran, or the sanctuary found in the sixth century by the followers of Severus' doctrine when fleeing from persecution in the Roman Empire.

Nevertheless, in a very different context, the Zoroastrian religion was a factor influencing Persian strategy. Of particular importance in the Iranian ideology of power was the Zoroastrian *ātaš warahrān*, 'victorious fire' (ŠKZ 22/17/39), a great sacred fire burning in the temple of Ādur Gušnasp in Azerbaijan, one of the three great fires of ancient Iran. Ādur Gušnasp belonged to the warrior estate (*Bundahišn* 18.23–4). A fire altar appears frequently on the reverse of coins minted by Sassanian kings. The king was expected above all to be a victorious warrior. Echoes of this ideology can be seen on monumental rock reliefs depicting the kings in the moment of victorious battle with the enemy, such as Ardaxšīr at Fīrūzābād or Warahrān II at Naqš-e Rostam. The motif of a warrior king who is extremely proficient with his weapons is a repetitive topic of decorations on Sassanian toreutics. The king is depicted hunting wild animals using various weapons: a spear, a bow or even a sword.[1]

As the Sassanians had seized power by overthrowing the Parthian dynasty of the Arsacids, victory also played a significant role in their legitimation of power. The king's victories over Rome were a sign of the benevolence of Ahura-Mazda, the Zoroastrian deity, and a confirmation of the Sassanians' rights to the throne of Iran through the god-granted *xwarrah*. The legitimation of Sassanian power in Iran was of particular importance in the north-western provinces. The memory of Parthian rule in Iran and of blood ties between the Armenian and the Iranian Arsacid families lived on in Armenia well into late antiquity (Procopius 2.1.32). This tradition culminated in the revolt of Warahrān VI Čōbēn, who in 590 declared that the fall of the Sassanids was imminent and that the kingdom must be returned to the rightful sovereigns, namely the Arsacids (*Šāh-nāma* 9, p. 29).

There is evidence that the Iranians had some notion of agreed rules of inter-polity behaviour, the breach of which could be punished by war. In *Res Gestae divi Saporis*, Šābuhr I stated as the reason for the war with Rome that 'Philip lied about Armenia'. And Šābuhr II, during the peace negotiations of AD 363, referred to the fact that he wanted to regain northern Mesopotamia, because until the treaty of 298 these lands had belonged to his ancestors.

Objectives (Ends)

Both political and economic objectives guided Sassanian strategy in warfare. Domestically, they needed to neutralise the opposition to their rule associated with the previous Arsacid dynasty; externally, they aimed to reclaim territories that had previously been linked to a Parthian state (Ṭabarī 823). The strongest bastion of resistance against the new Persian dynasty was Armenia, whose kings had kinship ties with the Arsacid rulers. The Sassanian kings also needed to strengthen their position in relation to the indigenous aristocracy by benefiting through taxation from the urbanisation and economic development of territories under direct royal rule.

The dynasty change in Iran was perceived as threatening in the Roman Empire (Herodian 6.2.2; Cassius Dio 80.3.4). But the Sassanians did not seek to annex Roman provinces, as the Western sources suggested they did. Based on Šābuhr I's title – *šāhān šāh ērān ud anērān*, 'the king of the kings of Aryans

---

1 New York, Metropolitan Museum of Art, inv. no. 1970.6; St Petersburg, State Hermitage Museum, inv. no. S-252; London, British Museum, inv. no. 124092, respectively.

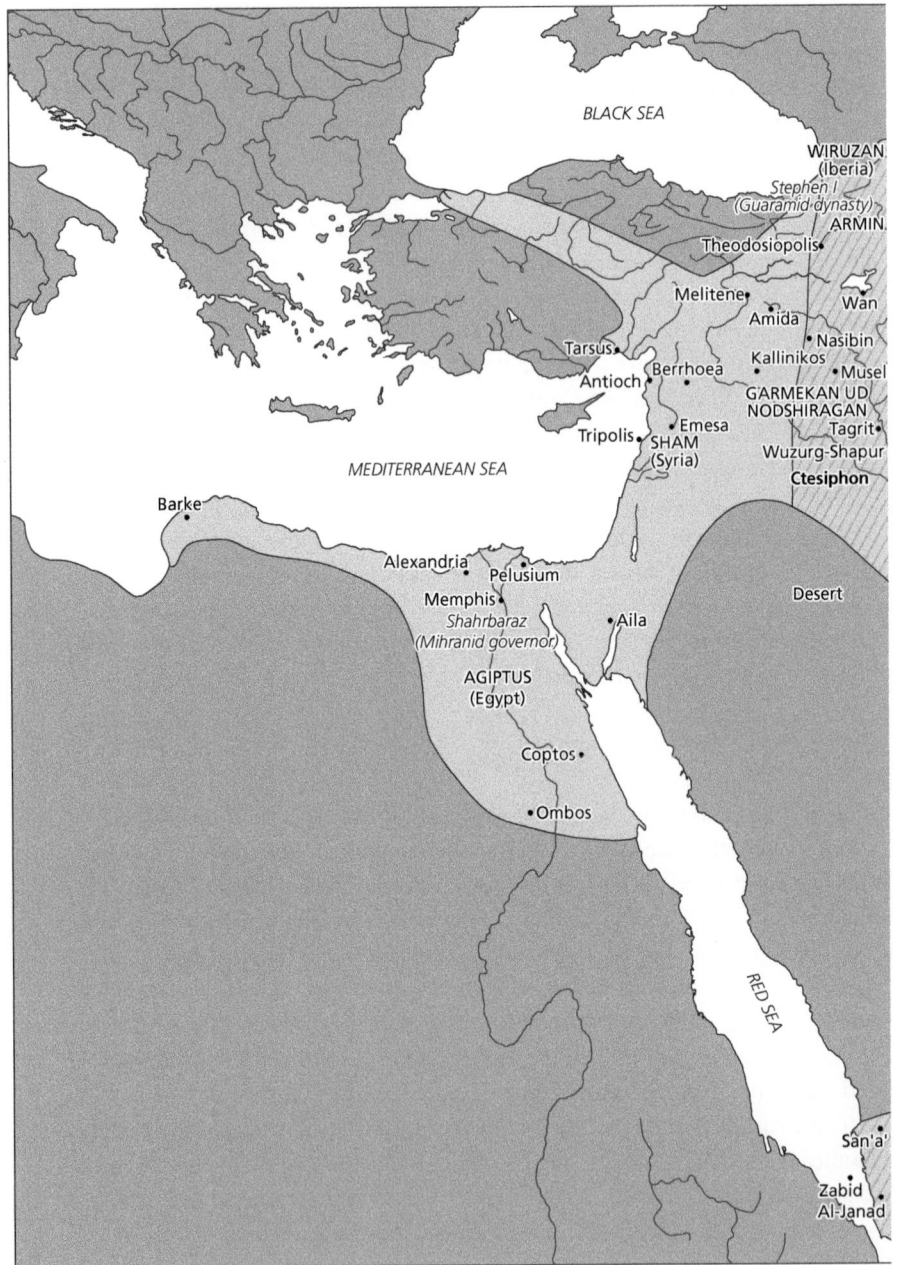

Map 9.1 Strategies of the Sassanian Persian Empire (AD 224–651)

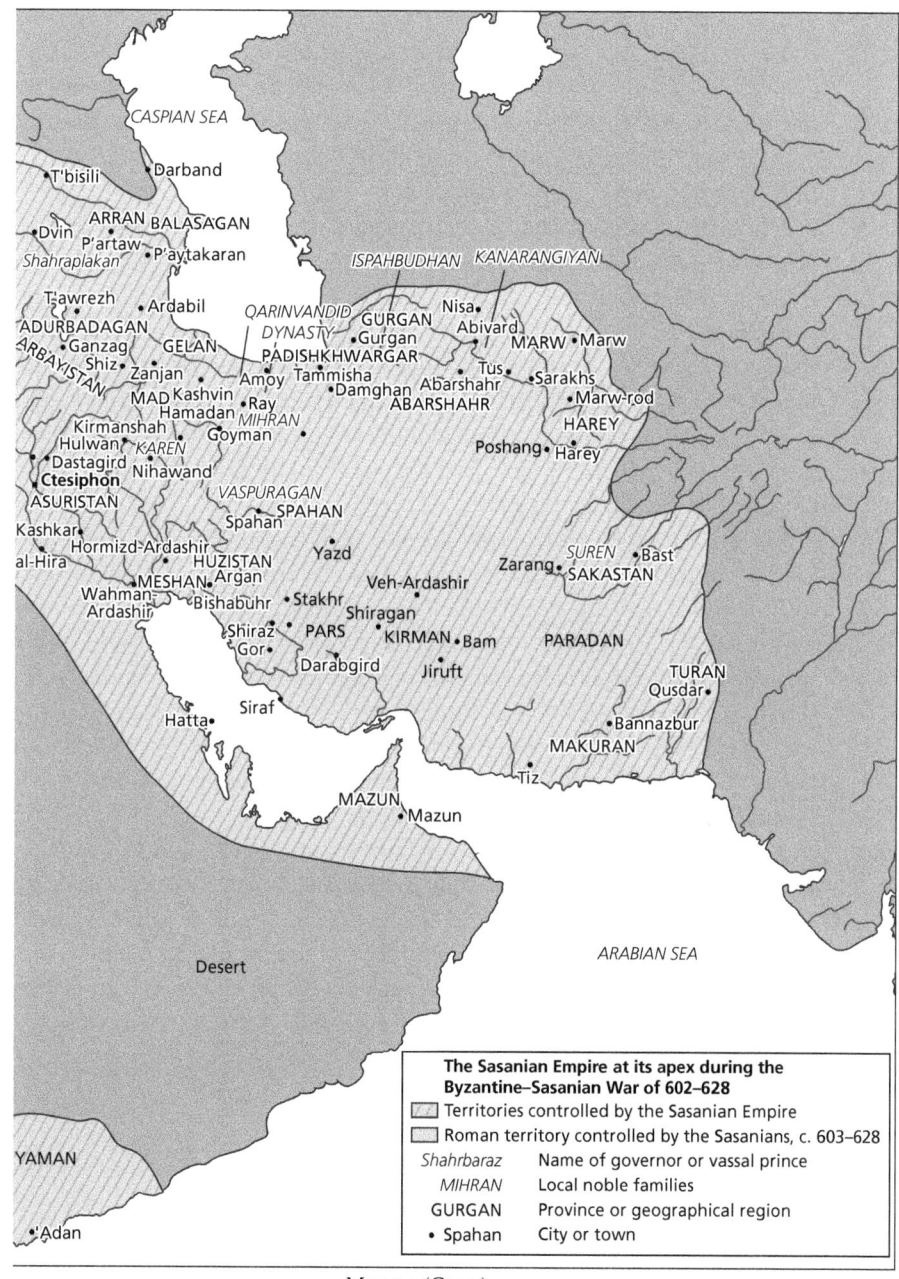

CASPIAN SEA

T'bisili •Darband

•Dvin ARRAN BALASAGAN
P'artaw •P'aytakaran
Shahraplakan

ISPAHBUDHAN KANARANGIYAN

T'awrezh •Ardabil QARINVANDID GURGAN Nisa•
ADURBADAGAN DYNASTY •Gurgan Abivard•
•Ganzag GELAN PADISHKHWARGAR MARW •Marw
Shiz• Zanjan • Amoy Tammisha Tus• •Sarakhs
MAD Kashvin •Damghan Abarshahr •Marw-rod
Kirmanshah Hamadan •Ray ABARSHAHR
Hulwan KAREN Goyman MIHRAN HAREY
•Dastagird Nihawand Poshang• Harey
•Ctesiphon VASPURAGAN
ASURISTAN SPAHAN
Kashkar• Spahan
Hormizd-Ardashir Yazd SUREN •Bast
al-Hira • HUZISTAN Argan Zarang• SAKASTAN
Wahman- MESHAN• Veh-Ardashir
Ardashir •Bishabuhr •Stakhr PARADAN
Shiraz• Shiragan
Gor• PARS •Bam TURAN
•Darabgird KIRMAN Qusdar•
Jiruft
Siraf •Bannazbur
Hatta• MAKURAN

•Tiz

MAZUN
•Mazun

Desert ARABIAN SEA

The Sasanian Empire at its apex during the Byzantine–Sasanian War of 602–628	
▨	Territories controlled by the Sasanian Empire
▥	Roman territory controlled by the Sasanians, c. 603–628
Shahrbaraz	Name of governor or vassal prince
MIHRAN	Local noble families
GURGAN	Province or geographical region
• Spahan	City or town

YAMAN

•'Adan

Map 9.1 (Cont.)

and non-Aryans' (ŠKZ 1/1/1) – it must be assumed that the Sassanians considered only Pārs, Media and Xūzestān the true native Iranian lands, so the first Sassanian attack on northern Mesopotamia was no attempt to restore the borders of the Achaemenid period. The aim seems to have been to destroy the Roman cities of Syria and deport their inhabitants into Iran (ŠKZ 20–21/15–16/34–35; Ṭabarī 827).

The first Sassanian rulers sought to control trade routes to the Far East, primarily to control the 'silk trade'. Even before overthrowing the Arsacids, Ardaxšīr had attacked al-Baḥrayn (Ṭabarī 820). It seems that, in the long run, Ardaxšīr planned to capture all of Arabia, and subsequently the entire maritime coastline of the Persian Gulf. His building activity, especially the founding of new cities (Ṭabarī 820), may be connected to this ambition, as it enabled the Sassanians to gain an autonomous source of tax revenue from them, in a relatively short time. The next step was the control of the route in Central Asia by seizing it from the Kushans.

Šābuhr I took firm control over the port of Spasinou Charax. This enabled him to monopolise trade in the Persian Gulf. After the destruction of Ḥaṭrā (in 240) and Dura Europos (in 256), Palmyra monopolised trade in Syria, but after its destruction by Roman emperor Aurelian in 272, the trade routes moved from the Euphrates to the Tigris, resulting in an enormous increase in the trade traffic of Nisibis. The Roman–Persian Peace of 298 made this city the only place for trade exchange between the two countries (Petrus Patricius frg. 14). Contested control over Nisibis determined Iran–Roman relations for centuries to come.

The Sassanian income gained from trade on the 'Silk Road' collapsed after Bactria was captured by the Huns in the mid-fourth century. Although Khusro I, in alliance with the Gök Türks, succeeded in breaking their power, in the absence of an Iranian–Turkish agreement on trade in raw silk, the Türks attempted to bypass Iran by an alternative route across the steppe to the Black Sea, which led to a reversal of alliances.

Means

Diplomatic and military actions were the Sassanians' basic means of pursuing strategic goals.

One of the greatest challenges faced by the Sassanian army was the vastness of the empire combined with limited military resources. The *šāhān šāh* was able to muster an army of around 120,000 to 150,000 men, including all possible provincial recruits, conscripts and auxiliaries, combined with the 'professional' core. The cavalry (the *aswārān*), recruited from Iranian nobles, divided into lancers and mounted archers (Ammianus Marcellinus 24.2.5, 25.12–18), remained the core of the Sassanian army throughout the empire's existence and was its main force. Light cavalry of the Sassanian army was recruited among the allied troops fighting under the command of their own chieftains, such as Chionites in the army of Šābuhr II in AD 359 (Ammianus Marcellinus 19.2.3). Western sources (such as Procopius 1.14.25) often spoke condescendingly of Sassanian infantry, calling them blind and worthless, but Ammianus Marcellinus (26.12.49) admiringly compared some units with Roman gladiators.

Early Sassanian siege warfare technology and tactics were most likely influenced by the Romans, but the Sassanians soon began to manufacture their own siege equipment (Ammianus Marcellinus 19.5.6). The Sassanian *spāh* utilised a number of different systems, including the engineered change of the flow of rivers, effected during Šābuhr's first siege of Nisibis in AD 337/338 (Theodoret, *Historia religiosa* 1.11–12).

To protect key border zones against incursions, the Sassanians constructed walls. The oldest was Šābuhr II's Wall of the Arabs in southern Mesopotamia, close to the city of Ḥira. Control of this area was delegated to the allies from the Naṣrid Arab clan. Three further walls were constructed at the turn of the fifth and sixth centuries. The Wall of Gorgān and the Wall of Tammīša, extending from the Caspian Sea to the Alborz and the north-eastern mountain chains of Persia, were directed against the Hephthalites. The Wall of Darband could stem nomadic incursions from beyond the Caucasus.

Generally the army was commanded by the *spāhbed* (chief of an army), but in especially endangered border areas a *marzbān* was appointed, an administrator who combined civilian and military competences. The title would be directly associated with a city, such as the *marzbān* of Nisibis (Acta Mar Ḳardaghi 5), or a particular territory, such as Armenia (*Epic Histories* 5. 38).

In the military reforms of the sixth century, the single commander (the *ērānspāhbed*) was replaced by four *spāhbeds* responsible directly to the king (Ṭabarī 894). Each of these four *spāhbeds* was assigned to one of the four quarters of the Sassanian empire, one to the north-east (*kust ī xwarāsān*), one to the south-east (*kust ī nēmrōz*), one to the south-west (*kust ī xwarbārān*) and one to the north-west (*kust ī Ādurbādagān*). The purpose was presumably to increase the operational flexibility of the Iranian army.

The Sassanians also pursued their strategic goals through alliances. The most durable of these was the agreement with the aforementioned Naṣrids of Ḥira, who protected Iran's south-western border throughout the Sassanian period. The situation on Iran's eastern border was far less stable. The nomadic powers there were periodically hostile or co-operative; allies could become enemies, as with the Gök Türks. The Sassanians, initially fighting against the Kidarite Huns and the Gilani, eventually concluded a treaty of alliance with them, taking advantage of their forces on the western front (Ammianus Marcellinus 17.5.1). In the fifth century, they tried to secure their eastern frontier by paying off the Hephthalites with tribute (Priscus, *Fragmenta* 6.41.3).

The Execution / Application of Strategy

After defeating the Parthian king Ardawān IV (216–224), Ardaxšīr launched his immediate attack against the Arab city of Ḥaṭrā and the kingdom of Armenia (Cassius Dio 80.3.2). This led to conflict with the Roman Empire (Herodian 6.2.5, 6.5.1–6.6.6; SHA, *Alex. Sev.* 61.8). Despite the capture of Ḥaṭrā, Ardaxšīr failed to break Parthian resistance in Armenia and Iberia, the ancient name of Eastern Georgia (Ammianus Marcellinus 25.7.9). Armenia was conquered by the Sassanian forces only in AD 252/253. On the western front, to achieve the primary objective of securing Ōhrmazd-Ardaxšīr's power in Armenia, the *šāhān šāh* conducted an attack on Syria and Cappadocia, which made it impossible simultaneously to send legions into Armenia, further shifting the zone of military action towards Roman territory.

Population transfers played an important role in Persian applied strategy. The inhabitants of Roman towns conquered by Šābuhr I were settled in provinces directly under the control of the Sassanians (Persis, Ḵūzestān and Āsōristān), which influenced the economic development of these areas, bringing additional income to the dynasty. Such relocations also affected the rebellious Arab tribes (Ṭabari 839) and the Armenians (*Epic Histories* 4.24, 4.54–5, 5.7). But Šābuhr II aimed not only to pacify the populations, but also to change the ethnic composition of northern Mesopotamia. This goal was achieved after the Persian conquest of Nisibis by the transfer of its inhabitants to territory now under Persian control, and, on the king's orders, Iranian people were settled in Nisibis (Ṭabarī 843).

The treaty of AD 298 accepted by Narseh (293–302) after defeat suffered at the hands of the Romans near Satala undid the achievements of Šābuhr I in northern Mesopotamia (transferring Nisibis to Rome) and the Caucasus region. Especially unfavourable for the Sassanians was restoration of the Arsacids on the throne of Armenia. Thus the aim of capturing Armenia and northern Mesopotamia was the dominant strategic goal of Sassanian military operations for another century. In 337, Šābuhr II began a long war to reconquer Nisibis and subdue Armenia. Depite several attempts (in 337, 346 and 350) the Iranian army was unable to achieve its main goal of capturing Nisibis (Theophanes A.M. 5837, A.M. 5841; Zosimos 3.8.2).

Nomadic invasions from central Asia forced Šābuhr to turn his attention to the east (Ammianus Marcellinus 14.3.1; 16.9.3). For several years, the military operations in Mesopotamia were stuck in a stalemate. Šābuhr pacified the threat from the east by concluding an alliance with the Kidarite Hunnic chief Grumbates (Ammianus Marcellinus 17.5.1).

After several failed attempts to directly capture Nisibis, Šābuhr II changed his strategy. In the early fourth century, other than Nisibis, Rome controlled a number of fortified places in northern Mesopotamia: Bezabde (which secured the strategic passes leading through the Taurus mountains into central Armenia), Singara (which controlled the crossing points of the Tigris river from the Adiabene direction) and Amida (which was to protect Greater Sophene). First, in 359, after a siege of seventy-three days, Šābuhr II captured Amida, and the following year took the two Roman strongholds Singara and Bezabde (Ammianus Marcellinus 19.9.9, 20.6.1–9, 20.7.1–15). With these actions he isolated the eastern Trans-Tigritania region; he could now attack Nisibis also from the north, simultaneously blocking off the Roman armies, and opening the road to Armenia for Iranian forces.

Šābuhr finally achieved his goal of capturing Nisibis after the disastrous Persian expedition of Julian the Apostate, when in 363 Julian's successor, Jovian, concluded an 'ignominious peace' surrendering his strongholds in north-east Mesopotamia (including Nisibis) and, with that, Roman influence in Armenia and Iberia. The integration of four-fifths of the south Caucasus into the Iranian sphere of influence gave it a clear strategic advantage.

The common threat from the Huns, who had occupied territories north of the Caucasus, led the Romans and the Persians to compromise. Armenia was partitioned as a result of an agreement in the 380s between Theodosius I (AD 378–395) and Šābuhr III (383–388). The appearance of the Huns in the Caucasus region forced the Sassanians to change their defence strategy. Securing the Caucasus passes (Darial and Derbent), through which the invaders had to pass to attack northern Mesopotamia, became the strategic priority. It is likely that the Roman empire, impressed by the size of the Hunnic invasion which sacked parts of Asia Minor and Syria in 395 (Socr. HE 6.1.7) reached an agreement with Iran to share in the cost of Iran's defence of the Caucasus. In AD 428, Warahrān V (420–439) introduced a military administration into

Armenia (the 'marzbanate'), turning the kingdom into an Iranian province, finally marking the end of Arsacid rule in Armenia. After the defeat of Pērōz in 484, Iran decided to turn its strategy towards the Huns from military to diplomatic action, providing tribute payments in return for immunity from Hun attacks.

The strategic situation on the western frontier changed dramatically when Kawād I unexpectedly entered northern Mesopotamia, capturing Amida in 502 (Ṭabarī 888). The Roman response was to build a new fortress, Dara, in close proximity to Nisibis. From 522 the Persian–Roman conflict in Caucasian Iberia and Lazica intensified (Procopius 1.11.29, 1.12.2–6.). Khusro continued the western orientation of his father's operations, attacking Roman Syria in 540, where he captured Antioch and, like Šābuhr I, deported its inhabitants (Procopius 2.8.1–35, 2.9.14–18), he also sent an army into the Caucasus region, which became the arena of Roman–Persian clashes for almost 100 years.

The climax of the military confrontations with Rome in the west was the reign of Khusro II (590–628). The *šāhān šāh* ceded most of the territory of Armenia and northern Mesopotamia to Rome in return for military assistance in his fight against the usurper Warahrān Čōbēn; he also agreed to divide Iberia (east Georgia) between Iran and Rome (Theophylact Simocatta 4.13.24; Sebeos 76, 84). These concessions were strategically unfavourable for Iran; its later rulers would strive to review the treaty. They seized their opportunity with the assassination of Emperor Maurice in 602. Within a few years, in 610, the Persian army occupied northern Mesopotamia, then conquered the major cities of the Roman east, including Antioch, Jerusalem and Chalcedon. The culmination of the campaign was the capture of Egypt in 618 (Ṭabarī 1002).

Not until 622 did Heraclius (610–641) launch a counteroffensive. The turning point in the war was the failed siege of Constantinople by allied Avar and Persian armies in 626. After his victory near Nineveh in 627 (Sebeos, 126) Heraclius reached Ctesiphon without any further resistance. The Iranian defeat at the battle of Nineveh was not strategically decisive, because the two main Persian armies in the west remained intact. Instead, crucial to ending the war and concluding the peace treaty in 630, which restored the *status quo ante bellum* in the Middle East, was the palace coup that resulted in the assassination of Khusro II (Ṭabarī 1044–5). The aristocratic families of Iran were not interested in expanding Iranian territory in the west as this would have strengthened their king's position.

Defending such an enormous area was a challenge, as was protecting it from centrifugal tendencies, typical of multi-ethnic states, generated also by the ambitions of local nobility, leaders and semi-independent local rulers. Despite these factors, the Iranian state managed to assure the territorial integrity of its core areas for four centuries, aside from some fluctuations of the borders both in the west and in the east, and some civil strife. The tool to achieve this was the army – mobile, efficient, disciplined and motivated. The durability of the structures of Sassanian Iran was determined as much by a kind of 'alliance' between the king and the great aristocratic families as by the army; when this collapsed at the end of the sixth century, the last Iranian empire ceased to exist soon after the assassination of Khusro II.

Historiographic Debates

The main scholarly debate concerns the military reforms of the sixth century. One of the debates concerns the creation of a standing army of crack units, the *asavarān*, by Khusro I, as postulated by Zeev Rubin. According to Rubin, this army was recruited among young nobles as well as from the *dahīgān* – a class of landed gentry considered inferior in rank to the *āzādān*.[2] This idea has been convincingly challenged by James Howard-Johnston, who believes that the introduction of a permanent 'professional' army was not a sixth-century innovation. He concluded that already from the reign of Ardaxšīr I, both infantry and cavalry 'were registered on state rolls and paid in cash'.[3] Stefan Hauser dates the creation of a standing army already to the Parthian period.[4]

---

2 Z. Rubin, 'The reforms of Khusro Anoshirvan', in A. Cameron (ed.), *The Byzantine and Early Islamic Near East*, Volume III: *States, Resources and Armies*, Papers of the Third Workshop on Late Antiquity and Early Islam (Princeton: Darwin Press, 1995), 227–98.

3 J. Howard-Johnston, 'The two great powers in late antiquity: a comparison', in Cameron, *States, Resources and Armies*, 157–226, 219.

4 S. Hauser, 'Was there no paid standing army? A fresh look on military and political institutions in the Arsacid Empire', in J. Tubach and M. Mode (eds), *Arms and Armour as Indicators of Cultural Transfer: The Steppes and the Ancient World from Hellenistic Times to the Early Middle Ages* (Wiesbaden: Reichert, 2006), 295–319.

10

The Rashidun, Umayyad (661–750) and Abbasid (750–1258) Caliphates

MEHDI KURGAN KADER

Sources

Few sources for this period illustrate Rashidun, Umayyad or Abbasid strategic decision making in any detail.[1] Foreign commentators knew little about the internal dynamics of the caliphate, and early Arab historians deemed the events outside the Muslim world unworthy of comment.[2] The majority of surviving works were not written by politicians or military men, but by Islamic scholars. Consequently, whilst the early chroniclers and historians of each respective period recorded events and anecdotes, they were far less concerned with strategy than with extolling and celebrating the glory of the rulers or detracting from their predecessors. Many of the authors had particular allegiances or were directly financed by the rulers.[3]

The history of the caliphate on the whole is rich in war; however, most historical sources provide little more than facts in the form of names, dates, places, victories and defeats, as well as accounts of domestic politics, to illustrate the existing strategic setting and environment within which military activity took place both inside and outside the caliphate. Contemporary scholarship has correlated these narratives and chronicles,[4] cross-referenced them and analysed them critically from the perspective of multiple

---

1 See K. Y. Blankinship, *The End of the Jihad State: The Reign of Hisham Ibn 'Abd al-Malik and the Collapse of the Umayyads* (New York: State University of New York Press, 1994), 247–72; C. F. Robinson, *Islamic Historiography* (Cambridge: Cambridge University Press, 2003), 3, 52, 131–8.

2 See H. Kennedy, *The Great Arab Conquests: How the Sword of Islam Changed the World We Live In* (London: Phoenix, 2007), 15–17, 30, 344–62; and W. E. Kaegi, *Byzantium and the Early Islamic Conquests*, (Cambridge: Cambridge University Press, 2000), 12.

3 See U. Martensson, 'Discourse and historical analysis: the case of al-Tabari's History of the Messengers and the Kings', *Journal of Islamic Studies* 16 (2005), 287–331; and A. S. Mourad, 'On early Islamic historiography: Abu Isma'il al-Azdi and his Futuh al-Sham (Conquests of Syria)', *Journal of the American Oriental Society*, 120:4, (2000), 577–93.

4 See F. M. Donner, *Narratives of Islamic Origins: The Beginnings of Islamic Historical Writing* (Princeton: Darwin Press, 1998), 230–48.

disciplines.[5] This information is sufficient to explore the political and strategic setting as a means to understand how domestic pressures informed and directed geopolitical objectives, policies and military activity.

Actors

Although later apocryphal traditions would claim that Muhammad prophesied four Rightly Guided Successors (*Khulafa al-Rashidun*), from which the Rashidun period derived its name, the development of Muslim political authority was anarchic. No formal legislation or religious guidance had been left for political succession prior to Muhammad's death in 632, making the succession to the position of the Caliph and by extension the caliphate a contest for power and legitimacy.

Originally, the vacuum of leadership was filled by the vote of a handful of Muhammad's closest companions to appoint Abu Bakr (d. 634) as Muhammad's *khalifah* (lit. 'successor'). The lack of support for the customary tribal policy of hereditary authority alienated members of Muhammad's own clan, Banu Hashim, creating an immediate tension within the Muslim body politic and a recurring source of internal dissidence. Furthermore, given the ad hoc appointment of Abu Bakr, with no precedent to validate his authority, widespread tribal rebellion spread, resulting in the Ridda Wars (632–633).

Abu Bakr, in his dying days, after consultation with his war council, appointed his chief political adviser 'Umar b. Khattab (d. 644) as his successor, overlooking the Banu Hashim again. Prior to his death, 'Umar gave instructions for a select committee which he appointed, to adjudicate his successor from a list of candidates he had recommended. 'Uthman b. 'Affan was duly appointed despite a candidate from Banu Hashim having been a contender. After twelve years in power, 'Uthman was deposed and murdered in 656, sparking the First Civil War in Islam, known as the Fitna. Successionist tribal politics and grievances since the death of Muhammad resurfaced.

'Ali ibn Abu Talib, the strongest contender with a claim to leadership within Banu Hashim, accepted the petitions of 'Uthman's executioners to take the seat of power. With the backing of his clan, he accepted. 'Ali's decision was contentious and provocative, with little to no support from the broader community of Muhammad's Companions and to the bitter resentment of

---

5 S. R. Humphreys, *Islamic History: A Framework for Inquiry* (London and New York: I. B. Tauris & Co. Ltd, 1991); M. K. Kader, 'On the origins and strategic dynamics of pre-legal jihad 610–680 C.E.', PhD thesis, King's College London (2016); and F. M. Donner, *The Early Islamic Conquests* (Princeton: Princeton University Press, 1981).

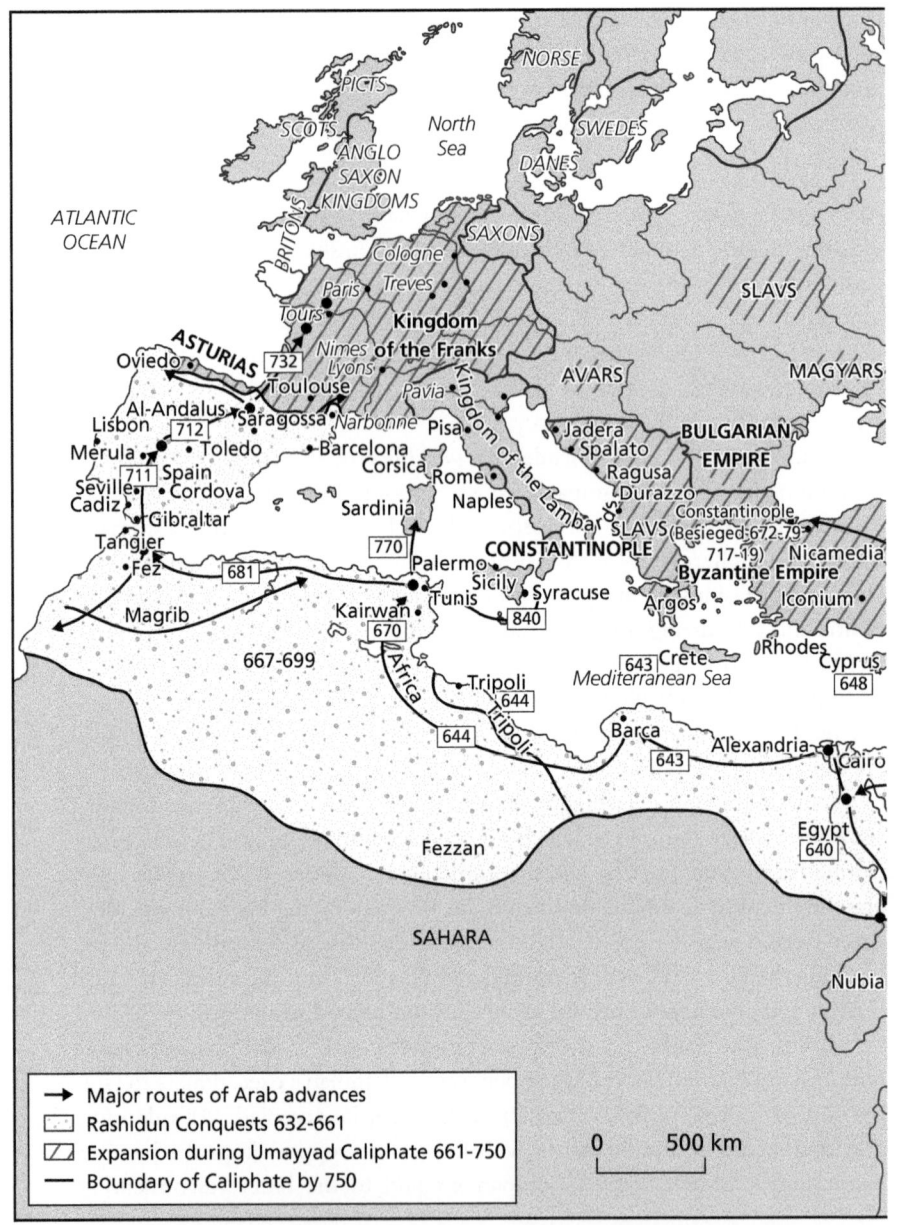

Map 10.1 Strategies of the Rashidun, Umayyad (661–750) and Abbasid (750–1258) caliphates. Redrawn with permission based on a map originally created by Map Archive (www.themaparchive.com).

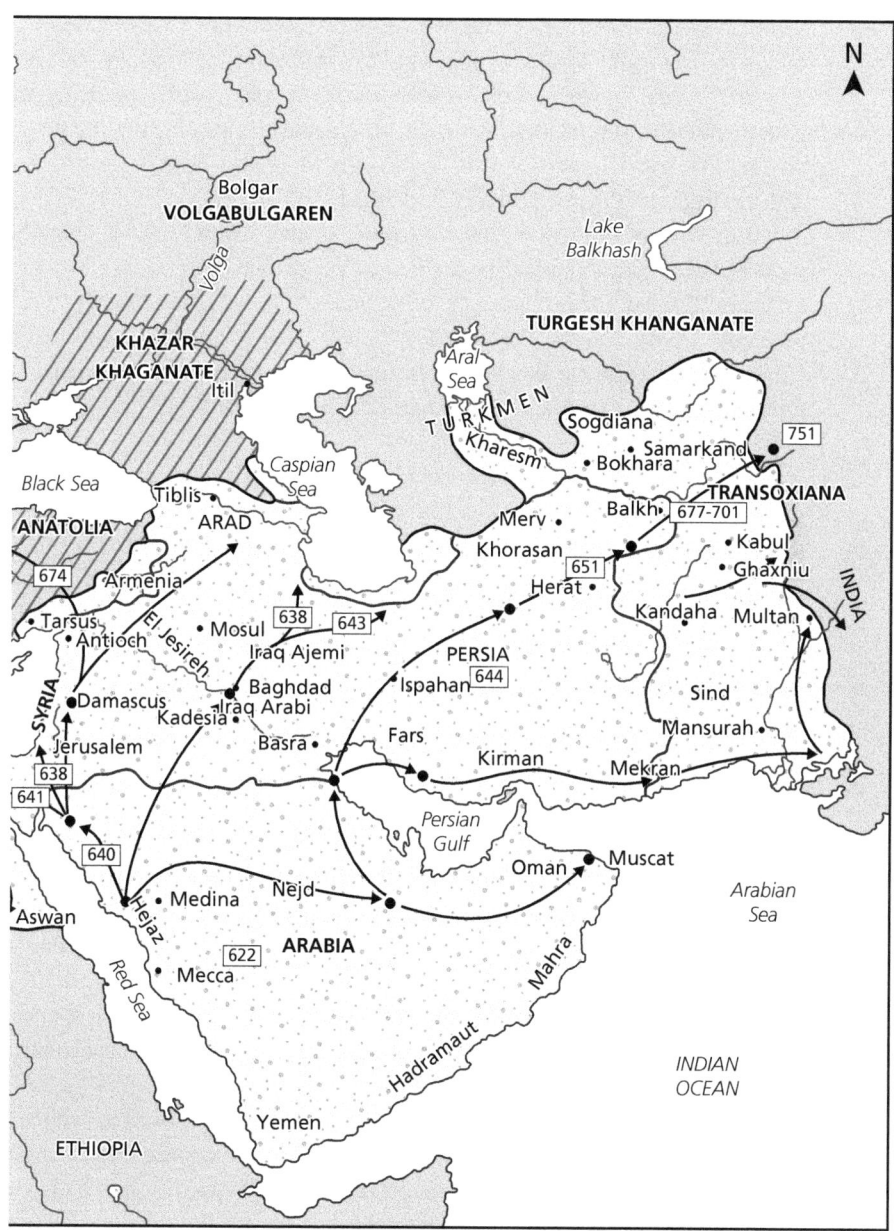

Map 10.1 (Cont.)

'Uthman's clan, Banu Umayyah, who sought retribution for the murder of their clansman and leader of the Muslim community. Mu'awiya ibn Abu Sufyan (d. 680), governor of Syria at the time, and 'Aisha (d. 678), the widow of Muhammad, led the military resistance against 'Ali's claims to power. The Fitna lasted for five years, with Mu'awiya emerging victorious and the beginning of the Umayyad caliphate.

Under Mu'awiya, a new dawn of political and military affairs unfolded, modelled after the vanquished Sassanids and the Byzantine Empire. In an attempt to ensure stability in the transition of power, Mu'awiya, following Byzantine precedent, made his son Yazid I (d. 683) heir. The caliphate itself from the Umayyad period onwards was a dynastic superstructure built upon religious foundations with hereditary monarchies claiming, and later vying for, the title of Caliph.

Neither the Qur'an nor Muhammad left any explicit guidance or religious injunctions for statecraft. The Rashidun and early Umayyad caliphs understood that political legitimacy would be gained by meeting particular expectations – the retention of a standard of leadership akin to Muhammad's, based on the teachings of the Qur'an. In doing so, the Caliph, like Roman emperors, assumed the persona of God's chosen representative, who was to be obeyed to the extent that he conformed to the Qur'an and to the teachings of Muhammad.

Means

In evaluating the military means available to the caliphs, the most taxing problem associated with the early campaigns of the Rashidun, Umayyad and Abbasid caliphates is that of numbers. The Arabic sources cite either contradictory or inconceivable figures – often both. Furthermore, the specific details concerning the composition of the armed forces, both infantry and navy, across all caliphates, as well as their military formations and battlefield tactics, weapons used and employment of cavalry and archers, are sparsely documented, and academic investigation of these areas is often speculative given the compromised state of the Arabic source materials.[6]

What can be written with some confidence is that the Rashidun caliphate inherited a force of tribal Bedouins, skilled in desert raiding and counter-raiding tactics and manoeuvres. Constant inter-tribal skirmishes had provided the Arab tribes with fighting experience before the advent of Islam, and during Muhammad's mission these tribes had developed even greater

---

6 See H. Kennedy, *The Armies of the Caliphs: Military and Society in the Early Islamic State* (London and New York: Routledge, 2001), 3, 19–21.

war-fighting experience. Although unified under Muhammad, tribes remained independent entities rather than an incorporated military force deployed by request of the Caliph. Each tribe would recruit fighters from within its own ranks, generally self-equipped for battle, and war booty was the primary material reward for participation.

The military experience and acumen of the Arabs escalated dramatically within the first decade of the Rashidun caliphate off the back of a series of highly successful campaigns of conquest into Iraq, Syria, Palestine and Egypt. The deployment of forces differed dramatically between campaigns. Academic estimates aside,[7] what is clear is that the Arabs accumulated a growing arsenal of weapons from the conquered, upgrading their existing swords, spears and armour as they went along.

Strategic success was also politically reinforced with the increase of the Muslim armed forces by the defection and conversion of Persian soldiers. The introduction of professional soldiers, including the elite troops and senior commanders of Yazdegerd III, undoubtedly served as a force multiplier, refining the operational and tactical prowess of the Muslim army. Greeks are also mentioned in the early Arab sources as participating in the Muslim conquest of Egypt, although the general tendency of these sources was to limit and downplay the influence of non-Arab allies in Arab victories.

A resettlement policy was employed during the caliphate of 'Umar, to manage and maintain control of the newly acquired non-mobile wealth from conquest, as well as the new populations now under Arab rule. The resettlement policy went hand in hand with the building of garrisons and the introduction of the *diwan*, a military roster, to register and pay salaries and pensions to the armed forces. The early stages of a naval fleet also began development during the caliphate of 'Uthman.

Restoration of war-fighting aims during the caliphate of Mu'awiya led to the restructuring of the Umayyad military, updating state apparatus to accommodate taxation, administration and bureaucracy. Mu'awiya's long-standing engagements with the Byzantines since his days as governor of Syria undoubtedly influenced the introduction of reforms to the Umayyad navy and infantry which copied not only their organisation, but also the introduction of drill and tactical manoeuvres adopted and learnt from the enemy.

7 Donner, *The Early Islamic Conquests*, 133–5, 221.

These reforms were the beginnings of an Umayyad state proper, distinct from the proto-state society of the Rashidun caliphate.[8] Resettlement policies continued, with infrastructure developed to house deployed troops and their families.[9]

During the Rashidun caliphate, the armed forces were operating within geographical proximity of Madina, the capital, which facilitated direct command-and-control communication between Madina and operational theatres of war. Consequently, the Rashidun caliphs exercised significant control over unfolding events. As the caliphate extended its territories, the need to decentralise military control ensued. The orders of the Caliph were executed through regional governors, local administration and military generals deployed in the field who would deputise commanders to lead specific expeditions or raids.[10]

Governors were chosen by the Caliph to maintain the local *diwan*, and to manage and collect taxation, and were responsible for order and security within their respective provinces. Regional military forces (*muqatila*) developed following resettlements, such as in Iraq, Egypt and later Khorasan, and were under the authority of the regional governor. Overall command of the armed forces remained decentralised throughout the period of the Umayyad caliphate, and the hierarchical structure of the *muqatila* remained informal, with status within tribes correlated to leadership and command appointments rather than to military experience.[11] The *muqatila* became increasingly diverse as local populations, converted or voluntarily enlisted, joined the ranks.

A noteworthy example is that of the Berbers. By 698, the Umayyads had effectively prised north Africa away from Byzantine control and pacified Berber resistance in the region. The Berber population's subjugation and subsequent conversion to Islam were not only a military victory but also an important political one. They reinforced the legitimacy of the Umayyad

---

8 See F. M. Donner and A. Cameron, 'Centralized authority and military autonomy in the early Islamic conquests', in A. Cameron (ed.), *The Byzantine and Early Islamic Near East*, Volume III: *States, Resources and Armies* (Princeton: The Darwin Press, Inc., 1995), 337–60.

9 See W. B. Hallaq, *Authority, Continuity and Change in Islamic Law* (Cambridge: Cambridge University Press, 2005), 31; M. G. S. Hodgson, *The Venture of Islam*, Volume I: *The Classical Age of Islam* (Chicago and London: The University of Chicago Press, 1977), 208–10; A. Qurbanov, 'Some aspects of the resettlement policy of the Arab Caliphate in Azerbaijan', *Caucasus & Globalization* 4:3–4 (2010), 114–19; Kader, 'Strategic Dynamics', 183–90; and Donner, *The Early Islamic Conquests*, 258, 266–7.

10 See H. Kennedy, *The Prophet and the Age of the Caliphate: The Islamic Near East from the Sixth to the Eleventh Century* (London: Longman, 1986).

11 Kennedy, *The Armies of the Caliphs*, 18–23, 30–51.

leaders in the eyes of their domestic populations. The Berbers instantly supplied the caliphate with additional troops for the north African armies to continue operations in the region, to great success.

Syrian troops (*ahl al-Sham*) formed the vanguard of the Umayyad military, loyal to the Umayyad house, constituting the most professional and the best-equipped force available to the Caliph. The Syrian troops were the first seeds of a standing army, usually deployed as battlegroups to augment regional governors and *muqatila* stationed outside Syria. They were authorised to act in concert and under command of the regional *muqatila* and to return to Syria following completion of their missions.

The distinction between the Syrian troops and the general armed forces of the Caliph is important. Throughout the Rashidun caliphate and well into the Umayyad, warfare was a default state of affairs. The Arabs were mobilised based on war-fighting needs and the distinction between soldier and civilian did not exist. Recruitment and incentive to fight were premised upon appeals to faith and material reward in the form of booty, one-off payments and later salaries based upon participation. Although many men would re-enlist continuously as a means of livelihood, there were also part-time fighters. Accordingly, the regional *diwan* registered the names of individual participants of the *muqatila* without accounting for returning fighters, resulting in inflated numbers.

The expense of continuous war-fighting, in terms of logistical supplies, military replacements, replenishing arms and maintaining garrisons, amongst other expenditures, inevitably depleted state resources. The Umayyad treasury became dependent on successful expansions to relieve state expenditure through the acquisition of booty, and the exploitation of the resources of the conquered. Financial crisis often ensued as dependence on booty was compounded by insufficient administrative infrastructure and fiscal measures, which provoked violent resistance within the caliphate. The costs of internal disturbance often persisted, offsetting the introduction of reforms intended to counterbalance and pacify public outcry.

The Abbasid caliphate broke with many of the warfighting policies of their predecessors, yet remained true to the organisational infrastructure of the Umayyads. Crucially, the collapse of the *ahl al-Sham* made way for the *ahl Khurasan* – the military troops of Khorasan, who became the vanguard military force of the Abbasids and fulfilled a similar role to their forerunners. Syrian troops were struck from the *diwan* and marginalised, occasionally employed on the frontiers or for otherwise undesirable campaigns.

A class of barons known as *quwwad* emerged early on in the Abbasid caliphate. These were permanently salaried military commanders with direct political ties to the ruling class. The *qa'id* (sing.) essentially performed the same functions as a tribal chief during the Umayyad caliphate (being responsible for recruiting fighters to the *diwan*, organising and mobilising his forces for military operations when necessary), and was similarly a hereditary role. A natural evolution and development in military technique continued as it had done throughout the Umayyad caliphate, though such incremental advances were unremarkable on the whole.

Causes of War

Explanations offered for the Rashidun and later Umayyad expansions have been largely of socio-economic persuasion, ranging from the desire for wealth to freedom from poverty, overpopulation or scarcity of resources – none of which sufficiently explain the speed and explosive impact which the rise of the caliphate had upon the region.[12] Alternatively, the modern preoccupation with jihad as *casus belli* for all forms of violence associated with Islam is fundamentally incorrect. The strategic setting itself is the obvious and most satisfactory explanation for the initial causes of war in the region.

Muhammad's rise to power in Arabia triggered a regional security dilemma that caused the regional powers to take precautions. Trade routes, particularly the frankincense distribution channels from southern Arabia to Byzantium, were compromised given the changing hands of power. Skirmishes took place around 629–630 between Muslims and the northern Arab nomadic tribes – the Ghassanid Arabs who were Byzantine vassals, and the Lakhmid tribes who were former Sassanid proxies around the grasslands that separated Arabia from the Fertile Crescent. Around the same time or shortly thereafter, the Muslims engaged a division of Byzantines, all suggesting that Muhammad was particularly concerned with the border security of northern Arabia. That Abu Bakr would later prioritise and implement a strategy against the northern Arab tribes that was in fact commanded by Muhammad prior to his death may well be plausible, though ultimately unprovable.

12 Donner, *The Early Islamic Conquests*, 267; Kader, 'Strategic Dynamics', 171–4; and J. W. Jandora, 'Developments in Islamic warfare: the early conquests', *Studia Islamica*, 64 (1986), 101–13.

Indeed, the caliphate of Abu Bakr, following the *Ridda* Wars and galvanised by their rapid successes, overran the northern Arab tribes and pressed on into Persian, then Byzantine territories, forcing full-scale military operations by each power on the counteroffensive. The caliphate of 'Umar continued operations with great success, eventually dominating the Sassanids and capturing vast territories from the Byzantines. By the third Rashidun caliph, 'Uthman, the caliphate had cemented itself as a stable regional power, replacing the Persians as Byzantium's main contender for power.

Continued Umayyad expansion was founded upon the earlier success of the Rashidun. The Umayyad inheritance to regional dominance by the swift accumulation of territorial power and the apparent hegemony the caliphate enjoyed made them the principal actor in the region, reinforcing the tension between the expectation of constant military action to maintain credibility and authority and the need to stabilise the inherited strategic environment. The Abbasid caliphate would also inherit the enemies and strategic environment of their predecessors. Policies intended to de-escalate tensions and rivalries were more often than not political rather than strategic, as the Abbasid Caliphate remained, at least initially, dependent upon a military (and enemies for the military to fight) – as had the Umayyads.

Aggressive security maximisation through polices of expansionism explains the mechanism by which the caliphate rose to power. Jihad was an ideology justifying warfare as a continuation of *Politik* by other means. The romanticism of jihad was propaganda politically encouraged to support recruitment and reinforce the political legitimacy and credibility of the ruling house of the caliphate, both Umayyad and Abbasid. The weaponisation of literature in an increasingly literate population, alongside the explosion of apocrypha in the *Hadith* traditions, cultivated – in concert with the nostalgia of the Rashidun caliphate – a fertile ground for military recruitment and support for military activities of the caliphates. The ninth-century development of Islamic legal doctrines which reinforced a perpetual state of war between Muslims and the rest of the world was the product of strategic escalation rather than substantive religious teachings that Muhammad had preached.

Adversaries

The main adversary of the Rashidun caliphate, following the defeat and collapse of the Sassanian Empire, became the Byzantine Empire. Maintaining the new balance of regional power was the consequence of having invited Byzantium as an opponent by the usurpation of former Byzantine territories, rather than Christendom. Later, the Umayyad caliphs, having bound themselves to a perpetual state of war, with no natural end, championed jihad to their domestic audiences. However, limited rather than unlimited warfare was demonstrably practised and the Umayyad caliphate – despite being aggressive security maximisers – had no expectation of converting the known world through Islam. Military activity at every border was, as a matter of policy, a strategic constant unless a truce had been agreed and was little influenced by religion.

Where resistance to occupation was met, intensive battle followed. Prisoners of war were held for ransom if not sold into slavery. Alternatively, in the absence of resistance, towns were rewarded with great leniency and religious tolerance, and the pre-existing ruling elite were given renewed political positions within local government and the promise of military protection. Conquered populations were not subject to forced conversion and taxes levied were lower than those charged by their predecessors. The Rashidun caliphs in particular were generally content to rule and collect taxes as long as there existed a low-threat environment.

Later ideological reforms during the Umayyad caliphates of Marwan I, 'Abd al-Malik, and 'Umar II (684–720) targeted religious communities. The Christian population, particularly in Syria and Egypt, had numerous religious freedoms restricted as part of a backlash following successive defeats by the Byzantines and civil strife within the caliphate. Diminishing religious tolerance toward non-Muslims included their disarmament, banning public displays of their faith and restrictions in clothing in order to distinguish themselves from Muslims.

Military expansions on all fronts had effectively halted during the First Civil War (656–661), as the domestic power struggle absorbed both the political will of the Muslim body politic and their military means.[13] In the aftermath, a host of resurgent adversaries were met on all fronts, or later joined the list of opponents the Umayyads would contend with. The preeminent and enduring adversary was again Byzantium, which towards the very end of the Umayyad period began to move from defence to counteroffensive, but the Turgesh Khaganate, the Khazars, the Visigoths, the Bulgars, the Berbers, the Mardaites and the Tang dynasty would all play a role as simultaneous warfare on all fronts was sustained. Many of these opponents would be inherited by the Abbasids to a lesser degree, except for

---

13 Kader, 'Strategic Dynamics', 227–38.

the Byzantine Empire, which in the ninth and early tenth centuries managed to embark on a last counteroffensive to reconquer some of its Middle Eastern lands lost to the Muslims.

Perhaps, most notably, since Muhammad's death, the Muslim community had always been in tension with itself over claims of authority and power. As a result, even more so than the Byzantines, the most frequent source of adversarial threat to the caliphate came from within. The political fallout of the *Ridda* Wars and of the First, Second and Third Civil Wars, as well as the constant threat of internal insurrection by vying tribal elements across the caliphate, all had considerable impact and influence over the course of military affairs – often more than external enemies had. In point of fact, the strategic priorities of the caliphate, from the Rashidun to the Abbasid, was often dictated by the fragile balance between internal stability and the strength of external adversaries.

Strategic Priorities

The policies and expansions of the Rashidun caliphate set off a domino effect of cascading strategic priorities that the Umayyad, and to a lesser degree the Abbasid, caliphates were bound to. How specifically the armed forces of the Rashidun caliphates fought, and how they were so successful in the face of improbable odds against overwhelmingly superior opponents, is perhaps the greatest mystery of early Islam. For this reason, the strategic priorities of Rashidun, which can be discerned, shall be presented here, with greater emphasis on the Umayyad execution of strategy and war-fighting later.

The caliphate of Abu Bakr (632–34) demonstrates a clear strategic prioritisation for security-maximising policies and military action. The commencement of these policies began following the pacification of Arabia during the *Ridda* Wars (632–633). Abu Bakr commissioned the brilliant military leader Khalid ibn al-Walid (d. 642) as commander-in-chief of the armed forces and gave him the sole directive to crush all forms of tribal insurrection and resistance to the authority of the new caliph. Khalid's swift and decisive victories firmly established Abu Bakr as the undisputed authority of Arabia.

The second priority of the overall strategy was border control. Under the command of Khalid, the caliphate indirectly drew first blood against Sassanid Iraq in 633, and then Byzantine Syria in 634, by striking at their proxies. The strategy had limited aims and was most likely not intended as a provocation of Byzantium or Persia. Nonetheless, by striking at the northern nomadic tribes, both powers were incited to retaliate following the successive defeats of their respective auxiliaries and perceived territorial encroachment.

Abu Bakr's war council, which included all later Rashidun caliphs, amongst others, undoubtedly influenced the offence-dominant strategic approaches of the later caliphs. Subsequent military priorities of the Rashidun caliphates were the strategic outcomes of the setting Abu Bakr had left for his successors, augmented by the introduction of a resettlement policy by 'Umar. In combination, the caliphate achieved total theatre domination in Iraq (636–637); Persia (642); and most of Syria, Armenia and Eastern Anatolia by 638. 'Umar continued the expansions into Egypt (640–642), north Africa (643), and Khorasan (643–644).

Originally, the act of resettling Arab Muslims into conquered territories was a colonial tactic in response to the threat of defeated populations being incited to rebel, or to sabotage the presence of the caliphate, as per the defeat of Yazdegerd III in 640, and his subsequent attempts to rally a revolt against the Arabs amongst the Persian populations that the caliphate now occupied. 'Umar, through the resettlement of Arab tribes, bound their loyalty to the caliphate through fiscal dependence and extended security. The strategic consequence for the resettlement was twofold: first, to secure the new territories through raw manpower (population redistribution) and military presence (garrisons), and second, to reduce logistical loads required for further military action. Subsequently, the policy created strategic strongholds that facilitated forward-operating bases for continued expansions or defensive containment actions.

The policies of extended security and resettlement directed by Abu Bakr and 'Umar respectively were the fundamental strategic priorities of the Rashidun with respect to the developing power and character of the caliphate. Later Rashidun caliphs followed the basic elements of both policies, with essentially one significant development – the beginnings of the acquisition of a navy. War with Byzantium in particular had impressed the need for an armada. Mu'awiya had been appointed governor of Syria by 'Umar, and had remained in place throughout the caliphate of 'Uthman (644–656). He was the strategic visionary who had first petitioned 'Umar for the need for a fleet. 'Umar had refused, desiring the seas as a buffer space between the caliphate and Byzantium rather than another theatre of operations.

Following the appointment of 'Uthman, Mu'awiya convinced the new caliph of the strategic need. Within a year, the new navy saw action in the defence of Alexandria in 645, from Byzantine attempts to recapture their former territory. The addition of sea power to the caliphate was an escalation of the security dilemma with Byzantium. It also signalled a shift of intent to project warfare across the seas, beginning during the caliphate of 'Uthman. The strategic prioritisation of sea power between 'Uthman's reign and the caliphate of Mu'awiya – that is, the Umayyad Caliphate – would have been a direct continuation, but for the events of the *Fitna*.

Although Umayyad strategic decision making is barely discussed in the classical Arabic sources, we can infer that the Umayyads' belief in the efficacy of violence suggests that they preferred constant war-fighting and expansion over regional stability, consistent with their estimate that they could success-fully annex neighbouring territories.[14] Caliphs tended to succeed each other between campaigns but inherited the problems of their predecessors, limiting the ability to make sweeping strategic changes. Mu'awiya prioritised balan-cing domestic civil–military relations and instituting a defensive strategy against external threats that might have become emboldened by the inter-ruption of expansions due to the First Civil War.[15]

In the midst of a Second *Fitna* (680–692) Caliph Marwan I (d. 685) launched a full-scale ideological campaign to reignite nostalgia of the Rashidun era. Internal dissent was vigilantly monitored and insurgencies were supressed militarily. Iraq in particular had become a hub for anti-Umayyad rebels, and the regional governor, al-Hajjaj ibn Yusuf, spearheaded the search-and-destroy policy in the east, with Syrian troops redeployed to the region to aid the effort. The Iraqi troops were mostly discharged and soldiers were only redrafted if they were willing to campaign on a more hostile frontier such as Khorasan and Sind. The demilitarisation and occupation of Iraq, with a purpose-built garrison known as *al-Wasit* to house the Syrian troops, was and would remain a long-standing security expense to the treasury, but was deemed a strategic priority nonetheless.

Similarly, 'Abd al-Malik (685–705), the fifth Umayyad caliph, weakened by civil war, recovering from defeat at Constantinople and still at war with Byzantine and Mardaite forces, prioritised stability in the form of a ten-year truce with the Byzantines in 689. Constantinople was able to impose humili-ating conditions, but in return the Byzantines relocated 12,000 Mardaite fighters from Syria to Armenia, effectively ending the Umayyad campaigns against Mardaites which had been ongoing since 678. The truce allowed 'Abd al-Malik to concentrate on suppressing continued political opposition and rebellion in his own lands.

---

14 See M. Bonner, 'Some observations concerning the early development of jihad on the Arab–Byzantine frontier', *Studia Islamica*, 75 (1992), 5–31.

15 Kader, 'Strategic Dynamics', 261–77.

The eighth Umayyad caliph, 'Umar II (d. 720), in the face of a second defeat outside Constantinople, and defeat at the hands of the Chinese Tang in Transoxiana, inherited the aggressive power-maximising strategy of his predecessors which had compromised the caliphate both politically and militarily. Under the threat of a shifting balance of power irrevocably in favour of the resilient Byzantines, 'Umar II abandoned the iconic Umayyad cult of the offensive, and prioritised a new strategy of security maximisation in the belief that defensive operations rather than offensive would favour stability and Umayyad survival. Between 718 and 720, 'Umar II ordered a cessation of all offensive military operations around Umayyad territories. This was the first time in Umayyad history that offensive operations were voluntarily terminated, demonstrating a reversal of strategic priorities.

In the early period of the Abbasid caliphate, the relationship between policy and strategy disintegrated due to the fragmentation of the caliphate into multiple power centres. Autonomous and semi-autonomous polities quickly emerged across the caliphate, each with an independent set of political aims and military agendas, with no grand strategy reflective of the Abbasid central administration. Moreover, two distinct consequences of the fall of the Umayyad caliphate systemically crippled the Abbasid potential for strategic decision making and contributed to its fragmentation.

The first concerns the end of any official grand strategy, more specifically the ability of the Abbasid central administration to form and direct state-wide policy. Following the civil wars of 740–750, the shared religious identity which had unified the caliphate was permanently shattered, which in turn decisively ended the political unity of the Muslims. A satellite pro-Umayyad succession-ist movement in Spain claimed independence in 756; the Idrisids claimed independence in Morrocco in 788, the north African territories of Tunisia and parts of southern Italy under the authority of the Aghlabids were semi-autonomous by 800. By 892, the Khorasan and Transoxiana territories were fully autonomous from Abbasid control, united under the Samanids. The Saffarids seceded in the Persian province after 870; the territories of Egypt were lost to the Fatimids by 969, and territories in Iraq switched hands in 945 and 1055 between Buyid control and the Seljuks respectively.

Second, the executive authority of the Caliph to authorise war-fighting was enduringly compromised. The Abbasids, relative to their predecessors, made only minor local conquests before their fragmentation. The rise of internal competition for political authority and successionist movements incurred territorial losses alongside new claims to legitimate authority, and usurped the monopoly of violence from the Caliph. Without executive control over the refined military instrument wielded by the Umayyads, the Abbasids, bar a few exceptions, could not wage war on multiple frontiers, and all expansion ceased.

Execution of Strategy

The Umayyad caliphate was constantly engaged in warfare along several fronts simultaneously. Aside from Byzantium, long-standing opponents were the Turgesh Khaganate at the Transcaucasia frontiers, the Khazars and the Tang dynasty in central Asia, and the Berbers and Visigoths in north Africa and Spain respectively. The lack of early decisive victories in these theatres prolonged campaigns that were politically motivated rather than strategic necessities. Umayyad strategy was bound to a policy of expansionism – generating revenue to feed the military and domestic infrastructure of the caliphate – whilst maintaining credibility as the legitimate heirs of the Rashidun. Umayyad war-fighting lacked any consistent operational or tactical patterns worthy of analysis other than the need not to cede defeat.

The lack of opportunities for booty and plunder due to stagnant operational theatres, hand in hand with continuous exhausting campaigning of little strategic value, and accompanying disastrous military defeats, continuously hit the morale of deployed troops. Bitter and resentful at their treatment, troops became hostile to the central government and refused to be deployed. Discriminatory practices within the military further divided the religious cohesion that had initially founded it, particularly the racial and ethnic divides which the Umayyad Arab leadership promoted.

Non-Arab troops were frequently deployed in hostile environments and their Arab counterparts were deliberately exposed to less hostile theatres. Military stipends paid to the Arab troops were initially not available to the non-Arabs, who were paid through their share of the booty. When the grievances of the non-Arab troops fell upon deaf ears after multiple attempts to have them addressed, internal revolt ensued. The Great Berber Revolt (740–743) effectively stripped political control of the military instrument from the Umayyad leadership and sent shock waves throughout the caliphate.

The contest with Byzantium was the exception, and serves as the case which best identifies the Umayyad execution of strategy. The initial successes of the Rashidun against the Byzantines established a long-term contest of attritional war-fighting on all fronts to regain the strategic advantage lost by either side. The Byzantines, a more experienced war-making empire, frequently made use of advanced weapon systems, proxies and alliances as force multipliers against the fledgling Umayyad caliphate.

The Umayyad fixation with the conquest of Constantinople was at the heart of the conflict with Byzantium, but their strategy also included stripping the empire of its provinces. Encouraged by the Rashiduns' earlier successes, the Umayyads struck at Rhodes between 672 and 673, and at Cyzicus in 675, establishing both as forward operating bases to blockade Constantinople. However, the ensuing naval campaigns in the Aegean and around Constantinople ended in devastating defeats. Emperor Constantine IV employed Greek fire, a liquid incendiary weapon projected by hose and nozzle against enemy ships, which staved off successive Umayyad attempts to conquer Constantinople in the campaign of 674–678.

In 688 the Umayyads were forced to conclude a truce with the Byzantines and withdraw from their garrisons along the Byzantine coastlands between 679 and 680. To make matters worse, the retreating naval fleet was all but destroyed by storms off the southern coast of Sillyon. The loss of the fleet effectively denied the Umayyads any further tactical ability to project maritime force in the region. The Byzantine counteroffensive by sea, following the first Umayyad failure to sack Constantinople, reached Syria unopposed and was aided by the Mardaites, an autonomous population of Christians in the Syrian mountains who had resisted absorption into Umayyad territory. In turn, the caliphate undertook campaigns against the Mardaites, albeit with minimal gains, damaging the Caliph's credibility. Mu'awiya was forced to settle for a thirty-year tributary truce also with the Mardaites.

Byzantine forces also allied with the Berber king Caecilius from the exarchate of Carthage, to ambush and defeat the Umayyad forces, at the Battle of Vescera at Thabudeos in 682. The alliance reversed the earlier successes of the Umayyads in key strategic regions of Byzacena (eastern Tunisia) and Khorasan, and forced them to withdraw from the Tunisian territories.

In 692, Emperor Justinian II broke the truce of 688, and during ensuing skirmishes, such as the Battle of Sebastopolis, the Umayyads inflicted successive defeats on the Byzantines as the strategic advantage shifted back to the caliphate. Umayyad penetration continued into Asia Minor, with a series of territorial acquisitions in Armenia and deeper penetration of the Byzantine borderlands. From 712 onwards, the Umayyads sacked numerous Byzantine towns and forts. Under Caliph Sulayman I's leadership (715–717), assaults on the Byzantines, who had been racked by the civil strife of the Twenty Years' Anarchy (695–717), continued. Resources were redirected at attacking

Constantinople, the Byzantine centre of gravity, once more. The Byzantine leadership in turn prepared for war.

The joint Umayyad land and sea offensive began in 716, penetrating Asia Minor and occupying the western coastlands. By 717, Umayyad land forces had built a strangling double circumvallation around the walls of Constantinople, beginning the Second Siege of Constantinople that would last into the following year, leaving the sea the only point for supply to the city. On the sea front, the restored Umayyad navy completed the full blockade. Once again, the Umayyad fleet could not match Byzantine fire-power, as Greek fire was employed with great success. The besieging infantry was attacked by Byzantium's Bulgar allies, inflicting heavy damage. Moreover, during the winter months of 717–718, famine and epidemics decimated the Umayyad army. Reinforcements were sent by Sulayman but were defeated once more by the Bulgars. In 718, the Umayyads, under the new caliph, 'Umar II, dispatched further reinforcements from Africa and Egypt to Asia Minor – two fleets plus infantry – only to have them all destroyed, ending Umayyad offensive operations in the region. Uncharacteristically, the Byzantines did not exploit the window of opportunity to strike back at their defeated enemy. They engaged in attritional skirmishes with the Umayyads rather than seeking any decisive gains. The Taurus mountains of Asia Minor came to demarcate a frontier, heavily fortified by each side, with a buffer zone between the two opponents.

The failed siege was fraught with repercussions for the Umayyads, most notably for the credibility of the Caliph. Vast economic resources had been lost through defeat and a diminishing treasury must have been of great concern. The military, the quintessential icon of Umayyad power, had shown itself to be overextended. Both army and navy were severely weakened, to the point of inviting threats to their own borders.

Once more seduced by the cult of the offensive, following a series of tactical victories into central Anatolia, the tenth Umayyad caliph, Hisham ibn Abd al-Malik (d. 743), commissioned the largest offensive force of his reign (724–743) to strike at the Byzantines. What followed, at the Battle of Akroinon in 740, was a decisive victory for the Byzantines under Emperor Leo III, and a strategic disaster for the Umayyads. Subsequently Leo, and later his son, Constantine V, launched counteroffensive campaigns against the Umayyads. Increasingly fragile domestic stability, coupled with exhaustion and over-extension of the military, are the best explanations for the recurrent course of the Umayyad–Byzantine contest, with the Byzantines more often on the ascendant.

The political disintegration of the Umayyad caliphate had already blunted the military instrument, and Abbasid attempts to renew defensive campaigns on the frontiers and against the Byzantines in particular cannot be considered in the same vein as that under the expansionist drive of the Rashidun or the Umayyads. Abbasid strategy preferred to appease opponents such as the Byzantines as a strategic effort to recuperate and create buffer space when threatened. Furthermore, no significant territorial gains or advancement in warfare occurred which might warrant specific strategic comment on this contest.

More broadly, the Abbasids were able to avoid the recurrent strategic engagements of the Umayyads through lessons learnt and having benefited from the Umayyad victories and territorial acquisitions which had effectively neutralised many potential threats to the new caliphate. Thus the Abbasids enjoyed a relatively low-threat environment, despite the generally militarily weakened and battered empire they inherited. War-weariness and economic stress dictated many strategic decisions, as did numerous revolts, yet the caliphate still possessed a relatively strong domestic powerbase. Time and opportunity, a luxury that the Umayyads never possessed, allowed the Abbasids to address internal sociopolitical problems.

Despite these opportunities, the Abbasids squandered their vast territorial and ideological resources with remarkable haste, lacking consistency, internal management, political leadership and strategic judgement.[16] Whilst the Abbasid caliphate would continue to rule, at least in name, until 1517, by 1258, during the Mongol Hülegü Khan's sacking of Baghdad, the caliphate had lost the strategic initiative on most fronts, and there was diminishing support for a defence-dominant military stance against most regional opponents. With no legitimating doctrine, or shared existential threat to unify grand strategic objectives, the Abbasid caliphate was permanently defanged.

Historiographic Debates

The labelling of the 'Rashidun' caliphate was a ninth-century Islamic revisionist attempt to reframe and selectively account for political succession and the violent internal struggles between the Companions of the Prophet.[17] Muslim historians,

---

16 See A. Black, *The History of Islamic Political Thought: From the Prophet to the Present* (Edinburgh: Edinburgh University Press, 2011), 30.
17 See W. Madelung, *The Succession to Muhammad: A Study of the Early Caliphate* (Cambridge: Cambridge University Press, 1997), 1–2; P. Crone, *God's Rule, Government and Islam: Six Centuries of Medieval Islamic Political Thought* (New York: Columbia University Press, 2004), 1–3; Donner, *The Early Islamic Conquests*, 82.

especially Ibn Khaldun, framed the Rashidun period as an era of divine providence, driven by the righteousness of Muhammad's Companions, who faithfully adhered to the sharia. The Umayyads were described as actors driven by the natural demands and vicissitudes of politics, to attain and preserve power.[18] By sanitising the politico-strategic events of the thirty years before the Umayyads, and thereby distinguishing the Rashidun caliphs as embodying pious political authority par excellence, Islamic legal scholarship would later reinforce this binary construction of history, to project and infer a secondary set of legal precedents after the Qur'an and the practice of Muhammad in matters of war and statecraft.

In contrast, modern scholarship has been concerned with the causes of the Rashidun expansions, overlooking the principal strategic factors we have elaborated upon, preferring Malthusian assumptions that survival drove conquest over security. Hugh Kennedy, like Reuven Firestone, supports the popular 'ecological thesis' that,[19] following Abu Bakr's politico-strategic consolidation of Arabia following the *Ridda* wars; the Arabs were deprived of inter-tribal plunder and raiding opportunities, inviting the scarcity of resources within the Arabian peninsula upon themselves and the threat of tribal implosion and the re-emergence of competition.[20]

Fred Donner and Montgomery Watt have both contested the ecological thesis as counterfactual speculation where the evidence is lacking. In a rare instance of surviving early sources, there is evidence for the opposite of the ecological thesis: hunger and overpopulation were not an issue or a threat.[21] The expansions only increased sufficient food supplies and the general economic health of the region with the distribution of additional agricultural produce and livestock gathered from taxation and territorial gains.[22]

The early historiographical debates among Arabic authors were overtly political. The memory of the Umayyad house and their accomplishments was controversial, as the early Muslim historians battled to recount their activities praising the jihad of the Muslims but keen not to attribute victories solely to the leadership of the Umayyads. This debate occurred between two historical genres divided on issues of religious identity and often written within the same work of an author, the *Futuh* and the *Fitna*.

---

18 See Ibn Khaldun, *The Muqaddimah: An Introduction to History*, Volume I: trans. Franz Rosenthal (New York: Princeton University Press, 1980), 423–4.
19 Donner, 'Centralized authority', 342.
20 See R. Firestone, *Jihad: The Origin of Holy War in Islam* (Oxford: Oxford University Press, 1999), 124–5; Kennedy, *The Great Arab Conquests*, 56–7.
21 Donner, *The Early Islamic Conquests*, 267.
22 See M. Watt, *Muhammad at Mecca* (Oxford: Clarendon Press, 1953), 3–4.

Of the most recognised works are those written by Abu Isma'il al-Azdi (d. 810), *Futuh al Sham* (The Opening of the Levant); al-Waqidi (d. 822–3), *Kitab Futuhat al-Sham* (The Liberation of the Levant); Ibn Abd al-Hakam (d. 871), *Futuh al-Misr* (The Opening of Egypt); al-Baladhuri (d. 892), *Kitab al-Futuh al-Buldan* (The Liberation of the [non-Muslim] Lands); and, most famously, the pro-Abbasid historian Muhammad b. Jarir al-Tabari's (d. 923) *Kitab Tarikh al-Rasul wa al-Muluk* (The Complete History of the Messenger and Kings) – all published in various editions by various Arabic publishing houses.

The *Futuh* literature focused on the conquests of the Rashidun era, emphasising providentialism and on the righteousness of individuals associated with the actions of conquest. This body of work was thematically similar to the Umayyad claims of political legitimacy based on a doctrine of war-fighting and policies of expansionism. The historicising and genealogical legitimation of individuals, families or tribes, to rule by virtue of 'divine right' as the *axis mundi* on earth, was used by pro-Umayyad authors to legitimise Umayyad leadership and justify military aggression and the domination of conquered lands and peoples as following the example of their pious predecessors, the Rashidun.[23]

The *Fitna* literature concerned the events of the First Civil War, and seemed predominately written to counterbalance and discredit Umayyad claims to 'divine right' and to promote the successionist tribal politics and grievances held since the *Fitna*. This genre in particular would become extremely politicised as the Islamic community developed, to disgrace the Umayyad political leadership, justify politico-military resistance to the Umayyad house, and eventually celebrate the triumphalism associated with the Abbasid Revolution in 750 by its supporters.[24]

Contemporary scholarship, less influenced by the religious problems of identity and memory, have concentrated on the technical problems of reconstructing history, politics and strategy. In particular, they focused on the socio-political explanations for the military events and the civil wars that served as hiatuses for war-fighting.[25] Kennedy considers the reign of the Caliph Hisham ibn 'Abd al-Malik as the weak link which led to the fragmentation of the empire.[26] Patricia Crone emphasised the appearance of a new class of generals who sought power outside the Umayyad tribal-based regime;[27] whilst Julius Wellhausen

---

23 Kennedy, *Arab Conquests*, 15–17.   24 Donner, *Narratives of Islamic Origins*, 177–91.
25 Blankinship, *The End of the Jihad State*, 4–5.
26 Kennedy, *The Prophet and the Age of the Caliphate*, pp.112–16.
27 See P. Crone, *Slaves on Horses: The Evolution of the Islamic Polity* (New York: Cambridge University Press, 1980), 46–8, 55–7, 61; also P. Crone, 'Were the Qays and the Yemen of the Umayyad period political parties?', *Der Islam*, 71 (1994), 95–111.

highlighted internal and external sociopolitical problems as the prime cause of the Umayyad downfall – internally the tribal wrangling of the Arabs, and externally the growing dissatisfaction of the emergent second-class non-Arab Muslims (*mawali*), especially in Khorasan.[28]

M. A. Shaban agrees with the external problems detailed by Wellhausen and also emphasises the problems created by the resettlement and assimilation of Arab tribes in Khorasan, producing revolutionaries who would oppose the Umayyad house.[29] In Khalid Blankinship's analysis of the Umayyad collapse, the various domestic problems were exacerbated by an unprecedented series of external military defeats and disasters inflicted by regional powers. Blankinship's analysis of the failure of policy seems to be the initial catalyst for the later developments that Kennedy, Crone, Wellhausen and Shaban identify as the drivers for the Umayyad collapse.

Blankinship concedes their arguments as the later constituents that escalate the internal disintegration.[30] But his conclusion, which explains the failure of the Umayyad caliphate in terms of other causes, such as socio-economic collapse, domestic politics or the result of external military superiority gaining the upper hand, points to failures in strategic decision making and poor judgement in the utility of the war-fighting doctrine. The link between military success and the political security of the caliphate was, in the case of the Umayyads, direct. Revolution was the price of military failure, with new policies aimed at renewing military success following every change of administration. The strategic failure to recognise the inescapable consequences of overextension, coupled with stagnating foreign and domestic policies, escalated friction externally and internally until it became unmanageable. Means and ends were unbalanced, and the military instrument became increasingly less subordinate to policy.

---

28 See J. Wellhausen, *The Arab Kingdom and Its Fall*, trans. M. Graham Weir (Calcutta: University of Calcutta, 1927), 495–500, 557–9.

29 M. A. Shaban, *Islamic History* A.D. *600–750* (A.H.*132*): *A New Interpretation* (Cambridge: Cambridge University Press, 1971), 170–9; and M. A. Shaban, *The 'Abbasid Revolution* (Cambridge: Cambridge University Press, 1970), 158.

30 Blankinship, *The End of the Jihad State*, 9, 241.

Byzantine Strategy (AD 630–1204)

GEORGIOS CHATZELIS

The eastern part of the Roman Empire, which survived the western part by nearly a millennium, gradually transformed itself into a culturally distinct entity that also developed its own strategies of survival under the constant pressures of foreign invasion. Roughly speaking, between the seventh and ninth centuries, the Eastern Roman Empire, referred to as the Byzantine Empire, was on the defensive, sometimes struggling for its very survival, against the Arabs in the east and the various Turkish and Slavic tribes in the Balkans. From the tenth century to the mid-eleventh, Byzantium turned to the offensive, reclaiming part of its lost territory as well as extending its influence and suzerainty over other polities. From the eleventh century, Byzantium was heavily challenged by Turkish tribes in Asia Minor, but, despite some permanent setbacks, it managed to recover and to play a significant, sometimes dominant, role in the international political and military scene until 1180. The following quarter-century saw a decline in the prestige of the emperor in Constantinople and of his capabilities to tip the balance in favour of the empire, a procedure which culminated in the diversion of the Fourth Crusade against Constantinople and the capture of the latter by the Latins.

Sources

The main sources for the study of Byzantine strategy are historical narratives and military manuals. Although Byzantine historians usually recorded military events, they employed various literary and rhetorical devices. Sometimes, they were ill-informed and biased, while their testimony seems to have been partly based on lost official military bulletins and promotional biographies of famous generals. This raises questions about how accurately aspects pertaining to strategy can be reconstructed, but a comparative reading of Byzantine historical narratives with Arab, Armenian, Latin and Slavonic accounts can address many of these difficulties. Military manuals, on the other hand, were solely focused on the prescription of strategy and tactics. Some were introductory and generic, like the *Taktika* of Emperor Leo VI (886–912),[1] the *Sylloge Tacticorum* (c. 930)[2] and the *Praecepta Militaria* of Nikephoros II Phokas (c. 963–969),[3] while others were specialised, such as the *De Velitatione Bellica* (after 969),[4] which centred around guerrilla warfare. While these treatises constitute an invaluable source of information, their adherence to past models and their occasionally idealised and complicated recommendations leave the historian wondering about their practicality and the applicability of their advice during military operations.

Other sources include promotional and commemorative works which celebrated military undertakings, such as poems, imperial orations and inscriptions. Manuals on the geography, administration and foreign affairs of the empire, such as the *De Administrando Imperio* of Constantine VII (945–959),[5] highlight the principles of Byzantine strategic goals. Last but not least, administrative lists and inventories associated with expeditions, lead seals of military and civil officials, hordes of coins found in frontier areas, and remains of fortifications add to the picture of Byzantine military organisation and the financial and logistical preparations which came with the pursuit of the empire's aims.

Actors

The emperor was the ultimate military authority in Byzantium. Emperors like Nikephoros II, John I (969–976), Basil II (976–1025), Alexios I (1081–1118), John II (1118–1143) and Manuel I (1143–1180) led their own armies into battle,

---

1 Leo VI the Wise, Τακτικά / *Taktika* (c. 900) in *The Taktika of Leo VI* (ed. and trans. G. Dennis) (Washington, DC: Dumbarton Oaks, 2014).

2 Pseudo Leo VI the Wise, Συλλογή Τακτικῶν/ *Sylloge Tacticorum*, in *Sylloge Tacticorum Que Olim 'Inedita Leonis Tactica Dicebatur* (ed. A. Dain) (Paris: Les Belles Lettres, 1938); G. Chatzelis and J. Harris, *A Tenth-Century Byzantine Military Manual: The Sylloge Tacticorum* (London: Routledge, 2017).

3 Nikephoros II Phokas, Στρατηγικὴ Ἔκθεσις καὶ Σύνταξις/ *Praecepta Militaria* (c. 963), in E. McGeer (ed. and trans.), *Sowing the Dragon's Teeth: Byzantine Warfare in the Tenth Century* (Washington, DC: Dumbarton Oaks, 1995).

4 Nikephoros II Phokas, Περὶ παραδρομῆς/ *De Velitatione*, in *Le Traité Sur la Guérilla de l'empereur Nicéphore Phocas (963–969)* (ed. and trans. G. Dagron and H. Mihăescu) (Paris: Eds du CNRS, 1999).

5 Emperor Constantine VII, Πρὸς τὸν ἴδιον υἱὸν Ῥωμανόν/ *De Administrando Imperio*, in *Constantine Porphyrogenitus: De Administrando Imperio* (ed. and trans. G. Moravcsik and R. J. H. Jenkins) (Washington, DC: Dumbarton Oaks, 1967).

Map 11.1 Byzantine strategy (AD 630–1204). Redrawn based on a map in J. Haldon, *The Palgrave Atlas of Byzantine History* (London: Palgrave Macmillan, 2005), 60–1. Reproduced with permission of the Licensor through PLSclear.

while others, like Leo VI and Constantine VII, preferred to stay at the palace and to delegate such tasks to their subordinates, though without omitting to demonstrate their authority alternatively, such as by compiling treatises on

Map 11.1 (Cont.)

warfare and/or haranguing their troops by letter, by sending good wishes and promises for reward and promotion, and by highlighting their regret that due to *force majeure* they had not been able to join the campaign.

When emperors did not assume supreme command, the task usually fell to a relative who held the honorary title of *kaisar*, or to a trusted man holding the highest-ranking military office, such as the *domestikos ton scholon* (such as John Kourkouas and Leo Phokas) or the *megas domestikos* (such as John Axouch). Lower-ranking men put in charge of a military district (*strategoi* and *doukes*) enjoyed relative initiative on how to pursue foreign policy and strategy. Sometimes, these worked in harmony with the emperor, like the *doux* of Dalmatia who, in the reign of Manuel I, was responsible for seeking support for the Byzantine cause in Italy and Hungary. On other occasions, however, they preferred to carve their own role, like the *doux* of Antioch, Damian Dalassenos, who, most probably opposing Basil II's wishes, backed Tyre's rebellion against the Fatimids. Once more on a local level, governors and commanders of notable cities could also affect strategic planning, a good example being the reluctance of some of these officials to resist the Arabs at fortified centres, which undermined the response plan of Herakleios I (610–641).

The supreme commander (emperor or otherwise) was not left alone at the helm. Ideally, the right course of action would be implemented after reading reports from allies, spies, pro-Byzantine aristocrats in foreign countries and governors of outposts at the frontier. For instance, the commander of Cherson in Crimea assumed the task of informing the capital of the movements of the nomads in the steppes to ensure the security of the Balkans, the Caucasus and the Black Sea. Councils of war also contributed to decision making. The sources speak of prominent military and civil officials taking part in such meetings and offering advice on the right course of action. It seems that treatises and documents (stored in the baggage train and in the palace) on weather, geography, history, warfare, logistics, permanent military camps and stations and even fortune telling (such as apocalyptic traditions, dream interpretation, occurrences, astrology) also played their part.

Adversaries

The prime theatres of war were the Balkans, the Caucasus, northern Mesopotamia and Syria and Asia Minor. The Byzantines were also active in Italy and Sicily but usually with limited means. Between the seventh and tenth centuries, the main enemies of the Byzantines were the Arabs. Some Arabs, however, were ex-soldiers and allies of the empire, employed to suppress the raids of their fellow people. Both the Arabs who were on friendly terms with Byzantium and those who raided it were aware of the poor military position in which the wars of 602–628 had left the Byzantines and the Sassanids, and, united by Islam and the promise of booty, riches and conquests, by 698 they had deprived the Byzantines of all their possessions in north Africa, Egypt, Palestine, Syria, Armenia and Cilicia. Up to 718 the Byzantines were struggling for their survival, but by the tenth century and the early eleventh they had managed to counterattack and recover many of their losses.

Simultaneously with the Arabs, the Byzantines had to face the Slavic tribes, who crossed the Danube (c. 580), penetrated Byzantine territory and settled in it, as far as the Peloponnese. Initially, they lived in autonomous enclaves (*sklaviniai*) exhibiting loose political organisation at best, but in the ninth and tenth centuries they were mostly converted to Christianity and integrated into the imperial political, social and military organisation. The most dangerous of these peoples were the Bulgars. Although originally not of Slavic origin, they subdued the Slavic tribes of the Danube and, under Asparukh, settled themselves on Byzantine soil, creating an independent Bulgar polity around Pliska (c. 681). After their establishment, the Bulgars continued to raid and subjugate imperial territory mainly in Macedonia and Thrace. A series of offensive campaigns conducted by John I Tzimiskes and Basil II dealt with this threat and resulted in the annexation of the Bulgar kingdom into the empire. In 1185, taking advantage of the crisis that followed the succession of Manuel I, the Bulgars and the Vlachs gained their independence from the Byzantines and established a new kingdom.

Various other tribes and peoples, mainly of Turkish origin – the Avars, Khazars, Magyars (Hungarians), Pechenegs, Ouzes and Cumans – and others not, such as the Rus' – moved and settled between the rivers Dnieper and Don and the Carpathian basin. These peoples had mixed relations with the empire. Sometimes they raided Byzantine territory, mainly in the lower Danube, Thrace and Macedonia, with the exception of the Rus', who, with their light navy, raided around Constantinople and Bithynia in Asia Minor. On other occasions, they formed alliances with the Byzantines, providing intelligence and campaigning against imperial enemies. These arrangements sometimes backfired, for the empire's allies often conquered enemy territory, expanded their influence and pushed other tribes southwards towards Byzantium. They also allied themselves with Byzantium's enemies (such as the Bulgars), preventing the empire from getting the upper hand easily. From these peoples, the Khazars, Rus' and Magyars established the most lasting and influential polities.

From 1038 onwards, the Byzantines had to face various Turkish tribes in Asia Minor, closely or loosely connected to the Seljuks. From the 1070s the situation became increasingly dangerous, with the Turks controlling large parts of imperial territory in Asia Minor, either as enemies of the empire or by joining it as allies in civil wars. The First Crusade gave the Byzantines a breathing space and the situation had largely crystallised by around 1130. The Byzantines controlled western Asia Minor and the south coastland, as well as the region of the Pontus, which sometimes eluded imperial control and became independent. The Seljuks, on the other hand, established themselves in central Anatolia with Konya as their centre, while other emirates appeared in Cappadocia and Armenia, the most important being the Danishmandid emirate.

Simultaneously with the Turkish pressure in Asia Minor, the Byzantines faced Norman advances in the west. Entering the scene as mercenaries to assist the Lombard cause against the Byzantines (1016), they gradually offered their services also to the Byzantines and to the western (Holy Roman) emperors, gaining renown, experience of local power structures and vacuums, and a good knowledge of the tactics and military organisation of their masters. Finally, getting hold of the strategic fortress of Melfi (1041), they extended their rule in all directions and by 1091 dominated most of south Italy and Sicily. Having consolidated their authority, they turned their attention eastwards and begun to raid and to challenge Byzantine authority in Illyria, the Ionian Sea, Macedonia and Antioch.

Means

The Byzantines employed a variety of means to gain the upper hand against their adversaries. For Michael Psellos, an eleventh-century Byzantine historian, philosopher and courtier, two such means were the most significant factors which 'sustained the hegemony of the Romans, namely, our system of honours and our wealth'.[6]

Despite their occasional setbacks, the Byzantines kept their imperial ideals alive as a source of culture, values and international legitimation for neighbouring peoples. Military occupation was only one way for them to pacify and control adjacent regions. Alternative means included diplomatic marriages, permission for foreign tribes to settle in decimated and depopulated imperial lands, and the enticement of prominent foreign potentates and bestowal on them of imperial court titles. Foreign aristocrats were offered

6 Michael Psellos, Χρονογραφία / Chronographia, 6.29, in Michaelis Pselli Chronographia (ed. D. R. Reinsch) (Berlin: De Gruyter, 2014); Michael Psellos, Fourteen Byzantine Rulers: The Chronographia of Michael Psellos (trans. E. R. A. Sewter) (Harmondsworth: Penguin, 1979).

baptism and awarded Byzantine titles and offices, received stipends and luxurious gifts including fabrics and robes (in accordance with their rank), and were entrusted with the government of their own or other regions in the name of the emperor, and henceforth owed military service to him. Thus foreign potentates enhanced their prestige, status and legitimacy among the local aristocracy, and imperial authority appeared neither alien nor subversive to the locals. For example, Leo VI (886–910) awarded Krikorikios, the Armenian prince of Taron, the rank of *magistros* (the fifth-highest dignity of the empire), a yearly sum of 1,440 gold coins and a luxurious house in Constantinople, in the hopes that other Armenian potentates would be induced to offer their submission too.[7] Centuries later, in the reign of John II and Manuel I, we still find Byzantium controlling areas of interest through potentates, such as Dobronja in Dalmatia and Béla III (1172–1196) in Hungary.

The Byzantines imposed an order on the world surrounding them, expressed through a hierarchy of states (either established or adaptable) at the summit of which was the Byzantine emperor, the only true emperor in the world, perceived as the 'spiritual father' of all foreign kings and rulers. Next came the 'spiritual brothers' (the western emperors), the 'spiritual children' (allies and subordinates, such as the Bulgars) and so on. This 'commonwealth', conceived basically as one of peaceful cohabitation, served Byzantine interests well when the empire enjoyed victories, prosperity and elevated international prestige. When the above elements were absent, however, this structure usually yielded little practical benefit, with local potentates seeking either independence or alternative sources of legitimation (such as the Pope or the western emperor). Consequently, it comes as no surprise that the crumbling of Byzantine might and international standing after the death of Manuel I resulted in serious territorial losses (such as the emergence of a new Bulgar–Vlach state and the capture of Constantinople).

Where did the empire find the resources to finance both such a system and its armies? The Arab conquests left Byzantium in a dire economic situation; it is estimated that the Byzantines lost two-thirds of their revenues, while yearly land and sea raids contributed to economic decadence. The state responded to these challenges with various measures, and from the mid-ninth century onwards economic and demographic growth became evident. Herakleios I, Leo III (717–741) and Nikephoros I (802–811) initiated a census of the population and cultivated lands to facilitate taxation (either fiscal or in kind), while new taxes were invented (or broadened), such as the household tax

---

7 Constantine VII, *De Administrando*, 43.61–87.

(*kapnikon*). The remaining fertile areas (such as Thrace and western Asia Minor) acted as the new 'granaries' of the empire, with emperors such as Constantine V (741–775) taking care to resettle peoples in them (such as Slavs in Asia Minor and Armenians and Syrians in Thrace). Other emperors confiscated papal lands in Calabria and Sicily, and the properties of monasteries following deviant religious practices. To respond to the crisis better, many Byzantines changed their cultivation patterns, partly favouring cereals (over olive trees and grapes) and a pastoral economy. The aforementioned measures, together with the taxation of international Mediterranean and Black Sea trade, a state monopoly on some products (such as salt, iron, gold, silk, arms), legislation regarding land, and, from the eleventh century onwards, the culmination in the growth of cities and the manufacture of luxury and everyday goods constituted some of the means by which the Byzantines secured their flow of money.

The Byzantines also relied on their army, adapting its organisation, tactics and troops according to their strategic needs. The dramatic crisis of the seventh century brought about significant changes which have long been debated by scholars. The current consensus is that after 636 the remaining field armies withdrew or moved to Anatolia to fight for the survival of the empire: the *comes obsequii* (officer of the palatine troops) moved from the capital to north-west Asia Minor, the *magister militum per Thracias* (general of the field army of Thrace) moved from Thrace to western Asia Minor, the *magistri militum per orientem* (generals of the eastern field army) retreated to south-east Asia Minor and the *magister militum per Armeniam* (general of the field army of Armenia) settled in north-east Asia Minor. In the southern Balkans, command of the *caravisiani* was established by 654. The resettling of these armies and commands evolved into the establishment of large military districts (*strategiai*) and, by the reign of Nikephoros I, into *themata*, military and administrative units under the command of a *strategos*, supervised by the central authority in Constantinople. By the tenth century, military service in the *themata* was clearly associated with the holding of land labelled as military; that is, land which was cultivated by the soldier and his family for sustenance and for covering military expenses (such as mounts, arms and armour). One also finds smaller independent military commands around the frontier called *kleisourarchiai* whose duty it was to supervise passes and harass and ambush the enemy. The *themata* were gradually reduced in size, partly to enable more rapid mobilisation, and partly for political reasons, while newly annexed territories were organised in *akritika* (frontier) *themata*, commanded by the so-called lesser *strategoi* (military commanders), whose districts were limited to a relatively small area around an important fortress. From the 960s onwards, the annexed areas turned into *doukata* or *katepanata* under the authority of a *doux* or *katepano* (such as of Mesopotamia, Antioch, Iberia, Edessa, Vaspourakan, Bulgaria), with this new organisation also dominating older districts in Thrace and Macedonia (like Adrianople and Thessaloniki). The main roles of the armies of the *themata* were to conduct raids and defend the empire against enemy incursions.

In the reign of Constantine V (741–775), the Byzantines created a new elite force, the *tagmata*. These troops were under the direct jurisdiction of the central authority, commanded by the *domestikos of the scholai*, and were better trained, provisioned and equipped than the regular army, which often performed badly in pitched battles against Arabs and Bulgars. Their command was split in two in the reign of Romanos II (959–963), forming the *domestikos* of the east and the *domestikos* of the west, and allowing forces to operate on two fronts simultaneously, if needed. By the late tenth century, new regiments were created and, mainly to serve the offensive needs of the empire, some were stationed on the frontiers under the command of a *doux* or *katepano* who also commanded the regular army of his region. These developments coincide not only with the Byzantine counterattack in the east and in the Balkans, but also with the evolution of tactics and the appearance of new specialised troops, better suited to offensive operations (such as the *menavlatoi* – infantry specialised in repelling heavy cavalry, and the *kataphraktoi* – specialised heavy cavalry designed to charge enemy formations head-on). The same century saw a decline in the importance of the army of the *themata*, with central government preferring to hire professionals in lieu of relying on conscripted soldiers. Around the mid-eleventh century, the regular army of the *themata* was so degenerate that Romanos IV Diogenes's attempts to revive it were unsuccessful.

Gradually, already from the tenth but more prominently from the eleventh century, the Byzantines relied heavily on mercenary and professional troops. While new *tagmata* appeared in this period (such as the Varangians of Basil II and the Archontopouloi of Alexios I), these and the old ones seem to have disappeared after the 1090s. The imperial army now comprised many foreigners. Some were hired as mercenaries, others were sent by allied rulers and potentates, while still others provided military service having defected and/or settled in imperial lands, such as the Pechenegs in the reign of Constantine IX (1042–1055). We thus find references to Armenians, Saracens, Rus', Normans, Germans, Franks, Anglo-Saxons, Turks, Serbs, Hungarians, Bulgars and Cumans serving in the Byzantine army. Nevertheless, professional native units continued to be employed, mainly from Macedonia, Thrace and Thessaly, but also from Anatolia. The vacuum created by the disappearance of the *themata* and their defensive role was partly remedied by the dynasty of the Komnenoi. The army continued to be organised in districts (*doukata* and *katepanata*), but *themata* and fortresses were re-established or created from scratch (such as Thrakesion, Neokastra), commanded by the *doukes* and the *kastrophylakes* (castle guards). Land and military service was also partly re-established through an institution which provided individuals with public revenues from an area in return for the provision of troops.

The Byzantines also invested in technological innovations, in part to impress foreign visitors: the emperor received vassals or foreign dignitaries in the throne room which contained various automata (mechanical birds and beasts) and artificial trees, while the throne stood on an elevating platform. Two other innovations were more of military value. The first was the fire telegraph. It transmitted reports of enemy numbers and operations from the frontier all the way to Constantinople, functioning as a warning system along the way. The second was the Byzantine flamethrower. This device cast a flammable mixture known as Greek fire through a siphon, either portable or fixed on towers or ships. Greek fire was unquenchable by water. Other flammable mixtures were poured into big earthen vessels and catapulted against the enemy by siege engines, while others in small pots could serve in ways similar to hand grenades.

Causes and Objectives of War

Byzantium's objectives regarding warfare were shaped both by imperial ideology and by realpolitik. Byzantine political ideology perceived Byzantium as the true heir of the Roman Empire, and the emperor as God's representative on earth, destined to restore peace and order to the earthly world. Simultaneously, however, the Byzantines demonstrated flexibility, making short-term compromises if it fitted the circumstances while promoting their ideals by force if necessary, but also indirectly through diplomacy, the grant of court titles, or the dispatch of missionary expeditions. Fighting for peace and defence – which was thought to include the liberation of lost previously Roman territories – was central to Byzantine thinking: only these intentions were just and could find grace in the eyes of God, whose assistance was expected.

Hard-pressed on more than one frontier and often short of manpower, the empire usually sought to neutralise incoming threats with the least possible losses. Restoration of old and construction of new fortified centres, coupled with the repopulation of sensitive areas with foreign peoples or populations from other districts, contributed to the security of Byzantine holdings and the availability of troops.

The defence of the empire was realised in four main ways: (a) appeasement, (b) counterbalance, (c) deep defence and (d) reactive defence. The first was usually employed when Byzantium was relatively weak (recently defeated or fighting on another front). It entailed anything from payments of cash (single payments or yearly tributes) to the signing of a truce or peace treaty, and from ceding frontier fortresses to abstaining from restoring them. For instance, from 806, Nikephoros I paid 30,000 gold coins to the Arabs yearly in exchange for a truce which enabled him to campaign freely against the Bulgars.

The second method entailed forming alliances (either short- or long-term) in order to counterweight Byzantium's enemies and restore a balance of power. The Byzantines mostly employed this tactic either when operations had resulted in a stalemate or when they could not afford to deploy considerable manpower at a front. Peoples residing in the steppes (such as Ouzes, Pechenegs, Magyars or Rus') and in the Balkans (such as Serbs) were usually asked to campaign against an enemy polity. Thus the Magyars, the Serbs and the Rus' were employed against the Bulgars (894–896, 965) and the Pechenegs were to act against the Rus'. On other occasions, the empire sought to win over members of enemy coalitions to downsize a pending threat. In 924, for example, the Byzantines outbid Symeon I's offer to the Fatimids for an alliance and a joint naval and military operation against Constantinople, winning over the Fatimids and neutralising the peril of a dangerous siege of the capital.

Deep defence, coupled with guerrilla tactics, was most successfully employed against the Arabs in Asia Minor between around 720 and 970, though not without military, civilian, and financial losses. For the strategy to yield maximum benefits, the Byzantines remained constantly informed about enemy raids and their routes. People, mobile possessions, crops, food supplies and livestock were ideally moved to fortified locations in advance, while fodder and crops which could readily fall into the hands of the enemy were burned. As a response to the plunder of the countryside and of less fortified sites, the Byzantine army ambushed the invaders at appropriate occasions (such as at night, while foraging or while establishing camps) and defended key fortresses and cities along the most strategic routes. The final confrontation usually took place when the Arabs were exiting Byzantine territory, the imperial troops having occupied, blocked and barricaded the mountain

GEORGIOS CHATZELIS

passes in advance to ambush and trap the enemy. Fatigued and burdened by the campaign, by spoils and by the lack of supplies, the enemy was annihilated, and booty and prisoners were reclaimed.[8]

Reactive defence, on the other hand, entailed moving regional and palatine troops in order to stop invasions and raids preferably at the border or, if not possible, in a pitched battle around the threatened areas. While Byzantine strategic theory usually perceived pitched battles as extremely risky, Byzantine commanders were sometimes eager to face the enemy in battle and to put a quick end to his advances and destruction. Defensive pitched battles were predominantly fought against the Bulgars and Hungarians in the Balkans, and against the Turks in Asia Minor. The results of these confrontations were sometimes inconclusive or disheartening for the Byzantines. The unsuccessful attempts to confront Krum, the *khan* of the Bulgars (803 and 814), as well as the limited results of Romanos IV Diogenes's campaigns against the Turks (1068 and 1069), are demonstrative of this fact.

When the empire recovered its strength, the Byzantines launched offensive operations. The ultimate nature of these operations was often defensive, both ideologically (restoring lost territory to the empire), and strategically (increasing the security of the frontier and restoring the balance of power). Byzantine offensive operations were mostly undertaken to meet one or more of the following four basic objectives: (a) destruction of enemy polities, (b) reclaiming lost territory, (c) attritional warfare and (d) installation of a pro-Byzantine regime. As far as the first objective is concerned, only rarely did the Byzantines seek to eradicate enemy polities, for they understood that the fluid political landscape and the migrations of nomad tribes might result in exchanging a lesser evil for a greater one. An exception to the rule was Nikephoros I's campaign against the Bulgars (811) and Manuel I's failed attempt at the battle of Myriokephalon (1176) to conquer Konya, the capital of the sultanate of Rum. The more modest objective of restoring part of lost territory was more popular. The targets were usually districts of key strategic, economic and ideological significance, often used as bases by Byzantium's enemies since they controlled major routes and passes and dominated fertile plains. During the high point of Byzantine expansion in the east (*c.* 930–1031), it was exactly such sites which the Byzantines restored to the empire.

On other occasions, the Byzantines conducted a war of attrition, advancing the imperial cause through other means. For instance, the Byzantines raided enemy territory to extract booty, to capture prisoners and livestock

8 Nikephoros II Phokas, *De Velitatione.*

and to damage the enemy's economic and military potential. Some raids aimed at inflicting damage on lesser sites in case the Byzantines failed to storm and capture primary ones. Others were punitive, seeking to avenge hostile operations or to distract enemy invaders and compel them to withdraw from imperial territory. During such raids, captured cities and fortresses were looted, demolished and abandoned, while treaties were often imposed on them, enforcing non-belligerence, a military alliance and/or buffer-state status. Given that the signing of treaties was standard practice, an additional purpose of such warfare was to show the flag deep in enemy territory and increase the chances of obtaining favourable agreements without investing much time, money and manpower. Byzantine expansion in the east during the reign of Romanos I (919–944) and Constantine VII is demonstrative of this strategy. A good example of the installation of a pro-Byzantine regime constitutes Manuel I's attempts to secure Stephen IV (1163–1165) of Hungary on the throne, in the hopes that he would restore some land to the Empire and act as a buffer to prevent the western emperor from extending his influence to Hungary and the Balkans.

Priorities

Byzantium's priorities were mainly dictated by strategy, geography, ideology and economy. While, theoretically speaking, all former lands previously belonging to the Eastern Roman Empire were important to the Byzantines, some areas enjoyed more continuous interest than others. From the time of Arab conquests to the reign of Manuel I, the Byzantines gave precedence to coastal areas. These, acting as military/naval bases and trading centres, could easily be supplied and relieved by the sea. Cherson in Crimea, and Mesembria (modern Nesebăr) on the western coast of the Black Sea, are examples of such centres, which, along with the Pontic cities, contributed to the Byzantine security network, controlling communications and movements of troops and reducing the chances of successful naval attempts against Constantinople. Further west, the cities of Dalmatia and Illyria (such as Ragusa, Corfu and Dyrrachion/Durrës) monitored the movement of armies and supplies from Italy and acted as bases and fortified centres for both offensive and defensive operations. Land communications were also critical. The Byzantines sought to control the valleys of the Nestos and Strymon rivers not only because they were fertile, but also because they provided easy access into Balkan territory. Accordingly, dominion over the main highways was another priority. The Via Egnatia connected Constantinople with Thessaloniki and ended in

Dyrrachion, while another road passed through Constantinople, Andrianople, Serdica (Sofia), Naissos (Niš) and Singidunum (Belgrade). Sites along these routes were of primary significance. In the eleventh century, Dyrrachion and Naissos were each a seat of a *doux* and played a key role during Byzantine operations against the Normans, the Serb insurgents (usually backed by the Hungarians) and the Cumans.

Natural obstacles were also of strategic importance to the Byzantines. More specifically, rivers hindered invaders and enabled imperial armies and supplies to be shipped quickly, bypassing potentially difficult mountainous terrain. The river Danube is perhaps the most characteristic example. From the late tenth century to the late twelfth, the Byzantines organised their western frontier across this river, restoring key fortresses, towns and piers along its stream (such as Belgrade and Dristra / Silistra). In addition, mountain ranges and defiles greatly assisted the defence of a region, constituting natural barriers, choke points and suitable areas for the appliance of guerrilla warfare. Control of the Haemus mountains (Stara Planina) was of seminal importance since they blocked and monitored movements towards Constantinople and the fertile plains of Thrace and Macedonia, while the Taurus and Anti-Taurus mountains and their passes were key to the defence of Anatolia.

Similarly, the regions of Armenia and Georgia were considered significant both for the defence of Anatolia and the Black Sea and for offensive campaigns. They monitored access to the Caucasus, the routes to central and northern Anatolia and movements towards northern Mesopotamia and Syria. The *De Administrando Imperio* treats the strategic importance of this region extensively and explains why the Byzantines invested heavily in it. The Byzantines sought primarily to ally with Armenian potentates against the Arabs for offensive and defensive purposes. To this end, they recognised and militarily supported the appointment of an Armenian 'prince of princes' who, however, had to recognise the overlordship of the Byzantine emperor explicitly or implicitly. The latter sent him a crown and gave the 'prince of princes' quite a high rank in the Byzantine 'commonwealth', addressing him as son of the emperor and sending him imperial letters with a seal worth three gold coins (the most prestigious being a seal worth four gold coins). On top of that, Armenian and Georgian kings were awarded with the prestigious title *kouropalates* (the third-highest rank) and received from the emperor the rich salary which accompanied the dignity. The more the Byzantines were able to defeat the Arabs, the better their chances of securing the friendship of the Armenians. Gradually, the friendly relations between Byzantium and Armenia led many hard-pressed

Armenian potentates to exchange their holdings in Armenia for lands, titles and offices within the empire, and to the annexation of Armenian provinces.

Despite these fixed strategic considerations, the Byzantines shifted their priorities in accordance with the current international and domestic situation. Avoiding war on two fronts simultaneously remained a strategic principle, with the Byzantines practising three main methods to alternate their efforts. The first, already covered above, entailed the appeasement of an adversary on one front while transferring manpower and funds to another. The second was to take advantage of the adversaries' relative weakness. For instance, the civil war in the Arab caliphate allowed Constans II (641–668) to move his attention to the Balkans and launch a campaign in southern Thrace against the *sklaviniai* (658), restoring Byzantine authority and communications and compelling the Slavs to pay taxes and enrol in the imperial army. The final method involved an alliance with an ex-adversary and the enlistment of his assistance in the fighting of a new one. A good example is Alexios I's alliance with the Turks, whereby the Byzantines recognised an independent Turkish polity in Nicaea under Sulaymān ibn Qutlumush in return for peace and the dispatch of Turkish forces to assist the Byzantines against the Norman invaders (1081).

While most emperors focused their attention on a specific front for strategic and military purposes, others did so mainly for reasons of self-promotion. For instance, a critical account of Romanos III's reign (1028–1034) stressed that the emperor undertook operations against Aleppo only to prove himself and to acquire glory.[9] Another example is how relatively inconclusive campaigns were celebrated as major victories by Constantine VII with a view to augmenting his legitimacy, prestige and popularity, as well as to highlight God's favour. Manuel I's plans to launch offensive operations against Egypt (1169 and 1177) served to enhance his profile among the Crusader states and to demonstrate that the Byzantines, despite their long-lasting alliances with non-Christians, were the true champions of Christianity and claimants to the former imperial territory.

Execution / Application of Strategy

The Eastern Front

Menaced by the plague, by Slavic tribes in the Balkans and by military and economic debility from continuous warfare with the Sassanids, the Byzantines had to face various united Arab tribes, some of whom were

---

9 Michael Psellos, *Chronographia*, 7.132–43.

ex-allies or mercenaries of Byzantium. In the absence of natural barriers in Syria, Egypt and Palestine, Herakleios I mainly sought to halt the enemy at fortified centres and to avoid pitched battles. This strategy proved largely unsuccessful for political, religious, ethnic and military reasons. For instance, local commanders underestimated the enemy and, overlooking imperial orders and their inexperience in fighting the Arabs, they engaged in open battle with disastrous results (usually defeated by ambush or feigned retreat). Herakleios I, on the other hand, was unable to dispatch relief forces to most besieged cities, rendering them reluctant to resist. Considerably outnumbered, garrisons preferred to accept the favourable terms of the besiegers than to risk defeat, enslavement and death. Terms were skilfully adapted and aimed accordingly, since the Arabs had been in contact with the empire for centuries and were familiar with Byzantium's internal tensions.

The biggest turning point was the battle of Jābiya-Yarmūk (636) where the defeat of the Byzantines marked the end of organised defence and, by 640, the fall of Palestine, Syria and Mesopotamia. The imperial army withdrew to Anatolia across the natural barrier of the Taurus mountain range. Although Byzantine garrisons and expeditionary forces continued to offer some resistance, by 661 the Arabs had conquered Egypt, built a fleet, conquered Cyprus and, after a series of partly successful raids, persuaded the Armenians to become vassals of the Muslim caliphate.

Despite the occasional successful incursions deep into Anatolia, its conquest was a challenging endeavour for the Arabs, due to harsh mountainous terrain, climate, logistics and relative homogeneity between centre and periphery. Instead, the Arabs aimed at the subjugation of the Byzantine Empire by attacking Constantinople itself. A series of failed expeditions against the impregnable capital were organised between 654 and 718. Although attempts to stop the Arab fleet around the Lycian coast failed, Arab naval forces were unable to enter Constantinople's eastern harbour in the Golden Horn and were destroyed at the Sea of Marmara (due to Greek fire, unfamiliarity with local currents and weather, defections and lack of supplies). Arab troops marched to Chalcedon (across the Asian coast from Constantinople) and captured bases around the capital (such as Cyzikos and Abydos), but were forced to abandon the cause, retreating either leisurely, plundering on the way back, or hastily, after being defeated by the Bulgars and the Byzantines in Thrace and Anatolia.

The next two centuries were characterised by defence, fortification and consolidation. Raids continued to take place in both directions, up to three times a year, with both adversaries seeking plunder above all. Through treaties, looting and destruction of fortifications, the Byzantines aimed to pacify and control important fortified sites along strategic routes and major frontier cities, used as bases for seasonal raids (such as Tarsos, Melitene, Theodosioupolis, Marash, Samosata and al-Hadath). Such sites were repeatedly taken, destroyed and recaptured. Arab fleets operated extensively in the Mediterranean, capturing major islands and coastal cities (such as Crete and Sicily in the 820s) and raiding others (such as Lemnos and Thessaloniki in 902–904). Save for a few pitched battles (such as the Battle of Akroinon in 740), the Byzantines mainly resorted to a guerrilla defensive strategy. They intentionally turned the so-called 'outer zone' or marches of Asia Minor (the Taurus and Anti-Taurus mountains) into a devastated no man's land and obstacle to enemy communications and supplies. This strategy seems to have been abandoned by the tenth century, when we find signs of resettlement, of trade and growth in this area. The 'middle zone' in the heart of Asia Minor consisted of fortified cities and fortresses, and the final zone (west and north-west Asia Minor) was mainly used for agriculture and tax revenues. The years from 927 to 1067 mark the culmination of Byzantine expansion in the east. The increase of elite specialised troops, more refined tactics and a long-lasting peace with the Bulgars, coupled with new threats faced by the Abbasids and Ḥamdānids (such as nomad raids, fragmentation and internal strife), allowed the Byzantines to prevail. Although raids and looting continued, key sites were now permanently annexed by the Byzantines, like Melitene (934), Theodosioupolis (949), Samosata (958), Crete (961), Tarsos (965), Antioch (969) and Laodikeia (in Syria, 975). In the reign of Basil II, Aleppo became tributary to the Byzantines. South of Aleppo lay the territories of the Fatimid caliph, with whom the Byzantines were mostly allied, in this way securing the eastern front after centuries of instability.

Continuous Byzantine attempts to win the Armenians back only bore notable results after 915–928. The Byzantines successfully supported Ashot II (914–929) and secured the alliance of Armenian and Georgian potentates. The culmination of close ties was the annexation of some Armenian principalities, offered to the Byzantines by their potentates in exchange for imperial titles, lands and offices. The Byzantines occupied Kamacha and Keltzin (c. 886–912), the district of Taron (c. 966–970), Vaspurakan (c. 1019–1022), Tao (1022), Ani (1045) and Kars (1065), with either little or no bloodshed.

The Byzantines struck similar deals with non-Christian potentates. A fruitful example is the surrender of Edessa to Byzantium (1031–1032) by Sulayman, its governor. Byzantine–Muslim deals were not always honest and profitable, though. For instance, Nasr ibn Musharraf persuaded the *doux* of

Antioch to build him a fortress in the mountainous area between Tripoli and Laodikeia (in Syria, 1028) in order to check Muslim advances, in exchange for money, the title of *patrikios* (the seventh-highest rank) and the command of 1,000 soldiers. Nevertheless, once the fortress was complete, Nasr occupied and ruled it independently with the assistance of Muslim troops.

From 1038 onwards, the biggest threats in the east were the Turks and Turkmen tribes. The latter subjugated various Muslim buffer states of Byzantium along the frontier in Azerbaijan, Diyar Bakr and Syria, and raided Byzantine territory repeatedly and extensively, first in the area of newly annexed Armenia (such as Vaspurakan) and gradually up to the Aegean coast. Most of these operations were raids, aiming at the extraction of booty and payments, not at permanent occupation of cities and fortresses. The highly mobile and dispersed Turkish bands quickly managed to dominate the Byzantine countryside and roads, but only started to control cities and fortresses, sometimes with the assistance of the local aristocracy, after extensive Byzantine civil wars and cuts in military spending (*c.* 1059–1081). Consequently, the imperial frontier was severely neglected and weakened, and military administration collapsed. At best, centralised organised defence was replaced with local initiatives. On less favourable occasions, however, high-ranking imperial officials – Byzantines, Latins, Armenians and Georgians – rebelled against central authority, appropriated imperial territory and at times surrendered their holdings to the Turks or worked with them to capture the throne (such as Robert Crispin, *c.* 1069; Philaretos Brachamios, *c.* 1071–1087; Roussel de Bailleul, *c.* 1073; Nikephoros III, *c.* 1078). This allowed the Turks to capture key strategic sites, such as Ani (1064), Artāh (1068) Khelat and Manzikert (1070). While some joined the Byzantines (especially during civil wars) in exchange for money, ranks and titles, they never abandoned the cities and fortresses they were given to garrison. Defensive operations were characterised by blunders, disagreements, tensions between the military aristocracy and a lack of co-ordination, rendering the organisation of an effective defensive guerrilla strategy (previously employed against the Arabs) difficult at best. This strategy was seldom used against the Turks, and mostly by local potentates who had the advantage of co-ordinating their forces better. The Byzantines mainly favoured the passive defence of fortified sites. Troops usually stayed within the walls, protecting the locals and waiting for allied (such as Georgians), imperial and mercenary forces from Anatolia and the Balkans. This strategy yielded some fruit and several advances were repelled (such as in Manzikert, Baberd/Paipert and Basean).

The alternative method entailed pursuing enemy detachments and forcing a pitched battle upon them, usually around their main points of entrance (such as Lake Van and Manzikert). Some of these operations failed, partly or completely (such as the Battle of Kapetron/Hasankale in 1048, and the Battle of Manzikert in 1071), while others were relatively successful, such as Romanos IV's initial operations against the Turks (1068–1070). Romanos IV repelled attacks against Antioch and Cilicia, trapped and annihilated Turkish detachments, and even captured some fortresses (Artah and Manjib).

The biggest problem with the Byzantine approach, however, was that both strategies allowed the highly dispersed Turks to bypass imperial armies and heavily fortified centres, to dominate the roads and the countryside around them, and to raid any less heavily defended district. By 1081, Alexios I, pressed by the impending Norman campaign against the western regions of the empire, was forced to officially recognise the lordship of Sulaymān in Nicaea and Nicomedia, constituting him an independent authority in an area previous belonging to Byzantium. By the time of the First Crusade (1096–1099), the Turks possessed western and central Anatolia and the entire area between the Caucasus mountains and Cappadocia, including Antioch and Edessa (save for some Byzantine enclaves in Pontus and Byzantine–Armenian lordships in Cilicia).

To reverse the situation, the Byzantines sought to restore imperial rule by fulfilling three objectives: (a) drive the Turks from the coasts, (b) push them further inland and (c) destroy their polities. The first objective began to be realised by Alexios I, who secured the Asian coasts opposite Constantinople, recovered Nicomedia (1090) and Nicaea (1097, along with the troops of the First Crusade) and erected the key fortress of Sidera between Lake Baane and the Sangarios river, significantly blocking Turkish movements westwards. The Turkish defeat at the Battle of Dorylaion (1097) weakened the fighting spirit of Turkish polities which could no longer count on the assistance of relief armies, enabling Alexios I to restore all coastal areas from Bithynia to Seleucia and to gain recognition of Byzantine overlordship over some areas of Cilicia ruled by Armenian potentates. The consolidation of these conquests was among the priorities of the Byzantines from 1113 onwards. Cities and fortresses were rebuilt, repopulated and built from scratch to fend off Turkish invasions, to control the roads and to allow agriculture to prosper (such as Lopadion Adramyttion/Edremit, Philadelphia, Malagina, Pithykas, Chiara and Pergamon). Some of the latter were even organised to the *thema* of Neokastra (1162–1173). Further to the south-east coast, Cyprus, Attaleia, Kourikon/Kizkalesi and Seleucia were also fortified or refortified to act as firm and long-lasting bases, controlling communications, supplies and trade to Cilicia and Antioch.

Although John II recaptured Tarsus, Adana, Mopsuestia and Anazarbos (1137) from the Armenians, most of these holdings were lost to the Armenian prince Toros II (1144/1145–1169). Failing to pacify the mountain districts of Cilicia, the Byzantines settled for Toros II's recognition of imperial overlordship in the area. Similarly, the Byzantines failed to achieve a direct occupation of Syria and Antioch but forced the Crusader states to recognise their vassalage to the Byzantine emperor.

The Battle of Dorylaion (1097) was key to the realisation of the second objective. Alexios I restored inland districts, stopping at Philomelion, west of Konya. John II (1118–1143) recaptured Laodikeia and Sozopolis in Pamphylia (1119–1120), which secured the routes to Philomelion and the coasts in the south, and took hold of Kastamona and Gangra (1132–1133), neutralising enemy bases and securing routes to the Black Sea. Manuel I aimed to restore Cappadocia through an alliance with his former enemy, Kilig Arslan, against the Danishmendids. Manuel I supported Kilig Arslan's cause in return for restoring all conquered territories to the empire, only to see these territories being occupied by Kilig Arslan himself. This debacle prompted Manuel I to fortify Dorylaion and Soublaion (1175), which dominated the main roads to Konya, and to attempt an attack on Konya itself. Despite gathering an impressive army, Manuel I was defeated at the narrow passes of Myriokephalon (1176), barely escaping captivity. Peace negotiations with Kilig Arslan compelled Manuel I to destroy Dorylaion and Soublaion, but only the latter was razed. Despite the defeat, the Byzantines were able to repel Turkish raids and invasions and to maintain the status quo. Instead, the greatest threat to Byzantine security lay on the western front.

The Western Front

Along with the Arabs and Turks in Anatolia and the Levant, and the Franks and Lombards in Italy and Sicily, the Byzantines were forced to deal with the Slavs and the Bulgars, who had established themselves in Moesia, the Black Sea region south of the Danube. The Byzantines regarded any area south of the Danube as imperial territory and struggled to reassert their authority, as well as to restore strategic sites, fertile valleys, manpower and tax income to the empire. Being pressured on other fronts, the Byzantines usually offered concessions (such as payment of tribute) to the Bulgars. When the international setting allowed it, however, the Byzantines aimed at repelling raiding expeditions which sometimes reached as far as Constantinople, restoring and reconstructing strategic fortresses and bases (such as Constanteia), and even seeking to annex the Bulgar polity to the empire. Anchialos (Pomorie), Mesembria (Nesebăr), Develtos (Burgas) and Markellai (Krumovo) were among the most strategic sites, frequently changing hands and experiencing numerous conflicts. To enhance imperial security, the Byzantines attempted to draw Bulgaria into their sphere of influence. An alliance of Boris I (852–889) with the Franks and his agreement to accept missionaries from Rome troubled the Byzantines greatly. As a response they attacked Bulgaria (863) and compelled Boris I to accept orthodox Christianity. Krum I (803–814) and Symeon I (893–927) were among the most dangerous opponents, seeking imperial recognition, killing a Byzantine emperor in action (the death of Nikephoros I at the Vărbica Pass in 811), defeating the Byzantines numerous times (such as Versinikia in 813, Boulgarophygon in 896 and Acheloos and Katasyrtai in 917) and raiding extensively in Thrace, Macedonia and Greece. By the end of the eighth century and the beginning of the ninth, as a response to the Bulgar threat, the Byzantines organised the districts of Macedonia, Strymon and Thessaloniki into *themata*. In the first half of the tenth century, the *thema* of Strymon was enhanced with the addition of a *kleisoura* in the Rupel Pass.

Shortly before Symeon I's death, the Byzantines concluded a long peace treaty with the Bulgars, whereby some fortified centres were restored to the empire in exchange for a yearly tribute. The watershed of 927 marks the almost unhindered focus of Byzantine manpower and funds against the Arabs and the gradual domination of the eastern front. Nikephoros II reconsidered the status quo with the Bulgars after their failure to stop Magyar raids from reaching Byzantium. Preferring to avoid the Haemus passes and to remain focused in the east, Nikephoros II called the Rus', who by now had established themselves in Kiev and were allied to Byzantium, to invade and raid Bulgaria from the north. Aiming to become emperor, Kalokyros, the *strategos* of Cherson, ruined the negotiations, urging Svyatoslav (945–971) to occupy Bulgaria in return for supporting him. By 969–970 Svyatoslav had secured Bulgaria and begun to attack imperial territory. The Byzantines counterattacked under John I and took Preslav and, after joint land and naval operations, Dorostolon/Silistra (971).

Taking advantage of the extensive civil wars during the reign of Basil II, some aristocrats (Byzantine, Armenian or Bulgar) rebelled in western Macedonia (976), the most renowned of them being the so-called Bulgarian Samuel (997–1014). By 995, the rebels secured Macedonian Edessa and a band of towns from Pliska, Vidin and Sofia to Dyrrachion (modern Durrës), carrying out raids throughout Macedonia, Thessaly and all the way to Corinth. They deprived Basil II of supplies, ambushing and destroying his army at the passes of the Gates of Trajan (986). The Byzantines dealt the first serious blow to Samuel in 996. Nikephoros Ouranos forded the swollen Sperchios river, successfully attacked the enemy camp at night and then proceeded to reoccupy key fortresses and cities in Greece. Around the year 1000, Basil II, after settling affairs on the eastern front, campaigned against Sofia once more, capturing the city and the surrounding fortresses. Samuel's lands were now cut into two as Byzantine commanders annexed Presthlavitza, Preslav and Pliska. A ten-year Byzantine–Fatimid truce concluded in 1001 allowed Basil II to focus his man-power entirely on the western front. In two years, Basil II recovered key cities on Via Egnatia and besieged Vidin. Samuel conducted a raid on Adrianople in the hopes of distracting imperial troops away from Vidin, which fell to the Byzantines in 1002, followed by Naissos and Skopje a year later. The com-mander of the latter exchanged it for the gift of imperial titles, as did the commander of Dyrrakhion in around 1005. In 1014 Basil II returned to the offensive, seeking to control all the roads and passes to the Strymon valley. He won a battle at the passes of Kleidion and allegedly blinded 15,000 prisoners of war as retaliation, blinding being a common punishment for rebels desiring to appropriate the imperial title. The current consensus is that these numbers are vastly exaggerated, while some argue that the story is suspect altogether. After the battle, surrounding fortresses surrendered. The death of Samuel allowed the Byzantines to take Bitola, Prilep and Shtip. The imperial army captured many prisoners, turned them into soldiers and settled them in Thrace and Armenia. The fall of Müglen followed (the Byzantines diverted the stream of the Moglenitza river and undermined its walls), and then Enotia, Sosk and Ostrovo. By 1018, despite some debacles, Basil II had annexed or accepted the surrender of all the remaining cities and fortresses that had rebelled in regions located in western modern Bulgaria, central and southern modern North Macedonia, north-western modern Greece and central and southern modern Albania, in return for money, ranks and titles, and reinstated the empire's frontier at the Danube. Most of the fortifications around the Danube were restored by John I and Basil II. From 1018, the area had been organised militarily into one district called Boulgaria under the command of a *doux*.

Around 1037, the invasions of Pechenegs and Ouzes compelled the Byzantines to organise separately the eastern part (between the lower Danube and the Haemus) into the district of Paradounavon/Paristrion, under a *doux* or *katepano*. The nomads laid waste to many small fortresses in the lower Danube, reaching as far as Thrace and Thessaloniki (in 1032–1036,

1046–1053 and 1053–1072). Failing to check the Pechenegs in pitched battles, the Byzantines relied on heavily fortified centres, located on riverbanks and at strategic junctions in the mainland (such as Dinogetia, Păcuiul lui Soare, Isaccea, Presthlavitza, Sofia and Stara Zagora), the garrisons of which launched ambushes and surprise attacks against the wandering invaders. Lesser forts were neglected and abandoned. To prevent easy plundering, once again the Byzantines resorted to the creation of marches, wastelands between the Moesian plain and the Haemus mountains. Where these measures failed, the Byzantines came to terms with the invaders. The nomads were allowed to settle within the empire, usually by the Danube. They were converted to Christianity and their chieftains and troops were enlisted for military service, in exchange for payment and titles. A Pecheneg revolt (1072–1091) against imperial rule turned into extensive raiding, sometimes with Hungarian assistance and that of fellow Pecheneg tribes north of the Danube. The raiders reached Thrace several times (such as in 1077, 1086 and 1087), but they were annihilated by Emperor Alexios I Komnenos at Levounion (1091). Although Alexios recovered Paradounavon, he confronted future raids (such as by the Cumans) at the Haemus passes, demonstrating the strategic value of these sites.[10]

Another major threat for Byzantine dominion in the Balkans was the Normans. Having established themselves in southern Italy and Sicily, they launched several campaigns against Byzantium (such as in 1081–1083, 1084–1085 and 1107–1108). These operations had some common features. The Normans disembarked and aimed at securing the area around Aulona, Corfu and Cephalonia. Alexios I called upon the Venetians, his allies and vassals, to attack the Norman fleet in exchange for trading privileges and the award of imperial ranks and titles (such as *protosebastos*, the fifth-highest rank, and *doux* of Dalmatia and Croatia). The prime Norman targets were Illyria, Epirus, Macedonia (with Dyrrachion and Thessaloniki being the biggest prizes) and fortified centres around the Via Egnatia. Byzantine attempts to deal with the Normans in a pitched battle largely failed (such as at Dyrrachion and Ioannina) but indirect approaches saved the day. Ambushes and blockades at mountain passes (such as around Larrisa and Dyrrachion), coupled with famine, disease and attempts to win over Norman lords, compelled the Normans to abandon their campaign and seek peace.

---

10 Anna Komnene, *Ἀλεξιάς/Alexiad*, 7.4–6., in *Anna Comnenae Alexias* (ed. D. R. Reinsch, A. Kambylis and F. Kolovou) (Berlin: De Gruyter, 2001), *Anna Komnene Alexiad* (trans. E. R. A. Sewter and P. Frankopan) (London: Penguin, 2009).

The death of Manuel I and the tyrannical reign of Andronikos I (1183–1185) reversed the situation. Byzantine aristocrats fled to Sicily while others unreluctantly co-operated with the tyrant. William II of Sicily (1153–1189) took advantage of the situation and invaded Byzantium (1185–1186). Dyrrachion and the Dalmatian cities surrendered to him, allowing neither time for naval operations nor for the occupation of mountain passes. The Normans marched to Thessaloniki almost unhindered. The city fell after a brief but violent siege. After pillaging it, the Normans occupied the Strymon valley and pushed towards the capital. They were finally defeated at Mosynopolis and Strymon, and forced to abandon Thessaloniki and Dyrrachion.

The most decisive advances against the empire in the Balkans were achieved by the Hungarians, Serbs, Vlachs and Bulgarians, and the Latins of the Fourth Crusade. From 1071 to 1167, Hungary contested the Byzantines for hegemony in the Balkans but with few lasting results. Although the Hungarians repeatedly interfered with Byzantine affairs in Serbia and Dalmatia, either aiming to control these areas directly or to stir up and back up revolts, the Byzantines maintained the status quo. Belgrade, Braničevo and Niš were repeatedly threatened and restored to the empire, with Manuel I upgrading their fortifications and expanding them. Isaac II Angelos (1185–1195 and 1203–1204) married Béla III's daughter and made peace with the Hungarians, at the cost of acknowledging the Hungarian annexation of Dalmatia, maintaining, in exchange, control over Belgrade and Niš.

Soon, however, a Bulgar–Vlach revolt in the Haemus mountains (1185) proved fatal for Byzantium's hegemony in the area. Most of the rebels seem to have had military experience, serving as garrison troops in defiles (*kleisourai*) and as separate regiments in imperial armies. They occupied impregnable mountain fortresses and established themselves around Tǎrnovo, fighting along with the Cumans in order to form an independent Bulgar–Vlach polity. Controlling the passes, they inflicted devastating defeats on Byzantine armies (such as at Trjavna Pass in 1190), raided imperial territory and extended their holdings to Moesia in the north and the Strymon valley in the south. By 1202 they had occupied key sites from Belgrade to Constanteia (modern Constanţa in Romania) and from Mesembria (modern Nesebǎr) to Skopje. The disintegration of Byzantine political stability, prestige and military might, and the depletion of the imperial coffers, allowed leading figures of the Fourth Crusade to interfere in imperial succession disputes and to capture Constantinople (1204).

12

Strategies in the Wars of Western Europe, 476–c. 1000

JOHN FRANCE

Strategy, by which leaders 'set objectives, establish priorities among them, and allocate resources to them, whether or not they develop or keep to long-range systematic plans',[1] is a word not often used in connection with the early medieval period in which war is often seen as mere feud or the gathering of loot. It was only in the 1960s that historians began to understand warfare in the Middle Ages.[2]

Sources

The period between *c.* 476 and *c.* 1000 is known as the 'Dark Ages' largely because source material is scarce and limited. The only manual of war known in this period was the *De Re Militari* of Vegetius.[3] Freculph of Lisieux presented a copy of Vegetius's work to Charles the Bald (843–877) in the hope that it might be of practical use. Rabanus Maurus made an abbreviation in about 856 at the request of Lothar II (855–869).[4] It is, however, doubtful whether any of these was actually used as a practical

---

1 K. Kagan, 'Redefining Roman grand strategy', *Journal of Military History*, 70 (2006), 333–62, 348.

2 J. Beeler, 'Towards a re-evaluation of medieval English generalship', *Journal of British Studies*, 3 (1963), 1–10; J. F. Verbruggen, *The Art of Warfare in Western Europe during the Middle Ages* (first published in Dutch as *De Krijskskunst in West-Europa in de Middeleeuwen Ice tot begin xive eeuw* (Brussels: Koninklijke, 1954), but first available in English trans. S. Willard and R. W. Southern) (Amsterdam: North Holland, 1977) with an expanded edition coming later (Woodbridge: Boydell, 1997), 276–350.

3 C. Lang (ed.), *Vegetii Epitoma Rei Militaris* (Leipzig: Teubner, 1885), which was translated by N. P. Milner, *Vegetius: Epitome of Military Science* (Liverpool: Liverpool University Press, 1993).

4 Freculphi, MGH Epp. 5: 618–19, for the context of which see R. McKitterick, 'Charles the Bald (823–77) and his library: the patronage of learning', *English Historical Review*, 95 (1980), 31 [28–47]; Rabanus Maurus, 'De procinctu Romanae militia' (ed. E. Dümmler), *Zeitschrift für deutches Alterthum*, 15 (1872), 443–51.

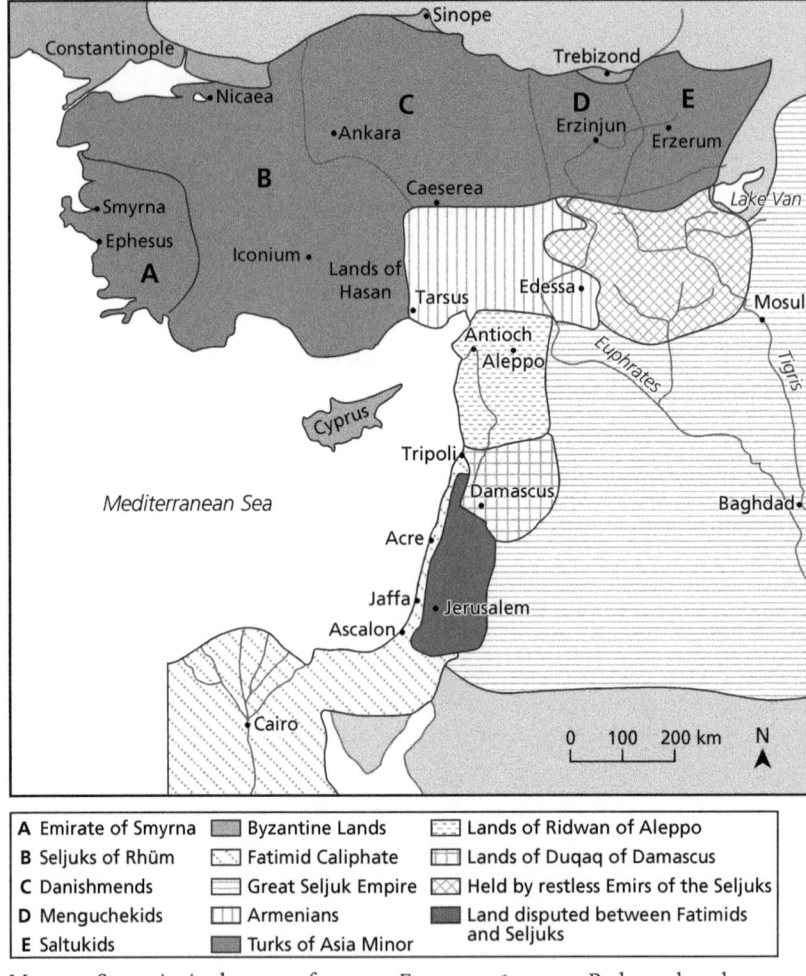

Map 12.1 Strategies in the wars of western Europe, 476–c. 1000. Redrawn based on a map in J. France, *Victory in the East: A Military History of the First Crusade* (Cambridge: Cambridge University Press, 1994), 109.

guide.[5] There is one work which focuses on a military event, the siege of Paris 885–886.[6]

5 C. Allmand, *The De Re Militari of Vegetius: The Reception, Transmission and Legacy of a Roman Text in the Middle Ages* (Cambridge: Cambridge University Press, 2011); B. S. Bachrach, 'The practical use of Vegetius's De Re Militari during the early Middle Ages', *Historian*, 47 (1985), 239–55.
6 Abbon, *Siège de Paris par les normands* (ed. H. Waquet) (Paris: Belles Lettres, 1942), trans. Nirmal Dass, *Attacks on Paris: The Bella Parisiacae Urbis of Abbo of Saint-Germain* (Leuven: Peeters, 2007).

Record sources for the post-Roman period are very limited. Amongst them are law codes, but these are often very difficult to use. There was a brief efflorescence of record sources in the high Carolingian period, but otherwise the historian is largely dependent upon chroniclers of varying degrees of reliability and upon saints' lives and theological works. The chronicles of the immediate post-Roman period were produced well after 476 and were largely written by clerics. Since they were drawn from the same elite as the warriors and often shared their pride in glory, this does not necessarily mean they knew nothing of war. But they had other preoccupations, often seeking to reveal divine providence.

Early medieval writers were often centred on particular peoples, though Byzantine writers, notably Procopius, are sometimes helpful.[7] The Goths were chronicled by Jordanes, an Eastern Roman administrator of Gothic origins writing in 551, and the famous Isidore of Seville (560–636).[8] Gregory of Tours (538–594) wrote a *History of the Franks* which is our chief source for knowledge of the early history of this people.[9] What we know of the early Anglo-Saxons is dominated by Bede, whose work was completed by 731.[10] Paul the Deacon wrote a history of his Lombard people towards the end of the eighth century.[11]

The Carolingian family who ruled the Franks after 714 were immensely conscious of the way in which the past could be manipulated to influence the present. The *Annales Mettenses Priores* harnesses conventional views of divine providence to the particular end of showing that the Merovingians were ineffectual and undeserving, that their displacement by the Carolingians was part of God's providence, and that the new dynasty ruled as true Frankish kings.[12] The *Royal Frankish Annals* were constructed at the court of Charlemagne and present a triumphal account of military campaigns. After Charlemagne's death a reviser provided

---

7 W. A. Goffart, *Narrators of Barbarian History (AD 550–800): Jordanes, Gregory of Tours, Bede and Paul the Deacon* (Princeton: Princeton University Press, 1980); Averil Cameron, *Procopius and the Sixth Century* (London: Routledge, 1985).

8 Jordanes, *History of the Goths* (ed. H. Wolfram, trans. J. Dunlap) (Berkeley: University of California Press, 1990); Isidore of Seville, *Historia Gothorum*, MGH Auctores Antiquissimi 11: 241–303.

9 Gregory of Tours, *History of the Franks* (trans. L. Thorpe) (Harmondsworth: Penguin, 1974).

10 Bede, *The Ecclesiastical History of the English People* (ed. J. McClure and R. Collins) (Oxford: Oxford University Press, 1994).

11 Paul the Deacon, *Historia Langobardorum*, Volume 1 (Hannover: MGH SRG, 1878), 241–303; trans. P. I. Pretta, *History of the Lombards* (Terni: Tektime, 2020).

12 *Annales Mettenses Priores* (ed. B. von Simson) (Hannover: MGH SRG, 1905); J. Fried, *Charlemagne* (trans. P. Lewis from a 2013 German original) (Cambridge, MA: Harvard, 2016), 7.

additional, sometimes revealing, information about mistakes and defeats.[13] The royal annals were only part of a great flood of letters, theological writing and royal legislation, the capitularies, which formed part of Charlemagne's attempt to establish good administration and order in his empire.[14] The collapse of this polity led to a bifurcation in the writing of chronicles between what became the French kingdom[15] and the German Empire, which embraced northern Italy.[16] In the British Isles the *Anglo-Saxon Chronicle* was a grand narrative, but it originated at the court of King Alfred (871–899) of Wessex, whose dynasty is made central to its history. However, from his time onwards we have administrative records like the *Burghal Hidage*, many of which provide some insight into military matters.[17] Local and more restricted works were produced and became commoner as Europe in the tenth century became richer. None of this material, though infused with military events, is centred on war or reveals much about strategic ideas.

Actors

The barbarians broke into the Western Empire to improve their lot, and their strategy was essentially that of a protection racket. In 410 the Visigoths were negotiating terms with Rome, and when discussions collapsed they sacked the city. But subsequently they entered into complicated relationships with the ebbing Roman power so that Europe at the end of the fifth century was a place of extraordinarily complex and fluid political relationships. In Italy the barbarian general Odoacer became king in 476. He was displaced by Theoderic, a general in East Rome, who led his Ostrogoths into Italy, becoming king in 493. He imposed strong

13 Charlemagne's wars are recorded in the *Annales Regni Francorum*, 741–828 (ed. F. Kurze) (Hannover: MGH SRG, 1895); trans. B. W. Scholz and B. Rogers, *Carolingian Chronicles* (Ann Arbor: University of Michigan, 1972), 37–125.

14 P. E. Dutton, *Carolingian Civilization: A Reader* (North York, ON: Broadview, 1993).

15 *Annals of St Bertin* (ed. J. L. Nelson) (Manchester: Manchester University Press, 2004); Flodoard, *Annals 919–66* (ed. S. Fanning and B. S. Bachrach) (North York, ON: Broadview, 2004); Richer of Saint-Rémi, *Histories* (ed. J. Lake), 2 vols (Washington, DC: Dumbarton Oaks, 2011).

16 Regino of Prüm, *Chronicle* (trans. S. MacLean) (Manchester: Manchester University Press, 2009); Widukind, *Rerum Gestarum Saxonicarum libri* III (ed. P. Hirsch) (Hannover: MGH SRG, 1935); Thietmar of Merseburg, *Chronicon*, trans. in D. A. Warner, *Ottonian Germany* (Manchester: Manchester University Press, 2001).

17 *The Anglo-Saxon Chronicle* (trans. M. J. Swanton) (New York: Routledge, 1998), year 894; and on Alfred's wider strategy R. Lavelle, *Alfred's Wars: Sources and Interpretations of Anglo-Saxon Warfare in the Viking Age* (Woodbridge: Boydell, 2010).

government there until his death in 526, when a succession struggle broke out. The Eastern Roman emperor Justinian (527–565), having reconquered north Africa from the Vandals, invaded Italy, precipitating a long and bitter war. The Lombards from the Danube intervened and by the end of the sixth century ruled almost all of northern Italy, and seized the duchies of Spoleto and Benevento.[18] The Visigoths had been persuaded to go to Aquitaine and Spain, from where they expelled the Vandals to north Africa.[19] The Franks from east of the Rhine were pagan despite long contact with Rome. They united under Clovis (481–511), conquered the Roman kingdom of Soissons and imposed themselves on Gaul north of the Loire. In 507 Clovis defeated the Visigoths of Aquitaine and established Frankish rule there. His conversion to Catholic Christianity strengthened his government in the Frankish lands and probably made his rule acceptable to the native population of Aquitaine, for the Visigoths were Arian heretics. The Visigoths then fled into Spain and set about a full conquest there. In Britain the Anglo-Saxon incursion resulted in a mix of native and Germanic kingdoms, destroying the fabric of Roman government.[20] In the early seventh century the rise of Islam weakened Byzantium, whose conquests in the west, except for vestiges in Italy, faded.

Everywhere the complex Roman system of government weakened, and this had military consequences. Rome collected taxes and paid its army, but the disruptions caused by conquests and reconquests demanded a simpler system. The barbarian kings settled land upon their followers, but this was not done on an egalitarian basis. The invaders were not tribes but accretions of small groups, each with its own opportunistic leader, who followed some figure like Theoderic, who promised to bring them to better things. Childeric, Clovis's father, had a Hun, Wiomad, amongst his intimate followers.[21] The Lombards, who appeared later, were 'a wide ethnic stock'.[22] In Britain the conquerors are described as Anglo-Saxons and Jutes.[23] Opportunist groups adopted the culture and outlook of the leader

---

18 N. Christie, *The Lombards* (Oxford: Blackwell, 1995).
19 P. Heather, 'The creation of the Visigoths', in P. Heather, *The Visigoths: From the Migration Period to the Seventh Century* (Woodbridge: Boydell, 1999), 41–92.
20 S. S. Evans, *The Lords of Battle: Image and Reality of the Comitatus in Dark-Age Britain* (Woodbridge: Boydell, 1997), 17–18.
21 A. C. Murray, *From Roman to Merovingian Gaul: A Reader* (Toronto: UTP, 2008), trans. of Fredgar's *Chronicle*, 87.
22 N. Christie, *The Lombards* (Oxford: Blackwell, 1995), 86.
23 Evans, *Lords of Battle*, 17–18.

and his group. In this way a sense of identity emerged – this was ethnogenesis.[24]

The chief men were allocated much greater lands than their humbler followers. These great men had personal guards, professional bully-boys, who formed the core of their following. They and the lesser men soon married into the Gallo-Roman aristocracy and gentry, who themselves kept armed followers, so that the army ceased to be an ethnic group and was distinguished by being landholders, great and small. And because the Roman administration had withdrawn, these chief followers took over the counties ensuring that all government was militarised.

Kings enjoyed prestige and great wealth as well as residual administrative organs whose offices they could distribute by way of royal patronage. And they could adjudicate in disputes and offer legitimate titles. But their authority was conditional, for the military elite monopolised all organs of power and, therefore, had to be consulted and persuaded.[25] Assemblies of important men (*placitum*, pl. *placita*) were crucial in the formation of policy and usually came together at the same time as the army.

In this context armies were not institutions with a permanent life, but short-lived entities gathered by negotiation. The formation of strategy was, therefore, a complex process and much depended on the personality of the king. In 639 the child-king Sigebert III was forced by his great men to fight the Thuringians, who won the ensuing battle, leaving him weeping as he fled on his horse.[26] At the other end of the scale Charlemagne could almost always get his way, but even he was very careful to consult his great men with very regular meetings of the *placitum*.

Kings usually led armies. In 496 Clovis and his Salian Franks allied with King Sigebert of the Ripuarian Franks to defeat the neighbouring Alemanni at the battle of Tolbiac. At Vouillé, Clovis, in the thick of the fight, was nearly killed. Charlemagne often, though not always, led his armies personally, while the foundation of the glory of the Capetian kings of France was Odo's defence of Paris against the Vikings in 885–886. In a highly militarised society, leadership in war was essential for royal prestige.

24 S. Ghosh, *Writing the Barbarian Past. Studies in Early Medieval Historical Narrative* (Leiden: Brill, 2016), 1–38.

25 G. Halsall, *Warfare and Society in the Barbarian West, 450–900* (London: Routledge, 2003), 20–39.

26 J. M. Wallace-Hadrill (ed.), *The Fourth Book of the Chronicle of Fredegar with Its Continuations* (London: Praeger, 1960), 4. 87, 73–4.

The Franks were the most powerful people in Europe. They were unusually homogeneous, for northern Gaul between Rhine and Loire lacked great Roman estates and they were numerous enough to dominate it entirely, and from there to exercise control over southern Gaul and much of western Germany. They were far removed from Byzantium, which had destabilised their neighbours. The success of their Merovingian royal family generated prestige and created loyalty. Clovis divided his lands between his four sons, propagating partible inheritance, which would be the rule in his Merovingian house for almost its whole existence. Between his death in around 511 and 679 there were only twenty-two years when the Franks were ruled by a single king. The land of Frankish conquest, the *regnum Francorum*, was most commonly divided into three units, Austrasia (land of the East Franks), Neustria (land of the West Franks) and Burgundy; parts of Aquitaine and Provence were allocated between the rulers of these on an ad hoc basis. The kings were commonly at war with one another, but it is hard to see any strategic purpose, as distinct from momentary opportunism, in these conflicts, though successful war produced lands and loot, solidifying support for a king. The Franks were loyal to the Merovingian house. By contrast, in Visigothic Spain no single dynasty was ever established and the monarchy became elective, producing destructive rivalries for the throne amongst the elite. Fredegar commented on the 'Gothic weakness for dethroning their kings'.[27] Similarly in the Lombard kingdom the monarchy was elective amongst the Lombard dukes.[28]

Kings had no monopoly on violence, and a series of child monarchs in the Merovingian house provoked a bloody struggle for power between great aristocrats, leading to the rise of the Carolingian family to rule of the *regnum Francorum* in the person of Charles Martel (714–741).[29] In the late ninth century, conflict between the various kings weakened monarchs, who had to bid for support. Then early deaths in the Carolingian family opened the way for the accession of Odo, count of Paris, whose dynasty, the Capetians, contested kingship amongst the West Franks till they established the dynasty in the eleventh century.[30] In short, wars were in large part intestine, but recognised by all as wars.

Churchmen, especially bishops, regarded a king as a guarantor of peace and order, and Charlemagne, who understood the need for literacy and

27 Wallace-Hadrill, *The Fourth Book of the Chronicle of Fredegar*, Book 4, Chapter 82, 70.
28 P. Delogu, 'Lombard and Carolingian Italy', in R. McKitterick (ed.), *The New Cambridge Medieval History*, Volume II: *700–900* (Cambridge: Cambridge University Press, 1995), 290–319.
29 P. Fouracre, *The Age of Charles Martel* (Harlow: Pearson, 2000).
30 E. James, *The Origins of France: From Clovis to the Capetians 500–1000* (Basingstoke: Macmillan, 1982), 157–60.

regular administration, consciously cultivated the relationship. His son, Louis the Pious (814–840), sought a genuinely centralised empire, but aristocratic resistance brought his ambitions to nothing.[31] His quarrelling sons concluded the Treaty of Verdun of 843, by which Lothar remained emperor, holding a belt of lands stretching from Italy to the North Sea, while Louis (843–876) held the lands of the East Franks (Germany) and Charles the Bald the lands of the West Franks (France). Nominally all remained part of the Frankish empire, but bitter rivalries and failures of succession produced wars comparable to those between the Merovingians.[32] However, the intimate fusion of church and state persisted and was justified as a necessary guarantee of the social order:

> If anyone who is ignorant of the divine dispensation objects to a bishop ruling the people and facing dangers of war and argues that he is responsible only for their souls, the answer is obvious: it is only by doing these things that the guardian and teacher of the Faithful brings to them the rare gift of peace and saves them from the darkness in which there is no light.[33]

Means

The law codes of the barbarian kings insist that all freemen could be called to the army, and this was certainly true in the period of the invasions. Figures are very rare. Procopius says that the Vandals numbered 80,000 plus women and children.[34] At the other end of the scale Ine of Wessex defined a *here*, an army, as any number of armed men over thirty-five.[35] In 589 a Frankish army was ambushed in southern France and, according to Gregory of Tours, all but wiped out, losing 5,000 killed and 2,000 taken prisoner. Isidore of Seville says that this army numbered 60,000.[36] It is hardly surprising that historians have differed sharply on this question. In the depressed economy of post-Roman Europe, with its small scattered populations, supporting a large army would

31 R. McKitterick, *Charlemagne: The Formation of a European Identity* (Cambridge: Cambridge University Press, 2008); P. Goodman and R. Collins (eds), *Charlemagne's Heir: New Perspectives on the Reign of Louis the Pious (814–40)* (Oxford: Clarendon,1990).
32 R. Collins, *Early Medieval Europe* (London: Macmillan, 1991), 318–43.
33 Ruotger, *Vita Sancti Brunonis, Coloniensis Archiepiscopi (953–65)*, PL 134: 937–77 or MGH SS 4: 252–6.
34 Procopius, *The Secret History* (trans. G. A. Williamson) (Harmondsworth: Penguin, 1966), 18. 15 131.
35 'Dooms of Ine', in C. Stephenson and F. G. Marcham (eds), *Sources of English Constitutional History* (London: Harper, 1937), 7.
36 Halsall, *Warfare and Society*, 121.

have been very difficult. In the later seventh and eighth centuries, as things improved, the potential would have been greater. Charlemagne united Europe and we know he sometimes put two or three armies into the field. But even in the Byzantine Empire, better organised and more developed than the west, single armies of 4,000 were thought large, and 12,000 was exceptional.[37] These figures should be regarded as maximal for western Europe.

In this period the army was a gathering of retinues, amongst which the greatest was normally that of the king. He could draw on his own guard and the lesser landowners on his own territories. But vast areas of land were held by aristocrats whose loyalty to the king was conditional, and they had similar forces. The most important amongst them, the counts and dukes, gathered armies for the king, whose royal servants they technically were under the Merovingians. Both under them and under the Carolingians, all free men could be summoned to the host. Especially Charlemagne sometimes raised substantial numbers. But there was always some reluctance to serve. Charlemagne often specified that people should club together to provide one well-equipped soldier, pointing to the high costs of war. And the king's appeal, mediated through great men, could be used by them in their own interests. In the later stages of Charlemagne's reign, ordinary freemen complained bitterly that magnates were manipulating the call-up, forcing men to go again and again to war until they were impoverished and forced to surrender their freedom. Even under this greatest of monarchs, royal power was abused. And gathering armies needed the consent of the great.[38]

Early medieval armies consisted of both cavalry and infantry. Procopius thought that the Franks of the sixth century had few mounted men, but perhaps he was comparing them with Byzantine forces, whose cavalry element was large, while the Lombards were famous as horsemen. The law codes clearly expected men of substance to come to the host with horses, along with mail armour, shields, spears and swords. But they were not necessarily just specialised cavalry, for Charlemagne specified that they had to bring bows and arrows, which were all that was required of the poorest. This underlines the real distinction in the army. The personal retainers of the king and his great men were well equipped and practised in war. And in an age when fighting was a matter of athletic skill this was very important. Regino of Prüm noted that in a battle near his abbey in 882 the Vikings

37 J. Haldon, *Warfare, State and Society in the Byzantine World 565–1204* (London: UCL, 1999), 99–103.
38 J. France, 'The composition and raising of the armies of Charlemagne', *Journal of Medieval Military History*, 1 (2002), 61–82.

massacred 'a crowd of common people, not so much unarmed as bereft of military training'.[39] This is not to say that the mass of infantry were useless. Charlemagne's long campaigns in Saxony turned on seizing and holding strongpoints, which demanded plenty of labour in dangerous circumstances.

In a famous letter Charlemagne ordered that Fulrad should come to the host with all his cavalrymen fully armoured, together with plenty of carts which would carry 'axes and stone-cutting tools, augers, trenching tools, iron spades' and three months' rations for each man.[40] Even in his capitulary, *De Villis*, much concerned with the good management of the royal estates, Charlemagne insisted that weapons kept on them should be in good order, and barrels be provided for the use of the army.[41] And as a corollary of having a well-armed force he prohibited the export of weapons and mail shirts, which might fall into the hands of his enemies.[42]

But technological advantage was limited; western Europeans had more iron than others, but not different weapons. The key change in armies in the tenth century was the consequence of political change. The West Frankish kingdom became sharply divided into the two royal lines of Carolingians and Capetians, who found it easier to raise small and well-equipped forces of mounted all-purpose soldiers than to train and mobilise masses. The East Franks formed a German Empire which dominated Italy. They faced raiding horsemen from the steppes of western Asia, so they too needed cavalry which could be quickly mobilised. Contemporaries referred to armies as being made up of *milites et pedites*. The term *milites* simply means soldiers, but the contrast with *pedites* emphasises that a particular kind of soldier had usurped the title – the knight. Elite soldiers, closely allied to the leaders of society, had long dominated warfare and this is emphasised by the linguistic change.

Knights were very effective warriors, but because they were raised from the landholdings of kings and great men they were used to fighting in small groups. This pattern was imposed by the fragmented nature of landholdings. They were all-purpose warriors, fighting on horseback or on foot, as siege often required, but lacked military discipline. Indeed 'chivalry', which characterised their lifestyle, emphasised individual courage, skill and loyalty rather than discipline. This lack of cohesion when major forces gathered was

39 Regino of Prüm, *Chronicle* (trans. S. MacLean) (Manchester: Manchester University Press, 2009), 185.

40 A. Boretius (ed.), *Monumenta Germaniae Historiae, Legum* (Hanover: MGH, 1883), 168.

41 Boretius, *Monumenta Germaniae Historiae, Legum, De Villis*, Clause 42, at 87, and Clause 68, at 89.

42 Boretius, *Monumenta Germaniae Historiae, Legum*, capitulary of Thionville of 806, at 142.

a powerful disincentive to battle where chance in any case was a formidable factor. Even in the petty warfare of squabbling French aristocrats infantry were essential. In battle, especially stiffened with knights, they provided mass, assisted in the business of ravaging, provided services like horse-coping, and were vital in the heavy labour of siege.

Infantry had limited armour, perhaps an iron helmet and sometimes a shield, and usually wielded the spear or the bow and arrow. The spear was equally the prime weapon of the cavalry, but their chainmail was of better quality, combined with a shield and steel cap. The sword was the very symbol of the knight's vocation. Horses which had to carry all this were soon exhausted by fast movement, so these armies had limited manoeuvrability and in battle relied on close order for the close-quarter butchery which was the business of war.

Adversaries

Western Europeans most commonly fought amongst themselves or rather similar enemies. The contests between Merovingian kings were somewhat ritualistic. Cities changed hands, usually with little trouble. Gregory of Tours records changes of rule in his city as of less significance than his feud with Leudast, its count.[43] But sometimes this rivalry swelled into an ugly climax and large-scale confrontation. In 612 Theuderic of Burgundy fought Theudebert II of Austrasia at Zülpich and 'the carnage on both sides was such that in the fighting line there was no room for the slain to fall down'. After the battle Theuderic captured his rival and his baby son, and 'a soldier took him by the heels and dashed out his brains on a stone'.[44] In 871 Alfred (then prince) confronted the Vikings at Ashdown in an infantry battle in the same kind of close formation which seems to have been the norm for infantry forces.[45]

In Italy the Goths at first capitulated before the well-organised and disciplined armies of East Rome, but recovered to fight a long war before going down to defeat. The Lombards then conquered much of Italy as East Rome became preoccupied with eastern wars. In Spain the Visigoths in 711 fell to the Muslims of north Africa.[46] The arrival of Islam in Spain introduced a new

---

43 Gregory of Tours, *History of the Franks* (trans. L. Thorpe) (London: Penguin, 1974), 314–22.

44 Wallace-Hadrill, *The Fourth Book of the Chronicle of Fredegar*, 32.

45 Asser, *Life of Alfred* (Harmondsworth: Penguin, 1983), 77.

46 R. Collins, *Early Medieval Spain: Unity in Diversity 400–1000* (London: Macmillan, 1995), 36–51.

kind of enemy, one inspired by ideology. During the lifetime and after the death of Muhammad, conquest was part of the mission he had entrusted to his followers of expanding the *Dar al-Islam* and it provided a fine excuse for the ambitions of any Islamic potentate. In 733 the governor of Islamic Spain, 'Abd ar-Rahman, was tempted by the fighting in the Frankish world between Charles Martel and his enemies to lead a raid into Aquitaine. Charles defeated the Arabs at Moussais-la-Bataille north-east of Poitiers. The Franks, we are told, 'Remained immobile like a wall, holding together like a glacier in the cold regions'.[47] This sounds very like the tight infantry mass noted at Zülpich in 612 and Ashdown in 871. There were certainly cavalry in these armies, but they became much more important later in those of the Carolingians and their enemies. Charlemagne insisted that substantial men bring horses to the host. He employed small fast-moving cavalry units (*scara*) to strike at his enemies. One of these *scara* came to grief against the Saxons in an encounter on the Süntel mountain.[48] Undoubtedly the rising prosperity of Europe at this time made possible the raising of more horses. But new enemies increased the importance of cavalry.

The German kingdom was threatened by the settlement of the Magyars, a steppe people in the great Hungarian plain which could support clouds of light horse. Speed of movement and the hitting power of their bows enabled them to defeat western armies, leading to looting or demands for protection money. This was particularly effective because the great dukes of Germany were divided, and elected Henry of Saxony (919–936) as king with little authority outside his duchy. He received no support from them when the Hungarians attacked Saxony in 924, forcing him to pay tribute. His strategy was to create fortified refuges across his duchy, establishing stud farms for horses and giving land to increase the number of soldiers who could afford mounts. There was no room in Germany, or indeed elsewhere in Europe, to create clouds of light horsemen, so his were heavy armoured cavalry. In 933 he renounced his tribute and the Hungarians invaded. But they found little loot, and when brought to battle at the Riade Henry ordered his cavalry,

> When you begin your charge no one should attempt to ride ahead of the others, even if he has a faster mount, but each of you should cover one another with your shields and take the first enemy arrow. Then you should

---

47 P. Wolf, *Conquerors and Chroniclers of Early Medieval Spain* (Liverpool: Liverpool University Press, 1990), 180.

48 *Annales Regni Francorum*, year 782, in B. W. Scholz and B. Rogers (trans.), *Carolingian Chronicles* (Ann Arbor: University of Michigan, 1972), 59–61.

impel yourselves vigorously at full gallop, so that he cannot launch a second arrow before feeling the wounds inflicted by your arms.[49]

In 955 Henry's son, Otto I (936–973), finally destroyed the Hungarian threat at the battle of the Lech.[50]

In the west the Vikings were also highly mobile. At first adventurous young Scandinavians took ships along trade routes, prepared for commerce or killing as appropriate in isolated raids. Once raiding was established as profitable, participants would look to leaders who chose their targets intelligently. Thus a great army landed in East Anglia, the weakest of the English kingdoms, in 865, and attacked Northumbria, which was divided by civil war. In 879 another major army arrived in England, recognised that resistance had hardened, and attacked France, where there were more opportunities. Charles the Bald, whose West Frankish kingdom was exposed to raids along its river systems, ordered the building of fortified bridges, notably that at Pîtres, and summoned soldiers with horses to defend the realm.[51] But he faced resistance from the great, on whom the costs of these measures fell:

> And no one, neither counts nor any agent of the realm, through violence or through any wicked trick or through any undue force whatsoever, is to take the property or the horses of such Franks, so that they may not be able to join the army.[52]

Noble resistance undermined the efforts of Charles, for the powerful seemed to have decided that their own resources were sufficient to deal with the threat. The long siege of Paris by the Vikings in 885–886 ushered in a period of major Viking assaults on the West Franks, but they were largely beaten off by the great lords; only the settlement in what we know as Normandy established a permanent presence. By contrast, Alfred of Wessex adopted the same strategy with much more success. He granted lands to increase the number of armed and armoured soldiers called *thegns*. And, as recorded in the Burghal Hidage, he fortified existing towns and even

---

49 *Antapadosis* ('tit for tat'), found in Liudprand of Cremona, *Complete Works* (trans. P. Squatriti) (Washington, DC: Catholic University of America, 2007), Book 2, Chapter 31, 70.

50 C. R. Bowlus, *The Battle of the Lechfeld and Its Aftermath, August 955* (Aldershot: Ashgate, 2006).

51 *Annals of St Bertin* (ed. J. L. Nelson) (Manchester: Manchester University Press, 1991–), year 869, 153–4.

52 B. E. Hill, 'Charles the Bald's "Edict of Pîtres" (864): a translation and commentary', MA thesis, University of Minnesota (2013), 26.

founded new ones – the 'burh' system, demanding that one man from every hide of land should go to defend them. But in addition, 'The king had divided his army into two parts; so that they were always half at home, half out; besides the men that should maintain the towns.'[53]

This was a terrible burden on England, so that by the late tenth century the strategy had been abandoned. At the same time Denmark emerged as a state and the English realm was conquered and absorbed into a Scandinavian empire by the early eleventh century.[54]

Causes of Wars

The fundamental cause of war was that the collapse of Rome gave birth to a highly militarised society in which authority was placed in the hands of kings and great men for whom violence was a way of life. Successful kingship rested on leadership in war and the profits it could bring, which consolidated rule. This was replicated at the level of great men, counts and dukes who saw violence as the way to protect themselves. For lesser men, military status guaranteed their position in local society. Many of the barbarian kingdoms, notably the Vandals of Africa and the Visigoths of Spain, had no time to merge with existing populations before they were swept away by powerful external forces, while the Lombards flourished only because Byzantium was weakened and Italy exhausted by long and bitter wars. The petty Anglo-Saxon and native principalities of the British Isles saw one another as existential threats. It is of the utmost importance to recognise the effect of succeeding waves of conquest and reconquest in the fifth and sixth centuries, and their radical effect upon the nature of European society.

The peoples of what had previously been the Roman Empire were, however, richer than their neighbours, the Slavs, Hungarians, Vikings, Arabs and later Turks, tempting their predatory instincts. But perhaps the greatest cause of war was aristocratic faction and ambition. The great in Merovingian times were rivals for royal patronage, and this developed into the wars which led to the rise of the Carolingian family. The failure of Charlemagne and Louis the Pious to centralise power meant that aristocratic privilege had to be respected. Amongst the East Franks, as we have seen, Henry of Saxony emerged as a shrewd king and was followed by a series of strong and able rulers who were able to establish the

---

53 *The Anglo-Saxon Chronicle*, year 894; R. Lavelle, *Alfred's Wars: Sources and Interpretations of Anglo-Saxon Warfare in the Viking Age* (Woodbridge: Boydell, 2010).

54 P. Stafford, *Unification and Conquest: A Political and Social History of England in the Tenth and Eleventh Centuries* (London: Arnold, 1989).

monarchy. This, however, was only achieved by respecting the rights of the great aristocrats so there was always tension and disorder, and at moments of crisis like the accession of the child Otto III (983–1002) something like civil war threatened.[55] England grew out of the small realm of Wessex and was more tightly controlled, but outside the south, which the kings inhabited, royal interference was limited and by the late tenth century the power of the great *thegns* was very evident.

Underlying aristocratic tension was another cause of conflict, especially in France and Italy: in tenth-century France the families of Carolingian and Capetian disputed the throne, while in Italy there were numerous fractured polities. The lands of the wealthy were not discreet blocks, but scattered assemblages, often widely separated, for they had been acquired by the accidents of grant, purchase, inheritance, marriage and outright seizure. Each lord's land interpenetrated with those of many others. In the absence of anyone able to enforce judgements, violence was inevitable. Chivalry, the ethos of aristocratic society, is shot through with a sense of entitlement, entitlement to use violence and to honour its use as a true manifestation of worth.[56]

Premises Underlying Strategic Decisions

Our sources rarely provide much insight into the thinking behind military action, and sometimes what they do tell us reflects the thinking of their authors rather than that of the actors. The *Royal Frankish Annals* tell us that in 791 Charlemagne decided on the expedition against the Avars, a steppe people in what is now the Hungarian plain, 'because of the excessive and intolerable outrage committed by the Avars against the Holy Church and the Christian people'.[57] The campaign met with various setbacks until, in 796, Duke Eric of Friuli took advantage of divisions amongst the Avars to overrun their famous 'Rings' and seize a great booty. The emphasis in the *Royal Frankish Annals* is then on the booty and gifts to the great, with no mention of the Christian church and people.[58] On this occasion Charlemagne was very concerned to give a religious significance to his expedition, so we need not be

---

55 J. Gillingham, *The Kingdom of Germany in the High Middle Ages* (London: Historical Association Pamphlet G. 77, 1971); G. Barraclough, *The Origins of Modern Germany* (Oxford: Blackwell, 1957), 60–3.

56 R. Kaeuper, *Chivalry and Violence in Medieval Europe* (Oxford: Oxford University Press, 1999).

57 *Annales Regni Francorum*, year 791.   58 *Annales Regni Francorum*, year 796.

unduly cynical about his plans.[59] Moreover, this fed into his wider strategy of alliance with the church, which demanded that, at the very least, a religious gloss should be put upon events. There is no doubt that the *Annals* offer us a gloss profoundly influenced by the need to present the king's action in the best possible light.

Perhaps the best insight into strategic thinking can be found in Gregory of Tours's remark about Clovis, who 'encompassed the death of many other kings and blood relations of his whom he suspected of conspiring against his kingdom. Thus he spread his dominion over all the Franks and, indeed, the whole of Gaul.'[60]

Dynastic ambition and security were the driving forces of the chief actors in early medieval war. Kings were expected to show leadership in war, to share the hardship of the soldiers, and to distribute the loot brought by success. Concern for the security of their personal position and that of their chosen progeny runs like a golden thread throughout the period. Their great followers had to choose who to follow, for how long and subject to what conditions, if they were to guarantee their own success and the establishment of their progeny. This was especially important because laws of inheritance were not clearly defined, and while descent might be royal, succession could be unclear. The Agilolfing dukes of Bavaria were long established in the duchy and aspired to independence, and even perhaps royalty. Duke Tassilo was doubly dangerous because he was the son of Pepin's sister and his marriage into the Lombard royal house gave him additional royal connections in Italy. His strivings for independence were ultimately quashed by Charlemagne, who went to extraordinary lengths to have the duke condemned by the Pope and mobilised no less than four armies to achieve his end.[61]

In the late ninth century, western Europe saw a fundamental divergence between the East and West Franks. The Saxon dynasty claimed to rule as the heirs of the Carolingians and, as they saw it, the Roman emperors. This fed into their concern that the southern dukes might acquire control in Italy and thus create powerful new entities. In 963 Otto I (936–973) seized Rome and was crowned emperor, Otto II (973–983) attempted to subjugate all south Italy but was defeated at Cap Colonna in 982, and his son Otto III (983–1002) is

59 D. S. Bachrach, *Religion and the Conduct of War c. 300–c. 1215* (Woodbridge: Boydell, 2003).
60 Gregory of Tours, *History of the Franks*, Book 2, Chapter 42, 158.
61 *Annales Regni Francorum*, years 787–788.

credited with the slogan *Renovatio Romanorum Imperii*, a real effort to move the basis of Ottonian government to Rome.[62]

By contrast, amongst the West Franks, two 'royal' houses competed for the throne. The impoverished monarchy ceased to have any patronage. This enhanced the importance of landholdings, which were becoming more valuable as peasants drove into the wastelands. This meant the emergence of a strategy of building up territory and the annexation to it of the 'honours', the offices originally granted by the monarchy which thereby became clearly hereditary. This process had been going on for centuries, for as we have seen even under such a powerful king as Charlemagne lords used their offices for their own benefit. However, with the eclipse of monarchy the power of this higher aristocracy became very clear. The French monarch became one of the competing 'princes' who dominated France. Strong aristocrats emerged all over Europe, with varying intensity, but in the realm of the East Franks (what later became Germany) and England monarchy retained a greater degree of centralised authority (patronage).

Priorities

For the kings of Europe it was essential to exploit weaknesses amongst their neighbours in order to demonstrate their strength and to offer profit to their greater followers, who, like junior *mafiosi*, were allowed their own quarrels. Merovingian kings warred almost ritualistically amongst themselves. When East Rome tried to reconquer Italy the Franks made agreements with the emperors, or attacked their armies, opportunistically. The pattern of war in the sixth to eighth centuries is deeply confusing. The Carolingians were no less driven by personal and dynastic considerations, but they understood the need for stable and literate government in which church and monarchy marched together. Their emphasis on external warfare enabled them to exercise a degree of control over their factious aristocrats. The structural framework for which they laid the foundations endured, but in a rather more decentralised form than they had envisaged. The outstanding priority of the militarised elite was to protect their ascendancy in the social order as well as exploiting every opportunity for aggrandisement.

---

62 Barraclough, *Origins of Modern Germany*, 24–45.

Execution / Application

The reative social fluidity of early medieval Europe changed with the breakdown of the Carolingian empire because its great men were determined to assert their monopoly of the direction of violence, thereby creating a more rigidly hierarchical society. In the 840s East Frankish aristocrats crushed the *stellinga* revolt of poorer freemen restive at their domination.[63] The Viking threat was not enough to make the West Frankish nobles rally to the monarchy, and indeed their priorities were quite different, as the following passage shows:

> The Danes ravaged the places beyond the Scheldt. Some of the common people living between the Seine and the Loire formed a sworn association amongst themselves and fought bravely against the Danes on the Seine. But because their association had been made without due consideration, they were easily slain by our more powerful people [i.e. the nobility].[64]

The assertion of an aristocratic monopoly of violence gave birth to chivalry, a self-centred justification of entitlement.

In the west the new emphasis on landownership in an age of bitter competition led to a strategy of castle building. In place of the wooden manor houses, France became studded with earthwork and timber castles which were intended to overawe their peasants and deter rivals. Fulk the Black (987–1040) of Anjou inherited dispersed lands along the Loire which he united at the expense of his neighbours by constructing powerful castles, some of stone. For castles were not merely defensive: they served as bases for the lord's bully-boys, the knights.

These sociopolitical developments changed the balance of warfare. There are only three modes of war: battle, siege and economic warfare, which is ravaging.

Battle was not an inviting prospect for small elite armies and with the eclipse of the Viking threat in the 940s such confrontations became rare. Castles, where a defeated enemy could seek refuge, inclined commanders against battle. Ravaging undermined the enemy and fed your own men. The concomitant of this was improvement in siege techniques. At the siege of Paris 884–885, the Vikings used siege towers to overtop the fortifications, and catapults to cast

---

63 E. J. Goldberg, 'Popular revolt, dynastic politics and aristocratic factionalism in the early Middle Ages: the Saxon *stellinga* reconsidered', *Speculum*, 70 (1995), 467–501.
64 *Annals of St Bertin*, year 859, 89.

stones and lead balls. By the end of the tenth century major assaults on towns and castles frequently deployed such methods.[65]

Historiographic Debates

Until very recently it was thought that Charles Martel invented the mounted warrior we call the knight. He certainly gave church land to soldiers. This, it was thought, enabled them to afford horses and armour, and Charles and his Carolingian descendants to pursue a cavalry strategy which gave them supremacy over all other peoples.[66] It was considered likely that he was driven to this in order to combat the Arabs of Spain who, it was surmised, had a largely mounted army. It was thanks to his newly invented cavalry that he defeated them at Poitiers, although the best evidence suggests that the Franks at this battle fought on foot. Some important writers, like Oman, Delbrück and Lot, rejected the notion of a sudden invention of the knight, but accepted the supremacy of the heavily armed cavalryman who they thought had evolved through Merovingian times.[67] The notion of cavalry supremacy was reinforced in 1962 by White, who suggested that the adoption of the stirrup gave stability in the saddle, enabling the knight to fight effectively.[68] However, it is now accepted that wealthier soldiers always had ridden to war and many kings appropriated church lands in olrder to have new lands to distribute to their followers. Debate about when the mass charge with couched lance emerged has focused on the turn of the eleventh and twelfth centuries.[69]

---

65 J. France, 'La guerre dans la France féodale à la fin du ıxe et au xe siècle', *Revue belge d'histoire militaire*, 23 (1979), 177–93, 183–5.

66 H. Brunner, 'Der Reiterdienst und die Anfänge des Lehnwesens', *Zeitschrift der Savigny-Stiftung für Rechtsgeschichte, Germanistische Abteilung*, 8 (1887), 1–38; K. Devries, *Medieval Military Technology* (North York, ON: Broadview, 1992), 95–110.

67 C. Oman, *The Art of War in the Middle Ages 378–1485*, 2 vols (London: Methuen, 1924); H. Delbrück, *Geschichte der Kriegskunst im Rahmen der politischen Geschichte*, 6 vols (Berlin, 1920–32), of which the third volume of 1923 was translated by W. J. Renfroe Jr as *History of the Art of War within the Framework of Political History*, Volume III: *The Middle Ages* (Lincoln: University of Nebraska Press, 1982); F. Lot, *L'art militaire et les armées au moyen âge en Europe et dans le proche orient*, 2 vols (Paris: Payot, 1946).

68 L. White, *Medieval Technology and Social Change* (Oxford: Oxford University Press, 1962), 6–11.

69 D. J. A. Ross, 'L'originalité de "Turoldus": Le maniement de lance', *Cahiers de civilisation médiévale*, 6 (1963), 127–38; V. Cirlot, 'Techniques guerrières en Catalogne féodale: Le maniement de la lance', *Cahiers de civilisation médiévale*, 28 (1985), 36–43; J. Flori, 'Encore l'usage de la lance: La technique du combat chevaleresque vers l'an 1000', *Cahiers de civilisation médiévale*, 31 (1988), 213–40.

The reason for the enthusiastic reception and long life of this idea is that historians have always been dazzled by the achievements of Charlemagne, the 'Father of Europe', who created a great empire embracing almost all of western Europe.[70] The 'Brunner thesis' provided a single explanation for his success and for the growth of 'feudalism'. It was not demolished until the works of Bachrach and Bullough in 1970 which were given currency by Contamine (1984).[71] Nobody doubts that cavalry were an important element in Carolingian armies, but it is widely accepted that infantry were also vital, and that Charlemagne's careful attention to organisation and logistics was crucial.

70 Notable laudatory modern treatments of the emperor are D. A. Bullough, 'Europae pater: Charlemagne and his achievement in the light of recent scholarship', English Historical Review, 85 (1970), 59–105; A. Barbero, Charlemagne: Father of a Continent (trans. A. Cameron of a 2000 Italian original) (New Haven: Yale University Press, 2004); R. McKitterick, Charlemagne: The Formation of a European Identity (Cambridge: Cambridge University Press, 2008). By contrast, H. Fichtenau, The Carolingian Empire (trans. by P. Munz from a 1949 German original) (Oxford: Blackwell: 1957).
71 Bullough, 'Europae Pater', 84–90; B. S. Bachrach, 'Charles Martel, shock combat, the stirrup and feudalism', Studies in Medieval and Renaissance History, 7 (1970), 47–75; B. S. Bachrach, Merovingian Military Organization, 481–751 (London: Oxford University Press, 1972).

13

Latin Christendom in the Later Middle Ages

SOPHIE THÉRÈSE AMBLER

Sources

Over the period from 1000 to 1500, narrative and documentary sources were created and survive in increasing abundance to illuminate strategy and means. Chronicles were produced within monasteries, at royal courts and in cities to chart the histories of communities, from towns to kingdoms. Expedition narratives also flourished as a genre, in the aftermath of the First Crusade (1096–1099). The *Gesta Francorum* was seemingly written by a participant in that campaign.[1] It begins with the launch of the expedition by Pope Urban II (1088–1099) at Clermont in 1095, charts the movement of crusader forces through the Byzantine Empire towards Jerusalem, describing battles and sieges, and culminates in the capture of the holy city. This became a model for narrative history.[2] Histories could also be crafted around the deeds of individuals, often monarchs. Narrative histories were often shaped by the sense of a historical or divine agenda or the need to flatter powerful men. Narratives can be read alongside other sources: for instance, the planning of crusades can be glimpsed in the charters (records of grants of lands and privileges) in which knights sold lands to finance their campaigns.[3]

From the beginning of the thirteenth century, a Europe-wide boom in record keeping offers a new level of insight into the planning and execution of operations, as government institutions produced increasing quantities of correspondence, financial accounts and contracts. The scale of bureaucratic

---

1 R. Hill (ed. and trans.), *Gesta Francorum et Aliorum Hierosolimitanorum* (London: Nelson, 1962).
2 Odo of Deuil, *De profectione Ludovici VII in Orientem* (ed. and trans. V. G. Berry) (New York: W. W. Norton, 1948).
3 G. Constable, 'Medieval charters as a source for the history of the crusades', in P. W. Edbury (ed.), *Crusade and Settlement: Papers Read at the First Conference of the Society for the Study of the Crusades and the Latin East and Presented to R. C. Smail* (Cardiff: University College of Cardiff Press, 1985), 73–89.

growth in England was ingeniously charted by Michael Clanchy through the quantity of sealing wax used by the royal chancery per week, which rose from 3.6 pounds in the mid-1220s to almost thirty-two pounds in the late 1260s.[4] Many governments also began to keep central copies of outgoing correspondence: the English royal chancery from the accession of King John (1199–1216), the papal chancery from the enthronement of Pope Innocent III (1198–1216). The increase in the sources available to historians from here is dramatic. While 303 of Innocent III's letters survive, 730 survive for the shorter pontificate of Innocent IV (1243–1254). In France, some 2,000 letters can be attributed to the administration of King Philip II Augustus (1180–1223), and some 15,000 to that of his grandson King Philip IV the Fair (1285–1314).[5] As Christian rulers conquered the southern reaches of the Iberian peninsula, they brought the (Islamic) paper industry under their control. Paper was much cheaper than parchment, so copies could be kept of government documents on a new scale. The registers of James I of Aragon, who conquered Játiva (the principal site of paper production in Valencia) by the mid-thirteenth century, number twenty-four and contain around 10,000 documents.[6] The registers of his great-grandson, Alfonso IV the Benign of Aragon (1327–1336) number ninety-three.[7] Such government records of the later Middle Ages illuminate matters from diplomatic relations to the planning and financing of campaigns, and the raising of armies.

Still, much has been lost in the passage of time and, occasionally, in singular disasters. In 1526, an attempted evacuation of the royal archive of Hungary after defeat against the Turks ended when the barge transporting the archive from Buda up the Danube to Bratislava sunk en route. The major part of Scotland's medieval archive was lost as the result of its removal by English conquerors, first King Edward I of England (1272–1307) and then Oliver Cromwell in 1650. The archive was to be returned to Scotland in 1660, but one of the two ships transporting it was wrecked. The archive of the Knights Templar in the Holy Land has vanished, having probably survived the fall of the Crusader States to the Mamluks in 1291 and the evacuation to Cyprus, as well as the order's dissolution in 1312, only to perish in the Ottoman invasion of Cyprus in 1571.

4 M. T. Clanchy, *From Memory to Written Record: England 1066–1307*, 2nd ed. (Oxford: Wiley, 1993), 59.

5 Clanchy, *From Memory to Written Record*, 61.

6 R. I. Burns, 'The paper revolution in Europe: Crusader Valencia's paper industry: A technological and behavioral breakthrough', *Pacific Historical Review*, 50 (1981), 1–30, 7.

7 L. J. McCrank, 'Documenting reconquest and reform: the growth of archives in the medieval crown of Aragon', *Society of American Archivists*, 56 (1993), 256–318, 295.

Actors

Europe was characterised by a multiplicity of polities of varied political structures, but the majority were unified by membership of the Catholic Church. Indeed, by the end of the twelfth century, Latin Christendom (those polities that at least nominally recognised papal authority and followed the Latin liturgy) had doubled in size. Frontiers were pushed forward in the Holy Land, Sicily and the Iberian Peninsula (territories that had been conquered and settled by Islamic rulers centuries earlier). Latin Christianity was implanted in Scandinavia and the Baltic, which had hitherto held to polytheistic paganism.[8] As this suggests, the papacy was the most powerful strategic actor. Popes were elected to provide leadership of Latin Christendom. They wielded the spiritual authority to launch the major multi-polity, long-distance expeditions necessary to confront Islamic rule, incentivising would-be participants with spiritual benefits, and commanded the international communications networks needed to publicise them. They were the legal superior of Latin Christendom's rulers, with the right to make and depose kings and intervene in disputes between or within polities. They could thus consolidate growth in the twelfth century by authorising the creation of new monarchies in Jerusalem, Sicily and Portugal, and in the thirteenth century in the Baltic by the establishment of the theocratic state of Christian Prussia under the Teutonic Knights. The pre-eminent role of the papacy, particularly between the mid-eleventh century and the late thirteenth, enabled strategy making on a near-global scale.

Within polities, established hierarchies and political processes offered customary means of establishing goals and planning their achievement. Whilst monarchy (rule by an individual, whether a king, a duke or a count) was the most common form of government, decision making was generally collective. Even anointed kings were expected to seek the advice of their leading men before taking important decisions, especially in planning wars, because such men were entitled to be consulted on matters that would impact them significantly. The process of 'taking counsel' was also intended to prevent rash decisions and ascertain the most productive course, and was seen as an essential part of good rulership; chroniclers and biographers were keen to note this in order to highlight a ruler's virtue. In his autobiography, James I of Aragon describes in expansive detail the process by which the conquest of Majorca was agreed upon

8 R. Bartlett, *The Making of Europe: Conquest, Colonization and Cultural Change, 950–1350* (London: Penguin, 1994), 5–23.

and planned.[9] James gathered his nobles in November 1228 at Tarragona, where they put the prospect to him; he then summoned a general assembly of the archbishop, 'the bishops, the abbots and the nobles . . . together with the citizens of Catalonia' to meet at his palace in Barcelona the following month. There he made a speech, requiring the advice of his assembled men

> in three things: first, that we may establish peace in our land; second, that we may be able to serve Our Lord in this voyage that we wish to make to the kingdom of Majorca and the other islands that pertain to it; and third, that we may accomplish this action to the honour of God.

Representatives of the prelates, nobles and cities deliberated amongst their cohorts for three days, while James held a 'secret council' with his noblemen, who urged him to undertake the conquest. At the appointed time, various named representatives of the three contingents stood in turn, offering their endorsement of the campaign and agreeing taxes to pay for it, and the number of knights or ships they could contribute. The conquest had been a goal of Catalan rulers for at least a century: Majorca and its neighbours were wealthy and offered control of the western Mediterranean seas, while winning lands from the *Dar al-Islam*, the Abode of Islam, would fulfil James's duty to bring them back into Christendom (the *Reconquista*). Still, the emphasis of the royal author himself on the consensual nature of the decision-making process highlights the importance placed upon it by the political community, as well as illuminating who was involved in such a decision and how.

On campaign, the same principle of consultative decision making applied, but smaller groups were involved. These comprised the chief noblemen of the expedition and, on crusading campaigns, representatives of the Templars and Hospitallers, and a papal legate if one was attached to the expedition. In 1192, King Richard I the Lionheart of England (1189–1199) had to decide whether to march on Jerusalem, the avowed goal of the Third Crusade. The Hospitallers and Templars, drawing from their local knowledge, made their position clear: Jerusalem was probably unobtainable and certainly impossible to hold.[10] Coming under pressure from the rank and file and French barons in his army to besiege Jerusalem, Richard reminded them that

---

9 James I of Aragon, *The Book of Deeds of James I of Aragon: A Translation of the Medieval Catalan Llibre dels Fets* (trans. D. Smith and H. Buffery) (Farnham: Ashgate, 2010), 69–78.
10 Ambroise, *The History of the Holy War* (ed. M. Ailes and M. Barber), 2 vols (Woodbridge: Boydell, 2003), ll. 7675–7702, 7746–65.

they did not know the country and 'must work through those who live in the land . . . and through the advice of the Templars, with the agreement of the Hospitallers' (according to Ambroise, the expedition's participant narrator). He established a council of twenty, composed equally of Templars, Hospitallers, Syrian knights and French barons, to decide the army's goal.[11] In 1249, once the forces of the Seventh Crusade had taken Damietta, Louis IX of France (1226–1270) 'summoned all the barons in the army in order to determine which route he should take, whether to Alexandria or Cairo' (as described by his biographer and crusade participant John of Joinville). The Count of Brittany and the majority favoured Alexandria, because its harbour would enable them to establish a new supply line. But Robert, Count of Artois, one of Louis's brothers, argued for Cairo, 'since it was the capital of the whole kingdom of Egypt, and . . . he who wishes to kill the serpent must first crush the head'.[12] Louis followed Robert's advice – as it turned out, with disastrous results. En route to Cairo the crusaders were defeated at the Battle of Mansurah (1250): Robert, whose rash charge had precipitated the battle, was killed together with a great many others, while Louis was taken prisoner.

Adversaries

There were a multiplicity of conflicts and adversaries both in the heartlands of western Christendom and on its frontiers. These can be crudely divided between intra- and inter-cultural wars: conflicts in which the adversaries were Latin Christians whose leaders shared the habitus of the chivalric elite, and those in which Latin Christians battled against enemies of another faith and culture who seemed to present a military and existential threat to Christendom itself. In some conflicts the two overlapped, when holy wars were waged within Europe against heretics or Christian rulers deemed to have threatened the church.

The monarchs of England and France were at war sporadically and then almost continually between the twelfth century and the mid-fifteenth, at first over competing territorial ambitions. A cross-channel dominion was created by the conquest of England by William, Duke of Normandy, in 1066, and was expanded at the accession of Henry II of England (1154–1189). Henry had inherited the duchy of Normandy; the counties of Anjou, Maine and

---

11 Ambroise, *History of the Holy War*, ll. 10124–96.

12 John of Joinville, 'The life of Saint Louis', in C. Smith (ed. and trans.), *Joinville and Villehardouin: Chronicles of the Crusades* (London: Penguin, 2008), 137–336, 190 (para. 183).

Touraine; and suzerainty over the duchy of Brittainy. His marriage to the great heiress Eleanor of Aquitaine brought him Poitou and Gascony. At the turn of the thirteenth century, the territory of the Capetian kings of France was small compared to that of the Angevin kings of England, with direct Capetian rule encompassing only a small region centred on Paris. Philip II, however, conquered the great majority of Angevin territories and his grandson, Louis IX, took Poitou in 1224, so that Henry III of England (1216–1272) was left only with Gascony and the Channel Islands. Despite their competing claims, conflict between the two royal houses was far from inevitable. Richard I of England and Philip II of France had been friends, and Richard was betrothed to Philip's sister, Alice. Relations broke down partly because of Richard's attempts to outdo Philip on the Third Crusade, and partly because Richard rejected Alice (although on the understandable grounds that she had slept with his father, Henry II). Peace between England and France was thus averted, and Richard's untimely death and the accession of his less capable brother, King John, opened the door for French territorial aggression. A new era of harmony was established following Henry III of England's failed Continental campaigns in the middle years of the thirteenth century: he and Louis IX had married sisters (heirs to the house of Provence) and became brothers-in-law and allies.

In the fourteenth century, their successors embarked on what was to become known as the Hundred Years War (1337–1453), this time over competing claims to the crown of France. King Edward III of England (1327–1377) staked his hereditary claim to the French crown after Charles IV of France (1322–1328) died without a direct male heir, but the crown went to Philip of Valois. As Philip VI of France (1328–1350), he confiscated Edward's possessions in south-west France. Edward declared himself king of France in 1340 and, with the help of his son, the Black Prince, achieved several victories over the following three decades. Other polities were pulled into the conflict, with Edward securing allies across the Low Countries and the French enjoying an alliance with the Scots. The Black Prince also became involved in a civil war in the Iberian peninsula, on the side of Pedro II the Cruel of Castile (1350–1366 and 1367–1369). He led an Anglo-Gascon force over the Pyrenees in 1367, and at the Battle of Nájera defeated an army of Castilian and Aragonese troops supported by Franco-Breton and Genoese mercenaries. The Anglo-French war was renewed by Henry V of England (1413–1422), taking advantage of civil conflict in France between the Burgundian and Armagnac factions. Henry invaded France and won a famous victory at the Battle of Agincourt (1415), going on to conquer Normandy. With Burgundian support, he married Catherine, daughter of Charles VI of France (1380–1422), and was recognised as Charles's successor. This might have presaged an era of Anglo-French peace, albeit on terms highly favourable to the English king. But the deaths of both Henry V and Charles VI in 1422 opened the way for the Armagnacs to promote the cause of Charles VI's natural heir, the dauphin Charles. In 1429 the dauphin's cause was transformed by the apparently miraculous intervention of Joan of Arc, who led the French to victory at the Siege of Orléans and saw the dauphin crowned as Charles VII (1429–1461). In 1449 Charles retook Normandy and captured Gascony, sealing his victory at the Battle of Castillon in 1453. Only Calais remained under English dominion, held until 1558. The conflict between England and France, and their respective allies, thus dominated much of this period.

This was not by any means the only intra-cultural war of the era. For instance, the Hohenstaufen dynasty became embroiled in a conflict with the papacy in the thirteenth century. Frederick II, king of Germany from 1212 and Holy Roman Emperor from 1220, inherited the kingdom of Sicily and set about asserting imperial power in northern Italy, before threatening the papacy's own territories in central Italy. Pope Innocent IV deposed Frederick at the Council of Lyon in 1245, and the papacy went on to wage a war to oust the Hohenstaufen from its power base in southern Italy, licensing first Henry III of England and then Charles, Count of Anjou, a brother of Louis IX of France, to conquer the kingdom of Sicily on its behalf and rule there as king of Sicily (1266–1285). Participating in these wars and others were Pisa, Genoa and Venice. The wealth and power of the maritime republics grew in concert with Latin Christendom, their shipbuilding industries providing the fleets for crusades and their own controlling trade routes and outposts from the Balearic Islands to southern France and Italy, the Byzantine Empire, the Holy Land, Egypt and north-west Africa. The three maritime powers competed against each other for market share, through trade agreements with various rulers and open war on land and sea. Wars were also waged in the northern reaches of Europe, particularly over mercantile interests. Between the mid-twelfth century and the mid-seventeenth, trade across the North Sea and the Baltic Sea was dominated by the Hanse, a network of Germanic traders and towns (the most important of which was Lübeck) co-operating for the purpose of profitable trade. In response to privateer attacks on English merchant vessels, Edward IV of England (1461–1470 and 1471–1483) revoked the Hanse's trading privileges in his kingdom, prompting the Hanse to launch a maritime war against England in 1469.

At the same time, vast reserves of military energy were directed against the enemies of Christendom, principally the Abode of Islam. In 1095, an appeal from the Byzantine emperor for aid against the Seljuk Turks moved Urban II to launch the First Crusade. The crusaders defeated the Seljuks but relations with the Byzantine emperor were tense, with the crusaders refusing to deliver Antioch (formerly a Byzantine possession) when they wrested it from Seljuk hands. The Muslim revanche of the following century was led by Saladin, who took over Fatimid Egypt and then Zangid Syria in the 1170s, commanding vast resources to take on the Crusader States of the Middle East. He inflicted a cataclysmic defeat on Christian forces at the Battle of Hattin in 1187, before taking Jerusalem. The Third Crusade, led by Richard I of England and Philip II of France, sought to challenge Saladin's grip on the Holy Land, with some success. Saladin's dynasty, the Ayyubids, were overthrown in a coup by their slave soldiers, the Mamluks, in 1250, in the course of the Seventh Crusade. The Mamluk sultan, Baybars, waged a devastating campaign against the Crusader States and, in 1291, under al-Ashraf Khalil, the Mamluks took the last remaining Christian stronghold, Acre.

This brought to an end almost two centuries of Latin Christian government in the Holy Land, and the regular dispatch to the Middle East and north Africa of Europe's warriors both in small bands and in major multi-polity expeditions. Hopes of reclaiming the Holy Land were still cherished in Europe in the following century, encouraged by possession of Cyprus and Rhodes, the former taken by Richard I of England during the Third Crusade, the latter conquered from the Byzantine Empire by the Hospitallers in the early 1300s. Sporadic campaigns were launched, including one to Mamluk Alexandria led by Peter I of Cyprus (1359–1369) in 1365, although, after sacking the city, the crusaders withdrew with their plunder.

Meanwhile, increasing crusading energy was channelled into Baltic campaigns. Since the twelfth century the Latin Church had targeted this pagan region through evangelisation and holy war: the West Slavs of Mecklenburg and Brandenburg were incorporated into Latin Christendom in the twelfth century, and Estonia, Livonia and Prussia in the thirteenth. Lithuania's pagans resisted absorption into Latin Christendom and forged a large and powerful state. By the mid-fourteenth century, this had become a regular destination for crusaders from western Europe, who were hosted by the Teutonic Knights for seasonal campaigns. These continued even after Lithuania's grand duke converted to Christianity in 1386 (when he married the queen of Poland), before tailing off in the fifteenth century.

Western Christendom also confronted a new threat from the Mongols, who emerged as an all-conquering force in the early decades of the thirteenth century. Their armies swept across China and threatened Christian territories in the Holy Land (they were stopped by Baybars at the Battle of Ayn Jalut in 1260) and eastern Europe. Mongol forces took Kiev in 1240 and Cracow in 1241, before conducting a campaign of devastation across the kingdom of Hungary. Europe's rulers were alive to the danger (both Innocent IV and Louis IX of France sent diplomatic envoys to the Mongols), but the ongoing conflict between Frederick II and the papacy threatened to open Europe to Mongol invasion. In the end the Mongols withdrew, either as a result of internal divisions or because the devastation of Hungary left its lands unable to support their armies, but Hungary and Poland still suffered from Mongol attacks in the following decades.

Throughout the period, Christian rulers of the Iberian peninsula were engaged in the *Reconquista* of territory from the Muslim rulers of the south. It culminated in the campaigns of Queen Isabella I of Castile (1474–1504) and Ferdinand II of Aragon (1479–1516), which in 1492 secured the territory of the Nasrid Emirate of Granada, the last remaining Muslim polity in Europe.

Cultures of War and Motivations to Fight: Historiographic Debates and Sources

In both intra- and inter-cultural conflicts, facets of the culture shared by the military and ecclesiastical elite of Latin Christendom created the conditions for war and encouraged the participation of individuals. These included a sense of religious mission and a military culture that prized conquest, prowess and matching the achievements of ancestors. In a society in which the spiritual and the secular were not divisible according to modern conceptions, these factors tended to be present in all conflicts in various measures, and were generally seen as compatible.

To some extent a culture of conquest encouraged knights to push forward Latin Christendom's frontiers. Many leaders of the First Crusade were related to participants in the Norman conquests of Sicily and England of the 1060s. The knightly generation of the 1090s could thus draw from practical experience of large-scale campaigns, but were also encouraged to consider a venture of their own to compare in scale and risk (and therefore renown) with those of their fathers. The precedents of conquest could also reassure them that such highly risky expeditions could succeed, and could bring lands and glory for their leaders. Thus 'material questions, land, plunder, worldly success and martial honour' were an integral part of knightly culture in the age of the First Crusade.[13]

---

13 K. Kjær, 'Conquests, family traditions and the First Crusade', *Journal of Medieval History*, 45 (2019), 553–79, 579.

Map 13.1 Strategies in Latin Christendom in the later Middle Ages 1000–1500

But religious motivation was crucial from the beginning, and especially so in the ensuing crusades, where almost invariably cost hugely outweighed any

Map 13.1 (Cont.)

economic benefit for crusaders. The materialist view popular in the middle
decades of the twentieth century – that crusading was motivated exclusively by

imperialist mentalities and the desire to accrue lands and moveable wealth – was shown to be untenable in the 1980s by Jonathan Riley-Smith, amongst whose work the seminal article 'Crusading as an act of love' showed the prevalence of *caritas* (self-sacrificing, generous love for God and fellow Christians) in crusade sermons.[14] Charters issued by crusading knights evidence their belief that in fighting for the church they would atone for their sin, their acceptance of their likely death on campaign, and the significant financial outlays they made to finance their expeditions.[15] Indeed, the cost of mounting campaigns was monumental, and for many knights could require the sale or mortgage of precious hereditable land at home. Rulers bankrolling expeditions were required to dedicate state resources on a massive scale: Louis IX of France laid out perhaps 1.5 million pounds *tournois* for the Seventh Crusade, at a time when the Crown's annual income was around 250,000 pounds. Such outlays were an investment: the return was spiritual, not economic, capital.

More broadly, it is now generally recognised that the church's great achievement from the late eleventh century was to turn the energies of the military elite away from internecine conflict and towards the frontiers of Christendom. In so doing it offered knights, who held a profound sense of the sinfulness of their profession when shedding Christian blood, an opportunity to use their skills and bellicose temperaments in the service of the church and to achieve salvation. For crusaders, the theology of holy war encouraged the shedding not only of enemy blood but also of their own. The belief that those who died as sworn crusaders on expedition were martyrs, whose death earned their place in heaven beside the saints, emerged amongst the earliest crusaders – so much is attested by the *Gesta Francorum*.[16] In the twelfth and thirteenth centuries, the death of knightly combatants was far more likely fighting on Christendom's frontiers than in its heartlands, where knights were largely protected by ransoming culture. Participant accounts show just how costly crusading was in terms of lives lost, whether in battle or through disease or deprivation – for kings as much as the lowliest crusaders.[17] Crucially, the crusading cause and its spiritual merit were woven into life at home through liturgy: the masses, prayers, hymns and processions shared by all Christians, male and female of every status, across Latin Christendom. Cecilia Gaposchkin has revealed how liturgy 'embedded the aspirations of

14 J. Riley-Smith, 'Crusading as an act of love', *History*, 65 (1980), 177–92.
15 Constable, 'Medieval charters'.
16 S. Niskanen, 'The origins of the *Gesta Francorum* and two related texts: their textual and literary character', *Sacris Erudiri*, 51 (2012), 287–316, 305–9.
17 See, for instance, Joinville, 'The life of Saint Louis', 199–245 (paras 216–405).

crusade into the fabric of Western culture', making it 'one of the mechanisms that constructed the Latin West as a crusading society, defined ... by ... a general and ongoing commitment to warring with the infidel'.[18]

At the same time, profound spiritual motivations for crusading went hand in hand with aspects of chivalric culture that encouraged all military endeavours. Values such as loyalty, forbearance, hardihood, largesse, the duty to defend the weak, and honour were embedded in elite culture through the histories and *chansons de geste* on which young nobles were raised and which were sung in the feasting hall, contributing to the 'noble habitus'.[19] All warfare offered the opportunity for knights to demonstrate these virtues, including the crusades. And whilst knights might hope to emulate the deeds and virtues of the knightly heroes of history and literature, they also looked to their own fathers and ancestors as exemplars. 'Family memory' of earlier crusading was passed down across the generations in the twelfth and thirteenth centuries, through texts, tales and objects, so that new generations were exhorted to 'follow in the footsteps' of their renowned forebears.[20] Across the period, spiritual and chivalric motivations could be combined unproblematically. As Thibault, Count of Champagne and leader of the Barons' Crusade of the late 1230s, explained in one of his poems,

> Lords, know this: whoever will not now go to that land where God died and rose again ... will find it hard ever to go to heaven ... Soon those valiant young men who love God and the honour of this world, who wisely wish to proceed towards God, will set out on their way; and the snotty-nosed fainthearts and the lechers will stay behind ... Whoever does not aid God at least once in his lifetime, and at so little cost, loses the glory of the world.[21]

Objectives and Prioritisation

The underlying goal of the papacy, in concert with Europe's secular rulers, especially between the later eleventh century and the later thirteenth, was the expansion of Latin Christendom into those regions that had been under

---

18 M. C. Gaposchkin, *Invisible Weapons: Liturgy and the Making of Crusade Ideology* (Ithaca and London: Cornell University Press, 2017), 7, 12.

19 D. Crouch, *The Birth of the Nobility: Constructing Aristocracy in England and France, 900–1300* (Harlow: Longman Pearson, 2005), 46–80.

20 N. Paul, *To Follow in their Footsteps: The Crusades and Family Memory in the High Middle Ages* (Ithaca and London: Cornell University Press, 2012).

21 Thibaut de Champagne, 'Seignor, sachiez, qui or ne s'an ira', trans. from *Troubadours, Trouvères and the Crusades*, at https://warwick.ac.uk/fac/arts/modernlanguages/research/french/crusades/texts/of/rs6/page1.

Muslim or pagan rule and the security of Christian territories. The jewel in the crown was Jerusalem, whose centrality in Christian (as well as Islamic and Jewish) faith meant that its possession was the chief objective of the age. It is not certain that the taking of Jerusalem was named as the goal of the First Crusade by Urban II (as opposed or in addition to the security of the Byzantine Empire), because reports of the Pope's sermon were produced years later, perhaps with the benefit of hindsight.[22] From the perspective of the early 1100s, however, the *Gesta Francorum* frames the capture of Jerusalem and the ability of Christians to visit its holy sites as the goal of the First Crusaders themselves.[23] The city was lost to Saladin in 1187, and its reclamation was the ultimate goal of crusading efforts over the following century. But it was also clear that Christendom would need to secure other territories to support the achievement of that goal. Thus, while the Third Crusade was intended to take Jerusalem, Richard I of England captured the island of Cyprus en route to the Holy Land, and aided the capture of the port city of Acre in 1191 (both sites would be critical in facilitating future Christian expeditions, Acre until its fall to the Mamluks in 1291 and Cyprus until its fall to the Ottomans in 1571).

From the early twelfth century, it was recognised that possession of Egypt (then held by the Fatimid Caliphate) would underpin the long-term security of the Crusader States, given its economic might and control of trade routes, and the military threat its forces posed. Five attempts to take Egypt were made by Amalric I of Jerusalem (1163–1174). Saladin's seizure of Fatimid Egypt and then Zangid Syria in the 1170s made the objective more urgent, since he now commanded vast resources and could move troops from one territory to the next and attack the Crusader States by land from all sides. There was a tension, however, between the recognised strategic need to take Egypt and the allure of securing Jerusalem. The council of Templars, Hospitallers and Syrian and French knights established by Richard I of England in 1192 had advised an attempt on Egypt, but the bulk of the crusader army would not consider any destination but Jerusalem.[24] Egypt was named as the destination for the ill-fated Fourth Crusade, when French crusade leaders contracted the city state of Venice in 1201 to provide a transport fleet, but this was kept secret from the rank and file of the army, for fear they would only want to participate in a campaign to the Holy Land. The Fourth Crusade was

---

22 E. Peters (ed.), *The First Crusade: The Chronicles of Fulcher of Chartres and other Source Materials*, 2nd ed. (Philadelphia: University of Pennsylvania Press, 1998), 25–37.

23 *Gesta Francorum*, 87–103; Niskanen, '*Gesta Francorum*', 299–302.

24 Ambroise, *The History of the Holy War*, ll. 10185–200.

notoriously diverted after the crusaders failed to fulfil the terms of the 1201 treaty and accepted Venice's plans for recouping its lost investment, first targeting the Christian city of Zara on the Dalmatian coast and then Byzantine Constantinople, which city the crusaders eventually sacked before installing a Latin emperor on the throne. But a renewed attempt to pursue the Egyptian strategy was made with the Fifth Crusade, which headed for Ayyubid Egypt in 1218. The crusaders took Damietta, but their advance up the Nile delta ended in disaster, and they were forced to surrender the city in 1221 in return for their safe withdrawal. The Seventh Crusade, led by Louis IX of France, also targeted Ayyubid Egypt (although the Ayyubids were overthrown by the Mamluks during the course of the war). This expedition also took Damietta but ultimately ended in failure, at the Battle of Mansurah, in 1250. Egypt was a sound strategic objective, and the failure to take it would undermine the efforts of Latin Christendom's leaders to achieve the ultimate goal of securing the Holy Land, as actors were well aware. In the event the situation was especially perilous, since the Mamluks, fresh from their seizure of power in Egypt, would sweep all before them and ultimately bring down the last bastion of the Crusader States, Acre, in 1291.

Meanwhile, the papacy and secular rulers were balancing the security of the Holy Land with other objectives closer to home. Innocent III, after the setback of the Fourth Crusade, co-ordinated two major campaigns in the early thirteenth century – the 'reconquest' of the Iberian Peninsula from the Almohad caliphate and the Albigensian Crusade against the so-called Cathar heretics of Languedoc – at the same time as planning the next attempt on Egypt (what would be the Fifth Crusade, launched by his successor). Since the mid-twelfth century, popes had set the security of Christian Iberia on a par with that of the Holy Land by offering equal spiritual benefits for participants. In 1212, Innocent III ordered liturgical processions across Europe for the Iberian cause and paused the Albigensian Crusade, diverting troops across the Pyrenees to join the combined forces of the kings of Castile, Aragon, Navarre and Portugal. This vast coalition secured a pivotal victory at the Battle of Las Navas de Tolosa, in 1212.[25]

The fall of the Crusader States at the end of the thirteenth century refocused the ambitions of Europe's elite. While there had always been intra-cultural wars within Europe, it is hard to imagine such a protracted conflict as the Hundred Years War before the fourteenth century, given the drain on

---

25 J. Bird, E. Peters and J. M. Powell (eds), *Crusade and Christendom: Annotated Documents in Translation from Innocent III to the Fall of Acre, 1187–1291* (Philadelphia: University of Pennsylvania Press, 2013), 82–95.

financial, human and emotional resources brought by crusading expeditions. Even before the fall of Acre, England's kings were newly ambitious in extending their dominion, enabled by systems of credit that made the financing of campaigns more efficient, and increasingly sophisticated means of raising armies. Edward I of England (1272–1307) set out to conquer first Wales and then Scotland, creating what Sir Rees Davies termed 'the first English Empire'. Determined campaigns brought Wales under English rule in 1282, with the killing of the last native prince of Wales, Llywelyn ap Gruffudd. Edward's dreams of rule over Wales and Scotland were fuelled by the legends of King Arthur. In 1284, he celebrated his victory at Nefyn, in north-west Wales, site of the supposed discovery of the prophecies of Merlin, and went on to build across the region a string of castles, the greatest of which, Caernarfon, was designed to call to mind imperial Constantinople.[26] The practical benefits of conquering Wales were also recognised, with Edward able to draw on a new pool of manpower. The English king advanced into Scotland in 1298, towards eventual victory at the Battle of Falkirk, at the head of probably the greatest army hitherto seen in the Atlantic Archipelago: 26,000 infantry and 3,000 cavalry. Over 10,000 of the infantrymen were raised from Wales.

The conquest of Scotland, a sovereign kingdom, was legally problematic and Edward strove to provide justification for his ambition. In 1291, as he began to intrude himself into Scottish affairs, he commanded the monasteries of England, 'scrutinize your chronicles, and [send] everything which you find there concerning those things which touch our kingdom and the governance of Scotland'. This enabled Edward to instruct Scottish prelates and magnates on the historicity of his claim to dominion over their kingdom.[27] Resistance was led by Robert I of Scotland (1306–1329). With comparably small financial and military resources, Robert employed the infantry tactics that had begun to transform warfare in the early 1300s, bringing down the English cavalry at the Battle of Bannockburn in 1314. In 1320, together with his prelates and magnates, he appealed to the Pope, in the document known as the Declaration of Arbroath. They contradicted Edward's claims by establishing the historicity of the Scottish nation and aligning the English king with past tyrants deposed by the papacy, and justified continued military resistance by pronouncing Robert 'another Maccabaeus' (the Old Testament warrior whom the church held up as

---

26 R. R. Davies, *The First English Empire: Power and Identities in the British Isles 1093–1343* (Oxford: Oxford University Press, 2000), 31–2.

27 A. Taylor, 'Recalling Anglo-Scottish relations in 1291: historical knowledge, monastic memory and the Edwardian inquests', in A. M. Spencer and C. Watkins (eds), *Thirteenth Century England*, Volume XVI (Woodbridge: Boydell, 2017), 173–206, 173–4.

a model for crusaders) and underlining his legitimacy as king of Scots.[28] 'As long as a hundred of us remain alive', they famously proclaimed, 'never will we on any conditions be subjected to the lordship of the English. It is in truth not for glory, nor riches, nor honours that we are fighting, but for freedom alone, which no honest man gives up but with life itself'. Actors on both sides, then, saw themselves as heirs of a historic, biblical and legendary past that could help to form and certainly to justify their objectives. In Scotland, this process was intertwined with a growing Scottish national identity: for much of the thirteenth century, the political and learned elite had not necessarily regarded themselves as Scottish;[29] by 1320, after decades of English aggression, it had produced one of the most famous declarations of national identity and political sovereignty in Western history.

Means

Military Means

In the Middle Ages, as in antiquity, the estimations of army sizes in narrative sources need to be taken with a heavy dose of salt; along with composition and organisation, it varied greatly across the period. In general, armies were not standing armies but raised for particular campaigns. The papacy had no military resources of its own, and so raised armies for crusades from across Christendom by appealing directly to rulers and broadcasting calls to the faithful. Determining the size of forces based only on chronicle estimates is notoriously problematic, but those of the major crusading expeditions were certainly huge by any standard, indeed sometimes too large. In calling the Second Crusade in 1145, Pope Eugenius III (1145–1153) aimed to form a compact and well-equipped force composed mostly of knights, but the preaching campaign led by Bernard of Clairvaux was so successful that the force was vast and included many unskilled participants. Ill discipline and pressure on markets caused tension with the Byzantines as the army, opting to follow literally in the footsteps of the First Crusaders by taking a landward

---

28 'Declaration of Arbroath', text and translation compiled from scholarly editions available via the National Records of Scotland at www.nrscotland.gov.uk/files/research/declar ation-of-arbroath/declaration-of-arbroath-transcription-and-translation.pdf; S. Tebbit, 'Papal pronouncements on legitimate lordship and the formulation of nationhood in early fourteenth-century Scottish writings', *Journal of Medieval History*, 40 (2014), 44–62, 46, 55–61.

29 D. Broun, 'Defining Scotland and the Scots before the wars of independence', in D. Broun, R. J. Finlay and M. Lynch (eds), *Image and Identity: The Making and Re- making of Scotland through the Ages* (Edinburgh: John Donald, 1998), 4–17.

route, traversed imperial territory, and the crusaders came to ruin trying to navigate the passes of Mount Cadmus while under attack. With the lessons of the Second Crusade learned, later major expeditions were borne across the Mediterranean in fleets provided mostly by the maritime republics. For the Third Crusade, Philip II of France paid the Genoese to carry his 6,500 knights and 1,300 squires to Acre. The 1201 contract with French leaders of the Fourth Crusade required Venice to provide more than 200 transport ships for 94,000 silver marks, entailing a massive shipbuilding operation. The number of ships required turned out to be a huge overestimation, which threatened to bankrupt Venice. The size of the army led by Louis IX of France on the Seventh Crusade, estimated from chroniclers' accounts and some surviving records, was perhaps 15,000, of whom 2,500 to 2,800 were knights. For their transport, Louis contracted thirty-six ships himself from Genoa and Marseilles, and subsidised transport contracts made by various of his barons. The chosen port of embarkation in 1248 was Aigues-Mortes, hitherto a village: in the space of under four years, Louis invested heavily in its development in order to establish a port controlled by the Capetian kings.

The need to create a stable, well-resourced and proficient force to ensure the security of the Crusader States was addressed in the early twelfth century with the creation of the Knights Templar and Hospitaller, monastic orders dedicated to the military defence of Christendom. Supported by donations from the faithful, they built a significant landed base across Europe and the Holy Land to finance their operations. The orders' core knightly combatants were distinguished on the whole by their unparalleled skills, knowledge and experience, and were supported by their many non-combatant members. These were, effectively, the standing armies of crusading Christendom. They were thus central to any crusading campaign, but also bore heavy losses, especially as they did not flee the field. Our figures here are more reliable than in most cases, because of the compact nature of the orders and their reporting of casualty figures. In the twelfth century, the Templars' standing force in the Kingdom of Jerusalem might have numbered 300 knights; in the calamitous defeats by Saladin of 1187, the order lost 290 knights, and 280 were killed at the Battle of Mansurah in 1250.[30] The Templars were dissolved in 1312 and their possessions transferred to the Hospitallers, who in the later Middle Ages became a major naval power and in the sixteenth century led resistance against the Ottomans.

30 M. Barber, *The New Knighthood* (Cambridge: Cambridge University Press, 1994), 230, 232.

Unlike expeditions to the Holy Land and north Africa, those within Europe, especially in the first half of the period, were generally short and seasonal. Armies were thus commonly raised for fixed terms (customarily forty days) by systems of feudal obligation. Magnates and prelates provided a certain number of knights for their ruler when required, and settlements provided a number of infantrymen proportionate to population size. Rulers supplemented such forces by hiring paid troops, so that mercenaries (that is, men who served for pay without a particular tie to the ruler hiring them) were a normal part of warfare across the period. In the later Middle Ages, armies were increasingly professionalised, in the sense that troops were raised within polities according to agreed terms and served for pay. The English state developed a system for contracting armies in the fourteenth century, in support of its protracted wars against Scotland and France. A formal, written agreement (an indenture) set out the number and type of troops a nobleman was to supply for a campaign, and under what terms they would serve. Surviving indentures and other documentation, such as muster rolls, allow historians to trace the repeated and regular service of many individuals, as well as the changing composition of armies. For instance, the proportion of archers to men-at-arms in the English army rose from one to one in the fourteenth century to three to one under Henry V for the Agincourt campaign of 1415, because archers were relatively cheap and prodigiously effective. These records also allow a degree of certainty in gauging army sizes: for the 1415 campaign, Henry V agreed indentures with around 320 noblemen to raise around 12,000 troops for a year. Troops were borne across the English Channel by merchant vessels requisitioned from English ports. In this way Edward III of England could raise fleets of between 400 and 700 vessels; Henry V's Agincourt campaign probably required some 450 English merchant vessels, together with over 250 hired foreign ships.

Rulers operated in the longer term by forging alliances to secure peace, territory or military aid. The optimum form was an arranged marriage, since these could serve objectives over decades and even generations, with parties holding a personal stake in the outcome. Henry III of England faced civil war in the 1260s but was saved partly by marriage alliances made earlier in his reign. His queen, Eleanor of Provence, worked with her sister Marguerite, queen of France, and brother-in-law, Louis IX of France, to raise an armada and act in concert with the papacy to reclaim Henry's throne. Henry was also aided by Alexander III of Scotland (1249–1286), who had married Henry's daughter, Margaret, in 1251. Thus France and Scotland – two powers that could have disrupted the prospects of the English crown, as they had during the reign of King John and would do again in the Hundred Years War – were Henry's invaluable allies. Written treaties also served to secure military alliances and trading privileges. These were numerous in the case of the maritime republics, who agreed commercial treaties with Christian rulers across the Mediterranean and with Islamic rulers in north Africa. Meanwhile, intermittent attempts were made to secure peace between them. Pope Honorius III (1216–1227) established a peace between Genoa and Pisa, and Genoa and Venice, to enable the Fifth Crusade: both Pisa and Venice thus contributed galleys to the expedition and Venice imposed a trade embargo on Egypt.

Non-military Means

Beyond employing military force, legal means of pursuing objectives were also available, especially in the case of the papacy, whose legal authority was elevated above that of secular rulers in the later eleventh century. This enabled popes to shape political structures on the ground to support the expansion of Latin Christendom. As we have seen, twelfth-century popes had created new frontier kingdoms in Jerusalem, Sicily and Portugal. In the early thirteenth century, Innocent III redrew diocesan boundaries in the Iberian peninsula so that episcopal territories would cut across multiple kingdoms. His plan was to create a supra-regnal episcopate that, unbeholden to regnal divisions, could unite secular leaders in the pursuit of the crusade. In 1245, Innocent IV responded to complaints from the bishops and barons of Portugal that their king, Sancho II, was inadequate and failing to prosecute the crusade by pronouncing Sancho *rex inutilis* (literally 'useless king', a designation in canon law) in order to remove him from power. The Pope could also seek to compel obstructive rulers by excommunication, denying them the sacraments and enjoining fellow Christians to shun them, thus undermining their authority. Innocent III excommunicated King John of England in 1209 when the king refused to admit the Pope's candidate to the archbishopric of Canterbury. John submitted in 1213, was absolved, and further offered England as a papal fief, gaining special papal protection. Legates sent by the Pope, bearing his full authority, were crucial in saving the kingdom for John and his son Henry III in the civil wars of 1215–1217 and 1263–1267, excommunicating rebels and helping to lead the royal revanche. The papacy could also incentivise Christians to contribute to its causes, by offering spiritual benefits to those taking part in its sanctioned crusades, as well as the legal protection for their lands that would enable them to leave their dominions for extended periods.

Both ecclesiastical and secular rulers across Latin Christendom also employed spiritual means to pursue their objectives. Whilst they marshalled their financial and military resources, they knew well that factors beyond their own control could determine outcomes. Whilst a (modern) atheist actor might call these 'luck', a member of the faithful would attribute them to divine intervention and, recognising that God favours the righteous, would see the winning of his favour as critical to success. For this purpose the church mobilised entire populations, utilising the networks that connected the Pope – through cardinals, archbishops, bishops and deans – to parish clergy. Collective prayers, processions, fasting and masses could, as we have seen, serve to embed crusading ideology and encourage military, financial and emotional support for expeditions. But, first and foremost, these were what Honorius III called 'invisible weapons'.[31] When news reached the papal court of the annihilation of Christian forces by Saladin at the Battle of Hattin in 1187, the instantaneous response, set out in the papal proclamation *Audita Tremendi*, was to establish a liturgical campaign that would summon the entire Christian faithful to repentance, to be enacted across Christendom with the greatest urgency.[32] This was the priority not only because an expedition to confront Saladin would take months to organise, but also because such an expedition would have no effect unless divine favour could be reclaimed. All the Christian faithful were thus responsible for the security of the Holy Land.[33] On a smaller scale, the same principle applied within polities, and similar means were employed to mobilise populations to win divine support. Edward I of England, for instance, utilised ecclesiastical networks within his kingdom both to issue official justifications and accounts of his wars and to request prayers and processions in support of the kingdom's cause, and the same system was used extensively by Edward III in his war against France.[34]

---

31 Whence the title of Gaposchkin, *Invisible Weapons*.
32 'Audita Tremendi', in Bird, Peters and Powell, *Crusade and Christendom*, 4–9.
33 T. W. Smith, '*Audita Tremendi* and the call for the Third Crusade reconsidered, 1187–88', *Viator*, 49 (2018), 63–101, 86.
34 D. S. Bachrach, 'The Ecclesia Anglicana goes to war: prayers, propaganda, and conquest during the reign of Edward I of England, 1272–1307', *Albion*, 36 (2004), 393–406.

14

Chinggis Khan and the Mongol Empire,
AD 1206 to 1368

TIMOTHY MAY

Sources

The study of Mongol strategy faces the same basic problem that one encounters when dealing with any aspect of the Mongol Empire: languages. As David Morgan wrote,

> The sources available to the historian are in Mongolian, Chinese, Persian, Arabic, Turkish, Japanese, Russian, Armenian, Georgian, Latin, and other languages. No one can hope to be able to read more than a fraction of them in the original. Then there is the cultural difficulty. Even if we could read the sources in all these languages, could we be sure that we had understood them correctly? The societies of medieval China, Islam, Europe, and the steppe peoples were all different from one another; their historical writing has different assumptions and different conventions, and is underlain by quite different patterns of thought.[1]

The matter is further complicated as Mongol strategy can only be deduced and inferred from the sources. Most chronicles, such as from the Armenian, Georgian, Japanese, Korean, Arabic, Latin and Rus' sources, are useful for understanding the events of particular regional campaigns. Rarely do they provide direct insight to strategy. Even the sources closest to the Mongol perspective, such as inscriptions and the *Secret History of the Mongols*, do not provide a lucid understanding of Mongol strategy. Again, careful analysis must be given and then compared with other sources to ascertain the Mongols' actual intent.

Chinese and Persian sources remain the most important sources for the study of Mongol strategy due to volume and their tendency to consider events across the entire empire. From the Chinese sources, numerous biographies in the *Yuan Shi* provide details on campaigns and strategic decisions,

---

1 D. Morgan, *The Mongols*, 2nd ed. (Malden, MA: Blackwell, 2007), 5.

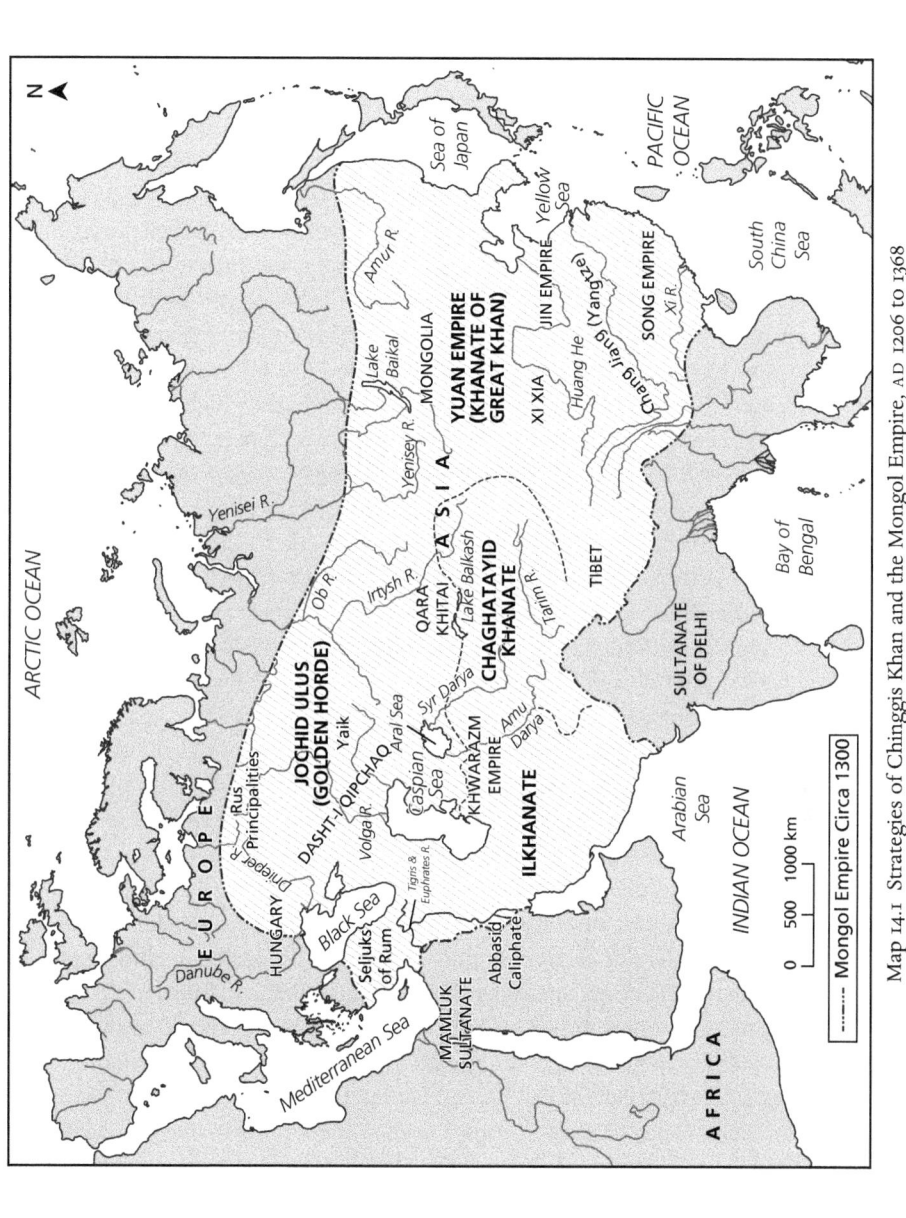

Map 14.1 Strategies of Chinggis Khan and the Mongol Empire, AD 1206 to 1368

but a complete picture of a single campaign must often be assembled like a puzzle from various entries of the participants. The *Shengwu Qin Zhenglu* (The Campaigns of the Holy Warrior (Chinggis Khan)) is clearly Mongolian in idiom, although the source only remains in Chinese. Still, it provides us with an account of Chinggis Khan's campaigns in China as well as his rise in the steppes of Mongolia, but lacks the more personal details of the *Secret History*. Of course, other official sources, reports, inscriptions and gazetteers provide supporting information as well.

The Persian sources are more direct. Like the *Yuan Shi*, at times direct information regarding Mongol strategy is apparent due to the number of Persians who wrote while serving in the Mongol government, such as Juwaynī, who wrote the *Jahan-i Gusha,* which provides great detail about events from 1210 to 1256. Waṣṣāf provides a continuation of Juwaynī's account. Rashid al-Din, wrote the *Jami' al-Tawarikh,* which drew heavily on Juwaynī and the *Shengwu Qin Zhenglu,* but also adds new information. Other Persian sources, such as *Akhbar-i Mughulan* by Shīrāzī, provide new details, but again from within the Mongol Empire. Jūzjānī, who fled the Mongols and wrote from the safety of the Delhi Sultanate due to the Mongol invasions, also provides a copious amount of information on many Mongol campaigns, particularly in central Asia and Iran.

While most Arabic sources were written from outside the Mongol Empire, a few do provide a broader picture than just regional events, thus assisting in understanding Mongol strategy. The earliest is Ibn al-Athīr's (d. 1233) voluminous *Al- Kāmil fī al-Tārīkh* and Muhammad al-Nasawī's *Sīrat Sultan Jalāl al-Din Mankobirtī.* Both tell of the invasion of the Islamic world by the Mongols, but include events outside the Islamic Empire, providing context for why the Mongols made certain decisions. From the later part of the thirteenth century, a number of Arabic sources emerge, primarily in the Mamlūk Sultanate. Of particular importance is al-Umarī's encyclopedia, which contains a considerable section on the Mongols. Additionally, al-Nuwayrī wrote a separate treatise on the Mongols within his *Nihāyat al-'arab.*

While few of the travel sources provide copious information on strategy and military matters, all comment on it. Furthermore, the information from various correspondents can be corroborated in other accounts, if not in the chronicles. Thus Chinese accounts such as the reports in the *Mengda Beilu* of Zhao Gong (a Song general) and the *Heida shi lüe* of Peng Daya and Xu Ting (Song envoys) balance those of the Franciscan friars, William of Rubruck and John de Plano Carpini, and even those of the well-known travellers such as Marco Polo and Ibn Battuta. Carpini is instructive as not only is he clear on the Mongols' intent (to conquer Europe), but he also includes suggestions as to how to repel the Mongols. While some have dismissed his ideas, they are actually quite sound. Although it is unlikely that someone listened to his ideas, as Plano Carpini was a Franciscan friar, they still demonstrate a competent understanding of Mongol warfare. While he did not witness Mongol military actions, it is clear that he spoke with those who had.

Too many sources exist to be discussed, but those mentioned are essential to understanding the development and application of strategy by the Mongols.

Actors

The Mongol Qa'ans – the title for the rulers of the Mongol Empire after Chinggis Khan – were arguably the most powerful rulers in the medieval world, yet they were not autocrats. While they could command vast armies to march against enemies and issue edicts, they did not act alone, particularly in the realm of strategy. The main strategic discussions took place at a *quriltai* or congress that included not only the Mongol Qa'an, but various Mongol princes, generals, ministers and even queens. As the ultimate executor of authority, the Qa'an made final decisions, but an important characteristic of any nomadic ruler was his ability to seek and listen to the counsel of his subordinate leaders. A ruler who ignored their counsel risked dissent and even a coup.

Even Chinggis Khan did not act independently on strategic planning. He heeded the advice of his subordinates, which sometimes contradicted his initial ideas.[2] The practice can be traced to Chinggis Khan's early days. After the wife of Temüjin (the man who became Chinggis Khan) was kidnapped by the Merkit, he turned to his suzerain, Toghril, the khan of the Kereit confederation. The *Secret History of the Mongols* reveals much about the campaign planning process in an indirect manner and that developing war plans was a consultative process between a khan (military leader) and his subordinates. They discussed troop numbers and routes, and also set a schedule to co-ordinate their efforts.[3] Adhering to the schedule was import-ant, as the commander had to consider logistics such as pasture availability for their horses and other livestock. Another contemporary of the planning process was connected with the Battle of Chakirma'ut (1204) against the Naiman, which was the last battle for Temüjin's dominance over Mongolia. The *Secret History* depicts both the Naiman and the Mongols

---

2 For an example, see *The Secret History of the Mongols* (trans. I. de Rachewiltz) (Leiden: Brill, 2004), 165.

3 *The Secret History of the Mongols*, 34–9.

discussing strategies and tactics, as well as logistical concerns.[4] Later Qa'ans proceeded in much the same way. While the ruler always retained the final decision, they listened to the counsel of others so that they considered different perspectives and opinions, including thoughts on possible outcomes as well as factors that the ruler may not have considered. The process did not change significantly in the post-dissolution era either.

Although a Qa'an might lead a campaign, the various Mongol princes also participated, whether serving as nominal commanders or as actual campaign leaders. Additionally, they provided troops from their own retinues. As the Mongol empire often operated as a family business, the princes had a stake in any campaign; if they did not receive an allotment of territories, they still received people or even *qubi* (shares) through the revenues of a distant market, village or city. The prince's status determined the amount of influence they had in any *quriltai*. Senior princes always had a respected voice. Typically, each branch of the family had a designated representative who spoke for their respective branch.

The Mongol queens, particularly the senior or primary wife, carried substantial weight at any *quriltai*. While they typically did not advise on military matters, they voiced their opinions to the Qa'an. Furthermore, as the queens directed the affairs of the *ordo* or camp, they, in effect, supervised much of the logistical support of the military. In such a capacity, they often had better knowledge of the status of supplies, the condition of the livestock and so on. Every prince's situation was mirrored with a similar arrangement.[5]

As indicated earlier, the *noyans* or commanders participated in strategic planning. This included voicing their opinions on the target, on developing a schedule and on army composition. Only the highest-ranking *noyans* had significant input, including devising operational plans as well as strategic goals. In the days of Chinggis Khan, these were often his most trusted (even above family members) advisers.[6] Gradually, as the empire developed, certain generals or *noyans* became *ulugh-amirs* or *qarachu begs* – the highest-ranking members of the military aristocracy. These individuals, especially after the dissolution of the empire, became increasingly influential.

The final category of actors were the ministers of state. As with the queens, they expressed their concerns on how a campaign might affect the affairs of state, as with Qubilai and Japan and then again with Java. In both cases, the

---

4 *The Secret History of the Mongols*, 111–18.
5 B. De Nicola, *Women in Mongol Iran: The Khātūns, 1206–1335* (Edinburgh: Edinburgh University Press, 2017), 130–7.
6 T. May, *The Mongol Art of War* (Barnsley: Pen & Sword, 2016), 86–99.

ministers presented a case that it was not economically prudent and carried other risks such as rebellion.[7] These examples align with earlier instances in which ministers are depicted as dissuading the ruler from massacres. While often literary tropes, they nonetheless depict the ministers of state presenting the economic considerations for a particular campaign.

Adversaries

The Mongols' adversaries were many and varied. They ranged from nomads who fought similarly to the Mongols to sedentary states with greater armies and resources. Yet these advantages typically proved insufficient to overcome the Mongols. Still, Mongol military success was easy. The variety of foes and terrain in which they fought proved that the Mongols were versatile as well as tenacious in all their military endeavours. The numerous adversaries of the Mongols only grew as they expanded, and the conquests slowed as they expanded, not only due to the tenacious defence of their opponents, but also due to the numerous civil wars that occurred within the empire after the dissolution of the United Empire or Yeke Monggol Ulus in 1260. In these wars, the Mongols faced other Mongols, with decisive, border-altering victories being infrequent.

Other steppe nomads served as the foremost opponent of the Mongols. Chinggis Khan's rise to power and unification of the Mongolian plateau was against other nomads who fought and operated in a fashion similar to the Mongols. Thus the Mongols had to develop new tactics and strategies to provide an advantage over the Tatar, Kereit, Merkit and Naiman confederations. Once they expanded beyond Mongolia, the Mongols then encountered new nomadic foes. Most of these were in the Dasht-i Qipchaq or Qipchaq steppe that stretched from the Carpathian mountains to the Altai and Tianshan mountains. Despite covering a vast amount of territory, the Qipchaqs were not united but actually comprised four or five confederations across the Dasht-i Qipchaq. Additionally, the Qipchaqs often served as allies and mercenaries among the sedentary states on the fringe of the steppes, such as the Khwārazmian Empire, Georgia and the Rus', even serving in the Jin empire in north China and Manchuria.

In addition to the nomads, the Mongols fought semi-nomadic groups as well. Dwelling in the Siberian regions north of Mongolia, they were

---

7 M. Rossabi, *Khubilai Khan: His Life and Times*, 2nd ed. (Berkeley: University of California Press, 2009), 212; T. May, *The Mongol Empire* (Edinburgh: Edinburgh University Press, 2018), 198, 202.

collectively known as the Forest People or Hoyin Irgen, and stretched from the Yenisei basin to Lake Baikal. While they initially submitted in 1207–1209, they later rebelled in 1216 and threatened the fabric of Mongol rule. The Hoyin Irgen consisted of numerous groups ranging from small tribal groupings to the Qirghiz confederation in the Yenisei river basin. We have few details about the Mongol conquests of the Tungus tribes east of Lake Baikal, but we know the Mongols extended their rule into that region as well, particularly as the Mongol homeland was in the Kerulen–Onan river basin. As the Mongols expanded westward, they also dominated many other Siberian groups and may have extended their control and influence to the Arctic Ocean if even only indirectly through control of the fur trade.

The Mongols achieved control of the fur trade with their defeat of Bulghar, a Muslim city state at the confluence of the Kama and Volga rivers. The Bulghars led a coalition, consisting of nomads such as the Qipchaqs and Bashkirs as well as semi-nomadic groups such as the Burtas and various Mordvin groups, against Mongol penetration across the Yaik (Ural) river. The final major semi-nomadic group were the As or Alans, who inhabited mountain fortresses in the northern Caucasus region as well as the steppes. As with the Qipchaqs, the Mongols conquered them in the Great Western Campaign in 1236–1240. Resistance, however, continued, as noted by William of Rubruck in the 1250s.[8]

Although the Mongols conquered all of what comprises modern China, several kingdoms comprised this region. The most prominent were Xi Xia (1038–1127), the Jin empire located in today's northern China and Manchuria (1125–1234), and the Song empire to its south (906–1279). Xi Xia, which became the first sedentary state the Mongols invaded, was a mix of Han Chinese and Turko-Mongol nomads with a Tibetan ruling elite known as the Tangut. Thus, while they primarily relied on their fortifications, they could muster sizeable armies of cavalry and infantry.

After the unification of Mongolia, the Jin empire became the Mongols' primary adversary. Ruled by the Jurchen, a Manchurian people of semi-nomadic origins, they possessed an army of 600,000 men. The Jin were the dominant military power prior to the rise of the Mongols, not only in numbers, but also in implementation. Besides their primary armies of cavalry, they had nomadic auxiliaries and numerous infantry levies of Han Chinese. Furthermore, their cities possessed impressive fortifications. Despite Mongol

---

8 William of Rubruck, *The Mission of Friar William of Rubruck* (trans. P. Jackson) (Indianapolis: Hackett, 2009), 259.

dominance on the battlefield, the tenacious defence and resiliency of the Jin empire continued the war until 1234, when the Mongols finally captured the last Jin stronghold and the final emperor committed suicide.

The Song empire, which was south of the Jin empire, aided the Mongols against the Jin. This relationship ended in 1234 when the Jin fell and the Song attempted to regain territory previously lost to the Jin. In addition to being the wealthiest and most technologically advanced state in the thirteenth century, the Song's wealth, vast population, supply networks and system of mountain fortresses, protected by their riverine navy, gave the Song the ability to seemingly prolong the war for forty-five years.

To the west was the Khwārazmian Empire, the most powerful Islamic state in the thirteenth century, boasting an army of 400,000, including many nomads from the steppes. Although powerful and dominating most of the Islamic world from the Zagros mountains in Iran to the Hindu Kush and from the Persian Gulf to the Syr Darya, it was a new empire, with much of its territory only recently conquered by Muhammad II Khwarazmshah (1200–1223).

As the Mongols expanded from Iran and into Transcaucasia, they encountered the Armenian and Georgian principalities. To the east, the Mongols also expanded into Koryŏ. The commonality was that all three states lacked the capability to resist the Mongol armies and largely fought a static war from their fortresses in the hope that the Mongols would exhaust themselves and depart. They did not. While Armenia and Georgia submitted, Koryŏ would submit and then attempt to reassert their independence periodically, with the mainland suffering while the court directed resistance from Kwangha Island. Similarly, the Nizari Ismailis also depended on their mountain fortresses in Mazandaran and Quhistan to resist the Mongols.

With the expansion across the Volga, the Mongols encountered the Rus'. The Rus' lacked a cohesive unity and did little to prepare for the Mongol onslaught. From the Rus' principalities and the Pontic steppes, the Mongols could now invade central Europe. The two primary powers they encountered were Hungary and Poland. Hungary boasted one of the finest armies in Europe and was well informed about the Mongols. As with Hungary, Poland relied heavily on feudal barons and their knights. Poland, a lesser threat, lacked the centralised authority that Hungary possessed, no matter how imperfect.

As with Europe, in the Middle East, the Mongols did not encounter the large empires that they met in east Asia and central Asia. Instead, they faced smaller principalities in northern Iraq and Syria, many of whom had connections with the Abbasid Caliphate in Baghdad, the Ayyubid Confederation in Syria and Egypt, or the Seljuk Sultanate in Anatolia. While some co-ordination existed, these principalities lacked a charismatic leader to unify the region, even if temporarily.

Two other Muslim powers, founded by mamluks, or 'slave soldiers', became stalwart opponents of the Mongols. In Egypt, the Mamluk Sultanate liberated Syria from the Mongols while the Delhi Sultanate shielded northern India. Although the Mongols attempted few concerted efforts to conquer northern India, they raided the region frequently, thus forcing the Delhi Sultanate to prioritise its defence over its only expansionist goals. Meanwhile, the Mamluks in Egypt and Syria became quite adept at defending against the Mongol invasions of Syria.

On the frontiers of Mongol rule in the east, Japan proved to be a particularly difficult opponent due to weather and the tenacious defence by the samurai. Meanwhile, in south-east Asia, the Mongols also found mixed results. Their invasions of Dai Viet, Champa and Burma in south-east Asia demonstrated their power, but climate, economics and terrain, had as much influence on Mongol success and failure as their opponents' military activities.

Causes of War

Despite the later concept of Heaven's Will, that Tengri (Heaven) had decreed that Chinggis Khan and his heirs should rule the world, there is little evidence that an ambition to rule the world motivated Chinggis Khan's campaigns. This concept developed after his death and was projected back upon his life as a means of legitimising the conquests and Chinggisid rule, as well as understanding the success of the Mongols.

The actual causes of war were many but became more focused over time. The wars that led to the unification of Mongolia largely consisted of feuds, some of which existed prior to Chinggis Khan's birth, with the Tatars and Merkit. Additionally, as the Mongols rose in power, success bred fear and jealousy, which led former allies to war with each other as with the Mongols and the Kereit. The final conflict with Naiman was for domination of the Mongolian plateau as the Naiman and the Mongols were the two remaining tribal confederations of any significance.

The Mongol victory initiated new conflicts as they expanded. Rather than global conquest, Chinggis Khan initially sought to stabilise his nascent realm by eliminating defeated tribal leaders and neutralising sedentary threats on the frontier. The Jin empire and Xi Xia both used proxies from the steppe to exert influence among the nomads. Additionally, Chinggis Khan's new state largely comprised groups who only recently had been hereditary enemies. By unleashing them on an outside entity, it allowed his army to take their aggression out on someone else instead of each other, as well as forging a more cohesive identity through pillaging. The warriors fought a common enemy and pillaged, thus gaining goods and wealth instead of remaining in Mongolia and idle and perhaps ruminating on past grievances. Originally, the Mongols were content with submission and tribute and did not seek occupation, as demonstrated with Xi Xia in 1208.

The cause of the war with the Jin had some justification in past grievances dating back generations before Chinggis Khan's birth. Yet Chinggis Khan had also been a client of the Jin empire and had benefited from their protection at times. Still, when a new emperor came to the throne, for whom he held no respect, Chinggis Khan rebelled. There is no indication that he sought to conquer the Jin initially, but rather to nullify their threat to Mongolia. While the Mongols were initially satisfied with raiding, they gradually had to penetrate deeper into the Jin empire. Despite opportunities to do so, the Jin refused to submit to the Mongols; thus war continued until 1234.

In addition to old grievances and pillaging, the Mongols also engaged in war to protect vassals and to punish crimes committed against the empire. After the Naiman prince Güchülüg, a refugee from Mongolia, usurped the throne in Qara Khitai, the incident did not trigger an immediate reaction by the Mongols. Yet, after he pressured Mongol vassals among the Uighurs and Qarluqs, who had submitted to Chinggis Khan in 1209 and 1211 respectively, to return their allegiance to Qara Khitai, the Mongols reacted. With the acquisition of Qara Khitai, the Mongols now bordered the Khwārazmian Empire in central Asia. The cause of the Khwārazmian War is clear-cut and incontrovertible. Chinggis Khan attempted to initiate commercial relations, but the Khwārazmians massacred a Mongol-sponsored caravan in the town of Otrar in 1218 over charges of espionage. Avarice was the likely motive. After diplomatic efforts failed to resolve the matter, Chinggis Khan abandoned the Jin campaign to punish the Khwārazmian Empire.

Rebellions always necessitated a reaction. While the Mongols attempted to resolve rebellions diplomatically, when those efforts failed retaliation was swift and rarely restrained, as in the case of Xi Xia, which rebelled in 1223 and whose ruling dynasty was eradicated in 1227. While not as severe, the ruling elite among the Qori-Tümed also was disposed of after the Hoyin Irgen rebellion was crushed in 1218. Other rebellions would be dealt with in similar manner.

After the death of Chinggis Khan, a new element entered the Mongols' strategic vision – an ideology of world domination. This idea was simple and easily proven from the Mongol perspective. It was allegedly a shaman, Teb

Tenggeri, who first spread the foundation myth that the Köke Möngke Tengri or Blue Eternal Heaven had bequeathed the earth to Chinggis Khan and his descendants. Thus all should submit to the Mongols; not to do so meant the defiance of Heaven's Will and thus the offender was a rebel. While the Mongols were not aware that Chinggis Khan had conquered more territory than any single leader in history, they certainly knew that he had accomplished something spectacular and undeniable in his lifetime. Thus, during the reign of Ögödei Qa'an (1229–1241) and his successor Güyük Qa'an (1246–1248), as well as Möngke Qa'an, Heaven's Will became the underlying rationale for Mongol expansion. To avoid an invasion, all a ruler had to do was submit and come before the Qa'an and demonstrate obeisance. After this, the Mongols then expected tribute and that they then provide troops and/or supplies when called upon.

Heaven's Will essentially created conditions for perpetual war, and this sense of mission and entitlement changed little when, from the second half of the thirteenth century, the Mongols were progressively converted to Islam and Buddhism. The temporary diversions to their expansionism were succession fights among themselves. While Heaven's Will was the stated *casus belli*, other factors also come into play. As Chinggis Khan had set the precedent of hunting enemy leaders, the pursuit of them led to new invasions, such as into the Middle East, Europe and south-east Asia. A key factor included the necessity to gain more territory for the ever-expanding Chinggisid family, or *altan urugh*, as appanages. Some wars appear isolated, yet were actually part of larger operations, such as the connection between the invasion of Armenia and Georgia with the conquest of the Dasht-i Qipchaq. Other events were quite clear, such as the invasion of Dali to open another front against the Song empire. Campaigns of punishment, such as the genocidal destruction of the Nizari Ismailis after rumours emerged that they sought to assassinate Möngke Qa'an.[9] Yet Heaven's Will or Tenggerism remained the overriding cause. Other factors simply served to prioritise campaigns.

With Möngke Qa'an's death in Sichuan in 1259, the empire slipped into civil war. The underlying tensions among the Chinggisids, caused in no small part by the ramifications of the Toluid revolution, which brought Möngke to the throne, erupted. If the succession process had proceeded smoothly, perhaps nothing would have occurred, but civil war erupted between Qubilai and his brother Ariq Böke over the throne after Qubilai attempted to usurp it. While Qubilai ultimately won, the war permitted other issues to

---

9 Rubruck, *The Mission of Friar William of Rubruck*, 222.

fester and soon most of the wars fought by the Mongols were against each other, typically over territory.[10] As a result, border wars between the Mongol patrimonies became a frequent occurrence, but usually resulted in insignificant changes.

Despite their internal issues, the Mongols did not forsake the ideology of Heaven's Will and continued to expand when they could. Qubilai, as the usurper of the throne of the Qa'an, needed conquests to bolster his legitimacy. Thus finishing the conquest of the Song empire and imposing Heaven's Will carried great importance for him. Yet in the midst of this campaign, Qubilai also embarked on an invasion of Japan in 1274. While often construed as an attempt to conquer the island, this invasion targeted Hakata, the primary trading port that the Song used. In short, he attempted to strangle the economy of the Song, which played an important role in buttressing Song resistance to the Mongols.

Despite his conquest of the Song empire in 1279, Qubilai still faced challenges not only from internal rebellion but also from Mongols in central Asia who dismissed his legitimacy as Qa'an. To mitigate such challenges, not only did he war with them, but also he sought to conquer new territories to establish his legitimacy through Heaven's Will. Thus invasions of Dai Viet, Champa, Japan, Pagan (today's Myanmar) and Java occurred with mixed results.

Meanwhile, in the west, the Ilkhanid Mongols in the Middle East repeatedly attempted to reconquer Syria in 1260, which they lost as part of the fallout of Möngke's death. The distractions of the succession struggle and then conflicts with the Jochids and Chaghatayids prevented the Mongols from decisively dealing with the Mamluks. Meanwhile, the Jochids in the Dasht-i Qipchaq focused on claiming Azerbaijan. They invaded central Europe on occasion. While European sources viewed these as efforts of conquest, these actions were actually raids. Those in central Asia nibbled at their fellow Mongol borders and made advances towards India, but these appear largely as plundering expeditions rather attempts at conquest.

Objectives

Chinggis Khan's successors had the clear objective of global conquest fuelled by the concept of Heaven's Will, which developed after Chinggis Khan's

10 P. Jackson, 'The dissolution of the Mongol Empire', *Central Asiatic Journal*, 22 (1978), 186–244.

death. Yet, prior to his death, the Mongols' objectives were more limited. Chinggis Khan's primary goal in all his campaigns was to ensure that the Mongol Empire did not fragment due to outside forces.

A part of this, and a consideration for all campaigns, was to provide for his followers, a key responsibility for any steppe leader. Yet he also sought to eliminate threats that could destabilise Mongolia. These threats came in two overlapping forms. The first was to eliminate competing aristocratic lineages that could challenge the ascendancy of the *altan urugh*, the family of Chinggis Khan, as the legitimate rulers of the steppes. Thus, pursuit of any refugees from the nomadic aristocracy was crucial.[11] Any of them served as potential rallying points for those discontent with Chinggis Khan's rule. The Mongol forays into Xi Xia and across the Altai mountains served this purpose. The second threat came from potential interference in Mongolia by neighbouring sedentary powers.

Qara Khitai, Xi Xia, and the Jin empire all maintained relations with various steppe leaders. The Jin empire in particular followed the traditional policy of 'using barbarians to control barbarians', thus they supported certain leaders and then switched their support should one become too powerful. Indeed, Jin support was crucial to Chinggis Khan's rise to power, thus he well understood how they could turn against him. Both Herbert Franke and H. D. Martin proposed that Chinggis Khan initiated hostilities with the Jin to end their influence (and meddling).[12] His invasions in 1209 first sought to neutralise any military threat to his rule, not only by drawing frontier groups to his side, but also by seizing control of the mountain passes that led to the steppes. Over time, however, Chinggis Khan found himself conquering the Jin territory as his armies marched deeper into the region to secure plunder. Furthermore, many locations and leaders within the Jin empire submitted and even switched sides, attracted by the charisma of Chinggis Khan and the fact that he seemed a more competent leader than the Jin emperor. Other factors also came into play as the Mongols certainly sought to punish the Jin for past defeats and executions of Mongol leaders as well.

---

11 R. Dunnell, 'The Hsi Hsia', in Herbert Franke and Denis Twitchett (eds.), *The Cambridge History of China, Volume VI: Alien Regimes and Border States, 907–1368* (Cambridge: Cambridge University Press, 1994), 154–214, 164.

12 H. Franke, 'The Chin dynasty', in Herbert Franke and Denis Twitchett, *The Cambridge History of China*, Volume VI: *Alien Regimes and Border States*, 215–320, 251; H. D. Martin, *The Rise of Chingis Khan and His Conquest of North China* (New York: Octagon Books, 1971), 114–15.

When the Mongols invaded the Khwārazmian empire, it was a war of retribution. They sought not only to retrieve the pillaged caravan goods, but also to punish the Khwārazmians so that they could never be a threat to the Mongols again. Although the Mongols did not conquer and incorporate the entire realm, they did such significant damage that it destroyed the Khwārazmian Empire. Surviving princes could only attempt to restore it from the fringes and hopefully away from Mongol eyes.

Chinggis Khan's final campaign was also a war of retribution as Xi Xia rebelled. While he initially attempted to resolve the matter peacefully, which required the ruling dynasty to send hostages, this failed. With no other choice, he resolved to incorporate the kingdom fully into the Mongol Empire, which also meant the elimination of the ruling dynasty. This became a standard objective of all rebellions and conquests. Unless the rulers submitted, they were to be destroyed.

Upon the death of Chinggis Khan, the Mongols possessed an empire that stretched from the Yaik (Ural) and Amu Darya rivers to the Sea of Japan. To his successors, such accomplishments could only be rationalised by Chinggis Khan and, by extension, his successors having the favour of Köke Möngke Tengri, or the Blue Eternal Heaven. Thus their ultimate objective was always the submission of their opponents, yet other strategic goals existed as well.

While the Mongols often invaded regions, even in the post-Chinggis era, they did not always occupy those regions. Rather, they created buffer zones and neutralised powers that could challenge their dominance in a neighbouring region. The invasion of Hungary appears to have fit this mould. While the Mongols stayed there a year, they withdrew completely after devastating the realm. A similar pattern can be found in Mongol operations while securing Transcaucasia and elsewhere. This allowed them to gradually incorporate new territory without overextending their resources.

Also, the Mongols sometimes invaded one area in order to weaken another target. Attacks on Dali and Dai Viet in the 1250s had the initial intent not only of forcing those states to accept Mongol rule, but also of their permitting Mongol troops to operate against the Song through their territory. Similarly, the invasion of Armenia and Georgia in the late 1230s coincided with operations in the Dasht-i Qipchaq and eliminated an escape route for the Qipchaq nomads.

The overriding objective of any campaign, however, was the submission of the opponent. If submission did not occur, that ruler was in rebellion against Heaven's Will, thus necessitating destruction.

Available Means

It should not be surprising that force was the primary means of achieving the Mongol Empire's strategic objectives. In most cases, force was used as a last resort. The first action was diplomacy, as the Mongols preferred to receive the submission and co-operation voluntarily. Thus envoys visited targets and demanded submission. Harming an envoy was an automatic act of war. Of course, actual application of violence also led to situations when implied use of force proved beneficial as well, causing some locations to submit immediately. Initially, however, the Mongols had to be wary of overextension due to limited resources, not only in manpower, but also in equipment, as in the early thirteenth century Mongolia possessed limited production means.

After the unification of Mongolia in 1206, the Mongol military consisted of approximately 95,000 men. Yet these armies grew rapidly, as by the late 1250s, it is estimated, the Mongols had an army of a million, not including sedentary forces, which certainly equalled that number. As the Mongols gained the submission of new nomadic groups, these were then incorporated into the Mongol military. Part of the terms of submission included the expectation of providing troops and supplies when called upon. At times, as in the case of Xi Xia, and later in Koryŏ, the demands could become excessive.

When the Mongols applied violence, their typical means of implementing strategy revolved around armies of two types. The first were the large armies of conquest, which drew upon the retinues of various princes from across the empire. Such forces were used against the Jin, Song and Khwārazm, and in the Western Campaign which conquered the Dasht-i Qipchaq and invaded Europe. The second type of army used to implement Mongol strategy was the *tamma*. The *tamma* was typically stationed on the frontier, often between steppe and sown, although this was truly a matter of ensuring that pasture was available to support the army.[13] The *tamma* army consisted of troops from the branches of the Mongol Empire. The commander, or *tammachi*, received his appointment from the Qa'an and reported to the Qa'an. Whereas the armies of conquest returned to their home pastures at the end of a campaign, the *tamma* stayed where they were assigned. Only when the frontier moved, as territory became incorporated under civil authority, did the *tamma* then relocate.[14] Thus being assigned to a *tamma* was a duty for life.

13 P. D. Buell, 'Kalmyk Tanggaci people: thoughts on the mechanics and impact of Mongol expansion', *Mongolian Studies*, 6 (1980), 45–7.
14 T. May, 'Mongol conquest strategy in the Middle East', in B. De Nicola and C. Melville (eds), *Mongols' Middle East: Continuity and Transformation in Ilkhanid Iran* (Leiden: Brill, 2016), 11–37.

The *tamma*'s duty was to extend Mongol influence by whatever means necessary, using force as well as intimidation. The *tamma* conducted raids and even campaigns of conquest, albeit on a smaller scale. Local troops who had accepted Mongol dominion augmented the *tamma* on the battlefield. Occasionally the *tamma* received reinforcements, but often they remained in a location for generations. For instance, the *tamma* established in Afghanistan in 1230 are the ancestors of the modern Hazara people.

Forces of other types were created as necessary; for instance, against the Song Empire, Qubilai constructed first a riverine navy and then an oceanic one. While largely manned by non-Mongols, the Mongols quickly adapted to this new mode of warfare and applied steppe tactics to the water.

Process of Prioritisation

In terms of invasion, the Mongols had had two primary priorities. The first was to destroy any field army and the second was to eliminate the enemy's leadership. The first gave the Mongols the opportunity to then pillage and plunder at will. Additionally, it provided them the luxury to besiege cities and fortresses at will. As the empire expanded under the ideology of Heaven's Will, however, the real strategic dilemma was how to prioritise their enemies, and then determine the subset of priorities besides the destruction of an opponent's military capabilities.

In the early phases of the campaign against the Jin empire, while some Mongol forces sought the enemy armies, other forces targeted the pastures of the imperial stud to deny the Jin horses. The Mongols also sought to control the mountain passes leading into Mongolia. As the war progressed, Chinggis Khan isolated sections of the Jin empire, preventing the Jin from effectively marshalling their resources. Meanwhile, against the Khwārazmian Empire, Chinggis Khan first sought to punish the governor of Otrar for the massacre, then to recover the caravan goods at Bukhara, and finally, to eradicate the Khwārazmian Empire as a threat. These three separate priorities overlapped, but could be acted upon independently.

During Ögödei's reign priorities shifted to fit the mantle of Heaven's Will. While the primary priority was the final destruction of the Jin empire, he also dispatched a *tamma* under Chormaqan Noyan to Iran to bring stability and prevent any restoration of the Khwārazmian Empire. In the great Western Campaign, the priorities were to secure territories for the Jochids. While this campaign is often depicted as an effort to conquer the Rus' and Europe, in truth the Mongols sought to bring the Qipchaq nomads under their control as well as the Bulghar, which had been engaged in hostilities with the

Mongols since the late 1220s. The conquest of Rus' was truly icing on the cake of the conquest of the Qipchaqs, who were not only sometimes allies of the Rus', but also a far more potent military force from the Mongol perspective. In many ways, the invasion of Europe was simply to protect their frontier by creating a buffer zone while the Mongols secured their new territories.

During Möngke's reign, the priority shifted to the Song empire, and to that end, he sought to open multiple fronts. While he and other forces attacked from the northern frontier, Qubilai was sent with an army to open a western front in Dali. Qubilai's general, Uriyangqadai, then sought to do the same from Dai Viet to attack the Song from the south.

In the Middle East, only a few polities remained outside Mongol control. While all sent tribute, some had not shown formal obeisance. Hülegü's priority was the Nizaris, who sought to eliminate Möngke and had hopes of challenging Mongol rule. Hülegü was sent with a large army to bring security to the region as well as to eliminate the Nizaris in what amounted to a genocidal campaign, and then to reduce the Abbasid Caliphate and any other recalcitrant power that failed to submit.

The dissolution of the Mongol Empire in 1260 led to civil wars. The primary goal for all of the Mongol states was to maintain their territories. Any additional conquests, whether the Song empire or perhaps Syria, could only take place when the conditions permitted. For instance, a rebellion in Mongolia and Manchuria by Mongol princes forced Qubilai Qa'an largely to halt his operations against the Song empire. Meanwhile, the Ilkhans lowered the priority of regaining Syria due to defending against Jochid and Chaghatayid incursions.

Execution or Application

The application or execution of strategy is often vastly different from the theoretical aspect of planning and formulating a strategy for invasion, or of even adhering to the tenets of an agreed grand strategy. In this regard, the Mongols were no different from any other state.

As part of Chinggis Khan's initial strategy, he eliminated competing aristocratic lines. To this end, he sent forces into Xi Xia to hunt for Senggüm of the Kereit. Part of the rationale for sending Jochi to the Hoyin Irgen territories in 1207 surely was to neutralise them as a base of operations for the Naiman and the Merkit. Then he personally led an army in 1208 to defeat the Merkit and Naiman at the Irtysh river. While he did not invade Qara Khitai in pursuit of Güchülüg, Mongol troops under Sübe'edei pursued the Merkit into Qangli territory north of the Aral Sea to neutralise them.

Meanwhile, Mongol operations encouraged the Qarluqs, the city of Almaliq and the Uighurs to offer their submission to Chinggis Khan.

These operations also gave Chinggis Khan an outlet for his recently unified state to seek riches, as well as to work out their aggression. Furthermore, the incursions into Xi Xia demonstrated that Xi Xia possessed riches that could be exploited. As with the Jin empire, Chinggis Khan never sought to occupy it. He routinely withdrew to Mongolia while campaigning against the Jin empire. While he left troops there, he relied more on local forces such as Khitan and Han forces that joined him. These troops allowed him to use his main army where needed, such as to deal with rebellions or invade central Asia. Once he realised that the Jin empire was no longer a major threat, he left a force to contain and, if possible, subdue it.

The Khwārazmian War is an astounding display of all aspects of Mongol strategy and tactics. The Mongols prioritised capturing Otrar, where the massacre took place, and with retrieving the stolen treasure from Bukhara. To this end, Mongol forces attacked Otrar while other forces entered Mawarannahr to prevent the Khwārazmians from consolidating against the Mongols or coming to the relief of Otrar. This allowed Chinggis Khan to disappear into the Kizil Kum desert and then reappear outside Bukhara 300 miles deep into Khwārazmian territory. After securing Mawarannahr, Mongol forces invaded Khurasan and Badakhshan while another task force pursued Sultan Muhammad II, thus preventing him from rallying against the Mongols. The Mongols made the war one against local forces, rather than against a co-ordinated imperial effort. After the news of the Xi Xia rebellion in 1223, Chinggis Khan withdrew and only kept Mawarannahr. His armies had, however, devastated Afghanistan and Khurasan, thus creating a buffer between his empire and any other force.

As would become standard practice, the Mongols massacred those who resisted, although they permitted a few survivors to escape. Those who submitted were spared and their possessions went unmolested after a tribute payment. Word spread and, given the option, many submitted rather than risk massacre. Ultimately, what most did not realise was that the Mongols were less focused on territory, and more concerned about the population. In essence, they viewed the population as livestock to be controlled. When culling was necessary, they did so with massacres. Otherwise, they preferred an intact population, particularly with skilled labor.

With Chinggis Khan's death, the Mongols soon had a new ruler in Ögödei, who also sought to destroy the Jin empire. Chinggis Khan's campaigns served as a blueprint for what became the tsunami strategy, in which the Mongols invaded an area and caused immense damage, reducing fortresses and armies.[15] Then they withdrew and only retained a portion of the territory. The destruction created a buffer between the Mongol territory and others. Furthermore, the zone usually declined in terms of agricultural or industrial production and reverted to pasture, which also benefited the Mongol armies. From here, *tamma* forces could operate and extend Mongol control gradually. When necessary, a large army of conquest would then come and reduce those too powerful for the limited forces of the *tamma*. This occurred repeatedly in the post-Chinggis Khan empire, albeit with some modifications. Ultimately, the execution of the tsunami strategy prevented the Mongols from overextending their forces while also allowing them to expand on multiple fronts.

Major Historical Debates

The early debates on Mongol strategy centred around whether the Mongols actually possessed strategy or whether they simply overwhelmed through superior numbers. This discussion had largely disappeared by the late twentieth century as Thomas Allsen conclusively demonstrated that, over time, the Mongols did succeed, not by throwing waves and waves of men at their opponents, but rather by being able to mobilise more men and resources due to the care they put into the organisation of the empire.[16] This largely ceased, but led to a shift in more regional concerns. For instance, from the mid-twentieth century, it was advanced that the conquest of Xi Xia was largely a practice run for the inevitable invasion and planned conquest of the Jin empire.[17] Furthermore, it was also necessary to protect the Mongol flank while they invaded Jin.[18] Both made assumptions that close analysis of the evidence easily disproves. Indeed, Owen Lattimore made a convincing argument that Chinggis Khan's strategy did not seek the conquest of China.[19] Yet, like the idea of the strength of numbers, the idea that the nomads had to conquer China has a foundational basis in how the Mongols were viewed: barbarians who largely thought to pillage and who coveted control of the wealthier civilisations on their borders. This

15 T. May, 'Grand strategy in the Mongol Empire', *Acta Historica Mongolici*, 16 (2017), 78–105.
16 T. T. Allsen, *Mongol Imperialism* (Berkeley: University of California Press, 1987), 189–90.
17 Martin, *Rise of Chingis Khan*, 115.   18 Morgan, *The Mongols*, 57.
19 O. Lattimore, 'The geography of Chingis Khan', *Geographical Journal*, 129:1 (1963), 6–7.

view assumes a Whiggish interpretation of history and of nomadism as an inferior mode of life and economy.

While tactical concerns were the primary theme of the lively debates between John Masson Smith Jr and Reuven Amitai, the whole gamut of military concerns, including strategy, came into play. Their discussions also included the importance of logistical considerations in strategy. Thus, for the nomadic cavalry, the availability of sufficient pasture and water for their horses had considerable impact on strategic deliberations.[20] While their focus rested on the encounters between the Mamluks and the Mongols in Syria, the lessons derived could also be applied elsewhere.

Two other themes in the study of Mongol strategy seem cyclical. The first is how environmental or climatic conditions affected Mongol expansion. In the twentieth century and even prior, scholars assumed that the desiccation of the steppes caused nomadic irruptions out of Mongolia as the nomads sought new and better pastures. Debate has since shifted due to clear evidence of a wetter period, which allowed the steppes to flourish and thereby establish conditions for increased herd sizes, and thus wealth and population in the steppes. Thus the Mongols then expanded due to increased population and wealth.[21] Because of this new evidence, climatic factors have spurred a new interest in understanding the Mongol withdrawal from Hungary. The standard explanation was that the death of Ögödei Khan in 1241 led to the Mongol evacuation in 1242. Yet scholars have never been completely satisfied with the explanation, as the Mongols had established overwhelming domination of the kingdom. Arguments centred on pasture, political intrigues and other factors. Now, climatic issues have been manifested with spirited debates on whether they played a role and also how they impacted the region.[22]

---

20 See J. Masson Smith Jr, 'Mongol society and military in the Middle East: antecedents and adaptations', in Y. Lev (ed.), *War and Society in the Eastern Mediterranean, 7th and 15th Centuries* (Leiden: Brill, 1996), 249–66.

21 N. Pederson, A. E. Hessl, N. Baatarbileg, K. J. Anchukaitis and N. Di Cosmo, 'Pluvials, droughts, the Mongol Empire, and modern Mongolia', *Proceedings of the National Academy of Sciences of the United States of America*, 111:12 (25 March 2014), 4375–9, 4375.

22 G. S. Rogers, 'An examination of historians' explanations for the Mongol withdrawal from central Europe', *East European Quarterly*, 30 (1996), 3–26; U. Büngten and N. Di Cosmo, 'Climatic and environmental aspects of the Mongol withdrawal from Hungary in 1242 CE', *Scientific Reports*, 6 (2016), 25606; Z. Pinke, Laszlo Ferenczi, Beatrix Romhányi and József Laszlovszky, 'Climate of doubt: a re-evaluation of Büntgen and Di Cosmo's environmental hypothesis for the Mongol withdrawal from Hungary, 1242 CE', *Scientific Reports*, 7 (2017), 12695.

15

Hindu and Buddhist Polities
of Premodern/Early Modern Mainland
South-East Asia (1100–1800)

TASSAPA UMAVIJANI

Introduction

The premodern/early modern polities of mainland south-east Asia had always been warlike. Brahmin Hinduism and Buddhism influenced the three prominent powers of this region: the Khmer Empire (802–1431) and the Siamese and Burmese kingdoms. The successive Siamese kingdoms from Ayutthaya (1350–1767), Thonburi (1767–1782) and Rattanakosin or Bangkok (1782–present) continually fought the Burmese kingdoms: the Taungoo Empire (1510–1752) and then the Konbaung Dynasty (1752–1885). Similar in culture, the smaller kingdoms of the Champa, Lanna and Lan Xang engaged in similar power struggles.

Under the continual military expansion of ambitious monarchs, the Khmer, the Siamese and the Burmese turned the smaller kingdoms around them into vassals and extracted tribute payments. There was barely any ideologically based mechanism to restrain them, no regional 'order' valuing peace. The languages of the educated classes of these 'Indic' polities of south-east Asia were marked by Sanskrit (much as European languages all contain many Latin and Greek words and concepts). They were strongly influenced in their statecraft and political ideology by the self-aggrandising concept of *cakravati* – the universal ruler. This had spread from India with Hinduism and Buddhism.

Thus, with similar military cultures and objectives, the kindred peoples of south-east Asia fought mainly against one another. From the twelfth century to the nineteenth, before machines replaced muscle power and before the world's population increased exponentially, manpower was precious, and the war aims of the rulers were to increase the population under their rule and to exact tribute. The former was done by forcing conquered enemy populations to resettle in the victor's domains to increase the size of the workforce and generate

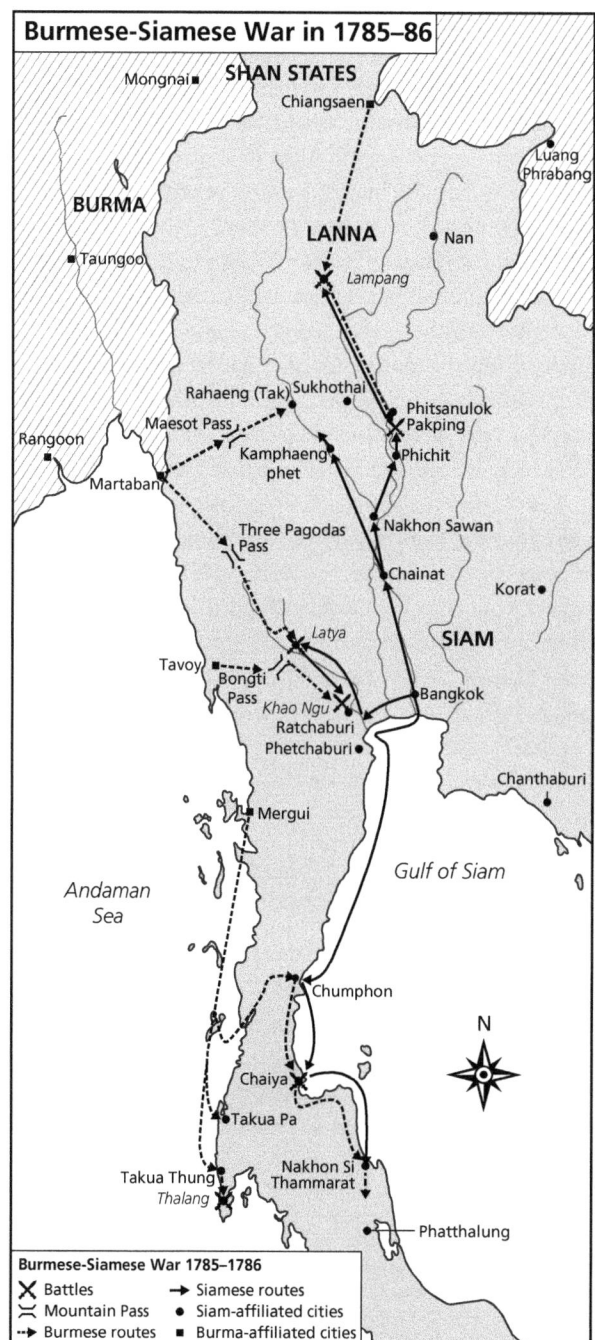

Burmese-Siamese War in 1785–86

Map 15.1 The Burmese marching routes against Ayutthaya in 1765–1767. Redrawn based on a map called 'Map of Burmese–Siamese War (1785–1786)' (Biggie 943 845 39, Wikimedia, CC-BY-SA-4.0).

economic growth. With constant commercial interactions with Chinese, Europeans and other foreigners, the south-east Asian polities imported foreign military techniques and mercenaries to increase their military capabilities.

Thus the Khmer Empire battled the Chams in a series of wars between 1128 and 1230 for their mastery over the Indochinese region. From the fourteenth century onwards, the Siamese kingdom of Ayutthaya consolidated its power in the Chao Phraya river basin, then expanded against the declining Khmer Empire that culminated in the collapse of Angkor Wat in 1431. Ayutthaya then contested with its Tai-speaking counterpart, Lanna, which caused a series of wars from the mid-fifteenth century to the mid-sixteenth (1442–1545). The Burmese Taungoo Empire, grown powerful after the struggles with the Mons, assaulted Ayutthaya and conquered it in 1569. After the Siamese wars of liberation by King Naresuan the Great in 1584, the protracted war between the Taungoo Empire and Ayutthaya Siam led to internal rebellions that threw Taungoo into disarray and decline. The Restored Taungoo Empire (1597–1752) suffered constant military challenges from the Shan, the Mons, the Siamese and Manipuri, eventually bringing about its collapse. Amidst the chaos, the new Burmese dynasty under King Alaungpaya rose to power and restored Burma's power, then mobilised manpower throughout Burma and its vassal polities to destroy Ayutthaya in 1767. When the Siamese polity was restored, its capital moved to Thonburi and then Rattanakosin (Bangkok); the new Siamese kingdoms sought to put all the population in the Tai-speaking world, as well as the Cambodians, under Siam's dominion to withstand future invasions from Konbaung Burma, especially after the major wars in 1785–1786.

Sources

The south-east Asian historiography of this period focused on the glorified deeds of monarchs, including their deeds in war. Depictions of military campaigns are abundant in the Bayon bas-reliefs and inscriptions depicting the Khmer Empire's amphibious expedition against Champa of 1190–1230.[1] The Chinese travellers Ma Tuan-lin and Zhou Daguan have left ethnographic accounts of the region and of how the Khmer Empire waged wars and how the armed forces were mobilised.[2]

---

1 M. Jacq-Hergoualc'h and M. Smithies, *The Armies of Angkor: Military Structure and Weaponry of the Khmers* (Bangkok: Orchid Press, 2007), 110–37.

2 Ma Tuan-lin, *Ethnographie des peuples étrangers à la Chine: Ouvrage composé au XIIIe siècle de notre ère* (London: H. Georg, E. Leroux and Trübner, 1876); D. Zhou, *A Record of Cambodia: The Land and Its People* (trans. Peter Harris) (Chiang Mai: Silkworm Books, 2007).

Siamese and Burmese accounts give us clues about applied strategy, even if no text deals as directly with the subject as Kautilya's *Arthashastra* in India or Sunzi's *Art of War* in China. Traditional south-east Asian historiography consists mainly of official chronicles and annals focusing on the kings, with their military exploits at the centre. In a culture rich in heritage from Hinduism and influential secular Indian literature such as the *Arthashastra*, kings were supposed to be part of the *kshatriya* or warrior order of society, and war was their constant occupation.[3]

Most of these sources are not accounts produced by military writers. At best they compiled campaign reports and correspondence that the royal scholars incorporated into their chronicles. We find some details of battles and stratagems in the *Phra Ratchapongsawadan*, the royal chronicles of the Siamese kingdoms. Their accuracy is questionable, and some of them are heavily biased. Some contain problematic revisions with underlying political agendas, aimed at undermining the legitimacy of earlier, vanquished dynasties.[4] Even so, they give us insight into the practice of strategy and other aspects of military affairs.

Poems commemorating the king's military deeds in the early part of the period in which Siam was ruled from the capital, Ayutthaya (1350–1767), the *Lilit Yuan Phai* or the defeat of the Yuan,[5] referring to the Lanna Tai kingdom of modern northern Thailand, constitute further primary sources recounting battles in the fifteenth century. The Burmese shared a similar tradition of writing chronicles and annals that elucidate how their wars were waged. There are the *Yazawin* royal chronicles of the Burmese dynasties, the *Ayedawbon Kyans* that elucidate military campaigns and some stratagems performed in past wars, and the *Mawgun*, the 'record of memorable moment' that recounts a story of specific military campaigns, notably the sack of Ayutthaya in 1767.[6]

Then, on the Siamese side, there are the *Pongsawadan* and *Tamnan* chronicles, and the chronicles of warfare compiled by Prince Damrong Rajanubhab (1862–1943), *Pongsawadan Thai Rop Pama* or *The Chronicle of Our Wars with the Burmese*.[7] The latter contain the prince's modern commentaries on the conduct of

3 Kautilya, *The Arthashastra* (ed. L. N. Rangarajan) (New Delhi: Penguin Books India, 1992), 676.
4 H. James, 'The fall of Ayutthaya: a reassessment', *Journal of Burma Studies*, 5 (2000), 75–108.
5 C. Phra Khlang (Hon), *Lilit Yuan Phai/ Lilit Petch Mongkut Chabab Chao Phraya Phra Khlang (Hon) (The Yuan Phai Poems on the Fall of Lanna and Lilit Petch Mongkut Poems Compiled by Chao Phraya Phra Khlang (Hon))*, (Bangkok: Phra Chan Publishing House, 1966).
6 Cui" Sūjā Mraṅ", *The Portrayal of the Battle of Ayutthaya in Myanmar Literature* (ed. Sunēt and Chutintharānon and C. J. Baker) (Bangkok, Institute of Asian Studies, Chulalongkorn University, 2011).
7 Prince Damrong Rajanubhab, *Pongsaowadarn Rueng Thai Rop Phama (The Chronicle of Our Wars with the Burmese)* (Bangkok: Matichon, 2013).

war, but the contents are largely those of the traditional accounts that could be considered both primary and secondary sources on the Burmese–Siamese wars. Then a work based on original sources by K. S. R. Kulab provides fruitful details on the conduct of war and strategies in the Annam–Siam Yuth,[8] recounting the later military contests between Siam and Vietnam over the Indochinese vassal polities between 1833 and 1845. It can be argued that these compilations of original sources offer the most comprehensive details of military affairs for the Siamese.

Apart from the Chinese, there are also accounts by European travellers and diplomats. For the Siamese kingdom of Ayutthaya, the works of the Portuguese mercenary and adventurer Fernão Mendes Pinto;[9] the Dutch East India Company's representative in Ayutthaya, Jeremias van Vliet;[10] and the French diplomat Simon de la Loubère, who visited Ayutthaya between the years 1687 and 1688,[11] shed light on the Siamese wars of expansion. We learn how the Siamese organised their armed forces, get estimates of their size and find clues to their strategic choices.

There is also a Siamese equivalent to a field manual, the *Tamra Pichai Songkhram*.[12] According to the royal Ayutthaya chronicles, it was composed in 1498 during the reign of King Ramathibodi II.[13] This book of stratagems illustrates the customary operational arts and ruses that could be used against adversaries, dealing with tactical rather than strategic matters. Nevertheless, the term *yutthasad* is now used as the Thai translation of 'strategy' in the modern century sense, for which there is no other word in Siamese military writing. The Siamese did, however, possess another term: *pichai songkhram* – 'how to prevail in warfare'. As in Europe, these and other works concerned the tactical level of military

8 K. S. R. Kulap and Bōdindēchā (Sing), *Annam–Siam Yuth waduai kansongkhram rawang Thai Lao Khmen lae Yuan (The Annam–Siam War: On Wars between the Thais, the Laotians, the Khmers and the Vietnamese)* (Bangkok: Kosit Printing Press, 2007).

9 F. M. Pinto, *Peregrinação (The Compilation of Journeys and Accounts by Mendes Pinto)* (trans. Sant T. Komolbutr, Nanthana Wornaetiwong and Singhadēchākun' Charat) (Bangkok: Silpakorn, 2005).

10 J. van Vliet, *Rūam banthuk prawattisāt 'Ayutthayā khǭng Fān Flīt (Wan Walit) (A Compilation of Historical Accounts by Jeremias van Vliet)* (Bangkok: Krom Sinlapākǭn, 2005).

11 S. de La Loubère, *A New Historical Relation of the Kingdom of Siam* (London: Printed by F. L. for Tho. Horne, Francis Saunders, and Tho. Bennet, 1693).

12 Suriyawong et al., *Tamra Pichai Songkram khong Krom Silpakorn (The Pichai Songkram Military Manual by the Department of Fine Arts)* (Bangkok: Phra Chan Publishing House, 1969).

13 Čhakkaphatdiphong (Čhāt), *Phrarātchaphongsāwadān Krung Sī 'Ayutthayā: chabap Phra Čhakkaphatdiphong (The Royal Chronicles of Krung Sri Ayutthaya)* (Bangkok: Kurusapa, 1998), 18.

operations, such as how to set up military outposts and camps, how to storm the enemy's fortified cities, how to set up military garrisons, how to configure forces for battle and how to improve the morale of one's soldiers or deceive the enemy in campaigns (including superstitious and magical elements in war) with *kolseuk* (stratagems). Thus working out what strategies were developed among the Indic mainland polities requires substantial interpretation based on the cultural frameworks that influenced their practices of strategy.

Actors

At the strategic level, the military hierarchy was centralised around the monarchs and their aristocratic councillors. Most of the strategic decisions were made by the kings; although the royal council of generals and advisers must have given advice, sources generally do not mention this. The kings were militaristic, in line with their ideology, which encouraged them to strive for divinely ordained universal monarchy. The warring monarchs, de facto *kshatriya* commanders-in-chief, might delegate power to generals and field commanders,[14] but many kings led their forces into battle. Due to the nature of the evidence we are led to believe that monarchs were the main or sole decision makers, as the chronicles dwell on their meritorious qualities, reflected especially in their mastery and luck in military affairs. We learn little about the personalities of other actors or interest groups besides the monarchs.

Ma Tuan-lin described Jayavarman VII's long-term war plan against the Chams, independent peoples with principalities in what is today central and southern Vietnam: the Khmer king 'decided to wreak terrible vengeance on his enemies, which he succeeded in doing after eighteen years of patient dissimulation'.[15] According to later Thai sources on Siamese warfare, the court issued a *damri* (royal decision). The royal chronicles of Ayutthaya record how King Maha Chakkraphat consulted with the council of his generals on how to use the combined forces of Ayutthaya and its vital ally, the city state of Phitsanulok, against Burmese forces, using cannon; the

---

14 P. Sitthithanyakij, *Čhŏmthap Thai læ 'ekkalak kānthahān khŏng phǣndin: nangsư̄ 'anusŏn 401 pī mahāwīrakam yutthahatthī nai Somdet Phra Narēsūan Mahārātčhao čhŏmthap Thai, 24 Makarākhom 2134–2535 (The Warring Thai King and the Military Identity of Thailand: Book Commemorating the 401st Anniversary of King Naresuan the Great Military Commander of Thailand, 24 January 1591–1992)* (Bangkok: Public Business Print, 1992), 51.

15 Ma, *Ethnographie*, 487; George Coedès, *The Indianized States of South-East Asia* (Honolulu: East-West Centre Press, 1968), 170.

council agreed.[16] On campaign, where the kings delegated authority, military commanders took decisions; the Siamese accounts tell us about key Burmese generals taking strategic decisions. For example, Maha Thiha Thura, a Burmese general serving under the Konbaung dynasty (1752–1885), resolved to capture the northern region of Siam to mobilise manpower and war materiel before launching a decisive Burmese invasion of Thonburi Siam in 1769.[17]

Generals and admirals had to fear extreme punishments if they took decisions and misjudged a situation. During the invasion of Tây Sơn Vietnam to assist Nguyen Anh, the Nguyen prince who allied himself with Bangkok after the Tây Sơn Rebellion captured Vietnam and founded the Tây Sơn dynasty (1778–1802), King Rama I of the Siamese Chakri dynasty (founded in 1782) ordered the immediate execution of his Admiral Phraya Nakhonsawan, who had allowed the Tây Sơn to retrieve captured war vessels and munitions after Siam's initial success in the expedition in 1785.[18] In the Siamese case, the king was no longer present on the battlefield in the nineteenth century but remained at the centre of the decision-making process in the capital, continuing to supervise generals at the front. In 1827, during Chao Anouvong's insurrection against Bangkok, King Rama III of Siam wrote a royal letter to consult with his field general, Bodin Decha, and other commanders whether or not they should burn and raze Vientiane to the ground, destroying the Laotian polity for good, to prevent future rebellions by the Laotian principalities.[19] This and other surviving correspondence illustrates that the monarch remained the supreme military commander in the south-east Asian Indic states.

Kings were polygamous, with a principal queen and many royal consorts. The succession between reigns could be a chaotic fight for the crown, occasionally leading to civil war. As for the Siamese, in the early Ayutthaya period during the fifteenth century, the king would assign his princes to govern the semi-independent *Mueng Lukelaung*, 'the Royal Heirs' Cities', situated away from the capital. This system made wars of succession more likely,[20] so it was abandoned by King Prasatthong (r. 1629–1656).[21] To ensure a smooth transition,

16 Čhakkaphatdiphong (Čhāt), *Phrarātchaphongsāwadān*, 49.
17 Damrong Rajanubhab, *Thai Rop Phama*, 481.
18 Chao Phraya Thiphākǫnwongmahākōsāthibǭdī (Kham) (ed.), *Phrarātchaphongsāwadān Krung Rattanakōsin: Ratchakān Thī 1–4* (The Royal Chronicles of Rattanakosin, King Rama I–IV (Nonthaburī: Samnakphim Sīpanyā, 2012), 102–3.
19 Kulap and Bǭdindēchā (Sing), *Annam–Siam Yuth*, 87.
20 Manop Thaworawatsakun, *Khunnang Ayutthaya* (*The Aristocracy of Ayutthaya*) (Bangkok: Thammasat University Press, 1993), 61–5.
21 Thaworawatsakun, *Khunnang Ayutthaya*, 96.

the Ayutthayan monarchs, such as King Ekathotsarot (r. 1605–1610), designated an heir apparent (*upparat*).[22] King Phetracha elevated the heir apparent to the position of viceroy, as *krom phra ratchawang bowon sathan mongkhon* (the Front Palace).[23] The Burmese kings chiefly appointed their eldest sons as *upparat*.[24] Both the Siamese and Burmese Crown princes or viceroys were heavily involved in making strategy; some of them were directly in charge in the strategic planning of campaigns. The *mahaupparat*, the grand Crown prince of King Nanda Bayin of Taungoo Burma, commanded the Burmese expeditionary armies in the invasion campaigns of Ayutthaya of 1590–1592.[25] One of the most competent military commanders and tacticians of Siam after the downfall of Ayutthaya was the viceroy Maha Sura Singhanat of the Chakri dynasty, who devised guerrilla tactics against Burmese supply trains and encampments, weakening the massive army of Konbaung Burma, leading to eventual Burmese defeat in the western theatre of the Burmese–Siamese War in 1785.[26]

Means

The Indic polities relied on intricate social stratification and aristocratic apparatus to dominate the populace, underpinned by a notion of divine monarchy. The polities' armies were formed mainly by the large-scale recruitment of male commoners, but stopping short of constant total mobilisation. Commoners were thought to have the duty to perform physical labour (including military service) for the upper classes, or to provide the upper classes with goods as tax in kind to evade such duties, a system referred to as 'corvée'. Thus poorly trained commoners formed a sort of militia. According to Zhou Daguan, a Chinese diplomat who visited Angkor in today's Cambodia in the year 1296, the majority of Angkor's soldiers were commoners recruited without proper training, for war against the Siamese.[27]

The Siamese had the vassal system, called the *phrai* ('servant') system: any male individual of the lower *na* (class of property holders) had to perform military service for at least six months in a year, according to the *khao duen ork duen* (regulation). Each lord (*munnai*) was required to send a certain number

---

22 Prince Damrong Rajanubhab, *Phra Ratchaopongsawadan Chabab Phra Ratchahatthalekha* (Bangkok: Siam Kolkarn Trading Co. Ltd, 1968), 417–18.

23 Damrong Rajanubhab, *Phra Ratchaopongsawadan Chabab Phra Ratchahatthalekha*, 500.

24 Damrong Rajanubhab, *Thai Rop Phama*, 87.

25 Damrong Rajanubhab, *Thai Rop Phama*, 129–45.

26 Klaus Wenk, *The Restoration of Thailand under Rama I, 1782–1809*, monographs and papers, Association for Asian Studies, University of Arizona, 1968, 52–5.

27 Zhou, *Record of Cambodia*, Chapter 39.

of soldiers to fight for the king, if called upon.[28] The high-ranking *munnai* aristocrats would command the *krom* (military divisions) as *chao krom* (division commander). *Sak Lek*, mass tattooing, marked males eligible to serve under this *phrai* system. In the nineteenth century, Siam also imposed the tattoo system on the Laotian population to control them.[29]

Similarly, the Burmese polities also practised compulsory recruitment (*ahmudan*), in many aspects more efficient than the Siamese *phrai* system. The *ahmudan* system mobilised men into platoons in a standing army also including specialist units such as musketeers, archers and cavalrymen. The more disciplined and better-trained Burmese *ahmudan* servicemen were concentrated within the provincial centre, where they enjoyed tax exemption and remuneration, and were provided with food rations.[30] In addition there were *athis* (commoners) who formed auxiliary forces.[31]

In wartime, these states could mobilise mass armies also from the peasantry of their vassal states. During peacetime, for fear of mutiny and rebellion, the kingdoms either demobilised these armies or maintained small professional forces and mercenaries to defend the court. The Khmer rulers, like the Eastern Roman emperors, had to fear insurgencies by their military to replace them. Only eight out of twenty-six rulers of Angkor were brothers or sons of the previous king; all the others owed their position not to dynastic succession but to a coup.[32] Similarly, in Siam there was no standing army before the nineteenth century.[33]

The armies of the Indic polities had semi-professional forces as their cadres. In the Siamese armies, these were royal guards or well-trained soldiers serving under the *phrai luang* (royal servicemen), forming part of the *krom* divisions, and foreign mercenaries.[34] Mendes Pinto recorded that in the campaign against Chiangmai, King Chairachathirat of

28 Kachon Sukhabanij, *Thanandon Phrai* (*The Status of the Common Man*) (Bangkok: The Historical Society, 2013), 17–19.
29 P. R. Pakawapan, 'Warfare and depopulation of the Trans-Mekong basin and the revival of Siam's economy' in M. W. Charney and K. Wellen (eds), *Warring Societies of Pre-colonial Southeast Asia: Local Cultures of Conflict Within a Regional Context* (Copenhagen: NIAS Press, 2017), 21–46.
30 Victor Lieberman, *Burmese Administrative Cycles: Anarchy and Conquest, c. 1580–1760* (Princeton: Princeton University Press, 1984), 97–102.
31 Lieberman, *Burmese Administrative Cycles*, 106–7.
32 D. P. T. Carter, 'Examination of ancient Khmer defensive warfare practices' (2015), at www.academia.edu/31872098/EXAMINATION_OF_ANCIENT_KHMER_DEFENSIVE_WARFARE_PRACTICES, 21–2.
33 N. A. Battye, *The Military, Government and Society in Siam, 1868–1910: Politics and Military Reform during the Reign of King Chulalongkorn* ([Ithaca, NY]:Battye, 1974), 10–11.
34 M. W. Charney, 'Southeast Asian Warfare, 1300–1900', *Handbook of Oriental Studies/ Handbuch der Orientalistik*, 16, Section 3, South-East Asia (Leiden: Brill, 2004), 226–7.

Ayutthaya enlisted 120 Portuguese mercenaries.[35] After the king's war against the Burmese at Chiang Kran in 1538, the Ayutthayan king allowed these Portuguese mercenaries to establish their community in Ayutthaya, where they spread Catholicism.[36] While they contributed superior military techniques, these forces could become unreliable. They later became power brokers in political unrest. Yamada Nagamasa, a Japanese mercenary captain who headed the Japanese community that lived within Ayutthaya, intervened in the royal succession of Siam, then in the late 1620s seized the southern city of Ligor (modern Nakhon Sri Thammarat in southern Thailand) before being poisoned. The Siamese army also recruited pardoned war prisoners: during the Anouvong Rebellion in 1827, Rama III ordered Siamese officials to unshackle the Burmese war prisoners and mobilise them into Bangkok's auxiliary forces.[37]

The number of forces reported in the premodern/early modern sources needs careful interpretation and contextual comprehension as evidence. With classic exaggeration intended to impress fellow Europeans, Mendes Pinto claimed that the sixteenth-century Burmese army of King Tabinshwehti of the Taungoo dynasty (r. 1530–1550) had 1,000 Portuguese mercenaries under the command of Diego Suarez D'Albergaria, along with supposedly 10,000 Turkish, Abyssinian, Moor and Malay mercenaries, who accompanied the massive forces that the king led in the Burmese invasion of Ayutthaya in 1548 – with considerable hyperbole, Pinto claimed they totalled 800,000 men.[38] More reliable accounts dating from the eighteenth century still suggests impressively large armies: the Siamese royal chronicles record that the Burmese armies sent to invade Siam by Bodawpaya numbered around 103,000 men.[39]

Besides foot soldiers, like the armies of South asia, the Indic polities also had horse cavalry and war elephant units. With sheer speed and manoeuvrability, cavalry played a vital role in raids on enemy camps, skirmishes and surprise attacks, whereas war elephants were effectively deployed against a mass of enemy infantry and fortified enemy positions. Well-trained war elephants were excellent weapon platforms for large crossbows and light cannon.[40] Both chargers and war elephants formed part of the centralised

---

35 Mendes Pinto, *Peregrinação*, 53.
36 Damrong Rajanubhab, *Phra Ratchaopongsawadan*, 307.
37 Kulap and Bōdindēchā (Sing), *Annam–Siam Yuth*, 40.
38 Mendes Pinto, *Peregrinação*, 89; Michael Charney, 'A reassessment of hyperbolic military statistics in some early modern Burmese texts', *Journal of the Economic and Social History of the Orient*, 46:2 (January 2003), 208–11.
39 Thiphākōnwongmahākōsāthibōdī (Kham), *Phrarātchaphongsāwadān Krung*, 141–4.
40 Jacq-Hergoualc'h and Smithies, *The Armies of Angkor*, 28–32.

nucleus of the royal armies: the Siamese *Three Seals Law* legal book tells us that the royal *krom* (division) was directly responsible for the procuring and maintenance of these service animals.[41]

Before the advent of firearms, the Khmer Empire enlisted Chinese crossbowmen; the overseas Chinese also introduced both the Chams and the Khmers to a ballista mounted on the back of an elephant during the siege of Angkor Wat and the subsequent wars.[42] Both the Siamese and the Burmese polities enjoyed the almost total control of firepower through their control of international trade, which in turn facilitated their professional cadres to control both the mass corvée levies and conquered populations. The evidence of Ayutthaya's use of firearms in the war against the Lanna kingdom's capital, Chiangmai, was depicted in the *Yuan Pai* poem; the Siamese carried harquebuses and arranged fired salvos against the Lanna forces in 1451.[43]

Cannon played a vital role in siege warfare against enemy capitals. Both the Siamese and the Burmese monarchies enjoyed technological advantages through international trade, with European adventurers and mercenaries importing European military technology and tactics. The royal governments' control of artillery facilitated political centralisation and the domination of vassals throughout their lands. To control the populace of a conquered area, mass casualties were initially inflicted in battles with great brutality, to facilitate the subsequent forced population resettlements. Crucially, these wars were fought not mainly to conquer territories; rather the belligerents sought to acquire more labour force.

Adversaries

The major Indic polities of mainland south-east Asia went to war to extend their *mandala* – their realm, their sphere of power and influence. A metaphoric interpretation articulated by Kautilya in his *Arthashastra*, this depicts relations between monarchs (and their polities) as circles devoid of fixed frontiers or other demarcation. Kautilya postulated that one's neighbours were one's enemies, and their neighbours on the other side were one's natural allies. In this system, all monarchs would seek to extend their *mandala* at the expense of their neighbours. Warfare was a highly normalised affair. Striving to become sole *cakravati*, kings saw it as their duty to win prestige through the expansion of their realm, as the rivals of neighbouring kings, their

41 Lingat Robert (trans.), *Kotmai Tra Sam Duang* (*The Three Seals Law*), Volume II (Bangkok: Kurusapa, 1962), 250–60.
42 Jacq-Hergoualc'h and Smithies, *The Armies of Angkor*, 28–35.
43 Phra Khlang (Hon), *Lilit Yuan Phai*, 36.

enemy–rivals. No supra-polity order bound them together to contain this trend towards war, which was endemic. Thus there were long and bitter wars between the Burmese and the Siamese, and between the latter and the Khmer.

In the East, the Cham people forming the Champa principalities constituted the primary threat to the Khmer Empire with their amphibious raids on the empire's southern shores which challenged Angkor's military might. The Chams did not have visible political or territorial objectives in invading the Khmer Empire other than that of pillaging the Cambodians with their powerful amphibious fleet.[44] Eventually, the Cham laid waste to Angkor itself; the Khmer retaliated with a massive campaign against the Cham people.

From the fifteenth century, the kingdom of Ayutthaya became the enemy of the Cambodians when these defected from Ayutthaya, an event referred to as the *Khmer prae paktr* or the defection or attitude change of the Khmers.[45] In the following century, after Ayutthaya's wars with Taungoo Burma, King Satha I of Cambodia in 1546 opportunistically attacked the enfeebled realm of Ayutthaya to plunder the population.[46] He continued to ravage Ayutthaya until Siamese king Naresuan the Great could turn the tables on him, in 1594 destroying Lovek, the capital of Cambodia after Angkor, with its populace being resettled in the Siamese domains.[47]

Enmity was not primarily a function of ethnic differences, but of the common heritage of the *cakravati* culture. Alongside these patterns, ethnic differences could also underpin competition over land and resources, with older forms of warfare persisting in the form of raids by tribal forces against sedentary polities, especially in the mountains of Burma. On the fringes of the *mandala* of the Burmese kings, the ethnic composition of the population was always diverse, and the kings faced constant challenges from the Mons, the Shan people, the Karens and others. The Burmese kings always sought to subjugate the tribes and polities surrounding their *mandala*. Whenever the central Burmese authority was weakened, smaller kingdoms and tribes could challenge it. After the wars with Ayutthaya in the late sixteenth century weakened the Taungoo dynasty and destabilised Burma, the restive population of Manipuri assaulted Burma on horseback.[48] As the Taungoo kingdom went into decline, the Mons in Pegu became increasingly powerful, challenging Burmese power.

---

44 D. P. Chandler, *A History of Cambodia*, 4th ed. (Boulder: Westview Press, 2008), 69.
45 S. Phakdīkham, *Khamēn rop Thai (The Wars between the Khmers and the Thais)* (Bangkok: Matichon, 2011), 96–100.
46 Damrong Rajanubhab, *Thai Rop Phama* 321–2.
47 Phakdīkham, *Khamēn rop Thai*, 197–213.
48 P. Surakiat, *Mīanmā-Sayāmyut* (Bangkok: Matichon, 2010), 152.

The Siamese tended to set upon the other polities to assert their dominance; the expansionist culture drove the king to venture on military expeditions to acquire more vassal polities.[49] One of the major wars between these Tai-speaking kingdoms was caused by a defection of Ayutthaya's former vassal polity, Phitsanulok, that had pledged loyalty to Lanna Chiangmai under the powerful northern king Tilokaraj (r. 1441–1487).[50] The Siamese monarchs pushed back against the northern Tai polity (the Lanna) that had expanded its sphere of influence into the regions of Ayutthaya's vassal in the upper central of provinces of modern Thailand. Ayutthaya waged wars against the northern Tai kingdom of Chiangmai to secure its control over the Laotian people, incorporating them into the tributary and labour system for Siam's prosperity. After the downfall of Ayutthaya in 1767, the Siamese successor polities continually expanded and absorbed other Tai polities surrounding it and became increasingly powerful in an effort to replenish manpower after the destruction of Ayutthaya as Siam's old *mandala* centre.

Causes and Purposes of Wars

All sides' understanding of inter-polity relations was one of structural hostility, with endemic wars. In the Indian tradition of political thought, the *cakravati* is the ideal universal ruler, the temporal representative of the Buddha. Buddhism had originally defined the universal ruler as benign and non-violent.[51] Despite the Buddhist teachings of peace and harmony, in order to become the sole, universal, ruler, the *cakravati*, in the larger geographic region, or at least to increase one's *mandala*, one had to subdue or eliminate all the rivals to this position. This logically led to wars in which polities defeating each other swallowed up the defeated party, while the Buddhist ideal of non-violence receded and was at best understood metaphysically. The strategic destruction of the enemy capital – the aim of the Burmese, Siamese and Khmer in many of their wars – had the purpose of destroying the core of the enemy's *mandala*. In the minds of the Indic rulers, territories were seen as reminiscent of 'galactic polities', as spheres or circles of political

49 Thaworawatsakun, *Khunnang Ayutthaya*, 52–7.
50 Phrayā Prachākitčhakōnračhak (Chǣm Bunnāk), *Phongsāwadān Yōnok* (Bangkok: Silpabarnakarn, 1961), 356.
51 S. J. Tambiah, *World Conqueror and World Renouncer: A Study of Buddhism and Polity in Thailand against a Historical Background* (Cambridge: Cambridge University Press, 1976), 42.

influence vaguely defined areas and the people dwelling in them.[52] The power sphere of the galactic polity also constituted the network of alliances with polities surrounding each *mandala*.[53] Polities of this region mainly waged wars over population and trade routes rather than aiming to capture land. The need to mark boundaries was not part of the mental approach. This became clear when the British Empire attempted to demarcate the boundaries with the Siamese after the First Anglo-Burmese War (1824–1826) as the Siamese continued to raid and opportunistically and forcefully captured population from the newly acquired British territories.[54]

Despite the shared Buddhist values of mercy and non-retribution, even towards murder and violence, Buddhism in this regional mix with Hindu traditions proved compatible with a militaristic society. Buddhism teaches that all lives are predestined due to *karma*. Thus, under the *karmic* system, power relations in this world are the constant cycles of suffering and retribution. In the long run, the Hindu–Buddhist polities of mainland south-east Asia fostered the self-aggrandising imperialistic design resembling that of the Western *gloire*, the pursuit of prestige through military contests.[55] Imperialistic in its essence, the *cakravati* teaching stipulated that a king with *bhune* (merit) and *paramita* (charisma) entitled him to impose power on other lesser monarchs, so that the dominant ruler could 'ride his chariot across the realm unchallenged', the literal meaning of *cakravati* ('the rolling wheels').[56] *Bhune* and *paramita* are comparable to Machiavelli's *virtù* and *fortuna*, in that those who possessed enough of these attributes could seize the initiative and vanquish their enemies, whereas those who ran out of the meritorious *bhune* or were *sin bhune*, 'fallen from grace', would become prey to other more meritorious and charismatic kings. This brought about highly unilateral inter-state relations between the large and militarily powerful polities and the weaker ones who were fated to become subservient to them. The larger polities were considered to be morally superior and more meritorious and would save the people from poor governance.[57] As King Aluangpaya of Konbaung Burma laid siege to Ayutthaya in 1765, the Burmese king declared that he himself was *arimittiya*, the incarnation of

---

52 Tambiah, *World Conqueror and World Renouncer*, 102–7.
53 O. W. Wolters, *History, Culture, and Region in Southeast Asian Perspectives*, rev. ed. (Ithaca, NY: Southeast Asia Program Publications, Southeast Asia Program, Cornell University, 1999), 28.
54 Winichakul, *Siam Mapped*, 64–5.
55 J. Black, *War and the Cultural Turn* (Cambridge: Polity, 2012), 44–7.
56 S. Chutintaranond, *'Cakravartin': The Ideology of Traditional Warfare in Siam and Burma, 1548–1605* (Ann Arbor: Michigan University Press, 1990), 46.
57 C. J. Baker and Pasuk Phongpaichit, *A History of Thailand*, 3rd ed. (Cambridge: Cambridge University Press, 2014), 31.

the future Buddha, and called upon the Siamese to surrender unconditionally (the Siamese found his hyperbolic claim ridiculous).[58]

Claiming moral superiority, monarchs prevailing in war felt the 'responsibility to impose retribution' upon the morally inferior states. The weakened states were basically suffering *karmic* retribution for moral decline or for deeds from previous lifetimes, allowing them to suffer the current fates, which were predetermined.[59] This in turn justified the demand for tribute and manpower from the lesser vassal polities.

This went hand in hand with economic motivations: the victor aimed to exploit his population and natural resources. Military objectives were to acquire tribute payments, manpower and recognition of superiority.[60] The population density of this part of the world was relatively low; therefore the war aims of the polities were to capture and gather populace from enemy realms and to resettle them where labour was needed. Populations would thus frequently be moved to increase the labour force of the victorious polity. Thus the thirteen independent Tai-speaking kingdoms of south-east Asia were reduced to a mere four by war between 1340 and 1540.[61] Thereafter, the wars between Siam and Burma and Siam and Cambodia could be seen as serial retaliation. Raiding by land or by sea also continued to be a purpose of wars, leading to vendetta military campaigns.

True power came from the command over the displaced communities or distant vassals who sent annual tribute. The perception of territoriality lacked the notion of borders. Instead, it was imagined as overlapping spheres of influence of peer competitors who exercised power over the smaller vassal polities. The bigger polities attempted to conquer or plunder the vassal polities situated on the outer edges of their competitors' spheres. Allegiance and alliance for protection led to wars. The power struggle between Ayutthaya and Lanna was largely caused by the latter attacking Ayutthaya's key northern vassal polity. Any powerful kingdom would exploit any opportunity to wage war against weakened ones in the imperative to expand their *mandala* influence.

---

58 J. Kathirithamby-Wells, 'The age of transition: the mid-eighteenth to the early nineteenth centuries', in N. Tarling (ed.), *The Cambridge History of Southeast Asia*, Volume II (Cambridge: Cambridge University Press, 1992), 579–80.

59 K. Roy, *Hinduism and the Ethics of Warfare in South Asia: From Antiquity to the Present* (Cambridge: Cambridge University Press, 2012), 44.

60 T. Winichakul, *Siam Mapped: A History of the Geo-body of a Nation* (Chiang Mai: Silkworm Books, 1994), 81–2.

61 V. B. Lieberman, *Strange Parallels*, Volume I: *Integration of the Mainland: Southeast Asia in Global Context, c. 800–1830* (New York: Cambridge University Press, 2003), 248.

Alliances were at times confirmed by dynastic marriages, as in the alliance between Ayutthaya and Lan Xang against the Taungoo Empire through the planned wedding between King Setthathirath of Lan Xang and Princess Thep Kasattri, daughter of King Maha Chakkraphat. The plan was sabotaged by King Mahathammaracha of Phitsunulok, one-time vassal of Ayutthaya who defected and affiliated his realm to Taungoo Burma. The Burmese forces intercepted the princess, triggering war between Lan Xang and Phitsanulok that resulted in the Burmese invasion of Lan Xang.[62] Against the background of polygamy, intermarriage between the Indic polities did not bring about succession wars; if there were attempts to impose hegemony on vassals, the powerful kingdoms would assign governors or a Crown prince to rule these vassal states directly, as Konbaung Burma did to Chiangmai with a governor in 1725 after the bloody invasion,[63] and Thonburi Siam's similar attempt in Cambodia with his son in 1781.[64] In both cases, the cause of the war was not one of contested dynastic succession, but dispute over vassals among expansionist peer competitors.

Premises Underlying Strategic Decisions and Objectives

The strategic decisions of Indic rulers were dominated by the grand scheme of securing control over their *mandala* and extending it to become *cakravati* within an imperial perception that could vary from polity to polity. According to the *Arthashastra*, each polity had to maintain its *mandala* along with its population and aristocracy.[65] It describes the need for fortifications of the capital city, of towns and of frontiers. The south-east Asian polities, however, saw their frontiers as fluid or as boundary regions, such as the Tenasserim mountain range that marked the contact zone between the Siamese and the Burmese kingdoms, but the capitals, the cores of the *mandalas*, were clearly the centre of gravity and of settlement.

The Khmer Empire's defence was a highly centralised affair, above all to protect its capital and population from the raiding forces of Champa. After his imprisonment in Champa, King Jayavarman VII resolved to retaliate by launching a full-scale war of revenge against the Chams' pirate raids. His strategic aim was to deter future raids. At the end of this victorious campaign, he took the Cham king back to Cambodia as a hostage, then in 1190 divided the Champa polity. His (short-term) strategic success was secured by negotiating

62 D. K. Wyatt, *Thailand: A Short History* (Chiang Mai: Silkworm Books, 2004), 81.
63 Phrayā Prachākitčhakōnračhak (Chǣm Bunnāk), *Phongsāwadān Yōnok*, 457–58.
64 Phakdīkham, *Khamēn rop Thai*, 260–8.   65 Kautilya, *Arthashastra*, 119–21.

the neutrality of the neighbouring Dai Viet, a nice example of the strategic use of diplomacy.[66]

In general, most of the war aims were to weaken enemy polities or destroy them, so the *mandala* and *cakravati* of the ambitious monarchs would flourish at the expense of others. The devastated polities' manpower would be subsumed into the victors' power. Originally, the stronger polities either sought to control the manpower of the weaker polities from afar or turn them into sources of permanent tribute. When this led to endless wars of retribution aiming to reverse earlier defeats, the contesting polities would begin to aim for the annihilation of enemy polities in order to absorb their population permanently and dissolve their *mandala* once and for all. Thus Ayutthaya absorbed neighbouring Cambodian and Tai polities.[67]

Nonetheless, internal unrest among the ruling classes of Ayutthaya continually plagued the kingdom; there was a series of insurrections of pretenders to the throne commanding personal bodyguards and mercenary forces. Thus Ayutthaya lost its grip on some Tai polities, especially Lanna, which leaned towards the Burmese and later became Konbaung Burma's vital source of manpower against the Siamese.

After the destruction of Ayutthaya at the hands of the vastly superior Burmese forces of Konbaung Burma in 1767, its successors of the Thonburi and Rattanakosin periods (1768–1851) continually sought to reassert their control over the Tai populations to be able to mobilise them for the recurring Burmese wars. With the aim of restoring Siam's *mandala*, Siam became increasingly aggressive and assertive towards Laos and Cambodia, with Siam annexing and dissolving the smaller Indic polities. This programme led to decades of conflict in the Indochinese region from the Anouvong Insurrection in 1827 to the wars with Vietnam. The military disaster inflicted upon the late Ayutthaya state by Konbaung Burma traumatised the Siamese rulers, whose strategies became notoriously pre-emptive. In 1833, Siamese king Rama III, concerned about Vietnamese influence in Indo-China, decided to attack Nguyen Vietnam pre-emptively, seizing the opportunity when the Vietnamese were fighting against rebellions in the south.[68]

Conforming to the general pattern, both the Taungoo and the Konbaung dynasties who ruled Burma from the sixteenth century until the end of the nineteenth aimed strategically to subdue neighbouring polities with their various ethnicities in order to extend their *mandala*. Rulers of both the

66 Coedès, *The Indianized States of South-East Asia*, 170–1.
67 M. Thaworawatsakun, *Khunnang Ayutthaya*, 41.
68 Kulap and Bōdindēchā (Sing), *Annam–Siam Yuth*, 170–1.

Taungoo and Konbaung dynasties suppressed ethnic minorities to impose their power on Burmese and non-Burmese alike, drawing on the divine *paramita* of their *cakravati*. King Bayinnaung of the Taungoo Empire conquered the region that included the entirety of mainland south-east Asia, comprising Siam, Lanna, Lan Xang, Pegu, Arakan and other minor polities.[69] Konbaung Burma adopted an even grander strategy, taking on Qing China and the Mughal Empire, whereas the Siamese polities generally did not perceive Burma as a part of their *mandala*.[70] Burma's expansionist military expeditions of the eighteenth and nineteenth centuries would eventually lead to the clash with the British Empire in the First Anglo-Burmese War (1824–1826).

Priorities

Strategic prioritisation depended on the circumstances of each Indic polity. The priority was usually to ensure the survival of their *mandala* or power sphere, but any war seeking to enlarge it risked inversion and the destruction of one's own capital as the core of the *mandala*. The more they could strengthen their *mandala*, the more secure their centre. Thus the priority was to dominate their neighbours around the kingdom, turning them into *pratesaraj* (vassals or client polities). As the attitudes of the surrounding polities changed or defections to other major polities occurred, strong monarchs did not hesitate to wage punitive war against former clients and allies.

Beyond this basic pattern, prioritisation was a function of internal politics. The Khmer Empire and the Siamese kingdoms used force to keep populations within their sphere of influence subdued, and to capture or forcibly move populations from a peer competitor's *mandala*, to disperse or resettle the fleeing people and rebuild new communities within the conquered territories. The campaign against the Chams by Khmer king Jayavarman VII (r. 1181–1218) resulted in the Khmer Empire sacking Champa's capital city, subduing the rival Chams. This brought the Cham threat to an end and even led to tribute payments from Pagan Burma, according to Ma Tuan-lin's account.[71] The Siamese operated in similar strategic patterns by expanding their control over other Tai polities: in the Ayutthaya period, Siam invaded Cambodia to resettle large numbers of its subjects within Ayutthaya's sphere.[72] The ideal strategic aim was to subdue

---

69 P. Surakiat, *Mīanmā-Sayāmyut*, 281–2.

70 Sunait Chutitaranond, *Phama Rop Thai: Wadua Kansongkram Rawang Thai Kap Phama (Burmese Fought Thai: On War between Thai and Burmese)* (Bangkok: Matichon, 2013), 188–97.

71 L. P. Briggs, *The Ancient Khmer Empire* (Bangkok: White Lotus Press, 1999), 217.

72 Thaworawatsakun, *Khunnang Ayutthaya*, 72–4.

rivals' ruling classes and commoners alike. Annual gold and silver trees as tribute were the lucrative outcome. Following the destruction of Ayutthaya's *mandala*, Konbaung Burmese forces immediately deported the Siamese populace and resettled them in Burma. Population displacement, therefore, was a highly prioritised strategy.

This is reflected also in the response of General Bodin Decha under Siamese king Rama III after the abortive expedition against Nguyen Vietnam in 1833. Before retreating from the southern Vietnamese city of Chau Doc, the general resolved to raze the city, tearing down its walls and fortifications, and demolishing all commoners' settlements to prevent the Vietnamese from using the city as an outpost against Siam. He then relocated the Vietnamese population along with the Cambodians to Siam's eastern provinces, so they could be resettled at the fortified coastal city of Chanthaburi to withstand future Vietnamese naval raids.[73]

Application of Strategy

Turning on the concept of *mandala* and *cakravati*, the long-term strategy of expansion could be pursued directly by fighting wars, or indirectly by threatening to force smaller polities into submission. In wartime, the Burmese would muster a large army from their own polity and from all vassal polities and marshal supplies sufficient to conduct protracted siege warfare against enemy capitals. The Siamese in the sixteenth century withstood the Burmese invasion by fortifying Ayutthaya itself and creating defences in depth in its *mandala*, then waiting for the monsoon season to obstruct the Burmese forces with floods. In turn this would allow the Siamese forces to attack the surrounding Burmese with boats armed with cannon, while mobilising their allies to attack the Burmese camps and relieve their city from the siege. In 1569 and 1767, however, this strategy failed, and Ayutthaya fell to the Burmese, in the latter case spelling the end of its role as the capital of Siam. Konbaung Burma effectively mobilised amphibious forces and bombarded the Siamese city with cannon throughout the wet season, ultimately sacking Ayutthaya.[74]

Protecting or expanding their *mandala* could involve the creation of military outposts to secure key passages. The preparation of longer campaigns was complex, especially when it included the monsoon season. The more influence

---

73 Kulap and Bōdindēchā (Sing), *Annam–Siam Yuth*, 234–5, 317.
74 S. Chutitaranond, *Phama Rop Thai*, 253.

a polity had over war materiel and the vassals situated near the areas under the adversaries' rule, the more likely a strategic incursion was to succeed.[75]

The strategy of population displacement was applied increasingly, well into the nineteenth century. Enemy populations were forced into submission through violent repression. This policy included the systematic massacring of resisters, as the Burmese did when they seized Ayutthaya. The Siamese in turn had the term *klia klom*, meaning 'persuading one to pledge allegiance', effectively armed coercion taking the form of massacring the entire resistant community or deporting them to resettle them elsewhere. For example, Bangkok applied this policy to the Laotian cities of Houaphanh province in 1834 during the war against Vietnam in which the Laotians were attempting to escape from Siamese forces in the north.[76] The effort to keep the vassal polities' allegiance was central to Siam's strategy in the nineteenth century.[77]

Pitched battles were also important and at times decisive, although second in importance to the capture or destruction of enemy capitals and mass population displacement. Battles tended to occur in the context of sieges of enemy capitals. If defeated, defenders had to retreat inside the city walls or to other fortified positions. However, decisive battles might take the form of battles for decisive outposts along borders, before further incursions into enemy territory, or they might be fought over attempts to repatriate captured civilians. Thus King Naresuan the Great ambushed the army of the Taungoo Crown prince Nanda Bayin that marched to attack Ayutthaya in 1590 after small skirmishes as a ruse at the western frontier city of Khanchanaburi.[78] Following Naresuan, Maha Sura Singhanat, the viceroy of Rama I of Chakri Bangkok, successfully executed outpost siege warfare along with guerrilla harassments of the sizeable Konbaung Army under Bodawpaya's command that weakened the Burmese before the decisive battle that drove the defeated Burmese out in 1785.[79] These two cases combined the preclusive and pre-emptive defence against enemy expeditions that required protracted outpost siege warfare, and the eventual pitched battles to decide the outcomes of the campaigns. Thus battles became necessary as the defensive strategy changed from the defence in depth to preclusive outpost wars.

Naval forces were vital strategically as they offered quick and cheap lines of communication for the cumbersome armies of the polities. Apart from the

75 P. Surakiat, *Mianmā-Sayāmyut*, 279–81.
76 Thiphākọnwongmahākōsāthibọdī (Kham), *Phrarātchaphongsāwadān Krung*, 1150–1.
77 Kulap and Bōdindēchā (Sing), *Annam–Siam Yuth*.
78 Damrong Rajanubhab, *Thai Rop Phama*, 129–31.
79 Thiphākọnwongmahākōsāthibọdī (Kham), *Phrarātchaphongsāwadān Krung*, 149–51.

Khmers and Chams who were accustomed to riverine warfare and piratical raids, the Siamese and Burmese began to engage in maritime combat more often in the nineteenth century as Konbaung Burma sought to cut Siam's key southern provinces off from Bangkok. A key maritime battle took place as the Burmese attempted to take Phuket in 1809; the Siamese sent naval forces of junk galleys armed with cannon in response. The Siamese ships' firepower proved effective, forcing the Burmese to retreat.[80] Naval forces also served to transport war materiel. After losing most of the major ships and smaller vessels to the Vietnamese navy in an expedition against southern Vietnam in 1833, the Siamese could no longer control the city of Chau Doc and decided to withdraw before becoming overwhelmed by the combined land and naval forces of the Vietnamese.[81] While none of the Indic polities attempted to establish systematic control over the sea, they built riverine fortifications allowing them to collect taxes from merchantmen entering the ports for trade with the *mandala* centres. Anti-piracy naval forces joined arms with armed Chinese merchantmen that served as the court's trading contractors, especially against the Malay pirates.[82]

Historiographic Debates

The relevant historiography centres on 'externalist narratives' that emphasise cultural diffusion of Brahmin Hinduism and Buddhism from India, i.e. an 'Indianisation process', affecting sociocultural developments, especially state-craft, the legal system and concepts of kingship (the *cakravati* ideology).[83] By contrast, 'internalist narratives' apply a nineteenth-century European nationalist approach to south-east Asia, particularly to the Burmese–Siamese and the Khmer–Siamese wars, casting them not in terms of warring kings, but of eternally inimical nations. The demonisation of the adversaries is indeed a dominant theme in national narratives. Prince Damrong denounced the Burmese strategic annihilation of the Ayutthaya kingdom in 1767 as by 'the army of bandits'.[84]

Other historians are critical of these nationalist narratives; the works of Sunait Chutitaranond suggest that the concept of nation in Thai historiography was built around the premodern wars with the Burmese in the urge to fortify the idea of nationalism with Burma as enemy nation.[85] Pamaree Surakiat argues that by

---

80 Thiphākǭnwongmahākōsāthibǭdī (Kham), *Phrarātchaphongsāwadān Krung*, pp. 416–17.
81 Kulap and Bǭdindēchā (Sing), *Annam–Siam Yuth*, 233–7.
82 Thailand. Krom Sinlapākō'n, *Chotmāihēt Ratchakān Thī 3* (Bangkok: Krom Sinlapākō'n, 1987), 18–19.
83 D. G. E. Hall, *Prawattisāt 'Ēchīa Tawan'ǭk Chīangtai lem thī 1* (*A History of South-East Asia*, Volume 1) (trans. Warunyuphā Sanitwong Na 'Ayutthayā) (Bangkok: Thai Watana Panich Publishing, 1979), 23.
84 Damrong Rajanubhab, *Thai Rop Phama*, 338.   85 Chutitaranond, *Phama Rop Thai*, 44–6.

and by, the Burmese polities transformed the relationship between the dominant kingdom and other polities from patron–vassal relationships to aggressive centralisation under the *cakravati* ideology; thereby, Konbaung Burma did not hesitate to execute the decapitation of Ayutthaya to eradicate any competing *mandala* in the eyes of Konbaung Burma, unlike its predecessors.[86]

Despite Prince Damrong's denunciation of the 'Konbaung bandits' that sacked late Ayutthaya, the pattern of sporadic extermination of enemy capitals can be seen throughout the long period of premodern/early modern south-east Asian warfare. The Ayutthayan Siamese conducted the systematic destruction of Cambodian capitals (Angkor Wat, then Lovek) and abducted the population to their own capital. As we have seen, this strategy was followed by all the major Indic polities. Furthermore, as previously discussed, the strategic changes were influenced by the process of restoration of the Burmese Indic polity, which sought to project its absolute superiority over other polities, thus seeking to eradicate its rival in the region. The war aim was no longer to force others to become vassals but to destroy the core of the *mandala* and then drain the population to strengthen the newly flourished Burmese Empire. Interestingly enough, this approach of strategic annihilation had become prevalent in the late eighteenth century and the nineteenth for the Siamese, as the successors of Ayutthaya followed Konbaung Burma's approach by seeking to dissolve their former vassals' *mandalas* and establish their own centralised authority. Siam extended its power over the 'Tai world', which extended into Laos, Lanna and Cambodia. Bangkok divided and ruled the Laotian principalities, seizing their workforce to weaken Vientiane's position.[87] This became the cause of a series of nineteenth-century wars. After the Anouvong Rebellion in 1827, Siam destroyed Vientiane.

Over the centuries, the wars between the Indic polities thus became increasingly destructive and brutal. Atrocities were interpreted as the bad karma that all lives were born to suffer.

---

86 P. Surakiat, *Mīanmā-Sayāmyut*, 281–4.
87 Mayoury Ngaosyvathn, *Paths to Conflagration: Fifty Years of Diplomacy and Warfare in Laos, Thailand, and Vietnam, 1778–1828* (Ithaca: Southeast Asia Program Publications, 1998), 42–5.

16

Pre-Columbian and Early Historic Native American Warfare

PATRICIA M. LAMBERT

As in other world regions, warfare in pre-Columbian North America varied considerably in nature and scale across time and geographic space. In the diverse array of pre-state societies that peopled this landscape prehistorically, warfare was generally more personal and less formalised than in the state-level societies of Mesoamerica and the Andes region of South America, where state-sanctioned warfare could include elite warriors, formal military campaigns and complex war rituals.[1] Unlike in these state-level societies, however, where war was memorialised in epigraphic accounts or in detailed iconographic images, records are generally lacking for pre-Columbian North America and in consequence the deep history of warfare here has largely been reconstructed from the archaeological record, informed in part by written accounts of European explorers, missionaries and colonists, and the oral histories of Indigenous peoples. Nonetheless, this region offers an unparalleled opportunity to examine the nature of war in an array of political systems unique to those that form the corpus of this volume, providing a comparative framework for assessing the similarities and differences in the practice of war across a broad sociopolitical spectrum.

According to archaeological evidence, warfare in North America may be traced back to as early as 6,000 to 8,000 years ago. On the whole, warfare here was relatively small in scale for much of the preliterate period, though notable exceptions exist when viewed from the perspective of mortality rates.[2] This pattern changed in the last millennium before European contact, especially during the period from AD 1000 to 1500, when both the frequency

---

1 Patricia M. Lambert, 'The archaeology of war: a North American perspective', *Journal of Archaeological Research*, 10:3 (2002), 207–41. Andrew K. Scherer and John W. Verano (eds), *Embattled Bodies, Embattled Places: War in Pre-Columbian Mesoamerica and the Andes* (Washington, DC: Dumbarton Oaks).

2 Lambert, 'The archaeology of war'. Cave 7, a 2000-year-old Basketmaker II cemetery site in southeastern Utah, for example, contained the remains of around ninety-four people, of whom at least 27 per cent (40 per cent male) died by violence.

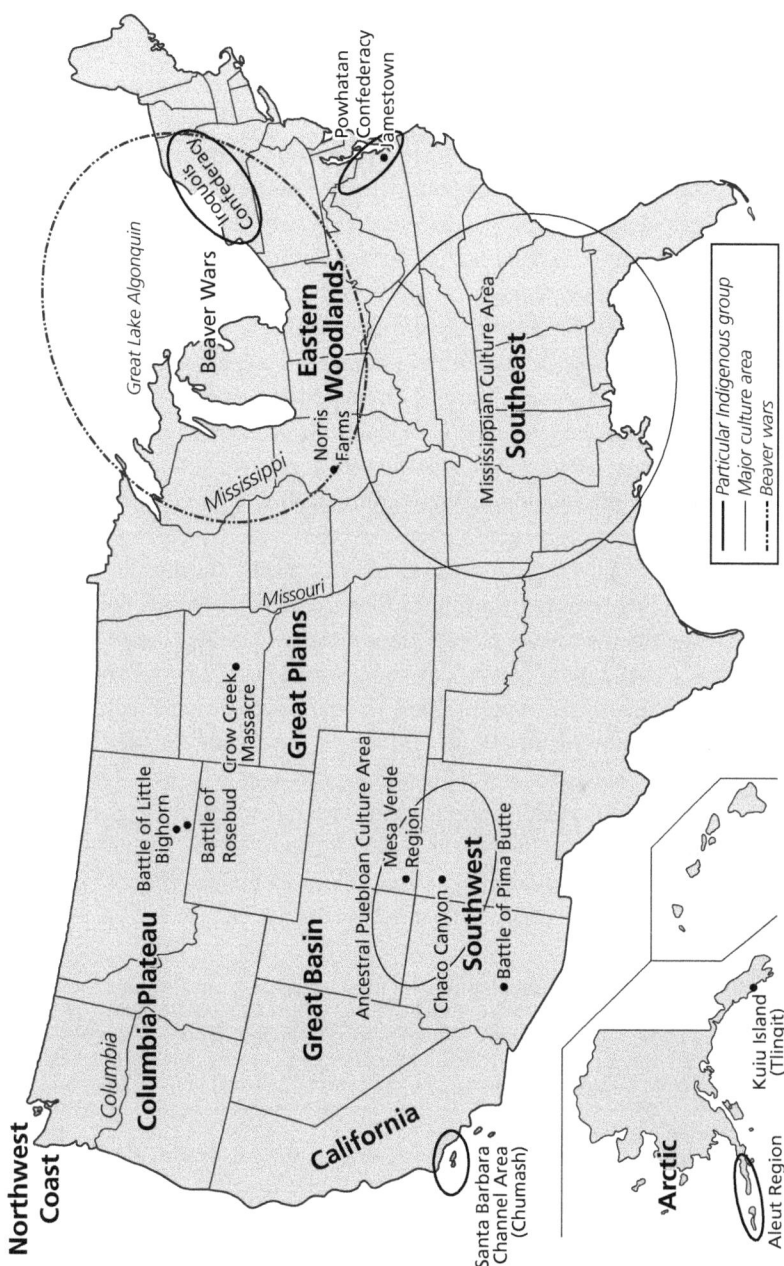

Map 16.1 Pre-Columbian and early historic Native American battles, wars and regional conflict (1000–1860)

Northwest
Coast

Columbia

Columbia Plateau

Battle of Little
Bighorn

Battle of
Rosebud

Crow Creek
Massacre

Great Plains

Great Basin

Missouri

Ancestral Puebloan Culture Area

Mesa Verde
Region

Chaco Canyon

Southwest

Battle of Pima Butte

California

Santa Barbara
Channel Area
(Chumash)

Mississippi

Norris
Farms

Eastern
Woodlands

Beaver Wars

Great Lake Algonquin

Iroquois
Confederacy

Powhatan
Confederacy
Jamestown

Mississippian Culture Area

Southeast

Arctic

Kuiu Island
(Tlingit)

Aleut Region

Particular Indigenous group
Major culture area
Beaver wars

and severity of war escalated across the continent.[3] It is from this period and the early years of European contact that much of our understanding of Indigenous North American warfare derives.

One of the most accessible types of archaeological information on war strategy pertains to defence, as defensive measures usually involve visible shifts in settlement configuration, size and location. Around 1250 in the Four Corners region of the American Southwest, for example, Ancestral Puebloan farmers shifted from dispersed hamlets on valley floors near agricultural fields to aggregated settlements on defensible hilltops or prominences, or into inaccessible rock shelters on steep cliff faces, indicating a change in settlement priorities towards increased defensibility.[4] Defensive architectural features, such as walls, palisades and towers, often appeared in conjunction with such settlement shifts, varying in accordance with unique landscape attributes and the raw materials available for construction. Line-of-sight visibility between settlements also played a role in strategic defence in some times and places, permitting communication between allies in times of war. This strategy appears to have been employed by Puebloan communities in the Kayenta region of northeastern Arizona during the thirteenth century, enabling remote communications among allies within and between valleys.[5] Viewshed was also an important priority for village locations on the Northwest Coast, where enemies came by sea and visibility over open water allowed residents to spot approaching war canoes in time to seek shelter in nearby redoubts or island refugia.[6] Many of these responses are strikingly similar to those seen in medieval Europe, for example, where castles and forts were built on hills, rocky outcrops and steep shorelines for defence and enhanced viewshed.

When defences failed, burned houses, unburied bodies, violent injuries in human skeletal remains and signs of trophy taking left a record of strategies

---

3 Patricia M. Lambert, 'Indigenous warfare in North America', in Burkhard Meissner, Kurt Raaflaub, Oliver Schmitt and Robin Yates (eds), *The Cambridge History of War*, Volume I: *War and the Ancient World* (Cambridge: Cambridge University Press, in press).

4 Jonathan Haas and Winifred Creamer, *Stress and Warfare among the Kayenta Anasazi of the Thirteenth Century* A.D. (Chicago: Field Museum of Natural History, 1993); Steven A. LeBlanc, *Prehistoric Warfare in the American Southwest* (Salt Lake City: University of Utah Press, 1999), 197–245.

5 Haas and Creamer, *Stress and Warfare among the Kayenta Anasazi*, 53–72; Patricia M. Lambert, 'War histories in evolutionary perspective: insights from prehistoric North America', in Todd K. Shackelford and Viviana A. Weekes-Shackelford (eds), *The Oxford Handbook of Evolutionary Perspectives on Violence, Homicide, and War* (New York: Oxford University Press, 2012), 324–38.

6 Kenneth M. Ames and Herbert D.G. Maschner, *Peoples of the Northwest Coast: Their Archaeology and Prehistory* (London: Thames and Hudson, 1999), 214–16.

employed by attackers.[7] These archaeological indicators have enabled estimates of the nature and scale of attacks, such as the devastating fourteenth-century massacre at Crow Creek on the northern Great Plains.[8]

Weaponry specific to warfare was less common in pre-Columbian North America than in some parts of the world, as warriors were community members drawn away from daily life when fighting forces were needed rather than professional soldiers in standing armies provisioned and equipped for prolonged military campaigns. Equipment such as spears, bows, atlatls and adzes used in battle might also be used for hunting or domestic activities, as men (and sometimes women) moved between their roles as warriors and providers. That said, war armaments have been identified in the archaeological record of some regions, such as bone and stone war clubs on the Northwest Coast;[9] tomahawks in Algonquian and Iroquoian areas of northeastern North America;[10] and Aleut clubs, shields and body armour on the lower Alaska peninsula.[11] The most common weapons of war across North America were probably various clubbing implements and the bow and arrow after its adoption in the first millennium AD. Osteological evidence such as stone points embedded in bone and depressed cranial vault fractures clearly document the use of these weapons for killing humans.[12] Despite the availability of similar technology, however, weapons of choice often varied by region: the bow and arrow for lethal conflict in coastal California, for example, versus shock weapons in the northern Southwest.[13]

Human skeletal remains have yielded some of the most definitive evidence for the existence and nature of war in pre-Columbian North America, providing information on weaponry and forms of engagement, as well as the age and sex of the dead and wounded, rates of violent

---

7 Lambert, 'The archaeology of war'.
8 P. Willey, *Prehistoric Warfare on the Great Plains* (New York: Garland, 1990); Douglas B. Bamforth, 'Climate, chronology and the course of war in the middle Missouri region of the North American Plains', in Elizabeth N. Arkush and Mark W. Allen (eds), *The Archaeology of Warfare: Prehistories of Raiding and Conquest* (Gainesville: University Press of Florida, 2006), 66–100. Note: based on complexities associated with dating the site, Bamforth has suggested that the raid may have occurred in the fifteenth century.
9 Ames and Maschner, *Peoples of the Northwest Coast*.
10 Colin F. Taylor, *Native American Weapons* (Norman: University of Oklahoma Press, 2001), 30.
11 Herbert D. G. Maschner and Katherine L. Reedy-Maschner, 'Raid, retreat, defend (repeat): the archaeology and ethnohistory of warfare on the north Pacific Rim', *Journal of Anthropological Archaeology*, 17 (1998), 19–51.
12 Patricia M. Lambert, 'The osteological evidence for indigenous warfare in North America', in R. J. Chacon and R. Mendoza (eds), *North American Indigenous Warfare and Ritualized Violence* (Tucson: University of Arizona Press, 2007), 202–21.
13 Lambert, 'War histories in evolutionary perspective'.

death,[14] and the scale of war at different times and places.[15] Osteological evidence for violent conflict has been documented across the continent from the earliest Americans, such as Kennewick Man, who sustained a non-lethal spear wound in his left hip some 9,000 years ago,[16] to inter-group conflicts during the American Indian Wars.[17]

The archaeological record is largely silent on the identities or capabilities of pre-Columbian war leaders and strategists. Great war leaders surely existed and would have wielded their power and influence on the sociopolitical landscape of the North American continent. At the time of the founding of Jamestown near Chesapeake Bay in 1607, for example, the paramount chief Powhatan was at the pinnacle of his power among the Algonquian peoples of eastern Virginia. With expansionist aspirations dating back to the inheritance of his father's paramount chiefdom in the late sixteenth century, Powhatan had incorporated thirty Indigenous nations into his polity by 1608 through violent conquest, colonisation, negotiation and charismatic leadership. His ways of war included light skirmishes, ambushes, surprise raids, direct assaults, prolonged sieges and more conventional open-field battles with warriors in formation, strategies variously employed against the English at Jamestown. Ultimately, his goals were the expansion of his power and reach through the conquest of neigh-bouring peoples and the acquisition of their territories and trade relations. While his subordinate chiefs were not forbidden from engaging in trade and conflict for their own interests, they were obligated to join forces with Powhatan when called upon to do so.[18] Chiefdoms existed throughout the Southeast from Virginia to Florida and west to the Mississippi valley as early as AD 900, so Powhatan's way of war, both its conduct and its motivations, may well have characterised warfare after 900 in this broad eastern sweep where chiefdoms structured the political landscape.[19]

Glimpses of powerful tribal leadership from the years that followed include the exploits of famous war leaders such as Chief Joseph (Nez Percé), Crazy

14 Lambert, 'The osteological evidence for indigenous warfare'.
15 It should be noted that small numbers of dead do not necessarily indicate small engagements. Organised battles among the Highland Dani involved hundreds of men, but few, if any, deaths. Robert Gardner, *Dead Birds* (Film Study Center of the Peabody Museum at Harvard University, Cambridge, MA, 1963).
16 James C. Chatters, 'Wild-type colonizers and high levels of violence among Paleoamericans', in Mark Allen and Terry Jones (eds), *Violence and Warfare among Hunter-Gatherers* (Walnut Creek: Left Coast Press, 2014), 70–96.
17 Lambert, 'The archaeology of war', 226, 228.
18 James D. Rice, 'War and politics: Powhatan expansionism and the problem of Native American warfare', *William and Mary Quarterly*, 77:1 (January 2020), 3–32.
19 David H. Dye, 'The transformation of Mississippian warfare: four case studies from the mid-South', in Arkush and Allen, *The Archaeology of Warfare*, 101–47.

Horse (Lakota) and Geronimo (Apache), who emerged to lead their people in a range of actions against the US military.[20] Cheyenne oral histories also preserve accounts of women warriors such as Buffalo Calf Road, a Northern Cheyenne woman whose act of bravery in rescuing her brother from the battlefield changed the course of the Battle of Rosebud (in 1876) in favour of her people; she went on to fight to victory alongside her husband Black Coyote in the Battle of Little Bighorn.[21] Priorities for Indigenous leaders in the American Indian Wars were relatively straightforward: to repel Euroamerican soldiers and settlers, to protect or reclaim traditional lands, to protect women and children and to avenge the dead. Their ways of war, however, would have been honed over centuries of intra- and intertribal conflict such as that in the late prehistory of the Missouri river basin, where the ancestors of the Mandan, Hidatsa and Arikara engaged in deadly conflict.[22]

Tribal leaders during the historic period also forged strategic alliances with Europeans against common foes when these suited their political and economic ends. In the Beaver Wars (1640–1701), for example, the Huron, Algonquins and Mohicans fought alongside the French against the Iroquois over trade in northern beaver pelts and other goods, while the Iroquois allied themselves with the Dutch to obtain guns to deploy against those groups. Such strategic alliances in war were not born of European contact, however, but had very deep roots in Indigenous North America's own political history.[23]

The identity of adversaries can also be challenging to ascertain for pre-Columbian warfare in North America. In the case of Powhatan, whose rule spanned the period of early European contact in Chesapeake Bay, opponents were most often other Algonquian chiefs who resisted or threatened his rule.[24] In the case of attacks for which there are no written records, however, aggressors seldom left signature traces, and thus remain unknown. That said, conflict within versus between ethnically distinct groups can often be differentiated.

20 See Albert Britt, Great Indian Chiefs: A Study of Indian Leaders in the Two Hundred Year Struggle to Stop the White Advance (New York: Whittlesey House McGraw-Hill Book Company, Inc., 1938).
21 Rosemary Agnito and Joseph Agnito, 'Resurrecting history's forgotten women: a case study from the Cheyenne Indians', Frontiers: A Journal of Women Studies, 6:3 (Autumn 1981), 8–16.
22 Bamforth, 'Climate, chronology and the course of war'.
23 Neal Salisbury, 'The Indians' Old World: Native Americans and the coming of Europeans', William and Mary Quarterly, 53:3 (July 1996), 450–7.
24 Rice, 'War and politics'.

In the Chumash heartland of southern California, for example, conflict among the maritime fisher–foragers of the region primarily involved other Chumash communities, a pattern well documented for the early historic period in villages along the Santa Barbara mainland coast. At the time of European contact the Chumash were organised into hereditary chiefdoms,[25] and inter-village conflict documented during this period may in part reflect the machinations of aspiring leaders or kin groups, though long-standing patterns of amity and enmity were clearly in evidence. Violence in the Santa Barbara Channel area can be traced back to some of the earliest, band-level societies around 7,000 to 10,000 years ago, and episodes of small-scale tribal warfare appear to have occurred sporadically for millennia thereafter. War began to escalate after AD 500 and appears to have been endemic over much of the period from AD 600 to 1300 on the populous Santa Barbara mainland coast and offshore islands of Santa Rosa and Santa Cruz. About 10 per cent of all individuals (and over 20 per cent of adult males) from cemeteries dating to this period show injuries from spears or arrows – mostly lethal – demonstrating just how deadly this small-scale war could be. This period was character-ised by highly variable climatic conditions punctuated by episodes of severe drought, so climate-induced resource stress likely played a role in escalating violence in the region. A shift from spears to the bow and arrow as the primary weapon of war around AD 900 would have changed the way war was conducted and may also have contributed to higher rates of lethal violence between AD 950 and 1300.[26]

Tribal warfare in Ancestral Puebloan societies of the northern Southwest also appears to have involved other Puebloan groups.[27] Following a period of relative peace from AD 900 to 1150 (after centuries of fairly low-level warfare), warfare began to increase in frequency and severity amidst a severe and prolonged drought from 1130 to 1180.[28] Around 1150 in the Mesa Verde region of southwestern Colorado, for example, an isolated farming community on

25 John R. Johnson, 'Ethnohistoric descriptions of Chumash warfare', in Richard J. Chacon and Ruben G. Mendoza (eds), *North American Indigenous Warfare* (Tucson: University of Arizona Press, 2007), 87. Lynn Gamble, *The Chumash World at European Contact: Power, Trade, and Feasting among Complex Hunter-Gatherers* (Berkeley: University of California Press, 2008).

26 Lambert, *War and Peace on the Western Front*; Lambert, 'Indigenous warfare in North America'.

27 Kristen A. Kuckelman, 'The depopulation of Sand Canyon Pueblo, a large ancestral pueblo village in Southwestern Colorado', *American Antiquity*, 75 (2010), 497–525.

28 Steven LeBlanc, *Prehistoric Warfare in the American Southwest* (Salt Lake City: University of Utah Press, 1999); Haas and Creamer, *Stress and Warfare among the Kayenta Anasazi*, 53–72.

the southern piedmont of Sleeping Ute Mountain was attacked and at least twenty-four residents, including men, women and children, were killed and their bodies cannibalised. Similar events appear to have occurred in several other Puebloan communities in the region between 1150 and 1175. The occurrence of these attacks in the middle of a fifty-year drought suggests that food shortages were a driving force for intercommunity strife, likely exacerbated by social instability associated with the arrival of immigrants from the south during the twelfth-century abandonment of the Puebloan cultural epicentre at Chaco Canyon in north-western New Mexico.[29]

Warfare engulfed the Four Corners region between 1250 and 1300 in association with cooling temperatures, environmental degradation and severe drought that led to the failure of maize crops and increasing inability to sustain domestic turkey flocks – a crucial source of animal protein. During these years Puebloan peoples throughout the region moved to highly defensible locations and built walls, towers and tunnels for additional protection; some headed south in search of more propitious farming conditions as depopulation of the region began.[30] However, even large, well-fortified settlements such as Sand Canyon Pueblo in the Mesa Verde region, with massive walls and towers surrounding a village with hundreds of rooms and some 500 residents at the height of its occupation, were ultimately breached. Attacked around 1280 amidst the 'Great Drought' of 1276–1299 and a heavily degraded subsistence base, at least thirty-five of the residents who remained at the pueblo were killed and some of them scalped, their bodies left on rooftops, dumped in rooms, sprawled on floors or scattered in abandonment contexts. Other pueblos in the vicinity experienced a similar fate, including Castle Rock Pueblo about four miles from Sand Canyon Pueblo.[31] The attack around 1285 at Castle Rock, a partially fortified village of approximately fifteen households (around 100 people), left at least forty-one people dead, their bodies sprawled on floors and rooftops. As at Sand Canyon Pueblo, climate-induced food stress likely played a role in the catastrophic attack that ended the occupation of this village.[32]

---

29 Brian R. Billman, Patricia M. Lambert and Banks Leonard, 'Warfare, cannibalism, and drought on the Colorado Plateau in the twelfth century A.D.', *American Antiquity*, 65 (2000), 145–78.

30 LeBlanc, *Prehistoric Warfare in the American Southwest*, 197–276; Kuckelman, 'The depopulation of Sand Canyon Pueblo'.

31 Kuckelman, 'The depopulation of Sand Canyon Pueblo'.

32 Kristen A. Kuckelman, Ricky R. Lightfoot and Debra L. Martin, 'The bioarchaeology and taphonomy of violence at Castle Rock and Sand Canyon Pueblos, southwestern Colorado', *American Antiquity*, 67 (2002), 486–513; Kuckelman, 'The depopulation of Sand Canyon Pueblo'.

Highly lethal tribal conflict also emerged among sedentary farming groups in the Middle Missouri region of South Dakota in the next century following a northern migration of Caddoan speaking peoples (Initial Coalescent tradition) from the Central Plains into the Missouri trench around 1300. Their arrival into a region already occupied by Siouan peoples (Middle Missouri tradition) was met with hostility and an increasing investment in defensive architecture. Whereas sporadic warfare among smaller Middle Missouri villages and towns had occurred before this time, the fourteenth-century massacre at Crow Creek, a large Initial Coalescent town with ditch and palisade fortifications, appears to have been a full-scale, annihilative raid by a coalition of resident groups or possibly other Coalescent groups competing for limited arable land. Nearly 500 people were killed in the attack, most of them scalped and their bodies disposed of in a mass grave on the edge of the settlement. People of all ages and both sexes were killed, although young men were differentially targeted and some young women were apparently taken captive. A documented association between periods of village fortification, poor health and drought suggests that climate played a role in escalating violence in this region and possibly also in this event.[33]

To the north on the Northwest Coast (Oregon to Southeast Alaska), stratified hunter-gatherer societies of the historic era (1775–1855) engaged in inter-group warfare over revenge, honour, status, plunder, territorial gain and slaving. Internal quarrels over women could also lead to group fissioning and ultimately to clan warfare.[34] The most common forms of war were surprise attacks and raids, and the capture of slaves for labour and ransom was both a common outcome of such attacks and a reason for going to war, especially among the more northerly groups.[35] Powerful and high-ranking war leaders are known to have led their lineages and clans on long-distance raids (over 600 kilometres in some cases) involving hundreds of warriors in dozens of sixty-foot war canoes,[36] although, in pre-contact times, targets for slaving were often closer to home.[37] Notably, historically documented patterns of war began to emerge after AD 500 on the northern Northwest Coast,

---

33 Bamforth, 'Climate, chronology and the course of war'. Douglas B. Bamforth, 'What do we know about warfare on the Great Plains?', in Andrew J. Clark and Douglas B. Bamforth (eds), *Archaeological Perspectives on Warfare on the Great Plains* (Boulder: University of Colorado Press, 2018), 3–34.
34 Ames and Maschner, *Peoples of the Northwest Coast*, 195–209; Leland Donald, *Aboriginal Slavery on the Northwest Coast of North America* (Berkeley: University of California Press, 1997), 27, 33, 105.
35 Donald, *Aboriginal Slavery on the Northwest Coast of North America*, 27.
36 Ames and Maschner, *Peoples of the Northwest Coast*, 195.
37 Donald, *Aboriginal Slavery on the Northwest Coast of North America*, 106–7.

concurrent with the appearance of the bow and arrow. This cultural transition is recognised in the archaeological record of the Tlingit of Kuiu Island, Alaska, by a change from a settlement pattern favouring ready access to open-water resources to one prioritising defensibility and good viewshed, the appearance of larger houses and villages indicating population aggregation, and a shift in subsistence activities towards those that could be undertaken in large groups or closer to home. Warfare continued after European contact, when targets came to include European soldiers and traders that threatened clan territories and trade relations.[38]

Intertribal conflict is also well documented in the nineteenth-century battle at Pima Butte on the Gila river in southern Arizona, the last major battle fought between Indigenous Americans and one for which both Euroamerican and Native American histories preserve a fairly concordant record. According to these accounts, a large coalition of Yumans and their Mohave, Yavapai and Apache allies travelled up to 160 miles from their respective homelands along the Colorado river in late August of 1857 to attack their traditional enemy the Maricopa. Though the Yumans and Maricopa were culturally similar in language and part-time farming economy, a long history of enmity between the groups and an ongoing cycle of revenge warfare was likely the impetus for this attack, although the Yuman leader Chief Hawk was also motivated by his own political aspirations. The Yuman-led war expedition was initially successful in attacking a Maricopa village near Pima Butte, but their dwindling coalition was soon routed by the Maricopa with the aid of their Pima allies, who surrounded the Yuma contingent and slaughtered them almost to the last man, the Yuma refusing to yield to their sworn enemy.[39] According to a Mohave version of events, seven Yavapai, sixty Mohave and all but two of the Yuma contingent of eighty-two ultimately fell in the battle – while the Apache, most Yavapai and some Mohave allies fled before the slaughter.[40] This battle appears to have been the culmination, rather than the initiation, of hostilities among these desert peoples and it likely represents a long-standing pattern of war in this region.

There were many causes of war in pre-contact North America, including honour, revenge, trade and territorial disputes, status striving, wealth

38 Ames and Maschner, *Peoples of the Northwest Coast*, 199, 210–17.
39 Clifton B. Kroeber and Bernard L. Fontana, *Massacre on the Gila: An Account of the Last Major Battle between American Indians with Reflections on the Origin of War* (Tucson: The University of Arizona Press, 1986).
40 Alfred L Kroeber, 'The Mohave: concrete life', *Handbook of the Indians of California, Bulletin of the Bureau of American Ethnology*, 78 (Washington, DC: Government Printing Office, 1925), 726–53.

acquisition, chiefly aspirations and slaving, as noted above. That said, an overarching stimulus for escalating warfare during the centuries when it is most evident in the North American archaeological record (1000–1400) appears to have been climate change – and in particular drought in the arid West in association with the Medieval Climatic Anomaly (c. 950–1400).[41] Palaeoclimatic data from tree rings, lake sediments and other climate indicators document prolonged episodes of drought in southern California, the Southwest and the northern Great Plains during this period,[42] and the archaeological evidence for severe drought as a significant cause of war is strongest for these regions.[43]

Indigenous warfare in North America has not traditionally been seen as very formal or deadly, primarily because there were no state-level societies to support standing armies, and intertribal conflict has had the reputation of being relatively small in scale and not very lethal.[44] However, as noted above, there are indications from a number of North American regions that this war could, in fact, be very deadly, sometimes engage hundreds of warriors, and be motivated by the same kinds of causal factors as seen in state-level warfare. The paramount chief Powhatan could readily assemble a large force for an open-field battle, frontal assault or ambush as his needs or wants dictated, and his siege warfare against the English nearly eradicated the Jamestown colony in its early years.[45] In southern Arizona, both Yuma and Maricopa leaders were able to muster hundreds of warriors to their cause to engage in highly lethal conflict.[46] It seems likely that the forces responsible for deadly attacks such as those at Sand Canyon Pueblo and Crow Creek during the pre-Columbian period also comprised large coalitions, structured by alliances and motivated by the nature of historic relations with targeted communities. Even apparently smaller-scale

41 Henry Diaz, Ricardo Trigo, Malcolm Hughes, Michael Mann, Elena Xoplaki and David Barriopedro, 'Spatial and temporal characteristics of climate in medieval times revisited', Bulletin of the American Meteorological Society, November 2011, 1487–1500.
42 Jeffrey S. Dean and Carla R. Van West, 'Environment–behavior relationships in southwestern Colorado', in Mark D. Varian and Richard H. Wilshusen (eds), Seeking the Center Place: Archaeology and Ancient Communities in the Mesa Verde Region (Salt Lake City: University of Utah Press, 2002), 81–99; Mark L. Raab and Daniel O. Larson, 'Medieval Climatic Anomaly and punctuated cultural evolution in coastal southern California', American Antiquity, 62 (1997), 319–36; Bamforth, 'Climate, chronology and the course of war', 71–3, 81.
43 Bamforth, 'Climate, chronology and the course of war'; Lambert, 'War histories in evolutionary perspective'; LeBlanc, Prehistoric Warfare in the American Southwest, 309–12.
44 Lawrence Keeley, War before Civilization (New York: Oxford University Press, 1996), 3–24; Rice, 'War and politics'.
45 Rice, 'War and politics'.   46 Kroeber and Fontana, Massacre on the Gila, 11–32.

warfare, however, such as that documented at the fortified Oneota town of Norris Farms in Illinois in around 1300, could be very deadly in the long run. Here, killings from surprise attacks on small and vulnerable work parties resulted in the deaths of at least a third of the adult population over time.[47] The percentage of people killed in small raids and ambushes thus could rival the death rates reported for wars in more politically complex societies elsewhere in the world,[48] and this warfare should therefore be understood as strategic, serious and formative. The social landscape of Indigenous North America was shaped by centuries of war before the first European ships made landfall and this history surely influenced the nature of social interactions and the course of war in the years that followed their arrival.

47 George Milner, Eve Anderson and Virginia G. Smith, 'Warfare in late prehistoric west central Illinois', *American Antiquity*, 56:4 (1991), 581–603.
48 Keeley, *War before Civilization*, 83–97.

17

Ottoman Expansionism, 1300–1823

MESUT UYAR

The Rise of the Ottoman Empire

The Ottoman Empire was one of the greatest and longest-lasting empires of the world and it was the last Mediterranean empire. At its zenith in the seventeenth century it occupied an area that stretched from the southern and eastern shores of the Mediterranean to the Caspian Sea and from Poland in the north to the Indian Ocean in the south. Even though certain provinces – like Hungary, the Danubian principalities and the Caucasian and Iranian frontier regions – experienced almost continuous warfare, most of the other provinces enjoyed long periods of peace and prosperity thanks to the efficiency of the Ottoman bureaucracy. The empire was more bureaucratic than military. Instead of imposing a clean break with the past, as it established itself, it preserved or transformed existing administrative systems into systems of its own.

The rise of the Ottoman Empire from an obscure small political entity is one of the most important phenomena of the late medieval period. Turcoman tribes entered recorded history in the eleventh century when they left their central Asian homeland and began to migrate to the Middle East. Several settled on land they had prised away from the Byzantine Empire, including Asia Minor, where they formed *beyliks* or emirates. One of their leaders, Osman I Gazi ('Fighter of the Faith', d. *c.* 1325), founded a dynasty named after him, with further expansionist ambitions. His descendant Sultan Mehmed II Fatih ('the Conqueror'), transformed the Osmanlı or Ottoman *beylik* into an empire. He set out to conquer the remaining territory controlled by Constantinople and, above all, the city itself, and adopted a strategy to achieve this. After two years of long political, economic and military preparations, Mehmed II besieged and conquered Constantinople on 29 May 1453. Mehmed II declared himself caesar and set out to conquer remaining Byzantine enclaves in Trebizond and the Peloponnese peninsula.

Moreover, seeing himself as the successor of the Roman Empire, like Justinian whose equestrian statue in Constantinople he melted down, he then espoused the strategic aim of bringing all the lands that had once belonged to the Roman Empire under his control. This strategic aim guided his successors for the following centuries, and even when further expansion proved impossible after the turning point of the second siege of Vienna in 1683, the dream remained alive.

Sources

Ottoman historians first wrote about their early history and the foundation of their *beylik* in the late fifteenth century. The earliest accounts of the Ottomans survive in the Byzantine chronicles, but do not provide concrete and sound information. Instead, there are only occasional entries about different aspects of the Ottoman emirate, which create more questions than answers as Byzantine authors tried to imitate ancient great works and literary styles at the expense of reality when it did not fit. For example, they rarely called the Ottomans 'Turks' but instead referred to them as 'Persians' (as Persians had been the enemy 'other' for Hellenes and Romans since antiquity) or simply 'Barbarians'. Our Byzantine sources are heavily contaminated with legends, which themselves reflected a Byzantine perception of war that saw nearly all military activities from the perspective of a struggle between Good and Evil.[1]

After the end of the fifteenth century, we have more and better indigenous and foreign sources. The Ottoman chroniclers ironed out problems within earlier written accounts (now lost) and oral recollections, and wrote down more consistent and harmonious histories.[2] But neither do they provide details to construct the Ottoman understanding and application of strategy. Ottoman soldiers did not record their experiences, or produce military manuals, drill books and other tactical or technical works until the late eighteenth century. In short, we cannot get much information about Ottoman warfare, let alone strategy, from Ottoman sources alone.[3]

By capturing critical ports of the Mediterranean, the straits (the Bosporus and the Dardanelles) and other places of maritime importance, the Ottomans appeared on the radar of Italian city states. Thus there are many documents

---

1 C. Imber, *The Ottoman Empire 1300–1481* (İstanbul: Isis Pres, 1990), 1–4.
2 V. L. Ménage, *Neshri's History of the Ottomans* (Oxford: Oxford University Press, 1964).
3 E. İhsanoğlu, Ramazan Şeşen, Serdar Bekar and Gülcan Gündüz, *History of Military Art and Science Literature during the Ottoman Period*, Volume 1 (İstanbul: IRCICA, 2004), xv–xviii, lv–lxv.

about them in the archives of Venice, Genoa and Florence. Modern scholars have gradually begun to publish their contents. We also have memoirs of some captured Europeans who served the Ottomans as soldiers or slaves. Nevertheless, they also lack precious details about strategic decisions that we are looking for.[4]

Ottoman warfare and military systems became a serious area of study thanks to Habsburg generals like Lazarus von Schwendi and Raimondo Montecuccoli. The Habsburgs fought against the Ottomans for centuries. They tried not only to understand the Ottomans but also to devise responsive strategies, arguably preparing the way for the turn of the tide of Ottoman expansion after 1683 and the slow reconquest of the previously Christian lands of south-eastern Europe.[5]

Actors

During the foundation period, Turcoman chieftains, march lords and powerful vizier families were part of the decision-making process. The Ottoman sultans followed the centuries-old nomadic custom of collective decision making until Mehmed II. Viziers, generals and sometimes march lords were influential in decision making and in designing strategy. As governors of distant provinces, the *sehzade*s (Ottoman princes), by contrast, seldom participated in making policy or strategy. There were exceptions, as in the example of Selim I, called Yavuz ('the Grim', r. 1512–1520). Selim as a prince was very unhappy about his father Bayezid II's foreign and domestic policy and his exclusion from the decision-making process. Selim rebelled against his father in 1510 and after a brief struggle acceded to the throne.

The nomadic type of collective decision making came to an end after the conquest of Constantinople in 1453. Henceforth the Ottoman sultan was, in theory, the absolute ruler of his realm. Mehmed II purged Turkish aristocracy and curbed the power of march lords and governors. He effectively centralised decision and strategy making under his authority, leaving only a few advisers in the process. Mehmed II replaced Turkish aristocrats with *kuls*

---

4 K. Mihailović, *Memoirs of a Janissary* (trans. Benjamin Stolz) (Ann Arbor: University of Michigan Press, 1975).

5 G. Rothenberg, 'Maurice of Nassau, Gustavus Adolphus, Raimondo Montecuccoli, and the "military revolution" of the seventeenth century', in P. Paret (ed.), *Makers of Modern Strategy: From Machiavelli to the Nuclear Age* (Princeton: Princeton University Press, 1986), 32–63; B. Heuser, 'Lazarus Schwendi, Raimondo Montecuccoli and the Turkish wars: peaceful coexistence or rollback?', in B. Heuser, *Strategy before Clausewitz: Linking Warfare and Statecraft, 1400–1830* (Abingdon: Routledge, 2017), 136–67.

(military–administrative slaves). Like the Janissaries, they were products of child levy (*devşirme*) from the various areas now ruled by the Ottomans, educated and trained to serve the Ottoman Empire. These measures greatly increased the authority of the Sultan. Selim I and Süleyman I, called Kanuni ('the Lawgiver', better known in the West as 'the Magnificent', r. 1520–1566), followed their grandfather's centralised and authoritarian system. However, *kuls* and the palace regained power slowly in the following decades and became real power brokers after the seventeenth century. Even the most powerful and charismatic sultans like Mehmed II and Süleyman I knew the restricted nature of their rule.

Until the seventeenth century, the sultans, with the chief exception of Bayezid II, almost always led their armies into battle. Their martial prowess and achievements were instrumental in establishing their authority and control. If the Sultan did not assume command of the expeditionary force, his chief vizier or one of the high-ranking and trusted viziers would take over the responsibility as *serdar* (commander). The Ottoman princes initially used to command troops during campaigns in order to gain experience, but after rebellions and succession crises involving princes and their armies this practice came to an end.[6]

During the last years of the long reign of Süleyman I, Grand Vizier Sokullu Mehmed Pasha gained the confidence of the Sultan and thereby became immensely powerful. The new Sultan, Selim II, called Sarı ('the Blond', r. 1566–1574), was a very weak character and left all duties and responsibilities of governance to Mehmed Pasha. From the reign of Selim II onwards, sultans spent most of their time resident in their palace in Kostantiniyye, as Constantinople was now officially referred to. This radical change not only empowered the pashas but also sultans' wives and concubines, and the eunuchs and other key palace officials. Viziers and governor generals had to gain the support of palace factions in order to preserve their positions and gain promotion. Contrary to common misconceptions, inclusion of these new actors into the decision- and strategy-making processes improved and rationalised those processes. The whims and erratic behaviour of the charismatic sultans had come to an end with more actors involved in governing. However, the new system increased political competition and, sporadically, violence.[7]

---

6 M. Uyar and E. J. Erickson, *A Military History of the Ottomans* (Santa Barbara: ABC-Clio, 2009), 32–79.

7 C. Finkel, *Osman's Dream: The Story of the Ottoman Empire 1300–1923* (New York: Basic Books, 2005).

Governors of frontier provinces acted autonomously to deal with crises and sudden attacks by using their conventional troops and militia. Perpetual conflicts against the Habsburgs in the west and the Safavids in the east during the sixteenth and seventeenth centuries were instrumental in increasing the role and power of these governors who led campaigns. Of course, they needed protectors and sponsors to make their voices heard from afar in the capital. Therefore their autonomy was more limited than contemporary accounts suggested.[8]

The Ottoman footprint was very light in distant provinces like Iraq, Egypt, Libya, Tunis and Algeria. During the late seventeenth century most of these provinces gained autonomy under local dynasties and acted like independent states, thus, for example, generating the problem of the so-called 'Barbary pirates'. However, they still needed Ottoman weapons and military experts and officers to keep up with their regional rivals. Mahmud II managed to eliminate most of these local dynasties and re-established central control over them during the early years of the nineteenth century, with the chief exception of Egypt.

Adversaries

When the tribe following Osman I first formed a settled emirate, this was located at the north-west of the Turkish–Byzantine march lands of Bithynia. Although the Byzantine Empire was initially its largest rival, it was not the most dangerous one and actually the weakest. Bigger fellow Turcoman emirates posed a greater danger. Luckily for the Ottomans the bigger and more powerful emirates became targets of the Ilkhanids, the Seljukids and the crusaders several times, while the Ottomans stayed away from these dangerous attacks and, consequently, benefited from their results. Initially, the Ottoman attacks against the Byzantines were conducted without a master plan or strategy, but did follow a general pattern. The early Ottoman sultans assigned frontier regions or marches to regional governors or march lords who were also military leaders, and ordered them to conduct continuous raids and attacks. From time to time the Byzantines managed to inflict serious defeats but they had no means to counter this onslaught. After crossing into Europe at Gallipoli in 1354, over the following century the Ottomans conquered Constantinople's remaining hinterland both in

---

8 M. R. Hickok, *Ottoman Military Government in Eighteenth-Century Bosnia* (Leiden: Brill, 1997).

Europe and in Asia, reducing it from an empire to a city state and eventually capturing it in 1453. Yet in the intervening century, the Byzantines from time to time caused much damage, as during the Ottoman interregnum (1402–1413), when the succession of Bayezid was fought over by his sons.[9]

In the late fourteenth century, the Christian Balkan states were weak and constantly fighting each other. With some luck, the Ottomans were able to inflict a serious defeat on the Serbian army in Černomen in 1371, and more famously at Kosovo Polje in 1389. These defeats greatly weakened the only regional power capable of resisting Ottoman advances. At the same time many Byzantine, Serbian and Bulgarian magnates officially became vassals of the Ottomans. From now on the Ottomans exploited the military potential of their Balkan vassals to the limit and if any of them showed insubordination their territory was immediately ransacked or even conquered by the march lords.

The Hungarians did not realise the threat the Ottomans posed until very late. They also failed to mobilise other European powers effectively. Only Hungarian general Hunyadi Janos (c. 1406–1456) understood the inherent weaknesses of the Ottoman military at the operational and tactical levels. He launched attacks on the European domains of the Ottomans using a window of opportunity created by the seasonal nature of Ottoman campaigning and demobilisation. He saved Belgrade from an attack by Mehmed II and won some startling victories. But even the smart Hunyadi underestimated the pragmatism and adaptability of the Ottomans, who quickly copied Hungarian tactics and techniques. Consequently, he suffered two defeats (1444 and 1448) at the hands of the Ottomans, resulting in the deaths not only of thousands of experienced soldiers but also of Hungarian king Vladislav I.[10] A last encounter between Hungarians and Ottomans at Mohacs in 1526 again resulted in a Hungarian defeat and the death of another Hungarian king, Lajos II, with the Hungarian crown and the mission to free Hungary, now almost entirely under Ottoman control, inherited by the Habsburgs, who became the Ottomans' chief adversaries in Europe. Habsburg generals such as Lazarus von Schwendi knew that they had limited chances against the Ottomans in pitched battle. So the Habsburgs launched a large construction campaign of renovating old fortresses and building new ones based on the latest flat designs (*alla moderna*), thereby drastically transforming the Western

---

9 Imber, *The Ottoman Empire*, 15–116; S. Vryonis Jr, *The Decline of Medieval Hellenism in Asia Minor and the Process of Islamization from the Eleventh through the Fifteenth Century* (Berkeley: University of California Press, 1971).

10 Imber, *The Ottoman Empire*, 91–141.

theatre of war. The Ottomans had no choice but to build their own network of fortresses. What followed were no longer short and decisive campaigns but long and arduous wars of attrition, often without a clear outcome.[11]

In Asia the Ottomans initially faced Turcoman emirates. Although they suffered some problems in conquering their territories due to the reluctance of their soldiers to fight against fellow Turcoman warriors, they overcame this by making use of Balkan Christians. The real troubles started when the Ottoman armies reached the borders of Egypt and Iran. The Egyptian Mamluks defeated the Ottomans three times in a row whereas the Iranian Safavids incited the Turcoman tribes to full rebellion. Selim I destroyed the Mamluk threat after two pitched battles and conquered Syria, Egypt and Hejaz, including Mecca and Medina, the holiest cities of Islam. The Safavids survived the defeats inflicted upon them by the Ottomans but permanently lost east Anatolia and some parts of the Caucasus.[12]

Their place as chief rival in the area of the Black Sea and central Asia was filled by Russia, which also had expansionist ambitions. The last two centuries of the Ottoman Empire thus saw it fighting mainly defensive wars against the Habsburgs and the Russian Romanovs in the west and the north, while its north African provinces were captured by the French and the British in the nineteenth century. That century also saw indigenous independence movements turn into wars of independence in Greece and later Bulgaria, with external backing not only from Russia but also from Britain and France.

Causes and Objectives of War

Along with the other Turcoman tribes, the Ottomans wanted to capture a new homeland and found a large powerful state. They had converted to Islam but the central place of religion in the Ottoman world view did not distort the Ottoman governing elite's understanding of the world as a whole, at least until the mid-eighteenth century. Material gains motivated their warriors and every victory increased the number of their followers. They made effective use of Islam to achieve, justify and legitimise their political aims.

In the process of empire formation, commercial aims played an important role. The control of trade routes, critical harbours and passes, and the

---

11 R. Murphey, *Ottoman Warfare, 1500–1700* (New Brunswick: Rutgers University Press, 1999), 6–11.

12 S. Har-El, *Struggle for Domination in the Middle East: The Ottoman–Mamluk War 1485–94* (Leiden: Brill, 1995).

expulsion of potentially dangerous powers, were the main motives behind some of the major Ottoman military expeditions and conquests. Three primary old trade routes linked Asia to Europe, all of which came together in the eastern Mediterranean. The Ottomans gained control of the northern route that passed through the Black Sea by the conquests of Constantinople and Trebizond (1461). Half a century later, the Ottoman leadership turned its military might against Syria (1516), Egypt (1517) and Yemen (1520); thereby the southern route came under its control. The next target was the central route passing through the Persian Gulf and Baghdad. The Ottomans had no major difficulties in capturing Baghdad (1534) and Basra (1554). Not surprisingly one of the important reasons behind the conquests of Algeria (1533), Tunis (1535) and Tripoli (Libya, 1553) was the desire to control trade routes, this time Afro-European ones. Spanish king Philip II tried to recapture Tripoli, but his armada was ambushed and destroyed by the Ottoman fleet in Djerba in May 1560.[13]

The Ottoman expeditions against the Portuguese in the Indian Ocean are also important, in order to appreciate both the Ottoman military capacity and structural limitations, but also the global view, concept, aims and strategy of the governing elite. Western European nations were trying to find an alternative route to India, bypassing old routes under Italian and Muslim control. The Portuguese tried to monopolise commercial access to India by blockading old trade routes. The Mamluks had shown feeble resistance against the Portuguese naval onslaught of 1503–1505. Simultaneously with the Mamluks, several Muslim emirates and trade colonies sought Ottoman help. Furthermore, frequent Portuguese naval incursions seriously undermined the security of the Islamic holy cities. The Ottoman administration capitalised on these developments, seeing them as golden opportunities to expand their sphere of influence into Mamluk domains.

The Ottomans initially sent military experts and weapons. Yet the Ottoman military advisers and assistants did not alter the situation. The Portuguese beat the Mamluks and their local allies in every confrontation. Therefore it is no great wonder that, when the Ottomans captured Egypt, all parties (including Venetians, whose monopoly on the spice trade was threatened by the Portuguese) welcomed the development. By securing the Red Sea and establishing a powerful presence in the Persian Gulf the Ottomans gained a strategic advantage over the Portuguese, which they immediately

---

13 P. Brummett, *Ottoman Seapower and Levantine Diplomacy in the Age of Discovery* (Albany: State University of New York Press, 1994).

capitalised on. The Ottoman navy launched a series of attacks against the Portuguese – starting from 1538. Although they managed to push the Portuguese out of the Red Sea, their attempts to do the same in the southern Persian Gulf and the Indian Ocean failed.

Means

The early Ottomans inherited central Asian steppe nomadic, Islamic and Byzantine traditions. By blending this heritage into a unique form, they were able to overcome their rivals and occupy the eastern Balkans and Anatolia. From their nomadic origins, they underwent several radical transformations which enabled them to compete on favourable terms with the best armies of the day. As the world's dominant military machine from 1500 to the mid-1700s, the Ottoman army led the way in military institutions, organisational structures, technology and tactics. In much-reduced stature thereafter, it nevertheless remained a considerable force to be counted in the balance of power until the Ottoman Empire's dissolution in 1918.

To begin with, the sudden expansion of the Ottoman emirate between 1352 and 1402 created serious problems not only of consolidation and integration, but also of protecting newly conquered regions from reconquest by their previous owners. Introduction of the Ottoman administrative and financial system needed time. The Ottomans did not have the numerical strength and power to control conquered territories at all times. Although the administration tried to resettle Turcoman tribes from Anatolia the surplus population quickly dried up.

The only viable solution was winning the active support or collaboration of the subject nations by providing incentives and better living conditions than before. The Ottoman sultans were pragmatic enough to use the services of renegades and mercenaries, and were able to develop coexistence and cohabit-ation mechanisms, being tolerant enough to accommodate all religious and ethnic groups and pragmatic enough to borrow and learn useful institutions and methods from the enemy. This relative tolerance of their subject peoples, where Greek Orthodoxy and Roman Catholicism were extremely intolerant of deviant confessions and repeatedly persecuted 'heretics' and Jews, was the main instrument of soft power wielded by the Ottoman Empire. By creating local allies and collaborators, and encouraging religious conversion, they managed to hold the conquered territories. Local aristocracies and the other natural leaders of conquered societies were very important in this respect. They had the means to keep locals loyal and law-abiding by mediating the relationship. Moreover, they had valuable military skills and potential. In most cases the Ottomans eliminated the royal families and higher aristocracy but preserved the mid- and low-level aristocratic families by awarding them with land grants (better known as *timar*) in exchange for their former feudal domains, their loyalty and their service. The deliberate employment of the local military and administrators in their home territories as intermediate bodies created a peaceful atmosphere for transformation of the region according to the needs of the Ottoman system. Additionally, the elimination of the old feudal system created incentives for the Christian peasant population to support the Ottomans. In this way the Ottomans purposefully used the wide-ranging peasants' protests and the age-old struggle between peasants and feudal lords for their own benefit. In the meantime, many Christian *sipahi*s (soldiers) converted to Islam and were reassigned to other parts of the empire in order to cut their connections with their country of origin. The Ottomans invested in auxiliary corps to repair Roman roads and bridges, providing transport for the troops and their baggage. Most of these were native Balkan people. For example, semi-nomadic Vlachs were employed as mule and ox cart drivers, whereas members of the old military classes were transformed into local security forces, guarding bridges and mountain passes and hunting bandits.

Different regions were handled differently, largely in keeping with local customs and traditions.[14] The Ottomans employed divergent methods to absorb other military classes in Asia and Africa. In a sense the Ottomans enhanced effective centralised state control without making large changes in people's lives.[15] The empire was tolerant in accommodating, to a certain extent, the assimilation of various cultures and ethnic groups into its patrimonial realm. While the empire's military elite included a disproportional number of ethnic Turks, the Ottoman administration emerged as the engine in the creation of a multi-ethnic, multi-religious and multicultural empire by granting minorities some degree of self-rule. It was the diversity of geography, population and cultures that was not only the empire's unique identity, but also its strength and endurance. In the sixteenth and seventeenth centuries, thousands of mercenaries were deployed for war along the Hungarian border regions, whereas tribal warriors gained power in the east. Additionally, more and more troops were left behind after the end of campaigns in order to counter out-of-season attacks.

14 M. Greene, *A Shared World: Christians and Muslims in the Early Modern Mediterranean* (Princeton: Princeton University Press, 2000), 4–10, 40–4.
15 P. F. Sugar, *Southeastern Europe under Ottoman Rule, 1354–1804* (Seattle: University of Washington Press, 1977).

The Ottomans successfully transformed their mostly nomadic army into a complex mixture of conventional, mercenary and auxiliary armed forces. The Turcoman tribal horsemen were reorganised and put under hierarchical command and control under the name of *timarlı sipahi* (timaroit cavalry). During the last decades of the sixteenth century, these numbered around 100,000, of whom about 40,000 to 50,000 would have been available on any one campaign.

However, they failed to create an effective conventional infantry corps from the Turkish peasants and nomads. The age-old Islamic military slave system inspired the Ottomans to found Janissary corps which depended on a new mode of recruitment, the infamous child tribute system called the *devşirme*. The main idea behind this new recruitment mode was the forced tribute of selected children from their Christian families, who were then used as military slaves after a long training period that included cultural and religious training in addition to military training. The Janissary corps was not the only infantry corps created by the early Ottoman commanders but it was the first modern regular infantry in the Ottoman army. As royal guards they had the privilege of wearing elaborate white hats and they became the elite of the elite, and subsequently the most famous and powerful corps of the entire Ottoman military.[16]

The Janissaries were, at the beginning, numerically small – probably around 1,000 strong – and as an elite unit they were very precious and expensive. By 1560 they had increased to 13,357, and at the beginning of the seventeenth century their numbers peaked at over 35,000. The sultan's 'household corps' or cavalry (*kapıkulu*) grew from 100 when first constituted at the end of the fourteenth century to 8,000 men in the mid-fifteenth century and then to 20,869 men in 1609. Artillerists deployed in battles grew in number from 250 in 1453 to 2,827 at the end of the sixteenth century.

But the army also needed large infantry units that were expendable and easy to replace. The solution was to introduce a semi-mercenary infantry corps of soldiers called *azabs* – literally 'bachelors'. The Sultan decided the numbers of *azabs* needed for each campaign and allocated the requirements between provinces. The governors then collected the necessary financial assets to raise the allocated numbers of *azabs* from the population. Initially *azabs* were part-time soldiers who were called up or who volunteered for a certain campaign, but in time, due to the nature of prolonged and constant

16 İ. Hakkı Uzunçarşılı, *Osmanlı Devleti Teşkilatından Kapukulu Ocakları*, Volume I (Ankara: Türk Tarih Kurumu Basımevi, 1988).

campaigning, most *azabs* became semi-mercenaries, who broke all bonds with their villages and migrated to the provincial cities looking for employment on a continuous basis.

Azabs were essentially light infantrymen and their main weapon was the composite bow. They habitually performed dangerous duties, fought in the front lines and were tasked with wearing down the enemy. For this reason, their casualty rates were very high but their rewards were commensurately high. In addition to their salary the *azabs* were exempt from taxes during the campaign. Occasionally, for heroic combat achievements and meritorious service, they were awarded *timar* or permanent employment in the army – and most then became guards in frontier castles. Even though the *azabs* were essentially mercenaries (due to the constant campaigns, strong state control and lack of independent *condottieri*-type captains) they acted more like the full-time soldiers of the age. They did not have loyalty to their units and their only common bond was the quest for a salaried job and looting. But, in any event, the process of urban unemployment after demobilisation made them the precursors of the real Ottoman mercenary system that was born after the mid-sixteenth century with the spread of handheld firearms.

Due to their nomadic origins, the Ottomans, initially, had no maritime capability or interest. This was a serious structural limitation. They needed ships to cross the Dardanelles and protect their newly conquered coastline. But they were lucky. The Byzantine emperor Andronicus II disbanded his navy, as a cost-cutting measure, forcing Byzantine sailors to seek employment in the Turcoman emirates. Some emirates, like Karesi and Aydın, already had fleets which were later incorporated into the brand-new Ottoman navy. Consequently, the Ottomans easily crossed the Dardanelles and damaged the Italian sea trade. Although they rehabilitated old Byzantine dockyards and hired more captains and sailors, establishing naval supremacy needed more effort and time.

In terms of weapons technology, the Ottomans were pioneers rather than imitators. The Ottoman leadership came to understand the potential and importance of firearms in a remarkably short time. However, they insisted on keeping composite bows while most European nations (a notable exception was the English insistence on keeping the longbow up until 1589) discontinued the old missile weapons that required long and continuous training because they could replace them with easier-to-use firearms. A rare blend of pragmatism and conservatism played an important role in this decision. The Ottomans were very attached to their traditional main weapon, while early firearms (arquebuses and matchlock muskets) were often unreliable and slow

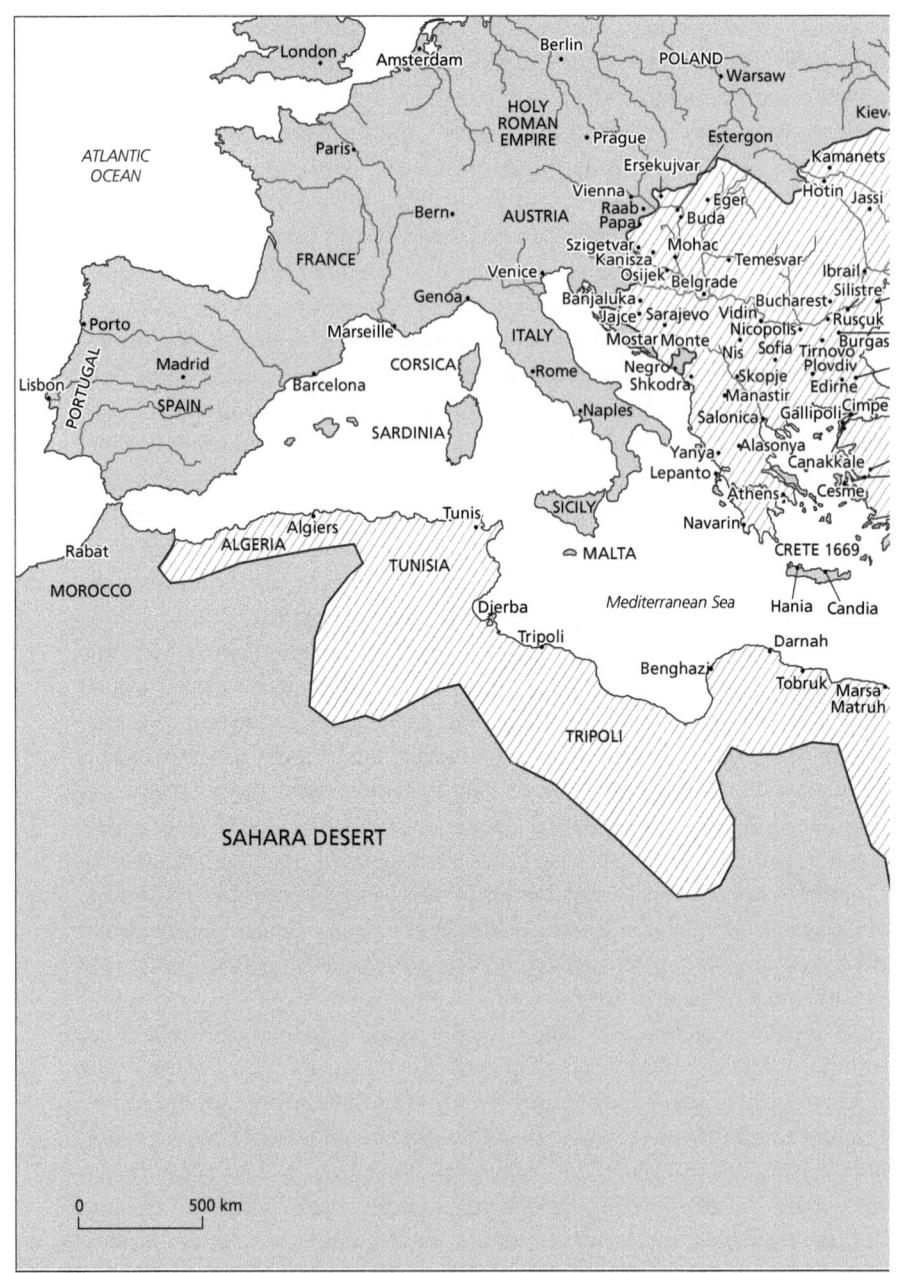

Map 17.1 Ottoman strategy

Map 17.1 (Cont.)

to recharge. Composite bows were accurate and reliable and had a high rate of fire (nine to ten shots per minute as against one shot every two to three minutes). A well-trained archer also had greater effective range, up to 300 metres, whereas hitting a target with a firearm farther than seventy metres was pure coincidence. Thus by retaining the composite bow along with firearms, the Ottomans had a comparative advantage over their adversaries.

Always open to trade with non-Muslims,[17] the Ottoman Empire also played a crucial role in the diffusion of firearms and firearm technology, though not always intentionally. Persia acquired firearms from the Ottomans, initially as war booty but mainly with the help of deserters and mercenaries and also through illicit trade. Ottoman-trained mercenary musketeers, so-called *Rumi*, became sought-after soldiers, not only in Persia but also in central Asia, Afghanistan and India. They altered local power balances by providing services to different conflicting sides. After the uncontrolled diffusion of firearms to the east, the Ottoman sultans began to send parties of guns, technicians and soldiers to various Islamic states. Even though none of these parties was big, they were still effective. Ottoman aid improved the capabilities of the Uzbeks against Persia and the Aceh Sultanate in Sumatra against Portugal. Official Ottoman military advisory teams and profit-oriented mercenaries played an even more important role in north Africa. Their aid to Morocco proved to be a crucial factor in its resisting a Portuguese invasion. In some cases, however, Ottoman military help turned out to be counterproductive, as also in the case of Morocco. With Ottoman technology and know-how, Moroccans were able to defeat the Portuguese and extend their influence deep into the Sahara. But they also successfully blocked Ottoman expansion into the far western regions of north Africa. In addition to these Islamic lands, some non-Muslim countries, such as China, received Ottoman firearms through indirect means.[18]

Despite their great success in bringing down Constantinople with cannon of unprecedented size, Ottoman armies had difficulties with siegecraft. A lack of an effective infantry corps and the absence of a technical corps were the main reasons behind this deficiency. Ruse, surprise, insider collaboration and, sometimes, natural disasters were the only means to capture fortified places in a short time. Otherwise, they had no choice other than to blockade all the

---

17 M. Bulut, 'The Ottoman approach to the western Europeans in the Levant during the early modern period', *Middle Eastern Studies*, 44:2 (March 2008), 259–69.

18 G. Agoston, *Guns for the Sultan: Military Power and the Weapons Industry in the Ottoman Empire* (Cambridge: Cambridge University Press, 2005), 190–205; K. Chase, *Firearms: A Global History to 1700* (Cambridge: Cambridge University Press, 2003), 24, 73–4.

approaches to fortifications, forcing villagers to seek refuge within them and starving them into surrender. This method, obviously, was time-consuming and costly. Only after the foundation of the Kapıkulu Ocakları (the court military slave corps), with their famous subunit, the Janissaries, were the Ottomans capable of conducting effective sieges and pitched battles.[19]

Priorities

The main priority of the early Ottomans was to increase their domain and numbers of fighters without irritating major powers. They not only needed continuous expansion but also kept their warriors busy and satisfied. This was so important that the sultans frequently lent them out as mercenaries to the Byzantines. Of course, this practice came to an end when the Ottomans became a major Balkan power. The early sultans knew the shortcomings of their Turcoman cavalry. They repeatedly defeated local Byzantine magnates.

Expanding towards the west to conquer the territories of the old Roman/Byzantine Empire was the main strategic aim of the Ottomans, as we have seen. To do so, the Ottoman leaders kept up the pressure on their Balkan rivals. Capturing strategic fortresses and controlling critical terrain on the old Roman military roads were given importance to facilitate the rapid movement of expeditionary forces.

After the stabilisation of borders in the west and the east, avoidance of two-front wars became the major priority. The resilience of the Iranian Safavids and the danger they posed put the Ottomans in a difficult strategic situation. The Ottomans found themselves facing two serious rivals on two distant fronts: the Habsburgs in the west and the Safavids in the east. Additionally, they were completely different types of enemy. But the Ottomans did not have the luxury of raising two separate armies, one for each theatre. So the same army had to face these diverse enemies, sometimes at the same time. The Ottoman administration wanted to abolish the timaroit cavalry and instead invest in more infantry and artillery units. But they needed cavalry to fight against the Safavid Turcoman cavalry. This necessity was instrumental in disrupting the plans to create a European-style army until the end of the eighteenth century.

There was no way to end the small wars on both fronts. On their western frontier, the continuous low-level warfare led to the militarisation of the border region, drawing increasingly on local resources. But this was not

---

19 Uyar and Erickson, *A Military History of the Ottomans*, 15–21.

possible on the Iranian border, where tribes were the power brokers. Keeping them loyal and obedient was not only difficult but also financially ruinous. The Ottoman Empire's western expansion came to an end after continuous wars on the Hungarian frontier had drained its human and financial resources. Only after the collapse of the authority of the state of Iran in the mid-eighteenth century was the eastern question temporarily resolved. Fifty years later, the Russians became the next great adversary, this time in the Caucasus; throughout the nineteenth century, the Ottoman Empire had to factor the Russian desire to gain free access to the straits into their strategic prioritisation. Ultimately, the Ottomans faced increasing resistance and rebellions from their subject people, resulting in a loss of revenue on the one hand and ever-increasing financial burdens of war on the other.[20]

The Execution / Application of Strategy

At the beginning, the Ottoman Emirate which was located on the Byzantine border was one of several small emirates born out of the disintegration of the Anatolian Seljukids. The Ottomans and other emirates were conducting continuous raids into Byzantine domains from every direction. These decentralised, constant and unpredictable raids by numerous chieftains were instrumental in the collapse of the Byzantine defences. There was also a relentless and sometimes vicious competition between them. The future success of the Ottomans was due to lessons learned during this competition and every opportunity was used to gain more territory, booty and fame. In the beginning Ottomans were very slow compared with some others. But their slowness turned out to be an advantage in the long run because they spent more time on state building internally, while externally escaping the wrath of outside powers. Certainly this was not a deliberate strategy. The Ottomans used their instincts better and they were very lucky.

Interestingly, the Byzantine emperors and aristocrats increasingly depended on the services of their deadly Turkish enemies as mercenaries against the Serbians and Bulgarians, and from time to time for their own internecine fights. Thanks to these employment opportunities the Ottomans not only gained substantial amounts of money but also learned the weakness of the Byzantines and the Balkan states and became familiar with the terrain. Therefore, when they finally crossed the Dardanelles in the 1360s they

---

20 C. Finkel, *The Government of Warfare: The Ottoman Military Campaigns in Hungary, 1593–1606* (Vienna: VWGÖ, 1988).

managed to penetrate deep into western Thrace and Bulgaria following strategic advance routes without much difficulty. At the same time many Byzantine, Serbian and Bulgarian magnates officially became vassals of the Ottomans. From now on the Ottomans exploited the military potential of their Balkan vassals to the limit.

The European powers discovered the danger of the Ottomans very late. King Sigismund of Hungary was able to convince several important European monarchs of the idea of a crusade. This crusading army, however, which mainly consisted of Hungarians and French, was completely crushed at Nicopolis on 25 September 1396. The large number of Christian losses included many famous knights, and subsequent horrendous accounts by the participants deterred western European monarchs from further engagements with the Ottomans in the Balkans and eastern Europe, leaving this region at their mercy.

From the very beginning the Ottomans struggled to legitimise their expansion against fellow Turcoman emirates. Ottoman soldiers were hesitant to fight against emirate soldiers who were seen as comrades and, at the same time, opportunities for material gain and looting were very limited in Anatolia due to strict regulations in Islamic law. Murad I and his son Bayezid I solved this important shortcoming by using some of his new Christian vassals' military potential and standing army units. In this manner the Ottomans captured most of the territories of the neighbouring emirates easily. However, these easy conquests came at a heavy price. The Ottomans were very unpopular among large segments of the Anatolian population, and they sought the help of Timur (Tamerlane). Timur was the self-made sultan of a great central Asian Turcoman state, who had just finished the conquest of Iran, becoming the neighbour of the Ottomans. Timur defeated the Ottoman army in a set-piece battle in Ankara on 28 July 1402.

Some of the former emirates were restored, Bayezid's sons immediately engaged in a civil war and the country was unofficially divided into three parts. The twelve-year interregnum (1402–1413) saw vicious internecine fighting. It looked as if the Ottoman state would come to an end. Despite this vulnerable situation the European domains of the sultanate remained quiet. The Balkan principalities and foreign powers like Hungary were unable to take advantage of this ideal opportunity to push back the Turkish conquests. Most of the sultanate's Christian subjects remained loyal and did not rebel. It is evident that the Ottomans managed to establish an enduring legitimate political and administrative system that had the support of the majority of the population. Shortly after the end of the civil war the Ottomans were able to counter the Hungarian-led east European and Balkan league in Varna (1444) and Kosovo (1448).

The conquest of Constantinople in 1453 was seen by the Christian and Muslim worlds as the realisation of apocalyptic oracles and as the beginning of a new era. Why did the city fall after withstanding dozens of sieges over hundreds of years? The common answer is because of the giant cannon and successful introduction of firearms into the Ottoman military. Obviously cannon and firearms played important roles but the real reason behind the victory was skilful military organisation backed by an efficient administrative and financial system. Although their wars caused great bloodshed, destruction and upheaval, the Ottomans were quick to establish order and peace and start rebuilding. For example, Mehmed II the Conqueror spent enormous effort and money in repopulating and redesigning Constantinople to create a fitting capital for his empire. The city was in terrible shape after decades of neglect and the long and bloody siege but in a relatively short time it once again became the biggest city in Europe and certainly the most cosmopolitan one.

During the siege of Constantinople, the Ottoman navy failed to breach the chain closing off the entrance to the Golden Horn and was unable to enforce the blockade effectively. Mehmed II invested in a navy and managed to support his expeditionary forces efficiently and even captured Otranto, the heel of the Italian peninsula, in 1481. Interestingly the Ottomans never felt the need to create specific naval units and used regular land forces instead. The *sipahi*s were always the most numerous troops on any naval expedition.

The real naval leap was achieved in 1517 when pirates in Algiers under the leadership of Barbarossa Hayreddin entered Ottoman service. The pirates came from all Mediterranean nations, chief among them Turks, Greeks, Italians and Maltese. They were very talented and experienced captains and sailors. Ottoman financial and material support increased their fleet, manpower and, most importantly, ambition. When Barbarossa became the chief admiral of the Ottoman navy in 1533, he employed more pirates. Employment of pirates provided not only naval capacity but also flexibility. The Ottomans were able to employ them wherever there was need, including the Red Sea and the Indian Ocean. Furthermore, the regenerated Ottoman navy put the most dangerous enemy of the empire, the Habsburgs, at bay. In 1538, Barbarossa soundly defeated the Habsburg and Venetian armada near Preveza. To make matters worse for the Habsburgs, the joint Ottoman–French fleet captured Nice in 1543.

In the sixteenth century, initial failures to drive the Portuguese out of the Red Sea did not discourage the Ottoman governing elite and commanders on the ground. Grand Vizier Sokullu Mehmed Pasha and his protégés tried to overcome this impasse by drastically altering the status quo. They revived the idea of a canal to join the Red Sea with the Mediterranean (following nearly the same path as the modern Suez Canal), not only to enable the navy to sail directly from its main base but also to revive commerce. Unfortunately for the empire the project was terminated immediately after the initial groundwork. The priorities of other theatres of operations (especially Hungary), increasing competition with the Safavids of Iran and the Mughals of India and ever-present internecine fights between small Muslim entities were instrumental in curtailing the Ottoman military presence in the region. In the end both Ottomans and Portuguese unofficially had to recognise each other's sphere of influence and tried to consolidate their bases and network of alliances.[21]

For most modern commentators the Ottoman military effort to expel the Portuguese from the Indian Ocean was an overly ambitious and faulty decision. They are right to point out the technological constraints such as the Mediterranean galleys' poor design for the job of continuous control of the high seas or the Ottoman military's difficulty in conducting operations far from its main support bases. However, they tend to ignore great achievements, like establishing absolute control of the Red Sea and the northern Persian Gulf, the enormous prestige of protecting the traditional realm of Islam (including guarding the holy cities) and restoring the volume of traditional trade up until the mid-seventeenth century with relatively modest commitments. It was not Portugal, which was soundly defeated by the Dutch navy at Amboyna in 1605, but the Netherlands and Britain that would bypass Ottoman-controlled trade routes during the second half of the seventeenth century.

In the meantime, excepting Morocco, the whole Mediterranean coastline of Africa was conquered and this time the Ottoman onslaught targeted the big islands of the Mediterranean. Malta withstood a four-month Ottoman siege in 1565, but Rhodes (1522) and Cyprus (1571) did not. After a long series of victories, the overconfident Ottoman navy was seriously beaten in Lepanto in 1571. Although the Habsburgs and Venetians did not get what they had wanted, it was still a serious blow. The Ottomans lost nearly 200 ships and suffered around 30,000 casualties. Sokullu Mehmed Pasha, in record time,

---

21 G. Casale, *The Ottoman Age of Exploration* (Oxford: Oxford University Press, 2010).

constructed a new fleet of ships but the Ottoman Empire had no means to replace the loss of experienced sailors. The Lepanto defeat definitely ended Ottoman plans to control the western Mediterranean. But it was Ottoman leaders who destroyed the navy by cutting its budget year after year, thereby causing its slow death.

Key Debates

The end of the sixteenth century has been generally seen by scholars as the end of Ottoman military superiority and the beginning of stagnation and eventual decline. According to these authors, an influx of American silver and an associated price revolution, demographic pressures, the rise of western European military states, and economic hegemony were instrumental in the corruption of the classical Ottoman military–administrative system. In turn, the Ottoman Empire simply did not have the means to compete with the western Europeans, who were undergoing a wide-ranging political, socio-economic and technological transformation – and consequently, its decline was a foregone conclusion.[22] This line of scholarship grew out of the inaccurate views of contemporary observers of the Ottoman Empire, combined with well-established Eurocentric tendencies to apply different standards to the Islamic and non-western Ottoman Empire. It should not come as a surprise that the so-called 'long and inevitable decline' became, and remains, the dominant theme of received Ottoman history from the beginning of the seventeenth century.

From the military perspective, 'declinists' have difficulty in explaining the Ottoman victories and military successes – other than pointing out factors such as unusual leadership, geographical difficulties or simple luck. This difficulty is even more evident when trying to explain the relative ease with which the Ottoman government overcame serious military defeats and setbacks, including the battle of Lepanto (1571), the fall of Baghdad (1623) and the long campaign for Crete (1645–1669, 1684–1699). In this period, an ever-resourceful government continued to overcome its problems by creative or pragmatic methods. Admittedly, sometimes the solutions themselves were instrumental in the creation of even larger secondary problems.

---

22 İ. Hakkı Uzunçarşılı, *Osmanlı Tarihi*, Volume III, Section 2 (Ankara: Türk Tarih Kurumu Basımevi, 1983), 270–88; H. İnalcık and D. Quataert (eds), *An Economic and Social History of the Ottoman Empire, 1300–1914* (Cambridge: Cambridge University Press, 1994); Ö. Lütfi Barkan and Justin McCarthy, 'The price revolution of the sixteenth century: a turning point in the economic history of the Near East', *International Journal of Middle East Studies*, 6:1 (January 1975), 3–28.

The theory of decline is also unable to explain the rapid transformation of the Ottoman military against the threat raised by Habsburg Austria or its ability to fight on the eastern and western frontiers at the same time. In truth, following contemporary European trends, the Ottoman military transformed itself slowly but decisively by increasing its size, introducing new firearms en masse and increasingly making use of siege and countersiege operations. Obviously a totally new approach is needed to explain the Ottoman military of the seventeenth century, but the first focus must be on the increased capability of the Ottoman military's logistic and manpower systems in order to explain why this period should be labelled a 'transformation' rather than a 'decline'.[23]

It is certainly wrong to attribute the surprising victories and territorial expansion against several strong rivals only to military might. The Ottoman military of the classical period was neither 'nearly perfect' nor simply a good imitator, which are the two opposite views that come from both traditional academic and popular works about this subject. The real classical Ottoman military achieved great victories but also suffered defeats; it did imitate European models and experiences but managed to produce original concepts and practices that were, in turn, imitated by the Europeans. The Ottoman military was, overall, an effective force relative to its principal opponents and proved capable of providing viable military capability in support of the political objectives of the Ottoman Empire.[24]

The Decline of the Ottoman Empire

On 12 September 1683, within reach of a spectacular victory, the Ottoman army suffered a disastrous defeat at the hands of Poles and Austrians outside Vienna. The expedition against Vienna had been the biggest military effort but it was not the only one. The empire had been fighting on several fronts – in Asia to the east and in Europe and north Africa to the west – continuously for nearly a century, therefore this last defeat, following sixteen years after that against the Holy Alliance (Austria, the Polish–Lithuanian Commonwealth, Venice, Russia and the Papacy), was simply too much. When Emperor Mustafa II signed the Treaty of Karlowitz in 1699, the Ottoman army had lost a trained

23 V. Aksan, *Ottoman Wars 1700–1870: An Empire Besieged* (Harlow: Pearson, Longman, 2007); Metin Kunt, *The Sultan's Servants: The Transformation of Ottoman Provincial Government, 1550–1650* (New York: Columbia University Press, 1983).

24 Murphey, *Ottoman Warfare*, 185–92; Agoston, *Guns for the Sultan*, 8–60, 192–5.

and battle-hardened cadre of the transformed military without any chance of renewal by a new cadre.[25]

Against all odds the empire did not collapse but survived for another two centuries (outliving, in fact, most of its main adversaries) by transforming its military and civil bureaucracy to adapt to developments in the West. Obviously, the transformation, adaptation and reform processes were laden with inconsistencies, contradictions, corruption and half-hearted efforts, but these attempts eventually gave the empire a new life.

The profound dilemma for the Ottoman Empire was that the military and administrative reforms required to resist Western expansion and to ensure the integrity of the empire turned out to be a double-edged sword requiring enormous financial resources and provoking intense domestic and foreign hostility, thereby weakening the entire state further. Moreover, and unfortunately for the empire, most of the reformers were ill-equipped to understand the relationship between the failure of military reforms and the overall inadequacy of the politico-administrative structure, the agrarian economy and the social fabric. When western Europe was experiencing the Industrial Revolution – thanks to large coal deposits in Britain and France and the enormous resources of the Americas and other dominions – in the second half of the eighteenth century the Ottomans were trying to protect their domains against the Russians and, to a certain extent, the Austrians. Continuous wars put a heavy burden on the economy and state finances, which caused more internal unrest and more economic and social problems. Despite wars and rebellions, the Ottomans managed to survive into the modern era, whereas the Mughals of India and the Safavids of Persia collapsed and disintegrated.

25 J. Stoye, *The Siege of Vienna* (London: Collins, 1964).

18

Strategy in the Wars of Pre-colonial Sub-Saharan Africa

JOHN BURTON KEGEL AND GIACOMO MACOLA

Introduction

African military history remains 'perhaps the last bastion of the kind of distorted Eurocentric scholarship that characterised African studies' before the decolonisation wave of the 1960s.[1] This is especially true of the pre-colonial period, on account of both the sparseness and the limitations of the sources available for study. Both in tactical and in strategic terms, African pre-colonial warfare (insofar as it can be reconstructed) was as complex as warfare in any other historical setting. The standard causes of war – ideology, territorial conquest or the control of wealth and trade – are just as pertinent. The consequences of war, which can include state formation or political fragmentation, follow similar patterns too. We propose to substantiate our argument by exploring a number of regional case studies organised in a loose chronological order: early modern warfare in the empires of the Sahel; Dahomian warfare in the context of the Atlantic slave trade; Zulu and Ngoni warfare in southern Africa; and, finally, central African warfare in the age of warlords.

The Sources

Most of sub-Saharan Africa remained without writing until colonisation, thereby depriving historians of their conventional sources. Such pre-colonial written sources as do exist were more often than not produced 'by outsiders for outsiders'.[2] Examples of the genre are the writings of the European traders who operated around Whydah in the eighteenth and nineteenth centuries or those of the slightly later missionary observers of Garenganze (see below). Sources of this nature, of course, pose problems,

---

1 R. J. Reid, *War in Pre-colonial Eastern Africa* (London: James Curry, 2007), 3.
2 Reid, *War in Pre-colonial Eastern Africa*, 14.

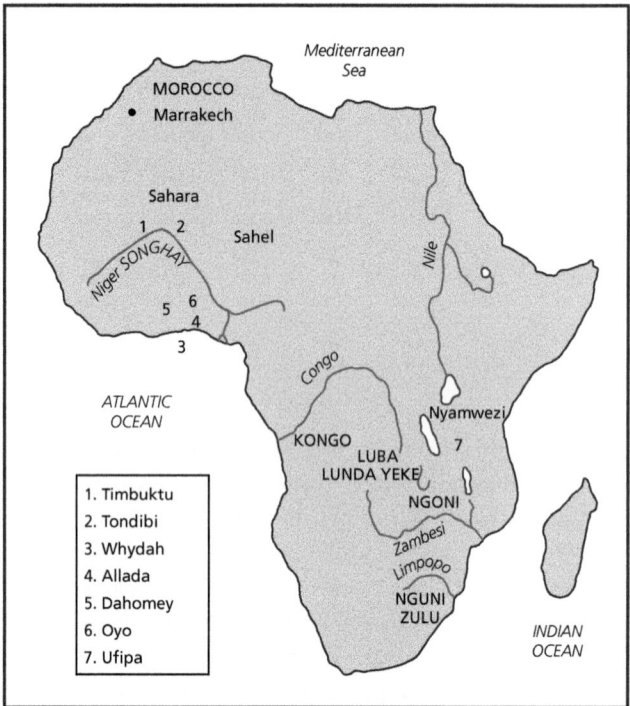

Map 18.1 Strategy in the wars of pre-colonial sub-Saharan Africa

many of which stem from the racial and 'orientalist' biases which frequently pervade them. They nonetheless have their use; however full of prejudice, one can 'hear a multitude of African voices' when reading them carefully.[3]

Historians of pre-colonial Africa can draw on sources of two other types. First is archaeological evidence, although it too can be sparse.[4] While the stone cities of the Ethiopian Highlands, the middle Nile or Great Zimbabwe have stood the test of time, settlements built using organic material have survived much less well. Moreover, while archaeological evidence might

---

3 R. J. Reid, 'Violence and its sources: European witnesses to the military revolution in nineteenth-century eastern Africa', in P. S. Landau (ed.), *The Power of Doubt: Essays in Honor of David Henige* (Madison: Parallel Press, University of Wisconsin Libraries, 2011), 45.

4 For a good introduction to the topic, see G. Connah, *African Civilizations: Precolonial Cities and States in Tropical Africa. An Archaeological Perspective* (Cambridge: Cambridge University Press, 1987).

throw light on past practices of war, it hardly lends itself to divining the intentions of strategists and tacticians. To an extent, the same is true of the second type of evidence: oral tradition, defined as 'verbal testimonies which are reported statements concerning the past'.[5] This loose definition has the advantage of including several disparate forms: chiefly and royal narratives and genealogies, of course, but also epics, poems, songs, proverbs, slogans, historical tales and so on. However, the selectivity of oral traditions, and their responsiveness to present-day circumstances,[6] mean that they are seldom sufficiently detailed to elucidate the inner workings of the military apparatus of the polities by which such traditions have been preserved.

The Actors

Oral traditions tend to ascribe strategic decision making to individual rulers, while the internal debates which must have accompanied military pursuits and the actors involved in them remain very largely beyond our gaze. The unevenness and the limitations of our source material prevent a comprehensive discussion of the subcontinent's strategy makers. Even so, as the regional examples discussed in the next four sections clarify, there is no reason to suppose that, in determining the allocation of resources for military purposes, African rulers did not avail themselves of the expert advice provided by the members of their courts, their military commanders (who were at times the leaders of standing armies but who could also consist of territorial governors entrusted with the temporary mobilisation of men in their respective districts) and their spiritual advisers. The latter offered counsel not so much on strategic matters as on the omens of an impending expedition or the will of the gods and the ancestors.

The common imbrication of religion and warfare, as well as the existence of fora for collective decision making, are also borne out by the case of the Nyiginya kingdom of present-day Rwanda. There, the king (*mwami*) is known to have relied on allies from within his lineage group and chosen warriors for political support and military advice.[7] 'The Way of War', one of the kingdom's epic

---

5 J. Vansina, *Oral Tradition: A Study in Historical Methodology* (London: Routledge and K. Paul, 1965), 19.

6 W. G. Clarence-Smith, 'A note on the "Ecole des *Annales*" and the historiography of Africa', *History in Africa*, 4 (1977), 275–81.

7 J. Vansina, *Antecedents to Modern Rwanda: The Nyiginya Kingdom* (Madison: University of Wisconsin Press, 2004).

poems dating to perhaps 1750–1850, describes both the ritual and the practical preparations for combat. A passage, in particular, explains how the *mwami* sets off for battle with his warriors, dynastic poets and musicians:

> When he will arrive at the above-mentioned place,
> Where the warriors are gathered and practice,
> We set the plan of operations
> For the day of the attack.[8]

Early Modern Warfare in the Sahel

Warfare in the Sahara, the Sahel and Sudan has long been driven by religion and trade. War, religion and trade have, in turn, had profound effects on state formation. Particularly important in this regard is the literature on the role of horses and cavalry in trading and slaving.[9] Raiding was a key form of warfare on the border between the Sahara desert and the Sahel, as it tends to be wherever nomadic pastoralists and sedentary agriculturalists meet.[10] One of the major causes of these raids was the value of slaves in the trans-Saharan trade. However, there was a clear difference between this steady decentralised warfare, which was wholly tactical, and larger conflicts in which we recognise true strategic decision making on the part of state actors. This, of course, is not to say that low-level raids could not be incorporated into strategic thinking when necessary, not least because 'smaller operations were often preparation for larger ones, or perhaps a substitute in situations where one country did not wish to risk larger engagements'.[11] A clear example of strategic confrontation is the invasion of Songhay, in present-day Mali, by the Moroccan sultan Ahmad I al-Mansur Sa'did. This large-scale operation is well documented in the Timbuktu Chronicles and several other minor written sources and captures a key technological and political moment in the history of the Sahel.

---

8 M. d'Hertefelt and A. Coupez, *La royauté sacrée de l'ancien Rwanda: Texte, traduction et commentaire de son rituel* (Tervuren: MRAC, 1964), 163.

9 See, e.g., H. J. Fisher, 'He swalloweth the ground with fierceness and rage: the horse in the central Sudan. ı Its introduction', *Journal of African History*, 13:3 (1972), 367–88; H. J. Fisher, 'He swalloweth the ground with fierceness and rage: the horse in the central Sudan. ıı Its use', *Journal of African History*, 14:3 (1973), 355–79.

10 E. A. McDougall, 'The view from Awdaghust: war, trade and social change in the southwestern Sahara, from the eighth to the fifteenth century', *Journal of African History*, 26:1 (1985), 1–31, 13.

11 J. K. Thornton, *Warfare in Atlantic Africa 1500–1800* (London: UCL Press, 2003), 33.

By the end of the sixteenth century, the Sa'did dynasty, which controlled much of modern-day Morocco, was under growing pressure from the resurgent Christian Iberian kingdoms to its north and the advancing Ottoman Empire to its east. Searching for ways to reinforce the fiscal basis of his state, al-Mansur became interested in an intelligence report from his spies which announced that the Songhay kingdom was in 'wretched circumstances . . . powerless.'[12] In December 1589, he sent a letter to the king of Songhay, Ishaq II, demanding taxes on a sub-Saharan salt mine under the latter's control. Ishaq promptly refused, and so the sultan decided to resort to military force to capture the trading hub of Timbuktu and the gold mines beyond it. He hoped that the capture of the city would allow the Sa'did to control the trans-Saharan trade, diverting it into Morocco, and thus gain access to the gold and salt they needed to finance wars in the Mediterranean. To undertake the campaign, the general in charge, Judar Pasha, would have to cross the Sahara with an army and emerge from it fresh enough to do battle against the forces of Songhay, including its formidable cavalry. Despite the obvious difficulties, the sultan underpinned with arguments his belief in the success of such an undertaking. When asked by his religious advisers how they would overcome the Songhay cavalry, al-Mansur replied,

As for former dynasties which, you say, never contemplated such a project as mine . . . their armies were composed only of horsemen armed with spears, and of bowmen; gunpowder was unknown to them, and so were firearms and their terrifying effect. Today the Sudanese have only spears and swords, weapons which will be useless against my modern arms. It will, therefore, be easy for us to wage a successful war against these people and prevail over them.[13]

In addition, the Songhay kingdom was still recovering from a civil war which had only ended the previous year, something the Moroccan spies would undoubtedly have reported to al-Mansur.[14] An anonymous Spaniard who lived in Marrakech, perhaps to gather intelligence for King Philip II, wrote about the extensive preparations which the sultan made before his army departed from the city. The Moroccan forces numbered about 4,000

12 J. Hunwick, *Timbuktu & the Songhay Empire: Al-Sa'dī's Ta'rīkh Al-sūdān down to 1613 and Other Contemporary Documents* (Leiden: Brill, 2003), 187.
13 Quoted in L. Kaba, 'Archers, musketeers, and mosquitoes: the Moroccan invasion of the Sudan and the Songhay resistance (1591–1612)', *Journal of African History*, 22:4 (1981), 457–75, 463.
14 N. Levtzion, 'The western Maghrib and Sudan', in R. Oliver (ed.), *The Cambridge History of Africa*, Volume III: *From c. 1050 to c. 1600* (Cambridge: Cambridge University Press, 1977), 441.

veteran soldiers armed with muskets and blunderbusses. There also was a small contingent of cavalry. The whole force was supported by a vast supply train. Besides gunpowder, the army carried '10,000 camel loads' of dates, wheat, oats and water.[15] On 16 October 1590, Judar Pasha's forces started their journey across the desert.

King Ishaq II's response to the invasion is difficult to reconstruct from available source material. He seems to have undertaken three concrete steps. First, he called for his allies on the fringes of the desert to deny water to the invaders by closing the wells on their route. However, treachery might have prevented this from happening, as the Moroccan army emerged from the Sahara largely unscathed. Second, he used canoes to carry out a surprise attack on the Moroccan army as it was encamped on the banks of the Niger river. 'One night, as they were camped in these woods [along the Niger], a large number of Blacks came from the river on boats ... they bravely attacked Jawdar's camp ... The musketeers immediately ran towards them, and with a few salvoes killed many ... forcing the others to retire.'[16] Third, Ishaq mustered his army and faced Judar Pasha in battle at Tondibi. Although all sources agree that the Moroccans were heavily outnumbered, their firepower seems to have carried the day. Although the Moroccan army claimed the field, victory did not give Sultan al-Mansur what he had hoped for. A fierce Songhay insurgency which lasted until 1617, combined with the treacherous journey through the Sahara which Moroccan reinforcements had to make, meant that 'by 1630 the Sultans' authority had become nominal',[17] and that the Moroccan strategy of territorial conquest and economic exploitation had failed, its technological edge notwithstanding.

Dahomey, Grand Strategy and the Atlantic Slave Trade

Climate and geography are key to understanding African warfare. Whereas cavalry was a formidable weapon in the Sahara and the Sahel, sleeping sickness, which is fatal to cattle and horses, limited its use in regions inhabited by the tsetse fly. In practice, this meant that cavalry was not a viable tactical asset along the rainforest-covered Atlantic coast. The only exception to this rule was the Benin Gap, where the savanna extended all

---

15 Hunwick, *Timbuktu & the Songhay Empire*, 319.
16 Hunwick, *Timbuktu & the Songhay Empire*, 321.
17 Kaba, 'Archers, musketeers, and mosquitoes', 473.

the way to the coast.[18] This allowed both infantry and cavalry to coexist there and gave rise to one of pre-colonial Africa's most potent military states.

The kingdom of Dahomey makes its first appearance in historical sources in the early eighteenth century as a slave-trading polity in the interior of the so-called Slave Coast (modern-day Benin). It was squeezed between the Oyo Empire, with its formidable cavalry, to the north, and the slave-trading cities of Allada and Whydah to the south. Dahomey's rise took place against the backdrop of an increase in the slave trade. In the 1640s, about 600 slaves were exported annually from the region, but, by the 1690s, the number had risen to around 10,000.[19] The Portuguese, Dutch and British traders paid the coastal African polities for their slaves with luxury goods and firearms. Although Dahomey had initially been a vassal or tributary of Allada, the balance of power had shifted by 1724, when the Dahomians had conquered Allada. In 1727, Dahomey's King Agaja demanded that the port of Whydah give his traders access to the coast. When the latter refused, the army of Dahomey invaded and conquered the city.[20] As Reid has pointed out, 'whether local expansionist violence merely coincided, in the first instance, with the expansion of the slave trade, or whether it was driven by the latter from the outset is perhaps a matter of speculation'. What is clear, however, is that 'the two processes quickly became indelibly interlinked.'[21] Under Dahomian rule, Whydah 'remained the largest port in the region'; in 1750, it was 'estimated to be exporting between 8,000 and 9,000 slaves annually.'[22]

The key to Dahomey's success was its professional and disciplined army, described in a 1730 French account as 'not numerous', but made up of 'select troops, both brave and well disciplined, led by a Prince full of valour and prudence, and under him by experienced officers ... obedient and submissive to their chiefs.' A few years earlier, the slave trader Snelgrave had been similarly impressed. In his view, Dahomian forces 'march[ed] in a much more regular Order than I have ever seen before [i.e. in Africa] ... [a] sight ... well worth seeing even by us Europeans'.[23] Access to the slave trade made this army even

---

18 Thornton, *Warfare in Atlantic Africa*, 55.
19 R. Law, *Ouidah: The Social History of a West African Slaving 'Port', 1727–1892* (Oxford: James Currey, 2004), 30.
20 R. Law, 'Dahomey and the slave trade: reflections on the historiography of the rise of Dahomey', *Journal of African History*, 27:2 (1986), 237–67, 244; R. Law, '"The common people were divided": monarchy, aristocracy and political factionalism in the kingdom of Whydah, 1671–1727', *International Journal of African Historical Studies*, 23:2 (1990), 201–29.
21 R. J. Reid, *Warfare in African History* (Cambridge: Cambridge University Press, 2012), 82.
22 Law, *Ouidah*, 125.   23 Both quoted in Law, 'Dahomey and the slave trade', 248.

more formidable, as it could now count on an ample supply of firearms, which in turn allowed it to carry out more wars and capture further slaves. However, its military did not make Dahomey invulnerable, and successive Oyo invasions, which seem to have been spearheaded by cavalry, in 1728, 1729 and 1730 forced it to pay regular tribute to the latter.[24]

Nonetheless, Dahomey's slave-trading economy flourished until 1794, when Revolutionary France abolished the practice. The Haitian Revolution and British Abolition in 1804 and 1807, respectively, reduced the trade even further.[25] Dahomey, like the Kongo kingdom further south, maintained close diplomatic relations with Western powers. It had sent diplomatic missions to Portugal, through Brazil, and the accompanying correspondence gives us an interesting insight into the strategic objectives of its rulers. In 1795 King Agonglo asked the governor of Bahia to designate Whydah the sole port from which Portuguese ships could buy slaves, cutting out other coastal competitors. Agonglo was rebuffed, but his successor, Adandozan, made a similar request in 1805.[26] However, Adandozan's arrogant attitude vis-à-vis the Portuguese, especially after the Portuguese king was forced to flee to Brazil in the face of Napoleon's invasion, and his bickering with a local merchant in the pay of Portugal, Francisco de Souza, cost him the throne.[27] In 1818, Adandozan's younger brother, Gezo, mounted a successful coup against him with de Souza's help. Gezo, clearly a more gifted diplomat than his brother had been, also succeeded in enlisting de Souza's help against the now tottering Oyo Empire. In 1823, Gezo's troops defeated the Oyo army in battle, carrying 'Dahomey to the peak of its military success',[28] and placing it in the ideal position to dominate the now technically illegal slave trade for decades to come. Although we do not know if firearms played a key role in the Dahomian defeat of Oyo, there is no doubt that a highly disciplined and drilled gun-wielding infantry would remain the backbone of the state's armed forces throughout the nineteenth century.[29]

In Dahomey's history, in sum, we can distinguish a grand strategic vision which lasted beyond the reign of a single king. The control of the slave trade, the firearms it provided and a strong martial identity created a powerful predatory

---

24 R. Law, 'A west African cavalry state: the kingdom of Oyo', *Journal of African History*, 16:1 (1975), 1–15.

25 A. L. Araujo, 'Dahomey, Portugal and Bahia: King Adandozan and the Atlantic slave trade', *Slavery & Abolition*, 33:1 (2012), 1–19, 4, 8–9.

26 Araujo, 'Dahomey, Portugal and Bahia', 4, 8, 12.

27 Araujo, 'Dahomey, Portugal and Bahia', 11.

28 Law, 'Dahomey and the slave trade', 252.

29 R. A. Kea, 'Firearms and warfare on the Gold and Slave Coasts from the sixteenth to the nineteenth centuries', *Journal of African History*, 12:2 (1971), 185–213.

state that dominated the region. However, when military might was unable to achieve the kingdom's objectives, its leaders showed a shrewd understanding of international diplomacy and tried, with varying degrees of success, to draw on the assistance of European interlopers.

Zulu and Ngoni Warfare in Southern Africa

The late eighteenth century was a turbulent period for the agro-pastoralist Nguni-speaking peoples of present-day KwaZulu-Natal. While historians have debated the causes of such conflicts,[30] their contribution to processes of political centralisation is hardly in doubt. Among the northern Nguni, state formation took a very distinctive form. Age sets, or *amabutho*, had been a feature of the social organisation of the region for decades, if not centuries. In their original form, the *amabutho* were groups of young men 'brought together by chiefs for short periods to be taken through the rites of circumcision, and perhaps to engage in certain services, such as hunting'.[31] In the deteriorating political landscape of the late eighteenth century, however, emerging local leaders transformed these age sets into labour and fighting detachments, thereby bringing into being increasingly permanent and professionalised armies. Thereafter, the *amabutho* became both a consequence and a cause of the growing levels of militarism among the northern Nguni.

Against this background, and that of prolonged drought exacerbating regional instability, the Zulu state gained power in the early nineteenth century. The consolidation and expansion of the Zulu kingdom in the lowveld of KwaZulu-Natal from the late 1810s is closely associated with the towering figure of Shaka, who not only systematised the *amabutho* system, now turned into 'a fully-fledged national army',[32] but also such pre-existing tactical innovations as the 'bull's horns' formation and the famous short stabbing assegai. Shaka was moved by personal ambition and the will to dominate his neighbours, but his wars of expansion were also shaped by deeper motives, of which he may have been but dimly aware. Ecological crisis led to fierce armed competition between chiefdoms. Warfare, in this context, was primarily intended to secure such lands as

---

30 See, e.g., C. Hamilton (ed.), *The Mfecane Aftermath: Reconstructive Debates in Southern African History* (Johannesburg: Witwatersrand University Press, 1995).

31 J. Wright, 'Turbulent times: political transformations in the north and east, 1760s–1830s', in C. Hamilton, B. K. Mbenga and R. Ross (eds), *The Cambridge History of South Africa*, Volume 1: *From Early Times to 1885* (Cambridge: Cambridge University Press, 2010), 221.

32 I. Knight, *The Anatomy of the Zulu Army from Shaka to Cetshwayo, 1818–1879* (London: Greenhill Books, 1995), 33.

could still support agro-pastoral pursuits, as well as the conscription of newly subjugated young men into Zulu regiments.

Zulu territorial expansion and systematic raiding – 'the quickest route to wealth for the state and the soldiers'[33] – drove several groups to seek refuge to the north of KwaZulu-Natal and across the Limpopo river. Their protagonists are best understood as highly mobile and heterogeneous military bands held together by personal loyalty to individual war leaders, such as Mzilikazi – who imposed his supremacy, first, over the Highveld and, then, in the late 1830s, over the rich pastures of today's south-western Zimbabwe – and Zwangendaba Jere, who led his followers as far north as Ufipa, in present-day south-western Tanzania, at about the same time.[34] These movements spread the new Nguni/Zulu principles of social and military organisation to territories where they had been previously unknown.

For example, the strategy of Zwangendaba's followers, roving bands now known as Ngoni, during their epic northward trek amounted to a kind of 'migrant brigandage' targeting sedentary communities for food, livestock and captives. The last of these were not normally sold on as slaves, but rather married, if female, or, if male, incorporated into the regiment system, which permitted their 'indoctrin[ation] into Ngoni ways':

> Men captives were drafted into the regiment appropriate to their apparent age, and boys were enrolled with their coevals. They were called upon to fight in the same way as their aristocratic comrades, and were offered the same prospects of promotion, both within the age-set system and in the segmentary organization, as a result of successful fighting.[35]

To describe the Ngoni socio-military structure, anthropologist John Barnes coined the term 'snowball state' – a state that came into being through the accretion of successive layers. Exacerbating the effects of the long-distance slave and ivory trades, the violence unleashed by the Ngoni prompted several unrelated people 'to adopt the Ngoni model, reorganising and arming for defence, and then for offence as well, thus sustaining the momentum of regional militarisation'.[36]

Upon Zwangendaba's death in Tanzania in about 1845, his 'snowball state' fragmented into several autonomous sections, at least two of which

---

33 E. A. Eldredge, 'Sources of conflict in southern Africa, c. 1800–30: the "Mfecane" reconsidered', *Journal of African History*, 33:1 (1992), 1–35, 31.

34 N. Etherington, *The Great Treks: The Transformation of Southern Africa, 1815–1854* (Harlow: Longman, 2001), 249–56, 277.

35 J. A. Barnes, *Politics in a Changing Society: A Political History of the Fort Jameson Ngoni* (London: Oxford University Press, 1954), 40.

36 Reid, *Warfare in African History*, 118.

eventually opted for a settled existence, giving rise to separate centralised kingdoms in present-day eastern Zambia and northern Malawi in the 1860s–1870s. Although this shift did not change the basic features of Ngoni militarism or the fundamental purposes of their wars, it did bring them into closer contact with long-distance traders from the Swahili coast. Thus Ngoni warfare became more commercially oriented, with ivory now featuring among the spoils of raids. The Ngoni's aversion to selling slaves, however, remained unchanged – as did their opposition to the military deployment of firearms, which continued to be regarded as a cowardly weapon that prevented young fighters of captive origins from reaping the rewards of bravery.[37]

Central African Warfare in the Age of Warlords

Source scarcity allows at best some broad generalisations for Central Africa. In the southern savanna, unlike in the sparsely inhabited Congo basin rainforest, expansive and centralised state systems – beginning with the Luba and Lunda kingdoms[38] – came into being from about 1700. Oral tradition implies that the most common strategic driver of war within these polities was the ambition to increase their tributary bases and wealth in people.[39] This explains why military expansion out of the Luba and Lunda heartland areas in present-day Katanga targeted favourable environments (for instance river banks and alluvial plains) that supported comparatively large agricultural and fishing populations, and districts endowed with scarce mineral resources (most notably salt, iron and copper). External commerce and the sale of slaves to Portuguese Angola became increasingly important for the Lunda over the course of the eighteenth century, but the accumulation of exportable commodities for the international market was not the primary aim of war.

Very little is known about tactics, other than that firearms played a minimal role in the wars of the central African interior. In the 1750s, the Angolan slave trader Manoel Correia Leitão, while describing the Lunda as 'terrestrial Eagles' who raided 'countries so remote from their Fatherland only to lord it over other peoples', also emphasised their dislike of guns, a

---

37 This argument is developed at greater length in G. Macola, *The Gun in Central Africa: A History of Technology and Politics* (Athens: Ohio University Press, 2016), Chapter 5.

38 For a brief introduction, see G. Macola, 'Luba–Lunda states', in J. MacKenzie (ed.), *Encyclopedia of Empire* (Chichester: Wiley–Blackwell, 2016), at https://onlinelibrary.w iley.com/doi/10.1002/9781118455074.wbeoe060.

39 T. Q. Reefe, *The Rainbow and the Kings: A History of the Luba Empire to 1891* (Berkeley and Los Angeles: University of California Press, 1981), 107; J. K. Thornton, *A History of West Central Africa to 1850* (Cambridge: Cambridge University Press, 2020), 231–2.

'handicap to valor' that inhibited hand-to-hand combat 'with a sword ... a leather shield which covers them completely and small spears'.[40] Neither the Luba nor the Lunda seem to have had professional standing armies (exceptions were made for small units of royal bodyguards), but rather called for the temporary mobilisation of commoners, who served as infantrymen under the leadership of territorial aristocrats doubling up as military commanders.[41] This – as well as the pressures of the agricultural timetable and the need to live off the land while on campaign – must go some way towards explaining the apparent brevity of large-scale military engagements and also the crucial political importance of persuasion, blandishment and religious backing, rather than violence and force, in fostering peripheral integration.

This changed in the nineteenth century with the full incorporation of the southern savanna into global networks of trade built around the exchange of ivory and slaves for imported guns, cloth and beads. As the old elites failed to keep up with the unprecedented levels of militarisation ushered in by booming commerce and its aggressive spearheads, their erstwhile place was often usurped by new 'warlord states' characterised by an 'intimate association between political leadership and military command'.[42] Within them,

> power rested less on religious sanction and economic redistribution than on their leaders' personal achievements, successful involvement in commerce, and sheer military force. The diffusion of firearms and their recasting into primary means of military and economic domination were often central to these processes of political realignment, which also drew some of their impetus from the related emergence of semi-professional standing armies of brutalized young men.[43]

As a result of these far-reaching transformations, warfare became more and more central to the political economy of the region. Its strategic objectives changed, too, as it was now mainly – or even solely – aimed at securing the human and material commodities which stoked the external trade.

Warlord states – sometimes led by outsiders, sometimes by recycled members of the previous political order – spread all over the eastern half of today's Democratic Republic of the Congo. An early example of their

40 E. Sebestyen and J. Vansina (eds and trans.), 'Angola's eastern hinterland in the 1750s: a text edition and Translation of Manoel Correia Leitão's "Voyage" (1755–1756)', *History in Africa*, 26 (1999), 299–364, 347.
41 Reefe, *The Rainbow*, 108.   42 Reid, *Warfare in African History*, 116.
43 Macola, *The Gun in Central Africa*, 46.

functioning is provided by Garenganze, the state founded by Msiri and his followers (who became known as 'Yeke') in the 1850s.[44] Msiri, originally a Nyamwezi trader from present-day Tanzania, settled in southern Katanga, a savanna region that had previously formed the periphery of the Luba and the eastern Lunda states. As a parvenu shorn of local roots and legitimacy, Msiri had no option but to draw on foreign commerce to consolidate his power.[45] This is why newly subjugated Katangese communities were mercilessly preyed upon for slaves and ivory, the goods which attracted both Arab–Swahili and Ovimbundu long-distance operators to Bunkeya, Msiri's sprawling capital.

Msiri's *Raubwirtschaft* depended on the deployment of a network of territorial aristocrats and centrally appointed officials. The main duty of the latter and the armed bands which they controlled (according to German explorer Paul Reichard, Msiri could count upon as many as '2,000 or 3,000 flintlock muskets' in 1884[46]) was still tribute collection. Yeke exactions, however, were more burdensome than had been the case under the previous political dispensation, since Msiri is said to have instituted a 'system of compulsory production quotas' with a view to increasing his supplies of ivory and slaves.[47] Slaves were also obtained by means of systematic raids. More common than full-blown wars of expansion, these raids kept the Yeke military constantly occupied. The missionary Frederick S. Arnot was perfectly aware of the intimate relationship that obtained between external trade and warfare in Garenganze in the mid-1880s:

> War is, to a great extent, carried on for the sake of making captives; and on account of this the king has often difficulty in restraining his soldiers from extending their raiding expeditions mercilessly, when once he has banded them together to attack any chief . . . Large numbers of slaves are brought into the capital every year by returning war parties, and are sold chiefly to Arab traders from Zanzibar and to Ovimbundu traders from Bihé [in Angola].[48]

Yeke pressures and their exclusive reliance on hard power generated much local hostility. Eventually, in 1891, this erupted into an open rebellion, which the

44 H. Legros, *Chasseurs d'ivoire: Une histoire du Royaume Yeke du Shaba (Zaïre)* (Brussels: Éditions de l'Université de Bruxelles, 1996), 28–9.

45 A. D. Roberts, 'Firearms in north-eastern Zambia before 1900', *Transafrican Journal of History*, 1:2 (1971), 3–21, 13.

46 Quoted in Roberts, 'Firearms in north-eastern Zambia', 9.

47 Legros, *Chasseurs d'ivoire*, 110.

48 F. S. Arnot, *Garenganze or Seven Years' Pioneer Mission Work in Central Africa* (London: James E. Hawkins, 1889), 242–3.

Yeke of Mukanda Bantu (the late Msiri's son and successor) proved able to overcome only through an alliance with the newly arrived forces of the Congo Free State.[49]

The Causes and Objectives of Warfare

Although the *immediate* causes of conflict in sub-Saharan Africa varied from region to region and from time to time, our four examples point to the existence of a close relationship between warfare and the economy.

In at least three of our four case studies, the key economic driver of conflict was the ambition to take part in international circuits of exchange and to accumulate exportable commodities for the market. In the sixteenth century, the aim of Moroccan sultan Ahmad I al-Mansur Sa'did was to gain control of the trans-Saharan salt and gold trade to finance his wars against his enemies to the north and east. While there may have been a religious aspect to his invasion, this was surely of secondary importance.[50] Not only were the elites of Songhay fellow Muslims, but if the sultan had specifically wanted to tackle unbelievers, he could more easily have fought the Spanish and Portuguese – and avoided a long journey through one of the most inhospitable deserts in the world. The case of Dahomey is similar, since access to the coast and the flourishing slave port of Whydah was the ultimate strategic objective of King Agaja's thrust to the south in the 1720s. In the southern savanna of central Africa, the increased nineteenth-century demand for slaves and ivory emanating from both the Indian Ocean and the Atlantic coasts resulted in the collapse of old political structures and the concomitant rise to prominence of warlords, such as Msiri, who, once more, saw warfare as the quickest and most effective means to secure marketable commodities.

Commercial motivations, on the other hand, appear to have been less in evidence in early nineteenth-century southern Africa. In a context of ecological crisis – and even leaving aside Shaka's personality – the cause of warfare was territorial expansion into still fertile lands. The result, probably the objective of the campaigns, was the displacement of large groups of people. For the now landless and roving Ngoni, the warfare through which

---

49 G. Macola and J. Hogan, 'Guerrilla warfare in Katanga: The Sanga Rebellion of the 1890s and its suppression', *Small Wars & Insurgencies*, 30:4–5 (2019), 872–94.
50 For a more detailed discussion, see S. Cory, 'The man who would be caliph: a sixteenth-century sultan's bid for an African empire', *International Journal of African Historical Studies*, 42:2 (2009), 179–200.

the material and human resources of sedentary communities were appropriated was a matter of survival and of keeping the regiment system viable. It was only after some decades that it also became tied to processes of territorialisation and to external commercial interests.

Conclusion

The plight of students of strategy in much of pre-colonial Africa has been crisply summarised by Robert Smith:

> A consideration of past military strategy must begin with an attempt to understand the plans and ambitions which preceded it. History in such terms presents much difficulty since the motives of governments as well as of men are confused and changing, and often lie below the surface of consciousness. The difficulty is increased in the case of the history of non-literate peoples who have left behind few if any indications about their policy and the motives for their actions to supplement the possibly misleading record of 'what actually happened'.[51]

Even so, it would be misleading to make a case for some kind of African military exceptionalism. African wars had the same causes (conquest, trade, religion), the same means (technology, training of troops, reliance on allies, guerrilla warfare, intelligence) and the same outcomes (state formation, state collapse, social and institutional change) as European or Asian wars. And since the practice of strategy in Africa did not differ from that obtaining in other contexts, it must be approached by scholars with the same degree of diligence.

Sometimes, the lack of sources will pose insurmountable difficulties. More often, it will necessitate the adoption of imaginative research methodologies that combine the focused restudy of conventional written and oral sources with new evidence drawn from such disciplines as historical linguistics.[52] The effort is certainly worth making, if the tendency towards the 'foreshortening of African history' is to be resisted and if Africanist historians are to succeed in reconnecting the continent's deep past with the challenges of its present.[53]

---

51 R. S. Smith, *Warfare & Diplomacy in Pre-colonial West Africa* (Madison: University of Wisconsin Press, 2005), 120.
52 J. K. Thornton, 'Placing the military in Africa history: a reflection', *Journal of African Military History*, 1:1–2 (2017), 112–19.
53 R. J. Reid, 'Past and presentism: the "precolonial" and the foreshortening of African history', *Journal of African History* 52:2 (2011), 135–55.

19

Strategies of the Mughal Empire

PRATYAY NATH

The Mughal Empire was one of the biggest, richest and most powerful empires of the early modern world. The making of the empire was not a result of random historical events and processes; rather, it was the product of complex interplays between various strategies of the state and a diverse range of contingent factors. The Mughals did not have a single term with a meaning equivalent to 'strategy' in the modern sense. They did not, however, lack a strategic vision or understanding. Based on the dynamics of imperial expansion, the sequence of conquests, investments in various fields and the outcomes of military campaigns, it is possible to form an idea about this vision.

Sources

The most important source for studying the history of Mughal military strategy is the corpus of dynastic chronicles, biographies and autobiographies produced within the imperial courtly milieu. For most of their authors, description of military exploits was a means of extolling the greatness of the emperors and the dynasty. Hence descriptions of military campaigns feature prominently in most of these texts. But at the same time, none of these descriptions can be taken at face value. Most chroniclers wrote their texts far away from actual military campaigns. Their accounts, hence, were mostly based on second-hand information. Also, like some of their European medieval and early modern counterparts, these chroniclers narrated military matters in particular – often stylised – ways, using literary tropes, idioms and metaphors, with the express objective of glorifying Mughal rule.[1] Compared

---

1 For the politics of narrating wars under Akbar, see P. Nath, 'Narratives of Akbar's sieges and the construction of Mughal universal sovereignty', in J. Ostwald and A. Fischer-Katner (eds), *The World of the Siege: Representations of Early Modern Positional Warfare* (Leiden: Brill, 2019), 175–204.

to these court chronicles, sub-imperial texts – especially those written by generals operating on the ground – are more revealing, but relatively rare. One important text of this genre is Mirza Nathan's *Bahāristān-i Ghā'ibī*. Posted as a military commander on the empire's eastern frontier in the first quarter of the seventeenth century, the author provides a first-hand account of the unfolding of imperial strategy on the ground.

Perspectives different from these Mughal texts emerge from a variety of other sources. Several European travellers visited the Mughal Empire and left behind their observations. Some of them were closely associated with the imperial court for years. Consequently, their accounts often offer us alternative explanations of political and military events. The sixteenth and seventeenth centuries also saw an increasing proliferation of literature in a range of vernacular languages. Often produced within local or regional social milieus, these texts provide us with some idea about the effects of Mughal strategies. Finally, we are fortunate still to have many extant material remains from the Mughal period. South Asia is dotted with forts, palaces and other buildings that form an integral part of the Mughal past. They help us visualise the implementation of imperial strategy and augment the information we gather from literary accounts.

Actors

Who shaped Mughal strategies? Imperial biographies and dynastic chronicles suggest that all major military and strategic decisions were taken by the emperors. No doubt this was true in many cases. Most emperors led military campaigns themselves. As strong monarchs and able strategists, it is obvious that they took many of the strategic decisions themselves. Yet, at all times, they were also advised by members of the highest nobility. Early on in his rule, Akbar (r. 1556–1605) created four ministerial offices to supervise military, financial, religious and household matters. Emperors relied on the counsel of such ministers as well as senior military commanders. Elite Mughal women also had considerable influence over emperors, and, in turn, over their political decisions. Exceptional women like Nur Jahan, the wife of Jahangir (r. 1605–1627), also wielded considerable political authority herself and decisively shaped statecraft for several years.[2] Finally, Mughal princes exercised substantial authority and could influence imperial strategies. For

2 E. B. Findly, *Nur Jahan: Empress of Mughal India* (New York and Oxford: Oxford University Press, 1993); R. Lal, *Empress: The Astonishing Reign of Nur Jahan* (New York: W. W. Norton & Company, 2018).

instance, as a prince and governor (*ṣūbadār*) of Deccan, Aurangzeb (r. 1658–1707) moulded imperial policy towards the Deccan sultanates. While his father, Emperor Shah Jahan (r. 1628–1657) adopted a generally moderate position, Aurangzeb vigorously lobbied for outright conquest and annexation of these states in the 1650s.

Occasional pieces of information also make it clear that commanders operating on the ground played a significant role in shaping strategy. Commanders like Shaista Khan, Jai Singh, Bahadur Khan and Diler Khan, for example, significantly shaped the course of Mughal expansion in the Deccan under Aurangzeb through the 1660s and 1670s.[3] The occasional reference in contemporary sources indicates that commanders could also act on their own sometimes. The first Mughal intrusion into the hill kingdom of Tripura in north-eastern India in the early seventeenth century, for instance, was a result of the personal enterprise and ambition of a commander named Abdul Wahid. Posted at the nearby outpost (*thāna*) of Bhalwa, he sent his son with an army to plunder the kingdom. This invasion was motivated by the lure of personal financial gain as well as the prospect of making the outpost of Bhalwa more secure.[4] In course of campaigns, we find decisions being taken by war councils.[5] At the end of the day, imperial orders often did not serve more than a broad mandate. Commanders operating on the ground and far away from the imperial court would often interpret this mandate creatively. Their own ambitions and agenda, as well as the immediate context of unfolding events, would shape this interpretation considerably. If the decisions taken by them resulted in military conquests and the expansion of imperial territory and authority, these achievements could then be appropriated by imperial chroniclers and projected as the expected results of well-thought-out strategic decisions made by the emperors.

Adversaries

The most important adversaries of the Mughals in the early years were the Afghans. Traditionally pastoralists and horse traders, they had come to dominate north Indian politics in the course of the fifteenth century. Around the time of the advent of the armies of Babur (r. 1526–1530), the Afghans were

---

3 S. Chandra, 'The Deccan policy of the Mughals (ii): under Aurangzeb', *Indian Historical Review*, 5 (1979), 135–51.
4 M. Nathan, *Bahāristān-i Ghā'ibī*, JS 60–2, Jadunath Sarkar Collection, National Library, Kolkata, JS61, 166b.
5 See, for instance, Nathan, *Bahāristān-i Ghā'ibī*, JS60, 62b–63a.

vying with the Rajput kingdoms of western India for control over Hindustan.[6] Babur's victories against the Afghan armies of the Lodi sultanate at Panipat (1526) and an Afghan–Rajput coalition at Khanua (1527) quashed these political ambitions temporarily. As the Mughals began to establish themselves, the Afghans scattered; many withdrew towards the east. Soon, they found a new leader in a young and energetic Sur Afghan chieftain called Sher Khan. Following an invasion of Bengal, he led the Afghans to two consecutive victories against Humayun (r. 1530–1540 and 1555–1556) in 1539 and 1540. He crowned himself the ruler of Hindustan under the name Sher Shah and drove Humayun out of north India. As king, he introduced a variety of administrative measures that held the promise of creating a centralised and durable Afghan state. Following his premature death in 1545, his son Islam Khan ruled for the next eight years; but he failed to materialise the promise held out by his father's rule. Following his demise, Humayun recaptured Delhi in 1555 and re-established his dynasty in Hindustan. At the time of his untimely death and his son Akbar's coronation the next year, various Afghan groups still lay scattered across north India, especially its eastern parts.

Another major adversary whom Akbar and his successors had to negotiate with were the various chieftains of south Asia. This was an extremely diverse group whom Mughal texts refer to as zamīndārs (lit. 'land-holders'). The heterogeneity of this largely rural aristocracy ranged from petty chieftains with authority over a few villages to powerful rulers of substantial kingdoms. Most of them had their own private armies.[7] Out of these, the most notable group were the Rajput kings of western India. Their clans had originated from humble, often pastoralist, backgrounds. By the beginning of the sixteenth century, several powerful clans had emerged with considerable command over fortifications and armed forces, as well as material and cultural resources. It was one of these Rajput rulers, the Sisodiya king Sangram Singh, who led the Afghan–Rajput coalition against Babur in 1527. For the emergent Mughal Empire under Akbar, these Rajput kings held the possibility of becoming a major threat if not contained early.

South Asia of the mid-sixteenth century also had several independent sultanates. In the west, Gujarat was under a powerful and enterprising ruler called Bahadur Shah. In the early sixteenth century, the sultanate

---

6 For the Mughals, the geographical term 'Hindustan' largely signified the north Indian plains, comprising the Punjab plains and the Gangetic basin.

7 S. N. Hasan, 'The position of the Zamindars in the Mughal Empire', *Indian Economic and Social History Review*, 1 (1964), 107–19; I. Habib, *The Agrarian System of Mughal India, 1556–1707* (New Delhi: Oxford University Press, [1963] 1999), 169–229.

received military aid from the Ottoman Empire in its efforts to curb increasing Portuguese influence in the Indian Ocean. Humayun conquered Gujarat briefly in 1535–1536, but Bahadur Shah quickly regained control over the region. However, following his untimely death in 1537, the sultanate entered a phase of instability and factionalism. In the north, Kashmir had been ruled by a Muslim sultanate since 1346. In 1555, the region passed again under the control of the Kashmiri dynasty of the Chaks. In central India, Baz Bahadur, the son and successor of the Sur governor of Malwa, declared himself an independent monarch around the time of Akbar's accession.

The most powerful sultanates, however, lay in the Deccan. These were Khandesh, Berar, Ahmadnagar, Bijapur and Golconda. Most of them had emerged out of the ashes of the medieval sultanate of the Bahamanis at the close of the fifteenth century. The nobility in most of these states comprised Afghan and Deccani Sunni Muslims as well as Persian Shias. There were also many Abyssinian military slaves, many of whom wielded considerable power. This cosmopolitan urban nobility ruled in alliance with the rural aristocracy – Maratha *deshmukhs* in the west and Telugu chieftains in the east. Rulers like Ibrahim Qutb Shah (r. 1550–1580) of Golconda and Ibrahim Adil Shah II (r. 1580–1626) of Bijapur forged accommodative and cosmopolitan reigns that patronised art, culture and vernacular languages. Aside from employing large numbers of Persian immigrants, many of these sultanates also maintained close political, religious and cultural ties with the Safavid Empire of Iran. Sultans of Bijapur and Golconda even recognised the political suzerainty of the Safavid dynasty. The Deccan frontier hence signified a political frontier between the domains of influence of the Mughals and the Safavids.[8]

In the 1660s, a new threat to Mughal imperialism appeared in the Deccan: the Marathas. Traditionally, Maratha chieftains would render military service in the armies of the Deccan sultanates. However, in the mid-seventeenth century, a young and charismatic leader named Shivaji Bhonsla broke away from the control of the Bijapur sultanate and carved out an expanding domain of influence in the Western Ghats. His growing power was fuelled by a string of formidable hill fortresses, a considerable number of Maratha *deshmukhs* and Brahmin administrators, and an ambition to create an independent kingdom. Rapidly expanding his power and resources through

---

8 M. Alam and S. Subrahmanyam, 'The Deccan frontier and Mughal expansion, ca. 1600: contemporary perspectives', *Journal of the Economic and Social History of the Orient*, 47 (2004), 357–89.

plunder, taxation and new conquests, Shivaji presented a formidable challenge to the Mughal Empire by the 1660s.

The empire faced two formidable adversaries in the north-west – the Uzbeks of Turan and the Safavids of Iran. Of these, the Uzbeks were a major steppe power of early modern central Asia. They had conquered most of the erstwhile Timurid lands by the early sixteenth century, reducing Timurid princes like Babur to political refugees. Even after the emergence of the Mughal Empire in south Asia, the nearby presence of the Uzbeks always threatened imperial control over the city of Kabul, the gateway to central Asia. The Mughal relationship with the Safavid dynasty of Persia was more complex. Founded in the early sixteenth century, the Safavid dynasty proved to be a saviour of the first two Mughal monarchs in their days of hardship. During the 1510s, Babur accepted Safavid political and spiritual hegemony in return for the first Safavid ruler Shah Ismail's military support for him against his arch-enemy, the Uzbek ruler Shaibani Khan. Three decades later, Ismail's son and successor Shah Tahmasp sheltered Humayun as he landed up at the Safavid court as a political refugee following his defeats at the hands of the Afghan chieftain Sher Khan Sur in north India. In the following years, Safavid military assistance proved valuable for him in reconquering parts of his lost domains and returning to north India in 1555.

In the following years, the Safavids took great pleasure in highlighting this symbolic victory over the Mughals. The Safavids were also always keen on proclaiming their cultural superiority over the eastern Islamic lands, where most dynasties, just as the Mughals, had adopted the Persian language and culture. Aside from these ideological tensions, the two dynasties constantly vied for the control of the frontier fortress of Kandahar. The close ties of the Safavids with the Deccan sultanates also created political tensions once the Mughals started expanding into the peninsula. All this created a complicated relationship between the two powers, marked by cordiality on the surface but strong rivalry beneath it.[9]

In the north-east, Mughal armies encountered the powerful Ahom kingdom, founded by Shan people who had migrated into the Brahmaputra valley from upper Myanmar since the fourteenth century. Ahom society was organised around levies on labour and produce, whereby the ruler could mobilise the entire male population as soldiers. Assam abounded in

---

9 E. Koch, 'How the Mughal *padshahs* referenced Iran in their visual construction of universal rule', in P. F. Bang and D. Kołodziejczyk (eds), *Universal Empire: A Comparative Approach to Imperial Culture and Representation in Eurasian History* (Cambridge: Cambridge University Press, 2012), 194–209.

elephants, which figured prominently in Ahom warfare. Living alongside the numerous rivers of Assam – most notably the mighty Brahmaputra – also made them adept at riverine warfare. These fundamentally different dynamics of political economy and military techniques posed a substantial challenge for Mughal expansion in the course of the seventeenth century.

Finally, the Mughals had a complicated relationship with the various European powers that started founding their own settlements in south Asia from the early sixteenth century. Centred in Goa, the Portuguese imperial venture had a strong presence on India's western littoral. In the east, they founded an official trading outpost in Hugli in western Bengal in the 1570s. Further east, Portuguese pirates and renegades seized the port of Chittagong and settled down in the south-eastern reaches of the Bengal delta. For much of the seventeenth century, they posed a grave threat to the newly founded Mughal establishment in Bengal. In alliance with the neighbouring Arakan kingdom, they became a major naval threat in these areas. By the late seventeenth century, other European powers, most notably the British and the French, started making their presence felt across the Indian coastline.

Causes and Objectives

In the Mughal Empire, military conflict was the result of a diverse range of causes. Political factors often provided the immediate contexts for military expeditions. They would sometimes take the form of retaliation in response to the subversion of Mughal political authority. For instance, military action against Daud Khan Karrani, the Afghan ruler of Bihar and western Bengal, in 1574 was precipitated by the latter's refusal to accept Mughal suzerainty, unlike his father Suleiman Karrani. This upset the political status quo that his father had maintained.[10] The empire also took advantage of political instability in neighbouring kingdoms to mount invasions against them. In the 1640s, Nazar Muhammad Khan, the Uzbek ruler of Balkh, was plagued by a civil war against his son Abdul Aziz. When the khan asked Shah Jahan for assistance, the latter used this opportunity to mount a full-scale invasion of Balkh in 1646.[11] Aside from such political events, imperial wars were also fuelled by other more long-term considerations, as the examples below

---

10 A. Fazl, *Akbar-nāma* (ed. Maulawi Abdur Rahim), 3 vols. (Calcutta, Asiatic Society of Bengal, 1873–87), Volume III, 69–70.
11 M. A. Ali, 'The objectives behind the Mughal expedition into Balkh and Badakhshan 1646–47', *Proceedings of the India History Congress*, 29 (1967), 162–8.

illustrate. Nevertheless, almost all campaigns resulted from a multiplicity of causes and objectives.

Violence was not usually justified in the name of any particular community or religion, as was the case in much of the early modern world. In fact, the Mughals seldom fought wars in the name of religion. Rather, wars were legitimised in the name of the abstract concept of justice (*'adl*). Although Sunni Muslims themselves, Mughal emperors were usually conceptualised as divinely mandated universal sovereigns, whose prime duty was to establish justice, harmony and order across the world; war and military violence were seen as unavoidable means of achieving that. Imperial chronicles justify the waging of war in different situations by saying that this is what justice demanded.[12] The merit of such rhetoric was that, divorced from any association with a specific community, the concept of justice yielded itself to be interpreted differently by different actors and in different contexts. This is one of the cultural forces that helped the Mughals to bind their disparate armed forces together.[13]

Economic considerations played a major role in prompting the early conquest of the Punjab plains and the Gangetic basin under Akbar. This vast region comprised some of the most fertile lands of the Indian subcontinent. For centuries, land revenue levied on the thriving agriculture of these parts had served as the most important source of income for north Indian states. Additionally, these plains were studded with towns and cities that acted as important centres of non-agricultural production and trans-regional trade. For the nascent Mughal state, seizing control of these plains was indeed vital to secure a sound economic basis for itself.

Often an important factor behind campaigns, strategic considerations could emerge as the defining motivation. For instance, they shaped the long-standing contest between the Mughals and the Safavids over the fort of Kandahar. It lay right on the frontier of the two empires. Together with neighbouring forts like Bust and Zamindawar, Kandahar comprised a strategic stronghold that both the empires coveted. For the Mughals, holding Kandahar was important in ensuring protection against potential Safavid aggression. Failing to hold it shrank imperial control substantially, making Multan and Bhakkar in the Indus basin the outermost frontier towns. This was because the roads to

---

12 See, for example, K. N. Ahmad, *Ṭabaqāt-i Akbarī* (ed. B. De), 3 vols. (Calcutta, Asiatic Society of Bengal, 1931), Volume I, 151.

13 P. Nath, '"The Wrath of God": Legitimisation and Limits of Military Violence in Early Modern South Asia', in P. Wilson, E. Charters and M. Houllemare (eds), *A Global History of Violence in the Early Modern World* (Manchester: Manchester University Press, 2020), 161–76.

Kandahar from Multan and Bhakkar passed over arid and rugged terrain and very few major settlements. Together with Kabul, Kandahar was a vital part of Mughal geopolitics on the north-western frontier.

Finally, the case of the Mughal invasion of Balkh in 1646–1647 demonstrates the power of ideological motivations in precipitating military action. This invasion was triggered by the express desire of recovering the erstwhile Timurid lands from the Uzbeks. Alongside the loss of important Timurid political centres like Herat, Bukhara and Samarqand, the Uzbek conquests had also caused the loss of the homeland of Naqshbandi sufis, who shared close ties with Timur and his descendants. The sense of loss and trauma all this produced became an integral part of dynastic memory and ambition. It was Shah Jahan who converted this dynastic ambition into an actual military expedition using political tensions in the Uzbek khanate as an opportunity. The conquest of Balkh was supposed to be the first step towards the recovery of the erstwhile Timurid lands from the Uzbeks.[14]

Means

What enabled the Mughal state to execute its strategies? Conventional replies to this question point to military technology, especially gunpowder weaponry. However, while firearms did comprise an important component of Mughal warfare, scarcely did it alone bestow on Mughal armies a military advantage. The Mughal state did not exercise a monopoly over firearms. In fact, sheer technological superiority alone rarely accounted for Mughal military victories.[15] It is, hence, more fruitful to look at certain other facets of the state. These include the armed forces, the logistical workforce, the animal economy, means of supply and finance. More than technology, these factors played a crucial role in helping the Mughals pursue their strategic goals.

The Mughal state fielded huge armies. In 1581, for instance, Akbar mustered 50,000 cavalry in addition to 500 elephants and camels, and a large infantry, to fight his half-brother and political rival Mirza Muhammad Hakim.[16] In 1599, he mobilised an army of 80,000 for the invasion of the Ahmadnagar sultanate.[17] Some 50,000

---

14 R. C. Foltz, 'The Mughal occupation of Balkh 1646–1647', *Journal of Islamic Studies*, 7 (1996), 49–61.

15 D. E. Streusand, *The Formation of the Mughal Empire* (New Delhi: Oxford University Press, 1989), 51–69.

16 A. Monserrate, *The Commentary of Father Monserrate, S.J. on His Journey to the Court of Akbar* (trans. J. S. Hoyland) (London: Oxford University Press, 1922), 83.

17 J. F. Richards: *The New Cambridge History of India*, Volume 1.5: *The Mughal Empire* (Cambridge: Cambridge University Press, [1993] 2001), 54.

cavalry were dispatched along with 10,000 infantry, including gunners and artillerymen, for the conquest of Balkh in 1646.[18] The army sent under Prince Aurangzeb to besiege the fort of Kandahar in 1649 had similar numbers.[19]

Out of this, the cavalry had a centralised organisation. Its commanders were a diverse lot. It began with an original group of Turks and Uzbeks. To this, Akbar added an increasing number of Persians, Indian Muslims and Rajputs. In the course of imperial expansion, other chieftains were co-opted from different parts of south Asia. This group of commanders of different statures was organised by Akbar in 1573–1574 through military ranks (sing. *manṣab*) and fixed salaries, which often came in the form of revenue assignments (sing. *jāgīr*). In 1596–1597, the *manṣab* was further broken down into *zāt* (the rank of a commander in the official hierarchy) and *sawār* (the number of horsemen he was expected to muster). In this centralised military organisation, every commander – at the head of his troops, raised largely from his own community – was directly under the authority of the emperor.[20] The infantry – mainly artillerymen, matchlockmen and foot archers – largely comprised peasant soldiers, recruited from the bustling military labour market of Hindustan. The ranks of artillerymen included many immigrant military professionals, especially from the Ottoman Empire and western Europe.

Aside from armed forces, military campaigns also relied heavily on the logistical workforce. In sieges, the task of building siegeworks like mines and saps fell on carpenters, stonecutters and other labourers. In forested areas, armies needed woodcutters to go in front, cutting down trees and creating a path. In areas with rugged terrain, pioneers and workmen also became very important for levelling the ground and creating a road for the main army. In Bengal, boatmen were indispensable for manning riverine vessels and manoeuvring the artillery on them. Most of these logistical workmen would be recruited by imperial armies on a temporary basis, often from the theatre of war itself. Aside from them, the state also maintained a huge number of workers for various perennial duties – caring for war animals, manufacturing weapons, attending to the camp and so on. Mughal conquests were as much

18 A. H. Lahori, *Bādshāh-nāma* (ed. M. K. Ahmad and Abdul Rahim), 2 vols. (Calcutta: Asiatic Society of Bengal, 1867–1868), Volume II, 482–4.
19 J. Sarkar, *History of Aurangzeb*, 5 vols. (Calcutta: M. C. Sarkar & Sons, 1912), Volume I, 151.
20 M. A. Ali, *The Mughal Nobility under Aurangzeb* (New Delhi: Oxford University Press, [1966] 2001); J. Gommans, *Mughal Warfare: Indian Frontiers and High Roads to Empire, 1500–1700* (London and New York: Routledge, 2002), 81–8.

the result of the concerted work of this large logistical corps as of the military performance of the armed forces.[21]

Mughal military capabilities also depended heavily on the careful management of a variegated animal economy. Imperial armies used large numbers of horses as mounts for their cavalry in combat, while mules and cattle were used as beasts of burden. Camels and elephants found use in both logistics and combat. Mobilising these animals in thousands was a matter of complex co-ordination. Horses would be imported in bulk from west and central Asia. Elephants would be gathered from the forests that covered large parts of south Asia during this time. Cattle were available widely across the subcontinent. Camels had to be mobilised from Rajasthan and Sind, while mules were often imported from distant lands like west Asia. The process of purchasing, gathering, training, feeding and deploying these animals went a long way in enabling Mughal armies to campaign, fight and, in turn, conquer.

Mughal ability to pursue strategic objectives also derived from their ability to efficiently handle military logistics and finance. For supply, the state relied squarely on the services of the Banjara. These were nomadic pastoralists, who travelled with armed caravans of thousands of pack animals at a time, transporting primarily food grains from surplus to deficient areas. In most of the Indian subcontinent, Banjaras would travel with armies on the march, supplying them with rations and supplies. Thanks to them, imperial forces did not have to carry their supplies around in most of south Asia.

As for finance, the Mughal state benefited from the thriving cash nexus and banking networks of early modern south Asia. This cash nexus had emerged in north India by the early fourteenth century under the Delhi sultanate. The Mughals developed this further by collecting land revenue in cash across large portions of their empire. This was facilitated by a centralising fiscal apparatus, a robust currency system and the pouring in of New World silver. A sophisticated network of transfer and remittance of credit also existed in the form of bills of exchange (sing. *hūndī*), operated by specialised money-lending and moneychanging communities like the Sarrafs.[22]

---

21 P. Nath, 'War and the non-elite: towards a people's history of the Mughal Empire', *Medieval History Journal*, 25:1 (2022), 127–58.

22 J. F. Richards, 'Mughal state finance and premodern world economy', *Comparative Studies in Society and History*, 23 (1981), 285–308; I. Habib, 'The system of bills of exchange ("hundis") in the Mughal Empire', *Proceedings of the Indian History Congress*, 33 (1971), 290–303.

Priorities

One of the top priorities of Mughal military strategy was to control routes of communication. This included both land routes and rivers. In the course of military campaigns, these routes enabled Mughal armies to penetrate different regions. Control over routes was necessary not only for the unhindered mobility of troops, but also for maintaining a steady flow of supplies. Hence taking over the control of existing routes or forging new ones played a vital role in military campaigns. This was, however, much easier in regions with flat open terrain – like the Punjab plains and the Gangetic basin – than in other parts. In the Afghan region, for instance, the terrain was dominated by hills, defiles and ravines. Taking control of roads was laborious business here. Contemporary descriptions of Mughal campaigns in these parts, hence, are peppered with mentions of dogged road-building activities. In cases where wide roads did not exist, or where they did but Mughal armies failed to assume control of them, new roads had to be created. This was the case, for instance, in the forests of Assam. Here, military campaigns involved the cutting down of some of the vegetation to create roads for armies to proceed. The military and strategic importance of controlling routes of communication was indicated not only by these actions of Mughal armies, but also by those of their adversaries. They repeatedly contested imperial control over these routes in the course of wars and insurgencies.

What was the mechanism of exercising this control? A careful analysis of the course of military campaigns bears out a clear answer – forts. Across the length and breadth of the Mughal Empire, fortified strongholds of various types stood on routes of communication. Since the early days of the empire, Mughal monarchs had invested their time and energy in capturing forts. Fort commanders who surrendered would usually be pardoned and often co-opted into the imperial officialdom. However, they would rarely be allowed to retain their forts, which would be brought instead under the direct authority of the Mughal emperor. After their acquisition or construction, forts would be placed under the command of imperial officers (sing. *qal'adār*) who would report directly to the emperor. This made Mughal forts the points of concentration of military power and political authority. Garrisoned in such forts, Mughal troops exercised command over nearby routes of communication as well as the neighbouring countryside. While the former ensured the smooth flow of troops and traders, the latter secured the process of revenue exaction. Akbar built major forts at Agra, Lahore, Allahabad and Ajmer – all located on important nodal points of communication. The network of these four major fortresses can be considered 'a protective framework of Mughal imperial power'.[23] Apart from this, smaller forts were built at other points of intersection of important routes. A case in point is the fort of Attock that Akbar built at the crossroads of the Indus river and the road connecting Kabul with Lahore. Finally, in the course of military campaigns, imperial armies also regularly established smaller military outposts (sing. *thāna*). They helped the troops defend their position against hostile armies and exercise command over nearby routes. Among the rivers of Bengal, for instance, several such forts were constructed out of mud, later reinforced with brick, at nodal points of riverine communication.

Alongside being rooted in the permanence of such fortified locations that studded the length and breadth of the empire, imperial strategy also made great use of royal mobility as a mechanism of the exercise of power. Mughal emperors were itinerant monarchs. Estimates put the regnal periods in mobile military camps between 1556 and 1707 or 1739 at 35 to 40 per cent. Unlike some other early modern powers like the Ottomans, the Mughals did not have a fixed capital. The capital would be wherever the imperial residence was, be it the mobile camp or a stationary palace fort. Mobility comprised a vital part of governance and statecraft. On tour, emperors would spend time hunting, exploring the realm, watching over commanders and chieftains, forging new alliances with local powers and co-ordinating military campaigns. Royal mobility was so vital to the exercise of power in the Mughal Empire that Aurangzeb's increasingly sedentary habits during his Deccan campaigns from 1681 severely eroded imperial authority and contributed to the fragmentation of the empire.[24]

Finally, Mughal strategy prioritised an extremely accommodative diplomatic approach, aided by an open-ended attitude to military violence. Notwithstanding various subtle shifts in imperial ideology over time, the enduring presence of the doctrine of universal sovereignty enabled Mughal strategic vision to remain committed to an accommodative and flexible diplomatic posture. This universalism allowed the state to employ anybody and everybody willing to become a part of the imperial project. For the Mughals, the faith of an individual or a community seldom mattered in fighting or co-opting them. In building alliances, Mughal emperors developed the practice of marrying into local communities irrespective of their faith. Thus Babur married into Muslim Afghan communities as the ruler of Kabul, while Akbar started the process of forging

23 Richards, *The Mughal Empire*, 28.   24 Gommans, *Mughal Warfare*, 100–11.

matrimonial ties with Hindu Rajput houses of western India. These marriages were always unidirectional, in the sense that the Mughal household would take in women from other communities, but would never offer its own women to them. Consequently, giving women in marriage to an emperor or a prince symbolised subjugation to the empire. Such marriages would usually be accompanied by the induction of some leading male members of the community into Mughal officialdom. These members would be showered with gifts and were given an official rank and salary. This would come with the responsibility of joining the Mughal armies on military expeditions as and when needed. From being local or regional chieftains, they would thus become partners of a major empire. This transformation would usually usher in a gradual increase in wealth, power and prestige for these chieftains, not only within the empire, but also in their own region. At the end of the day, building alliances – matrimonial or otherwise – was the usual way the empire expanded, much more than it did by annihilating its adversaries. Farhat Hasan's study of Gujarat shows that enduring Mughal conquests often emanated from the state's ability to incorporate members of the local society into its body politic and share its sovereignty and resources with them. In the countryside, expansion and governance relied squarely on the collaboration and support of the rural aristocracy. In such a paradigm, wars were frequent and violent, but more often used as a tool for subjugation and co-option than for annihilation.

Application

The product of all these strategies was a powerful empire that embraced almost all of the Indian subcontinent at its apex at the close of the seventeenth century. The process of empire building under Akbar started centring Mughal bases in Delhi and Agra. Following the victory in the Second Battle of Panipat (1556), Mughal armies drove their Afghan rivals in various directions, especially eastward, through a series of skirmishes. By 1559, imperial control had extended eastward up to the Gorakhpur–Jaunpur belt in eastern Uttar Pradesh. This enabled them to capture the towns and cities as well as the routes of communication in the Punjab plains and the Gangetic basin early on in Akbar's rule. Based in these, the state gradually consolidated its hold over the countryside and began extracting land revenue. However, in order to consolidate its hold over these vast north Indian plains, its western and southern flanks needed to be secured. Seemingly with this objective, Mughal armies conquered Malwa and Garha Katanga in central India in 1561 and 1564 respectively. In Rajasthan in the west, Akbar followed a strategy of carrot and stick. By forging matrimonial alliances in some cases and using military force in others, he managed to neutralise several important Rajput kingdoms in the course of the 1560s.[25]

These conquests and alliances in central and western India opened up the two major routes connecting the Gangetic basin with the Gujarat littoral. Taking advantage of political instability in the Gujarat sultanate, Akbar invaded the region in 1572. His armies conquered the capital city, Ahmadabad; the port of Surat; and several other important towns. At one stroke, these conquests helped the Mughals connect the economically prosperous Gangetic basin with the Indian Ocean through the ports of the Gujarat littoral. Distance from the imperial heartland, however, meant that imperial armies took more than two decades to subjugate the various chieftains of the region completely and bring it under firm control.[26]

Further west, war also broke out in Bhakkar in Sind in 1571. Far from the imperial heartland in north India, Punjab emerged as the main launch pad of these campaigns. After a brief period of hostilities, Bhakkar fell to the Mughals. Imperial armies took the war further south to Thatta in 1591. With the ruler of Thatta surrendering the next year, the entire Indus basin came under Mughal control. The economically prosperous region of Punjab was thereby united with ports like Lahari Bandar at the mouth of the Indus under a single political regime. This brought great economic benefits to the empire in subsequent years. Command over the Indus river, as well as over cities on it like Bhakkar, Lakhi and Sehwan, also opened new westward routes, most importantly to Kandahar.[27]

The 1570s also saw an eastward push along the Gangetic basin. In 1574, Mughal forces captured Patna in Bihar, and Tanda in western Bengal. In the process, they drove the Afghans of the area into Bengal and Orissa. Like the Gujarat littoral in the west, the Orissa littoral in the east took another two decades to be subjugated properly. Conquering Bengal proved to be even more challenging. It took imperial armies four decades to dominate all of the region. Even after that, the south-eastern stretches of the delta remained under the control of Portuguese pirates until 1666, when a Mughal army finally conquered the port of Chittagong and secured that area. In the north-east, the empire sought expansion first into Kamrup and then into Assam in

---

25 Streusand, *The Formation of the Mughal Empire*, 51–81; Nath, *Climate of Conquest*, 10–53.

26 F. Hasan, *State and Locality in Mughal India: Power Relations in Western India c. 1572–1730* (New Delhi: Cambridge University Press, 2006), 20–30.

27 F. Z. Bilgrami, 'The Mughal annexation of Sind: a diplomatic and military history', in I. Habib (ed.), *Akbar and His India* (New Delhi: Oxford University Press, [1997] 2007), 33–54.

the Brahmaputra basin. Between 1613 and 1682, imperial armies fought four major wars against the Ahom kingdom, but failed to secure any lasting territorial gain. A major defeat in Assam in 1671 and the loss of Kamrup in 1682 marked the end of Mughal ambition in this region.

In 1585, Akbar annexed Kabul and the next year his armies conquered the Srinagar valley in Kashmir. These inaugurated the long – and essentially incomplete – process of Mughal pacification of the Afghan region. The Afghan tribes put up a determined resistance against Mughal authority. They exploited the rugged and broken terrain to attack imperial forces time and again, especially in narrow mountain passes. While over time some Yusufzai, Dilzak and Afridi Afghans joined the imperial ranks, the rest continued to fight the empire through much of the seventeenth century. The latter tried to counter this by building new forts and establishing military outposts to secure the Lahore–Kabul road, which was vital for the flow of both troops and overland commerce. Beyond this route, the countryside was dominated largely by the Afghans owing to the inability of Mughal forces to negotiate the rugged terrain of the area beyond a certain point. Similarly, imperial expansion in Kashmir remained limited beyond the Srinagar valley owing to the long winters, arid countryside and mountainous terrain. However, south of Kashmir, Mughal forces did make inroads into other parts of the Himalayan foothills. These included the subjugation of Mankot (1557), Nagarkot (1573), Bandhu (1574), Jammu (1601) and Kangra (1620).

Two major bouts of war broke out on the north-western frontier under Shah Jahan. In 1646, he sent his son Murad Bakhsh at the head of a huge army to invade Badakhshan and Balkh. After encountering some resistance initially, the imperial army managed to occupy both its targets. As Nazar Muhammad Khan, the Uzbek ruler of Balkh, fled the city, a triumphant Murad Bakhsh claimed it in the name of his father. However, Mughal difficulties increased rapidly after this. The aridity of the region, the cold and snowy winter and the relentless resistance of Uzbek troops forced the imperial army eventually to hand the city back to Nazar Muhammad Khan in October 1647. The return march proved disastrous for the Mughals as cold temperatures and snows on the one hand and Uzbek attacks on the other claimed the lives of thousands of soldiers and animals.[28] Unlike this isolated war in Balkh, Kandahar remained a thorny issue between the mid-sixteenth century and the mid-seventeenth, as it repeatedly changed hands between the Mughals and the Safavids. Full-scale war broke out in 1648 with its

28 Foltz, 'The Mughal occupation of Balkh'; Gommans, *Mughal Warfare*, 179–87; Nath, *Climate of Conquest*, 99–108.

occupation by the Safavid shah. In retaliation, Shah Jahan had the fort besieged three times between 1649 and 1653. All three sieges, however, failed. Even more than in Balkh, logistical challenges proved to be insurmountable in the Kandahar campaigns. The aridity, snowy winters, rugged terrain, transport difficulties and sheer distance from Hindustan made it impossible for Mughal armies to take the fort. After 1653, Kandahar remained under Safavid control until the fall of the dynasty in the early eighteenth century.

In the Deccan, the Mughals fought a long-drawn-out war of attrition since Akbar's invasion of Ahmadnagar in 1595. The sultanate ceded Berar to the Mughal Empire in 1596. This was followed by Mughal occupation of the fort of Ahmadnagar (1600) and Asirgarh (1601). Under Jahangir, Mughal ambitions in the Deccan were largely frustrated by the resistance offered by Malik Ambar and Raju Deccani, both commanders of the Ahmadnagar sultanate. During the reign of Shah Jahan, the Mughals reached an understanding with the sultanates of Bijapur and Golconda, whereby the territory of Ahmadnagar was partitioned between the Mughals and Bijapur. Following this, the two sultanates accepted Mughal suzerainty in return for a free pass to expand southward, which they did rapidly in the subsequent years. This, however, eventually triggered Mughal anxiety and led to an invasion against Bijapur in 1656 and against Golconda in 1657. The invasions ended in a treaty in 1657, whereby both the sultanates were made to cede some territory, even though Prince Aurangzeb advocated annexation.

Once Aurangzeb became emperor himself in 1658, however, the situation changed drastically owing to the emergence of Maratha power in the 1660s. Shivaji's meteoric rise made dealing with the Marathas the top priority of Mughal strategy. Aurangzeb left no stone unturned in the process, including allying with the sultanates against the Maratha ruler. From the early 1660s to the late 1680s, successive Mughal generals fought the Marathas with varying success. But in the meantime, the sultanate of Bijapur itself began to crumble internally after 1672. In 1680, Shivaji died. Following these events, Aurangzeb arrived in the Deccan himself in 1681, and led the Mughal conquest of Bijapur (1686) and Golconda (1687). He also had Shivaji's son Shambhaji captured and executed in 1689. The territories of Bijapur, Golconda and the Maratha kingdom were annexed to the Mughal Empire, increasing its territorial extent by 221,107 square miles, or a fourth of its total area.[29]

---

29 Richards, *The Mughal Empire*, 223; Gommans, *Mughal Warfare*, 187–97; S. Chandra, 'The Deccan policy of the Mughals (i): up to Shah Jahan', *Indian Historical Review*, 4 (1978), 326–35; Chandra, 'Deccan policy of the Mughals (ii)'.

These hard-earned victories could not, however, prevent the erosion of imperial authority that was already under way. In western Deccan, Mughal authority faced a strong challenge from Maratha power, which refused to die down. Empowered by numerous hill fortresses, decentralised authority and mobile units of light cavalry, the Marathas dominated this region even as Aurangzeb annexed all of Deccan into his empire. Maratha armies found support in Berar and Khandesh, and started raiding Gujarat and Malwa by the early years of the eighteenth century. Around the same time, European powers also became powerful and confident enough to challenge Mughal authority in coastal areas. Finally, the long absence of the emperor from north India took its toll. Local powers like the Jats rose up in open rebellion against imperial authority. Following Aurangzeb's death in 1707, Mughal power rapidly fragmented away all across south Asia.[30]

Conclusion

The discussions of the preceding sections should help us debunk the idea of a fixed Mughal strategic culture. Mughal strategic concerns were diverse and context-specific. They were broadly guided by the dynastic ideology of universal sovereignty, although this itself went through subtle shifts over time. This ideology was articulated time and again through royal titles, dynastic chronicles, courtly rituals, miniature paintings and imperial architecture. In turn, it produced an inclusive and accommodative diplomatic posture, whereby the state was willing to co-opt anybody and everybody, as long as they accepted Mughal suzerainty and were willing to serve the emperor loyally. Alongside this, there were some enduring strategic priorities – controlling forts, commanding routes, garnering local collaboration and legitimising military violence in terms of the idea of justice. To these ends, the state marshalled its military means – armed forces, logistical workers, animals, supply networks, finance and technology.

Beyond this, imperial strategies were flexible and adaptive. Their translation into actual territorial expansion was a complex and dynamic process. It was shaped by factors as diverse as economic prospects, military considerations, the ability to forge alliances, the natural environment, diplomacy, internal law and order, the cultural climate, the personality of the main actors and, last but not least, sheer chance. Not even the territorial form that the

---

30 For a collection of various perspectives on the fragmentation of the Mughal Empire, see M. Bhargava (ed.), *The Decline of the Mughal Empire* (New Delhi: Oxford University Press, 2014).

empire assumed was a part of a predefined Mughal strategic vision. After it conquered north India, the Mughals tried to expand periodically in four major directions: north, north-west, east and south. As it happened, it met with limited success and periodically suffered major losses in the first three directions. It was only in the fourth direction – the south – that it met with considerable success, although, even there, expansion came at a heavy cost through a century-long war of attrition. The formation of the empire was thus a product of the way historical processes unravelled with a heterogeneous mix of success and failure in terms of the implementation of its strategies in different regions.

20

China, 1368–1911

KENNETH M. SWOPE

Introduction

The Ming (1368–1644) and Qing (1644–1911) dynasties, grouped together here as encompassing the late imperial period, mark the apex of China's strategic tradition and represent the accumulated wisdom of the previous eras. Much that has already been said about those periods can be applied here. However, there are a number of important distinctions to be made. The world was a far different place by the time the peasant rebel founder of the Ming, Zhu Yuanzhang, wrested power from the Mongol Yuan and established his own empire, reigning as Emperor Hongwu (r. 1368–1398), which translates as 'Overflowing Martial Brilliance'. In the aftermath of the great Mongol conquests the disparate regions of the globe were growing more interconnected and these links would only increase over the ensuing centuries. Thus while the Ming and Qing were confronted by the same strategic challenges as their forebears, they also faced an array of new strategic challenges. That both dynasties nevertheless lasted so long is a testament to the flexibility of China's strategic traditions, as well as to the adaptability and creativity of the Ming and Qing strategy makers. Constantly under pressure from multiple directions, they managed to prevail most of the time by the flexible application of grand strategy, with lessons derived from the past but jiggered for contemporary conditions and, of course, interpreted by an ever-changing set of decision makers.

Despite geostrategic constants, one should not expect to find a single coherent grand strategy employed consistently for as long a period as the one covered herein. Different organisational cultures competed: on the one hand, civil officials, trained in the classics referenced in Peter Lorge's chapter above in this volume, tended to quote these and repeat platitudes about good government and the transformative power of moral rule. Military officials, on the other hand, as well as many of the Ming and Qing emperors themselves, were wont to place much more stock in practical battlefield experience. The Qing emperor Kangxi (r. 1662–1722), for example, famously stated,

> In war, it's experience of action that matters. The so-called Seven Military Classics are full of nonsense about water and fire, lucky omens and advice on the weather, all at random and contradicting each other. I told my officials once that if you followed these books, you'd never win a battle … All one needs is an inflexible will and careful planning.[1]

Moreover, the personalities of individual monarchs and their advisers and executives played significant roles in how specific strategies were devised or implemented.[2] This being said, a single overarching theme dominated their efforts to remain supreme in the east Asian, and to a lesser extent central Asian, worlds. This is simply explained as 'manifesting awe'.[3]

The Chinese term *wei* (威), variously translated as 'awe/awesome' or 'majesty/majestic', recurs frequently in the military classics in a variety of contexts. For example, the *Taigong's Six Secret Teachings* references the need for rulers not to relinquish control of agriculture, industry and commerce to others, lest they lose their awesomeness.[4] Another of the classics, *The Methods of the Sima*, advises the ruler to accumulate awesomeness in order to 'prevent transgressions and change intentions'.[5] Even more significantly for the present discussion, one finds repeated references to the need to maintain one's awesomeness in actual policy memorials written during the Ming and Qing and in court deliberations regarding warfare. Ming policy makers sometimes referred to their inability to maintain the proper level of awesomeness as being key to their inability to control troublesome steppe rulers and polities.[6] When crushing domestic rebels, both the Ming and Qing deliberately made use of superior technology, most notably firearms, as well as recruiting troops of multiple ethnicities from across the vast empire, as a way to overawe their foes. In discussing their dilemmas vis-à-vis the Western imperialist powers

1 Cited in J. D. Spence, *Emperor of China: A Self-portrait of K'ang-hsi* (New York: Vintage Books, 1974), 22.
2 K. M. Swope, *A Dragon's Head and a Serpent's Tail: Ming China and the First Great East Asian War, 1592–1598* (Norman: University of Oklahoma Press, 2009); D. M. Robinson, *Ming China and Its Allies: Imperial Rule in Eurasia* (Cambridge: Cambridge University Press, 2020); and J. W. Dardess, *More Than the Great Wall: The Northern Frontier and Ming National Security, 1368–1644* (Lanham, MD: Rowman & Littlefield, 2020).
3 K. M. Swope, 'Manifesting awe: grand strategy and imperial leadership in the Ming dynasty', *Journal of Military History*, 79:3 (July 2015), 597–634.
4 See R. D. Sawyer (trans.), *The Seven Military Classics of Ancient China* (Boulder: Westview Press, 1993), 46.
5 Sawyer, *Seven Military Classics*, 136.   6 Dardess, *More Than the Great Wall*, 189.

in the late nineteenth century, Qing commentators pointed to having lost their awesomeness. Tellingly, once the Qing finished spectacularly crushing a series of massive domestic uprisings and recovering huge swathes of lost territory in central Asia from a would-be empire builder who had hitched his wagon to the Ottomans, the Russians and British India without success, some Qing officials declared that they had in fact recovered their awesomeness.[7] Albeit only for a while, it seems. Nonetheless, the remainder of this chapter shall explore how the Ming and Qing took the nebulous concept of 'manifesting awe' and transformed it into a viable strategy for building and maintaining an empire.

Sources

Historians of the late imperial period are unquestionably blessed when it comes to sources. For the Ming period alone there are probably more surviving primary sources than for all of the previous dynasties combined. The surviving sources for the Qing are even more voluminous, likely exceeding the Ming by a magnitude of five or more. The reasons for this include their relative proximity in time, but also the explosion of printing and the increase in literacy in the era under consideration, which sparked interest in all types of literature, including both official and unofficial, or private, histories. These sources enable historians to get a far more sophisticated and nuanced understanding of how strategy and policy debates unfolded, though much is dependent, as always, upon the sources one consults.[8]

To name just the most important, these include the Veritable Records (*shilu*) and the official dynastic histories (*shi*) of the Ming and Qing dynasties.[9] The Veritable Records are based on archival documents, memorials from officials and court diaries, many of which have not survived in complete

---

7 Yixin and Chen Banrui (comps), *Qinding pingding Shaan-Gan-Xinjiang hui (fei) fanglue* (Campaign History of the Pacification of the Muslim Bandits of Shaanxi, Gansu and Xinjiang) 30 vols (Taipei: Chengwen chubanshe, 1968).

8 L.-H. Foon Ming and W. Franke, *Annotated Sources of Ming History: Including Southern Ming and Works on Neighboring Lands, 1368–1661*, 2 vols (Kuala Lumpur: University of Malaya Press, 2011); L. Struve, *The Ming–Qing Conflict: A Historiography and Source Guide* (Ann Arbor: Association for Asian Studies, 1998); E. Wilkinson, *Chinese History: A New Manual*, 5th ed. (Cambridge, MA: Harvard University Press, 2018).

9 Yao Guangxiao et al. (comps), *Ming shilu* (Veritable Records of the Ming Dynasty), 133 vols + 50 vols of appendices (Taipei: Lishi yuyan yanjiusuo, 1966); *Qing Shilu* (Qing Veritable Records), 60 vols (Beijing: Zhonghua shuju, 1987); Zhang Tingyu et al. (comps), *Ming shi* (History of the Ming Dynasty), 12 vols (Taipei: Dingwen shuju, 1994); Zhao Erxun et al. (comps) *Qing shigao* (Draft History of the Qing), 4 vols (Beijing: Zhonghua shuju, 1997).

form. They are organised chronologically by the emperors' reigns and can thus be useful for tracing the evolution of strategy over time. They must be used with caution however, as they are framed in accordance with the biases of their respective compilers. The dynastic histories are more general and shorter, but very useful for getting the broad picture through reading the basic annals (*benji*) sections that constitute chronicles for the reigns of the emperors. Additionally, the dynastic histories consist primarily of biographies of notable individuals from famous generals to peasant rebels, so they are invaluable for researching the human elements in the strategy debates. Along these lines, researchers of the Ming and Qing are also well served by the *Dictionary of Ming Biography* and *Eminent Chinese of the Qing Period*, two expansive reference works that also contain copious documentation of primary sources pertaining to the individuals in question.[10]

The Ming and Qing dynasties are also noted for the proliferation of privately written or unofficial histories, many of which relied upon materials that are no longer extant. These include both topical works (*jishi benmo*) and chronologically ordered texts, some of which contain extensive annotations referencing the sources used.[11] Such works can be particularly useful in examining specific events that might otherwise be buried in the morass of entries one encounters in sources such as the Veritable Records or allow one to gain a local perspective on national events. For example, Qin Xiangye and Chen Zhongying's account of the Qing campaigns against the Taiping rebels in Zhejiang province provides meticulous details on the planning and execution of both the military campaigns themselves and efforts to rehabilitate local society and the economy in the aftermath of the war.[12] Additionally, they can provide a perspective divorced from that of the central government.

Particularly salient for the topic at hand are the collected works of Ming and Qing military officials. These include a wide array of documents including memorials to the throne, official communications with other officials, directives from the emperor himself, private letters and even poetry. They are often invaluable for adding detail and ascertaining specific policy and

---

10 L. Carrington Goodrich and Chaoying Fang (eds), *Dictionary of Ming Biography*, 2 vols (New York: Columbia University Press, 1976); and A. W. Hummel (ed.), *Eminent Chinese of the Qing Period*, revised ed.(Great Barrington, MA: Berkshire, 2018).

11 E.g. *Lidai jishi benmo* (Compilation of Topical Histories), 2 vols (Beijing: Zhonghua shuju, 1997); Xia Xie, *Ming tongjian* (Mirror of the Ming), 5 vols (Taipei: Xinan shuju, 1982); and Tan Qian, *Guoque* (Outline History of the Dynasty), 10 vols (Taipei: Dingwen shuju, 1978).

12 Qin Xiangye and Chen Zhongying, *Ping Zhe jilüe* (Record of the Pacification of Zhejiang) (Taipei: Wenhai chubanshe, 1968).

strategy recommendations, and give us different individuals' perspectives, which can be extremely valuable when researching a faction-ridden topic such as the late Ming arguments over frontier policy vis-à-vis the rising Manchu threat.[13] Additionally, there are also compilations of so-called 'statecraft memorials' that were put together to provide insights and advice for officials facing practical problems by providing evidence in the form of policy documents culled from the past.[14]

Still another useful type of source is the campaign history. In the Ming period, these tended to be compiled by private individuals, both to glorify the military accomplishments of the empire and the ruler, and to serve as inspiration and practical guidance regarding current military affairs.[15] The Qing, as noted by Joanna Waley-Cohen and others, explicitly embraced the martial side of their heritage to an extent not previously seen, and this included the creation of a new government office devoted to preserving military campaign records, known as *fanglüe*. These voluminous compilations contain detailed records on every aspect of military operations, including details on planning, costs, logistics and post-conflict reconstruction efforts.

Also of use to those interested in policy debates are the so-called 'capital gazettes', known in Chinese variously as *dibao, dichao* and *jingbao*. These contained official news from the government in the form of published announcements, edicts and news on current affairs. Intended for circulation amongst bureaucrats only, they found their way into general circulation and constituted an important news source particularly for metropolitan areas. By the late nineteenth century, Western news sources such as the *North China Herald* regularly translated excerpts from the gazette for their readers. Finally, there are many compilations of historical materials pertaining to specific wars and uprisings culled from various government archives.[16]

13 E.g. Xiong Tingbi, *Xiong Tingbi ji* (Collected Works of Xiong Tingbi) (Beijing: Xueyuan chubanshe, 2010); Yuan Chonghuan, *Yuan Chonghuan ji* (Collected Works of Yuan Chonghuan) (Shanghai: Shanghai guji chubanshe, 2014); and Sun Chengzong, *Sun Chengzong ji* (Collected Works of Sun Chengzong) (Beijing: Xueyuan chubanshe, 2014).

14 E.g. Chen Zilong (comp.), *Huang Ming jingshi wenbian* (Statecraft Compilation of Materials from the August Ming), 6 vols (Beijing: Zhonghua shuju, 1997); and Zhonghua shuju (comp.), *Qing jingshi wenbian* (Compilation of Qing Statecraft Memorials), 3 vols (Beijing: Zhonghua shuju, 1992).

15 E.g. Mao Ruizheng, *Wanli san da zheng kao* (A Study of the Three Great Campaigns of the Wanli Emperor) (Taipei: Wenhai chubanshe, 1971); and Zhuge Yuansheng, *Liangchao pingrang lu* (Record of the Pacification Campaigns of Two Emperors) (Taipei: Taiwan xuesheng shuju, 1969).

16 E.g. Chinese People's University and No. 1 Historical Archives (comps), *Qingdai nongmin zhanzheng ziliao xuanbian* (Compilation of Historical Materials Pertaining to Peasant Wars in the Qing Dynasty), 3 vols (Beijing: Renmin daxue chubanshe, 1984).

Actors

Because he was literally a paranoid control freak, Hongwu (1328–1398), the founding emperor of the Ming dynasty, eliminated the position of prime minister, executing the man who occupied that position along with some 30,000 of his alleged friends, associates and co-conspirators in a bloody purge that set the tone for subsequent Ming imperial governance.[17] He also dissolved the post of chief military commissioner, creating five chief military commissions, each headed by a varying number of commissioners-in-chief in an effort to consolidate imperial power and fragment that of potential challengers.[18] While this did have the intended effect of concentrating authority in the emperor's hands, it also put a great deal of stress upon him and had long-reaching consequences for decision-making and the formulation of strategy, for most emperors were not nearly as energetic as the founder and his (usurper) son Yongle (r. 1403–1424). Several came to the throne as children and therefore required regencies, which typically consisted of their mothers, tutors, grand secretaries (who often came to fill the post of prime minister in a de facto manner) and eunuchs. Grand strategy under both the Ming and the Qing was usually formulated by the so-called Nine Chief Ministers (*da jiu qing*), which generally, but not always, denoted the heads of the Six Ministries, the censors-in-chief of the Censorate, the chief minister of the Court of Judicial Review, and the transmission commissioner of the Office of Transmission.[19] This was done in conjunction with the monarch as well as select relatives and imperial favourites, often including eunuchs. The degree to which the emperors themselves were involved varied in accordance with their individual predilections and personalities.[20]

As foreign conquerors with their distinctive military and leadership traditions, the Qing dynasty added its own dimensions and figures to the decision-making process. First and foremost were members of the Manchu imperial clan, who frequently served as regents or advisers to the Qing

17 The official in question was Hu Weiyong (d. 1380). For a biography that includes references to relevant primary sources, see Goodrich and Fang, *Dictionary of Ming Biography*, 638–41.

18 C. O. Hucker, *A Dictionary of Official Titles in Imperial China* (Stanford: Stanford University Press, 1985).

19 Hucker, *A Dictionary of Official Titles*, 176. This could vary in the Qing. The Six Ministries or Boards were Rites, Revenue, Personnel, War, Justice and Public Works.

20 Swope, 'Manifesting awe'; and Dardess, *More Than the Great Wall*; J. Waley-Cohen, *The Culture of War in China*; and P. Perdue, *China Marches West: The Qing Conquest of Central Eurasia* (Cambridge, MA: Harvard University Press, 2005).

emperors, as well as trusted battlefield commanders. They also had privileged access to the throne by means of having the right to send secret communications directly to the emperor. On the whole they played a much larger role in the making of strategy right up to the end of the Qing dynasty than their Ming forebears had. The Qing also created the Imperial Household Department (*neiwu fu*), which functioned as an Inner Court that served as a liaison with the Outer Court, particularly the Grand Council (*junji chu*), which was established in 1730 to handle military emergencies.[21] Additionally, in 1861 the Qing created a new office, generally known the Zongli Yamen, specifically for the purpose of conducting foreign relations with the Western imperialist powers. This office was typically headed by one or more imperial princes with their distinctive agendas and factions. Finally, in both the Ming and the Qing, officials of all ranks were allowed to submit policy memorials to the throne which might carry significant impact if they attracted attention from the proper quarters. In the late imperial period, policy makers had a significant reservoir of both institutional assistance and informal advice to draw upon, informed by precedents accumulated over many centuries of imperial governance. While on the surface such arrangements and even the articulation of strategy itself might seem rather timeless, the primary sources reveal that a wide array of flexible strategies to ever-evolving challenges emerged.

Lurking Fears: Enemies of the State

While there were common recurrent foes and threats, other challenges arose in response to the changing domestic and international environments. The major security threats were as follows:

1. the Mongols and other steppe peoples,
2. maintaining secure borders,
3. bandits and peasant rebels,
4. sectarian uprisings,
5. countering coastal threats and piracy,
6. maintaining order amongst tributary vassals along all the borders and in central Asia,
7. controlling the Jurchens in north-east Asia (for the Ming),
8. Muslim uprisings (for the Qing),

---

21 B. Bartlett, *Monarchs and Ministers: The Grand Council in Mid-Ch'ing China, 1723–1820* (Berkeley: University of California Press, 1990).

9. minority uprisings along the frontiers,
10. dealing with the Western imperialist powers and
11. countering troop mutinies.

Superficially it appears that the Ming and Qing were battling the same old foes as previous dynasties. Of course, many of these threats overlapped and reinforced one another. A local sectarian uprising could trigger a much larger movement and then morph into a full-blown peasant uprising. A troop mutiny might be occasioned by lax delivery of salaries and supplies for carrying out military operations against the Mongols or other groups on the steppe. Peasant rebellions might arise as a result of natural disasters or due to increased taxes levied to fund military operations. Minority uprisings of peoples such as the Miao were often the result of excessive tax or labour obligations or due to the expansion of the frontier, in a pattern replicated in expanding empires the world over. In the case of the so-called Manchu invasion of the mid-seventeenth century, it was initially a regional war between the Latter Jin state created by Nurhaci (1559–1626) that evolved in response to the Ming government in Beijing being defeated by domestic peasant rebels, leading the last Ming emperor to commit suicide. A traitorous Ming general, who ironically later rebelled against his new Qing masters, led the Manchu forces into the capital and then spear-headed one major arm of the Qing advance over the next two decades, eventually capturing and executing the last Ming claimant, the hapless Emperor Yongli (r. 1647–1662), who was extracted from a curious house arrest in Burma.[22] Therefore it is important to remember that strategy was often predicated on responses to cascading series of events and was not simply a matter of consulting some military classic or consulting records of a previous war for strategies that had previously been successful.

The Ming and Qing empires were ever-expanding, not unlike their Russian or Ottoman counterparts, and this brought them into constant conflict with a wide array of foes. Yet institutions such as the so-called tributary system were deliberately flexible and allowed both sides an array of options to resolve external difficulties, including peaceful ones.[23]

---

22 K. M. Swope, *On the Trail of the Yellow Tiger: War, Trauma, and Social Dislocation in Southwest China during the Ming–Qing Transition* (Lincoln: University of Nebraska Press, 2018).
23 D. C. Kang, *East Asia before the West: Five Centuries of Trade and Tribute* (New York: Columbia University Press, 2010).

Causes of Wars

Individual leaders' ambitions could play a key role in causing wars on both sides. While Chinese sources written in both the Ming and the Qing tend to focus on factors such as 'Mongol greed' in provoking wars with their respective empires, successful campaigns against the Mongols in particular could confer considerable prestige upon the monarch. Certainly Yongle realised this and his many campaigns into the steppe were likely also spurred on by the circumstances of his rise to the throne. But his immediate successors also sought glory on the steppe. The Zhengtong Emperor (r. 1436–1449), in particularly disastrous fashion, got himself captured and subsequently deposed only to be restored after the aforementioned era of house arrest, reigning as Tianshun for several more years (1457–1464).[24] Later Ming emperors also devoted much of their time to solving the Mongol threat, which they eventually did, for the most part, by investing powerful chieftains with princely titles and increasing legitimate trading opportunities while simultaneously launching offensive military operations to deny the Mongols valuable resources such as sheep and horses. Conversely, for their part, central Asian nomad leaders often gained status amongst their followers by distributing booty, trade goods or titles procured from the Ming and Qing empires. But when specific rulers attempted to build their own empires, these would be contested and eventually defeated by the Ming or the Qing. In the end, it was the ability of the high Qing rulers to combine the logistical capacities of the Chinese bureaucratic state with their own skill and experience in steppe warfare that resulted in the utter annihilation of the Mongol Zunghar Empire.[25]

Internally, the imperial institutions successfully prevented imperial family members from challenging the ruling monarch. With the exception of the usurpation of the Prince of Yan who became the Yongle Emperor in 1403, there were no other cases of regicide in the Ming or Qing and only a couple of minor princely uprisings, as well as one rather odd case of an emperor being deposed and returning to the throne after several years of house arrest. By contrast, there were many internal rebellions and sectarian or religious uprisings, usually caused by local conditions, extended natural disasters and increased taxation. Official corruption, which was endemic to both the Ming and the Qing, frequently exacerbated such problems.[26] During the reign of

24 Dardess, *More Than the Great Wall*, 157–218.   25 Perdue, *China Marches West*.
26 J. W. Tong, *Disorder under Heaven: Collective Violence in the Ming Dynasty* (Stanford: Stanford University Press, 1991).

the Emperor Wanli (r. 1573–1620), eunuch tax collectors were blamed for unrest in some cities, though recent scholarship has cast new light on these activities.[27] The widespread incidents of piracy in both the Ming and the Qing were connected to broader regional events and economic conditions. The Ming eventually solved the problem through a combination of more effective military action and a relaxation of trade restrictions. In the Qing it was a combination of the end of war in Vietnam and a co-opting of the leaders of the pirate confederations that ended the threat.

Encroachment upon traditional living areas by Han Chinese settlers could lead to war in frontier regions, as could excessive tax obligations, whether in labour, products or military service, since these obligations were often placed upon certain minority groups who were considered 'savage' or martial by the Han majority. During the Qing period, as government control extended further and more intrusively into regions predominately inhabited by Muslims, both Turkic and of other ethnicities, religious and cultural disputes often arose. These turned into full-scale rebellions increasingly as the Qing went on, sometimes leading to horrific reprisals. By the late Qing, there were the added pressures brought by the intrusions of the Western imperialist powers that directly or indirectly helped sparked the largest civil war in world history in terms of casualties, the religiously inspired Taiping Rebellion of 1851–1866. This event coincided with the diffuse Nian Rebellion (1851–1868) that raged across north and central China, and with Muslim disturbances in the south-west, the north-west and central Asia. All these movements had specific proximate causes, but they came to exacerbate and reinforce one another as the Qing scrambled to respond.

Outright invasions constitute another category of late imperial warfare but these were surprisingly uncommon undoubtedly due to the ability of the Ming and the Qing to effectively inspire awe. Certainly in the early to mid-Ming there were ambitious empire builders on the steppe who sought to restore the Mongol Yuan or create some approximation of it. But none really came close to succeeding. Other central Asian city states contented themselves with maintaining regional influence and had neither the inclination nor the ability to challenge the Ming. There was the so-called Manchu invasion of China, but, as noted above, that was a response to an opportunity rather than part of a long-term strategic plan. It succeeded largely because of the co-

---

27 The traditional interpretation of the eunuch tax revolts can be found in Gu Yingtai, *Mingshi jishi benmo* (Topical History of the Ming), included in the *Lidai jishi benmo* compilation cited above, 2386–2390. The revisionist account is H. Miller, *State versus Gentry in Late Ming Dynasty China, 1572–1644* (New York: Palgrave, 2008).

operation of the Chinese themselves, who constituted the bulk of the Qing armies after 1644 as well as serving in many of the key leadership and strategy posts. The Qing defeated the Zunghars in the eighteenth century, but that was largely a central Asian affair; the Zunghars presented little threat to invade and topple the Qing or replace it in east Asia. The Qing fought numerous border conflicts with the Russians and their south and south-east Asian neighbours, but these posed no existential threat to the Qing itself, with the possible exception of the Russians in the late nineteenth century, though even then they lacked the ability to do more than swallow up territory. In fact what was most important to the Russians, not unlike the other late nineteenth-century imperialist powers, was the extraction of additional trade concessions from the tottering Qing state.

As with the Romans, a final reason for late imperial conflicts was the commitment to protect China's tributary allies and interests. The Ming intervention in Vietnam in the early fifteenth century was initially conceived as an effort to restore a deposed ruler and only morphed into a colonial project later.[28] Throughout the Ming period, Ming emperors authorised interventions into central Asia or the steppe, backing or opposing various Mongol chieftains, Turkic rulers of oases cities and the like. They also co-operated with the Koreans to keep the Jurchens (later the Manchus) divided and reasonably loyal for more than 200 years.[29] In this respect the Ming were following in the footsteps of their Mongol predecessors and surprisingly proved more successful in negotiating the vagaries of steppe politics, at least with respect to maintaining their overall supremacy in the region. By far the greatest challenge to the Ming tributary order came in 1592 when the newly victorious overlord of Japan, Toyotomi Hideyoshi (1536–1598), launched a massive invasion of Korea, which he intended to use as a springboard for the conquest of China. Twice the Ming sent tens of thousands of troops and spent millions of ounces of silver in defending their tributary vassal, eventually gaining a victory in a war that was poorly managed yet successful enough that it helped preserve Chinese hegemony in east Asia for another three centuries.

---

28 Gu Yingtai, *Mingshi jishi benmo*, 2210–16, for a late Ming account of the Ming intervention in Vietnam, or Annam as it was known to the Ming. For a modern study of the Sino-Vietnamese relationship over the course of the Ming, see K. Baldanza, *Ming China and Vietnam: Negotiating Borders in Early Modern Asia* (Cambridge: Cambridge University Press, 2016).

29 Robinson, *Ming China and Its Allies.*

The Qing proved similarly active in defending its tributary vassals, as well as in extending its reach further territorially than the Ming in this respect. For example, the Qing formally extended their control over Tibet and then used that as a springboard for later operations in central Asia.[30] Over the course of the eighteenth century, in addition to wiping out the Zunghars, the Qing extended much tighter control over the city states and oasis polities of central Asia, bringing all of the so-called Silk Road into China's orbit for the first time in history. This brought new challenges in the form of new ethnic minorities and many Sufi Muslims, whose rebellions would become a recurrent source of trouble for the Qing dynasty that culminated in the great military campaigns of Zuo Zongtang (1812–1885) in the 1870s, resulting in the formal incorporation of these lands into the empire as the province of Xinjiang in 1884.[31] The repercussions of that action are still being felt today in the region. The Qing also intervened in Burma, Nepal and Vietnam in the eighteenth century. And two of its most fateful wars, the Sino-French War of 1884–1885 and the Sino-Japanese War of 1894–1895, effectively marked the termination of the tributary order in east Asia. The latter two wars in particular marked a curious conflation of the traditional tributary perspective with a desire to maintain the empire and prove to the other imperialists that the Qing could keep up with them. In any case, the war with the French proved to be more successful than the later one, even if the long-term ramifications were essentially the same for the Qing.[32]

Objectives

In a nutshell the main objective of the Ming and Qing rulers and their advisers was to maintain hegemony across east and central Asia. For the most part it can be said that they were both remarkably successful. There were only four major inter-state wars between 1368 and 1850: the Ming

30 Yingcong Dai, *The Sichuan Frontier and Tibet: Imperial Strategy in the Early Qing* (Seattle: University of Washington Press, 2010).

31 Li Fanwen (comp.), *Xi Huimin qiyi yanjiu ziliao huibian* (Compilation of Historical Materials on Muslim Rebellions in Northwest China) (Yinxiang: Ningxia renmin chubanshe, 1992). For modern studies, see Hodong Kim, *Holy War in China: The Muslim Rebellion and the State in Chinese Central Asia, 1864–1877* (Stanford: Stanford University Press, 2004); Zuo Zongtang, *Zuo Zongtang quanji* (Complete Works of Zuo Zongtang), 15 vols (Changsha: Yuelu shushe, 2014); and K. M. Swope, *Struggle for Empire in Nineteenth-Century China: The Military Career of Zuo Zongtang* (Annapolis: Naval Institute Press, 2024).

32 S. C. M. Paine, *The Sino-Japanese War, 1894–1895: Perceptions, Power, and Primacy* (Cambridge: Cambridge University Press, 2005); B. C. Davis, *Imperial Bandits: Outlaws and Rebels in the China–Vietnam Borderlands* (Seattle: University of Washington Press, 2017).

interventions in Vietnam and Korea, the Ming–Qing War(s), and the Qing war with the Zunghars. Of these, only the Ming–Qing war resulted in the overthrow of a dynasty. One would be hard pressed to find any other place in the world where the hegemonic power can claim such a record.[33] Domestically the Ming and Qing were generally stable and prosperous, with sizeable harvests and high standards of living despite markedly low rates of taxation for much of the period under consideration. Of course there were domestic rebellions of all shapes and sizes. Some involved hundreds of thousands of rebels and equally large (or larger) forces on the government side. But the vast majority ended up being quelled and the state thereby achieved its objective of retaining power and restoring order. Even on the heels of the massive devastating Taiping Rebellion, which claimed some 30 million lives, the Qing had the wherewithal to stamp out the pesky Nian rebels and then embark upon a decade-long campaign to defeat a loosely linked series of Muslim rebellions before negotiating the withdrawal of Russia from a large swathe of the Yili valley that it had occupied in the early 1870s. So on the macro level one has to conclude that the overall strategy of the Ming and Qing brain trusts was sound.

On the individual or micro levels, our assessment might be more mixed. Wars could be waged for spurious or petty reasons. Both official careers and imperial reputations could be made or broken by successful or failed military campaigns; in this, the Ming and Qing emperors and statesmen resemble their Eurasian peers. The Ming and especially the late Qing dynasties were set on expanding their realm to new lands to settle their peoples, and get their hands on new resources. Indeed, many Han statecraft scholars saw central Asia as a 'promised land' which only needed the 'right people' there to cultivate and exploit its resources.[34] Certainly Zuo Zongtang's rosy reports to the Qing court in the aftermath of his victories in central Asia bespeak a confident Han chauvinist imperialism that animated late Qing discourse.

Means

For most of their respective existences the Ming and Qing reaped the benefits of being the wealthiest empire on the planet, buttressed by the world's oldest and most sophisticated functioning bureaucracy. These advantages were not

33 Kang, *East Asia before the West*.
34 P. Lavelle, *The Profits of Nature: Colonial Development and the Quest for Resources in Nineteenth-Century China* (New York: Columbia University Press, 2020).

The Qing Empire, circa 1850

Uliastai
OUTER MONGOLIA

Yili•
Ürümqi•

BUKHARA

XINJIANG

GANSU

Kashgar

Xining•

QINGHAI

TIBET
(XIZANG)

SICHUAN

Xigaze•   •Lhasa

NEPAL

BHUTAN

Dali• Yunnan
YUNNAN

INDIA

BURMA

SIAM

VIETNAM

Bay of Bengal

Map 20.1 Strategies of Ming and Qing China. Redrawn based on a map originally drawn by Glynn Seal.

insignificant. On the eve of their invasion of Korea in 1592 it might be argued that the Japanese possessed the best land fighting force in the world. Its soldiers had been at war for over a century. Its leading commanders had hundreds of years of military experience between them. They were equipped

Map 20.1 (Cont.)

with advanced weaponry, including large numbers of arquebus muskets. Yet they were defeated by the Ming and their Korean allies, with their superior technology, logistics and seemingly endless resource base. Throughout the conflict Ming negotiators stressed the size of their country and the resources at their command, even though relatively few of these were actually brought to Korea. But Hideyoshi's commanders were convinced. Even after scoring a surprising victory over the allied forces at the fortress of Ulsan in the winter of 1597–1598, Hideyoshi's generals implored him to withdraw from Korea, arguing that there was no way they could compete with the Ming over the long haul. Megalomaniac though he was, Hideyoshi eventually agreed and, contrary to popular belief, the troops were recalled months before his death in the autumn of 1598.

Also in domestic or frontier uprisings the Ming and Qing relied upon a combination of overwhelming numerical force, superior technology, better training and psychological warfare to overawe their opponents. For example, the Ming amassed some 240,000 troops to finally crush the rebellion of the Miao leader Yang Yinglong in the summer of 1600, shortly after the conclusion of the war in Korea.[35] Such forces would typically come from all over the empire, including Mongol units and some made up of various minority groups such as the so-called 'Wolf Troops' of Guizhou province, which had a reputation for ferocity and were sometimes hired as bodyguards by civil officials. The Ming considered such groups 'martial races', not unlike how the Greeks, Romans, Habsburgs, British and French conceptualised certain ethnicities they hired to fight for them. Under the Qing dynasty, domestic uprisings were typically handled by the Chinese Green Standard forces, but in times of great need the elite Manchu and Mongol banners could be brought in as well, though these troops commanded higher salaries and enjoyed other perks. But the rationale behind such deployments was the same. The empire had myriad forces and peoples under its control and they could bring a vast array of troops with different skill sets to bear against their foes. Regular troops were often supplemented by local militia forces. By the late Qing new professionalised armies that combined traditional and modern Western equipment, training and tactics came to the fore and proved invaluable in crushing the Taiping, Nian and Muslim rebellions. The most famous of these were the Huai, Xiang and Chu armies of Zeng Guofan (1811–1872), Li Hongzhang (1823–1901) and Zuo Zongtang respectively.

There was a generally persistent effort to deploy superior military technology against both domestic and foreign foes. The Ming were the world's first gunpowder empire. They created the world's first firearms training divisions in 1420. Firearms proved critical in the initial conquest of

35 Mao Ruizheng, *Wanli san da zheng kao*; and Zhuge Yuansheng, *Liang chao pingrang lu* (Pacification Campaigns of Two Reigns), 1606 repr. (Shanghai: Shanghai guji chubanshe, 2002); Li Hualong, *Ping Bo quanshu* (Complete Records of the Pacification of Bozhou), 6 vols (Changsha: Shangwu yinshuguan, 1937).

Vietnam, though Ming advantages were later negated by virtue of the Vietnamese capturing and copying guns to use against the Ming. In the war against Japan in Korea, the Ming and the Koreans used superior naval technologies and more powerful cannon to eventually drive the Japanese from the Korean peninsula, most famously dislodging the Japanese from the city of Pyongyang in early 1593 in a battle that lasted just a few hours thanks to the overwhelming power of Ming cannons. The Manchus later eagerly recruited Chinese and Korean gunners and artillery experts to aid their war against the Ming and it was superiority in firearms that helped the Ming loyalist movement hold out against the Qing invaders for some two decades. The Qing would subsequently combine superior firearms with Chinese logistics and planning to bring the steppe nomads to heel for the first time in China's long history. Unfortunately for them, the Qing entered an era of comparative peace and were disinclined to continue to advance their technologies (having no serious challengers) just as the Europeans were entering their Industrial Revolution phase.[36]

Both the Ming and the Qing also cultivated allies to facilitate their hegemony. This was done largely through the instruments of the tributary system whereby rulers would be given titles and trade privileges in exchange for pledges of loyalty. Although such pledges could indeed be tenuous, the Ming and Qing could almost invariably outspend any potential rivals for loyalty and in effect give recipients better deals than they might get from others. And there was always the credible threat of military force. When regional disputes arose, the Chinese dynasties might intervene on one side or the other, tipping the balance. They could also use the threat of bringing more tributaries into a given conflict as the Chinese negotiators did when threatening the Japanese during their invasion of Korea. The Ming officials repeatedly told the Koreans and the Japanese that more help was coming from Siam and other tributaries, even though this was not entirely true. (In fact, an offer to invade Japan by the king of Siam was rejected by the Ming court.)

Martial spectacles such as military parades, and commemorating war through the erection of steles and the commissioning of battle paintings, were also ways in which the Ming and Qing manifested awe. Events such as military parades and royal hunts were referenced in poems and private writings, the authors often noting the sheer majesty and fear created by

---

36 T. Andrade, *The Gunpowder Age: China, Military Innovation, and the Rise of the West in World History* (Princeton: Princeton University Press, 2016), 237–96.

virtue of the image of thousands of armoured soldiers in formation. As the Ming writer Xia Yuanji notes in one poem,

> Armies from the four quarters
> A million fierce warriors
> Assemble in the capital city
> Awe-inspiring and overflowing with spirit
> [They are lined up] in a fish-scale array,
> Martial and majestic,
> They merit the name tiger-runners.[37]

Displays such as this were clearly intended to impress the dynasty's subjects and overawe its potential enemies. Since these were typically held in the capital city, there is no doubt that foreign dignitaries and spies would also have been able to witness such spectacles and report back to their respective leaders. Imperial tours of the countryside, conducted most notably by the early Qing emperors, constituted yet another such display of imperial majesty intended to convey the power and reach of the imperial state.[38] Likewise the conspicuous display of war paintings and battle trophies in the imperial residence and the erection of victory monuments throughout the countryside served as visible reminders of the potential costs of resisting Chinese/Manchu rule.

With respect to what is generally termed 'soft power', the Ming and Qing are rather different from their European counterparts. The Chinese, as a general rule, did not conduct marriage alliances with neighbouring powers as that would be unbecoming for the self-styled Son of Heaven and would undermine the explicitly hierarchical nature of the tributary system. Hideyoshi requested a Ming princess as part of his demands for peace in the 1590s and was explicitly ignored. The early Qing emperors offered royal princesses as wives or concubines to prominent Ming generals in the 1620s and 1630s in order to entice their defection, and this practice was continued with respect to Mongol and central Asian leaders. The Ming and Qing did use titles and tributary gifts to great effect however, adroitly playing off potential foes and rivals against one another. They made strategic alliances with steppe leaders and afforded local leaders a great deal of latitude in managing their own affairs so long as they kept the peace. The Ming and Korean governments co-operated in military operations against the Jurchens. Finally, the Qing went to great efforts to cultivate other symbols of legitimacy for their

37 Full text in Robinson, *Martial Spectacles*, 180.
38 M. G. Chang, *A Court on Horseback: Imperial Touring and the Construction of Qing Rule, 1680–1785* (Cambridge, MA: Harvard University Press, 2007).

disparate subjects, portraying themselves as ideal Chakravartin Buddhist monarchs in a pattern that would not be unfamiliar to students of south Asian history.[39]

Prioritising Strategy Resources and Objectives

As suggested above, there was generally a hierarchy of strategic priorities, though Ming and Qing policy makers were generally flexible enough to shift priorities in accordance with changing circumstances. For most of the period under consideration here, the primary strategic threat to the empire came from central Asia. Thus the lion's share of resources, as most famously evidenced by the construction of the Great Wall, were generally devoted to the north and north-west. The Ming records are replete with debates over competing strategies for managing the frontier and relations with the Mongol polities, and scholarly interpretations of these debates and what they say about Ming grand strategy, strategic culture and strategic priorities vary widely.[40] The Mongol threat gone, in the mid-sixteenth century Ming policy debates shifted towards the south-east coast and the looming problem of the so-called Japanese Dwarf Pirates (*wokou*), which sparked a veritable cottage industry of strategic publications. Similar spikes would occur during the crisis in Korea in the 1590s and again in the 1620s with the twin threats of the Jurchen/Manchus and the peasant rebels.

In the Qing dynasty, at least according to some scholars, there appears to have been a more personalised prioritisation of strategic threats, allegedly due to the presence of a 'steppe mentality' that emphasised personal vendettas.[41] There also appears to have been a more sustained interest in aggressive military expansion, most notably into central Asia, over the first century and more of Qing rule. Once the Qing's war aims preordained by destiny were realised, strategic priorities shifted towards the maintenance of law and order across the far-flung realm. Unfortunately, the very success of the Qing facilitated a steady increase in corruption that ended up having a seriously deleterious effect on military performance and obfuscated the efforts of strategy makers in the capital.[42] Once the military challenges

---

39 P. K. Crossley, *A Translucent Mirror: History and Identity in Qing Imperial Ideology* (Berkeley: University of California Press, 2002).

40 Robinson, *Ming China and Its Allies*; Dardess, *More Than the Great Wall*; A. Waldron, *The Great Wall of China: From History to Myth* (Cambridge: Cambridge University Press, 1990); Swope, 'Manifesting awe'.

41 Perdue, *China Marches West*.

42 Yingcong Dai, *The White Lotus War: Rebellion and Suppression in Late Imperial China* (Seattle: University of Washington Press, 2019).

multiplied in the late Qing period, debates over strategic priorities intensified and were sometimes played out on the public stage, perhaps most famously in the debate over coastal defence versus the recovery of central Asian territory lost to the Muslim rebels and the Russians in the 1870s. After impassioned pleas from Zuo Zongtang in favour of the central Asian campaign and Li Hongzhang in favour of coastal defence, the powerful Dowager Empress Cixi (1835–1908) and her advisers ruled in favour of Zuo's proposal and the Qing embarked upon a campaign that resulted in the formal annexation of the lands in question to the empire as the province of Xinjiang. But while this campaign proved successful, there would be significant fallout on the naval front over the next two decades, though perhaps due more to factional infighting than to outright strategic gaffes. In the late imperial milieu strategic priorities were very much subject to the whims of specific monarchs and the ever-changing constellations of advisers in their midst, whatever their intrinsic merits.

Execution and Outcomes

In the broadest sense, the old narrative of stasis and decline that was applied to the late imperial Chinese state in the latter stages of Western imperialism and its aftermath needs to be firmly rejected. Given their abilities not only to persist but to remain the hegemonic power in east Asia for more than five centuries, the Ming and Qing must be regarded as among the most successful empires in world history. Despite their many incessant military challenges spread across thousands of miles in every conceivable terrain, they managed to keep order and afford the majority of their subjects living standards that would be the envy of most of their contemporaries. Strategists had a wealth of precedents and advice to draw upon and they did so while also retaining their flexibility and initiative in pursuing new strategies when necessary. Of course, as in any political order, particularly monarchies, much was dependent upon individual initiative, personality and predilections. Implementation of policy depended upon having sufficient support in various levels of the sprawling bureaucracy as well as having competent commanders in the field to execute said policy.

With respect to outcomes, perhaps the best way of evaluating the overall success of the Ming and the Qing is to simply glance at a map. The People's Republic of China essentially comprises the territory that was fully integrated into the empire under the Ming and Qing, with the notable exceptions of Outer

Mongolia and Taiwan (the Republic of China, still claimed by the mainland). No other empire achieved so much territorial consistency over six centuries.

Historiographic Debates

The relative constancy of China's enemies has led some to falsely believe that China's rulers were not martially inclined and / or were content to simply use the least-violent means possible in order to preserve the general status quo. Chinese writers in particular tend to downplay the imperial aspects of these dynasties, some even going so far as to claim that the Chinese dynasties were not imperialistic at all.[43] By contrast, Western scholars seldom consider the Chinese empires in this light. In fact, as noted above, the Ming and Qing empires were consistently expansionist. While contemporary Chinese historians and certainly officials in the imperial era tended to emphasise the great natural and material wealth of the empire and how that made it a target for the greedy neighbours around it, more recent scholarship suggests that the desire for expanding resources, particularly with respect for developing lands where the expanding population could settle, proved a key incentive for military actions, especially in the late Qing.

The emergence of the so-called 'New Qing History' field has opened up the study of the military culture of the Qing dynasty, a development that in turn sparked a much greater interest in the dynamics of military culture and military activity in the preceding Ming dynasty.[44] Previously, there was little interest in the personalities and personal preferences of emperors and their advisers, another area in which great advances have been made in recent research. Scholars continue to debate the respective effects of culture and 'national psychology' upon decision-making processes, but it seems to this writer that such efforts are doomed to fail because they cannot capture the complexity of the situations the Ming and Qing confronted, or account for the multifarious cultural influences upon military and strategic culture in late imperial China.

43 Li Aiyong, 'New Qing History and the problem of "Chinese empire": another impact and response?', *Contemporary Chinese Thought*, 47:1 (2016), 13–29.
44 J. Waley-Cohen, 'The New Qing History', *Radical History Review*, 88 (Winter 2004), 193–206; J. Waley-Cohen, *The Culture of War in China: Empire and the Military under the Qing Dynasty* (London: I. B. Tauris, 2006); D. M. Robinson, *Martial Spectacles of the Ming Court* (Cambridge, MA: Harvard University Press, 2013).

Early Modern Europe: The Habsburgs and Their Enemies, 1519–1659

DAVID PARROTT

While the word 'strategy' was not used in its modern sense during the sixteenth and seventeenth centuries, we have plenty of evidence from an array of formal and informal source material that the relationship between available resources, competing aims and geopolitical realities was understood and conceptualised by European rulers, statesmen and military commanders. Strategic priorities may have turned out with hindsight to have been mistaken, but they were priorities nonetheless and were acted upon, thus fulfilling the definition of 'strategy' underlying this collection. Focusing attention on the Habsburg dynasty in the period from 1500 to 1660 reveals with particular clarity this practical engagement with strategy. Habsburg concerns with the maintenance of the territorial integrity of their uniquely extensive realms and the ability to face down threats from other powers involved huge problems of command and control, and strategic thinking on a global geopolitical scale.

Charles V and the Practice of Strategy

Through a remarkable series of dynastic inheritances which began in 1506 with the Burgundian territories of the Franche-Comté, the county of Luxembourg and the various lordships of the Netherlands, Charles of Habsburg became successively ruler of the kingdoms of Castile and Aragon, Naples and Sicily, and the Habsburg territories in Austria and Alsace. In 1519 he was elected Holy Roman Emperor, which gave him juridical rights and political influence over all the German states of the empire and territories in north and central Italy. The combination of a windfall of family inheritances and the votes of the German electoral college had brought together the most powerful agglomeration of territorial rule and political authority seen since the fall of the Roman Empire. Following the practice of his contemporaries, and to avoid confusion with his distinct role as Holy Roman Emperor, I will refer to the totality of these territories as Charles's *monarchía*.

Sources

The most obvious source for Charles's strategic thinking is the autobiographical memoir of his reign from 1516 to 1548, now accepted as genuinely by the emperor.[1] More directly related to strategy are two important documents, written by Charles himself to his son Philip: the 'secret instructions' of 1543 and the 'political testament' – or policy evaluation – of 1548.[2] These are focused upon the qualities and strengths of key figures on whom the emperor and his heir would rely for government in their territories, the resources and defensive capabilities of these territories, and the principal threats requiring prioritisation. Then, a vast quantity of private correspondence between Charles, his extended family and his closest councillors survives, as well as formal administrative records. The 'nerve centre' of Charles's *monarchía* was Castile, whose central administration was precociously bureaucratic in its use of specialised councils to report in writing to the emperor, his representatives and councillors. Well over a century before France developed similar processes, the minutes of conciliar meetings were recorded and archived, and these provide an extensive documentary record of policy making, resource mobilisation and political coordination. From 1516, the postal network that the family had slowly been knitting together between north Italy and the Holy Roman Empire developed under the emperor's authority into a European postal system enabling the movement of unprecedented amounts of paper as well as money and troops.

Actors

The emperor himself was the key player in managing this vast composite monarchy. As supreme sovereign authority, he made all final decisions concerning the waging of war and making of peace with his enemies, the prioritising of his resources, and when and where to raise armies. Accepting the logic of being the ruler of multiple, separate territories, he spent his

---

1 J. Kervyn de Lettenhove, *The Autobiography of the Emperor Charles V. Recently Discovered in the Portuguese Language by Baron Kervyn de Lettenhove* (London: Longoman, 1862); and see G. Parker, *Emperor: A New Life of Charles V* (New Haven: Yale University Press, 2019), 534–7.
2 Both discussed in Parker, *Emperor*, 288–93, 408–14.

Dominions of the
House of Habsburg

Amsterdam
The Hague
NETHERLANDS
Bruges
R.Rhine
Antwerp
Cologne
Calais
Ghent
Brussels
Liege
Arras
Mainx
Luxemburg
Trier
Rouen
Metx
R. Paris
Strassburg
LORRAINE
Seine
Troyes
Freiburg
Dijon
Basel
R. Loire
Besançon
Charolais
Bern
FRANCE
SWISS
FRANCHE-CONTÉ
CONFEDERATION
Lyons
SAVOY
MILAN
Bordeaux
R. Garonne
Avignon
Bayonne
R. Rhone
Marseilles
Leon
Toulouse
Braganza
Burgos
Pampeluna
Braga
NAVARRE
Perpignan
Oporito
Valladolid
R. Douro
Saragossa
CORSICA
Salamanca
Barcelona
PORTUGAL
Madrid
ARAGON
SPAIN
R. Ebro
Lisbon
R. Tagus
Toledo
BALEARIC ISLES
SARDINIA
Badajox
R. Guadalquivir
Seville
Cadix
Granada
Cartagena
Tangier
Ceuta
Bona
Oran

Map 21.1 Strategies of the early modern Habsburgs and their enemies, 1519–1659

Map 21.1 (Cont.)

adult life at the head of a peripatetic court, moving from one major city to another across his *monarchia*. Given that his own presence could only be irregular, in crucial areas of his territories he relied heavily on his relatives. Most notably, his brother Ferdinand acted as both Charles's representative in the Austrian lands and the dominant Habsburg presence in the empire, while his son Philip from 1543 acted as his regent in Spain. In the Netherlands his aunt, Margaret, provided a consistent Habsburg presence until her death in 1530, when she was succeeded by Charles's sister, Maria of Hungary. Beyond a network of relatives by blood or marriage, Charles drew on an impressive cadre of ministers such as Mercurino Gattinara, Francisco de Los Cobos and Nicholas Perrenot de Granvelle. All of these members of his family and ministers were executors of Charles's authority, and he regularly overruled their advice, even their decisions, when they conflicted with his own political assessments. The same could be said of his political and military allies, who were never allowed to forget that the emperor enjoyed diplomatic pre-eminence in all international negotiations. Even the papacy's claims to spiritual authority and leadership could be countered both by Charles's claims as the Holy Roman Emperor – the secular 'sword' of Christendom – and by his possession of a formidable resource base. He was to force the reluctant Pope Clement VII to crown him Holy Roman Emperor at Bologna in 1530, only three years after his disorderly troops had sacked Rome.

Resources

As is evident from the previous survey, ultimate sovereignty was concentrated in Charles's own hands. He alone made decisions about peace and war; ordered and authorised the raising of armies and navies to undertake his policies; and requested taxes, loans and other financial obligations to meet their costs. Beyond this, however, Charles's decision making needed to draw on the willingness of his greater subjects to co-operate in making his decisions effective, above all providing the money that was required to pay for the armies and the foreign policy. There was no single tax system across Charles's territories; each state had its evolved political traditions in which formal representative institutions might be more or less directly involved in negotiating tax burdens. The semi-sovereign princes and estates of the Holy Roman Empire already collected taxes from their subjects; their taxes to the emperor were portrayed as 'donations' to meet specified needs – above all, collective defence from the Ottomans.

Much depended on effective persuasion, rather than coercion. The key challenge in Charles's *monarchia* was mutuality: could, for example, the Netherlands be persuaded to pay higher taxes to allow Charles to defend Naples from the Ottomans?[3] Any failure persuasively to justify demands for resources in terms that the local elites in the monarchy would accept brought the threat of non-compliance or outright rebellion, notably seen in Spain in the early 1520s, or in Ghent in 1541.[4]

Despite these rare challenges, Charles achieved high levels of fiscal and military mobilisation thanks to his personality and leadership, both intimately linked to ideas of providential imperialism. To ruling elites educated into reverence for the heritage of classical antiquity, Charles and his *monarchia* were imperial Rome rejuvenated.[5] The 'soft power' of imperial allusions and symbolism, and ideas of 'universal monarchy' and the 'great enterprise', were strongly marketed by those around Charles, and seem to have been successful in creating several generations of subjects, from aristocratic elites down to ordinary soldiers, who were prepared to go the extra mile for the emperor in facing hardship, inadequate support, personal expenditure and danger.

Means

Charles's capacity to raise both armies and navies, at short notice and throughout his reign, was admired by contemporaries. Multinational campaign armies were drawn together under Charles's aegis during the 1540s and 1550s, and his ability to field armies on this scale fuelled a wider European military inflation in these decades. There was no formal standing army under Charles, though the regular involvement of some of his states in warfare led to the creation of some de facto permanent units of troops, most notably the elite regiments, the *tercios viejos* of Castile and Naples. Elsewhere military resource mobilisation could seem haphazard and last-moment, but Charles was a typical early modern ruler who lacked the coercive and administrative apparatus to ensure regular high levels of income or to maintain large, permanent armed forces. Moreover his ability, through his extensive *monarchia* and his access to finance, to tap a huge multinational market in

3 J. Elliott, 'A Europe of composite monarchies', *Past and Present*, 137 (1992), 48–71.
4 A. Espinosa: *The Empire of the Cities: Emperor Charles V, the Comunero Revolt and the Transformation of the Spanish System* (Leiden: Brill, 2009).
5 F. Yates, *Astraea: The Imperial Theme in the Sixteenth Century* (London: Routledge 1975); T. Dandelet, *The Renaissance of Empire in Early Modern Europe* (Cambridge: Cambridge University Press, 2014); A. Molinié-Bertrand and J.-P. Duviols (eds), *Charles Quint et la monarchie universelle* (Paris: Presses universitaires de la Sorbonne, 2001).

mercenaries gave him both flexibility and assurance that he could raise experienced, high-quality troops, many of them experienced veterans, when he needed. Speaking about the 'overall size' of Charles's armed forces is thus meaningless, since the scale of mobilisation and the types of troops raised would vary substantially from campaign to campaign. More generally, Charles undoubtedly presided over and facilitated significant military inflation, and the typical campaign army of 20,000–30,000 men in the 1510s and 1520s had grown to 40,000–50,000 by the last decade of his reign. Moreover, these forces would be supported by other troops operating as detachments and garrisons in the lower-priority campaign theatres.

Adversaries

Of the threats to Charles's territories, the greatest were posed by the Ottoman Empire and France. The Ottomans offered a challenge in the two key areas of south-eastern Europe and the Mediterranean. The Ottoman victory at Mohács in 1626 over the combined forces of Hungary and Bohemia had been followed by their establishment of a vassal state in the southern part of Hungary. Paradoxically, the Habsburgs were initially the largest territorial winners from the Ottoman victory, with the future Holy Roman Emperor Ferdinand I succeeding his Jagellonian brother-in-law Louis, king of Bohemia and Hungary, who died in the battle. But the Ottoman victory at Mohács marked a century and a half of unchallenged Ottoman domination of southeastern Europe, from Sarajevo and Budapest to the Crimea. Only after the second unsuccessful Ottoman siege of Vienna in 1683 did the Habsburgs slowly roll back these Ottoman conquests.

In addition to this threat on land, the Ottomans sought to extend their naval power and conquests into the Mediterranean, threatening the seaborne communications on which Charles's *monarchia* depended. Ottoman military pressure shifted between these two theatres during these decades. Meanwhile, in the west, the king of France aggressively confronted the Habsburg *monarchia* throughout Charles's reign: Charles's composite monarchy included a mass of territories, from the North Sea to the Pyrenees, stretched out along the northern, eastern and southern frontiers of France. Depending on perspective and propaganda, this could either be presented as the 'encirclement' of France by a hostile continental superpower, or a concentrated threat posed by a powerful and populous French superstate to a set of small, vulnerable and overextended Habsburg territories scattered round its fringes. There was also a personal, emotional element to the rivalry: the young and dynastically ambitious Francis I (r. 1515–1547) had been snubbed in his candidature as Holy Roman Emperor in 1519. Six years later he had been defeated and captured at the Battle of Pavia while campaigning in north Italy. Charles's price for his release was to be the humiliating surrender of the French province of Burgundy in order to reconstitute the Burgundian duchy, which had been dismembered following the defeat and death of Charles's ancestor, Duke Charles the Bold, in 1477. Repudiating the peace terms the moment he regained France, the price of Francis's broken oath was paid by his two sons, one of whom was the future King Henri II (1547–1559), who endured stringent Spanish captivity from 1526 until finally ransomed in 1530. Successive French kings saw their attempts to challenge and undermine the power of the emperor in personal as well as geopolitical terms.[6]

Besides his two great enemies, Charles faced a large number of second-rank powers, whose support could be useful in achieving his strategic aims, and whose opposition, when aligned with his enemies, could be a considerable hindrance. One consequence of the Italian wars since 1494 was a political fluidity in which Italian rulers would align themselves opportunistically with the interventionist powers of France, Spain or emperor to seek local advantages. The fluctuating and opportunistic shifts in the alliances of Italian rulers would persist until the Habsburgs managed to tip the balance of military and political power sufficiently in their favour that none of them would envisage future gains from allying with France. This was not fully achieved until the reign of Charles's successor, Philip II, but by the 1540s a group of Italian states – Genoa, Mantua, Florence – had come to accept a permanent alignment with the Habsburgs.[7]

At the outset of his reign, Charles was reasonably confident that he could keep the German rulers of the Holy Roman Empire onside: respect for the authority of the emperor as sovereign overlord, and concern at the progress of the Ottomans, who had besieged Vienna in 1529, could ensure their loyalty and commitment to Charles's larger strategic aims. However, that assurance was progressively eroded as successive princes adopted Lutheran church reforms and moved from initial protests against church corruption into outright religious schism from the Catholic Church. Charles's initial responses to calls for reform were not unsympathetic; as the secular head of Christendom, he was attracted to the possibility of a compromise that

---

6 R. J. Knecht, *Renaissance Warrior and Patron: The Reign of Francis I* (Cambridge: Cambridge University Press, 1994); F. Baumgartner, *Henry II, King of France 1547–1559* (Durham, NC: Duke University Press, 1988).

7 M. Mallett and C. Shaw, *The Italian Wars, 1494–1559: War, State and Society in Early Modern Europe*, 2nd ed. (Abingdon: Routledge, 2019).

would heal the breach between Lutherans and Catholics. Yet as the challenge from Protestantism became more uncompromising and widespread, and the theological stance of the Catholic Church moved increasingly towards confrontation, Charles's approach to the Protestant princes changed. Recognising the extent to which the demands for religious concessions would represent both a political threat to imperial authority and bring the prospect of Italian-style bargaining for support from his enemies to advance their princely ambitions, Charles came increasingly to define Protestantism as inimical to his authority.

In other cases of independent second-rank states, notably England and Denmark, Charles recognised again the need to keep them away from alliances with France, or in the case of Denmark from too close association with fellow Lutheran princes in the empire. England provided Charles with an unexpected political bonus via the military delusions of King Henry VIII, whose desire to reignite the Hundred Years War locked him into virtually permanent enmity with France.

Objectives

If *conservación* was one watchword for a composite monarchy that had much more to lose from conflict and international turbulence than it stood to gain, the other dominating theme in the formulation of strategy was *reputación*. Charles V's inheritance was an extreme manifestation of a European international system shaped by dynasticism.[8] Dynastic assumptions charged the ownership of territory with emotional considerations of family prestige and obligation. A strong reluctance to concede anything that was part of the dynastic inheritance was compounded by the other key 'reputational' argument: that any sign of military or diplomatic weakness or reluctance to defend any part of the *monarchía* would precipitate a larger collapse in control and power projection. The domino theory of inter-state strategy might have been created for the Habsburgs. On some few occasions, however, Charles thought beyond these constraints to contemplate actions like the discussions of 1544–1545 which proposed the transfer of the Milanese to the younger son of Francis I in a bid to secure a stable Great Power settlement in Italy.

These exceptional moments indicate that dynastic interests were not Charles's only strategic motivation. The maintenance of communications and the movement of resources through the various states of the *monarchía* was also a high priority. Controlling routes and sea lanes meant maintaining

8 L. Bély, *La société des princes, XVIe–XVIIIe siècles* (Paris: Fayard, 1999); H. Rowen, *The King's State: Proprietary Dynasticism in Early Modern France* (New Brunswick, NJ: Rutger's University Press, 1980).

close diplomatic and, where possible, family links with strategically important independent territories such as Genoa, Tuscany or Portugal. It might on occasion also dictate expensive pre-emptive warfare: Charles's successful campaign to take Tunis in 1535 and his disastrous failure to seize Algiers in 1541 were driven by the same concern to secure Western Mediterranean communications threatened by the activities of north African corsairs. The issue of securing communication and control became a still bigger problem from the 1520s when Charles's *monarchia* was extended through its Atlantic links to the Caribbean and the New World.

Finally, Charles's objectives also extended to confessional issues. Charles's election as Holy Roman Emperor placed him in the highest-ranking position in the European political hierarchy, but this status was a direct consequence of his role as the defender of Christendom, with a particular obligation to confront both external and internal threats to the established – Catholic – church. Self-representation, religious duty and a keen sense of providential obligation came together to shape Charles's attitudes to the threats posed by the Ottoman Empire, and by the rise of Lutheranism and other Protestant sects in his territories.

Prioritisation

How did Charles prioritise, and how did he seek to achieve his objectives? The pressures exerted by his main opponents varied in intensity, and at crucial moments coincided, but could then diminish for reasons that were not directly within Charles's control. In 1529 Charles agonised over the threat to Italy posed by a renewed French invasion supported by Venice, Rome and Tuscany, while simultaneously receiving letters from his brother calling for military assistance in the face of the vast Ottoman army that had appeared before the gates of Vienna. In these situations, little more than gambler's instinct could condition responses: Charles decided to remain in Italy, smashed the French invading army and precipitated the collapse of the hostile Italian League; meanwhile successful resistance was offered to the Ottoman army, which had arrived outside Vienna late in the campaign season and at the outer limits of its logistical range. In less immediate form this decision reflected Charles's broader hierarchy of strategic prioritisation. France was consistently regarded as the most immediate challenge, and the defence of the Italian territories, for reasons of both situation and prestige, was prioritised over Flanders, the Pyrenean frontier or the empire. The threat posed by the Ottomans was ranked immediately after France. Only when threats from France and the Ottoman Empire could be neutralised was Charles prepared to consider a move against other challenges – notably the German Lutheran princes whom he finally confronted with military force in 1546–1547.

Execution: Success and Failure

Charles's practical strategy to defend his *monarchía* relied heavily on 'offensive defence'. Assertive military action offered the possibility of cutting through what were usually composite challenges to his states; providing a vital breakthrough in one theatre would buy time and resources to tackle challenges in others. In this readiness to turn to warfare Charles enjoyed much good fortune. From La Bicocca in 1522 to Saint-Quentin in 1557, Habsburg armies won a remarkable series of victories over their opponents. This success in battle was not just good luck: it was underpinned by his ability to draw on supplies of experienced soldiers from Germany, Spain and Naples, and the high quality of his foremost military commanders.

Yet this willingness to 'give war a chance', even when it led to apparently decisive successes in battles or campaigns – Pavia in 1525, Mühlberg in 1547 – did not produce the lasting strategic benefits that Charles anticipated. In part this was related to the nature of warfare in the first half of the sixteenth century. No European state, even the most powerful, was able to wage warfare for any continuous length of time. Reliance on experienced, highly skilled veteran troops as the primary means to achieve and maintain the military advantage had created a huge, and hugely expensive, mercenary market. Strategy was conditioned by the expectation that warfare would involve colossal direct expenditure to meet the costs of armies: states borrowed heavily to finance one or two campaigns, and in doing so exhausted their ability to access further credit. As a result, and by implicit mutual consent, two or at most three successive campaigns would be followed rapidly by treaties and periods of uneasy peace. When, for a sequence of contingent reasons, the conflict that started in 1552 between Charles's territories, France and a range of French allies continued uninterrupted until 1559 the financial consequences for both France and Charles were catastrophic, leading both states to bankruptcy – universal debt-rescheduling – by 1557.[9]

Unwillingness or inability to fund protracted military activity constrained war as a political tool, but Charles did not always recognise this. We have seen how the humiliating terms he imposed on Francis I after Pavia led the French king to repudiate the peace of Madrid, so that within a year Francis

---

9 J. Tracy, *Emperor Charles V, Impresario of War: Campaign Strategy, International Finance, and Domestic Politics* (Cambridge: Cambridge University Press, 2002), 91–113, 229–48.

was back with an army in Italy. Similarly, the harsh treatment imposed on the defeated Lutheran princes after Mühlberg in 1547 created resentment and unease even amongst those rulers who had supported Charles's campaign in 1547. Had Charles been able to maintain a continued military presence in the empire this would probably not have mattered, but the multinational forces he had led to victory over his enemies were rapidly demobilised. When providential good fortune seemed to favour him, Charles could succumb to both personal animosity and vindictiveness, allowing his ambition to achieve transformational goals to get in the way of consolidation.

Although Charles resorted to war readily, and with aims that were far more than simply defensive and reactive, both *conservacíon* and *reputacíon* also rested on willingness to use the possibilities of diplomacy to build and maintain relations with third-party states. His extraordinary status – the greatest ruler Europe had seen since the Roman emperors – could be turned to good account in the dynastic marriage market, and marriages were used to cement relations with Portugal, Denmark, England, Tuscany and Parma. France never managed to establish any kind of permanent league against the *monarchia*. Francis's and Henri's intermittent collaboration with successive Ottoman fleets in the western Mediterranean was a public-relations disaster, bringing only ephemeral military success to France while reinforcing Charles's status and prestige as the defender of Christendom. Henri II's operations in 1552 on behalf of the revolt of the Lutheran princes broke the political settlement that Charles had imposed on the empire in 1547, but the French annexation of the imperial bishoprics of Metz, Toul and Verdun reinforced the perception of German rulers that drawing foreign powers into imperial affairs was a costly and short-sighted expedient.

Physically broken at the time of his abdication in 1556, Charles could nonetheless consider that his practice of strategy had laid solid foundations for the survival of the Habsburg monarchies.[10] If he had failed to regain all the Burgundian territories of his ancestors, he had clarified the situation in Italy with a combination of secured territorial holdings and hegemonic control that would endure for well over a century. He upheld royal authority in Spain and in the Castilian territories of the New World.[11] Even in the Holy Roman Empire, where the failure to crush princely Lutheranism left an apparently dangerous hostage to fortune in a confessionally divided electoral college, Charles's performance of the role of emperor, the political culture that those

10 M. Rodríguez-Salgado, *The Changing Face of Empire: Charles V, Philip II and Habsburg Authority, 1551–1559* (Cambridge: Cambridge University Press, 1988).
11 H. Thomas, *The Golden Age: The Spanish Empire of Charles V* (London: Penguin, 2011).

around him had created and which enthused many of his elite subjects, contributed to a lasting 'default assumption' that the Habsburg family were the natural candidates for the imperial throne.

The Heritage of Charles V

By the early seventeenth century, much in the strategic landscape had changed for the Habsburgs. Whether or not Charles V had envisaged its permanence, his division of the *monarchia* at his 1556 abdication ceremony between his son Philip and his brother Ferdinand solidified in the ensuing decades. The Austrian branch, descended from his brother, gained the central European lands and asserted a presumptive claim as the Habsburg candidates for the imperial throne. Dynasticism had also taken a distinctive turn in the Austrian lands, where Ferdinand on his deathbed had permanently divided the hereditary lands between his three sons by establishing Habsburg cadet branches in Styria and the Tyrol. The interfamilial tensions that this was subsequently to generate weakened the dynasty's response to the political and religious demands of regional elites and external enemies.

Meanwhile the rest of the inheritance, ruled for four decades by Charles's son Philip (the second king of that name in Spain), ought to have enjoyed an unparalleled strategic opportunity. The French state was politically destabilised and reduced to insignificance in international relations by waves of religious and aristocratic revolt lasting from the early 1560s into the 1590s. The Ottoman Empire, after one of its most assertive decades in the Mediterranean in the 1560s, moved into a long period of detente following, but not necessarily caused by, the great Christian naval victory at Lepanto in 1571. When Ottoman pressure on Europe's frontiers resumed in the 1590s it was on the frontiers with the Austrian Habsburgs, not in the Mediterranean. Yet the opportunity was squandered by Philip, whose reluctance to adopt the peripatetic governing style of his father was coupled with a personality less capable of generating intense loyalty and commitment beyond his Castilian subjects. The Netherlands revolt was turned into an intractable and draining 'eighty years' of conflict by initially poor decision making and management of resources. The 'Invincible Armada' of 1588 and its successors of 1596 and 1597 failed at great expense to invade or achieve regime change in England. The diversion of military resources in the Netherlands required for the construction of these fleets halted the campaigning in the Low Countries which had brought a military solution to the revolt within grasp. It also hindered an early and forceful Habsburg intervention in France to strengthen the forces of the Catholic 'League' and to block the accession and consolidation of power by the Protestant Henri IV. These failures tend to overshadow Philip's palpable successes: making good his dynastic claim to the Portuguese throne and securing Portugal and its colonial territories in the early 1580s, and consolidating Castile's political control over its massive New World empire and resources. Still, the Spanish Habsburg monarchy at the opening of the seventeenth century had not turned the legacy of Charles V into a lasting predominance.[12]

Yet the position of the Spanish Habsburgs headed since 1598 by Philip III looked healthy in comparison with the worsening plight of their Austrian relatives. The religious settlement grudgingly conceded by Charles V – actually negotiated by his brother, Ferdinand – at Augsburg in 1555 had stabilised the relationship between Catholic and Lutheran rulers in the empire, and bought a couple of decades of religious peace. But a second wave of more radical Protestantism, spearheaded by Calvinist 'reformed' doctrines and practice, started to gain support amongst German princes not covered by the Catholic–Lutheran Peace of Augsburg. From the 1580s the Habsburgs needed to decide how far to engage with the resurgence of Counter-Reformation Catholicism, determined to roll back Protestant gains made over the previous half-century. In the empire, the rising tensions between 'reformed' Protestants and confrontational Catholics led to a series of confessionally charged political conflicts from the 1580s. The 'reformed' princes sought external support for a common Calvinist cause. There was now a very real threat that a crisis in the empire would draw in sympathetic states such as the Dutch Republic, England and France, whose ruler Henri IV had only recently converted from Calvinism. Europe stood on the brink of war in 1609–1610, as the dispute over the succession to the territories of the Duke of Kleve-Jülich assumed overtly confessional lines.[13]

This was the highly charged context in which future Habsburg strategy would need to be formulated, one in which the stakes for the survival of Habsburg power in the empire and in central Europe were much higher than under Charles V. And while the threat to the Austrian branch might be existential, the Spanish Habsburgs made little military progress and suffered

---

12 G. Parker, *Imprudent King: A New Life of Philip II* (New Haven and London: Yale University Press, 2014); G. Parker, *The Grand Strategy of Philip II* (New Haven: Yale University Press, 1998).

13 A. Anderson, *On the Verge of War: International Relations and the Jülich–Kleve Succession Crises (1609–1614)* (Boston: Humanities Press, 1999); G. Parker, 'The Dutch Revolt and the polarisation of international politics', in G. Parker and L. Smith (eds), *The General Crisis of the Seventeenth Century* (London: Routledge, 1978), 57–82.

financial exhaustion, leading Philip III and his ministers to concede a twelve-year truce with the Dutch in 1609 that left their future relationship issues unresolved. During the truce, the massive global expansion of Dutch maritime capacity became a direct threat to both the Castilian and Portuguese colonial empires, resource bases for the financing of European policy.

Habsburg Strategy and the Thirty Years War

Sources

Emperor Ferdinand II also left a testament (1621), showing that his concern for the political and religious integrity of the Habsburg lands was uppermost. His discussions, disputes with his ministers and advisers and decision making are recorded in formal administrative documents of meetings and discussions.[14] Extensive correspondence amongst those at the imperial court, and from the military commanders in the field to and from the emperor, also highlight questions of resources and prioritisation.[15] The most explicit discussions of Habsburg strategic prioritisation, discussed below, emerge under Ferdinand's son and successor, Ferdinand III, in his instructions to and correspondence with Maximilian von Trauttmannsdorff about the negotiating positions and the structured political priorities to be adopted at the Westphalia peace congresses.[16] In the case of the Spanish Habsburgs from the 1620s, the most extensive and direct source for the formulation of strategy comes from the memoranda and letters written by the Count-Duke of Olivares, especially to Philip IV and to the king's brother, Fernando, as governor of the Spanish Netherlands.[17] As with the Castilian imperial government of Charles V, bureaucratic conciliarism continues to generate a vast quantity of documentation relating to policy decisions and responding to letters and memoirs from imperial administrators, military

---

14 Typical of this, the translated memorandum written for Ferdinand by Prince Gundacker von Liechtenstein, 11 January 1634, concerning the decision to remove Albrecht Wallenstein from overall command of the imperial armies. P. Wilson, *The Thirty Years War: A Sourcebook* (Basingstoke: Palgrave Macmillam, 2010), 186–91.
15 See the extensive correspondence in the series of volumes edited by J. Koči, J. Polišenský and G. Čechová, *Documenta Bohemica Bellum Tricennale Illustratia*, 7 vols (Prague: Academia, 1971–81).
16 See especially M. Braubach and K. Repgen (eds), *Acta Pacis Westphalicae*, Series II, Abt A, *Die kaiserliche Correspondenzen*, 1643–48, 9 vols (Münster: Aschendorff, 1969–2013).
17 J. H. Elliott and J. F. de la Peña, *Memoriales y cartas del Conde Duque de Olivares*, 2 vols (Madrid: Ediciones Alfaguara, 1978–80), J. H. Elliott and F. Negredo (eds), *Memoriales y cartas del Conde Duque de Olivares: Correspondencia con el Cardenal Infante don Fernando (1635–1641)* (Madrid: Centro de Estudios Europa Hispánica, 2021).

commanders and local elites. The decision making surrounding the negotiations with the Dutch and the decision to reject French peace terms in 1648
are extensively documented in memoranda, conciliar discussions and
correspondence.[18]

Actors

The making of Habsburg strategy in the crucial years from 1620 lay ultimately
in the hands of two Habsburg cousins. In the east, Ferdinand II was originally
archduke of the Austrian territory of Styria, but the extinction of the main
branch of the Austrian Habsburgs with the death of Emperor Matthias in 1619
allowed Ferdinand to inherit the bulk of the Austrian lands, to be nominated
and elected king of Bohemia and Hungary in 1617, and elected Holy Roman
Emperor in 1619. In the south-west, in 1621 Philip IV was declared ruler over
all the territories of the Spanish *monarchía* in succession to his father.

The division of Charles's *monarchía* might have reduced the resources of
each branch of the Habsburg monarchy, but it did not challenge the enduring
assertion that sovereignty resided in the absolute right of the rulers to decide
on questions of war and peace, or to authorise the raising of armies. While
the individual German princes in the Holy Roman Empire could, and did,
raise armies on their own account, it was widely understood that such forces
should not be used against imperial authority. This did not stop some princes,
most notably Frederick V of the Palatinate (discussed below) seeking to
challenge the emperor's jurisdiction over legitimate force. Once defeated,
Frederick was charged with 'notorious imperial rebellion' and declared an
outlaw, and his princely territories and titles were confiscated and redistrib-
uted by the emperor. Other German princes were to suffer a similar fate
throughout the Thirty Years War. The great majority remained reluctant to
challenge the overall authority of the emperor.

The power of the Spanish monarch to decide on peace and war was no less
sacrosanct. An obvious case was Philip IV's unwavering determination never
to concede independence to the Portuguese, who had revolted against the
Spanish Crown in 1640. Only after Philip's death in 1665, and during the
regency of his son Carlos II, would the government in Madrid finally concede
independence to the Portuguese in 1668.

Behind the theoretically absolute decision-making powers of the Habsburg
rulers stood an array of both aristocratic and professional councillors and

---

18 A. Malcolm, *Royal Favouritism and the Governing Elite of the Spanish Monarchy, 1640–1668*
(Oxford: Oxford University Press, 2017), 181–205.

advisers. In the case of Emperor Ferdinand, some of his authority was mediated through the two major imperial courts in the Holy Roman Empire, the Reichshofrat (Imperial Aulic Court) and the Reichskammergericht (Imperial Cameral Court). The courts heard cases involving territorial and confessional disputes, appeals against decisions taken in princely courts and issues involving challenges to imperial authority. However, they lacked power to enforce decisions, and supported rather than underpinned the emperor's authority in the empire.

Ferdinand drew upon the advice and policy proposals of a range of close ministers and advisers, such as the princes of Eggenberg, Trauttmannsdorff or Stralendorf, and military commanders such as Ramboldo Collalto and Albrecht Wallenstein, all of whom were engaged in the process of policy making and prioritisation, and were often in open conflict with each other.[19] To pursue his strategic aims the emperor still needed the support of his greater subjects and their capacity to facilitate tax collection and mobilise military resources. The Catholic reconquest of Bohemia after 1620 defined a whole generation of Catholic ministers and military commanders who became heavily invested in the cause of the Catholics and the absolutist Habsburg monarchy.

In Spain, successful military collaboration with the Austrians to put down the Bohemian revolt which broke out in 1618 had run parallel with a lasting change in government policy and priorities. Philip III was succeeded by his son, and a new generation of ministers, the best-known being the Count-Duke of Olivares, consolidated their power and influence in government.

Resources and Means

Neither Ferdinand II nor Philip IV possessed much of the charisma of Charles V, and they were personally much less able to inspire selfless service from their greater subjects. But until 1640 the awareness that the collapse of the Habsburg monarchies would have drastic consequences for the long-established elites in all their constituent territories provided a strong incentive to collaborate actively with a strategy that aimed to maintain and strengthen the status quo by committing resources and support to the project for conserving the Habsburg monarchies. Eventually, the Count-Duke of Olivares disastrously overestimated his countrymen's willingness to support

---

19 R. Bireley, *Ferdinand II, Counter-Reformation Emperor, 1578–1637* (Cambridge: Cambridge University Press, 2014), 124–8. Wallenstein's disputes with the circle of Ferdinand's ministers in Vienna were notorious: P. Wilson, *Europe's Tragedy: A History of the Thirty Years War* (London: Allen Lane, 2009), 448–56.

the European strategy, provoking the simultaneous 1640 revolts of Catalonia and Portugal, which haemorrhaged the resources of the Spanish monarchy for over two decades.

In one crucial respect however, this high level of co-operation was less necessary than it had been a century before. The second half of the sixteenth century saw an evolution away from wars that were generally short and directly funded by the state. Both the French Wars of Religion and the Dutch Revolt were fought by de facto permanent military forces, engaged in military occupations as much as campaigns leading to battles and sieges. Lengthier periods of uninterrupted warfare provided greater opportunities for regular and reliable returns on private financial investment in warfare, with lower risk of default. By the Thirty Years War an elaborate system of military enterprise had evolved in which states, most notably the Austrian Habsburg monarchy, outsourced the great bulk of their war effort to military contractors, who absorbed recruitment and operating costs in return for the license to collect heavy military taxes – 'contributions' – from occupied territory. Though a few elite units might still be maintained directly on rulers' payrolls, outsourcing was the norm and the privatised system could mobilise resources that went far beyond the limited capacity of governments to collect taxation and raise credit on their own account. As the Thirty Years War demonstrated so devastatingly, wars could be waged on a larger scale and for far longer, and the occupation and asset stripping of territory became a formidable means to exert sustained political pressure on second-rank states.[20]

Until well into the second decade of the Thirty Years War, this evolving network of private–public military partnerships greatly assisted the Habsburgs. It allowed them successively to defeat the coalitions of Protestant German princes and the armies raised and maintained by the Dutch, English and Danes. By 1629 and the Peace of Lübeck the armies operated on behalf of the Austrian Habsburgs and their German Catholic allies stood triumphant in the Holy Roman Empire, while the Spanish seemed poised to achieve a far more favourable settlement with the Dutch.

Objectives

The Habsburgs needed a strategy for survival, and during the 1610s they established what would be their aims for the next four decades. It was based on two principles: a firm commitment to mutual support by both branches of

---

20 D. Parrott, *The Business of War: Military Enterprise and Military Revolution in Early Modern Europe* (Cambridge: Cambridge University Press, 2012).

the family, cemented by many intra-family marriages, and an equally firm commitment to the Catholic Counter-Reformation. Philip II of the Spanish branch had always been the champion of Catholicism and, resentful of his and his heirs' exclusion from the candidacy for the imperial throne, had regarded his cousins of the Austrian branch as crypto-Protestants and potential supporters of the Dutch rebels. The Oñate agreement of 1617 put an end to these tensions and committed both branches to military co-operation in the face of future challenges. With the 1619 election of Ferdinand II to the imperial throne, the Austrian branch was now headed by a figure whose commitment to militant Catholicism was absolute and linked to a providential sense of divinely inspired mission. The military co-operation between the two branches had massive geopolitical implications for future strategic decision making: axes of communication and vulnerable 'bridging' territories in the Habsburg European system needed to be defended and strengthened, above all the routes by which military support could be moved between the lands of the two powers.[21]

Equipped with these two fundamental principles the Habsburgs immediately confronted the huge threat posed by the revolt of 1618–1620 in Bohemia, the largest, richest and most strategically vital territory in the Austrian Habsburg monarchy. The separatist Calvinist rebels elected Frederick V of the Palatinate as the new king of Bohemia and appealed for external aid to a 'Protestant international' of German princes and foreign powers. This menaced almost every aspect of Habsburg policy. It threatened to elevate aggressive and confrontational Calvinism to be the predominant Protestant faith in the Holy Roman Empire, and challenged the Habsburgs' future grip on the imperial throne by decisively tipping the electoral college, four votes to three, against the Catholics. The Spanish Habsburgs, while preoccupied with the imminent end of the truce with the Dutch, acknowledged that the situation in central Europe took strategic precedence.[22]

Bohemian resistance collapsed in the face of military action by combined Habsburg forces, backed by a league of Catholic German princes: at the battle of the White Mountain in November 1620 the rebel army disintegrated, and victorious Habsburg troops entered Prague. The Rhenish territories of the

---

21 E. Straub, *Pax et Imperium: Spaniens Kampf um seine Friedensordnung in Europa zwischen 1617 und 1635* (Paderborn: Ferdinand Schoehnigh, 1980); P. Brightwell, 'The Spanish system and the Twelve Years' Truce', *English Historical Review*, 89 (1974), 270–92.

22 P. Brightwell, 'Spain and Bohemia: the decision to intervene 1619', *European Studies Review*, 12 (1982), 117–41, 371–99.

palatine elector were occupied by troops operating out of the Spanish Netherlands, and the network of landholdings allowing the movement of military resources between the Habsburg lands was greatly strengthened. Bohemia was reshaped from an elective monarchy into a hereditary Habsburg possession; confiscations and exile replaced a largely Protestant with an entirely Catholic ruling elite, who subsequently oversaw an uncompromising Catholic reformation. Frederick V was deposed and outlawed, and his electoral title was transferred to the Bavarian, Catholic, branch of the Wittelsbach family in return for the military support lent by the Duke of Bavaria during the revolt. Catholics now dominated the electoral college in the empire by five to two, and one of the five votes would henceforth be cast by the Habsburgs as hereditary kings of Bohemia.[23]

This was a transformational success for the Habsburg strategy of close military alliance, a complete reversal of the deteriorating situation during the first years of the century. Basic Habsburg strategic goals thereafter were clear: to solidify a remarkably favourable central European settlement and, in the case of the Spanish branch, to force a more favourable peace on the Dutch and to consolidate the security of the other territories in the *monarchia*.

The Adversaries

The rapid and remarkable success achieved through Habsburg military and political co-operation, in pursuit of a clear-sighted set of strategic goals, did not remain unchallenged. The expiry of the Dutch–Spanish 'Twelve Year Truce' in 1621 was followed by a surge of Dutch military and diplomatic activity, as they recognised the threat posed by the Habsburg successes. Dutch strategy after 1621 was shaped by the prospect that such successful Habsburg co-operation might now be applied against the republic. The principal Dutch response was to widen the conflict with the Spanish from the Netherlands into the Holy Roman Empire. The Dutch used diplomacy, money and military assistance both to subsidise German Protestant princes in challenges to the Habsburg settlement, and to encourage external powers – England, Denmark, Sweden – to intervene in the empire and to challenge Habsburg hegemonic pretensions.

The French Crown had been seeking since the late 1590s to turn the page on the decades of religious and aristocratic factionalism that had undermined France's international standing throughout the later sixteenth century. Further waves of unrest disrupted the minority of Louis XIII following the

---

23 Wilson, *Europe's Tragedy*.

1610 assassination of Henri IV, and this had contributed to the reluctance of France to make any commitment to the Bohemian rebels in 1619–1620. But the stabilising of Louis XIII's monarchy and the appointment of Cardinal Richelieu as the king's first minister in 1624 signalled the re-emergence of a directly confrontational approach to Habsburg military and political success.

The main strategic issue for France became whether Richelieu and Louis XIII could achieve their aim of challenging Habsburg hegemony by relying on cost-efficient and small-scale wars of choice, piecemeal territorial annexation, and diplomatic and financial support to other Habsburg enemies. This was Richelieu's chosen strategy from 1624 until 1635. However, in 1634 the crushing defeat of France's main military ally, Sweden, at the hands of a combined Austro-Spanish army outside Nördlingen in south Germany ended that option for France. Henceforth an anti-Habsburg strategy could only be sustained by France's all-out commitment to war against both Spain and Austria.[24]

The main factor which had enabled France to pursue limited war against the Habsburgs down to 1635 had been the success of the other great enemy of the Habsburgs, the Swedish monarchy and its army. Justified by geopolitical concerns for the security of the Baltic, and backed by French and Dutch diplomacy and finance, Gustavus Adolphus established a military bridgehead in north Germany in July 1630. Initially there had been little reason to expect that a Swedish military intervention in the Holy Roman Empire would prove any more successful than the failed intervention by the king of Denmark a few years earlier. But aided by some serious Habsburg military–political misjudgements discussed below, Gustavus was able to draw on enough Protestant support to buttress his army and win the decisive victory at Breitenfeld (September 1631), which secured a Swedish military presence across the empire.

The challenge to the establishment of a Habsburg European order thus came from the triangle of the Dutch Republic, France and Sweden. Notably absent from this group of enemies was the military power that had created the greatest strategic dilemmas for Charles V. The Ottoman Empire had suffered both structural and reputational damage from what has been termed Istanbul's own 'Thirty Years War' (1578–1611), when Ottoman troops fought, often simultaneously, against the Safavid Empire in the east, the Habsburgs

---

24 D. Parrott, *Richelieu's Army: War, Government and Society in France, 1624–42* (Cambridge: Cambridge University Press, 2001).

in Hungary during the indecisive 'Long Turkish War' of 1593–1606, and against waves of Celali revolts in eastern Anatolia and northern Syria (*c.* 1595–1610). The benefits to the Habsburgs of this circumstantial shift in Ottoman strategic priorities was one of the major factors behind both their success down to 1635 and their avoidance of disaster in the second part of the war.

Prioritisation and Execution

The triumph was short-lived. By 1645, the year in which the Westphalian peace congresses of Münster and Osnabrück began in earnest – albeit against a backdrop of continued warfare – the Habsburgs had almost entirely lost their military advantages, and were forced to make numerous tough concessions. They faced the same fundamental problems of strategic prioritisation that were seen under Charles V.

Success could breed complacency and over-ambitiousness. Goals which had not been part of any initial strategy seemed attainable and therefore desirable, despite the risks of jeopardising what had already been achieved. In the case of the Spanish branch, the decision from 1628 to contest the succession to the Mantuan territories in north Italy was a casebook study of strategic overreach. By 1628 one of Spain's primary goals had seemed within reach. A combination of their own military successes, especially the capture of the Dutch fortified city of Breda in 1626, and the spectacular achievements of Austrian armies in the empire, offered the real prospect of forcing a more favourable peace settlement upon the Dutch. Instead of pressing their advantage, the Spanish dissipated their own and Austrian Habsburg troops and resources in pursuit of an essentially secondary objective: the fight over the Mantuan succession, claimed by Charles de Gonzague-Nevers, a naturalised Frenchman whose relationship with the French Crown nonetheless ranged between cool and poisonous. Maintaining Spanish hegemony in Italy was certainly important, but Mantua was not essential to this. Eventually Philip IV and Olivares both failed to prevent Nevers's succession and lost their greatest opportunity to settle the Dutch conflict from a position of strength.[25]

Strategic hubris was not solely the prerogative of the Spanish Habsburgs. At precisely the moment when Olivares was ratcheting up the Spanish commitment to north Italy, Emperor Ferdinand II, counselled by his Jesuit confessor and inspired by military overconfidence and Catholic

---

25 J. Elliott, *Richelieu and Olivares* (Cambridge: Cambridge University Press, 1984), Chapter 4; R. Stradling, 'Olivares and the origins of the Franco-Spanish War 1627–1635', *English Historical Review*, 101 (1986), 68–94.

providentialism, imposed the 1629 Edict of Restitution on the empire. Regarded as controversial even by many Habsburg ministers, the edict reclaimed swathes of ecclesiastical territory across the empire that the emperor asserted had been appropriated by Protestant powers in contravention of the 1555 Peace of Augsburg. It united Calvinist and Lutheran princes in common outrage against the emperor, created a general unease about the extent of Habsburg assertiveness, and smoothed the way to Swedish military intervention. Again, from a situation in which he had defeated every opponent, this extension of war aims, compounded by the reduction of the emperor's forces as he conceded the Spanish call for assistance in north Italy, put all the previous Habsburg gains in jeopardy.

Some lessons were learnt from the subsequent years of military catastrophe. They were followed by a partial recovery which culminated in the remarkable Austro-Spanish victory at Nördlingen (1634). Yet the temptation to expand goals from the original war aims remained. The 1635 Peace of Prague sought to establish peace in the Holy Roman Empire through abandoning the goal of Catholic restitution. But it was fatally compromised by the Austrian Habsburgs' attempts partly to reverse it after a run of military success. Excluding some of the militarily active German rulers from the general imperial amnesty was to gamble that they would gain no external support. With the open intervention of France in the war, also in 1635, and the recovery of Sweden as a military power in the empire following their 1636 victory at Wittstock, the Habsburgs lost the gamble.

The failure to divide their enemies and to focus on clearly defined priorities came at a high cost, not least because the Habsburgs' opponents proved adept at using the same mechanisms of self-financing, attritional warfare in the empire that had brought the Habsburgs such advantages in the 1620s. The 1640 revolts of Catalonia and Portugal had an impact on the larger issue of shared burdens between the two Habsburg branches, the Spanish thereafter unable to provide either the financial subsidies or the troops that had bolstered the Austrian military position in previous decades.

That the Habsburgs emerged from the Westphalian peace negotiations without substantial losses and having made some important and lasting gains reflected a return to the focused prioritisation of their earlier policies. In a remarkable set of instructions written in October 1645 by Emperor Ferdinand III to his key plenipotentiary at Westphalia, Maximilian von Trauttmannsdorff, Ferdinand laid out a prioritisation which envisaged surrendering certain Habsburg advantages in the Holy Roman Empire to focus instead on core demands – the hereditary possession of Bohemia, and confirmation of Catholic hegemony across all of the Habsburg lands.[26]

For the Spanish Habsburgs the strategic priorities were equally stark. Confronted by too many enemies abroad and now within the peninsula, the Spanish reached a crucial decision. Helped by careless, overbearing French diplomacy which had antagonised France's allies, the Spanish made a separate peace with the Dutch in January 1648. The Dutch peace was a humiliation: the Spanish Habsburgs conceded everything that the renewal of war in 1621 had sought to revise. But with one enemy now eliminated, Spain could confront the greater strategic threat from France; the Franco-Spanish War continued for another eleven years.[27] It was a high-risk gamble, but in terms of strategic objectives it paid off. France collapsed into five years of civil war, the Fronde, from 1648 to 1652, and in the years following failed to recover the military superiority that she had enjoyed in the mid-1640s. The 1659 Peace of the Pyrenees largely allowed the Spanish monarchy to uphold the principle of *conservación*. The territories conceded – Roussillon and a scattering of places and territories on the Flanders frontier – fell far short of what France had been demanding in 1646–1647.

Conclusion

The Habsburgs were the great dynastic survivors of European history, and their ability to maintain their position was owed in no small part to the strategic decision making that took place between the time of Charles V's spectacular dynastic inheritance and the settlements that the Habsburgs and their negotiators achieved in the mid-seventeenth century. At numerous points, military and political events could have taken far more damaging turns, and certainly mistakes born of military overconfidence, dynastic pride and ambition, and of Catholic providentialism, litter this century and a half of policy making. Yet by prioritising key strategic aims and focusing military and diplomatic resources to secure these, the Habsburg monarchies managed to navigate a sea of powerful and aggressive enemies.

26 Instruction printed and translated in T. Helfferich, *The Essential Thirty Years War: A Documentary History* (Indianapolis: Hackett Publishing, 2009), 233–40.
27 Malcolm, *Royal Favouritism*, 185–90.

22

Naval Strategies[*]

ADRI VAN VLIET

Introduction

From the sixteenth century onwards, the Republic of the Seven United Provinces (Republiek der Zeven Verenigde Nederlanden), hereinafter referred to as the Dutch Republic, developed into a state that engaged in extensive maritime economic activities (fisheries, trade and whaling) and a vast trade network in Asia, Africa, the Caribbean and the Mediterranean, as well as North and South America. In the wake of these developments, the navy of the republic became involved in many conflicts throughout the early modern era. Sometimes such involvement was for conquest, but most of the time it was in defensive operations.

The defence and security policy of the republic and the associated construction, maintenance and deployment of the Dutch fleet and the Dutch army were determined by two complex factors. First, geography: the republic was a small country on the shores of the North Sea with barely any natural defences to the east or south. While other European powers could concentrate on either army or navy, both Spain and the republic needed both: to protect its trade and fishing, it needed a large war fleet, and to protect its territory, a substantial army and fortresses. Its peculiar territory necessitated large amounts of resources being spent on dykes and canals.[1]

There are five distinct levels to Dutch maritime operations before the nineteenth century: the grand strategic level, the military strategic level, the operational level, the tactical level and the technological level. There are no clear boundaries between these, as they tend to overlap. If we define grand strategy as

[*] Translated into English by Abel Vroegop.

1 M. van Alphen, Jan Hoffenaar, Alan Lemmers and Christiaan van der Spek, *Krijgsmacht en Handelsgeest: Om Het Machtsevenwicht in Europa 1648–1813* (Amsterdam: Boom, 2019), 457; A. Lambert, *Seapower States: Maritime Culture, Continental Empires and the Conflict That Made the Modern World* (London and New Haven: Yale University Press, 2019), 159–60.

the co-ordinated systematic development and deployment of economic, diplomatic, psychological and military means, as well as any other political tools of a state, its goal was to provide direction, co-ordination and making choices where resources were limited, whilst delegating detailed execution.

Naval strategy formed a part of this, with two dimensions: an offensive, focusing on the means of the enemy, and the defensive, which focused on the protection of one's own. At the time, an offensive strategy included naval battles, trade wars, blockades and amphibious operations. Defensive strategies were primarily engaged with convoying, patrolling and deterring enemy attacks by maintaining a 'fleet-in-being' while tying up enemy units.[2]

In this contribution we will explore, first, the Eighty Years War for Dutch independence from Spain (1568–1648), and second, the three wars between England and the republic in the second half of the seventeenth century.

Sources

Much potentially useful archival material was lost in a fire in The Hague in 1844. Strategic intentions have to be deduced in part from actions, which included attempts to secure the estuary of the Scheldt and the amphibious support of a few military land operations. More commonly, we see tactical responses to incidents. This stands in stark contrast to military action on land.

The few contemporaries in other countries who addressed naval warfare limited themselves to maritime tactics and did not pay any attention to grand strategic matters.[3] Even the later Dutch admirals, such as Maerten Harpertsz Tromp and Michiel de Ruyter, never wrote down any general reflections on what might be termed strategy. On the eve of the Four Days Battle (11–14 June 1666) against the English fleet, de Ruyter wrote to Grand Pensionary Johan de Witt (the chief executive of the Dutch Republic) (1625–1672),

> It would be good if one could put on paper how one should attack the enemy and his possessions at sea in an orderly manner, so it could be practised in a quick and Christian manner. But there are so many events that intervene that one cannot include all of them in writing, nor observe all of them in time.

2 J. B. Hattendorf, *Naval History and Maritime Strategy: Collected Essays* (Malabar: Krieger, 2000), 229–40; *Nederlandse Defensie Doctrine* (Zwolle, 2005), 17–20.
3 B. Heuser, *Strategy before Clausewitz* (Abingdon: Routledge, 2017), Chapters 4–6.

This lack of relevant literature was typical not only of the republic, but of most of Europe at the time.[4] Most of the naval officers were practical men. Professional officers' training, which focused on strategic thinking and theory development, did not appear in the republic until the end of the eighteenth century.[5]

Actors

Since the Union of Utrecht (1579), the Dutch Republic's strategic decision making was the competence of the States General (the bicameral legislature or parliament of the Dutch Republic). The seven sovereign provinces then delegated part of their military authority to this body. Yet this did not mean that the States General fully determined the strategy-making process. Although unanimity was required on important decisions in this body and each province had only one vote, the powerful province of Holland dominated policy making and prioritisation. It was the representative body of Holland, the Holland States, that drafted, debated and approved the policies to be considered by the States General, including strategic decisions on war. Even the instructions for the admirals were drafted by Holland. No decision could be taken at the meeting of the States General if Holland had not yet determined its position. Wealthy Holland as a maritime region par excellence made the protection of trade its highest priority, always agreeing that twice as much money was spent on the army as on the fleet.[6]

Yet the republic was not a centralised state. Holland's actual preponderance in decision making had to be reconciled with the formal equality of the other provinces. The process of strategy making and the prioritisation of resources and objectives required the support of different levels of government. The balance in the system was achieved by a shared ideology, which united powerful Holland and the weaker provinces in their struggle for freedom and faith, and the waging of a just war. This in turn legitimised the bridging of contradictions by making a strong appeal to public interest. Decisions taken at the highest level – in the States General – had to be accounted for in the individual provinces at the lowest

---

4 R. B. Prud'homme van Reine, *J. Hendrik van Kinsbergen 1735–1819, Admiraal en filantroop* (Amsterdam: De Bataafsche Leeuw, 1990), 43–4; R. B. Prud'homme van Reine, *Rechterhand van Nederland: Biografie van Michiel Adriaenszoon de Ruyter* (Amsterdam: De Bataafsche Leeuw, 1996), 276–8.
5 See G. Teitler, *The Genesis of the Professional Officers Corps* (Beverly Hills: Sage, 1977)
6 M. C. 't Hart, *The Making of a Bourgeois State: War, Politics and Finance during the Dutch Revolt* (Manchester: Manchester University Press, 1993), 61–2.

level. Consensus and the consultation of representatives with those they represented were required.[7]

The grand pensionary (*raadpensionaris*) was the chief executive. Especially Johan van Oldenbarnevelt during the Eighty Years War and Johan de Witt during the Anglo-Dutch Wars were the linchpin around whom everything revolved.[8] Oldenbarnevelt instigated the establishment of the Dutch East India Company (Vereenigde Oostindische Compagnie, VOC), and thus also took the fight against Spain and Portugal outside Europe. De Witt had an even greater say. In 1664 he secretly managed to order Michiel de Ruyter to sail to the west African coast and to reverse English conquests of the possessions in the Caribbean of the Dutch West India Company (Geoctrooieerde Westindische Compagnie, GWC), completely bypassing the States General. De Witt was also responsible for permitting tactical innovations during the four great naval battles of the Third Anglo-Dutch War.[9]

By contrast, the role of the stadholders in maritime affairs was limited. Although they held the rank of admiral general, the princes of the House of Orange who were appointed stadholder had little affinity with the fleet. Their main interest was the land army. They left the strategic choices and naval operations to the grand pensionary of Holland, the councils of admiralty and the highest flag officer.[10]

During the revolt against Spain, the component states of the Republic, especially Holland and to a lesser extent those of Zeeland, determined the maritime strategy in the States General. In the later seventeenth-century wars with England, by contrast, formulating strategy was left in the hands of the powerful grand pensionary of Holland, Johan de Witt, the only true maritime strategist of the republic. It was De Witt who managed to convince the other provinces to follow his overall strategy to terminate the wars with England and safeguard the prosperity of the republic. Under his inspiring leadership, the control and organisation of the navy was centralised and streamlined to an unprecedented degree. Relying especially on the rich and powerful Amsterdam

---

7 T. H. P. M. Thomassen, *Instrumenten van de Macht: De Staten-Generaal en hun Archieven 1576–1796* (The Hague 2015), 108–9.

8 Thomassen, *Instrumenten van de Macht*, 86–90.

9 J. R. Bruijn, *Varend Verleden: De Nederlandse Oorlogsvloot in de Zeventiende en Achttiende Eeuw* (Amsterdam: Balans, 1998), 116; B. Knapen, *De man en zijn staat: Johan van Oldenbarnevelt 1547–1619* (Amsterdam: Bert Bakker, 2005), 123–5; V. Vliet, 'Sijt gecommandeert te zeijlen na de Kust van Ghenee: expeditionair optreden op de kust van West-Afrika, 1664–1665', in V. Enthoven, H. den Heijer and H. Jordaan (eds), *Geweld in de West: Een militaire geschiedenis van de Nederlandse Atlantische wereld, 1600–1800* (Leiden: Brill, 2013), 245–73, 254–6.

10 Van Alphen et al., *Krijgsmacht en Handelsgeest*, 230–5.

admiralty, he managed to expand and maintain the fleet, making it second to none by the time of the second and third Anglo-Dutch Wars (1665–1667 and 1672–1674).[11]

The States General decided where and how to deploy the fleet, with Admiral De Ruyter fully accepting his military subordination to civilian government. As he noted in one of his last meetings before his death with the Council of the Amsterdam admiralty in 1675, 'The Lords do not have to ask me, but should command me. [Even] if I were commanded to raise the country's flag on a single ship, I would go to sea with it wherever the Noble States entrust [me to carry] their flag, [and] risk my life.'[12]

The military strategy of the admiralties and their admiral was subordinated to the political aims of the States General. It was the responsibility of the admiral to translate the political objectives and guidelines into achievable military objectives down to the tactical level.

In the Eighty Years War of independence, the self-proclaimed republic was pitted against its former ruler, the Habsburg scion Philip, who ruled Spain as King Philip II; it was long treated by the latter as a rebellion. The Dutch were variously supported by the English and French monarchs, Queen Elizabeth I and King Henri IV. The Anglo-Dutch Wars, however, were full inter-state wars, in which the republic dealt as an equal with, first, Oliver Cromwell's Commonwealth, and then the king of England and Scotland, and the king of France as main antagonists.

The Eighty Years War (1568–1648)

Causes and Objectives

The Eighty Years War (1568–1648) for the independence of the Protestant Dutch provinces from Philip's rule was caused by a combination of political, religious and economic grievances. Part of the nobility resisted the introduction of an absolutist and centralised government apparatus by Philip. His intolerance of Protestantism clashed with the traditional Dutch tolerance towards dissenters. New tax reforms and crop failures, state bankruptcy and the closure of the Sound caused spikes in prices and social unrest. Philip II tried to secure his position with an iron fist. A fight to the death ensued. The revolt developed into a civil war and eventually became a regular war. Both sides fought each other on land and at sea all over the globe.

---

11 A. P. van Vliet, 'Johan de Witt grondlegger van de Staatse oorlogsvloot', *Marineblad*, 124:8 (2014), 28–32.

12 G. Brandt, *Het Leven en Bedrijf van en Heere Michiel de Ruyter* (Amsterdam: 1687), 912.

The strategic goals set by the rebels at the beginning of the Dutch Revolt were initially very diverse. They fought to force Philip II to recognise city and provincial privileges, to reverse the centralisation efforts in the ecclesiastical domain and in the field of taxation, and to stop the persecution of heretics. Initially, the Dutch had no intention to claim independence. It was not until 1581 that the States General published the Plakkaat van Verlatinge (Placard of Abandonment) in which they indicated that they renounced their obedience to Philip II because of his tyranny. The provinces affiliated to the revolt chose to build their own state and defend it.[13]

The transit trade of the republic required the protection of shipping and sea fishing by using the old and proven means of convoying. Despite all sorts of internal discussions, the protection of merchantmen and fishermen remained more important than sea battles, patrols in coastal waters and the blockade of Flemish ports.[14]

Conduct

The insurgents faced superior army and naval units that managed to rally some cities and provinces to the Habsburg cause. The insurgents managed to build and consolidate a power base in Holland and Zeeland by defending fortified cities and flooding areas to create obstacles for the Spanish forces, making optimal use of the natural barriers in both regions. The river deltas, swampy countryside intersected with ditches and dikes, were poorly suited to large-scale battles and allowed guerrilla warfare. In addition, the insurgents managed to mobilise a flexible naval force that could be deployed in multiple ways: from eliminating enemy fleets and protecting trade and fishing to amphibious support for military operations on land.[15]

The naval branch of this insurgency, the Watergeuzen or 'Sea Beggars', was composed of a miscellaneous range of minor nobles, craftsmen, fisher-men, seamen and adventurers who had fled from the Low Countries in the spring of 1567 and the following winter to escape the reign of terror of Philip's general, the Duke of Alba. In English and East Frisian ports, these exiles fitted

---

13 S. Groenveld, *De Tachtigjarige Oorlog: Opstand en consolidatie in de Nederlanden (ca. 1560–1650)* (Zutphen: WalburgPers Algemeen, 2012), 115–16; Z. W. Sneller, *Unie van Utrecht en Plakkaat van Verlatinge: De wording van den Nederlandschen staat* (Rotterdam: Brusse, voor de Vereeniging voor Staatkunde van de Studenten der Nederlandsche Handelshoogeschool, 1929), 59–62.

14 Van Vliet, 'Foundation, organization and effects of the Dutch Navy (1568–1648)', in M. van der Hoeven (ed.), *Exercise of Arms: Warfare in the Netherlands (1568–1648)* (Leiden, New York and Cologne: Brill, 1997), 153–72, 158–61.

15 P. Groen (ed.), *The Eighty Years War: From Revolt to Regular War 1568–1648* (Leiden: Leiden University Press, 2019), 108–10.

out vessels which they could use to earn their living through piracy and privateering, while at the same time challenging Philip's control of the waters surrounding the Netherlands. In the first years of the revolt, the Sea Beggars fought Spanish men-of-war on the Zuiderzee, the Haarlemmermeer and the Zeeland streams. Their operations in the 1570s and 1580s fitted the definition of 'battle fleet strategy', 'sea control strategy' and 'strategy of sea denial' (according to the historian Jan Glete); all three are clearly recognisable patterns. These concepts are each clearly recognisable in the republic's Order of Command at Sea (Ordre op de beveilinge van de zee) of 1589.[16] Yet limited financial resources made it impossible for the rebels to maintain a strong blue-water navy and also to secure and protect merchant and fishing vessels and to conduct large-scale amphibious operations in support of military operations on land. The rebel provinces constantly had to adjust the balance between tasks and available resources. Luckily for the rebels, Spain had problems deploying its blue-water navy, the Armada del Mar Océano, in the North Sea due to the great distance between bases and the area of operations.[17]

This situation changed when Alexander Farnese, Duke of Parma, conquered large parts of the Flemish coast in 1583, and had ten warships built in Dunkirk, the so-called 'royal squadron'. He also managed to convince private shipowners to contribute vessels; thus the Dunkirk Privateers were born. During the further course of the Eighty Years War, this and the Spanish Armada de Flandes, or Flemish Navy, would demand all the attention of the Dutch Republic's navy.

Only twice was Spain able to bring in an invasion fleet to the North Sea. In 1588, the boisterously named 'Invincible Armed Fleet', La Armada Invencible, reached the Channel with the aim of dealing first with England (an ally of the rebels) and then with the rebels themselves.[18] The Dutch rebel navy was not involved in the real fighting. The armada proved quite vincible when it was scattered by the English and by storms. However, a squadron commanded by Lieutenant Admiral Justin of Nassau did prevent warships from Dunkirk joining the armada.[19] Two further Spanish armadas sailed forth from Spain in

16 J. Glete, *Navies and Nations: Warships, Navies and State Building in Europe and America, 1500–1860*, Volume 1 (Stockholm: Almqvist & Wiksell Internat, 1993), 56–9, 105–7; J. Glete, *Warfare at Sea, 1500–1650: Maritime Conflicts and the Transformation of Europe* (London: Routledge, 2000), 38–9.

17 Groen, *Eighty Years War*, 159.

18 Some current historians consider the term 'invincible' to be a product of later English propaganda. See 'The Spanish Armada', *Royal History's Biggest Fibs with Lucy Worsley*, Series 1, BBC 2, 5 September 2020.

19 C. Martin and G. Parker, *The Spanish Armada* (London: Hamish Hamilton, 1988); Van Vliet, *Bastaard van Oranje: Justinus van Nassau, Admiraal, Diplomaat & Gouverneur (1559–1631)* (Zutphen: Walburg Pers B.V, 2017), 66–72.

the 1590s but were prevented from reaching the Channel by adverse winds. A fourth armada that set out from Span four decades later was primarily intended to transport a Spanish army to the southern Netherlands, but it was destroyed in October 1639 at the Downs by Admiral Maerten Harperstz Tromp. This ended Spanish hegemony in western European waters: Spain no longer had a command of the sea. The naval battle at the Downs turned out to foreshadow the great naval battles of the later naval wars with England.[20]

From 1572 the English supported the Dutch rebels against Habsburg Spain with troops. At sea, they jointly fought Spanish maritime threats. Huguenot troops from France took part in military operations in the early stages of the revolt. In 1596 France, England and the republic concluded the Greenwich Treaty against Spain. Once France and England had made peace with Spain in 1598 and 1604 respectively, the republic was largely on its own, except for the French king Henry IV continuing to covertly send money and troops.

The Three Anglo-Dutch Wars (1652–1654, 1665–1667, 1672–1674)

Causes and Objectives

With the Eighty Years War ending in 1648, new conflicts arose paradoxically between the republic and England, who had supported the former so strongly against Spain. Despite being weakened by civil war and then its own republican period, England became the Dutch republic's chief trading competitor, and attempted to obstruct Dutch trade in three consecutive wars. With the enactment of the Navigation Act of 9 October 1651, Oliver Cromwell sought to protect English merchants' trade interests from cut-throat Dutch competition: the Act decreed that European products could only be transported to England by English ships or by ships from the country of origin. Thus an attack on the Dutch transport monopoly was launched. At the same time, England claimed sovereignty over its surrounding seas, the North Sea, the Channel and the Atlantic Ocean as far as its colonies in North America. The Dutch Republic, by contrast, insisted on the principle of the freedom of the seas (ironically, a line the English had taken previously during their own competition with Spain). All kinds of minor matters, such as the English insistence on inspecting Dutch ships for

---

20 R. Prud'homme van Reine, *Schittering en schandaal: Biografie van Maerten en Cornelis Tromp* (Amsterdam: Arbeiderspers, 2001), 73–86.

The Dutch Republic and the Southern Netherlands in 1648

Schiermonnikoog
Ameland
Emden
Terschelling
Vlieland
GRONINGEN
Leeuwarden
Groningen
Harlingen
Winschoten
Texel
FRIESLAND
WESTER-WOLDE
Steenwijk
DRENTHE
Medemblik
Enkhuizen
Coevorden
Hoorn
Alkmaar
Zwolle
Lingen
NORTH SEA
ZUIDERZEE
IJsel
Haarlem
Harderwijk
OVERIJSSEL
Amsterdam
Deventer
Leiden
UTRECHT
Amersfoort
Zutphen
The Hague
Gouda
Utrecht
GELRE
Groenlo
Delft
Arnhem
Doesburg
Rotterdam
Rhine
Hellevoetsluis
Dordrecht
Waal
Emmerik
Heusden
Nijmegen
Rees
Wesel
Zierikzee
Grave
Cleves
ZEELAND
Willemstad
s-Hertogenbosch
Middelburg
Breda
Vlissingen
Goes
STATES BRABANT GELDERLAND
Bergen op Zoom
Meuse
Venlo
BRABANT
Ostend
Sas van
Hulst
Antwerp
Roermond
Sluis
Gent
Bruges
Stevensweert
Nieuwpoort
Ghent
Mechelen
PRINCE-
Nete
STATES-
Dunkirk
VLAANDEREN
Scheldt
Demer
OVERMAAS
Cologne
Calais
Leuven
Maastricht
Ypres
Lys
Brussels
BISHOPRIC
LIM-
Aachen
Scheldt
Liège
BURG
(Aix-la-Chapelle)
Dender
Lille
Tournai
Meuse
TOURNAI
Mons
Charleroi
Namur
LIÈGE
ARTOIS
HAINAUT
NAMUR
STAVELOT-
Valenciennes
MALMEDY
Arras
Sambre
Cambrai
Dinant
CAMBRAI
Amiens
LUXEMBOURG
Saint-Quentin
Rocroi
Trier
Luxembourg
FRANCE

⚓ Admiralty headquarters
Area of the Dutch Republic
Generality Lands
Southern Netherlands

Reims

0   20   40 km

Metz

Map 22.1 Dutch naval strategies (1550–1800). Redrawn based on a map drawn by Netherlands Ministry of Defence.

the transport of contraband, and fishing rights in English and Scottish coastal waters, played a role.[21] Crucially, a mercantilist world view assumed that

---

21 B. Heuser, *Strategy before Clausewitz* (Abingdon: Routledge, 2018), 116–34.

world trade was finite and that one country's increase in trade was only possible at the expense of another's. As George Cock, a major Baltic Sea merchant and supplier to the Royal Navy, put it, 'the trade of the world is too little for us two, therefore one must drown'.[22] All these factors combined led to English public opinion turning increasingly against the Dutch.

Before 1650, the republic did not build offensive navies to establish command of the sea. This ambition only emerged when England aspired to gain full control of the Channel and thereby threatened the trade interests of the republic. Johan de Witt managed to shift priorities with the support of the powerful city of Amsterdam, making the Dutch Navy central to strategy. The old defensive convoy strategy gave way to an offensive maritime strategy aimed at command of the sea, sea control and the protection of power, to counter both Charles II's and Louis XIV's expansionist ambitions.[23]

Tactically, it was used to attack English squadrons, to protect Dutch merchant and fishing ships with convoys, to break barricades (the Battle of Ter Heijde, 1653, and the Battle of Kijkduin, 1673), to blockade the English coast (1667) and to humiliate Charles II by burning his fleet in harbour and carrying off his flagship (the Raid on the Medway, 1667). This multitude of tasks meant that in the first two Anglo-Dutch Wars, no clear choice could be made between an offensive and a defensive maritime strategy.

However, this was different during the third Anglo-Dutch War. The balance of forces had changed significantly. The Dutch Navy was now the weaker force, as the republic was attacked by sea and by land. The threat of invasion emanating from the combined Franco-English fleet and the numerical inequality forced a defensive strategy of sea denial. During these conflicts, the operational areas of the respective navies were primarily the North Sea, the Channel and the Mediterranean. Only occasionally did confrontations take place off the coasts of Africa, America, Asia and the Caribbean to secure the territorial and trade interests of the GWC and the VOC.[24]

22 P. M. Kennedy, *The Rise and Fall of British Naval Mastery* (London: Penguin, 1976), 47–67; G. Rommelse, *The Second Anglo-Dutch War (1665–1667)* (Hilversum: Uitgeverij Verloren, 2006), 46–50; Quote from Samuel Pepys, *The Diary of Samuel Pepys*, Volume v (ed. R. Latham and W. Matthews) (London: Bell & Hyman, 1971), 35. S. Pincus is the most vocal opponent to the economical explanation in his *Protestantism and Patriotism: Ideologies and the Making of English Foreign Policy, 1650–1668* (Cambridge: Cambridge University Press, 1996), 196–268.

23 Lambert, *Seapower States*, 161–2, 170–7.

24 J. B. Hattendorf, *Talking about Naval History* (Newport: Naval War College Press, 2011), 61; J. R. Jones, *The Anglo-Dutch Wars of the Seventeenth Century* (London: Routledge, 1996), 111, 115; E. Odegard, 'Merchant companies at war: the Anglo-Dutch Wars in Asia', in D. Ormrod and G. Rommelse (eds), *War, Trade and the State: Anglo-Dutch Conflict 1652–1689* (Woodbridge: Boydell Press, 2020), 230–47.

Conduct

In 1652 the first Anglo-Dutch War broke out over Admiral Maerten Tromp's reticence in offering the flag salute to admiral Robert Blake's squadron in the Channel, which provoked the latter to open fire. The English Commonwealth's fleet was more heavily armed than the Dutch from the outset, even though the Dutch fleet was more numerous, but had mostly older warships and hired merchant ships.[25]

Upon the restoration of the monarchy in England, King Charles II renewed the Navigation Act of 1651. Under his rule, England's hawkish courtiers and aristocratic naval officers searched for a new conflict. An English expedition against the property of the GWC in West Africa and the conquest of New Amsterdam (later New York) – in peacetime, *nota bene* – were the cause for the Second Anglo-Dutch War that began in March 1665.[26]

Only this time, the English fleet now had to deal with a peer opponent. The States General under the inspiring leadership of Johan de Witt had created a standing navy that, with capable fleet admirals such as Michiel de Ruyter and Cornelis Tromp, turned the tables on England. Lessons had been learned from the First Anglo-Dutch War, in which the weaknesses of the Dutch Navy had been shown: inferior ships or converted merchantmen and a lack of discipline and practice. The Dutch Navy not only grew but changed its tactics. Vice Admiral Maerten Tromp was the first to break with the traditional strategy of the republic. The previously predominant strategy – the protection of merchant shipping and fishing – was abandoned by Tromp on his own initiative. Instead he sought confrontation. The destruction of the enemy navy provided the best protection for merchant shipping and fishing. De Ruyter later continued Tromp's strategy. Boarding enemy ships became less important, and their sinking by cannon fire more so. An improved signalling system gave the central command of the fleet more control during a naval battle. Discipline made this new approach a success. Thanks to these changes, the republic managed to hold its own.[27] A peace favourable to the Dutch Republic was imposed in July 1667.[28]

On 1 June 1670, at Dover, Charles II signed a secret treaty with the French king Louis XIV against the republic. With French financial support, the English monarch hoped to sideline Parliament and increase his power. In return, he agreed to French predominance on the Continent and would contribute his fleet to support an attack on the republic. In March 1672,

---

25 J. R. Bruijn, *The Dutch Navy of the Seventeenth and Eighteenth Centuries* (St. John's: Liverpool University Press, 2011), 59–63.

26 Van Vliet, 'Sijt gecommandeert te zeijlen na de Kust van Ghenee'.

27 Van Vliet, 'Johan de Witt', 28–32.   28 Bruijn, *The Dutch Navy*, pp, 73–5.

a war broke out in which England, France and the archbishoprics of Münster and Cologne jointly tried to destroy the republic.[29]

During the conflicts with England, the Dutch Republic had varying allies. The republic's alliance with France (1662) gave it little actual military support. This was different with the Haags Verbond (1673), which brought the republic, Spain and Austria together in their fight against England and France.[30]

The new stadholder, William III of Orange (1650–1702), filled the political vacuum created in 1672 by the murder of Johan de Witt, for which he was partly responsible. After a disastrous start on land, the fortunes of the Anglo-Dutch War turned, and William was able to secure the territory of the republic. At sea, the Dutch war fleet, commanded by De Ruyter, was more successful from the outset. De Ruyter managed to check the combined Anglo-French fleet, preventing an invasion. Charles II's plans to turn himself into an absolutist monarch with the help of a victory over the Dutch had failed. He was forced to make peace with the republic in February 1674; Münster and Cologne followed. By contrast, the war with France dragged on until 1678.[31]

The Available Means

In the early modern period, in most western European countries, at least 70 to 90 per cent of state revenues were spent on the armed forces and on the payment of government debts incurred in previous wars. This also applied to the Dutch Republic. In general, expenditure on the army was twice as high as expenditure on the fleet. During the Anglo-Dutch Wars, however, the relationship was inverted.[32] Striking the right balance occupied Dutch strategy making from 1568 until 1795.[33]

---

29 J. Israel, *The Dutch Republic: Its Rise, Greatness, and Fall 1477–1806* (Oxford: Clarendon, 1995), 796–806; L. Panhuysen, *De Ware Vrijheid: De levens van Johan en Cornelis de Witt* (Amsterdam: Olympus, 2005), 374–7.

30 Van Alphen et al., *Krijgsmacht en Handelsgeest*, 53–4; Groenveld, *De Tachtigjarige Oorlog*, 138–40. For an overview of all alliances and treaties, see O. van Nimwegen, *The Dutch Army and the Military Revolutions 1588–1688* (Woodbridge: Boydell Press, 2010), 571–7.

31 Bruijn, *The Dutch Navy*, 75–7.

32 W. Veenstra, *Tussen Gewest en Generaliteit. Staatsvorming en Financiering van de Oorlog te Water in de Republiek der Verenigde Nederlanden, in Het Bijzonder Zeeland (1586–1795)* (Woubrugge: Vrije Universiteit Amsterdam, 2014), 29; K. Davids and M. 't Hart, 'The navy and the rise of the state: the case of the Netherlands, c. 1570–1810', in J. G. Backhaus (ed), *Navies and State Formation: The Schumpeter Hypothesis Revisited and Reflected* (Zurich: Lit Verlag, 2012), 278.

33 J. S. Bartstra, *Vlootherstel en legeraugumentatie 1770–1780* (Assen: s.n., 1952); Glete, *War and the State*, 157; H. Scott, 'The fiscal–military state and international rivalry during the

In the first years of the Dutch Revolt, it was mainly the provinces of Flanders, Zeeland and Holland that financed the war fleet. In addition, the States General encouraged private individuals to use their ships for privateering against the enemy. The fleet's equipment was eventually paid for from import and export duties (the so-called *convooien* and *licenten*) and from auction fees, booty and privateering with subsidies and loans. Although the Dutch Navy played an important supporting role in the fight against Spain, this naval force accounted for only 26 per cent of government expenditure, against 51.5 per cent for the army, which bore the brunt of the fighting, supported by English subsidies and English-paid forces.[34]

An important milestone in this process was the establishment of a naval budget in 1589, the Ordre op de beveilinge van de zee. Henceforth, every year the States General debated and determined the republic's naval posture and strategy. Strategic goals and tactical considerations were factored into this. The Council of State produced a detailed version of the naval budget in the Staat van Oorlog te Water (Statement on the Naval Forces), and the Generale Petitie (General Petition, a request to the States General for military funding). These included the numbers of blockade and convoy ships, the deployment of warships on inland waterways, salaries, the equipment requirements per admiralty and so on. Financing options were also included.[35]

From 14 June 1597, the States General established a regulation for the administration of the maritime activities of the state. Although the rule of 1597 was initially designed to apply only for one year, the system as a whole lasted until the end of the republic in 1795.[36] A set of 100 articles or ordinances provided for military justice, prices (war booty), finances, personnel and the procurement of equipment. The States General were confirmed as the highest authority in maritime affairs. Under their authority, the five admiralties in Rotterdam, Amsterdam, the Noorderkwartier (Hoorn/Enkhuizen), Zeeland (Middelburg) and Friesland (Dokkum until 1645, then Harlingen) carried out their instructions. Each admiralty financed its own shore organisation (offices, shipyards and warehouses); the purchase or hiring of merchant ships and their conversion; armament, equipment and supplies; and the possible construction of new ships.

---

long eighteenth century', in C. Storrs (ed.), *The Fiscal–Military State in Eighteenth-Century Europe: Essays in Honour of P. G. M. Dickens* (London: Routledge, 2009), 23–53.
34 't Hart, *The Making of a Bourgeois State*, 61–2.   35 Groen, *Eighty Years War*, 136, 214.
36 Van Vliet, 'Foundation, organization and effects of the Dutch Navy'. For the contents of the articles themselves, see L. Eekhout, *Het admiralenboek: Vlagofficieren van de Nederlandse marine 1382–1991* (Amsterdam: De Bataafsche Leeuw, 1992), 157–71.

They obtained the income from import and export rights on trade, from proceeds from privateering and from (targeted) subsidies from the States General. The income of the admiralties for the years from 1574 to 1680, as documented in the archives, amounted to an average of 3.1 million guilders annually. In 1628 and 1641 the total annual costs for the fleet, including personnel costs and shore organisation, amounted to over 4 million guilders. In 1652–1654 it was 6.3 million, in 1665–1667 12 million. A high point were the years 1781–1784, at 14.6 million guilders.[37]

In the early years of the Eighty Years War, the rebels' navy was composed of vessels hired from the merchant fleet. To supplement them, the five admiralties launched a large number of ships intended to form convoys for merchant and fishing vessels, to blockade Flemish ports loyal to Philip, to patrol the North Sea and the Channel, and to guard the Dutch estuaries. Faced with such a large number of tasks, in most years the republic's navy could not prevent Spain's Flemish Navy from making many victims among the fishermen of Holland and Zeeland. Expeditions against Spanish and Portuguese shipping and colonies funded by the States General were largely unsuccessful and caused the admiralties great losses. It was ultimately the VOC and GWC that successfully waged war against Philip's fleets outside Europe.[38]

When there was a strong sense of external threat, regional governments and populations were prepared to pay for a strong navy. But in peacetime the provinces, with the exception of Holland and Zeeland, did not provide enough money to maintain the required minimum strength. During the wars with England, the admiralties depended on extraordinary subsidies, derived from extra taxation. Standardised warships increasingly replaced hired merchantmen. The tonnage, the numbers of guns and the size of crews increased, enabling new tactics. The boarding battle was no longer the main objective. Line tactics became dominant, with a crucial role for the naval artillery.[39] In the span of two to three decades in the seventeenth

---

37 't Hart, *Bourgeois State*, 54, 174; W. Fritschy, *Public Finance of the Dutch Republic in Comparative Perspective: The Viability of an Early Modern Federal State (1570s–1795)* (Leiden: Brill, 2017), 150, 268; Veenstra, *Tussen Gewest en Generaliteit*, 136. Huygens ING The Hague, Database Provincial Finances of the Dutch Republic 1572–1795 (viewed 21 July 2020).

38 L. Sicking and A. van Vliet, '"Our Triumph of Holland": war, violence and the herring fishery of the Low Countries, c. 1400–1650', in L. Sicking and D. Abreu-Ferreira (eds), *Beyond the Catch: Fisheries of the North Atlantic, the North Sea and the Baltic, 900–1850* (Leiden: Brill, 2009), 354–60.

39 Van Alphen et al., *Krijgsmacht en Handelsgeest*, 294–302; Van Vliet, 'Foundation, organization and effects of the Dutch Navy', 164–5.

Table 22.1 Estimated size of the Dutch fleet and Spain's Flemish navies, 1585–1642

	Dutch fleet	Spain's Flemish Navy
1585	102	
1588		60
1596	140	
1597		22
1616	34	
1621	86	20
1628	124	19
1642	143	60

Source: A. van Vliet, *Vissers en Kapers: De Zeevisserij Vanuit het Maasmondgebied en de Duinkerker Kapers (ca. 1580–1648)* (The Hague: Stichting Hollandse Historische Reeks, 1994), 69–70, 185–6.

Table 22.2 The major European navies, 1660–1690, compared in numbers of warships and total displacement tonnage

	England		Dutch Republic		France	
	Number	Tons	Number	Tons	Number	Tons
1650	72	49,000	62	29,000	32	21,000
1655	133	90,000	101	64,000	23	18,000
1660	131	88,000	97	62,000	26	20,000
1665	143	102,000	115	81,000	47	36,000
1670	104	84,000	129	102,000	120	115,000
1675	110	95,000	110	88,000	134	138,000
1680	115	130,000	93	66,000	135	135,000
1685	117	136,000	95	86,000	133	140,000
1690	109	124,000	74	68,000	131	141,000

Source: J. Glete, *Navies and Nations: Warships, Navies and State Building in Europe and America, 1500–1860*, Volume II (Stockholm: Almqvist & Wiksell Internat, 1993), 550, 551, 575, 576, 639.

century, under the leadership and expertise of Grand Pensionary Johan de Witt, the republic managed to equip a fleet to rival the English Navy – despite England spending more money on its navy and the republic's additional requirement to maintain a large army.[40]

40 Fritschy, *Public Finance*, 265.

Epilogue

In 1688, with the Glorious Revolution and the coronation of stadholder William III of Orange as king of England and Scotland alongside his wife Mary II (the niece of Charles II), the balance of power in Europe between England, France and the Dutch Republic underwent a major change. This had enormous consequences for the strategic actions of the republic at sea and on land. Henceforth England and the republic were military allies working together as equals. William III, now king of England and Scotland, could thus develop a new grand strategy to achieve his primary political goal of curbing the expansion of the French king Louis XIV. From now on, England would lead any war at sea, with the Dutch war fleet playing a subordinate role (with an English-to-Dutch ratio of 5:3). In land warfare on the Continent the Dutch Republic would take the lead. The Dutch fleet gave way to the strategic priority of maintaining a large army and the construction of fortifications to secure the territory of the republic. Sea power was traded for territorial security.[41] Despite a few ups and downs this situation lasted until 1780.

The last Anglo-Dutch War (1781–1784) concludes our survey. At the time, the policy makers – the States General – constantly disagreed about whether the republic should have a pro-British or a pro-French foreign policy, and whether its strategy should be to prioritise territorial defence, using the army, or the defence of trade, which required the navy. There was no longer any question of a single, widely supported grand strategy. The republic was now largely dependent on other powers for its security.[42]

---

41 Van Alphen et al., *Krijgsmacht en Handelsgeest*, 70–1; Lambert, *Seapower States*, 197–200.
42 Van Alphen et al., *Krijgsmacht en Handelsgeest*, 64–5, 154.

23

The Strategy of Louis XIV

JAMEL OSTWALD

Louis XIV (r. 1661–1714) remains France's monarch most directly responsible for modern France's hexagonal frontiers. Not without reverses, over fifty years Louis consistently continued his predecessors' policy of territorial expansion by marriage and war. In the process, he transformed France into the dominant power on the European continent.

Sources

By the late seventeenth century, Louis XIV's court had created an administrative apparatus that managed several hundred thousand men across a dozen theatres of operation around the world. Managing and coordinating these disparate forces required an increasingly organised 'information state', with royal ministers relying on bureaucratic personnel in multiple departments (of state and of war, as well as espionage and civilian informants formed from personal client networks), connected with correspondents all over Europe. This information state created an avalanche of paper.[1] And yet no minutes were kept for the important debates about policy, so French strategic thinking is best approached through the court correspondence and planning paperwork which has survived in the Service historique de la défense (SHD) at Vincennes. As the number of enemies and theatres of operation increased, the volume of paper needed to manage these efforts expanded as well. Extant correspondence and memoranda from the Secretary of State for War's office grew from twenty-four volumes during Louis XIV's first war, the twelve-month War of Devolution (1667–1668), to over 1,000 volumes during his last, the War of the Spanish

---

1 L. Bély, *Espions et ambassadeurs: Au temps de Louis XIV* (Paris: Fayard, 1990); J. Rule and B. Trotter, *A World of Paper: Louis XIV, Colbert De Torcy, and the Rise of the Information State* (Montreal and Kingston: McGill-Queen's University Press, 2014).

Louis XIV's Major European Combats, 1667–1714

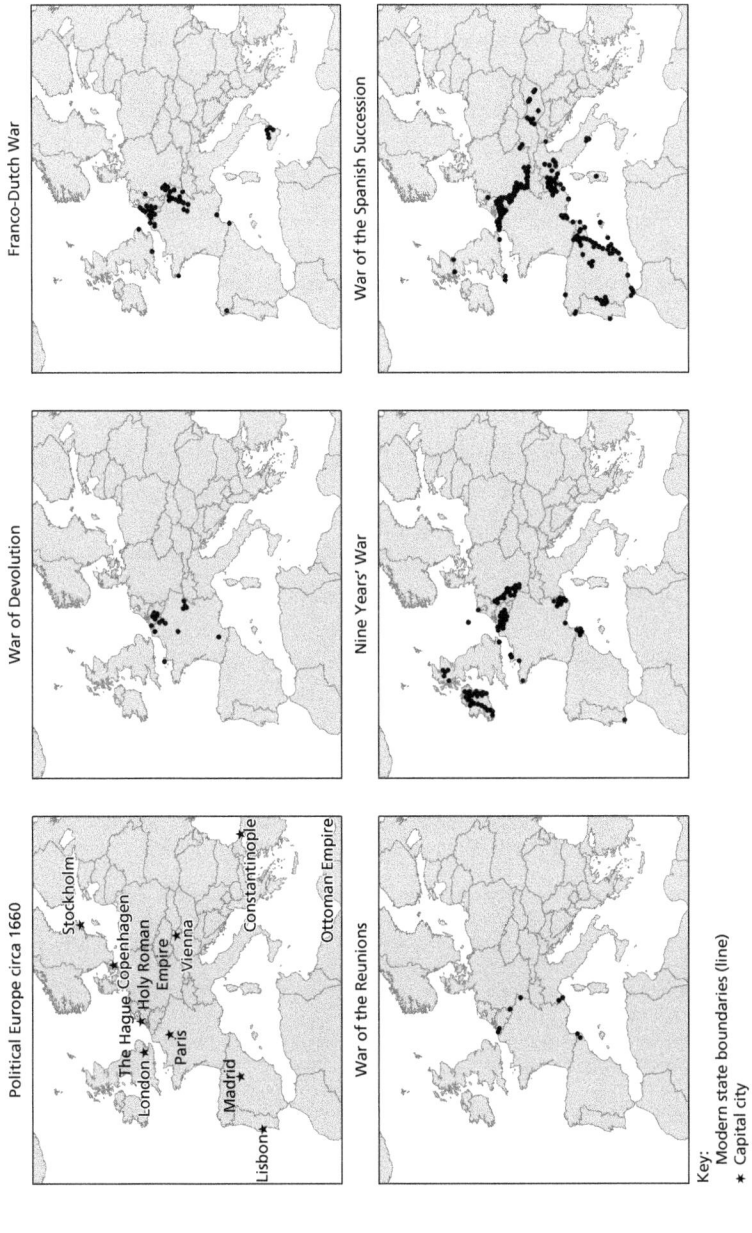

Franco-Dutch War

War of the Spanish Succession

Political Europe circa 1660

Stockholm

The Hague Copenhagen
London ★ ★ Holy Roman
Empire
Paris ★ Vienna ★

Madrid ★

Constantinople ★

Lisbon ★

Ottoman Empire

War of Devolution

Nine Years' War

War of the Reunions

Key:
— Modern state boundaries (line)
★ Capital city
• Military engagement

Map 23.1 The strategies of Louis XIV

Succession (1701–1714).[2] Among these, maps were an increasingly important tool for planning at all levels of war: tactical maps of battles and sieges abound, but also maps of entire theatres, indicating camp locations and march routes, as well as roads, rivers and permanent and field fortifications. Here, too, the SHD's map collection illustrates the growing scope of the Sun King's wars, from a single map preserved from the Devolution War to over 1,000 maps dealing with Louis's last conflict.[3]

These counts, however, only concern official correspondence, planning memoranda and documents in France's main archive for the French Army. Thousands of other documents can be found in numerous other libraries and public and personal archives throughout France.[4] Louis XIV's push to control and standardise military discipline led to innumerable directives on military regulations, as well as the publication of several collections of ordinances late in his reign.[5] The public sphere of Louis XIV's France was far more controlled than that of the Netherlands or England, though many pamphlets and several newspapers gave semi-official accounts of military actions.[6] Military treatises promising to divulge the secrets of the great captains for aspiring officers continued to be published, though it would only be in the later eighteenth century that veterans of the Sun King's last war began to reconceptualise the art of war.[7] Several participants published their memoirs after the war, and others published narratives of the campaigns later in the century, or in the next.[8] Several collections of court correspondence would also be published, and

2 Ministère de la guerre, *Inventaire sommaire des archives historiques (Archives anciennes, correspondance)*, 7 vols (Paris: Imprimerie nationale, 1898); L. Tuetey (ed.), *Catalogue général des manuscrits des bibliothèques publique de France: Archives de la guerre* (Paris: Librarie Plon, 1912).

3 C. Ponnou, M.-A. de Villèle and B. Fonck (eds), *Champs de bataille du Grand Siècle: Catalogue des cartes de l'Atlas historique jusqu'à la fin du règne de Louis XIV* (Paris: Archives et Culture, 2013).

4 Including the archives for the Marine, the Archives nationales, the Bibliothèque nationale de France, the diplomatic Ministère des affaires étrangères, various departmental and municipal archives in the respective theatres of operations, as well as private collections such as the Musée Condé de Chantilly.

5 *Reglemens et ordonnances du Roy pour les gens de guerre*, 15 vols (Paris: chez Frederic Leonard, 1691).

6 Newspapers: *Le Gazette de France*, *Le Mercure galant* and several French-language papers that were smuggled into France, such as the *Mercure historique et politique* and *L'esprit des cours de l'Europe*.

7 A. Manesson Mallet, *Les travaux de Mars, ou l'art de la guerre*, 3 vols (Paris, 1672); L. de Gaya, *L'art de la guerre, et la manière dont on la fait à présent* (Paris: chez Estienne Michalles, 1679).

8 C. S. de Quincy, *Histoire militaire du règne de Louis le Grand, Roy de France, où on trouve un détail de toutes les Batailles, Sièges, Combats particuliers, et généralement de toutes les actions de Guerre qui se sont passées pendant le cours de son Règne*, 7 vols (Paris: D. Mariette, 1726), Volume VIII: *L'art de la guerre ou Maximes et Instructions sur l'art Militaire*; J. S. de Quincy,

provide additional insight into the factional motivations behind various decisions.[9] Surviving fortifications and dozens of contemporary scale models (*les plans-relief*) constructed for Louis provide an important visualisation of the literal control of territory.[10] Many paintings, tapestries, equestrian statues and triumphal arches still exist as well, illustrating the importance of propaganda to Louis's strategic vision.

The Actors

It is not surprising that a king purported to have declared 'I am the State' would seek to monopolise military power within France. Louis XIV was the ultimate authority when it came to matters of war and peace. This control, however, required several generations of royal effort. Both his father, Louis XIII, and his father's prime minister, Cardinal Richelieu, had waged several short wars in the 1620s to subdue semi-autonomous Protestant Huguenots in western and southern France. They also razed the fortifications of noble strongholds and recalcitrant towns within the French interior, decreasing any temptation to revolt against the Crown. Fear of future successional strife was eliminated when a long-awaited heir to the throne, Louis XIV, was finally born in 1638. The heir apparent grew up during the Franco-Spanish War (1635–1659) and lived through a series of civil wars, the Frondes. He was raised for public service, which included education in the military arts. His father died in 1643 and Cardinal Richelieu six months earlier, leaving Louis XIV king at the age of five, under the regency of queen mother Anne of Austria, and Richelieu's successor, Cardinal Mazarin. Parisian crowds and, more importantly, powerful French nobles who commanded Spanish-funded armies against royalist forces in the Frondes threatened his position; several previous French kings had even been assassinated, including Louis's grandfather Henri IV in 1610. War, both internal and external, was central to Louis's childhood experience.

With Mazarin's death in 1661, Louis began his personal rule. The twenty-three-year-old declared that he would be his own chief minister. He continued

Mémoires du chevalier de Quincy (ed. Léon Lecestre), 3 vols (Paris: Librairie Renouard, H. Laurens, successeur, 1898).

9 H. Griffet (ed.), *Recueil de lettres, pour servir d'éclaircissement à l'histoire militaire du regne de Louis XIV*, 8 vols (The Hague and Paris: Antoine Boudet, 1760); Ph.-H. Grimoard (ed.), *Oeuvres de Louis XIV: Mémoires et pièces militaires*, Volumes III–IV (chez Treuttel et Würtz, 1806); F. E. de Vault and J. J. Germain Pelet (eds), *Mémoires militaires relatifs à la succession d'Espagne sous Louis XIV*, 11 vols (Paris: Imprimerie royale, 1835).

10 I. Warmoes, *Le musée des plans-reliefs: Maquettes historiques de villes fortifiées* (Paris: Éds du Patrimoine Centre des monuments nationaux, 2012).

Mazarin's policy of taming the elite nobles (*les grands*) by choosing his other ministers from robe nobles with a history of faithful bureaucratic service. For the entirety of his fifty-four-year reign, he would prioritise personal control over his government, especially regarding military affairs.

Yet as final arbiter of all major strategic decisions, Louis still had to rely upon innumerable assistants for information, advice and implementation. At the Cabinet level, these consisted foremost of the Secretary of State of War, the Secretary of State of the Navy, the Secretary of State of Foreign Affairs (diplomacy), and the controller general of finances. Historically, these positions had been held by powerful nobles and even royal princes, but Louis preferred candidates without independent power bases. He maintained most of the ministers bequeathed to him by Mazarin, who were divided between two competing families, the Le Telliers and the Colberts, although he would also bring in other families to balance these two ministerial dynasties and reorganise departments as he saw fit.

The Le Tellier family rose to dominate the French Army administration through their faithful and efficient service in military administration, the father, Michel, serving in Mazarin's ministry and during the Fronde, with his son François-Michel, the Marquis de Louvois, apprenticing under his father and then gradually taking over his father's role as Secretary of State of War starting in 1672. After Louvois's unexpected death in 1691, Louis continued the Le Tellier bureaucratic dynasty by appointing Louvois's twenty-three-year-old son the Marquis de Barbezieux to the post. Upon Barbezieux's death in 1701, however, Louis ended the Le Tellier ministerial dynasty by promoting his controller general of finances, Michel Chamillart, as Secretary of State of War. After Chamillart's resignation in 1709, Louis appointed one of his wife's favourites, Daniel Voisin, to the position.

During much of Louis's early reign, the Le Tellier clan competed for power and influence with the Colbert family, who controlled both royal finances and the navy. Jean-Baptiste Colbert (*le grand Colbert*) similarly served under Mazarin and was appointed Secretary of State of the Navy in 1662, and his fiscal effectiveness led to Louis appointing him controller-general of finances in 1665. Upon *le grand Colbert's* death in 1683, his son the Marquis de Seignelay was appointed to administer the navy. However, as with the army, Louis chose to prevent too much power and influence accumulating in a single family. Finances were given to Claude Le Pelletier, and upon Seignelay's death in 1690, Louis chose another family to administer the navy, the Phélypeaux de Pontchartrain family, first father Louis and then (in 1699) son Jérôme. Louis also sought to balance the Le Tellier and Colbert factions by dividing up the administration of fortifications within France: Colbert would manage the fortified ports as well as fortresses in the territories of old France (i.e. the interior provinces), while the Le Telliers would administer the fortifications of the recently conquered territories in the north, east and south-east.

Louis's wars were dependent on diplomacy, thus his head of foreign affairs was involved in major discussions of war and peace and was a particularly important source of intelligence. When Mazarin's appointee as Secretary of State of Foreign Affairs, Hugues de Lionne, died in 1671, Louis appointed a candidate from neither the Colbert nor the Le Tellier clan, the Marquis de Pomponne. However, Louis refused to let factional balance overrule talent, and once he became disenchanted with Pomponne's service, he placed *le grand Colbert*'s brother, the Marquis de Croissy, in charge of foreign affairs, and then Croissy's son, the Marquis de Torcy, in 1696.

Discussions of military strategy also required military expertise. Although Louis personally commanded his armies in Flanders from 1667 to 1692, he consistently leaned upon the expertise of more seasoned military men, promoting his favourites to the ultimate military distinction of *maréchal de France*. As with the ministers he inherited from Mazarin, Louis did not immediately create a new military command. The Marshal Turenne was France's towering military figure: he had proved himself one of France's greatest commanders during the Thirty Years War, sided with the royalist cause after a brief flirtation with the *frondeurs*, helped defeat Spain in the Franco-Spanish War, and was one of the young king's primary military tutors. He was elevated to the unique rank of *maréchal général de France*, commanding Louis's armies in the Low Countries and Germany during the War of Devolution and the Franco-Dutch War (1672–1678). But Louis made sure no one would acquire similar influence after Turenne died on the battlefield of Salzbach in 1675. The other dominant French commander of Louis's early reign, Louis II of Bourbon-Condé, Prince of the Blood, had famously defeated the Spanish at the Battle of Rocroi in 1643 and served France ably until he turned against Mazarin during the Fronde. Unlike Turenne, however, he continued in Spanish service for the remainder of the Franco-Spanish War. Louis eventually pardoned him after the Peace of the Pyrenees but would only return *le grand Condé* to military command in 1667. Condé would finally retire for good in 1676.

Louis appointed over fifty generals to be marshals of France over his long reign, though fewer than twenty shared this distinction at any one time.[11] All

---

11 F. El Hage, *Histoire des maréchaux de France à l'époque moderne* (Paris: Ministère de la défense, 2012).

but two came from ancient noble lineage, and all had significant military experience. Several were more noted for their political influence than for their talents in high command, and only eighteen commanded armies in the field. After the death of Turenne and the retirement of *le grand Condé*, the quality of this group declined. Commanders such as Luxembourg, Villars, Vendôme and Berwick all served more successfully than not, and the chief military engineer, Sébastien le Prestre de Vauban, provided expertise on fortifications and siegecraft. Other marshals, such as Tallard, Villeroi, La Feuillade and Marcin, would be responsible for most of Louis's major losses in his last war, leading many observers to rue the influence of court favouritism on the selection process. One of Louis's most important military advisers never acquired, however, the honour of a marshalate. This was the Marquis de Chamlay, who would be promoted to *maréchal général des logis* and was Louis's closest military adviser, particularly after the death of Louvois.

Who Were the Adversaries?

Each major war of Louis's drew in more opponents than the last. Looking across his many conflicts (see Map 23.1), Louis's most immediate, and persistent, enemies were the Spanish Habsburgs, a dynasty formed when Holy Roman Emperor Charles V retired in 1559 and distributed his Austrian dominions to his brother, and his far-flung Spanish holdings to his son. After the end of the Franco-Spanish War, Louis XIV, as the heir to the Bourbon dynasty, married the Spanish Habsburg princess Marie-Thérèse, allowing Louis XIV to eventually claim Spanish territories for their joint descendants when Spanish King Philip IV died in 1665. His young (and sickly) heir Carlos II, Marie-Thérèse's brother, ruled over 7 million subjects living in Castile, Granada, Leon, Aragon, Navarre and Catalonia, as well as in the many dispersed dynastic territories spread throughout the world. Louis, on behalf of his wife, and Carlos contested the inheritance of the fractious border territories of Roussillon (gained by France in 1659) and Catalonia along their shared border. Much of Spain's wealth came from its vast colonial empire, spanning from the south-eastern United States to South America to the Philippines, but Colbert could elicit only mild interest from Louis in the potential of overseas colonies. He had slightly more success convincing Louis to target Spanish ports in the western Mediterranean. More critical to Louis XIV's eye was the ring of isolated Spanish territories surrounding French soil – the Spanish Netherlands in the north, the Spanish duchy of Luxembourg in the north-east, and Franche-Comté to the east. Spain's

Italian territories, particularly the duchy of Milan, also held their appeal for a French king whose court was strongly influenced by Italian culture and numerous émigrés, including his own mentor Mazarin.[12]

The Austrian Habsburgs were another traditional rival of France. Austria's population was large, some 13 million people, and it was a composite monarchy of different polities. Though each ruler of the Holy Roman Empire, an empire with 15 million mostly German-speaking inhabitants, was elected by a college of German electors, Austrian Habsburgs had sat on the imperial throne since the fifteenth century. Their imperial stature gave them the most esteemed throne in Europe, yet due to the complex constitution of the empire, with its multiple checks and balances and representative imperial diet, emperors were forced delicately to navigate the interests of 300 fractious German polities of many different sizes, politics and confessions – principalities, duchies, bishoprics, city states and independent imperial knights, to name a few. The imperial diet (slowly) co-ordinated collective responses to external threats; armies raised to meet them included thousands of troops supplied by semi-independent German rulers, several of whom had their own dynastic territorial interests, including in land bordering on France. Emperors, as a result, had more control over the Austro-imperial armies (*kaiserliche Armeen*) than over the imperial armies (*Reichsarmeen*) ultimately controlled by the imperial diet.[13] Louis XIV never seriously pressed for the imperial crown, though he did portray himself as defender of German liberties against an overbearing Austrian emperor.[14]

The Dutch Republic, or the United Provinces of the Netherlands, was not ordained to become a central pillar of the anti-Louis XIV coalition. This small, highly urbanised state of less than 2 million people had become a commercial maritime power over the course of its eighty-year war of independence from Spain, an independence only formally recognised in 1648. Its central position connecting Continental markets and global trade networks, facilitated by their capture of Iberian colonies across the globe, led to two naval wars with England in the 1650s and 1660s. Thus the Netherlands shared two of France's traditional rivals, and the countries were allied with each other as late as 1667.

12 R. A. Stradling, *Spain's Struggle for Europe, 1598–1668* (London: Hambledon, 1993); C. Storrs, *The Resilience of the Spanish Monarchy 1665–1700* (New York, Oxford University Press, 2006).

13 See Chapter 24 in this volume.

14 D. Tollet (ed.), *Guerres et paix en Europe centrale aux époques moderne et contemporaine: Mélanges d'histoire des relations internationales offerts à Jean Bérenger* (Paris: Presses Paris Sorbonne, 2003).

They were, however, opposites in terms of political centralisation and religious toleration. The context for conflict lies in French expansionism and the Dutch fear of France's growing power along its southern border.[15] Louis's outrage that a 'nation of shopkeepers' whom he had supported in the past would dare to deny him further Spanish conquests in 1667 led to the Franco-Dutch War. Louis's invasion of Holland facilitated the rise of William III of Orange as de facto ruler within the Netherlands and forged a permanent enmity with the Dutch stadholder general.

Across the English Channel lay another long-time French foe, England. These two had a long history of conflict. For much of the seventeenth century, however, the two countries shared a hatred of the Spanish Habsburg hegemon. Charles II and his brother and successor James II both outed themselves as Catholics (the former wisely only on his deathbed). Through their mother, Henrietta Maria, they were grandsons of King Henri IV of France. These attributes made an alliance with their cousin Louis XIV a logical one, though domestically unpopular in England. The Glorious Revolution of 1688, initiated by James II's unpopularity and assisted by a Dutch invasion fleet, saw the overthrow of James and overturned the diplomatic landscape in the process. Now William III of Orange was not only the stadholder general of the Dutch United Provinces, but also William III king of England, Scotland and Ireland, courtesy of his marriage to Mary Stuart, James II's eldest Protestant daughter. Louis would continue to support, to his mind, the legitimate English Stuart ruler, but William's successes in the three kingdoms meant that by 1691 it was he, not Louis's ally, who controlled the wealthy English state's fiscal–military apparatus and ruled over its 6 million inhabitants. Louis would continue to support the claims of James II, then his son James III, from their French court in exile, even after William's death and the succession of Queen Anne.

France's geostrategic situation was also complicated by a variety of small to middling powers in its orbit. The Papal Comtat Venaissin (and its capital, Avignon) and the Principality of Orange were enclaves in southern France and were occupied multiple times. France also bordered fragmented imperial territories like the Archbishopric of Liège, the Palatinate of the Rhine, independent states like the Duchy of Lorraine, and dynastic conglomerations like Savoy–Piedmont in the western Alps. All these territories offered opportunities for an ambitious monarch like Louis XIV to win renown and expand his frontiers, but also drew in more distant powers.

---

15 See Chapter 25 in this volume.

Causes and Objectives of the Wars

The causes of war are both personal and systemic, predetermined and contingent. Contemporaries pointed to the inherent sinfulness of mankind and God's use of war to chastise the guilty, while almost all branches of Christianity recognised the possibility of just war. With a sense of entitlement, monarchs referred to war as the legitimate 'last argument of kings'. Modern historians begin their explanation with culture, specifically a pan-European political and social culture which gave individual monarchs personal dynastic claims to territory, gave them the ability to unilaterally declare war and peace, and gave them nobles who saw their own legitimation in waging war, all of whom acted within a culture of pervasive, violent masculinity that was only gradually being tamed.

At a diplomatic level, most of the wars of the early modern period involved questions of territorial control, and this usually came to the fore upon the death of the previous sovereign. Overlapping jurisdictions between rulers' territories led an earlier generation of scholars to argue that both Louis XIII and Louis XIV sought to acquire 'natural frontiers' for France, anchored on natural barriers such as the Rhine river. More recently, focus has been placed on dynasticism, and Louis's obsession to defend every ounce of his territory. The drive to defend and expand one's family holdings at all costs, the varying rules for succession in different territories, the frequency of diplomatic marriages, and the randomness of royal deaths that end royal lines, all combined with patchwork territories to create a multitude of points at which competing claims could be raised.

Thus most of Louis XIV's wars were wars of succession, usually pitting the rising Bourbon contestant against the declining Spanish Habsburgs. The long conflict between France and Spain had ended, at least officially, at the Peace of the Pyrenees in 1659, and was sealed with a diplomatic marriage intertwining the Bourbon and Spanish Habsburg houses. France won recognition of its gains from the Treaty of Westphalia, as well as the northern province of Artois, parts of Luxembourg and several towns in Flanders, in addition to Roussillon in the south-east. Louis XIV's wars involved the remaining Spanish territories encircling France. Louis's struggle with England from 1688 onward also encompassed the question whether the Williamite or Jacobite successors would sit on the British thrones.

At the level of individual behaviour, Louis XIV was one of the primary causes of his wars, the inevitable result of his repeated, unilateral aggressions. It was doubtful that a young French king, seeking *gloire* (reputation) and

thirsting for military action, would remain satisfied hearing about the victories of his elders.[16] Almost as soon as Louis took personal charge, he illustrated
his belligerent quest for *gloire* by threatening war against Spain and then
Rome over skirmishes with his diplomats. He sought military glory as his
fleet campaigned against the Barbary corsairs in Algeria, sent troops to fight
against the Terrible Turk in defence of Vienna, and marched a small army to
aid the Dutch against the Bishop of Münster, while his Atlantic fleet assisted
the Netherlands in the Second Anglo-Dutch War. All this by the fifth year of
his reign. When Philip IV died in 1665, Louis set his diplomats and jurists to
reinterpret local inheritance laws to apply to his wife's claims over a broad
range of Spanish territories. His surprising military success against the
Spanish in the War of Devolution quickly led to a Triple Alliance against
him to stop his further conquests. In turn, the Sun King expanded his list of
enemies by turning against one of these alliance members, the Netherlands.
Further military successes in 1672 led to an even larger coalition against
France. After the Treaty of Nijmegen ended this Franco-Dutch War, he
continued his aggressions in the 1680s against Spanish territories through
the reunions, while technically at peace.[17] He ordered his regional law courts
to form 'chambers of reunion' and unilaterally determine which foreign
territories in Lorraine, Alsace and Franche-Comté should be added to
France. He blockaded and besieged Spanish Luxembourg and bribed his
way to possession of the Italian fortress of Casale, violating the sovereignty
of Savoy lands in the process. This was hardly the way to reassure other states
of his pacific intent, particularly when he extended his reunions into the
kaleidoscope of German states along the Rhine and seized the strategically
important but neutral city of Strasbourg in 1681. The premeditated decision
to burn to the ground dozens of Rhenish towns in 1688–1689, while horrify-
ing, did not terrify the rest of Europe into submission and only increased the
number of states willing to join the League of Augsburg against France. And
after negotiating two treaties to partition the Spanish succession (without
involving the Austrian claimant), Louis then chose to accept Carlos II's will in
1700, which offered the entirety of the Spanish monarchy to his grandson.
Though Louis had realpolitik reasons for this decision, it further undermined
trust in negotiations. Worse, he then aggravated the Maritime Powers,
whom French diplomats had tried to keep neutral, with a whole series of
alarming decisions. He recognised James III as the true king of England over

16 'Gloire', in L. Bély (ed.), *Dictionnaire Louis XIV* (Paris: Bouquins, 2015), 572–3.
17 B. Jeanmougin, *Louis XIV à la conquête des Pays-Bas espagnols: La guerre oubliée (1678–1684)*
(Paris: Economica, 2005).

William III and then William's successor Queen Anne; he gave the monopoly of the Spanish slave trade to French merchants; he declared that his grandson – now Philip V of Spain – would not renounce his claims to the French throne; and he occupied the Spanish Netherlands and briefly imprisoned the Dutch troops who had been garrisoning in their Spanish barrier fortresses as a surety against French aggression. Time and again, the Sun King threatened war, negotiated in seeming bad faith, and refused to moderate his dynastic principles when a royal death presented another opportunity.

Other factors played their part in shaping Louis's wars, including religion. Although confessional differences as drivers for war had diminished by 1648, confessional hatred and mistrust lingered and came to the fore when they could reinforce other quarrels, including distrust between clergy loyal to the papacy and those more loyal to the monarch and 'gallicanism', the concept of a national French church controlled by the monarch, not by the Pope from afar. Most importantly, Louis's revocation of the Edict of Nantes, and the subsequent flight of more than 100,000 Huguenots from France, encouraged pan-Protestant anti-Louisquatorzianism as Huguenot refugees spread tales of Louis's barbarism, and offered the promise of a religious fifth column just waiting for a co-confessional invasion force. These refugees included thousands of French Huguenot soldiers, though their numbers were likely offset by Irish Catholics fleeing Williamite Ireland after 1691. Louis was flexible enough to support other confessions against his Catholic opponent, as when he encouraged Protestant Hungarians revolting against Austrian rule. In a similar vein, France had traditionally supported the Ottoman Turks, Muslims, against their Catholic Austrian rival. Here too, however, Louis's diplomatic relations with the Turks varied according to the situation: he briefly supported Vienna against an Ottoman invasion in 1663–1664, supported the relief attempt of the Turkish siege of Candia (Crete) in 1669, and also fought against Muslim Barbary corsairs in the 1660s and 1680s. More often, however, he encouraged the Ottoman sultans to attack Austrian lands, and sought to take military advantage of Austrian distraction in the east.

Finally, while we should not dismiss the importance of economic motivations in Louis XIV's wars, Louis clearly considered them subordinate to *gloire* and to his dynastic claims. Louis's wars were devastating to the royal fisc – the Franco-Dutch War destroyed the economic reforms Colbert had instituted, and each year of war required more fiscal exigencies that further weakened the Crown vis-à-vis its creditors. Through careful management and fiscal reforms, *le grand Colbert* had managed to whittle down some 450 million livres in royal debt to 250 million. By the end of the Sun King's many wars, Louis bequeathed to his great-grandson a royal debt of 2 billion livres, forty times the Crown's annual disposable revenues.[18] Fiscally, Louis's wars were a losing proposition for the Crown.

Ever the opportunist, Louis occupied and annexed territories in both wartime and peacetime, and not just Spanish territory. After searching for *gloire* in several one-off adventures, his major wars began with discrete Spanish territories on his northern frontier. But he quickly expanded his sights: no more than a few years of peace would pass between one treaty and the commencement of another conflict. After conquering his neighbours' territories, he then shifted to what he considered preventive and defensive wars, in which he embraced military coercion and occupation during periods of 'peace' and against neutral powers. By the late 1680s Louis has blustered, bullied and besieged himself into a corner, having convinced most of western and central Europe that he was an existential threat to European peace.

The Available Means

And yet, despite fighting much of western Europe for the last twenty-five years of his reign, Louis XIV was still able to pass a larger France on to his successor. That he was able to ward off invasion along his northern frontier until 1708, and retain so many of his conquests, is evidence of the resources he could extract from the French people. Economically, France benefited from a varied and fertile agricultural landscape, making it relatively self-sufficient in times of peace, with different parts of the country interacting with distinct economic regions of Europe. France's large territorial extent was mirrored by a similarly large population, though this was concentrated in the northern half of the country. With a population of approximately 18 million to 19 million people, its demographics dwarfed the other states of Europe. To draw on these resources, however, Louis XIV relied on an inefficient system of taxation which largely exempted the wealthiest members of French society. Colbert attempted to promote self-sufficiency in manufacturing and a surplus of exports, but his efforts to rationalise the tax system were short-circuited by Louis's wars, which required deficit spending and greater reliance on inefficient fiscal mechanisms such as selling venal offices as property and farming out tax collection. Yet given the large population and resources,

18 G. Rowlands, *The Financial Decline of a Great Power: War, Influence, and Money in Louis XIV's France* (Oxford: Oxford University Press, 2012), 236.

as well as the ability to convince the noble officer corps to subsidise his armies from their own pockets, even an inefficient fiscal regime allowed him to overmatch any other European power, and resist European coalitions for several decades. He was able to continue waging his wars, albeit at much reduced levels, even during two famines in 1693–1694 and 1709, which collectively led to the deaths of 1.5 million French subjects.

Half to four-fifths of the royal budget paid for war. Approximately 80 per cent of this money went to his primary military tool, the royal army.[19] The bulk of the forces were infantry, initially divided between pikemen and musketeers; French units gradually converted from pike to flintlock musket and bayonet, though this process was only completed in the first decade of the eighteenth century. The remaining troops were either cavalry, armed primarily with pistol and sword, or specialised troops like dragoons and grenadiers. Some fighters were mobile, lightly armed troops who, along with irregulars, were primarily responsible for devastating enemy lands as a form of economic attrition. Altogether, these units numbered some 60,000 men in 1661, but quickly rose to 135,000 for the War of Devolution, still short of the peak reached in the previous reign. Louis's ministers managed to regulate their finances and rationalise the administration of the troops so that by the time of the Franco-Dutch War, the French Army numbered a record 280,000 men on paper. After the Treaty of Nijmegen this number dropped to approximately 150,000 men, but this was similarly unprecedented for a French 'peacetime' force, and Louis would manage to maintain this sizeable standing army throughout the rest of his reign.[20] The expanded scope of the Nine Years War (1688–1697) led to France's peak manpower effort, some 420,000 theoretical effectives, though he was only able to arm some 380,000 men at the peak of the War of the Spanish Succession, in part by drafting local militia into the line army. Throughout his reign, about 70 per cent of these troops were raised within France, while the rest either came from mercenary states like the Swiss Confederation, or were émigré regiments like the Irish Brigade and the Wild Geese. These troops relied on black-powder artillery that had been refined over the previous century, while many of these troops would spend significant parts of their career garrisoning the many fortresses

---

19 R. Martin, 'The army of Louis XIV', in P. Sonnino (ed.), *The Reign of Louis XIV*, repr. (Atlantic Highlands: Humanities Press, 1991), 111–26.

20 J. Lynn, 'Revisiting the great fact of war and Bourbon absolutism: the growth of the French Army during the grand siècle', in E. García Hernán and D. Maffi (eds), *Guerra y Sociedad en la Monarquía Hispánica : Política, Estrategia y Cultura en la Europa Moderna (1500–1703)*, Volume 1 (Madrid: Editorial CSIC, 2006), 49–74.

constructed by Louis's corps of engineers, led by Vauban. Over the course of his fifty-year career, Louis's *commissaire général des fortifications* oversaw the construction or renovation of 170 fortified places all around France's borders.

Modern French monarchs had generally taken a greater interest in affairs on the European continent, rather than overseas.[21] Although France had more than 3,000 miles of coastline, its harbours tended to silt up. Only Francis I's harbour at the mouth of the Seine (Le Havre) was proximate to Paris. France's main naval bases in Brittany, Aquitaine and the Mediterranean were much more distant from the capital and its interests.[22] The primary naval facilities at Brest and Toulon faced the Atlantic and the Mediterranean respectively; combining the two fleets required circumnavigating the Spanish peninsula, which took time. French royal spending on its fleet never came close to rivalling army expenditures, averaging only 15 per cent of extraordinary military spending throughout the period, peaking at 20 per cent in 1695.[23] Nevertheless, continuing in the tradition of Cardinal Richelieu, celebrated as the founder of the modern French Navy, Colbert sought to develop the country's naval infrastructure and increase the size of the French battle fleet, notably ships of the line. In 1665 Louis had inherited some thirty-two such ships, which amounted to only a third of those available to England. By 1670, Colbert's construction programme had resulted in some eighty-four vessels, rivalling England's smaller fleet, and by 1675 French ships of the line outnumbered its nearest competitor by a quarter. Colbert's son and the Phélypeaux father-and-son duo continued to maintain and even increase these numbers, peaking at 119 vessels in 1695. This outpaced Dutch construction, but the French were unable to match the pace of English shipbuilding, and from 1700 onward the French battle fleet declined in size relative to the expanding Royal Navy.

For Louis, diplomacy was foremost a tool to prepare for war and facilitate his conquests. French agents gathered intelligence, while his diplomats sought to forestall potential (or dismantle real) enemy coalitions, to intimidate and bribe other powers, to distract his immediate enemies with diversions on other fronts, and to recruit middling powers to ally with him. Notably, the Sun King was unable, or unwilling, to groom any ally beyond

21 G. W. Symcox, 'The navy of Louis XIV', in Sonnino, *The Reign of Louis XIV*, 127–42; Daniel Dessert, *La Royale: Vaisseaux et marins du Roi Soleil* (Paris: Fayard, 1996).
22 G. Rowlands, 'Moving Mars: the logistical geography of Louis xiv's France', *French History*, 25:4 (2011), 492–514.
23 Olivier Chaline, *Les armées du roi: Le grand chantier* xviie–xviiie *siècle* (Paris: Armand Colin, 2016), 112–13, 181.

a single war, unlike his opponent William III. His inattention to the concerns of traditional allies, such as the Netherlands and Sweden, led to their disengagement from the French interest. Nevertheless, the well-trained French corps of diplomats served as a force multiplier: every agreement meant, at least for a time, one less enemy, or one less front to fight on, or one more strategic option, or one more provider of mercenary troops.

The Process of Prioritisation

For Louis XIV, the process of prioritising resources and objectives meant balancing spending on competing strategic resources (diplomacy, armies, navies and fortifications), as well as deciding which enemy to focus on, in which theatres of operations to conduct operations, and which military strategies to pursue. For all these, Versailles was the centre of military planning, particularly as the scope of France's wars grew and the king retired from active campaigning. The king, the Secretary of State of War, close royal advisers and the most trusted marshals spent the winter months planning future military operations, relying upon information provided by the various ministerial departments, collectively drawing upon their experience and upon projects submitted by a wide range of correspondents. Individual ministers recruited their own sources of intelligence, for information was valuable in the inter-ministerial competition for the king's ear. Military commanders and officers would also pass locally acquired information up the chain of command. The minister of foreign affairs provided the background of diplomatic developments and the latest (though still stale) intelligence from abroad. Military veterans were sometimes appointed to diplomatic posts, allowing them to provide a military judgement of the preparedness of their host country, and agents might be sent to reconnoitre potential routes and targets. Finances reported the latest estimates on royal income and expenditures. The Secretary of State of War was obviously at the centre of all discussions, and for missions involving a maritime component the Secretary of State of the Marine informed the king of the status of his navy and its capabilities. The Cabinet relied not only on its combined knowledge of the state of France and its enemies, but also on the unique experiences of various marshals in different theatres.[24] Befitting an absolute monarch, Louis and his innermost circle were the only ones to have the whole plan in mind,

---

24 L. Bély, *Les secrets de Louis XIV: Mystères d'État et pouvoir absolu* (Paris: Éditions Tallandier, 2013), 311–18; J.-Ph. Cénat, *Chamlay: Le stratège secret de Louis XIV* (Paris: Belin, 2011).

and as the campaigns unfolded, his military Cabinet, the centre of incoming information and outgoing orders, alone could see the forest for the trees – each theatre commander played a part in a much larger game.

Attendance at the *conseil d'en haut*, the council where the highest level of grand strategy was discussed, was solely at the king's discretion. Louis often excluded powerful military commanders from these meetings, so only the Secretaries of State of War, the Navy and Foreign Affairs were consistently invited, each defending their own and their department's perspectives and interests; bureaucratic politics was fully developed even then. These Cabinet ministers would naturally host numerous other meetings with their subordinates and peers, and Louis would individually meet with various stakeholders to gain information and advice. The actual application of such centralised decisions, however, required a much more complicated discussion, conducted across hundreds of miles and months of campaigning.

Louis and his Cabinet created and maintained the infrastructure necessary for war. They ordered the beginning of wars, and then prioritised theatres and provided plans for initial operations. Once a campaign began, however, Louis and his Secretaries generally recognised that the military commander on the scene had to take control. Louvois's domineering personality led to frequent attempts to micromanage military operations after the death of Turenne in 1675 through the reunions. But the Secretary of State of War's death in 1691 led to a loosening of *dictats* from court, which were replaced with even more lengthy lists of proposals. Theatre commanders were constantly reminded that they had the ultimate say, that all the plans and projects sent them from Versailles were only suggestions, though it was expected that they would explain their operational reasoning to the king. The result was that weak commanders would delay and keep asking for confirmation and clarification, while strong-willed commanders would often explain why Versailles's preferred option was too difficult to implement. Distance also influenced the degree of independence: in Iberia and Italy, there was no practical possibility of effective *guerre de cabinet* (cabinet war) since communication took a week or more in one direction. In Flanders and along the Rhine, a message might still require two to three days to deliver. Even when Louis took a more assertive approach after the War of the Spanish Succession turned increasingly desperate, he ultimately refused to dictate specific courses of action. In 1708, he went so far as to send Secretary Chamillart to the front to insist on attacking the Allied besieger's siege lines in order to prevent the fall of Lille. Chamillart's report convinced Louis that such an attempt was out of the question, and Louis backed down. Similarly in 1712, a desperate Louis pushed Marshal Villars to attack the enemy's main force in Flanders, but was forced to accept Villars's less risky attack on a large Dutch detachment at Denain.

At the broadest scale, Louis consistently prioritised his land forces over his naval forces, and terrestrial targets over enemy battle fleets. Colbert's and Seignelay's naval build-up allowed France to punch above its weight for a time, but this could not be sustained when France fought the Maritime Powers at the same time as it fought on land. French fleets, with ships in the North Sea, the English Channel, the Atlantic, the Caribbean and the Mediterranean, fought fewer than twenty battles against enemy ships over forty years of war.

The Execution / Application of Strategy

Looking across the wars of Louis XIV, certain strategic patterns emerge, even as the number of enemies and theatres of operation increased over time.[25] His monopolisation of military force within France meant that all his wars, except for a Huguenot uprising in the Cévennes between 1702 and 1704, were fought at or beyond his borders. The centralisation of diplomatic and military decision making within his hands meant that he could co-ordinate France's pre-war preparations against weak enemies in relative secrecy. The result was initial blitzkrieg campaigns at the outset of each war: 1667 in the Spanish Netherlands, 1668 and 1674 in Franche-Comté, 1672 in the Dutch Netherlands, 1683–1684 in Luxembourg and Alsace, 1688 along the Rhine, and the bloodless occupation of Spanish territories in 1701. Starting with the Franco-Dutch War, however, these rapid conquests quickly expanded into coalition wars of attrition. France's enemies eventually learned to match French military preparations, and formerly neutral powers joined growing anti-French coalitions once the French threat incontrovertibly manifested itself. This quickly resulted in more opponents for France and more contested theatres. By the Nine Years War, France fought almost alone against the rest of western and central Europe.

Although Louis's troops campaigned in over a dozen different theatres across his reign, the four main theatres were in Europe: the Low Countries, Germany, northern Italy and Iberia. While the exact prioritisation of theatre armies varied for any given campaign year, top priority was consistently

25 J. Lynn, 'A quest for glory: the formation of strategy under Louis XIV, 1661–1715', in W. Murray, M. Knox and A. Bernstein (eds), *The Making of Strategy: Rulers, States, and War* (Cambridge: Cambridge University Press, 1994), 178–204.

given to the theatres closest to Paris, and those under Spanish sovereignty. This meant the Low Countries foremost. Its fertile plains, dense population, economic development, lack of topographical obstructions and multitude of rivers running south–north all facilitated the maintenance of large field armies, some eventually numbering 100,000 troops. Plentiful grain and easy transport also allowed the massing of powerful artillery parks for large-scale siege warfare. Louis's long-term strategic priorities can, in fact, be approximated by the degree to which he fortified each part of his frontier. Vauban spent the 1670s–1690s shoring up the northern border, constructing the *pré carré*, a double line of twenty-seven fortresses stretching from the English Channel to the Ardennes. Overall, a third of Vauban's defensive projects defended the 400-mile border with the Spanish Netherlands.[26]

Next came the German theatre, where a jumble of imperial statelets and the Rhine river offered enticing opportunities for French expansion from 1673 onward. Here, Louis ordered Vauban to construct or renovate fortresses in an attempt to control passage across the Rhine, including at Philippsburg, Landau, Haguenau, Strasbourg and Alt- and Neuf-Brisach. France's 1702 alliance with Bavaria, and an Allied invasion of the Bavarian heartland in 1704, were the exception to this theatre's general Rhenish focus.

Apart from a Sicilian expedition in the 1670s, Louis's forces only engaged in Italy beginning in the Nine Years War, with fortification projects accelerating in the 1680s at Grenoble, Briançon, Mont-Dauphin and Antibes. Indecisive fighting in northern Italy during the Nine Years War gave way in the next war to brief French dominance after they occupied the lands of their erstwhile Savoy ally. The failed Bourbon siege of Turin in 1706, however, quickly led to the collapse of Bourbon positions and an Austria-dominated peninsula, though the Allies were unable to penetrate into French Provence after failing to capture Toulon the next year.

The least active of the four primary theatres was Iberian Spain. Other than the Catalonian border, it was only when his grandson took the Spanish throne that Louis sent French troops to fully engage in the theatre. Portugal's declaration of war against the Bourbons in 1703 opened a front along the arid Hispano-Portuguese border, while landings led to the Allied capture of Gibraltar (1704), and the rapid occupation of Catalonia and Valencia in 1706. With the assistance of the population, Philip V's forces would eventually expel Anglo-Dutch–imperial invaders from Spanish soil. Throughout the war, however, Louis held the Iberian theatre at arm's length – he could not control his

---

26 P. Griffith, *The Vauban Fortifications of France* (Oxford: Osprey Publishing, 2006), 13–20.

grandson or the Spanish grandees. He withdrew French troops from the theatre when pressed in the north, and even considered withdrawing financial support from his grandson when attempting to negotiate a peace with the Allies invading his northern frontier.

While the Flanders and German theatres received the bulk of Louis's attention, he also frequently ordered units to shift from one theatre to another. Success in the Low Countries might lead Louis to detach units to Germany once further Flanders conquests seemed unlikely, as in 1668 and 1673. However, as these conflicts ground on, Louis increasingly feared his ability to win a long war against the Austrian–imperial–Dutch–English alliance. In 1693 he abandoned his generally cautious approach of attacking in one theatre and remaining on the defensive in others. He ordered his commanders on three of the four fronts to go on the offensive, to convince them that France was still strong and encourage them to negotiate a peace.[27] But French battlefield victories at Landen/Neerwinden and Marsaglia, and the capture of several fortresses in multiple theatres, could not end the war, and it would drag on into 1697. In 1706, Louis gambled yet again, ordering his commanders in all four theatres to attack the enemy and shock them into negotiations. This time, the result was catastrophic. In Flanders, Villeroi offered battle and was utterly defeated at Ramillies – almost the entirety of the Spanish Netherlands surrendered to Allied forces within a few months. In the wake of Ramillies, the Duke of Vendôme was ordered to march from northern Italy to reinforce Flanders. Soon after, the Bourbon siege of Turin was broken by Prince Eugene of Savoy, and French forces were forced to evacuate all of Italy by year's end. Nevertheless, French troops consolidated their armies around their fortified borders, and with a shorter perimeter to defend, fought on for another eight years.

As these wars morphed into wars of attrition, as his army sizes grew beyond the capacity of royal coffers, and as his borders expanded, Louis increasingly struggled even to maintain his territory and his troops under arms. To make war pay for war, Louis occupied enemy and neutral territories on France's borders to pay for his own forces and weaken those of his enemies, often without declaring outright annexation.[28] He had already used military occupation against papal Avignon, Orange and Franche-Comté in the 1660s, and would use it in Lorraine, Luxembourg, parts of Alsace, Savoy,

27 R. Martin, '1693: the year of battles', *Proceedings of the Western Society for French History*, 31 (2003), 84–102.
28 Ph. McCluskey, *Absolute Monarchy on the Frontiers: Louis xiv's Military Occupations of Lorraine and Savoy* (Manchester: Manchester University Press, 2013).

Nice and the Spanish Netherlands as well. Perhaps because so many neighbouring regions were forced to host French troops for year after year, through war and peace, there was no consistent policy of occupation, other than to ensure that the inhabitants would pay for their occupation, and to create a buffer zone to protect French lands. In many cases, France would have to return these occupied lands at the peace, though not before destroying their fortifications and confiscating their arsenals. In almost every case, Louis would return to occupy them again in the next war. In several cases, they would be permanently annexed to the kingdom of France.

Enemy lands that were not occupied could still be devastated. Targeting enemy property and civilian inhabitants had been a constant of war for millennia, though the later phase of the Thirty Years War had witnessed some moderation with the conversion of outright devastation into a system of contributions, which avoided the inefficient destruction of resources and instead regularised it as a war tax. Throughout the Sun King's reign, Louis's armies demanded monetary contributions and requisitioned supplies on the spot, accounting for up to 20 per cent of an army's maintenance cost. French armies also ordered small parties of troops to devastate enemy lands as a form of economic attrition against the enemy's tax base, as a logistical attack on an enemy army's ability to feed itself, and as an attempt to terrorise the enemy population into submission. The Spanish Netherlands was repeatedly raided and plundered throughout the entire reign, Brussels was bombarded in 1695, there were widespread raids on Savoy during the Nine Years War, and rebellious areas of France's Cévennes region were also intentionally ruined during the Camisard revolt.[29] The devastation of the Palatinate was initially intended to shock the German Rhenish states into recognising the reunions, but once this failed, Louis and Louvois personally insisted on the utter destruction of dozens of towns. While Louis XIV's France was not the only combatant to explicitly pursue a policy to 'make the people cry out', as Louvois put it, it did so with a consistency and determination that made it stand out from its peers.

As the number of the Sun King's enemies grew, he increasingly sought to create as many diversions for them as possible. This put his diplomatic corps to good use, as French agents fomented distractions on other fronts. The Ottoman Porte was encouraged to fight along the Danube against Austria, and then French support shifted to Hungarian Protestant rebels under Ferenc

---

29 J.-Ph. Cénat, 'Le ravage du Palatinat: Politique de destruction, stratégie de cabinet et propagande au début de la guerre de la Ligue d'Augsbourg', *Revue historique*, 633:1 (2005), 97–132.

II Rákóczi, after the Ottomans signed the humbling peace of Karlowitz in 1699. French support for James II in Ireland and Scotland was largely an attempt to bog down William in the British Isles. Similarly, French diplomats tried to convince Sweden's Charles XII to attack Brandenburg–Prussia after his successes against Saxony, Poland and Russia, in hopes that German mercenary providers would be forced to withdraw their troops from western Europe. With so few allies, the French were not nearly as susceptible to this strategy, although the Allies did distract France by raiding and bombarding French ports.

The tactical glue which held Louis's military strategy together was positional warfare, which revolved around not the clash of armies in the open field, but the capture and control of bastioned fortifications. Louis never personally fought in a field battle, though he later regretted not doing so when he had the opportunity in 1676. He did, however, construct a network of fortifications around his borders, and plan and oversee dozens of sieges throughout his reign. These operations required detailed logistical planning (perfect for cabinet war), were generally successful, and usually entailed less risk than field battle. When a third or more of a theatre's forces were in garrison, fortresses served as force multipliers, blocking uncontested enemy advances by threatening supply lines, and could even delay a victorious foe for days or weeks. They also facilitated shifting troops between theatres and served as centres of occupation as well as bases from which raiding parties could devastate nearby enemy lands. The operational tempo of each theatre, and of regions within each theatre, was therefore largely defined by its fortification density. Flanders, the Rhine, Catalonia and northern Italy were all heavily fortified, and most of these campaigns revolved around sieges, occurring twice as often as field battles. Even when Louis's enemies defeated him in battle, his fortresses quickly blunted the enemy advance, and Louis would continue to fight on until exhaustion led to peace.

At sea, many of Louis's wars were fought over convoys, and few involved both sides' main battle fleets. French vessels in home waters primarily supported land operations, while all sides engaged in commerce raiding (*guerre de course*) against merchantmen. Once England and the Netherlands became enemies, the primary mission of France's two battle fleets consisted of defending the French coasts, though the strategic impact of a few dozen Allied amphibious descents against French territory was limited as much by the inherent limitations of the age of sail as by French defences. Louis's fleets had mixed success with their own descents, successfully landing James II and his supporters in Ireland in 1689 but failing to ignite a Jacobite uprising in

Scotland in 1708.[30] Most full-scale battles at sea were tactically indecisive, but the loss of a dozen ships of the line at La Hogue in 1692 and the famine of 1693–1694 led Louis to shift from direct confrontation back to commerce raiding. An attempt to dominate the Mediterranean, in conjunction with the Bourbon Spanish fleet, was checked at Málaga in 1704, and the Allied siege of the port of Toulon three years later forced the French to scuttle their Levant fleet in the harbour. Once again, Louis turned to sole reliance on a strategy of economic warfare at sea.

Historiographical Debates

The exact nature of Louis's military absolutism has been one of the more contentious historiographical issues over the past several decades. Guy Rowlands has argued that the military behemoth of Louis's late reign was made possible by the Crown's accommodation of the fiscal and familial interests of his noble officer corps,[31] while Hervé Drévillon has argued instead that Louis created a culture of honorable public service to entice his nobles into financial and physical sacrifices.[32] Both arguments reflect the increasing realisation that fiscal–military states, and the public–private partnerships undergirding them, were needed to sustain European states' largest enterprise, war.

Historians have long debated how much control Louis XIV actually exercised over his armies in the field, whether or not France conducted a cabinet war. Earlier stereotypes of an absolute monarch dictating individual army marches to all theatres has been abandoned along with other fictions of dictatorial rule. In its place, scholars have recognised the same process of negotiation between Crown and subjects, adjusted by context and personalities, that describes Louis's internal policies.[33]

The costs of war, who exactly paid them and the degree of control over troops also reflect a long-standing debate over how limited these military campaigns were. Historians have debated the issue for literally centuries,

---

30 G. Rowlands, 'The king's two arms: French amphibious warfare in the Mediterranean under Louis XIV, 1664 to 1697', in M. C. Fissel and D. J. B. Trim (eds), *Amphibious Warfare 1000–1700* (Leiden: Brill, 2006), 263–314.

31 G. Rowlands, *The Dynastic State and the Army under Louis XIV: Royal Service and Private Interest 1661–1701* (Cambridge: Cambridge University Press, 2002).

32 H. Drévillon, *L'impôt du sang: Le métier des armes sous Louis XIV* (Paris: Éditions Tallandier, 2005).

33 J.-Ph. Cénat, 'Le roi et la guerre', in Jean-Christian Petitfils (ed.), *Le siècle de Louis XIV* (Paris: Le Figaro histoire/Perrin, 2015), 372–91.

with recent historians both contesting the 'limited' nature of eighteenth-century warfare and questioning the 'total' nature of the Revolutionary and Napoleonic wars. As Louis's reliance on devastation and bombardment suggests, wars for politically limited objectives did not necessarily entail humanitarian concern for civilian populations.[34]

Conclusion

Louis XIV may indeed have 'loved war too much', as he is purported to have confessed on his deathbed. The military victories of his early reign fed his identification with the rising sun. His brilliance reached its apex in the 1680s, and his rise inevitably led to a reaction that led in turn to the decline of his fortunes over the second half of his reign – a fitting completion of the cyclical rising and setting of the sun. Throughout his reign, he consistently pursued a policy of territorial expansion against his neighbours, a goal perfectly matched by his combination of attritional tactics, positional warfare and systematic fortification. Whether the results were worth the price to France and the French people is up for debate, but one rarely questions the motivations of the sun.

---

34 B. Heuser, *War: A Genealogy of Western Ideas and Practices* (Oxford: Oxford University Press, 2022), 39 ff.

24

Hohenzollern Strategy under Frederick II

ADAM L. STORRING[*]

Introduction

King Frederick II ('Frederick the Great', r. 1740–1786) was perhaps the most notable of Brandenburg–Prussia's soldier-monarchs, doubling the size of his realm during his reign. Within months of his accession in 1740, Frederick took advantage of the weakness of the Austrian Habsburg Empire on the death of Emperor Charles VI to invade and occupy the wealthy Austrian province of Silesia, helping to touch off the broader War of the Austrian Succession (1740–1748). Having secured most of Silesia through the First Silesian War (1740–1742), Frederick fought the Second Silesian War (1744–1745) and then the Seven Years War (1756–1763) – also called the Third Silesian War – to hold onto his gain. In the latter conflict, Frederick avoided defeat in spite of facing a coalition of Austria, France, Russia, Sweden and the Holy Roman Empire. In 1772, he was able to take part in the First Partition of Poland along with Austria and Russia, gaining West Prussia as a land bridge between East Prussia and his core territories. Having altered the status quo to his advantage, Frederick then worked to maintain it, fighting the War of the Bavarian Succession (1778–1779) to prevent Austria from adding Bavaria to its territory.

The long eighteenth century saw aspirations for personal rule by princes, and Frederick sought to concentrate decision making in his own hands, making strategy dependent on the king's individual judgement. Frederick's invasion of Silesia, and his subsequent attempts to hold onto it and expand his dominions further, reflected his risk-taking personality and the way he chose to respond to circumstances. Frederick, however, enjoyed a much greater variety of strategic options than his predecessors because of the large army and well-stocked treasury bequeathed to him by his father, and this reflected the steady growth of states in this period and their increasing capacity to

* I am grateful to Brendan Simms and Peter Wilson, examiners of my doctoral dissertation, whose stimulating questions contributed much to this chapter.

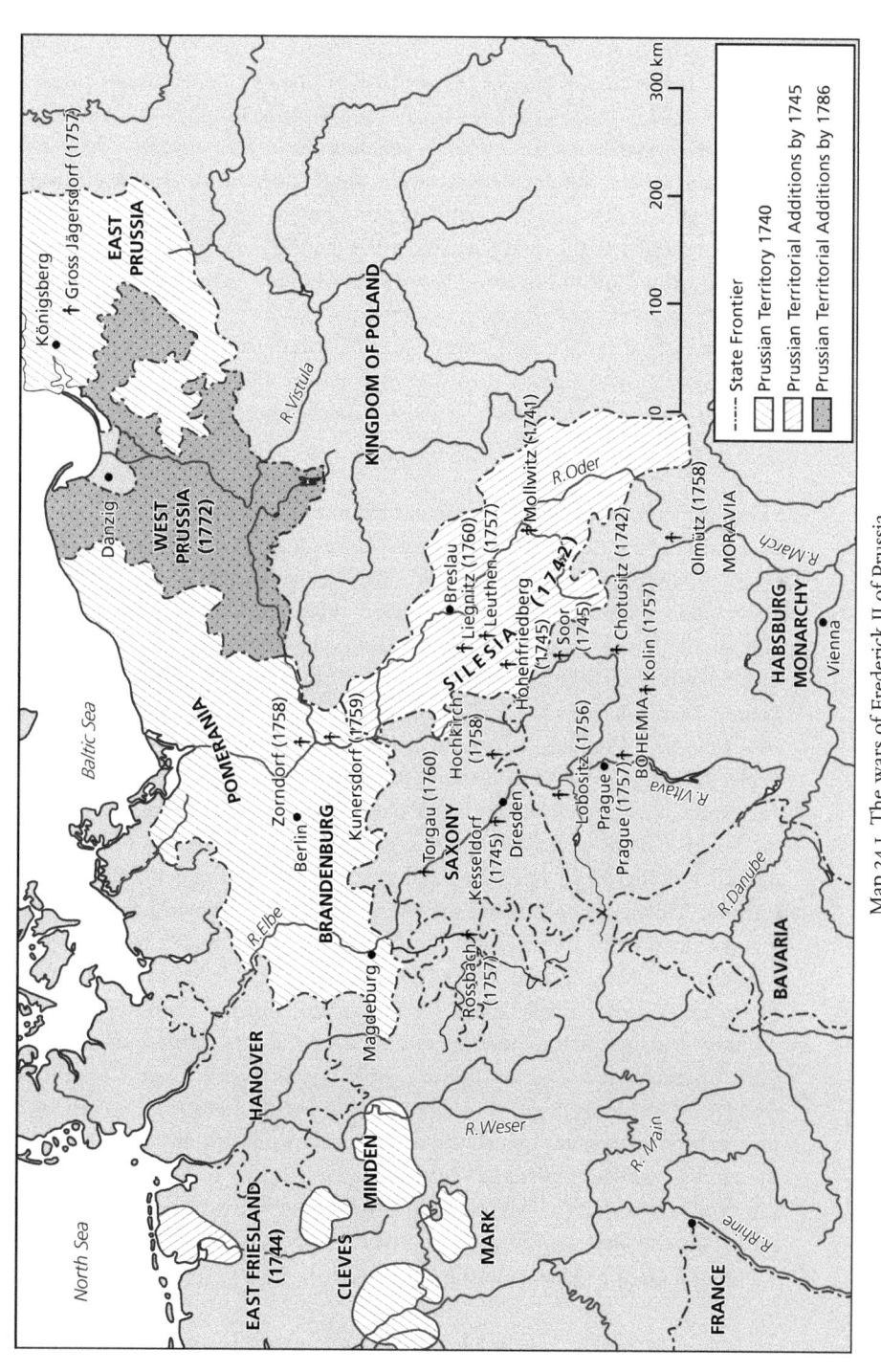

Map 24.1 The wars of Frederick II of Prussia

Legend:

- - - - - State Frontier

Prussian Territory 1740

Prussian Territorial Additions by 1745

Prussian Territorial Additions by 1786

0   100   200   300 km

Places and labels:

North Sea

Baltic Sea

Königsberg

† Gross Jägersdorf (1757)

EAST PRUSSIA

Danzig

WEST PRUSSIA (1772)

KINGDOM OF POLAND

R. Vistula

POMERANIA

Zorndorf (1758) †

† Kunersdorf (1759)

Berlin

BRANDENBURG

Magdeburg

R. Elbe

Breslau

Liegnitz (1760)

Leuthen (1757)

† Mollwitz (1741)

R. Oder

SILESIA (1742)

Hohenfriedberg (1745) †

† Soor (1745)

† Chotusitz (1742)

Olmütz (1758)

MORAVIA

R. March

Hochkirch (1758) †

† Kolin (1757)

BOHEMIA

Lobositz (1756) ●

Prague ●

Prague (1757) †

R. Vltava

HABSBURG MONARCHY

Vienna ●

Torgau (1760) †

SAXONY

Kesseldorf (1745) †

Dresden ●

Rossbach (1757) †

HANOVER

R. Weser

MINDEN

CLEVES

MARK

EAST FRIESLAND (1744)

R. Rhine

R. Main

R. Danube

BAVARIA

FRANCE

mobilise resources for war. The Hohenzollerns had for generations operated within a strategic context defined by the Holy Roman Empire, which covered all the German lands and within which a variety of princely dynasties competed for prominence under the overall hegemony of the Austrian Habsburgs. Successful Hohenzollern mobilisation of resources, however, made Frederick II the first German ruler in the early modern period to challenge the Habsburgs from a position of relative military parity. His successful gamble created a bipolar Germany, in which the two great powers of Austria and Prussia raised ever greater resources for their struggle against each other, far outstripping the other German states.

Sources

There are numerous published source editions for the reign of Frederick II, most notably the thirty volumes of the *Œuvres de Frédéric le Grand*, published between 1846 and 1856, and the forty-six volumes of the *Politische Correspondenz Friedrichs des Großen* (1879–1939). Both of these have been digitised and made available online, enabling researchers to search even for specific words across all the volumes.[1] Unfortunately, these are almost entirely writings *by Frederick*, often without the responses from his generals and ministers. This has led to a focus on the person of the Prussian king, neglecting other voices in Prussian policy making.

Research on the military history of Frederick's reign was long held back by the belief that the destruction of the Prussian Heeresarchiv in Potsdam by Allied bombing on 14 April 1945 had destroyed all of the relevant primary sources. This led to a reliance on older works written with access to the archive documents, particularly the German General Staff's multi-volume history of *Die Kriege Friedrichs des Großen* (1890–1914), which sought to paint Frederick as a Hohenzollern and German nationalist hero and to justify the military doctrine of imperial Germany. Since German reunification, however, historians have shown that the holdings of the Prussian Secret State Archive in Dahlem, Berlin, provide valuable perspectives on Prussian military history, as they contain all the correspondence to and from the Prussian monarchs – who administered the army personally – as well as the records of the civil administration. Members of many other German princely families served in the Prussian Army, and their archives also provide important source material for Prussian military history.

---

1 See http://friedrich.uni-trier.de.

The Actors

Frederick is famous for commanding his army personally, unifying political and military decision making. While he was the outstanding example of this in his generation, he was following broader contemporary trends. Since the mid-seventeenth century there had been ideas that monarchs should rule personally rather than relying on ministers, and King Frederick William I of Prussia (r. 1713–1740), for instance, moved away from Berlin (where his ministers were based) to Potsdam, conducting government business by letter and thus preventing ministers from exercising personal influence over the monarch. Frederick's personal military command reflected such practices, while also following the new ideas of the Enlightenment, which expected monarchs to demonstrate their greatness through merit rather than birth.

Advice from his generals could be important for Frederick, particularly in his early years on the throne, but only individuals who enjoyed his particular trust were invited to take part in discussions about going to war.[2] In October and November 1740, Frederick discussed his plans to acquire Silesia with his foreign minister, Heinrich von Podewils, and his new military favourite, Count Kurt Christoph von Schwerin, but excluded Prussia's most distinguished soldier, Prince Leopold I of Anhalt–Dessau. Frederick's intimate General Hans Karl von Winterfeldt helped to develop the plan that Frederick implemented in 1756, but was apparently not involved in the actual decision to go to war. Schwerin, who had gone in and out of favour, was this time also excluded from the planning process, although he was given the freedom to decide whether the final diplomatic reply from Vienna warranted an immediate military response by his army in Silesia.[3] In the course of the Seven Years War, with both Schwerin and Winterfeldt dead in battle, Frederick came to repose most trust in his brother Prince Henry. Although this did not normally extend to giving Henry a role in foreign affairs, the prince helped negotiate the First Partition of Poland with Catherine II of Russia.[4]

---

2 Adam L. Storring, 'Frederick the Great and the meanings of war, 1730–1755', unpublished PhD thesis, Cambridge University (2017), at www.repository.cam.ac.uk/handle/1810/277782), 224–78.

3 Dettlof von Schwerin, *Feldmarschall Schwerin: Ein Lebensbild aus Preußens großer Zeit* (Berlin: Verlag von E. G. Mittler & Sohn, 1928).

4 Generaldirecktion der Stiftung Preußische Schlösser und Gärten (ed.), *Prinz Heinrich von Preussen: Ein Europäer in Rheinsberg* (Munich and Berlin: Deutscher Kunstverlag, 2002).

Adversaries

Hohenzollern foreign policy had for generations taken place primarily within the Holy Roman Empire, and throughout his reign Frederick focused on supplanting the hegemony of the House of Habsburg within the German lands. The larger powers – France and Britain and later Russia – were important only in so far as they influenced this struggle between the traditional hegemon and the rising power.

The Holy Roman Empire functioned mainly by consensus under the leadership of the emperor, an office long held by the Austrian Habsburgs. The empire's systems for collective defence were used to raise military forces against, for instance, France and the Ottoman Empire. Like other German rulers, the Hohenzollerns sought over generations to benefit from the institutions of the empire while gaining as many advantages as possible for themselves, particularly at moments when the emperor was temporarily weak. They were in a comparatively strong position because, as rulers of Brandenburg, they were among the 'electors' who chose a new emperor. Thus, in 1700, when the Habsburgs were looking for support for war against France to assert their claims to the Spanish succession, Elector Frederick III of Brandenburg (r. 1688–1713) was able to get the emperor's agreement to crown himself 'King in Prussia', elevating him to royal status in the Hohenzollern territory of East Prussia.

The Hohenzollerns were, however, just one among a number of middle-ranking German dynasties. The electors of Hanover also attained royal status with the accession of Elector George Louis as King George I of Great Britain in 1714, but this actually reduced the importance of Hanover, as its rulers increasingly focused on Britain. Elector Charles Albert of Bavaria had married a daughter of the Habsburg Emperor Joseph I (r. 1705–1711), enabling him to claim the imperial crown in 1740 on the death of Charles VI and indeed to secure election as Emperor Charles VII in January 1742. Bavaria, however, lacked the military muscle to compete with Austria, and was soon overrun by Austrian forces. When Charles died in 1745, the imperial crown passed back to the Habsburgs.

Prussia's key opponent among the middle-ranking German states was Saxony. The Saxon elector Augustus the Strong had been elected King Augustus II of Poland in 1697, succeeded in 1733 by his son Augustus III, and the Wettin dynasty hoped to create a united Polish–Saxon monarchy, which would be linked geographically via a strip of the intervening Austrian province of Silesia. Frederick II's invasion of that province in 1740 was partly intended to scotch this. Saxony not only was very wealthy but also offered a direct invasion route into Brandenburg, with no natural boundaries or fortifications between it and Berlin. In his political testaments of 1752 and 1768 Frederick identified Saxony as the most important target for future Prussian expansion.[5]

Frederick II's key adversaries, however, were the Austrians. Alongside their position as Holy Roman emperors, the Habsburgs – the 'House of Austria' – ruled a giant empire stretching from the southern Netherlands to Transylvania, and including the Czech lands, Hungary, Croatia and northern Italy, as well as the lands of modern Austria. In the century before Frederick's accession, the Hohenzollerns had benefited from avoiding conflict with the Habsburgs. The Austrian failure to support Prussia's claims to the west German duchies of Jülich and Berg in the 1730s, however, alienated Frederick William I, while his son, the future Frederick II, chafed greatly as Austrian influence obliged him to marry a Brunswick princess rather than the British match proposed by his mother.

The year 1740 marked a point of extraordinary weakness for the Austrian Habsburg Empire, with its treasury exhausted after years of commitments that went far beyond its financial resources, and its army far below strength after defeat against the Ottoman Turks in 1737–1739. Charles VI had no male heir, and under the 'Pragmatic Sanction' he sought to exclude the two daughters of his elder brother Joseph I (married to the Bavarian and Saxon electors) from the succession. Instead, his daughter Maria Theresa (r. 1740–1780) would inherit the hereditary Austrian lands while her husband Francis Stephen of Lorraine became emperor. Frederick's decision to take advantage of this situation to conquer Silesia turned the remainder of his reign into a struggle with the Habsburgs, as the Prussian king sought to retain his prize while the Austrians focused all their attentions on trying, unsuccessfully, to defeat the Hohenzollern challenge and re-establish their dominance in the German lands.

Of the European Great Powers, the first to play an important role in Frederick's strategy was France, the greatest land power in Europe from the mid-seventeenth century. Immediately after his accession, Frederick sought an alliance with France, comparing himself with the Swedish king Gustavus Adolphus (r. 1611–1632), who had been France's ally in Germany against the Habsburgs in the Thirty Years War (1618–1648).[6] Frederick fought

5 Gustav Berthold Volz (ed.), *Die politischen Testamente Friedrichs des Grossen* (Berlin: Verlag von Reimar Hobbing, 1920), 61–3, 215–16, 219.

6 Johann Gustav Droysen et al. (eds), *Politische Correspondenz Friedrichs des Grossen*, 46 vols (Berlin: Verlag von Alexander Duncker, 1879–1939), Volume 1, 3–5.

alongside France during the War of the Austrian Succession and the French alliance was central to his foreign policy into the 1750s, but in the 'Diplomatic Revolution' of 1756 France allied with Austria, ending centuries of Franco-Habsburg struggle. The ensuing Seven Years War saw France's armies perform poorly in Germany and the war greatly damaged French prestige. France was in any case now primarily focused on its imperial rivalry with Britain, making it far less influential in central European politics in the second half of Frederick's reign.

Russia, in contrast, grew enormously in power and influence during the eighteenth century, playing a crucial role in Frederick's strategy from the 1760s onwards. Having risen to become the dominant power in the Baltic and eastern Europe during the reign (1682–1725) of Peter I, Russia in the mid-eighteenth century intervened for the first time in central European affairs, sending an auxiliary corps to Germany in 1735 during the War of the Polish Succession (1733–1735) and again in 1748 during the War of the Austrian Succession. The rise of Prussia threatened Russian interests, and in 1746 Empress Elizabeth (r. 1741–1762) made an alliance with Maria Theresa of Austria. In 1755, as war with France loomed, Britain contracted for a Russian observation corps to threaten Prussia – then France's ally – if it attacked Hanover. It was Frederick's desire to avoid this that led him in January 1756 to sign the Convention of Westminster with Britain, which in turn outraged the French, leading them to sign the Treaty of Versailles with Austria. Russia proved a dangerous enemy for Frederick during the Seven Years War, occupying East Prussia in early 1758, and moving its army across Poland to inflict frightful casualties on the Prussian troops at the battles of Zorndorf (25 August 1758), Kay (23 July 1759) and Kunersdorf (12 August 1759). The logistical difficulties of moving its armies over land across Poland, and the inability to acquire a port to supply them by sea, limited Russia's ability to strike into the Prussian heartland, but the capture of the port of Kolberg in December 1761 held out the prospect of overcoming these difficulties. The death of Empress Elizabeth on 5 January 1762, however, brought a volte-face in Russian policy, as the new Tsar Peter III idolised Frederick and swiftly concluded an alliance with him, returning East Prussia and sending a Russian army to fight on the Prussian side. Although Peter was quickly overthrown by his wife Catherine in July 1762, Frederick for the rest of his reign considered it vital to maintain good relations with Russia.

Britain became the most powerful European state during the eighteenth century, although its influence on central Europe was primarily indirect. While Britain's kings were concerned to protect Hanover from French attack, British statesmen used Continental allies to distract French attention from the naval and colonial struggle. In the War of the Austrian Succession, Britain reactivated its old Grand Alliance with Austria and the Dutch Republic against France, but the Prussian conquest of Silesia fundamentally changed the direction of Austrian policy, leaving them focused on maintaining their position within Germany rather than leading the empire against France. The 1756 Convention of Westminster was only a non-aggression pact between Britain and Prussia, but Frederick's victory over the French at Rossbach on 5 November 1757 turned him into a Protestant hero in Britain, leading to a formal alliance. An army of British and Protestant German troops, reinforced with some Prussian units and commanded by the Prussian Field Marshal Prince Ferdinand of Brunswick, held the French at bay in northern Germany for the remainder of the war, diverting huge French resources and helping to enable Britain's spectacular gains overseas. Britain's separate peace with France at the 1763 Treaty of Paris, however, left Frederick deeply embittered, and Britain found itself isolated on the European continent over the following decades.

Sweden had been an important power and a frequent enemy of Brandenburg–Prussia during the seventeenth century, but the Great Northern War (1700–1721) broke Swedish military power and their participation in the Seven Years War – as guarantor of the 1648 Peace of Westphalia – was little more than nominal. The Polish–Lithuanian Commonwealth, although still territorially massive, dividing Prussia's heartland from the isolated province of East Prussia, had become a negligible force in international relations, as the nobility – supported by Poland's powerful neighbours – prevented the establishment of any significant centralised state and army that might threaten their 'liberty'. The consequence was the three Partitions of Poland (1772, 1793 and 1795), during which Poland–Lithuania was swallowed by Austria, Prussia and Russia.

The Causes of Wars

Stephen Neff noted that statecraft in this period was 'strikingly rational' and 'just as strikingly amoral'.[7] 'Policy is the science of acting always by suitable means in accordance with one's interests', wrote Frederick: sometimes, 'the glory of the state obliges you to draw the sword'.[8] After the chaos of the

---

7 Stephen C. Neff, *War and the Law of Nations: A General History* (Cambridge: Cambridge University Press, 2005), 90.

8 Volz, *Die politischen Testamente*, 27, 76.

European religious and civil wars of the sixteenth century and the early seventeenth, the long eighteenth century saw an emphasis on strong states that could bring order, and military prowess was an important way for states to demonstrate this strength.[9]

The mid-eighteenth century also saw new developments in international relations. European states had been exhausted by the wars of King Louis XIV of France (r. 1643–1715), but the 1730s saw the rise of a new generation that was keen to assert their states' interests and win glory in war.[10] The period saw fierce colonial rivalry, and Anglo-French hostilities in North America from 1753 led both sides to seek European allies, touching off the Seven Years War in Europe. The 'rise of the Great Powers' also saw Austria, Prussia and Russia become much more powerful than other central European states, not only competing with each other but also collaborating to take territories from their weaker neighbours, particularly Poland–Lithuania and the Ottoman Empire.

Objectives

The most important objective of the European monarchical states during the long eighteenth century (roughly 1648–1789) was to achieve what King Frederick William I of Prussia called 'a great respect in the world'.[11] If his successor continued to pay and supply the army well, Frederick William promised, God would 'make his house formidable'.[12] Frederick II similarly had 'no doubt that the state will grow and aggrandise itself, and that with time Prussia will become one of the most considerable powers in Europe'.[13]

An important element in this was the accumulation of new territories, new subjects, greater state income and a larger army. Frederick William, for instance, made the pursuit of new 'territory and population' (landt und leutte) a key plank of his foreign policy.[14] The eighteenth century saw the first development of statistics, and Frederick II described the strength of the

---

9 Peter H. Wilson, *Absolutism in Central Europe* (London and New York: Routledge, 2000), 11–12, 15–16, 18, 35, 52–3, 60.

10 Armstrong Starkey, *War in the Age of Enlightenment, 1700–1789* (Westport, CT and London: Praeger, 2003), 12.

11 Richard Dietrich (ed.), *Die politischen Testamente der Hohenzollern* (Veröffentlichungen aus den Archiven Preussischer Kulturbesitz 20) (Cologne and Vienna: Böhlau Verlag, 1986), 224, 233.

12 Dietrich, *Die politischen Testamente*, 225   13 Volz, *Die politischen Testamente*, 65.

14 Gustav Berthold Volz, 'Friedrich Wilhelm I. und die preußischen Erbansprüche auf Schlesien', *Forschungen zur Brandenburgischen und Preußischen Geschichte*, 30 (1918), 59–67; Dietrich, *Die politischen Testamente*, 238, 241.

various states of Europe in terms of their population, annual revenue and numbers of soldiers and warships.[15] Military conquest was certainly not the only way to acquire new territories: inheritance was far more common. Territorial expansion was also not the only way to increase state revenues or the size of an army. The Hohenzollerns worked hard to stimulate the economy of their land, while the Habsburgs from the 1740s introduced substantial administrative reforms in order to increase their tax yields and thus fund stronger armed forces.

Glory and reputation were, however, just as important for sovereigns as concrete growth in the power of their states. Frederick, for instance, wrote that he decided to invade Silesia not only in order 'to augment the power of my house' but also 'to acquire reputation'.[16] This culminated in his ceremonial entry into Berlin on 28 December 1745 at the end of the Second Silesian War, when the official account claimed that the crowds shouted (in Latin) 'Long live Frederick the Great', reflecting Frederick's aim not only to add a wealthy and strategically important province to his domains but also to establish his own personal greatness.[17] Sovereigns could win glory through war, and Frederick took this considerably further by actually commanding his army in a series of victorious battles, establishing a military reputation that has endured even to the present day. Glory and reputation could, however, also be achieved outside the military realm. The Saxon Wettins, for instance, achieved great reputation through the magnificence of their court, and this gave them important influence in international relations.[18]

The Available Means

The aggressive, independent foreign policy of Frederick II was made possible by an impressive standing army built up steadily by his predecessors, which was proportionately much larger than that of other German states and – in the crisis of 1740 – was roughly equal to the real strength of the then badly undermanned and underfunded Austrian army. The Great Elector Frederick William of Brandenburg (r. 1640–1688), like other German rulers, had steadily established a standing army during the wars of Louis XIV, establishing

15 Max Posner (ed.), 'Frédéric II. Histoire de mon temps (Redaktion von 1746)', *Publicationen aus den K. preussischen Staatsarchiven*, 4 (1879), 161–211; Volz, *Die politischen Testamente*, 196–209.

16 Posner, 'Frédéric II. Histoire de mon temps', 214.

17 Jürgen Luh, *Der Große: Friedrich II. von Preußen* (Munich: Siedler Verlag, 2011), 60–2.

18 T. C. W. Blanning, *The Culture of Power and the Power of Culture: Old Regime Europe 1660–1789* (Oxford: Oxford University Press, 2002), 61–70.

permanent taxes that funded 40,000 troops by the death of King Frederick I in 1713. King Frederick William I virtually doubled this to around 80,000 by his death in 1740, funded partly by increased revenues but also by developing existing militia systems into the cantonal system by 1733, under which a proportion of Prussian subjects were conscripted into military service but most soldiers were in practice sent on leave for all but two months of training per year, allowing them to continue their civilian lives and employment and saving the state from paying them. This kind of compulsory recruitment coupled with extended leave was common in Germany and Scandinavia, and allowed states to raise armies despite limited financial resources.[19]

Frederick William I and his military intimate Prince Leopold I of Anhalt–Dessau also instilled in the Prussian army a culture of particularly rigorous performance of military duties. Regular annual training and reviews gave Prussian soldiers great facility with drill movements and, combined with their practice of marching in step, allowed them to manoeuvre much more easily on the battlefield than other contemporary armies. This enabled Frederick II frequently to execute flank attacks on the battlefield (his famous Oblique Order), or to march around the enemy and attack them from the rear (as at Zorndorf in 1758 and Torgau in 1760).

The Prussian army also benefited from well-organised logistics. A network of civilian magazines (to store grain in case of famine) also served military purposes. Prussia had better access than Austria to good-quality horses from Holstein in northern Germany and from eastern Europe, and also fed its horses better, making its cavalry more effective in battle. Prussia's supply system was well organised, with some 4,000 waggons allegedly accompanying Schwerin's army as it invaded Bohemia in 1757, and in the Seven Years War it deployed mobile ovens, which accompanied the armies and made it easier to bake bread.[20]

Prussian finances, however, were more limited. Unlike other 'fiscal–military states' like Britain, France and the Habsburg monarchy, which funded war primarily through taxes and borrowing, Prussian rulers in the eighteenth century were still reliant on their own private domains for one-third of state revenue. The process of persuading local estates (representative bodies) in the

19 Peter H. Wilson, 'Social militarization in eighteenth-century Germany', *German History*, 18 (2000), 1–39.
20 On Prussian logistics, see Marcus Warnke, *Logistik und friderizianische Kriegsführung: Eine Studie zur Verteilung, Mobilisierung und Wirkungsmächtigkeit militärisch relevanter Ressourcen im Siebenjährigen Krieg am Beispiel des Jahres 1757* (Berlin: Duncker & Humblot, 2018).

late seventeenth century to agree to taxes to support the army had been so fraught that Hohenzollern rulers throughout the eighteenth century did not feel able to impose significant new taxes, leaving them primarily reliant on population increases and the addition of new territories to provide increased revenues. Although Prussia's tax burden was proportionately comparable to that of Austria, it was far behind Britain's. While ordinary revenues were sufficient to support the army in peacetime, limited access to borrowing meant that the Prussians were reliant on cash reserves in their treasury to fund wartime expenditure, and these lasted only for one or two campaigns. To maintain a longer struggle, Prussia depended on alternative sources of revenue such as financial subsidies from the wealthier maritime powers and exactions from conquered territory.[21]

The second half of the eighteenth century saw a veritable arms race in central Europe, as all of the Great Powers steadily increased their state revenue and military establishments. The Prussian Army grew from around 80,000 in 1740 to 158,000 in 1777, and the Austrian Army from 108,000 to 220,000 in the same period.[22] The Seven Years War saw artillery take on a much greater role, as improved founding techniques enabled cannon to be lighter and thus more mobile, while new sights and the use of elevating screws made them more accurate. The Austrian artillery park grew from ninety-four field guns in 1745 to 1,060 in 1780, and Prussian expansion was comparable.[23]

The Process of Prioritisation

The strategic choices of Frederick II and his forebears revolved around how to respond to their state's comparative weakness on the international stage. They could pursue an independent foreign policy or they could seek to make gains by attaching Prussia to larger powers. The Great Elector secured the independence of East Prussia from Polish suzerainty in 1657 and conquered much of Pomerania from the Swedes, but at the 1679 Treaty of St Germain King Louis XIV of France humiliatingly forced him to give up most of his Pomeranian gains, underlining Brandenburg–Prussia's powerlessness in the face of larger powers. Elector Frederick III of Brandenburg (later King

---

21 On Prussian finances, see Peter H. Wilson, 'Prussia as a fiscal–military state, 1640–1806', in Christopher Storrs (ed.), *The Fiscal–Military State in Eighteenth-Century Europe: Essays in Honour of P. G. M. Dickson* (Farnham: Ashgate, 2009), 95–124.
22 T. C. W. Blanning, *The French Revolutionary Wars 1787–1802* (London etc.: Arnold, 1996), 10.
23 Hew Strachan, *European Armies and the Conduct of War* (London: George Allen & Unwin, 1983), 32–3.

Frederick I of Prussia) focused on alliance with Austria, the Netherlands and Britain against France in the Nine Years War (1688–1697) and the War of the Spanish Succession, thereby raising Prussia to royal status with Austrian support. King Frederick William I joined the coalition against Sweden at the end of the Great Northern War, thereby adding parts of Pomerania to his state. For most of his reign he cautiously maintained a close alliance with Austria, while doubling the size of the Prussian Army and building up a substantial financial reserve. It was this powerful army and well-stocked treasury that enabled Frederick II to act independently to conquer Silesia within months of his accession.

Like many other contemporary dynasties, the Hohenzollerns ruled over a composite monarchy of widely scattered territories, acquired primarily through inheritance. Historians have frequently claimed that this made the Hohenzollern territories uniquely vulnerable to attack, but their situation was common in early modern Europe.[24] Indeed, the Habsburg lands were even more widely dispersed, and it was the attempts of Charles VI to pursue an ambitious foreign policy in the southern Netherlands, Italy and the Balkans that so weakened Austria, leaving it exposed to Frederick's pre-emptive strike in 1740.

The long eighteenth century saw the 'dynastic state' – a state understood as the domains of a particular ruling family – gradually replaced by states whose power was conceived in terms of tax revenue and the size of their armies, with their territories often strategically grouped together. The Great Elector had attempted to divide his territories, which would have provided for his various sons but greatly weakened Brandenburg–Prussia's military power.[25] Frederick William I similarly focused on the acquisition of the duchies of Jülich and Berg in western Germany, territories to which the Hohenzollerns had well-founded dynastic claims but which could not have been defended as part of an independent foreign policy. His ambitions were stymied, however, by the failure of Austria in the 1730s to support Prussian claims, and his son Frederick took this as a lesson of Prussia's powerlessness when faced by coalitions of larger powers.[26]

The War of the Austrian Succession saw the multiple 'dynastic states' of Germany give way to two Great Powers, which were mobilising ever greater

24 E.g. Brendan Simms, *Europe: The Struggle for Supremacy, 1453 to the Present* (London etc.: Allen Lane, 2013), 45–8.
25 Dietrich, *Die politische Testamente*, 43–50.
26 Reinhold Koser (ed.), *Briefwechsel Friedrichs des Großen mit Grumbkow und Maupertius (1731–1759)* (Leipzig: Verlag von S. Hirzel, 1898), 59, 144, 146–9, 173–81; *Œuvres de Frédéric le Grand* (ed. J. D. E. Preuss), 30 vols (Berlin: R. Decker, 1846–1856), Volume 1, 56–7.

resources for war. The Bavarian Wittelsbachs went down to disastrous defeat trying to assert their dynastic claims to the Habsburg inheritance, while the Saxon Wettins utterly failed to convert their composite monarchy of Poland–Saxony and their claims to the Habsburg inheritance into concrete gains. In contrast, their successful mobilisation of resources made the Hohenzollerns the first German dynasty in the early modern period to challenge the Habsburgs from a position of something close to military parity. For both the Hohenzollerns and the Habsburgs the war was a signal to deprioritise their other territories, focusing instead on a bipolar struggle for supremacy within the Holy Roman Empire.

These developments were not inevitable, but reflected contingency and specific policy decisions. The Habsburgs had successfully mobilised the military forces of the Holy Roman Empire against threats from France and the Ottoman Empire in the late seventeenth century and the early eighteenth, and they again persuaded the princes of the empire to contribute substantial forces for war against the French in 1733–1735 and against the Ottomans in 1737–1739. The reign of Charles VI, however, saw a disastrous collapse not only of Austrian military power but also of their political position in the empire, as Charles alienated the Hohenzollerns by failing to support them over Jülich–Berg, while simultaneously trying to exclude the Bavarian Wittelsbachs and the Wettins from the Austrian succession.

That Prussia succeeded in challenging the Habsburgs was also not inevitable. Hohenzollern strategy over generations, like that of any other middle-ranking power, centred on taking advantage of favourable circumstances, and Frederick's seizure of Silesia was simply the most important example of this approach. Frederick also sought dynastic acquisitions elsewhere in Germany, and without the moment of extraordinary Habsburg weakness in 1740 he might have acted differently, although he had remarked for some years upon the growing weakness of the Austrian empire and the opportunities it offered, and came to the throne explicitly looking for a French alliance to take advantage of this.[27]

From the 1740s onwards, Prussia and Austria focused all their attentions against each other. During the Seven Years War, Frederick made no attempt to defend his western provinces and soon abandoned East Prussia as well, refusing even to visit the province for years after the war due to its co-operation with its Russian occupiers. In his 1768 political testament, Frederick described how he had made no plans at all to defend East Prussia or Cleves: 'never lose from view our true enemies: these are the Austrians. Therefore, it is against them that

27 Koser, *Briefwechsel Friedrichs mit Grumbkow*, 154, 156, 158–9, 163–4, 180; *Œuvres de Frédéric le Grand*, Volume VIII, 5–7, 18–20, 25.

I have directed all my measures'.[28] Brandenburg and even Berlin were scarcely fortified, with the Prussian government evacuated to Magdeburg during the Seven Years War, whereas Silesia bristled with fortresses. The Habsburgs sought to match Prussian resource mobilisation, and Holy Roman Emperor Joseph II (r. 1765–1790) and long-serving chancellor Wenzel Anton von Kaunitz repeatedly tried to exchange Bavaria for Austria's possessions in the southern Netherlands in order to create a single contiguous state.

Soft power – often expressed through magnificent display – continued to be important, however. To secure the prestige appropriate to a royal dynasty, Frederick I of Prussia had held an elaborate coronation ceremony and created a magnificent court modelled on that of Louis XIV.[29] Frederick William I turned away from courtly grandeur, and Frederick II claimed to follow suit, thereby adroitly aligning himself with Enlightenment criticism of luxury. In practice, he made skilful use of magnificent display when it suited him, building the grand New Palace in Potsdam 1763–1769 to show Prussia's continued strength after the Seven Years War. Frederick II also sought to emulate the cultural patronage of Louis XIV, culminating in the 1750 Berlin Carrousel, organised in imitation of the Sun King's carrousels in 1662 and 1664.[30] Frederick became so popular in French enlightened circles that, during the Seven Years War, the French cardinal Bernis lamented that 'our enemy, the king of Prussia, is loved to the point of madness'.[31] Frederick's patronage of French intellectuals – above all Voltaire – and his own activities as a writer and musician were just as important as his military victories in securing him greatness, both in his own time and subsequently, and these literary and cultural achievements should be seen as complementary, not in contradiction, to his military conquests.[32]

The Application of Strategy

Both statecraft and generalship in the long eighteenth century centred on the ability to exercise sound judgement in taking advantage of circumstances as they arose.[33] Frederick William I, for instance, advised his successor to 'profit'

28 Volz, *Die politischen Testamente*, 136.
29 Christopher Clark, 'When culture meets power: the Prussian coronation of 1701', in Hamish Scott and Brendan Simms (eds), *Cultures of Power in Europe during the Long Eighteenth Century* (Cambridge: Cambridge University Press, 2007), 15–35.
30 Thomas Biskup, *Friedrichs Größe: Inszenierung des Preußenkönigs in Fest und Zeremoniell 1740–1815* (Frankfurt and New York: Campus Verlag, 2012).
31 Blanning, *French Revolutionary Wars*, 23.   32 Luh, *Der Große*, 9–111.
33 On judgement in eighteenth-century generalship, see Adam L. Storring, 'Subjective practices of war: the Prussian Army and the Zorndorf campaign, 1758', *History of Science*, 60 (2022), 458–80.

from the strength of his army, which would allow him 'to hold the balance' in international relations.[34] While Frederick's decision to exploit Habsburg weakness in 1740 reflected the policy of his dynasty over generations, the way in which he responded to this opportunity reflected his own personality. Previous Prussian plans had envisaged the negotiated acquisition of Silesia, or part of it, in return for Prussian support of the Pragmatic Sanction, but Frederick instead seized it with a pre-emptive military strike.[35] This was only possible due to Prussia's greatly increased military power: none of his predecessors would have been able to contemplate waging war against the Austrians alone. It also reflected Frederick's lifelong inclination to take risks.[36] In this case, Frederick's judgement was vindicated, as his winter campaign to conquer Silesia in December 1740 and January 1741 anticipated all the plans of the other powers, and denied the Wettins the opportunity to link their domains in Saxony with their elected kingdom of Poland. The move carried great risks, however. In April 1741, the Austrian army of Count Wilhelm Reinhard von Neipperg cut off the Prussian forces in Upper Silesia – Frederick and Schwerin among them – forcing them to fight the ensuing battle at Mollwitz on 10 April with the Austrians across their lines of communication. At the beginning of the battle, the Austrian cavalry scattered their Prussian counterparts and Frederick was himself caught up in the rout and narrowly avoided capture as he fled the field.[37] If Neipperg had won at Mollwitz, or if the king had been killed or captured, the Hohenzollerns would have shared the fate of previous defeated opponents of the Habsburgs and Frederick William I's warnings to his successor to 'start no unjust war' would now be seen as prophetic.[38]

Frederick's strategy followed French examples. His quick dash across Silesia, bypassing the more strongly defended fortresses in order quickly to occupy most of the province, was inspired by his favourite book on the art of war: the *Mémoires* of Antoine de Pas, Marquis de Feuquières, a general under Louis XIV, who emphasised surprise attacks to seize a single territory and then hold it at a swift peace settlement. As Frederick remarked, 'our wars must be short and lively', and he had been able to observe this approach in French strategy during the War of the Polish Succession, where France

34 Dietrich, *Die politischen Testamente*, 241.
35 Volz, 'Die preußischen Erbansprüche auf Schlesien', 63–7.
36 Wolfgang Burgdorf, *Friedrich der Große: Ein biografisches Porträt* (Freiburg, Basel and Vienna: Herder, 2011), 7–11, 23.
37 Großer Generalstab, *Die Kriege Friedrichs des Großen. Erster Theil: Der Erste Schlesischer Krieg, 1740–1742*, 3 vols (Berlin: Ernst Siegfried Mittler und Sohn, 1890–1893), Volume 1, 362–425.
38 Dietrich, *Die politischen Testamente*, 239.

launched a surprise attack with overwhelming force and France's first minis-ter, Cardinal Fleury, then quickly ended the war through a peace settlement that secured the province of Lorraine.[39] In the same way, having achieved his main territorial objective, Frederick gladly left the war under the 11 June 1742 Treaty of Breslau, which granted him the bulk of Silesia, leaving the French and Bavarians to face the Austrians alone. Frederick re-entered the war in 1744, after the Austrians overran Bavaria and pushed to the Rhine itself, but victories at Hohenfriedberg (4 June 1745), Soor (30 September 1745) and Kesseldorf (15 December 1745) allowed him once again to make a separate peace at Dresden on 25 December 1745.

Frederick's focus on Austria, as he sought to hold onto his gain and prevent the Habsburgs recapturing Silesia, also chimed with the Prussian king's limited diplomatic horizons. Despite repeated requests, he had never been allowed to travel beyond the German lands as Crown prince, and he had little understand-ing of the imperial rivalry that now increasingly preoccupied Britain and France. Frederick believed that Franco-Habsburg antagonism would ensure that he always had a French ally, but his repeated abandonment of his allies during the War of the Austrian Succession had angered the French and, when Frederick's fear of Russian invasion led him to conclude the Convention of Westminster with Britain, Austrian chancellor Kaunitz was able to bring years of negotiations to fruition by agreeing the Treaty of Versailles with France. Intelligence reports made clear that, although the Franco-Austrian alliance was only defensive, Austria and Russia were mustering their forces to attack Prussia.

Hamish Scott noted that 'Frederick ... was probably psychologically incapable of riding out the crisis patiently and instead preferred to act'.[40] Frederick had identified Saxony as the next target of Prussian expansion, setting out plans to give the Saxon elector the Austrian province of Bohemia in compensation, and Winterfeldt had scouted the invasion routes into Saxony and Bohemia. Frederick sought to emulate the great 'conquerors' of history, especially Julius Caesar, and, having overrun Saxony in a lightning campaign from August to October 1756, he invaded Bohemia in spring 1757, trying to win his own personal Battle of Pharsalus (Caesar's victory over Pompey in 48 BC).[41] This time, however, Frederick's gamble failed, as he was

---

39 Adam L. Storring, '"The age of Louis XIV": Frederick the Great and French ways of war', *German History*, 38 (2020), 39–44.

40 H. M. Scott, *The Birth of a Great Power System, 1740–1815* (Harlow: Longman, 2006), 94.

41 Adam L. Storring, '"Our Age": Frederick the Great, classical warfare, and the uses and abuses of military history', *International Journal of Military History and Historiography*, 42 (2022), 344–9; Volz, *Die politischen Testamente*, 61–3.

defeated at Kolin on 18 June 1757 and forced to abandon his siege of Prague. Moreover, Frederick's invasion of Saxony not only activated the Franco-Austrian alliance but also led the Holy Roman Empire to place him under imperial 'execution', with the states of the empire contributing an army for service against Prussia. Sweden also entered the war, and Kaunitz wrote of 'the reduction of the house of Brandenburg to its primitive state of a small, very secondary power'.[42]

The strategy of seizing a province at the start of a war, however, which Frederick had learnt from Feuquières and Fleury, paid considerable dividends as Frederick plundered 48 million talers from Saxony during the war of attrition that now followed. Both Silesia and Saxony also had the advantage of being linked to the rest of Prussian territory by excellent river communications (respectively along the Oder and Elbe) that could be used for transporting supplies, and they were separated from Habsburg territories by mountain barriers that were logistically difficult for the Austrians to cross. The Russians and French also suffered great logistical problems, and their different political objectives prevented the allies combining sufficiently to land a decisive blow. Among the many battles that Frederick took the risk of fighting, the victory over the French at Rossbach brought him a formal alliance with Britain and subsidies of 27.64 million talers in 1758–1761. The unscrupulous Prussian king also exacted recruits and money from the smaller German states. These measures allowed Prussia to end the war with a substantial financial surplus, whereas near bankruptcy forced Austria to reduce the size of its army in 1761–1762.

Hamish Scott described the period after the Seven Years War as 'the second reign of Frederick II', and his foreign policy after 1763 was indeed substantially different from that beforehand. The king was well aware of how narrowly he had escaped defeat, and his focus throughout the rest of his reign was on maintaining the favourable status quo. Aware of the power of Russia, Frederick bent every effort to achieve a Russian alliance, which he successfully maintained from 1764 to 1781.[43] His army was now used primarily as a deterrent rather than a means for further conquests, and Frederick focused on raw numbers and impressive military reviews, which drew admiring observers from across Europe.[44]

42 Christopher Clark, *Iron Kingdom: The Rise and Downfall of Prussia, 1600–1947* (London: Penguin, 2006), 200.

43 H. M. Scott, '1763–1786: the second reign of Frederick the Great?', in Philip G. Dwyer (ed.), *The Rise of Prussia 1700–1830* (Harlow: Longman, 2000), 177–200.

44 D. E. Showalter, *The Wars of Frederick the Great* (London and New York: Longman, 1996), 321–52.

Frederick's focus on Germany had always included a keen awareness of the possibilities offered by the Holy Roman Empire, and throughout his life Frederick skilfully made use of the imperial institutions, particularly during the reign of the Wittelsbach Charles VII in 1742–1745. In 1748–1752, Frederick successfully blocked the election of Archduke Joseph as King of the Romans and thus prospective emperor. After 1763, as a 'satisfied power', and facing from 1765 a young Emperor Joseph II who aimed to emulate Frederick's military conquests and create an efficient Habsburg fiscal–military state, Frederick was able to mobilise German princes against Austria. He blocked two successive Austrian attempts to exchange Bavaria for the southern Netherlands, in 1778–1779 and 1784–1785, in the latter case founding a league of German princes (*Fürstenbund*) in 1785.

Frederick II also maintained strong links with a series of smaller German princes – particularly the houses of Brunswick, Hesse–Darmstadt, Hesse–Kassel and Württemberg. As well as marriage alliances, the Prussian rulers could offer these princes appointments as officers in the Prussian Army, whose prestige was greatly enhanced by Frederick II's victories. The Brunswick and Hesse–Kassel princes fought on the Anglo-Prussian side in the Seven Years War, helping secure Prussia's western flank against France. The small German princes, however, made an even more direct contribution to Prussian military power by providing several whole regiments, which were incorporated into the Prussian army in 1740–1745.

Conclusion

Prussia became a Great Power in 1740–1786 because its rulers had succeeded in making their state militarily strong enough to compete against the existing regional hegemon. Like many other early modern European states (including its Habsburg rival), Prussia was a composite monarchy of diverse territories held together by its ruling dynasty. Its rise reflected a broader process that saw states across Europe first establish standing armies in the second half of the seventeenth century and then raise increasingly greater and greater resources for war as the eighteenth century progressed. Without these resources, the successful wars under Frederick II would not have been possible, and indeed Prussia's tax base and credit were still limited by comparison with other 'fiscal–military states'. Frederick II's success turned the German political landscape from a multitude of dynastic states operating within the framework of the Holy Roman Empire into a bipolar world where two Great Powers – Austria and Prussia – far outstripped the others.

As a middle-sized German power, the Hohenzollerns had always been obliged to react to circumstances, trying to 'profit' from them as much as possible. Frederick II's invasions of Silesia in 1740 and Saxony and then Bohemia in 1756–1757 were the product of his own risk-taking personality and followed the example of France. The 1740 invasion in particular, however, also reflected a long-standing Hohenzollern tradition of using periods of Habsburg weakness to exact advantages for Prussia. In this case, Frederick's concentration of strategic decision making in his own hands placed a huge emphasis on his personal judgement in responding to circumstances and taking advantage of opportunities.

25

American Warfare in the Eighteenth Century

STEPHEN CONWAY

This chapter considers the strategic dimension of conflict in North America between the outbreak of fighting between the French and colonial Americans in the Ohio Valley in 1754 and the formal end of the War of American Independence in 1783. While this thirty-year period saw several local struggles between colonists and native peoples, the focus here is on the two major conflicts – the Seven Years War (1754–1760 in North America, 1756–1763 in Europe) and the War of Independence (1775–1783). Both wars were global struggles, extending well beyond North America – the Seven Years War from its outset, and the War of Independence from 1778, when the French became belligerents. Even so, the chapter will concentrate on the American aspects of these struggles, and only indirectly address the Caribbean, West African, European, and Asian dimensions. It will aspire to cover all the participants in the North American parts of the two wars – settlers, native peoples, and Europeans, particularly the British and the French.

Sources

How do we ascertain the strategies of the different belligerents? The task is especially difficult when we consider the native peoples involved in both wars, as we have no direct written testimony to illuminate their thinking. Native cultures were oral and visual rather than written; a major challenge for anyone trying to capture the perspective of North America's indigenous population at a distance of two hundred and fifty years or more. We are reliant, in their case, on the views of others (Creole or European allies or enemies) and what we can infer from their actions. But the problem of evidence is not confined to Native Americans. The challenges are considerable when we consider the other participants. For the American colonists (both French Canadian and British American), in the Seven Years War their strategic objectives were largely determined by metropolitan governments in Paris and London, though in both instances some degree of local decision

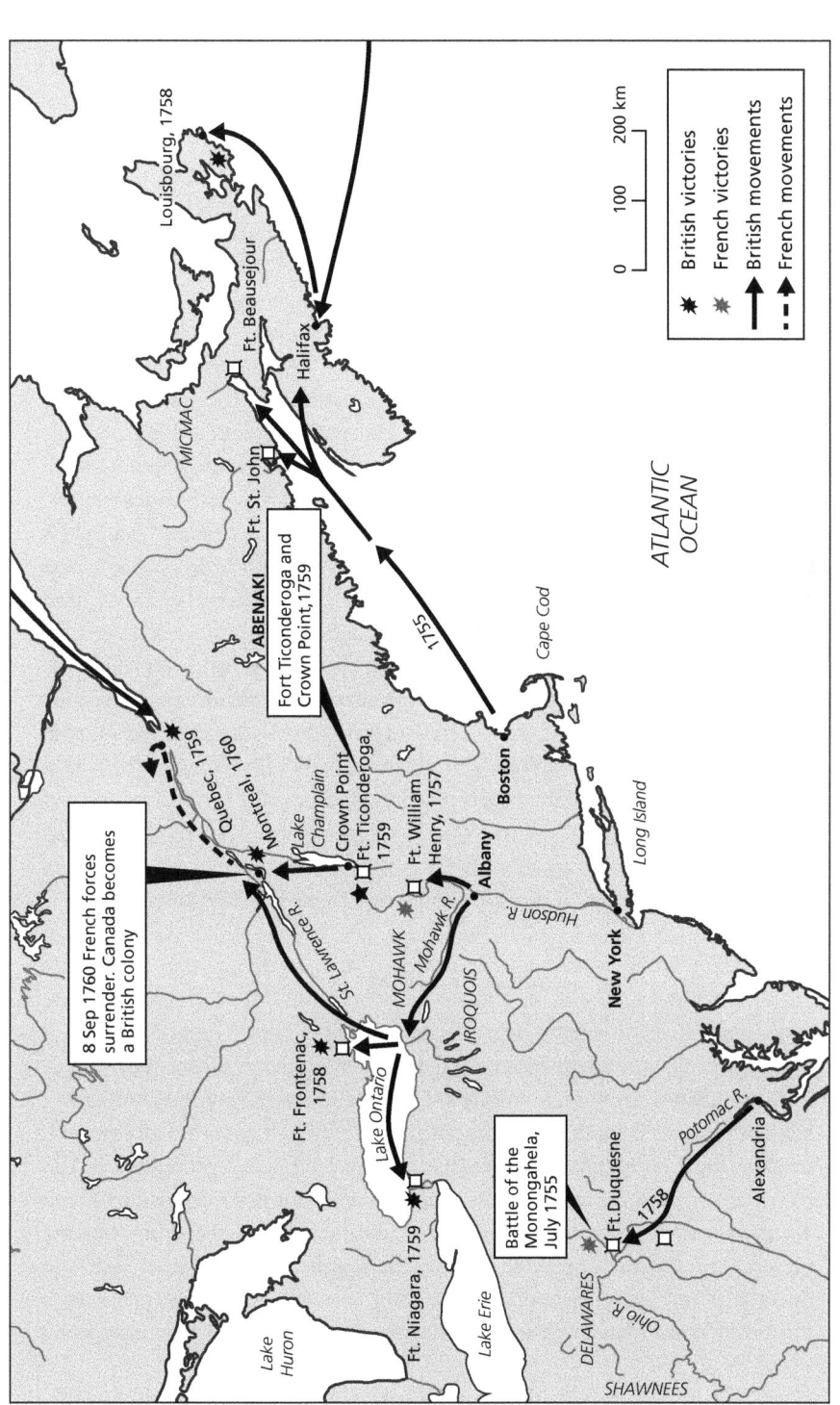

Map 25.1 American strategies in the eighteenth century. Redrawn based on a map in Michael Schaller et al., *American Horizons: U.S. History in a Global Context: To 1877* (Oxford: Oxford University Press, 2020), map 5–6. Reproduced with permission of the Licensor through PLSclear.

making was inevitable, given the distances from their respective mother countries. In the War of Independence, the Americans set up their own governments at state level and the Continental Congress assumed overall responsibility for setting military objectives. Tension between state and congressional authorities, as we will see, was a major problem for the American war effort. Again, however, a good deal of decision making rested with the commanders on the spot. The records of the different state governments, Congress and the commanders of the Continental Army that Congress created therefore form the source base for understanding the American side of the War of Independence. The enormous archive of George Washington's correspondence is a particularly rich and revealing source on both strategic objectives and outcomes in practice.

When we turn to the Europeans, cabinet minutes, which might tell us much about the objectives set by governments, survive only rarely. In their absence, we have the surviving correspondence between ministers and military and naval commanders in North America, in the French Archives de la marine in the Archives nationales, and the British Colonial Office papers in the United Kingdom National Archives. This correspondence gives us some inferential clues about strategic thinking. The private papers of participants can add to the official archival record. In the British case, for instance, the voluminous collection of the papers of William Pitt, the secretary of state who oversaw the war effort in North America in the Seven Years War, are immensely valuable, as are the almost equally large collection of the papers of Jeffrey Amherst, the British commander-in-chief from 1758 to 1763. For the War of Independence, the papers of General Thomas Gage tell us much about the beginning of hostilities, and the papers of General Sir Henry Clinton provide important insights into British strategy.

Decision Makers

Amongst Native Americans, tribal leaders set the strategic objectives of their different peoples, though loose confederations of tribes meant that several distinct Indian nations might follow a similar path. For the colonial Americans, legislatures agreed (or denied) requests from the British government for funds to raise local regiments. In this sense, colonial elected representatives had a crucial say over the deployment of manpower. But decision making about what we might call strategy (the term was not used at the time) was the preserve of British army commanders in North America, supervised and directed by ministers in London. The same was true on the French side in the Seven Years War. The French governor in Montreal had his own views on how the war should be fought, but ultimately the decision making rested with the commander of the French military forces in Canada, who received general instructions from Paris.

In the War of Independence, American strategy, while ultimately the work of officials appointed by Congress and subject to its approval, increasingly came to be determined by senior military commanders, especially Washington. For the French, Louis XVI's ministers seem to have debated the fundamental questions, notably whether to intervene or not, and if so, on whose side. Once they made the decision to join the war as American allies, the Comte de Vergennes, the strongest advocate of French involvement and the minister of foreign affairs, emerged as effective war minister. Even before formal intervention in 1778, he appears to have been the main advocate of more limited assistance to the Americans. On the British side, for most of the War of Independence the leading British war minister was Lord George Germain, the Secretary of State for the American Colonies from 1775 to 1782. His private papers, and his official letters to commanders across the Atlantic, suggest that he played a crucial role in the setting as well as the implementation of strategy. The king also played a part, taking seriously his role of head of state in wartime and seeking to influence the development of strategy at various points. We know, however, that strategic decisions, such as whether to concentrate naval forces in home waters or disperse them across the globe, were taken by the cabinet, which in the matter of naval deployments overrode the wishes of the first lord of the admiralty, the Earl of Sandwich.

Adversaries

In the Seven Years War, the conflict in North America pitted a modest force of French regular troops, French Canadians and their native allies against the far more numerous but divided British colonists, who were supported increasingly by native allies and by growing numbers of British regular troops. The Royal Navy also played a vital role in facilitating operations against French outposts such as Louisbourg on Cape Breton Island, the key to the St Lawrence estuary (1758) and then, sailing up the navigable St Lawrence river, at Quebec (1759). Spain entered the war in 1762, too late to help their French allies. Spanish efforts, furthermore, were focused on a campaign in Portugal and in defence of their exposed possessions in the Caribbean and the Philippines.

North America, as Spanish involvement in the war shows, was just one theatre amongst many. One aspect of the struggle, in which we can place North America, was a contest between Britain and France for dominance in the wider world. Besides North America, this contest was played out in the

Caribbean, West Africa, Europe (where the British paid for German allies and auxiliaries and committed ever larger numbers of their own troops from 1758) and South and East Asia. But the war also revolved around a separate but connected conflict – that between Prussia and Austria for superiority in central Europe and particularly the Holy Roman Empire. In 1756, because of the Diplomatic Revolution (or the reversal of long-standing alliances) Britain became an ally of Prussia and France of Austria. The British commitment to Germany was at least partly based on the need to show solidarity with the beleaguered Frederick II, also named the Great (who was very popular with the British public) by protecting his exposed western flank from French attack.[1]

The War of Independence began as a purely North American struggle, with the rebel colonies locked in conflict with the British Army and Navy. From early on, however, both sides received external support. The Americans drew on European money, munitions and military experts from the beginning of the conflict. From 1778, they were more openly assisted by French arms, first in the form of naval power, and from 1780 through direct military intervention when a French expeditionary force was despatched to the United States. The French troops, and French ships, proved decisive in the British defeat at Yorktown, Virginia, in 1781, the knockout blow from which the British Army in North America never recovered. The Spanish also joined the war in 1779, though technically as allies of France, not of the Americans. Spanish forces played an important role in tying down British troops in North America, campaigning successfully to capture the former Spanish possession of British West Florida.

The British themselves lacked a major European ally, making impossible any rerun of the Seven Years War, when the French had been obliged to commit most of their resources to the conflict in Europe, in order to defend their interests there, and the British had been able to focus on a colonial and maritime war. In the War of Independence, the tables were turned. It was the British who committed significant resources to a continental war (in North America) and the French who were able to deploy their expanded navy to capture scattered British possessions, especially in the West Indies, and threaten the British Isles with invasion. But though the British had no equivalent of Frederick the Great of Prussia to help them divert French power, they did receive important manpower reinforcements from other German states. Auxiliary troops from Hessen–Kassel, Hesse–Hanau,

---

1 For Frederick's popularity, see e.g. National Library of Ireland, Bruce Papers, Sermons of Rev. Samuel Bruce, 11 February 1757, 17 February 1758, 13 February 1761; [Anon.], *Reasons in Support of the War in Germany, in Answer to Considerations on the Present German War* (London: G. Woodfall, 1761), 49–55, 60.

Brunswick, Waldeck, Anhalt–Zerbst and Ansbach–Bayreuth (known collectively but inaccurately as 'the Hessians') augmented British forces in North
America and made possible the deployment of a larger field army than would
have been possible if Britain and Ireland had been the only sources of
manpower available to the British government.

North America also provided the British Army with reinforcements. Amongst
the settler population, a significant body of 'loyalists' emerged from 1776 –
Americans who could not accept a complete break with Britain and the rejection
of the British Crown. Organised in their own provincial regiments, these loyalists
became crucial to the British waging of the war, particularly in the south from
the end of 1778. Native Americans were no less important. While some fought
for the rebel forces, many more acted as allies to the British, attacking frontier
communities and causing considerable damage to the economy of the backcoun-
try. Still more controversially, the British recruited enslaved West Africans to
help their cause. For the most part, the British encouraged the flight of slaves to
their lines to undermine the rebel economy and compel the states to keep forces
at home to guard against the threat of large-scale slave insurrection. The British
also armed some slaves and used them as auxiliaries.

Causes

The two wars can be seen as the consequences of previous conflicts. The
Seven Years War owed much to the earlier War of the Austrian Succession
(1740–1748). That struggle had initiated the bitter enmity between Austria and
Prussia; Frederick the Great's unprovoked invasion of Austrian Silesia began
a contest between the two great German powers that was to last, with
various interruptions, until 1866, when Prussia finally and unambiguously
gained the ascendancy. The War of the Austrian Succession can also be seen
as a vital piece of the background to the Anglo-French contest in North
America that erupted in 1754. In part, the problem was the unresolved dispute
about the boundary between the French and British colonies, and particularly
between Nova Scotia and New France. But the events of the War of the
Austrian Succession played a part, too. The closing stages of the conflict had
seen the Royal Navy effectively blockade the Gulf of St Lawrence, cutting
New France off from France itself. In the absence of manufactures to trade
with native peoples for furs, the French saw the undermining of their
relationship with the tribes in their sphere of influence. Native peoples
increasingly gravitated towards the British colonists as trading partners, for
the simple reason that the British traders had the European manufactures

that the French Canadians lacked. To recover their relationship with the Native Americans (on whom they depended for military assistance against the more numerous British colonists), the French began to lay claim to the Ohio valley. At first, they simply planted metal plates in the ground to identify territory as belonging to the French Crown. When that failed to persuade the native peoples that the French were still a force to be respected, they started to build forts to make a statement about their power and significance.

While to the French in Canada the advance into the Ohio valley appeared as a defensive response to British aggression in trying to supplant them in the fur trade, to the British colonists the French fort-building programme seemed a clear and aggressive challenge. Both in North America and in London, the French presence in the Ohio valley was interpreted as an attempt to encircle the British colonies, by linking the French foothold in Louisiana with the French heartland in the St Lawrence valley.[2] Land speculators in the British colonies, furthermore, who had coveted the interior wilderness for their own money-making schemes, now saw their opportunities jeopardised. Colonial governments, many of which had ambitions to extend across the Appalachians, felt no less cramped by the French forward policy. Hence the opening shots of the conflict occurring in the Ohio valley, where the conflict was initially confined to a deployment of Virginian soldiers against the French, French Canadians and their native allies. It soon escalated into a much broader North American conflict, moving rapidly to the other legacy dispute from the previous war, the border between Nova Scotia and New France.

The War of Independence can also be seen as a fruit of the preceding war – in this case the Seven Years War. The loss of territory and influence that France and Spain experienced led them both to seek to recover their place by toppling the British from the position of dominance that they had acquired. The sense across Europe that Britain, rather than France, was now too powerful and a threat to the balance of power contributed to the difficulties that Britain had in securing European allies after the Seven Years War (though the manner of Britain's withdrawal from that conflict, deserting Prussia and ending its commitment to the German theatre, played at least as big a part). In North America itself, the Seven Years War also left an unfortunate legacy, which explains the outbreak of fighting between British Americans and Britons only fifteen years after the triumphal capture of Montreal and the surrender of all New France in 1760.

---

2 For the concerns of the Duke of Newcastle, the British Secretary of State, see British Library, Newcastle Papers, Add. MS 32,735, fol. 597.

Some historians argue that the British government's decision to annex French Canada was a great mistake. The French threat, they say, had helped to bind the colonies to Britain; without it, the ties loosened.[3] But if that were the long-term consequence, it was certainly not immediately apparent. In the aftermath of victory in 1760, colonial assemblies sent the new monarch, George III, loyal addresses that demonstrate a sense of Britishness that Americans shared, and a conviction that the successful wartime partnership could be continued into the peace.[4] What undermined these expectations was the British ministry's decision to base a peacetime army in North America from 1763.[5] The colonists saw no need for such a force, and soon made it clear that they would resist contributing to its cost through taxes levied on them by the British Parliament.[6] London's decision to keep a peacetime army in North America was partly based on the need to post troops in newly acquired Canada, where the loyalty of the French Catholic population could not be assumed. A garrison was also required in formerly Spanish Florida and along the frontier, to prevent settlers provoking the native peoples into further conflict (they had attacked British outposts and isolated frontier towns in 1763, in a desperate attempt to fend off the incursions they feared now that the French, their traditional allies, had been removed as a political and military presence). But the British government's main reason for wanting a peacetime army in North America almost certainly was as a mobile force that could be deployed against the French and Spanish in the Caribbean and Central America in the event of a renewed war with the Bourbon powers.[7] Much like the British Army in Ireland, it could act as a reinforcement to British military strength that was paid for by someone else – in the Irish case by the Irish taxpayer and in the American case (ministers hoped) by the colonists.

The outbreak of fighting, eleven years after the first parliamentary taxes were imposed on the Americans, shows that war was far from inevitable. There were many missed opportunities for a settlement, and the final clash owed more to fears of British authoritarianism and a threat to colonial

---

3 See e.g. the views of Laurence Henry Gipson, the great American imperial historian, as discussed in J. Shy, *A People Numerous and Armed: Reflections on the Military Struggle for American Independence* (Oxford: Oxford University Press, 1976), Chapter 5.

4 See e.g. M. Freiberg (ed.), *Journals of the House of Representatives of Massachusetts, xxxvii, pt. i, 1760–1761* (Boston: Massachusetts Historical Society, 1965), 115.

5 See e.g. J. Bullion, 'Securing the peace, the plan for the army, and the origins of the American Revolution', in K. W. Schweizer (ed.), *Lord Bute: Essays in Reinterpretation* (Leicester: University of Leicester Press, 1988), 17–39.

6 For American resistance, see e.g. M. Jensen (ed.), *English Historical Documents*, Volume IX: *American Colonial Documents to 1776* (London: Eyre & Spottiswoode, 1969), 659–98.

7 See S. Conway, *The British Army, 1714–1783: An Institutional History* (Barnsley: Pen & Sword Books, 2021), 29.

representative institutions than to the original issue of taxation. Even so, the Seven Years War, most historians agree, was the trigger that began the deterioration in relations that eventually led to war and independence.[8]

Objectives

For the British colonies, the Seven Years War was another contest against their French enemies. Access to land in the Ohio valley attracted land speculators and colonial governments keen to push their jurisdiction westwards across the Appalachians; unless the French were forced out of this territory, its exploitation by the British Americans would be hindered. The British government, for its part, decided in 1757–1758 to make the defeat of the French in Canada a major priority. Their thinking seems to have been more defensive than that of the Americans. Ministers saw security for the British colonies to the south of New France as vital for British interests.[9] Those colonies provided important raw materials for the metropolitan economy, and as their population increased they consumed larger and larger quantities of British manufactures. British troops and ships were accordingly committed to North America in ever greater numbers and separate armies converged on the French heartland of the St Lawrence valley from three different directions – from the estuary of the river in the east, from the Hudson–Champlain corridor to the south and from Lake Ontario in the west.

In the wider war, William Pitt presented the struggle in Germany as designed to aid the objective of vanquishing the French in North America.[10] But the truth was almost certainly more complex. British overseas gains were often not expected to be retained at the peace but traded in to obtain a withdrawal of French troops from western Germany, where no amount of British and allied effort seemed to be sufficient to displace them. Canada, of course, was retained; but many West Indian islands were restored to France as part of a comprehensive treaty of settlement in 1763.

For the French, the initial aim, as we have seen, was to restore their reputation amongst the native peoples by asserting themselves in the Ohio valley. When they achieved that objective in 1754–1755, they moved onto the

---

8 This is the case made convincingly by F. Anderson in his *Crucible of War: The Seven Years' War and the Fate of Empire in British North America, 1754–1766* (New York: Knopf, 2000).

9 See e.g. the cabinet's view in 1754: British Library, Newcastle Papers, Add. MS 33,029, fol. 124.

10 See his famous speech of 1762, in W. Cobbett and J. Wright (eds), *Parliamentary History of England*, 36 vols (London: Longman & Co., 1806–20), Volume xv, col. 1267.

offensive elsewhere, advancing in upper New York in 1756 and particularly in 1757, when they captured Fort William Henry. But that was the high-water mark of French advances; from 1758, they were forced into a largely defensive war, which aimed to parry the numerically superior British and colonial forces. Holding onto Canada would help sustain some of the French western ports that relied on Atlantic commerce, particularly the fur trade. It also acted as a check on British expansion in North America, which the government in Paris probably reckoned would increase British wealth and power. Even when the British captured Quebec in 1759, the French continued to resist with great determination, counterattacking and inflicting a reverse on the British outside the city the following year. We can surmise that the French hope was that by delaying the tightening of the British stranglehold for as long as possible the war in Europe would end before Montreal could be captured.

The American objective in 1775, at the start of the War of Independence, was not straightforward. Independence was repudiated by Congress itself that summer. What Congress seems to have sought was a better deal in the British Empire. It may well be that a limited war, intended simply to topple Lord North's government and bring in the Rockingham opposition, which had already shown its willingness to offer the Americans a return to the status quo of 1763, suited congressional purposes. But as it became increasingly clear that George III sided with his ministers and the claims of Parliament, American affection for the Crown diminished. The hope that the king would intervene to protect his American subjects faded and from July 1776 the colonists fought not for a reformed relationship with Britain, but for political separation.[11]

The perspective of the native peoples can be assessed mainly from their actions. The colonists' rebellion threatened further advances into the Native Americans' lands. In the early stages of the war, the native peoples largely backed the French, seeing them as the best means to prevent the encroachments of the British colonists on native lands. The French had been their principal allies before 1760, not least because the French Canadians were not committed to expanding settlement and sought a mutually beneficial relationship based on the fur trade, religious conversion and military alliance. The British colonists were seen as the enemy because they had obvious and consistent expansionary objectives. But once the conflict turned in favour of the British, in other words from 1758, native tribes increasingly gravitated towards their traditional enemies, or at least showed reluctance to give the

---

11 For American faith in the king, and its erosion, see E. Nelson, *The Royalist Revolution: Monarchy and the American Founding* (Cambridge, MA: Harvard University Press, 2014).

French unequivocal support. With the French no longer major players, native peoples looked to the British government as their best protector against the rapacious colonists to the east, especially after ministers in London tried to prevent westward expansion. Native American support for the British in the War of Independence was therefore as natural and as logical as Native American support for the French in previous conflicts.

The British government's objective in 1775 was clear – to subdue the American revolt and restore legitimate authority. The colonists were to be militarily defeated, then offered terms that Parliament had approved before the fighting started: as long as colonial assemblies raised the money required to pay for civil salaries and the army, Westminster would not exercise its right to tax.[12] Congress roundly rejected those terms in the summer of 1775, but they were still on the table when General William Howe and his elder brother Admiral Richard, Lord Howe, the British military and naval commanders in the 1776 campaign, held a commission entitling them to open discussions with the Americans after they had been vanquished in the field.

The king and his prime minister, Lord North, opposed the option of a naval blockade alone, which might in time have brought the colonists to seek terms, not least because George believed that the loyalists had to be supported and a purely naval strategy would take too long, whereas a knockout blow delivered by the army might bring the rebellion to a rapid close. The strategy for 1776 was to begin campaigning in the south, and then for three separate armies to converge in New York. In 1777, the approach was simplified; two armies were to rendezvous in the Hudson valley, cutting off irrecoverable New England from the other rebel colonies, which British ministers had high (and reasonable) hopes lacked the revolutionary fervour of the old Puritan colonies and feared the spread of Yankee democracy.

The defeat of a British field army in the autumn of 1777 at Saratoga, New York, forced a strategic reappraisal. Ministers in London now planned for a very different war, involving the French and probably their Spanish allies. Home defence became a priority, with Britain and Ireland exposed to the very real danger of invasion, or at least attack. America became much less of a priority. The government scaled back its ambitions. Recovery of the southern colonies now became the principal North American objective. The south was assumed to be full of loyalists, just waiting for a British lead to help restore royal authority. In essence, however, the war in America was

12 This was the policy agreed by Parliament in February 1775: see Jensen, *English Historical Documents*, Volume IX, 839–40.

continued largely for Caribbean ends; the importance of the southern colonies, Germain made clear, lay in their ability to sustain the West Indian islands with supplies.

For all this, the British were not thrown entirely on the defensive from 1778. They sought to attack the French West Indies, believing that if they undermined the contribution of the French islands to the French war machine, then the government in Paris would soon enter negotiations.[13] The same logic applied to the scattered and vulnerable Spanish Empire. British ministers hatched ambitious plans to take the war to Central America and the Philippines.[14] They also, somewhat recklessly, one might think, added to their list of European enemies by declaring war on the Dutch at the end of 1780. The Dutch had been sustaining the American, French and Spanish war efforts by carrying their overseas trade, and the London government reached the conclusion that it was better to have the Dutch as open enemies rather than allow them to support British enemies as neutrals.[15] Once the Dutch became belligerents, their trading posts across the globe faced British attack.

French ministers debated whether to support the Americans in a formal way in the spring of 1776, after having previously rejected the possibility that they might aid Britain, as a fellow European imperial power with a shared interest in seeing colonial revolts fail. Financial considerations encouraged the controller general of finances to recommend neutrality, but the hawks, led by Vergennes, argued that there would never be a better opportunity to reduce British power.[16] The French government may well have believed that if it could forge a durable alliance with the Americans, France would be able to benefit from Atlantic trade to the same extent as the British had in the past. But the French needed to know that the Americans were in earnest and would not patch things up with the British and return to their orbit. Hence their delay in formally beginning to negotiate with congressional delegates until independence had been declared. Thereafter, the French government planned to enter the war once it had built up its naval strength further, and, preferably, once it had persuaded the Spanish to become belligerents too.[17]

---

13 See S. Conway, *A Short History of the American Revolutionary War* (London: I. B. Tauris, 2013), 90.

14 P. S. Mackesy, *The War for America*, 2nd ed. (London: Longman, 1993), 373–5.

15 H. M. Scott, *British Foreign Policy in the Age of the American Revolution* (Oxford: Clarendon Press, 1990), 306–9.

16 J. R. Dull, *A Diplomatic History of the American Revolution* (New Haven: Yale University Press, 1985), 57–61.

17 Dull, *A Diplomatic History of the American Revolution*, 107.

For their part, the Spanish wanted to see a restoration of territory lost in 1763, especially Florida. But the government in Madrid had further ambitions, including in its list of war aims the recovery of Gibraltar and even Jamaica. It was not necessarily committed to achieving these objectives by joining the conflict as a French ally; if the British could make concessions, Spanish ministers would have been content to remain neutral. When such concessions were not forthcoming, the Spanish insisted on a joint Franco-Spanish attack on southern England as the price of their intervention. The aim was not a full-scale invasion, but a landing that would destabilise British public finances and force the British to come to terms before they could attack the vulnerable Spanish Empire.[18] The Dutch, who did not choose to enter the war, but had it thrust upon them, were largely concerned to hold what they had. A key Dutch objective, however, was to vindicate the rights of neutral carriers in wartime, which their government believed had been flouted by the Royal Navy.[19]

Means

In the Seven Years War, the French could call on much more limited human resources than their enemies. Even in 1760, the European population of New France was probably no more than 70,000; this compared with more than a million British settlers to the south.[20] A small number of French regular regiments (about 6,000 soldiers at best) boosted the military strength that the French Canadians could muster, and native tribes added more, making up in skills in wilderness warfare what they lacked in numbers. But there can be no doubt that their adversaries held a clear advantage in terms of manpower resources. True, the British colonies, with the exception of those in New England, were slow to mobilise and did so to a limited extent only. New England, especially Massachusetts, Connecticut and Rhode Island, raised spectacular numbers of troops from the beginning. In part this was because of the peculiar demographic and social structure of rural New England, with its marginal family farms and large surplus male population. It also owed much to the Protestant animosity of the New Englanders to the Catholic French and their semi-Catholicised native allies, as well as to a long-established tradition of mobilisation against a proximate and threatening

---

18 Dull, *A Diplomatic History of the American Revolution*, 108.
19 See S. Conway, *The War of American Independence, 1775–1783* (London: Edward Arnold, 1995), 66.
20 For the population of French Canada, see J. A. Dickinson, *A Short History of Quebec: A Socio-economic Perspective* (Toronto: McGill-Queen's University Press, 1988), 73.

enemy. But further south, further away from New France, the colonies were much more reluctant to put aside differences and commit to the common cause. It was this reluctance, manifested in the failure of the different colonial assemblies to endorse a Plan of Union agreed by delegates from various colonies who met in Albany, New York, in 1754, which encouraged the British government to send two regiments of regulars from Ireland to help clear the French from the Ohio valley. That initial military commitment was increased steadily, until by the final stages of the war in North America, some 25,000 regulars had been deployed.[21] By this stage, furthermore, concessions from the British government over status for American provincial officers and, more importantly, parliamentary subsidies to help pay for the raising of colonial regiments had unlocked the manpower potential of the British provinces south of New England. By the close of the conflict, as many provincial troops were in arms as regulars. This successful mobilisation of American manpower, which first became evident in 1758, played a crucial role in sealing the fate of New France. Once the manpower potential of the British colonies had been married to a significant commitment of regular troops from Britain and Ireland, it was only a matter of time before the French in Canada succumbed.

The War of Independence presents us with a more complicated picture. When fighting started in 1775, the advantage would seem to have lain with the British, who had a professional army and navy and an established system of public finance well able to pay for the waging of war. The Americans, by contrast, had to create an army and navy, and had to rely on contributions by the individual states to fund their war effort. Congress focused on the Continental Army, which started life as a rag-bag force of New England militiamen besieging the British in Boston. Washington's appointment as commander-in-chief was intended to symbolise the involvement of the south and to bring to the new army some of the discipline that Washington, as a squire from hierarchical Virginia, thought that the New Englanders lacked.[22] Unsurprisingly, money was short from the beginning, as many colonies (and then states) proved reluctant to commit resources to the common effort. Without a reliable tax income, Congress could not borrow heavily, and the solution, printing paper bills, while effective in the short term, eventually created a hyperinflation that proved ruinously damaging to the American economy.

---

21 See S. Brumwell, *Redcoats: The British Soldier and War in the Americas, 1755–1763* (Cambridge: Cambridge University Press, 2002), 24.
22 For Washington's disdain for the New England army at Boston in 1775, see J. C. Fitzpatrick (ed.), *The Writings of George Washington*, 39 vols (Washington, DC, Government Printing Office, 1931–44), Volume III, 450–1.

But the British had their challenges, too. Subduing a rebellion 3,000 miles from home was no easy undertaking in the age of sail and before refrigeration. The army, furthermore, was small by European standards and needed to be expanded rapidly to create a field force large enough to deliver a knockout blow to the rebel forces in the 1776 campaign. The king resisted pressure to recruit new regiments, believing that expanding existing regiments and hiring the services of foreign auxiliaries was the best way to assemble a large and serviceable army. Only when the French entered the war in 1778, and then the Spanish in 1779, did George relent and allow the creation of new regiments, which greatly expanded the ability of the army to wage a global struggle. Legislative concessions to Catholics, made in 1778 and again in 1782, owed much to a desire to encourage the remaining Catholic elite in Ireland to encourage their co-religionists to join the British Army. French and Spanish intervention also accelerated the British shipbuilding programme; naval expansion was dramatic from 1778. The sixty-six ships of the line in the Royal Navy in that year had risen to ninety-five by 1780. Even so, the British war effort in North America (and elsewhere) relied on people from beyond the British Isles. Besides the German auxiliaries, locally raised loyalist troops played an important part, especially from 1778, when the British regular presence in North America was reduced due to redeployments to the West Indies and home defence. Native Americans acted as a force multiplier on the frontier, as they had for the French in the Seven Years War. Slaves had arms put in their hands to aid British efforts at pacification.

France's population was twice that of Britain and Ireland combined, which gave it a great pool of domestic manpower on which it could call. But most of its enormous army remained at home. Apart from a modest expeditionary force sent to the United States in 1780 (just 5,500 troops), and French regiments brought up to North America from the Caribbean, the main French contribution was naval. The French Navy made up for the lack of an American fleet and offered a real challenge to the British Royal Navy, which had hitherto enjoyed complete control of the seaways. It was French naval growth in the years preceding French intervention in 1778 that made France such a formidable adversary for the British. By comparison, the Spanish played a minor part. Their troops, however, succeeded in reconquering West Florida for the Spanish Crown, and tied down British manpower that might have been employed against the Americans and French. The Dutch did not directly participate militarily in the war in North America, though their money, and that of the Spanish and French, helped to sustain the rebel war effort, and their islands in the Caribbean (especially St Eustatius) handled a good deal of the overseas trade of the United States before their capture by the British in 1781.

Priorities

We may not often have detailed evidence of strategic deliberations, but deployments can give us a good sense of strategic priorities. In the Seven Years War, the French government never devoted significant resources to the North American theatre. Its main focus, unsurprisingly for a nation with long land boundaries, was on Europe and defending its interests there.[23] Germany was for French ministers the principal area of concern, not North America. The British, by contrast, regarded North America as a strategic priority, as we can see from the commitment of an increasing amount of manpower and the determination to realise the full military potential of the British mainland colonies.[24] But, as we have seen, not all the overseas conquests that the British made were intended to be retained; as in previous conflicts, British governments sought extra-European acquisitions primarily as bargaining chips to trade in for French withdrawal from strategically important European territories (the Low Countries in the War of the Austrian Succession, western Germany in the Seven Years War). There was a lively public debate in Britain in 1760–1762 about whether Canada should be used in the same manner, or one or more of the French West Indian islands returned instead.[25] In the end, Guadeloupe and Martinique went back to France and Canada was retained, but perhaps as much because British sugar interests feared an overstocked home market than because Canada was prized as inherently valuable.

In the War of Independence, the British certainly prioritised recovery of the rebel colonies in the years from 1775 to 1777, though even then they mobilised resources in a rather limited way. From 1778, when they faced a much sterner challenge from France, then Spain, the British, as we have seen, redeployed their resources in a way that clearly indicates other priorities. Home defence, unsurprisingly, eclipsed the war in North America in the

---

23 The French government sent at most 6,600 troops to Canada, out of a total of 330,000 serving by the end of the war. Brumwell, *Redcoats*, 24.

24 See Anderson, *Crucible of War*, 212–14.

25 For a summary of the arguments, see P. Lawson, *The Imperial Challenge: Quebec and Britain in the Age of the American Revolution* (Montreal: McGill-Queen's University Press, 1989), 9–15.

allocation of resources, so did the West Indian islands. As the war globalised, the British government scaled back its ambitions in North America, yet increased them elsewhere, hoping to put pressure on their European enemies in all areas of the wider world where they had a presence. The cumulative effect was a much smaller proportion of British manpower and naval capacity focused on North America and a much greater proportion in other theatres of operation, from the Caribbean to the Mediterranean and from west Africa to south Asia. To give just one example: in July 1778, 41 per cent of the British Navy was deployed in North America; in July 1779 this had declined to just 9 per cent, while 49 per cent of the Royal Navy's ships were in European waters and 33 per cent in the West Indies.

For France, the War of Independence saw the reversal of the pattern of deployments in the previous conflict. Now the French government committed resources to an extra-European war, and carefully avoided involvement in a further Austro-Prussian conflict in 1778. North America may never have commanded a significant portion of France's great military potential, but its navy was at certain key moments deployed there in considerable strength. For the French ministers, as for the British, however, the West Indies took precedence. After Yorktown, Washington wanted the French Navy to help him capture the remaining British enclaves at Charleston, South Carolina and New York City. But the French fleet sailed away to the Caribbean, where the French government hoped to capture further British islands, including the biggest prize of all – Jamaica.

The Spanish government's priorities can likewise be discerned from its deployments. In North America, Florida was what mattered to Spanish ministers; its reconquest was accorded great importance. But recovering Jamaica was also a Spanish objective, to which troops and ships were devoted, and still more effort was put into bringing Minorca and Gibraltar back into Spanish control. For the Dutch, as we have seen, the war was almost wholly defensive; resources were used to prop up the Dutch position in west and south Africa, India and the East Indies. The British conquest of the Dutch West Indies occurred before the Dutch were even aware that war had been declared.

Outcomes

How successful were the various protagonists in achieving their strategic objectives? In the Seven Years War, the French lost Canada; but, as we have seen, it was never one of their priorities to keep it. Indeed, in many ways it was a drain on French resources and no attempt was subsequently made to regain it. For the native peoples who had been allies of the French, much more was at stake. French defeat exposed them to the British colonists, who they knew aspired to possess more of their lands. The removal of the French from the diplomatic equation, furthermore, narrowed native options. The kind of triangulation employed in the past was no longer achievable. The British government and its military forces emerged after the Seven Years War as the only possible protectors of native interests. For the French Canadians, most of whom grudgingly acquiesced in British rule after 1763, life seemed to have changed dramatically, but ended up remaining much the same as before the conquest. Concessions to traditional French Canadian property rights, religious practices and governing traditions, confirmed in the Quebec Act of 1774, played a part in nipping any insurrectionary tendencies in the bud.

For the British Americans, the end of New France was the reward for a successful mobilisation of resources. The co-ordinated three-pronged attack on French Canada, after a few setbacks (notably French general Montcalm's defensive victory near Ticonderoga, upper New York, in 1758) duly delivered victory in the autumn of 1760. Whether the British government's decision to keep Canada in 1763 turned out to be a wise one is a moot point; as we have seen, the removal of the French threat reduced the dependence of the colonies on British protection. In the short term, however, the war in North America was an undoubted British triumph and could be seen as part of a wider picture of success from 1758, when French preoccupation with continental Europe made it relatively easy for the British to mop up distant French dependencies, and then repeat the process with parts of the scattered Spanish Empire from 1762. Only in Germany did the French avoid heavy defeat; there they fought their enemies to a standstill and only the return of some of their lost islands in the West Indies induced them to evacuate Westphalia.

The successful implementation of British strategy in North America in the Seven Years War was not repeated in the next conflict. The concentration of force in the 1776 campaign led to some notable victories over the rebel forces, but General Howe, the British commander-in-chief, held back from delivering a knockout blow, partly for political reasons – he wanted to avoid reducing the chances of a post-war reconciliation – but also because he feared that a bloody victory would reduce his capacity to carry on operations when he was reliant on a 3,000-mile transatlantic supply route (and long wait) to secure reinforcements.[26] The three-pronged approach tried in 1776 did not

26 For Howe's inhibitions, see I. D. Gruber, *The Howe Brothers and the American Revolution* (Chapel Hill: University of North Carolina Press, 1972).

work. The army in the south arrived too late to support loyalists who rose prematurely; the southern army sailed north to rendezvous with the others in New York, but without having first restored royal authority in the southern colonies. The northern army advanced very slowly and stopped operations before bad weather hampered its move southwards. Only Howe's main army was in any sense successful. The 1777 campaign failed again to produce the desired result; this time, disastrously, a failure to co-ordinate the advance south of an army from Canada and an army marching north from New York City led to the isolation and enforced surrender of the northern army at Saratoga.

With that defeat, the best chance the British had of suppressing the American rebellion disappeared. French intervention (and the lack of major British allies in Europe to distract the French) made recovery of all the rebel colonies all but impossible. From 1778, the British government pursued a more limited southern strategy, designed to tap loyalist strength and to support the Caribbean economy. At first, it worked well; Savannah in Georgia was captured at the end of that year, and Charleston, South Carolina, fell in the spring of 1780. But subduing the southern provinces proved impossible. To stop help from further north sustaining local resistance, British forces advanced first into North Carolina and then into Virginia. But they left behind them a far from pacified country. At length, a second British field army was compelled to surrender at Yorktown, effectively ending the war in North America.

For the Americans, the main objective was secured, if not in 1781, then in the final peace settlement when the British government acknowledged the independence of the United States. But the outcome was not as disastrous for the British as it seemed in the immediate aftermath of Yorktown. The wider war turned in their favour from 1782, when they saved Jamaica, held on in Gibraltar, and even improved their situation in west Africa and south Asia. More importantly, perhaps, American independence did not prove the mortal blow to British power that government ministers, and much of the British public, had feared. The independent United States, from the mid-1790s, consumed British manufactures to a far higher value than in the colonial period. The Americans continued to send raw materials to Britain for processing, including, from the 1790s, cotton, the mainstay of Britain's Industrial Revolution. The Americans remained, then, in an essentially colonial economic relationship with Britain. The British, while enjoying the fruits of empire, saved on the administrative and military costs of trying to govern the mainland colonies. They lost the war, but arguably won the peace.

For the French, the outcome on one level was all they had hoped to see. French naval strength, combined with American and French armies on land, had snared the British at Yorktown, delivering a devasting blow to the British will to continue military operations in North America. But the French failed to reap the full reward for their commitment to the United States. The Franco-American alliance had never been more than a loveless marriage of convenience, with the two parties united only in their desire to defeat the British. Catholic and monarchical France made a strange bedfellow with Protestant and republican America. French hopes of supplanting Britain as the Americans' main trading partner faded rapidly once the peace was signed. Lord Shelburne, the shrewd British minister who negotiated the peace, offered the Americans generous terms, designed to drive a wedge between them and the French and encourage them to return to a British orientation. But, in truth, little encouragement was needed for the Americans to distance themselves from their allies. Once the French had served their purpose, the Americans dropped them like a hot brick. While still politically hostile to the British, the United States reverted to the pre-war commercial and cultural connections with the old mother country with remarkable ease. The French state, furthermore, racked up an enormous debt in helping the Americans (the controller general of finances had been right to urge caution in 1776). That debt, and its increase in the years that followed the war, led directly to the French financial crisis of the late 1780s that brought the old regime to the brink of collapse.

For the other European belligerents, the outcome was just as unfortunate. The Spanish reaped a whirlwind in the sense that the example of a successful colonial revolt helped to encourage their own colonies in Central and South America to seek their own freedom in the early nineteenth century. For the Dutch, the war was an unmitigated disaster, which led rapidly to internal turmoil, civil war and foreign occupation. But the biggest losers were perhaps the native peoples of North America. Without the British to hold back the westward expansion of the settler population, they were now exposed to the seemingly relentless desire of many Americans to take possession of lands to the west of the Appalachians.

Summary of Volume I

BEATRICE HEUSER AND ISABELLE DUYVESTEYN

Continuity and Change

The evolution of the application of strategy was not linear. We find recurring patterns across time, both within Europe and in other parts of the world, until (and sometimes beyond) that great turning point constituted by the French Wars of 1792–1815. The south-east Asian polities of the twelfth to nineteenth centuries applied strategy in ways reminiscent of the Guptas centuries earlier. From the accounts of the victims of their aggression, the nomadic Mongols and Turks in many respects resemble the Scythians, Sarmatians, Alans and Avars, Huns, Xiongnu and Uighurs who had previously spread east or west from the great steppes, all of whom specialised in raiding strategies. Some civilisations preferred pitched battles, others indirect approaches, some both.

There was continuity in some parts of the world, but in others there was a rise and decline in terms of the complexity and sophistication of many dimensions of social life, including warfare and the application of strategy. Societies in western Europe after the disintegration of the Roman Empire were far less sophisticated than their immediate Roman forebears, and resembled much earlier polities on the same continent. There are different views as to when western Europe emerged from these 'Dark Ages', whether around the year 1000, or with the twelfth-century Renaissance, or only in the following centuries. Eastern European polities were even less developed and only began to benefit from a larger civilisational upturn towards the end of the European 'Middle Ages'; for Russia, it is generally said that it entered modernity only with the reign of Peter the Great (1682–1725). Other parts of the world experienced rises and declines of standards of living, technological sophistication, complexity of warfare and strategy making. India clearly experienced a significant decline in the first millennium AD from which it was barely recovering when the Muslim incursions began. Many later cultures' warrior ethos would have impressed Homer or medieval Celtic or

528

Germanic bards, but was no match for Ottoman or European military organisation and technology in the sixteenth to nineteenth centuries. The Ottoman Empire produced a phenomenal war machine but from the later seventeenth century failed to keep up with further developments in western Europe, steadily declining thereafter until its demise with the First World War, despite injections of German practices in the late nineteenth century. China's societal decline in the eighteenth and especially in the nineteenth century, the 'century of humiliation', made it vulnerable to foreign exploitation and coercion by means of war.

Trying to make pronouncements on the evolution of strategy and its components around the globe thus does not lend itself easily to any chronological division, particularly not along the traditional European categories of 'antiquity', 'Middle Ages', and 'early modern history'. The overview presented here, emphasising patterns repeating themselves across time and space, has its own dangers, however, as it falls prey to the temptation to emphasise recurrent patterns at the expense of discontinuities. It is only fair to alert the reader to this.

Sources

Among sources across the civilisations we consider here, it is the diversity rather than the similarities that is pronounced. We find histories of wars in ancient Greece, Rome, and China. The histories of the Persian, Peloponnesian and Alexandrine wars were of unparalleled analytical quality and would become models for the subsequent millennia. Xenophon, Thucydides and Caesar, with their accounts of wars in which they had participated, left us further invaluable insights into the application of strategy. These eyewitness accounts give us better insights than many later second- or third-hand reports of warfare provided by religious men keen to detect the hand of God in success or failure. No surviving texts from other civilisations quite come up to their standard in terms of analysis of the nexus between political aims and considerations on how to apply them through military strategy, even if the term had not yet been invented. This is, of course, why, once the grip of religion had subsided, the heirs of this Graeco-Roman-Byzantine tradition were mentally disposed to conceptualise and analyse war with this secular logic.

Ancient Greece and Rome produced some manuals, partly lost, on military tactics, siege engines and other technical aspects of war. By contrast the Chinese works on war by Masters Sun (Sunzi), Wu (Wu Qi) or Xu, or the Indian work of Kautilya, included much that we would regard as philosophical or political as of importance at a strategic level. In the first millennium AD, only China and the Eastern Roman Empire took the exploration of this subject further. The latter produced the first works using the term 'strategy' in a way that encompasses higher, political aims.[1] Medieval western Europe, with a religiously dominated world view where victory in battle was seen as a divine judgement, not a function of skilful planning and execution, produced nothing of the sort.

The absence of historiographical sources for India for the first millennium AD is astonishing, and it seems that India had its own dark ages after the era that produced the works of Kautilya, Kamandaka (unless these should actually be dated to the third to eighth century AD) and Shukra.[2] The decline of western Europe in terms of technology and sophistication from the late fifth century is more easily explained. In many highly developed civilisations – think, for example, of pre-Islamic Persia or of the Roman and Byzantine empires – sources once existed that did not survive burning and looting by enemies. Thus for entire parts of the world, even where these were very sophisticated, we now need to rely upon their neighbours' accounts, a highly unsatisfactory situation.

The source base is much worse still for civilisations that lacked writing. Whether due to the loss of written evidence, or the illiteracy of these civilisations, most of the history of the neighbours of ancient Greece and Rome – those of Hannibal and the Carthaginians, those of the Persians, of Germanic tribes and invaders from the steppes, and of many other peoples – can only be reconstituted from Greek and Roman accounts, just as the history of the non-literary societies of sub-Saharan Africa, most of pre-Columbian America and Australasia can only be patched together most unsatisfactorily from archaeology or, later, from the accounts of foreign travellers. What is known about the Mongols and early Turkish tribes comes from the sources of countries invaded by them. The history of the Americas and of all of sub-Saharan Africa is shrouded in obscurity, as is that of large parts of Europe: no sources explain the causes for the great migrations that started in late antiquity and culminated with Viking/Norman conquests in the high Middle Ages, nor for the Slav expansion and the history of much of eastern Europe more generally before the tenth century. Architectural remains of fortifications found anywhere in the world *may* suggest a defensive strategy, but fortresses can serve to subdue and hold down conquered territories as much as defend against foreign invasions. Archaeological findings are precious, yet

1 See Beatrice Heuser, *The Evolution of Strategy* (Cambridge: Cambridge University Press, 2010), Chapter 1.
2 K. P. Mukerji, 'Fundamental categories of Hindu political thinking', *Indian Journal of Political Science*, 11:2 (April–June 1950), 1–12.

generally keep us guessing when they are not matched with written evidence. In the Americas, only the Mayans developed a system of writing; while impressive work has been done on their warfare, we cannot go much further than speculate on their strategic reasoning.[3] We have no written records on the subject for other parts of pre-Columbian America or for pre-colonial sub-Saharan Africa or Australia. Archaeological evidence at best suggests patterns of man-caused destruction (war) and construction (assumed to be peace), but does not reveal the ideational reasoning behind such actions. Neither the warfare of the peoples of the great plains in America, nor of large parts of sub-Saharan Africa, have left behind much by way of material evidence that might substitute for written records (see Chapters 17 and 19). No amount of even the most sympathetic archaeology can ever make up for the lack, or the loss, of accounts created at the time. We shall never be able to analyse the strategic aims and applied strategies of the inhabitants of pre-Columbian America or pre-colonial Africa or Australia in the same detail and complexity that is yielded by the accounts of Thucydides.

Where written sources do survive, China, Europe, India and south-east Asia, in the second millennium A D, royal chronicles would continue to furnish the main skeleton of historiography until well into 'modern' times. Archaeological evidence and more and better-preserved architectural remains complement these to some extent, and other forms of literature give us a feel of larger cultural contexts and values. The Hindu *Ramayana*; the Germanic Nibelungen Saga, Eddas and *Beowulf*; and the Celtic Gododdin and Arthurian cycles illustrate how layers of different cultures interacted, with the more pacific tendencies of Buddhism and Christianity being transformed by more bellicose traditions. However, the crass differences between historical events recorded by Gregory of Tours that inspired the Nibelungen Saga and the massive poetic licence we encounter in it must make us sceptical of the value of oral traditions elsewhere for the purposes of reconstructing strategy making and the values and reasoning behind it.

What seems specific to the Mediterranean world of the first millennium B C is the phenomenon of city states (Rome among them) that created some sort of consultative mechanism of policy making, including decisions to go to war (or to make peace) and on the conduct of war. We would find it again in the high and late Middle Ages in and around Italy and the Hanse cities, an association of city states similar to that of the Phoenicians' (Carthaginians) that hemmed in the Mediterranean in antiquity, and the late Medieval and early modern network of

---

3 Ross Hassig, *War and Society in Ancient Mesoamerica* (Santa Barbara: University of California Press, 1992), esp. 94–109.

the trading posts of Genoa and Venice around large areas of the Mediterranean. The social structure of these cities, dominated by a class of patricians–merchants, ruled by oligarchies or elected leaders like the doge, naturally engendered the need to articulate reasons for proposed courses of action, which find their echo in Thucydides' exceptional accounts of Athenian collective deliberations in prosecuting the Peloponnesian War. We also find allusions to, and later actual records of, such consultations in royal councils and then of parliaments in late Medieval and early modern kingdoms.

In India, south-east Asia and China, however, the source base for the history of the sixteenth to eighteenth centuries differed little, if at all, from the previous centuries, continuing to consist of royal chronicles, biographies of rulers and other works by court authors. Where a record-keeping administration was developed, archives were often degraded or destroyed by decay in a hot and humid climate (which also breeds termite infestations), or by fire, flood or war. In Europe and in the areas that would increasingly be controlled by Europeans, with the reintroduction of paper in the high Middle Ages, and then the invention of the printing press in the mid-fifteenth century, the number of sources produced grew, even if internal government documents continued to be written by hand until the typewriter made its way into offices at the end of the nineteenth century. For Europe this meant the exponential growth of a different category of sources: government and other records of all sorts which give us a more substantive knowledge of these periods, even when these archives were not all entirely reliable. Records on troop strengths, for example, were systematically inflated in many countries to deviate soldiers' pay into private pockets.

In short, all histories of warfare, and in our case of the practice of strategies, will be able to say more about Europe or about the rest of the world based on European sources, simply because there are more – and often more sophisticated and analytical – sources that have survived on this small continent than on others. Nevertheless, based on the available sources, the volume has offered as much detail and sophistication as possible about the practices around the globe, based on our academic standards for investigation.

The Strategy Makers

Throughout the two and a half millennia considered here, the polities that made and applied strategy were extremely varied and did not match nineteenth-century ideal types of 'the state' that today form the basis of most literature on political science and international relations, reason enough to challenge the utility of that literature as it applies to such a limited period of history, and such a limited area only: Europe. Polities ranged from individual tribes with leaders who barely qualified as kings (applying ancient Hebrew and Indo-European standards) to city states ruled by oligarchies of patricians; quasi-states or trading empires without substantial state territory, like the Phoenician or later the Hanse associations of port cities; the vast empire of the nomadic Mongols; the loosely interconnected Viking settlements; city states from ancient Thebes, to medieval and early modern Venice, to modern Singapore; semi-autonomous cities under the rule of a bishop or abbot; the Indic *mandala* polities revolving around a capital but without firm border areas. The main actors differed in each of these. Many city states in the Mediterranean region were governed by oligarchies or by a *demos* (people, even if this was interpreted narrowly to mean just a small proportion of the adult population, of course excluding women and slaves). In the second millennium AD, self-governing city states ruled often by oligarchies of patricians or guilds would be found not only in Italy but also to the north of the Alps, along the North Sea and Baltic coasts, and as semi-independent 'free imperial cities' within the Holy Roman Empire, or the rich and often rebellious cities of the Burgundian Netherlands. Not lending themselves to transformation into territorial states, most were later absorbed into such larger states; by the end of the Napoleonic Wars, Europe consisted of fewer, but territorially more consolidated, polities (monarchies, empires and other states) than at any time since the fall of Rome in AD 476.

In other polities, there was a supreme decision maker. Yet even autocrats, emperors or monarchs could rarely do entirely as they pleased, but were surrounded by counsellors, nobles, friends and relatives who offered advice and had a stake in whether or not it was followed. As Colin Gray rightly put it in the conclusions of a historical overview of strategy making, 'Strategy typically is developed by a process of dialogue and negotiation.'[4] In the Roman principate and dominate and subsequently in the Eastern Roman/Byzantine Empire, as in Persia, China and the Ottoman and Mughal empires, the emperor was the supreme decision maker but could not really afford to alienate other key potentates whom it was wise to consult in some fashion. In many polities, regional military commanders and administrators wielded considerable power, such as the lords of marches. In the Ottoman Empire, regional military commanders and administrators and other figures such as the sixteenth-century admiral Hayreddin Barbarossa or the late seventeenth-century vizier Mustapha Pasha devised strategies for campaigns and organised their application. If they

4 Colin S. Gray, 'Conclusions', in John Andreas Olsen and Colin S. Gray (eds), *The Practice of Strategy from Alexander the Great to the Present* (Oxford: Oxford University Press, 2011), 287–300, 292.

succeeded, a generous sultan would heap honours upon them. If they failed, they would be executed. Within the Ottoman armed forces, the elite Janissaries played a huge role in politics – occasionally, like the Byzantine armies before them in respect of their emperors, forcing abdications of sultans and staging rebellions or forcing the empire into military engagements, until they were dissolved in 1826. Russian tsars were surrounded by senior clergy and boyars, some with links through marriage to the ruling family. That rulers were expected to, but did not always, listen to advisers (often near-peer aristocrats with their own power base whom it was dangerous to alienate) seems to have obtained throughout; acting entirely autocratically usually got them into trouble.

In many parts of the world, times of great social unrest lent themselves to military commanders being acclaimed rulers (caesarism). Many dynasties across the globe owed their ascent to the military prowess of a founding father, a military-leader-turned-ruler. Many such monarchs wished to leave their realms to their progeny, whom they might train up to be worthy successors, including them in the policy- and strategy-making business at an early age.

Most strategy makers were men. As a polygamous society, ancient Egypt was exceptional in producing female rulers, but often alongside their brother–husbands; Hatshepsut (r. 1479–1458 BC) was the only one who ruled fully as a pharaoh. In other polygamous societies, women rarely played a part in making strategy or foreign policy, with exceptions being several Gupta queens, and the mothers of three Ottoman sultans. Polities practising monogamy from Carthage to Palmyra, and later from England and Scandinavia to Russia, also produced female rulers who took strategic decisions, even if they rarely, if ever, led their forces into combat, a task left by them (but also by many male rulers!) to military commanders. While the Amazon queen Hippolyta may be legendary and there is still some debate whether only women fought among the Amazons, Boudicca, queen of the Iceni, is a rare but historically documented exception. Women occasionally had influence on such matters as consorts or mistresses, or, more systematically, as widowed regent mothers of future rulers.

With the collapse of public administration in western Europe after the eclipse of Rome, the church for centuries assumed such functions, with crucial agency in the organisation and indeed the financing of wars. Both Christendom and Islam, like ancient Judaism, institutionalised the authority of religious leaders. Consequently, both church representatives and leading imams frequently had a voice in debates about war and strategy, in either restraining or escalatory ways. Most recently, we have seen the Russian Orthodox Church aligning explicitly with Putin's militaristic and expansionist strategies. Moreover, the church owned much land and other property, raised taxes and had other great revenues which it could make available for the financing of wars; in return, its higher prelates demanded a say in what was done with this money.

In Europe, the sixteenth to eighteenth centuries saw a transformation of the idea of statehood from one that served the interests of dynasties to one that served the interests of the entire populace. While the reality significantly lagged behind the theory until the watershed of the French Revolution, few states in this period were absolute monarchies, where the monarch could dispense with the need to persuade his diverse estates to support paying for war and recruiting soldiers. In the context of debates over the raising of such taxes, parliamentary records survive in various countries from the mid-fifteenth century or later, explicitly recording the rationale of strategies for war, alliances or peace, as given by monarchs or their representatives to their parliaments. Thus in Europe from about the fifteenth century, growing numbers of actors had an input into deliberations about strategic choices. Moreover, within the 'modern' states, professional bureaucracies slowly expanded, replacing the medieval clergy who in the Middle Ages had helped administer the realm. Making policy and strategy became an increasingly formalised, bureaucratic, consultative process. While monarchs might have had the last word, they relied on their bureaucracies to give them facts and figures, and to assure the financing and supplies of the armed forces while a growing military apparatus carried out the strategies. Increasingly, we find that the counsellors who gradually turned into ministers would debate different options, their positions often reflecting the narrower interests of their own government sectors – as Miles's Law put it in the twentieth century: where you stand depends on where you sit. On the eve of the French Revolution, Count Guibert complained,

> In almost all states of Europe, the different branches of administration are governed by particular ministers, whose interests and views jar, and are reciprocally detrimental to each other; each of them is occupied exclusively with his object. One might imagine the other departments belonged to a different nation.[5]

Enemies

A striking commonality is that all the regimes covered here had external and internal enemies. Intuitively, warfare between kindred tribes, populations or sometimes quite literally brothers fighting over dynastic succession rights is

5 Anon. [Guibert], *General Essay de Tactique* (London: chez les libraires associés, 1772), preface.

more puzzling than warfare with external enemies. In authoritarian and autocratic societies, where disputes could not be settled by democratic elections, the resort to force might seem the only way to settle them. Internal adversaries came in many forms. They included insurgents driven ideologically or by grievance (with or without leaders who might claim the crown or other supreme rule for themselves), secessionists and, in polities with a greater degree of role specialisation, internal challenges to the civilian power by the military. All civilisations we cover knew wars of dynastic succession, except that monogamy and primogeniture substantially reduced the number of potential contenders in the West. (In a polygamous context, Ottoman rulers solved the problem by killing all their brothers upon coming to power.) Monogamy could still lead to strife over succession when the succession of a child or a woman to kingship might tempt uncles or adult cousins to make a bid for power, entailing civil war. Personal and dynastic rivalries dominated medieval European warfare until the nineteenth century, when they were largely replaced by nationalist rivalries.

Wars between entities of much the same culture and similar populations were as prevalent – and not merely in Europe – as wars against truly 'other' enemies. While common around the world and through the ages, such wars between kindred tribes or polities tended to be denounced as particularly unnatural or sinful by philosophers and theologians. All systems of authority and their philosophers and lawyers tended to denigrate internal enemies (insurgents) as criminal and to focus in their theoretical and legal approach on 'equal' enemies as legitimate adversaries. Plato regretted the tendency of Greeks to fight against Greeks and thought only war against external enemies like the Persians amounted to 'proper war' or *polemos*; Roman authors found the civil wars particularly abhorrent (although not as upsetting as the slave revolts). Medieval Christendom differentiated between barons' feuds (which princes and the church sought over centuries to suppress and replace by a domestic system of administering justice), wars among Christian polities which were limited by a growing number of conventions, and wars against external aggressors to whom Christian polities were allowed to give as good as they got: here the gloves were off, and anything was allowed in response to the equally unrestricted warfare practised by the latter. Islam in theory outlawed wars between Muslims, remaining in lasting denial regarding the formation of separate state entities as Islam in theory recognised only a single *umma* (community of the faithful) under a single caliph. Yet philosophers and theologians themselves contributed to exacerbating such ideologically driven wars within or between neighbouring polities.

External foes could be territorially settled polities, usually neighbours, such as the Persians for the Greeks (and later Romans), or raiding parties of all sizes, from the Turkish *gazi* to the hosts of the Xiongnu that descended on the Chinese, and their nomadic successors, the Huns and Mongols who invaded the lands from China and India to the Middle East and Europe. Yet many early Chinese texts treating strategic and military affairs focus on an 'equal' adversary, a 'culturally like-minded opponent' (Graff, see Chapter 6), even when these were neither as frequent, nor as dangerous, as the devastating raids of the non-Chinese horsemen coming from central Asia.

In European dynastic wars, the competing dynasties' soldiers were not themselves seen as enemies if they surrendered or were captured: if they were not killed for practical reasons (looking after prisoners diverts manpower from the battle) they were generally held for ransom or exchanged for one's own captured soldiers, which increasingly became the practice from the seventeenth century. They might even be recruited into the other side's forces. Indeed, whole mercenary units might change sides if they were not paid by their first employers. Only if there was a religious dimension to the war and/or it was seen as a rebellion would individual soldiers be deliberately maltreated when captured. This stands out when one compares the conditions of surrender and retreat at the battles of Fontenoy and Culloden, held within a year of each other in 1745 and 1746: Protestant Hanoverian forces fought in both. Fontenoy was an inter-polity battle pitting British, Dutch, Hanoverian and other German forces against French forces; at Culloden, Scottish and Irish Catholics supported the Jacobite claim to the throne of the United Kingdom, held and defended, again, by Protestant Hanoverian forces that included Scots, English and Dutch contingents. At Fontenoy, the defeated army was allowed to withdraw with all honours and its arms; at Culloden, the victorious Hanoverians massacred the Jacobites both on and beyond the battlefield, executed or deported survivors, and imposed punitive repressive laws on the population as a whole.

The wartime strategies of all civilisations spared humble peasants and townsfolk only when it was in their interest not to lose their labour force and the products of their labour. But this was precisely a reason also to deal brutally with the enemy's subjects, to deprive an enemy of their productivity. In the Middle East and the Euro-Mediterranean world of antiquity, we have evidence of countless mass atrocities practised against enemy civilians. They clustered around three patterns: either a massacre of all, including women and children (or mass starvation through scorched-earth tactics); or a massacre of the men while women and children were carried off into slavery; or the enslavement of the productive part of the population, including suitable men (perhaps along with the summary execution of a limited number of enemy soldiers). This did not necessarily mean that these civilians were always themselves branded enemies (as the Hebrew Bible did on occasion): instead, they were seen mainly as property of the enemy ruler or dynasty, and it was them that one meant to harm by destroying or appropriating their property. For millennia, slavery was not a function of racism, but of a general disdain felt by ruling classes for their own and the enemy's commoners, who were reified – treated as objects, as chattel, not as fellow humans.[6]

There were also collective enmities, however: Rome inherited the long-lasting binary rivalry between Persians and Greeks. From the 630s this was replaced by that between Christians (Kafirs or Franks in Muslim parlance) and Muslims (Arabs, Persians, Turks, Mongols, Berbers, often indiscriminately referred to as 'Saracens', 'Paynim' or 'the Infidel' by Europeans). For the Muslim Rashidun, Umayyad and early Abbasid caliphates, as well as for the Seljuk and Ottoman Turks, the Byzantine Empire as the nearest, oldest and most prestigious outpost of Christianity was the main enemy.

On the Indian subcontinent, the fear of Muslim armies was such that the defenders of Hindu polities who were attacked by them undertook to fight to the death rather than surrender (*saka*), while there are multiple attested cases from the fourteenth century to the sixteenth of the women of these polities committing mass suicide by immolation (*jauhar*) to avoid rape and enslavement. This is reminiscent of the collective suicide of the citizens of Numantia in 133 BC and of the zealots of Masada in AD 74, all to escape Roman punishment and slavery.

Admittedly, when they met with no fighting resistance and with submissive compliance in the occupation, conquering Arabs and Turks often accepted regular payments of a tax (the *jizya*) in lieu of conversion. If civilians in captured territories were willing to convert, the Ottomans opened every career path to them, and a slave woman might become the mother of the future Sultan, a degree of tolerance that was rare within Christendom. Yet in Africa, the history of the confrontation of Arabs and black populations illustrates that discrimination existed despite the principles of the Koran by which all Muslims were the same unto Allah: Arabs were the slavers, black Africans the ware.

There was also mortal competition among Muslim tribes and leaders, including the Kurds, who with Saladin established themselves in and around Palestine, and the Mamluks in Egypt. We see this in the wars between the Ottoman

6 Beatrice Heuser, *War: A Genealogy of Western Ideas and Practices* (Oxford: Oxford University Press, 2022), 263–306.

Empire and Safavid Persia, followed by the Ottoman destruction and takeover of the Mamluk Empire. And the Muslim Mughal Empire of India also saw itself as at war with Muslim entities: the Afghans were their chief enemy, along with the sultanate of Deccan, and the Rajput kings, even before the Europeans began to encroach on the powers of local rulers as their trade emporia turned into colonies. Nor was Christian-on-Christian war less ferocious in all instances, as pre-Reformation Anglo-Norman clashes with the Welsh, the Scots, the Galwegians and the Irish illustrate.

Other enemy images existed from the Middle Ages, encapsulated, for example, by the French derogatory term *goddon* for the English in the Hundred Years War, derived from the latter's swearing, and more sprang up especially in the late nineteenth century and the early twentieth (with particularly gruesome characteristics attributed to 'the Hun', 'Ivan', 'the Turk', 'the Yellow Peril'). Such collective enmities were both the result of wars and contributors to subsequent ones. Passed on from generation to generation over centuries, they kept memories of enemy cruelty and one's own victimhood alive. Also on the side of invaders and occupiers, they passed on disdain for and fear of resistant subject peoples, regardless of skin colour.

While civilians were seen as chattel in all cultures until well into the second half of the second millennium A D, notwithstanding attempts by theologians or philosophers to protect them, they were very much seen as individual enemies in contexts of religious contention. Above all, the monotheistic religions furnished ample excuse for warfare against adherents of other religions. Thus Jews within Christendom, and in the Muslim world, the dozens of Christian denominations and some other faiths such as the Yezidis, were subject to repeated persecutions. While within the Ottoman Empire minorities of a different religion were tolerated for most of the time, and while there were periods when Jews were tolerated in European polities, before the French Revolution nothing mobilised animosity as widely as differences of confession or religion. While it might have required some convincing to inspire commoners to risk their lives for their sovereign lords, all seem to have found it immediately plausible that they should kill and risk being killed for their religious beliefs and their God. We thus see the brutal slaughtering of populations who refused to convert by the Muslims in the earlier centuries of Islamic conquest (and periodic lashings out against non-Muslim minorities throughout history, until the persecution of the Yezidis since the 2010s), the equally brutal excesses of some Byzantine armies and then the crusaders when recapturing formerly Christian cities (which by then had many Muslim and Jewish inhabitants), the Christian persecutions of Jews and of heretical communities like the

Albigensians in the thirteenth century, and then the confessional wars within Europe that started with the Hussite Wars in the early fifteenth century.

Causes and Aims of Wars

Migration, Booty, Conquest

The two simplest causes of war that can be traced back to antiquity, even to prehistory, and can be found in surviving primitive societies, are first, and most commonly, booty raids (and counterraids). Second but more rarely, there is mass migration. If the population density in the recipient areas had reached the level where the immigrants became a threat to the subsistence of the others, such mass migration (whether to escape famine or natural disaster, or as a knock-on effect of invasions once removed, or for reasons unknown) met with the resistance of those already settled in these lands; in other words, it caused war.[7] In the case of pre-Columbian North America, there is evidence that indigenous warfare was due to ecological changes which resulted in shortages of foodstuffs (Chapter 16). Also, in pre-colonial Africa, there are indications that ecological stress led to war between chiefdoms. In late imperial China natural disasters caused conflict and rebellion. On the flip side, when populations expanded, people hankered for more space: thus Greek city states established colonies. There were similar pressures in Europe prior to the plague in the mid-fourteenth century. The Ming and Qing empires aimed to maintain hegemony in central and east Asia, this was mixed with a quest for more territory to accommodate an ever-expanding population (Chapter 20).

Raids, like mass migration, can stem from famine and the need for food to survive, but can be transformed by the lust for movable booty or for land, or for both.[8] Booty, as we have noted, could be anything from grain, cattle, sheep, horses or portable objects to slaves. Land could be coveted for its resources, for its flourishing towns, for its strategic position on the way to something else, as an area to settle surplus populations, or merely to extend one's rule. The quest for booty as a motivation for going to war existed well into recent centuries. Guy Halsall has argued that in the European Dark Ages, north of the Alps, what little wealth existed was often carried along by armies if it was not stored in isolated abbeys; battles were in large part fought over its acquisition.[9] As professional

---

7 Paul Smith: 'Climate change, mass migration and the military response', *Orbis*, Fall 2007, 617–33; Nils Petter Gleditsch, *Wither the Weather; Climate Change and Conflict*, special issue of *Journal of Peace Research*, 49:1 (2012).

8 Azar Gat, *War in Human Civilisation* (Oxford: Oxford University Press, 2008), Part 3.

9 Guy Halsall, *Warfare and Society in the Barbarian West 450–900* (London: Routledge, 2003).

armies came into being in Europe later in the Middle Ages, they were often led by *condottieri* who acted as military entrepreneurs: they invested in their men and undertook to pay them, but then sought to retrieve their investment in any way possible. This would be mainly through the payment of those polities who hired them, but also the spoils of war.[10] Already in European antiquity there were rules about how booty was to be divided up between the polity (or prince), the captain and the soldiers. Medieval and modern European ordinances of war endlessly reiterated these principles, reflecting the centrality of booty to the war itself. The Spanish soldiers embarking on the subjugation of the Americas were under pressure to acquire movable goods as their captain conquistadores lent them arms and horses against contractual expectations to be paid back, and these means could only be acquired by making booty (and exploiting local populations through a form of serfdom).[11]

The victims of such raids would in turn go to war because of the wrong suffered, to retrieve property (whether this be land, slaves or booty) stolen by and to be recaptured from an enemy. That this was open to highly subjective interpretation, in the absence of a superior judge, tribunal or mediator, is clear: one need only to point to later Christian criticism of the earlier Roman narrative of having fought wars only in self-defence.[12] Many of the wars considered here arose from some rulers' desire to enlarge their sphere of power, but this was generally packaged in diverse ideologies and presented with equally diverse justifications. It is difficult to tell whether all leaders set on expansion thus sincerely believed they had a just cause. Apart from ecological stress, personal ambitions – what medieval philosophers called the lust for domination, *cupiditas dominandi* – feature prominently as a cause for war. In addition to the ideational definition of entire civilisations as enemies, there were many personal rivalries and enmities. Some had structural causes. The bicephaly that was created in the fourth century that divided authority in Christendom between the secular power of the emperor and the spiritual power of the Pope (or, in Constantinople, the patriarch) led to power struggles between several pairs or sets of them (as antipopes and anti-emperors were elected several times). A series of wars within the Holy Roman Empire pitted sub-entities (especially Italian city states)

---

10 F. Tallett and D. J. B. Trim (eds), *European Warfare, 1350–1750* (Cambridge: Cambridge University Press, 2010), esp. David Parrott, 'From military enterprise to standing armies: war, state, and society in western Europe, 1600–1700', 74–95.

11 Vitus Huber, *Beute und Conquista: Die politische Ökonomie der Eroberung Neuspaniens* (Frankfurt am Main: Campus, 2018).

12 Lactantius, *Divine Institutes* vi.ix.4f.

supporting the emperor (the 'Ghibbeline' faction) against those supporting the Pope (the 'Guelf' faction).

Then, all systems of dynastic monarchy generated frequent and ample opportunities for ambitious members of the ruling family to challenge the succession of another member. European dynastic marriage alliances, originally designed to cement peaceable relations, time and again, due to the gamble of fertility, turned into wars of dynastic succession. Whenever the slightest claim to the succession to any land arose, however tenuous, Christian princes believed it to be their duty to fight for it, as King Frederick II of Prussia bluntly told his heir.[13] French kings saw no contradiction in denying women the right to succeed to the French Crown and waging war for the rights of their wives to inherit foreign lands. Perhaps it is wrong always to look for detailed masterplans for conquest: many successful conquerors, like Alexander III of Macedon, Caesar, Frederick II of Prussia, Napoleon or indeed Hitler or Putin, may have had 'unclear endstates' in mind but widened their aims when the going was good.[14]

There was an interim solution stopping short of full-scale territorial expansion: the Sassanians sought to control trade routes in order to impose taxes on trade, a phenomenon also found locally in medieval Europe, where barons with strategically positioned castles, or towns, or abbeys extracted such payments; other civilisations such as periodically the Vikings and the Ottoman Turks developed the knack of attacking neighbouring areas to extract regular tribute payments, but not to occupy them permanently. Occupation could be costly in terms of occupying forces if the populations could not be persuaded to accept client status. Exacting a formal recognition of overlordship and regular tribute payments could be the mutually advantageous compromise.

Striving for and Resisting Universal Monarchy

Several of the more sophisticated civilisations of antiquity – Assyria, Persia, Macedon under Alexander III, then the Romans and the south and later south-east Asian polities – developed a claim to universal dominion, or at least dominion of the known world.[15] If there was anything outside this sphere of order (*kosmos*) and peace, it was seen as a sphere of chaos and

13 Frederick II of Prussia, 'Political Testament' of 1768, in Richard Dietrich (ed.), *Die politischen Testamente der Hohenzollern* (Cologne and Vienna: Böhlau, 1986), 650.
14 David Lonsdale, 'The campaigns of Alexander the Great', in Olsen and Gray, *The Practice of Strategy*, 14–35, 33; Charles Esdaile: "De-constructing the French Wars: Napoleon as anti-Strategist", *Journal of Strategic Studies*, 31:4 (2008), 512–52.
15 Roel Konijnendijk, 'Legitimization of war', in B. Jacobs and R. Rollinger (eds), *A Companion to the Achaemenid Persian Empire* (Malden, MA: Wiley-Blackwell, 2021), 1139–50; and see the relevant chapters in this volume.

anarchy that invited pacification (and thus conquest). Yahve is referred to in the Hebrew Bible as *Melech Malchei HaMelachim* ('the King of Kings of Kings'), and Achaemenid and Sassanian rulers saw themselves as the *Shahanshah* with the same meaning, which the Byzantines imported as *Basileus Basileōn*. All of these aspired to universal monarchy, or at least to supreme rule over the world as they knew it, as far as was feasible. The Romans articulated the ambition of ruling over the world somewhat more explicitly than anybody else, in spite of their ignorance of the existence of the Americas. It can be traced back to the second century BC, reached a first peak with Augustus and the writings of Vergil,[16] and gained additional momentum just as Rome was about to start its long decline, with the espousal of Christianity.

Islamic missionary zeal aside, Ottoman Sultan Mehmet II the Conqueror in the fifteenth century also harboured imperial ambitions: he not only wanted to take over what was left of the Byzantine Empire, but also claimed the imperial succession for himself. Proclaiming himself *qayser* (*caesar*), he and his successors wanted to conquer all the lands that had once belonged to Rome, or that now belonged to the Holy Roman Empire, hence their yearning to conquer Vienna (the Muscovite rulers would develop similar pretensions to be the heirs of Constantinople a century later).

Within Western Christendom, the idea of a restored Roman Empire had arisen from the ashes of Rome seven centuries earlier with Charlemagne, who nevertheless accepted the pre-eminence of the rulers of Constantinople (provided they were male). Under the Saxon emperors, the dream of a merger of the eastern and western empires and the *renovatio imperii Romanorum* was reborn briefly. The ideal of a single Christian republic lingered, as did the accusation levelled against Emperor Charles V, his son Philip II of Spain, Louis XIV of France and, with considerably more justification, Napoleon, that they were out to create an *imperium universalis* by fire and sword. Regional bids for hegemony were many, and the larger polities of Europe certainly wanted a say in the world's affairs, even if it remained hyperbole when a chancellor of Catherine II of Russia boasted that, in his time, not a single cannon in Europe had dared fire without the empress's permission.[17]

While Emperor Charles V was somewhat more modest in his ambitions than his chief servants, such as Mercurino Arborio de Gattinara, he provoked not only the French and English kings to compete with him for

---

16 Israel Shatzman, 'The Roman republic: from monarchy to Julius Caesar', in Olsen and Gray, *The Practice of Strategy*, 36–56, 44 f.

17 Count Nikita Panin, minister of Catherine the Great, in 1768, quoted in Simon Dixon, *Catherine the Great* (London: Profile Books, 2009), 187.

predominance, but also Ottoman Sultan Süleyman. The latter not only started calling himself Caliph (to the great chagrin of the last Abbasid Caliph, who died his prisoner in Kostantiniyye), but also marched on Vienna in conscious imitation of the progression of Charles's imperial coronation in Bologna, wearing a four-tiered crown evoking the three-tiered crown of the Pope plus the imperial crown.[18] In fact, the idea of a universal monarchy as a licence to conquer can be found throughout the Euro-Asiatic land mass. It is impressive how similar this ideal was to that the Hindu thinking we find in the writings of Kautilya in India. Later, we find it in the Islamic ideal of one worldwide Islamic polity under one sole Caliph, in the ideals driving the Mughal rulers of India and in the Indic polities of south-east Asia until the nineteenth century. We find similarities in the Mongol ideal of one empire under the Blue Heaven, on the basis of which they created the greatest land empire the world has known. We encounter a variant of the idea of universal monarchy also in China.

Wherever such a universal claim was made, it raised hackles, with push-back generally resulting in counterclaims and war. Any striving for domination, real or alleged, caused war just as much as did the resistance to it. In the European context, the French, English and Castilian kings, initially to rebuff papal interference in their domestic affairs, from around 1200 claimed sovereignty, *imperium*, supreme rule in their realm. They turned this also against the Holy Roman emperors who claimed, at the very least, to be first among equals, and occasionally tried to extend their rule over other rulers; wars ensued repeatedly from such jockeying for supremacy. Similarly, the aim of unifying China under one rule could only be pursued by war. Several of the wars of the Indian subcontinent resulted from quarrels about hierarchy and overlordship versus an equivalent to the insistence of European polities on their sovereignty. The defence of a polity's sovereignty against outside interference often resulted in war.

Insurgencies and Civil Wars

The concept of civil war and that of an insurgency to challenge rulers presupposes the existence of states or state-like entities. States came into being late in human history; indeed, they could disappear and re-emerge, yet war continued to exist. It is plausible to argue that a clear division between civil war (war between groupings belonging to a larger polity) and uprisings against rulers preceded the

---

18 Gábor Ágoston, 'The Ottomans: from frontier principality to empire', in Olsen and Gray, *The Practice of Strategy*, 105–31, 123.

establishment of states or empires, and that there were periods where clear distinctions between inter-polity and intra-polity wars were difficult to make. Moreover, the parties to intra-polity disputes often enough received help from without that polity, turning intestine wars into hybrids that included external strife.

Where polities had come into existence, on the whole their rulers sought to delegitimise any uprisings against them. And yet alongside the criminalisation of violent challenges to the government from within, there was also a tradition of justifying them if they met particular conditions. The Graeco-Roman tradition that survived into the European Middle Ages both in east and west already contained the idea of a social compact, allowing insurgency and tyrannicide in extreme cases of poor government. We find such ideas articulated again in Europe from the twelfth century. Even if the philosophical principles were lacking, the assumption seems to be common to most human societies, other than the most totalitarian, that rulers have to rule in the interest of their people, and practise good governance, or face deposition, however strong the myth of divinely ordained monarchy that protected them. We thus see examples of palace coups or wider insurgencies also in China and Persia that were explained in terms of poor governance.

The fear of coups was endemic in ancient China (see Chapters 1, 6). In the Chinese world of the first millennium A D, we see both internal and external wars, the former (like the An Lushan rebellion) sometimes involving the army – an interesting parallel with the Roman and later the Eastern Roman/Byzantine Empire, where armies often rose up against unpopular emperors to replace them with their favourite general. Coups also occurred in post-Augustan Rome, including its Byzantine successor, among the Mongols as they spread east and west across the great steppes, among the Turkic tribal leaders as they established themselves in the Middle East, in the south and south-east Asian Kingdoms, and in China. 'Inter-tribal skirmishes' within the greater Muslim polity, the *umma*, plagued the early caliphates. Japan was troubled almost exclusively by intestine wars in the period covered in this volume (except for two Mongol onslaughts in the thirteenth century and a thwarted Japanese attempt to conquer Korea in the late sixteenth).

Conversion by Force

The earlier polities of Asia, the Middle East and the Mediterranean basin seem not to have had any ambitions to convert others to their religion by the sword. This is true even for the monotheistic religion of the Israelites. Religion entered into their conflicts with the Romans when the latter sought to impose emperor worship on them, incompatible with the Hebrew and Christian worship of a sole jealous God. But war for the sake of conversion first entered the scene with Islam.[19] Mohammed's teaching included the injunction to spread Islam, by means of force, if there was resistance. Later, the Turkmen tribes that pushed into the Middle East from the eleventh century initially sought booty and new pastures for their herds. But once converted to Islam, like the Arabs before them, the Seljuk and then the Ottoman Turks discovered the cause and ambition to bring the known world into the *Dar al-Islam*, the House or Abode of Islam. It was also a Turkic dynasty, the Ghaznavids, who towards the year 1000 embarked on the conquest of India, followed by Muslim Afghan rulers in the thirteenth and fourteenth centuries who created the Delhi Sultanate and its successor states.

Christians had not initially fought wars for the purpose of exporting Christianity, even though fifth-century wars between Christians of different confessions gained additional justification from mutual accusations of heresy. Once the Prophet's green banner fluttered throughout the Middle East and all around the Mediterranean, however, reaching even into the Frankish realm north of the Pyrenees, we find some instances of Christians justifying aggression in terms of imposing Christianity, most notoriously Charlemagne's wars against the Saxons and the Baltic crusades. While individual theologians made the case that one could compel pagans by force to convert to Christianity, this concept remained alien to official Catholic doctrine, as summed up authoritatively by Gratian and Thomas Aquinas: no one was to be forced to accept Christianity.[20] Accordingly, the crusades, when properly authorised by popes and conducted according to their prescriptions, stood in continuity with the earlier wars of the liberation of formerly Roman (and thus Christian) territories under Justinian and Heraclius, and did not aim at forcible conversion. Admittedly, papal power was too feeble to control all the activities of the crusaders in the Middle East. Thus there are instances when crusaders, far from home, committed horrendous atrocities (definitely not authorised by Catholic doctrine), as at the capture of Jerusalem in 1099, or in 1204 when a whole crusade (the Fourth) deviated from the liberation of Jerusalem to the conquest and looting of the fellow Christian Byzantine Empire.

---

19 See e.g. John, Bishop of Nikiu, *Chronicle* (trans. R. H. Charles) (London: Text and Translation Society 1916), cxi–cxx.
20 There is one ignominious deviation from this pattern: Pope Nicholas V in 1452 allowed the enslavement of non-Christians in his Bull *Dum Diversas*, but it was revoked less than a century on.

The European Confessional Wars that commenced with the Hussite Wars of the early fifteenth century and reached their full strength in the sixteenth century and the first half of the seventeenth were in part fought over (religious) liberties, and in part to offset Habsburg power, in the belief that a balance of powers would be beneficial to all. These wars within Christendom straddled intra-state and inter-state wars, each side trying, first, to impose its reading of the Bible on all, and later to secure at least its own and its fellow confessionalists' religious liberties throughout Europe. They were particular to their times, even though the earlier rise and repressions of sects in late antiquity and in the Middle Ages presaged them; confessionally motivated uprisings in the United Kingdom to restore Catholic monarchs to the throne seized from them by Protestant rivals 1688–1746 were late aftershocks, with their late echoes in the multicausal Irish 'Troubles' of 1968–1999. Comparable confessional quarrels tortured the Islamic world, and seem to have broken out again in recent years. Outside the West, there seems to be much reluctance to build on the European experience that these can only be stopped from turning into war by keeping religion resolutely out of politics (a rare example was Mustafa Kemal Atatürk's Turkey). This lesson, essentially a compromise, was enshrined within the Holy Roman Empire in the Religious Peace of Augsburg of 1555, was largely ignored in the early 1600s which led to the Thirty Years War, and was reaffirmed at its end with the Westphalian Treaties of 1648.

Confessional differences blended into political disputes, with Protestantism in the seventeenth century going along with republicanism in the Netherlands and in the British Isles, and rejections of republican values during the French Revolution going along with a commitment to the monarchy and to the Catholic Church. Protestantism, with its emphasis on vernacular languages and 'national' churches, also furthered the cause of separatism from larger Catholic entities, giving rise to a proto-nationalism. This would herald the rise of wars pitting nations against one another, first crystallised in the Napoleonic Wars.

Just Cause

It seems that the notion that some justification for aggression was needed was not merely a Graeco-Roman heritage, even though modern international law stands in that tradition. The justification might be contrived, as when Alexander III of Macedon explained his war against Persia with the Persian burning of the Athenian Acropolis – a different polity altogether – a century and a half earlier (Arrian, *Anabasis*, III.xviii.11 f.). Or it might be a case for Sigmund Freud's couch, as when Russia's expansion over six centuries is justified in terms of the need for a buffer, after the traumatising Mongol invasions and occupation (often referred to as Tatar rule), or when Peter the Great, in proclaiming himself emperor and invoking his hope for peace, told his people that they must not diminish their military effort, in order to avoid the same fate that had befallen the Byzantine Empire.[21]

Some need for justifications for going to war existed also in ancient Persia.[22] The Buddhist polities of the Indian subcontinent adhered to the notion that war should only be defensive (see Chapter 8). This was offset, however, by the Hindu cult of the warrior that saw social prestige and indeed salvation coupled to fighting and risking one's life (or even succumbing in war), and provided the incentive for communities to raise themselves on the *varna* scale, which was possible only by dominating others. Even a civilisation with a quite separate ideational pedigree, such as ancient China, had ideas about just causes and just intentions of wars.[23]

By contrast, pre-Islamic Turkmen, Mongol and Germanic tribes seem to have pursued war without feeling the need to articulate a just cause. It is easy to interpret this as evidence of a 'Realist' world view in which 'the strong do what they can and the weak suffer what they must', as Thucydides put it (v.89). It is not evidence, however, that *all* polities and *all* rulers were *always* inclined to resort to war and expansion whenever the opportunity arose, at least not by military means and at the cost of many lives. The more pacific rulers and regimes have not, in general, left as great a mark on the historical accounts, as these tend to be about action, war and change, not about lasting peace and tranquillity.

Means

Kinetic Means

Warriors, Soldiers, Conscripts and Mercenaries

Recruitment of soldiers the world over would fall within a spectrum. At one end were peasants and townsfolk doubling as self-defence forces ('militias') and compulsory levies from among them when they were needed. This limited the time for their military service, as crops and other business needed to be tended to. Some polities, such as republican Rome and the Germanic

---

21 Quoted in Thierry Sarmant, 'Moi, Pierre, empereur', *L'Histoire*, 485–5 (July–August 2021), 30–45, 32.

22 Konijnendijk, 'Legitimization of war'.

23 D. A. Graff, 'The Chinese concept of righteous war', in H. M. Hensel (ed.), *The Prism of Just War: Asian and Western Perspectives on the Legitimate Use of Military Force* (Farnham: Ashgate, 2010), 195–216.

successor polities in the Western Roman Empire, made military campaigns an annual, seasonal business. Such levies and militias could not be expected to fight far from home. Even in the eighteenth century, French Count Guibert had learnt from his experience in the War Ministry that it was a challenge to get Frenchmen from 'the South of France to defend Flanders or Alsace, or the people of these provinces to protect the coasts of the Mediterranean or Gascony'.[24]

On the other end of the spectrum, there were professional forces. These tended to be, initially, small elite formations (a palace guard, the Persian 'spear bearers' and 'Immortals', the Roman Praetorian Guard), sometimes evolving into a dominant warrior caste or class. When permanent forces grew larger in number, they often included non-native units serving for pay. Republican Rome initially distinguished between Italian soldiers and the warriors of entire tribes contracted as auxiliaries or *foederati* in return for peace treaties, land or pay. Later, entire tribal units of warriors were integrated into an increasingly multinational Roman Army and rotated through the empire, to avoid identification with their regions of origin and the quarrels Rome might have with its inhabitants. Rome and the Chinese polities stand out as having had the most sophisticated state apparatus that allowed for extensive taxation, but also for wide recruitment, and sophisticated logistics to supply armies and move them around on well-built roads, by river or by sea. This made it possible for Rome, and later also China, to maintain professional forces that could be brought into action along and beyond their frontiers, far from home, to maintain fleets and to build and maintain fortifications and permanent camps.

Prior to the nineteenth century, there was no sharp distinction between a (foreign) professional soldier, what we now refer to as a mercenary and an (indigenous) professional soldier: criticism of the foreign professional, most famously articulated by Machiavelli, contrasted (unpaid) militias defending their own (Italian city) states and paid soldiers from elsewhere (in Italy and beyond) who had no emotional or material attachment to the city they defended. The advantages of militias were thus double: they were cheap and committed.

Early modern western European history produced the *condottiere*, and later the private military entrepreneur, who first emerged in the high Middle Ages and found work throughout Europe and even in south-east Asia (Chapter 15). While the king of France pioneered the creation of a standing army after the

24 Jacques-Antoine Hippolyte de Guibert, *De la force publique considérée par tous ses rapports* (Paris: Didot l'aîné, 1790), repr. in Comte de Guibert, *Stratégiques* (Paris: Herne, 1977), 613.

end of the Hundred Years War – drawing specifically on the direct taxation of the formerly Plantagenet provinces – many other states could follow only slowly. Thus the Thirty Years War was still largely fought by hired professionals.

Despite the proto-nationalism in France, Spain, England and Scotland that came into existence even before the French Revolution, fully professional soldiers were not expected necessarily to be native to the lands of the government they served: until the eighteenth century, Frenchmen fought in Prussia's armies; Welshmen and Scottish and Irish Jacobites offered their services to Continental powers, Dutchmen and Hanoverians fought for Protestant causes on both sides of the Channel, and Hessians, loaned by their duke to the king of England and Scotland, fought against the secessionists in America. Even Napoleon's Grande armée still included hundreds of thousands of foreign recruits. Meanwhile, Ottoman armies were recruited from any Muslim populations and thus were rarely, if ever, ethnically homogeneous – it is thus misleading to speak of 'Turkish' armies in this period. Only the rise of ethnic nationalism in the nineteenth century introduced disdain for professional soldiers merely on the basis that they were fighting for a polity with which they did not have ethnic bonds.

A further model was something of a compromise: the conscripted recruit who served for a distinct period of time based on allegiance to a prince or nation. Already in the late seventeenth century and the eighteenth some European polities had selectively recruited peasantry (more rarely townsfolk), often by lot, for several years' mandatory military service which made them, for that period, a more or less professional force.

Size

The sources of antiquity are notoriously unreliable when it comes to any quantitative evaluation of the means available. Ancient Chinese and Roman sources speak of hundreds of thousands of men being involved in battles, but figures may have been inflated for rhetorical effect, as already Thucydides suspected (Thucydides 1.10). The populations of ancient Greek city states were much smaller than many of the Chinese polities or the Roman Empire, and their armies must have been smaller still. For the wars of Philip II and Alexander III of Macedon, we see figures on their side of a few thousands, possibly going into low tens of thousands, while the numbers of Persians are supposed to have increased exponentially from 40,000 at the Battle of Granicus to over a million at Gaugamela – this smacks of poetic licence. In the following two centuries, Rome in its various wars mustered between close to 100,000 and 300,000 men for its wars. Under the principate and dominate, Rome's entire military force may have numbered around 300,000, and some higher figures are quoted; even so, Rome's forces were overstretched. In late antiquity, the Sassanians could bring 120,000 to 150,000 men to their campaigns; they, too, found it challenging to fend off invasions on their eastern and northern frontiers and also contend with the Roman Empire in the west. Individual battles will rarely, if ever, have seen forces of 100,000 on each side, but for some battles figures in the higher tens of thousands are plausible.

The dimensions of warfare in central Asia and in China easily exceeded those in most other parts of the world; as warfare in Europe shrank in numeric and geographical dimensions (if not in the violence used), armies in China continued to be numbered in the hundreds of thousands, especially in periods when one consolidated power predominated. The Mongol army supposedly grew from 95,000 – already a number no European polity could muster – in 1206 to a million by 1250; the Khwarazmian Emirate is said to have been able to raise 400,000 men in their army, and the Manchurian people 600,000. Archaeological traces of warfare in pre-Columbian America, by contrast, hint at population numbers and casualty figures more akin to prehistoric findings in Europe, with an entire population of a pueblo estimated at 500, of whom well under 100 would go into combat. The earliest Spanish conquistadores, Hernán Cortés and Francisco Pizarro, brought only 500 and 150 to 180 men respectively along with them, but recruited local enemies of the Incas and Aztecs with whom they achieved their astonishing victories.

Like China, Russia employed mass to offset its adversaries' superiority in terms of organisation and equipment until the Second World War. In Europe, army sizes that met in battle rose slowly from the medieval figures (usually in the low tens of thousands) that are still found in the Habsburg campaigns of the mid-sixteenth century. In China, the Ming and Qing dynasties amassed infantry forces that no European country could parallel until the times of Louis XIV of France, counted in many hundreds of thousands (even if actual battles often involved smaller numbers). Louis XIV raised by far the largest standing armies of the era for his wars, but the paper strength – 420,000 men in the Nine Years War (1688–1697) – differed considerably from the actual strength, estimated at a maximum of 250,000 to 350,000, and his battles were still fought by armies mainly in their tens of thousands.[25] In 1683, the second and last Ottoman attempt to capture

25 John Lynn, *The French Army of Louis XIV to 1688*, in Clifford J. Rogers and Ty Seidule (eds), *The West Point History of Warfare* (New York: Simon & Schuster, n.d.), Chapter 5.

Vienna saw an Ottoman force of 100,000 marching into Austria; the relief forces that defeated it in battle numbered around 70,000 to 75,000, of whom the Habsburg emperor was able to raise only 21,000 from his own lands.[26] The Mughals brought army strengths similar to those of European armies into battle – we read about 80,000 at the Mughal invasion of the Ahmadnagar Sultanate, or a combined cavalry-cum-infantry of 60,000 at the conquest of Balkh in 1646.

In the eighteenth century, Frederick II, with his famously large army in proportion to the rest of his population and lands, increased Prussia's forces from 80,000 men in 1740 to 158,000 in 1777. Meanwhile, the forces under the direct control of the Habsburg emperors rose from 108,000 to 220,000, as the Habsburgs by now had gained direct control of large swathes of eastern and south-eastern Europe that they had won back from the Turks. But again, numbers clashing in actual battles remained in the tens of thousands. The wars involving European settlers and European forces in America, if anything, involved even smaller numbers, with fewer than 10,000 on each side. Only in the Napoleonic Wars would battle strengths on a single side exceed the 100,000 mark, and thus return to the figures that could be mustered in Europe by the most performant polities of antiquity, or by the populations of central and east Asia. Again, we see here a reflection of the non-linearity of the evolution of warfare, especially in Europe.

Special Forces

Besides infantry and cavalry, and sometimes artillery, many of the bigger and richer polities hired special forces, who might double as the private guards of leaders able to pay them (usually from the taxation of their peasants or other revenues from their lands). Examples include Alexander III of Macedon's companions (the *hetairoi*), the Praetorian Guard of the Roman emperors, or Norsemen who were hired by the Byzantine emperors as their Varangian Guard. A development particular to Europe was that of the military orders, the 'monks of war', recruited to defend the Christian holy places in Palestine and the pilgrim routes to and from the Holy Land. Sworn to celibacy, this *militia Christi* in part created its own polities, on the Baltic Sea shores, in Malta and on several Greek islands, with their leaders playing important political roles, although formally subordinated to the papacy. They had some similarity with the Mamluks, originally slave soldiers of the Muslim world who in Egypt eventually overturned the rule of their employer and took power themselves, ruling from the thirteenth century to the early sixteenth, until Egypt fell to

26 Ágoston, 'The Ottomans', 127.

Ottoman expansionism. Mamluks still existed in the Middle East until the nineteenth century. The Turks had their equivalent in the Janissaries. From the fourteenth to seventeenth centuries, these had been recruited through the *devşirme*, a levy of Christian boys who would be taken from their parents, converted to Islam and trained as the Ottoman special soldiery. Later the Janissaries, now recruited from among the Muslim subjects of the Ottoman Empire, became a powerful political force, eventually deposing Sultan Selim III in the early nineteenth century, upon which a successor of Selim's, Mahmut II, disbanded them altogether in 1826. Specialist mercenary units continued to exist elsewhere. The Ming fielded Mongol units and groups drawn from special ethnicities thought of as being particularly martial – much as the Greeks, the Romans, the Byzantines, the Habsburgs and later the Russians would do.[27] This practice lived on in the nineteenth and twentieth centuries with the *sepoys* and *spahi*s and *askeri*s, and indeed the Gurkhas employed by the British and the Foreign Legion by the French.

Weapons and Weapons Systems

Until AD 1000 and in many areas for many centuries later, the means of land warfare were similar across the Euro-Asiatic land mass – swords, body armour, lances or pikes and shields seem to have been common to all these civilisations. We find two-wheeled horse-drawn chariots, accompanied by squads of foot soldiers, from China and India to the Middle East and all the way to Celtic Britain in the first millennium BC and then in the early centuries AD, after which they disappeared from Europe but not for a long time from Asia. Horse cavalry was used on all sides (the Americas are a case apart, as the horse was only introduced by Europeans with the conquistadores). China around AD 300 generated a small but highly significant technological innovation: the stirrup; it substantially strengthened the hold of riders on their mount and enabled them to carry out slashing and propelling movements with swords and spears without losing their balance or sliding off the horse. Unfortunately, not least for China, this innovation is thought to have spread by diffusion to its non-sedentary neighbours, who improved their combat forces to raid the sedentary cultures to their east, south, and west.

Some innovations were less technology-dependent but nevertheless effective: the Greek use of pikes in well-trained and well-ordered groups of men, the phalanx, or the Roman soldier's use of their shields to create a 'tortoise'

---

27 For a list of such ethnicities, see Capitaine Thomas-Antoine le Roy Grandmaison, *La petite guerre, ou traité du service des troupes légeres en campagne* (s.l.: s.n., 1756), Chapter 1.

formation for protection against arrows – both gave their respective armies a tactical edge over many adversaries. Similarly, the Indian use of elephants gave armies a tactical edge over adversaries who were merely on horseback or even on foot. The fourteenth and fifteenth centuries saw the emergence in several European countries of formations of pikemen who could hold their own in battle against armoured knights on horseback; some of them hired out their skills outside their native countries. This phenomenon would continue until the Thirty Years War and the Franco-Spanish War, when the last encounters of pikemen and cavalry took place. Pikemen were eventually made obsolete by their vulnerability to field artillery.

Levels of technological development began to diverge substantially in the second millennium AD. While the wheel was unknown to native Americans, and while, after the disintegration of the sophisticated trading system of the Roman Empire, Europe fell back technologically – a decline that only began to be reversed from the twelfth or thirteenth century onwards – east Asia remained technologically the most developed part of the world. After peaceful uses of the explosives they had discovered, the Chinese began to use them as gunpowder towards the end of the first millennium AD. The basic design of the cannon – dating back at least to the twelfth century – came to the Middle East and to Europe from Asia. The Ming empire (1368–1644) has been called the 'first gunpowder empire' and was first to create a firearm training division in 1420 (see Chapter 20). By the fourteenth century, Mamluks were using cannon in battle, and they began to appear on European battlefields; by the fifteenth century, cannon were having devastating effects used against curtain walls in siege warfare, with the fall of Constantinople due to a breach in its previously matchless fortifications, effected by bombardment. Japan had known gunpowder weapons before the Portuguese imported handheld guns in the sixteenth century, and subsequently retained their use by the upper warrior class while banning it among commoners.[28] Yet the development of handheld gunpowder weapons was slow to become more effective than bows and arrows.

The light cavalry of the people of the great steppes of Asia continued to press on all the surrounding areas, effecting previously unparalleled territorial conquests in terms of sheer size. The armies of eastern Europe and the Ottoman Empire, dominating the entire Middle East and most of north Africa, were different from those of western Europe, although they shared

---

28 Peter Lorge, *The Asian Military Revolution: From Gunpowder to the Bomb* (Cambridge: Cambridge University Press, 2008, 55 f., 62–4.

artillery. They were dominated by cavalry, both heavy and lightly armoured, still using composite bows but also handheld artillery.

By the fifteenth century, technology and mindset – European dynasties taking their competition from the European theatre to other parts of the world, and European entrepreneurs identifying business opportunities in new sources of raw materials and new markets – set the Europeans on a path of expansion to the rest of the world that would culminate only in the nineteenth century. When this was coupled with, on the one hand, a research-friendly culture that had shed the shackles of religious superstition, and, on the other, an increasingly standardised weapons industry, organised logistics and standing armies and navies, Europe left other civilisations behind in military–technological predominance.

Naval Forces

Unlike land warfare, naval warfare developed its full panoply of strategic options only in early modern times. Some key elements long precede this, however. Naval forces used to transport troops – either for ferrying or over longer distances (such as by the Vikings) – and naval battles near land go back to antiquity. Piracy existed throughout recorded history. Piracy was sanctified as *guerre de course*, with letters of marque bestowed upon captains by European polities since the fourteenth century, if not earlier. Until the Paris Declaration Respecting Maritime Law of 1856, naval warfare had an economic incentive even for regular navies and the states in whose employ they were: the crew that captured an enemy ship was allowed to keep part of the booty. The sea-based warlords who plied their trade around the islands of the Far East were among the first captains in the world to put cannon to use on their ships.[29] South-east Asian kingdoms were plagued by riverine piracy as well as by naval attacks on major ports and harbours. Also elsewhere on the globe, where estuaries and rivers were wide, piracy blended with extortion and taxation. At sea, too, rulers of polities struggled to impose a monopoly of the use of force. Some of the earliest documents referring to English monarchs' pretension to sovereign control of the Channel were complaints about piracy made by French trading communities, effectively asking them to act on their claims to maritime sovereignty.[30]

29 Lorge, *The Asian Military Revolution*, 57f.
30 Thomas Wemyss Fulton, *The Sovereignty of the Sea* (Edinburgh: William Blackwood & Sons, 1911).

Some early maritime polities, like Athens, had standing navies. Ancient Persia as much as sixteenth-century polities built ships for particular campaigns or hired them from allied or dependent polities. Well into the seventeenth century, European navies were raised mainly ad hoc, in part from existing fleets (as merchant vessels and men-o'-war were not yet of distinct construction). Philip II of Spain twice built a fleet to attack England in the late sixteenth century, while England well into the seventeenth relied on merchantmen that were hired for war. Only in the mid-seventeenth century did European states – the Netherlands ahead of all the others – begin to acquire their own navies for military purposes. China's taxation system allowed for the creation of both river fleets and the occasional blue-water fleet. Around the same time, the Ottomans also made good use of south-eastern Europe's rivers for their military logistics.

Ships evolved considerably from those floating bowls of Henry the Navigator, the Portuguese prince who discovered the Azores, to the cannon-laden men-o'-war of the eighteenth century. In the fifteenth century, only Ming China, with its huge bureaucratic apparatus and tax system, could afford such a great fleet as that of Chinese Admiral Zheng He, which was used to explore the Pacific and the Indian Ocean up to the shores of Africa, but China did not for another century develop a fleet for military purposes, and then of a size not much different to those of European powers in the following century.

It is thus only from the sixteenth century that, in combination with the compass, gunpowder and state sponsorship, naval warfare took off and began to encompass most of the strategies still known to navies today: naval blockades at source, interception of enemy shipping along lines of communication (the *guerre de course*) or near enemy harbours with distant or close blockade, the bombardment of crucial towns and cities on the coast from the sea, and naval battles usually near a port or straits (or *guerre d'escadre*). Queen Elizabeth's naval entrepreneurs explored all of these options in the Anglo-Spanish War of 1585–1604, and a few more, such as seizing and holding an enemy port, a forerunner of the later effected capture of Gibraltar.[31] Indeed, from this war onwards, wars could have components spanning the globe: by trying to cut the Spanish off from the revenue coming from their overseas' empire, the queen's captains took action on both sides of the Atlantic, and Sir Francis Drake may even have sailed to the west coast of America to lay claim to it on behalf of his queen.

31 Beatrice Heuser, *Strategy before Clausewitz* (Abingdon: Routledge, 2017), Chapters 4–6.

Ways had to be found to co-ordinate such wars when messages to and from the remote theatres of war would take weeks or months to arrive. Ships might engage in combat far from home only to find out belatedly that they were no longer at war. With its theatres of operations in North America and India and battles in the centre of Europe, the Seven Years' War was a first world war. This required a new level of central organisation, and navies the likes of which the world had not seen before. If global strategy was born in the Anglo-Spanish War, by the eighteenth century it was well and truly fledged.

Defensive Works and Fortifications

Traces of defensive technology – walls, fences, dikes, ditches and other obstacles – can be traced back to the Neolithic, with arguably the earliest example being the walls of Jericho, variously dated to between 8500 and 7500 B C. It is highly significant that from the first urban settlements, we find these accompanied by protective walls. The very word 'town' (often found in place names as '-ton') in English is linked to the Dutch *tuin* – enclosure, garden, and the German *Zaun*, fence, as the Anglo-Saxon term 'burgh' or 'borough' is with the German *Burg*, the Sanskrit *púra*, or the Thai *buri*, meaning castle, fortified place. It is thus not coincidental that we find place names of towns from Edinburgh or Loughborough in Britain, to Jodhpur or Jaipur in India, to Thonburi or Lopburi in Thailand, all featuring this particle. Similarly, the Celtic term for hillfort, *dun*, originally meaning 'hill', then 'fortification', can be found from Ireland and Scotland (Dunmore, Dunadd, Dunfermline, Dunblane) to France (Verdun, Châteaudun, Autun) and Germany (Tuntenhausen, originally Duntenhausen).

As Western Europeans after the fall of Rome forgot how to build fortifications, frontier walls and walled cities increased in number and extent in China. From around the year 1000, Europe was slowly catching up in other ways also: stone fortifications came back, castles sprang up and a variety of siege engines was invented or rediscovered from Roman precedents. The Byzantines in particular were masters in this art of *poliorkētikós*, the art of fortification and siegecraft in the Roman tradition, until this was overtaken by cannon. India also produced an impressive array of fortresses, mainly between the fourth century and the seventeenth, Kangra Fort being among the early examples, Mehrangarh Fort in Jodhpur and the main part of the Gwalior Fort being constructions of the fifteenth century, Agra Fort and the Red Fort in Delhi dating from the seventeenth.

The Romans owed their fame as engineers not only to their roads, aqueducts, waterborne transport networks and fortifications, but, crucial for our considerations, also to their siege engines: mobile towers would be brought up against curtain walls, and battering rams and onagers used to propel large stones or burning substances against and into enemy towns. But in this competition between offensive and defensive technology, the defence was the stronger until the arrival of gunpowder and cannon. This made much more profound adaptation necessary: fortifications turned from an emphasis on height with vertical 'curtain' walls and situations on natural or artificial hills to flatness and great depth. This transformation coincided with European colonial expansionism with the effect that such new fortifications *alla moderna* can be found from the Americas in the west to the Philippines and Macao in the east.

While cities have generally no longer been surrounded by permanent static defences since the late nineteenth century, longer walls have continued to be tools of strategy until the present. Earthworks, sometimes complemented by wooden palisades or stone walls, such as the Roman *limites*, Offa's Dyke or the Dannevirke, were matched in the twentieth century by the complex constructions dividing the two halves of Germany or the Korean peninsula, and later dividing the main territory of Israel from its occupied areas.

Beyond Kinetically Applied Strategy
Indirect Approaches

Another point of comparison for which we find evidence across time and space deserves mentioning. In war and in peace, the role of armed forces was not only to fight in war. Throughout history, a polity's forces under its central government had a deterrent role in peacetime: they were designed to keep insurgencies at bay as well as to deter external aggression or misbehaviour by neighbours, and, in the case of powers strong enough to do so, to reassure allies. We are told that inspiring 'awe' was important for the Chinese Ming and Qing dynasties, and while this was articulated especially by them (see Chapter 20), something quite similar can be seen in any military parade or public display of fighting power in military exercises, since those of Frederick II of Prussia. When the Grand Old Duke of York (presumably the Catholic brother and heir to King Charles II of England and Scotland) marched his men up and down hills, this was not to leave his mark on the nursery rhymes of the future, but to deter any invasion by Protestant forces – unsuccessfully, in the end, as he was overthrown by his own Protestant daughter and her Dutch husband in 1688.

The complexity of strategies varied greatly across the regions of the world. Economic incentives, concessions and tribute payments (in preference to war) were always components of strategy. And last, but not least, propaganda, deterrence and intimidation were instruments of strategy throughout recorded history. It was not just to brag but to coerce other cities into submission that Assyran king Aššurnasirpal II (883–859) on a stone inscription recorded the destruction of several cities:

> I besieged [and] conquered the city [of Tela]. I felled 3,000 of their fighting men with the sword. I burnt many captives from them. I captured many troops alive: from some I cut off their arms [and] hands; from others I cut off their nose, ears, [and] extremities. I gouged out the eyes of many troops . . . I hung their heads on trees around the city. I burnt their adolescent boys [and] girls. I razed, destroyed, burnt [and] consumed the city.[32]

Especially gruesome behaviour towards some enemy villages or cities *pour décourager les autres* can be found across the centuries. Xenophon, the fourth-century BC leader of a Greek army in Persian employ, recorded how, in Asia Minor, his Persian commander Seuthes burned the villages of a particular region 'to the ground, not leaving a single house standing, in order to strike terror into the other tribes to show them what would happen if they did not give in'. He then dispatched messengers to ensure that the other tribes knew that this would be coming to them if they did not submit to his will (Xenophon, *Anabasis* VII.4). The same approach of spreading terror would be used over and over during the Hundred Years War of the fourteenth and fifteenth centuries, when this strategic approach was known as the *chevauchée*. Coercion in that context would take the form of threatening towns and cities with extreme reprisals – sacking, burning and the killing, raping or, occasionally until the sixteenth century even among Christians, enslavement of citizens, if they were taken by force rather than surrendering. The infamous campaign through Italy of French King Charles VIII in 1494 followed that pattern: he brutally destroyed Mordano, the first Italian town to offer resistance, with the help of his new mobile cannon, after which other Italian cities surrendered to him without a fight.

This approach also underlay the reprisal killings that were practised not only, but especially widely, by the German armies in the First and Second World Wars, when snipers or other irregulars killed German soldiers. Executing hostages and burning down villages or towns that had (really or supposedly) given shelter to the irregulars had the larger aim of frightening others away from doing the same.

---

32 Amnon Altman, *Tracing the Earliest Recorded Concepts of International Law: The Ancient Near East, 2500–330 BCE* (Leiden: Martinus Nijnhoff, 2012), 176.

Diplomacy and Alliances

Non-kinetic elements of strategy included an adroit use of diplomacy (permanent missions were established from the sixteenth century), alliances, commercial incentives, tribute payments and the movement of populations by force or economic incentive. The Byzantines were the most inventive in this regard, ostensibly turning such payments into gracious presents made to predatory neighbours. This often had the adverse effect, however, of whetting the appetites of the recipients, with the result that they would come back for more or yearn to possess Constantinople, the luxurious capital city from which they flowed.

Alliances could be concluded for offensive or defensive purposes. The Greeks distinguished between a number of different types: eternal alliance by common descent or kinship (*syngenaia*), long-term alliances based on friendship (*philia*), or ad hoc alliances to fight a common enemy, which included the *symmachia* (between equals or unequal parties), the *epimachia* (purely defensive alliances) and other agreements.[33] Famous Greek examples are the Amphictyonic League of the seventh century BC which created a sort of security community (and notably not referred to as a mere *symmachia*),[34] and the Delian League of 478 BC headed by Athens in the fight against the Persians. Unsatisfactorily translated by the same English word, these different types of alliance tended to have a different durability.

Perhaps mainly on the lines of a *symmachia*, Rome had an elaborate system of alliances and agreements with neighbouring entities, and upheld the commitment to coming to an ally's defence (which tended to suit Rome's expansionist proclivities very nicely). They tended to have the additional benefit of securing auxiliary forces for the Roman army, or *socii*, the forces of allies. Chinese polities, especially in the Warring States period, were constantly forging alliances against common enemies.

'Realist' theoreticians of international relations would later offer the often quick demise of *symmachia*-type alliances (formed only to bring down a common enemy, but not based on common interests or values) as evidence that it was anarchy, not structure, that was the basis of all societies. In reality, more enduring alliance line-ups have existed in various periods and various parts of the world.

---

33 Wilhelm G. Grewe (ed.), *Fontes Historiae Iuris Gentium/Quellen zur Geschichte des Völkerrechts/Sources Relating to the History of the Law of Nations*, Volume I: *1380 BCE–1493* (Berlin and New York: Walter de Gruyter, 1995), 38–60.
34 Michael Whitby, 'Federalism, common peace, and the avoidance of war in fourth century Greece', *Annals of the Lothian Foundation*, 1 (1991), 71–94.

Sentiments of common values captured by *philia* have demonstrably had strong impacts on strategy making. Shared religion determined the line-up from the sixteenth century of Protestant versus Catholic polities, and of course, since the seventh century, of Christian versus Muslim. Even in the eighteenth century, where such religious line-ups were generally no longer articulated, de facto the sides taken in wars were largely determined by who was Protestant and who was Catholic.[35] Admittedly, there were exceptions, where *raison d'état* prevailed over common values. The French royal dynasty in its standing rivalry with the Habsburgs broke this pattern, reaching out even from the sixteenth century to the eighteenth to the Ottomans for joint operations against the Habsburg-dominated Holy Roman Empire, and in the following century allying with Protestants against the Habsburgs in the Thirty Years War. Protestant rulers of Transylvania preferred an asymmetric alliance with the Ottoman Sultan to vassalage to the Catholic Habsburgs. Russia, having become the sole Orthodox polity, had no natural religious allies in our period; in its attempts to push back the Catholic Polish–Lithuanian Empire and then Protestant Sweden, successive governments sought to create a 'northern system' of alliances with any polity with 'common interests', what Thucydides would have called a *epimachia* (as it was a defensive alliance), rather than an alliance founded on common values. Under Catherine the Great (r. 1762–1796), Russia's allies would be Denmark and Prussia, not a random alignment as she was born into German nobility and both Denmark and Prussia had German-speaking courts. Both the Danish and the Prussian kings were interested in keeping Sweden and Poland in check, and they were asked to keep Russia's (western) back free as Catherine embarked upon her campaigns against the Ottoman Empire. In many other contexts, the pattern of alliances joined by common values, here religious affiliation, obtained.

Alliances and peace settlements also included marriage alliances, underscoring the personal relations of colluding rulers. Of course, this had no place in city states ruled by oligarchies or 'democratically'. Even under the largely hereditary rule of the Roman principate, when the fiction of the election of each emperor was maintained, marriage with a foreign princess or even queen – Cleopatra VII, Berenice – was seen as unacceptable and in Julius Caesar's case contributed to his downfall. In civilisations with polygamy the women thus given or exchanged were nothing more than presents, the

---

35 Jeremy Black, 'Britain and the "Long" 18th century', in Olsen and Gray, *The Practice of Strategy*, 155–75, 162.

equivalent of the gift of a fine horse or work of art. This seems to have been the case when Han rulers sent their daughters to marry Xiongnu command-ers, or when Middle Eastern rulers sent their daughters (or horses) as gifts to augment the harems of Solomon or of Persian potentates. The polygamous Persian rulers were happy to accept foreign princesses among their women; Kawad, for example, married a chief's daughter of the White Huns. But given a choice, they kept their own daughters within the country, perhaps marry-ing them to aristocrats.[36] In Asia, dynastic marriages were more a tool to consolidate a peace agreement or even to create alliances, in China, for example, with chiefs of the Uighurs and Turks, to offset the enmity of other Uighur and Turkic tribes. For the Mughals the marriages were 'unidir-ectional': foreign women were accepted into the dynasty, but Mughal women were never married off to foreign potentates, reflecting a Mughal sense of superiority over the latter. Similarly, until the twentieth century, Thai royal princesses were not supposed to marry foreigners (or, for that matter, anybody of a lower rank, leaving little alternative to spinsterhood).

The monogamy that became part and parcel of Christianity turned dynas-tic marriages into transformative and sometimes very powerful tools. Byzantium also used its soft power and imperial marriages to draw numerous neighbouring tribes and polities into its sphere. Byzantine princesses travelled with a great entourage of Orthodox priests, teachers and artisans, thus bringing writing, texts and cultural artefacts (and baths) to their husbands' realms. In short, they changed cultures and exported political ideas. This was a strategic tool lacking entirely in the Muslim societies where even favourite wives or concubines had no *cultural* influence: even the most important wives of Ottoman sultans, for example, had been brought to the harem as foreign slaves, usually at an age far too young to have any education or cultural conditioning, and certainly lacking an entourage of scholars and artisans. Nor did they have powerful aristocratic or foreign royal families backing them and their children's claims to the succession. By contrast, such backing in the Christian context could be a force multiplier, or, as we have seen, it could become the cause of future wars.

Marriage diplomacy was famously taken to a new level by the Habsburg dynasty. Within only about a century, through marriage with heiresses rather than bloody military conquests, the Habsburgs, with their original lands in Austria, gained possession of the Hispanic peninsula (including in the

---

36 Katarzyna Maksymiuk, 'Marriage and divorce law in pre-Islamic Persia: legal status of the Sassanid woman (224–651 AD)', *Cogent Arts and Humanities*, 19:1 (2019), 170–200.

mid-sixteenth century even Portugal), Burgundy, the Burgundian Netherlands, Bohemia and Hungary (although most of the latter would be under Ottoman occupation until the eighteenth century). More still, they inherited the claims to overseas possessions which the Spanish and Portuguese monarchs had persuaded successive popes to grant them. By the time Charles II of Spain became Emperor Charles V of the Holy Roman Empire, the sun did not set on his lands. These overseas possessions he left to his son Philip, second king of Spain of that name, together with the Iberian peninsula and the Burgundian territories. Philip, in inheriting the Portuguese Crown and overseas possessions, augmented the lands of this empire truly to encircle the globe, which had previously been divided into two halves – one, the nearer, to be colonies Christianised by Portugal, the other (from the west of the Americas to the Philippines in the Far East, named after Philip, of course) by Spain. While the establishment of Spanish rule in the Americas was notoriously violent, the acquisition itself of all the European lands by inheritance constituted the greatest peaceful strategic expansion human history had known. This was understood by contemporaries and led to the famous quip *bella gerant alii; sed tu, felix Austria, nube* – others wage war, but you, lucky Austria, wed!

The French monarchs had followed the same course of action successfully at the outset of the modern era, when they managed to secure Brittany by marriage, and a century later Navarre by succession. The marriage alliance between Louis XIV and a Habsburg princess, however, engendered a long series of wars fought by the French king to claim his wife's inheritance in the Netherlands, and later, to claim the crown of Spain for his own grandson. The *renversement des alliances*, the reversal of alignment of France against the Habsburgs to being allies of the Habsburgs in the later eighteenth century, confirmed by the wedding of Empress Maria Theresa's daughter Marie Antoinette with the dauphin and future Louis XVI of France, again brought war, not peace, when Habsburg Austria mobilised against the French Revolutionaries to help restore the French monarchy.

Population Movements

Population transfers were tools of strategy in several ways: in anticipation of a coming conflict, one might transfer border populations, who for some reason might side with the enemy, from their traditional habitat to areas at the other end of one's empire, as the Byzantines did with the Paulicians or Bogomils. One might transfer populations of captured enemy towns from these disputed areas deep into one's own empire, as the Sassanian Persians did when they captured the Roman city of Dura Europos. Or one might enslave captured populations from conquered enemy territories and bring them into one's own realm to augment productivity, as Egyptians and Assyrians famously did with the Hebrews, and as the Greeks, Romans, Turks, Africans, Indians, south-east Asians and several pre-Columbian cultures did with captured enemy populations. This was a global phenomenon: it is not by accident that the themes of the Babylonian captivity or the Israelite slave population in Egypt appealed to slaves in the USA with their spirituals, but it was never only one 'race' that suffered from slavery, nor just one that inflicted it on another.

If there was a population surplus or a scarcity of land or other resources at home, one might, like Greek city states and Rome, export settlers into conquered areas to ensure their permanent pacification and acculturation, meanwhile augmenting these colonisers' chances of generating prosperity for themselves, and augmenting trade for all sides. Such population transfers usually took place before or mainly after wars, but were designed to have long-term strategic effects of pacifying and controlling disputed regions. Alternatively, the implantation of colonisers into newly conquered areas to assure their loyalty was common practice during the Arab and later Turkish conquests, just as it had been for ancient Greek cities or ancient Rome, which at the same time gave the colonisers opportunities to prosper. Russians were famous for it: both Peter the Great and Catherine the Great forcibly transferred subject peoples from one part of their growing empire to another (not always successfully: sometimes the areas where they were settled were so inhospitable that thousands of settlers either died of diseases or starvation or ran away), or invited volunteers from all over Europe to come and settle in remote provinces, in return for tax exemptions and other privileges. Thus we find Russian subjects but also foreigners settled in Siberia and German artisans invited to create a colony on the Volga, where they would live in a cultural bubble until the Second World War when Stalin, doubtful of their loyalty, deported them to Siberia, lest they side with the invading Wehrmacht.[37]

The Limitations of This Overview

Scholars run the risk of looking for coherence, logic and system where reality was more likely the result of ad-hockery, what seemed like a good idea at the time to charismatic leaders able to pull others along by the sheer force of

---

37 N. S. Kollmann, *The Russian Empire 1450–1801* (Oxford: Oxford University Press, 2017), 113–16, 161–3.

personality, without the rhyme or reason for which we are looking retrospectively. Explanations and justifications in the sparse records we have for most of the cultures surveyed here mostly post-dated the wars themselves. Their authors, the chroniclers and historiographers, were by definition members of educated elites like us in search of plausible narratives of causality and finality. Strategy, one suspects, was often not translated into coherently deduced military action, but into uneven application, due to unforeseen events in one part of the theatre of operations, with deviant actions of subunits (whether as a result of miscommunication or spontaneous decisions by commanders anywhere in the hierarchy), not to mention cases of indiscipline. We, like the chroniclers and historiographers upon whose works we draw, are likely to have imputed too much planning and coherence in what we have described. In reality, recurrent patterns of warfare sadly include that of bloodlust unleashed, of deliberate cruelty and delight taken in destruction and killing, at least as much as the pattern of using warfare as a considered instrument of policy.

Further Reading

NOTE: For literature cited in texts, see the footnotes of each chapter.

Sources

Ancient China

Liu An, *The Dao of the Military: Liu An's Art of War* (trans. Andrew Seth Meyer) (New York: Columbia University Press, 2012).

Milburn, Olivia, *The Glory of Yue: An Annotated Translation of the Yuejue shu* (Leiden: Brill, 2010).

Sunzi, *The Art of War: A New Translation* (trans. Michael Nylan) (New York: W. W. Norton and Company, 2020).

Greece 500–400 BC

Aeneas Tacticus, *How to Survive under Siege* (mid-fourth century BC) (trans. David Whitehead) (London: Bloomsbury, 2002).

Aeschines, *Perì tēs parapresbeías* (343 BC) (trans. C. D. Adams as Aeschines, *Speeches*, Loeb Classical Library) (Cambridge, MA: Harvard University Press, 1919).

Andocides, *Perì tēs pròs Lakedaimoníous eirēnēs* (*c.* 391 BC) (trans. K. J. Maidment in *Minor Attic Orators*, Volume i, Loeb Classical Library) (Cambridge, MA: Harvard University Press, 1941).

Demosthenes, *Hyper Ktēsiphōntos perì tou Stephánou* (330 BC) (trans. C. A. Vince and J. H. Vince as Demosthenes: *Orations*, Volume ii, Loeb Classical Library) (Cambridge, MA: Harvard University Press, 1926).

Demosthenes, *Katà Androtíōnos Paranómōn* (355–354 BC) (trans. J. H. Vince as Demosthenes: *Orations*, Volume iii, Loeb Classical Library) (Cambridge, MA: Harvard University Press, 1935).

Diodorus Siculus, *Historical Library* (late first century BC) (trans. C. H. Oldfather as *Diodorus of Sicily*, Loeb Classical Library) (Cambridge, MA: Harvard University Press, 1989).

Euripides, *Phoínissai* (408 BC) (trans. John Davie as Euripides, *The Bacchae and Other Plays* (Harmondsworth: Penguin Classics, 2006).

Herodotus, *The Histories* (*c.* 420 BC) (trans. Aubrey de Sélincourt (Harmondsworth: Penguin Classics, 2003).

Lysias, *Katà Agorátou endeíxeōs* (c. 399 BC) (trans. W. R. M. Lamb as *Lysias*, Loeb Classical Library) (Cambridge, MA: Harvard University Press, 1930).

Plato, *The Laws* (mid-fourth century BC) (trans. Tom Griffith and M. Schofield (Cambridge: Cambridge University Press, 2016).

Plutarch, *Cimon* (c. AD 100) (trans. Bernadotte Perrin as Plutarch, *Lives*, Volume 3, Loeb Classical Library) (Cambridge, MA: Harvard University Press, 1916).

Plutarch, *Pericles* (c. AD 100) (trans. Bernadotte Perrin as Plutarch, *Lives*, Volume II, Loeb Classical Library (Cambridge, MA: Harvard University Press, 1914).

Pseudo-Xenophon (the 'Old Oligarch'), *Athenaíōn politeia* (c. 422 BC) (trans. Robin Osborne as *The Old Oligarch* (London, LACTOR, 2017).

Thucydides, *The Peloponnesian War* (c. 400 BC) (trans. Martin Hammond) (Oxford: Oxford University Press, 2009).

Xenophon, *Anabasis* (mid-fourth century BC) (trans. Rex Warner as *The Persian Expedition*) (Harmondsworth: Penguin, 1949, repr. 1972).

Xenophon, *Memorabilia* (mid-fourth century BC) (trans. E. C. Marchant and J. Henderson as Xenophon, *Memorabilia, Oeconomicus, Symposium, Apology*, Loeb Classical Library) (Cambridge, MA: Harvard University Press, 2013).

Xenophon, *Hellenika* (mid-fourth century BC) (trans. J. Marincola and R. B. Strassler (London: Quercus, 2011).

Xenophon, *Cyropaedia* (mid-fourth century BC) (trans. Walter Miller, Loeb Classical Library) (Cambridge, MA: Harvard University Press, 1914).

Xenophon, *Lakedaimoniōn Politeia* (mid-fourth century BC) (trans. E. C. Marchant as Xenophon, *Scripta Minora*, Loeb Classical Library) (Cambridge, MA: Harvard University Press, 1968).

Xenophon, *Oeconomicus* (mid-fourth century BC) (trans. E. C. Marchant and J. Henderson as Xenophon, *Memorabilia, Oeconomicus, Symposium, Apology*, Loeb Classical Library) (Cambridge, MA: Harvard University Press, 2013).

Xenophon, *Póroi ē perì Prosódōn* (mid-fourth century BC) (trans. E. C. Marchant as Xenophon, *Scripta Minora*, Loeb Classical Library) (Cambridge, MA: Harvard University Press, 1968).

Philip II and Alexander III of Macedon

Arrian, *Anabasis* (mid-second century AD) (trans. M. Hammond as *Alexander the Great: The Anabasis and the Indica*) (Oxford: Oxford University Press, 2013).

Athenaeus, *Deipnosophistae* (late second century AD) (trans. S. D. Olson as *The Learned Banqueters*, Volume VI) (Cambridge, MA and London: Harvard University Press, 2010).

Cicero, *On the Republic* (54–51 BC) (trans. N. Rudd as *The Republic and The Laws*) (Oxford: Oxford University Press, 2008).

Demosthenes, *Philippic 1* (mid fourth century BC) (trans. R. Waterfield in Demosthenes, *Selected Speeches*) (Oxford: Oxford University Press, 2014).

Diodorus Siculus, *Bibliotheca* (late first century BC) (trans. R. Waterfield as *The Library*, Books 16–20) (Oxford: Oxford University Press, 2019).

Frontinus, *Strategems* (late first century AD) (trans. C. E. Bennett) (Cambridge, MA and London: Harvard University Press, 1989).

Justinus, *Epitome of Pompeius Trogus* (Trogus – end of the first century BC, Justin – probably late second/early third century AD) (trans. J. C. Yardley as Justin: *Epitome of the Philippic History of Pompeius Trogus*, Volume I (Oxford: Oxford University Press, 1997).

Orosius, *Seven Books of History against the Pagans* (early fifth century AD) (trans. A. T. Fear (Liverpool: Liverpool University Press, 2010).

Plutarch, *Life of Alexander* (late first/early second century AD) (trans. T. Duff and I. Scott-Kilvert in *The Age of Alexander*) (Harmondsworth: Penguin Books, 2012).

Plutarch, *Life of Aemilius Paullus* (late first/early second century AD) (trans. R. Waterfield in *Roman Lives: A Selection of Eight Lives*) (Oxford: Oxford University Press, 2008).

Plutarch, *Sayings of Kings and Generals* (late first/early second century AD) (trans. F. Cole Babbitt in *Moralia*, Volume III) (Cambridge, MA and London: Harvard University Press, 1931).

Plutarch, *The Fortune of Alexander* (late first/early second century AD) (trans. F. Cole Babbitt in *Moralia*, Volume IV (Cambridge, MA and London: Harvard University Press, 1936).

Polybius, *The Histories* (second century BC) (trans. R. Waterfield) (Oxford: Oxford University Press, 2010).

Quintus Curtius, *History of Alexander the Great* (probably mid-first century AD) (trans. J. C. Yardley as *The History of Alexander*) (Harmondsworth: Penguin Books, 1984).

Strabo, *Geography* (early first century AD) (trans. D. W. Roller as *The Geography of Strabo*) (Cambridge: Cambridge University Press, 2020).

Teispid and Achaemenid Persia (c. 550–330 BC)

Arrian, *Anabasis* (mid-second century AD) (trans. M. Hammond in *Alexander the Great: The Anabasis and the Indica*) (Oxford: Oxford University Press, 2013).

Quintus Curtius, *History of Alexander the Great* (probably mid-first century AD) (trans. J. C. Yardley as *The History of Alexander*) (Harmondsworth: Penguin Books, 1984).

Cyrus Cylinder (*c.* 539 BC), 'The text of the Cyrus Cylinder' (trans. H. Schaudig in M. R. Shayegan (ed.), *Cyrus the Great, Life and Lore*) (Boston: Ilex Foundation, 2019), 16–25.

Darius I, *Bisotun Inscription, Old Persian Version* (c. 520 BC, Old Persian Version) (trans. R. Schmitt in *The Bisitun Inscriptions of Darius the Great: Old Persian Text*) (London: School of Oriental and African Studies, 1991).

Darius I, Naqsh-e Rostam 'a' and 'b' inscriptions (late 6th–early 5th century BC) (trans. R. Schmitt in *The Old Persian Inscriptions of Naqsh-i Rustam and Persepolis*) (London: School of Oriental and African Studies, 2000).

Darius I, Susa 'e' inscription (late sixth century BC) (trans. R. Kent in *Old Persian: Grammar, Texts, Lexicon*, 2nd ed.) (New Haven: American Oriental Society, 1953).

Diodorus Siculus, *Bibliotheca* (late first century BC) (trans. C. H. Oldfather in *The Library of History*: Books XI–XV.19) (Cambridge, MA: Harvard University Press, 1954).

Hellenica Oxyrhynchia (*c.* 380 BC) (trans. P. McKechnie and S. Kern) (Warminster: Aris and Phillips, 1988).

Herodotus, *The Histories* (c. 420 BC) (trans. Aubrey de Sélincourt (Harmondsworth: Penguin Classics, 2003).

Isocrates, *Panegyricus* (c. 380 BC) (trans. A. N. W. Saunders in *Greek Political Oratory*) (Harmondsworth: Penguin Classics, 1970).

Nabonidus Chronicle (sixth century BC) (trans. A. K. Grayson in *Assyrian and Babylonian Chronicles*) (Locust Valley: J. J. Augustin, 1975).

Plutarch, *Life of Alexander* (late first/early second century AD) (trans. T. Duff and I. Scott-Kilvert in *The Age of Alexander*) (Harmondsworth: Penguin Books, 2012).

Xenophon, *Anabasis* (mid-fourth century BC) (trans. R. Waterfield (Oxford: Oxford University Press, 2009).

Xenophon, *Hellenika* (mid-fourth century BC) (trans. J. Marincola and R. B. Strassler (London: Quercus, 2011).

Xerxes, Persepolis 'h' ('Daiva') inscription (c. 475–465 BC) (trans. R. Schmitt in *The Old Persian Inscriptions of Naqsh-i Rustam and Persepolis*) (London, School of Oriental and African Studies, 2000).

Roman Empire

Agathias, *The Histories* (580) (trans. J. D. C. Frendo, Corpus Fontium Historiae Byzantinae 2A) (Berlin: De Gruyter, 1975).

Ammianus Marcellinus, *Res Gestae* (380) (trans. J. C. Rolfe), 3 vols (Cambridge, MA: Loeb, 1935–1939).

Appian, *Roman History* (150) (trans. Horace White), 4 vols (London and New York: Loeb, 1912–1913).

Cassius Dio, *Histories* (195–230) (trans. Earnest Cary, 9 vols. (Cambridge, MA: Loeb, 1914–1955).

Constantine Porphyrogennitus, appendix to *De Caerimoniis* (940) (trans. J. F. Haldon as Constantine Poryphyrogennitus, *Three Treatises on Imperial Military Expeditions*) (Vienna: Verlag der Österreichischen Akadamie der Wissenschaften, 1990).

Eusebius, *Life of Constantine* (340) (trans. A. Cameron and S. B. Hall) (Oxford: Oxford University Press, 1999).

Frontinus, *Stratagems* (90) (trans. Charles E. Bennett) (London and New York: Loeb, 1925).

John of Ephesus, *Ecclesiastical History* (580) (trans. R. Payne-Smith as *The Third Part of the Ecclesiastical History of John of Ephesus*) (Oxford: Oxford University Press, 1860).

John of Nikiu, *Chronicle* (645) (trans. R. H. Charles as *The Chronicle of John, Bishop of Nikiou*) (William and Norgate: London, 1916).

Josephus, *The Jewish War* (75) (abridged trans. Moses I. Finley) (New York: The New English Library, 1965).

Justinian, *Novels* (535–560) (trans. David J. D. Miller and Peter Sarris as *The 'Novels' of Justinian: A Complete Annotated Translation*) (Cambridge: Cambridge University Press, 2018).

Juvenal, *Satires* (130) (trans. Peter Green) (Penguin: Harmondsworth, 1974).

Malalas, *Chronicle* (565) (trans. Elizabeth Jeffreys, Michael Jeffreys and Roger Scott) (Melbourne: Byzantina Australiensia, 1986).

Menander Protector (590) (trans. Roger C. Blockley as *The History of Menander the Guardsman*) (Liverpool: ARCA 17, 1985).

Notitia Dignitatum (420) (trans. Roger Rees in *Diocletian and the Tetrarchy*) (Edinburgh: Edinburgh University Press, 2004), 139–46.

Panegyrici Latini (290–390) (trans. C. E. V. Nixon and B. S. Rogers as *In Praise of Later Roman Emperors: The Panegyrici Latini*) (Berkeley: University of California Press, 1994).

Prices Edict (301) (trans. Roger Rees in *Diocletian and the Tetrarchy*) (Edinburgh: Edinburgh University Press, 2004), 160–9.

Priscus, fragments (470) (trans. Roger C. Blockley in *The Fragmentary Classicising Historians of the Later Roman Empire: Eunapius, Olympiodorus, Priscus and Malchus*, 2 vols.) (Liverpool: Francis Cairns, 1983).

Procopius, *History of the Wars (540–55)* (trans. Anthony Kaldellis as *Prokopios, The Wars of Justinian*) (Indianapolis: Hackett, 2014).

Sebeos, *The Armenian History* (660) (trans. R. W. Thomson and J. Howard-Johnston as *The Armenian History Attributed to Sebeos*) (Liverpool: Translated Texts for Historians, 1999).

Suetonius, *Lives of the Caesars* (120) (trans. Anthony Birley) (Oxford: Oxford University Press, 2008).

Tacitus, *Agricola* (98) (trans. C. Edwards) (Oxford: Oxford University Press, 2009).

Tacitus, *Annals* (110–20) (trans. A. J. Woodman) (Indianapolis: Hackett, 2004).

Vergil, *Aeneid* (29–20 BC) (trans. David West) (London: Penguin, 2004).

Sassanian Iran

Abar Wizarisn, *On the Explanation of Chess and Backgammon: Abar Wizarisn i Catrang ud Nihisn New-Ardaxsir* (trans. T. Daryaee) (Boston: Brill, 2021).

Ammianus Marcellinus, *Res Gestae* (380) (trans. J. C. Rolfe as *Roman History*, vols. I–III, Loeb Classical Library) (Cambridge, MA: Harvard University Press, 1935–1939).

Cassius Dio (Cassius Dio Cocceianus), *Roman History* (195–230) (trans. E. Cary, vols. I–IX, Loeb Classical Library) (Cambridge, MA: Harvard University Press, 1914–1927).

The Epic Histories Attributed to P'awstos Buzand, Buzandaran Patmut'iwnk' (fourth–fifth centuries AD) (trans. N. G. Garsoïan) (Cambridge, MA: Harvard University Press, 1989).

Herodian, *History of the Empire from the Time of Marcus Aurelius* (AD 244) (trans. C. R. Whittaker, vols. I–II, Loeb Classical Library) (Cambridge, MA: Harvard University Press, 1969–1970).

Kârnâmak-i Artakhshîr Pâpakân: The Original Pahlavi Text, with Transliteration in Awesta Characters, trans. into English and Gujârati and Selections from the Shâhnâmeh (trans. E. K. Antia) (Bombay: Fort Printing Press, 1900).

Mar Kardaghi, *Acta Mar Ḳardaghi Assyriae praefecti qui sub Sapore II martyr occubuit syriace juxta manuscriptum Amidense una cum versione latina* (trans. J. B. Abbeloos) (Brussels: Société belge de librairie, 1890).

Menander, *The History of Menander the Guardsman* (mid-sixth century) (trans. R. C. Blockley) (Liverpool: Cairns, 1985).

Petrus Patricius, [works of] Petrus Patricius (mid-sixth century), in *Fragmenta Historicorum Graecorum*, Volume IV (ed. C. Müller) (Cambridge: Cambridge University Press, 2010).

Priscus, *Fragmenta Historicorum Graecorum* 4 (470) (ed. C. Müller) (Cambridge: Cambridge University Press, 2010).

Procopius, *History of the Wars* (540–555), Volumes I–V (trans. H. B. Dewing, Loeb Classical Library) (London and Cambridge, MA: Harvard University Press, 1914–1940).

Sah-nama, *Shahnameh: The Persian Book of Kings* (trans. D. Davis) (New York: Viking, 2006).

Sebeos, *The Armenian History* (660), Volumes I–II (trans. R. W. Thomson) (Liverpool: Liverpool University Press, 1999).

Scriptores Historiae Augustae, vols. I–III (trans. D. Magie, Loeb Classical Library) (London and Cambridge, MS, Harvard University Press, 1921–1932).

Šābuhr I, inscription at Ka'be-ye Zartošt, in M. Back, *Die sassanidischen Staatsinschriften: Studien zur Orthographie und Phonologie des Mittelpersischen der Inschriften zusammen mit einem etymologischen Index des mittelpersischen Wortgutes und einem Textcorpus der behandelten Inschriften* (Acta Iranica 18) (Leiden: Brill, 1978); English text: M. Sprengling, *Third Century Iran: Sapor and Kartir* (Chicago: University of Chicago Press, 1953).

Ṭabarī, *The History of al-Ṭabarī, Volume v: The Sāsānids, the Byzantines, the Lakhmids, and Yemen* (trans. C. E. Bosworth) (Albany: State University of New York, 1999).

Theodoret, *Historia Religiosa* (c. 450), in *Théodoret de Cyr, Histoire des moines de Syrie* (trans. into French by P. Canivet and A. Leroy-Molinghen) (Paris: Les Éditions du Cerf, 2013).

Theophanes, A. M. – *The Chronicle of Theophanes: Anni mundi, 6095–6305 (A.D. 602–813)* (trans. H. Turtledove) (Philadelphia, PA: University of Pennsylvania Press, 2011).

Theophylact Simmocatta, *The History* (c. 630) (trans. M. Whitby and M. Whitby) (Oxford: Clarendon Press, 1997).

Zosimus, *Historia Nova* (early sixth century) (trans. into French by F. Paschoud), *Histoire Nouvelle* (Paris: Belles lettres, 1971–1989).

Source Compilations in English Translation

Erskine, A., *Roman Imperialism* (Edinburgh: Edinburgh University Press, 2010).

Campbell, J. B., *The Roman Army, 31 BCE – CE 337: A Sourcebook* (Abingdon: Routledge, 1994) provides a very useful collection of translated texts.

Jandora, J. W., *Militarism in Arab Society: An Historiographical and Bibliographical Sourcebook* (Westport, CT: Greenwood Press, 1997).

Secondary Literature

General

Black, J., *Why Wars Happen* (London: Reaktion Books, 1998).

Corvisier, A., *Armies and Societies in Europe, 1494–1789* (trans. A. T. Siddall) (Bloomington: Indiana University Press, 1979).

Gooch, J. (ed.), *Armies in Europe* (London: Routledge, 1983).

Hartmann, A., and B. Heuser (eds), *War, Peace, and World Orders in European History* (London: Routledge, 2001).

Heuser, B., *The Evolution of Strategy: Thinking War from Antiquity to the Present* (Cambridge: Cambridge University Press, 2010).

Hill, C., *Grand Strategies: Literature, Statecraft, and World Order* (New Haven: Yale University Press, 2010).

Kortuem, H. (ed.), *Transcultural Wars from the Middle Ages to the 21st Century* (Berlin: Akademie Verlag, 2006).

Rogers, C., *Warfare and Military Organizations* (New York: Oxford University Press, 2010).

Strachan, H., *European Armies and the Conduct of War* (London: Allen and Unwin, 1983).

van Creveld, M., *The Transformation of War* (New York: Free Press, 1991).

Ancient China to AD 1127

Barfield, T. J., *The Perilous Frontier: Nomadic Empires and China, 221 BCE to CE 1757* (Oxford: Basil Blackwell, 1989).

Crespigny, R. de, *Imperial Warlord: A Biography of Cao Cao, 155–220 CE* (Sinica Leidensia, Volume XCIX) (Leiden and Boston: Brill, 2010).

Drompp, M. R., *Tang China and the Collapse of the Uighur Empire: A Documentary History* (Brill's Inner Asian Library, Volume XIII) (Leiden: Brill, 2005).

Fang, A. (trans. and annotated), *The Chronicle of the Three Kingdoms (220–265), Chapters 69–78 from the Tzu chih t'ung chien of Ssu-ma Kuang (1019–1086)* (ed. G. W. Baxter), 2 vols. (Cambridge, MA: Harvard University Press, 1952–1965).

Graff, D. A., *Medieval Chinese Warfare, 300–900* (London: Routledge, 2002).

Lewis, Mark Edward, *Sanctioned Violence in Early China* (New York: State University of New York Press, 1989).

Lorge, P., *The Reunification of China: Peace through War under the Song Dynasty* (Cambridge: Cambridge University Press, 2015).

McNeal, Robin, *Conquer and Govern: Early Chinese Military Texts from the Yi Zhou Shu* (Honolulu: University of Hawai'i Press, 2012).

Sawyer, R. D., and M.-C. Sawyer, *Zhuge Liang: Strategy, Achievements, and Writings* (North Charleston: CreateSpace Independent Publishing Platform, 2014).

Skaff, J. K., *Sui–Tang China and Its Turko-Mongol Neighbors: Culture, Power and Connections, 580–800* (Oxford: Oxford University Press, 2012).

Wang, Zhenping, *Tang China in Multi-polar Asia: A History of Diplomacy and War* (Honolulu: University of Hawai'i Press, 2013).

Wright, A. F., *The Sui Dynasty: The Unification of China, A.D. 581–617* (New York: Alfred A. Knopf, 1978).

Ancient Iran (Persia)

Börm, H., 'Die Grenzen des Großkönigs? Überlegungen zur arsakidisch–sasanidischen Politik gegenüber Rom', in F. Schleicher, T. Stickler and U. Hartmann (eds), *Iberien zwischen Rom und Iran: Beiträge zur Geschichte und Kultur Transkaukasiens in der Antike* (Stuttgart: Franz Steiner Verlag, 2019), 99–121.

Briant, P., *From Cyrus to Alexander: A History of the Persian Empire* (Winona Lake: Eisenbrauns, 2002).

Cawkwell, G., *The Greek Wars: The Failure of Persia* (Oxford: Oxford University Press, 2005).

Hyland, J. O., *Persian Interventions: The Achaemenid Empire, Athens, and Sparta 450–386 BCE* (Baltimore: Johns Hopkins University Press, 2018).

Jacobs, B., and R. Rollinger, *A Companion to the Achaemenid Persian Empire* (Malden: Wiley, 2021).

Manning, S., *Armed Force in the Teispid–Achaemenid Empire: Past Approaches, Future Prospects* (Stuttgart: Franz Steiner, 2021).

Ruzicka, S., *Trouble in the West: Egypt and the Persian Empire, 525–332* BCE (Oxford: Oxford University Press, 2012).

Tuplin, C., 'War and peace in Achaemenid imperial ideology', *Electrum*, 24 (2017), 31–54.

Howard-Johnston, J., 'The grand strategy of the Sasanian Empire', in C. Binder, H. Börm and A. Luther (eds), *Diwan: Untersuchungen zu Geschichte und Kultur des Nahen Ostens und des östlichen Mittelmeerraumes im Altertum. Festschrift für Josef Wiesehöfer zum 65. Geburtstag* (Duisburg: Wellem Verlag, 2016).

Jackson Bonner, M. R., *The Last Empire of Iran* (Piscataway: Gorgias Press, 2020).

Potts, D. T., 'Sasanian Iran and its northeastern frontier: offense, defense, and diplomatic entente', in N. di Cosmo and M. Maas (eds), *Empires and Exchanges in Eurasian Late Antiquity: Rome, China, Iran, and the Steppe, ca. 250–750* (Cambridge, Cambridge University Press, 2018), 287–301.

Rezakhani, K., *Reorienting the Sasanians: Eastern Iran in Late Antiquity* (Edinburgh: Edinburgh University Press, 2017).

Sauer, E. W. (ed.) *Sasanian Persia: Between Rome and the Steppes of Eurasia* (Edinburgh: Edinburgh University Press, 2017).

Ancient Greece

Borza, E. (ed.), *The Impact of Alexander the Great* (Hinsdale, IL: Dryden Press, 1974).

Brunt, P. A., 'Spartan policy and strategy in the Archidamian War', *Phoenix*, 19:4 (Winter 1965), 255–80.

Brunt, P. A., 'The aims of Alexander', *Greece and Rome*, 12 (1965), 205–15.

Caukwell, G., *Philip of Macedon* (London: Faber and Faber, 1978).

Foster, E., *Thucydides, Pericles and Periclean Imperialism* (Cambridge: Cambridge University Press, 2010).

Fuller, J. F. C., *The Generalship of Alexander the Great* (London: Eyre and Spottiswoode, 1958).

Goldsworthy, A., *Philip and Alexander: Kings and Conquerors* (London: Head of Zeus, 2020).

Hamilton, C. D., and P. Krentz (eds), *Polis and Polemos: Essays on Politics, War, and History in Ancient Greece in Honor of Donald Kagan* (Claremont, CA: Regina Books, 1997).

Hammond, N. G. L., *Alexander the Great: King, Commander and Statesman*, 2nd ed. (Park Ridge, NJ: Noyes, 1989).

Hanson, V. D. (ed.), *Makers of Ancient Strategy: From the Persian Wars to the Fall of Rome* (Princeton: Princeton University Press, 2010).

Hunt, P., *War, Peace, and Alliance in Demosthenes' Athens* (Cambridge: Cambridge University Press, 2010).

Konijnendijk, R., *Classical Greek Tactics: A Cultural History* (Leiden: Brill, 2018).

Konijnendijk, R., C. Kucewicz and M. Lloyd (eds), *A Companion to Greek Land Warfare: Beyond the Phalanx* (Leiden: Brill, forthcoming).

Lane Fox, R., *Alexander the Great* (London: Penguin, 2004).

Lendon, J. E., *Song of Wrath: The Peloponnesian War Begins* (New York: Basic Books, 2010).

Rawlings, L., *The Ancient Greeks at War* (Manchester: Manchester University Press, 2007).

Rusch, S. M., *Sparta at War: Strategy, Tactics, and Campaigns, 550–362* BCE (London: Frontline Books, 2011).

Sabin, P., H. van Wees and M. Whitby (eds), *The Cambridge History of Greek and Roman Warfare* I: *Greece, the Hellenistic World and the Rise of Rome* (Cambridge: Cambridge University Press, 2007).

van Wees, H., *Greek Warfare: Myths and Realities* (London: Duckworth, 2004).

Worthington, I., *By the Spear: Philip II, Alexander the Great, and the Rise and Fall of the Macedonian Empire* (Oxford: Oxford University Press, 2014).

Ancient Rome *(753* BC–AD *630)*

Burton, P. J., *Roman Imperialism* (Leiden: Brill, 2019).

Eckstein, A. M., *Mediterranean Anarchy, Interstate War and the Rise of Rome* (Berkeley: University of California Press, 2006).

Harris, W. V., *War and Imperialism in Republican Rome 327–70* BCE (Oxford: Clarendon, 1979).

Kagan, K., 'Redefining Roman grand strategy', *Journal of Military History*, 40 (2006), 350–4.

Luttwak, E., *The Grand Strategy of the Roman Empire: From the First Century* A.D. *to the Third* ([1976] London: Weidenfeld and Nicolson, 1999).

Luttwak, E. N., *The Grand Strategy of the Byzantine Empire* (Cambridge, MA: Harvard University Press, 2009).

Potter, D., *The Roman Empire at Bay,* CE *180–395* (London: Routledge, 2004).

Sabin, P., H. van Wees and M. Whitby (eds), *The Cambridge History of Greek and Roman Warfare* II. *Rome from the Late Republic to the Late Empire* (Cambridge: Cambridge University Press, 2007).

Whitby, M., *The Emperor Maurice and His Historian: Theophylact Simocatta on Persian and Balkan Warfare* (Oxford: Oxford University Press, 1988).

Whitby, M., 'War and state in late antiquity: some economic and political connections', in B. Meissner (ed.), *Krieg – Gesellschaft – Institutionen / War – Society – Institutions* (Stuttgart: Franz Steiner Verlag, 2005), 355–85.

Ancient India: *The Gupta Empire (*AD *400–500)*

Biswas, A., *The Political History of the Hunas in India* (New Delhi: Munshiram Manoharlal, 1973).

Kuwayama, S., 'The Hepthalites in Tokharistan and northwest India', in Xinru Liu (ed.), *India and Central Asia* (Ranikhet: Permanent Black, 2012), 90–102.

Maity, S. K., *Economic Life in Northern India in the Gupta Period* (New Delhi: Motilal Banarasidass, 1970).

Negi, J. S., 'Some points in early Gupta history', in J. S. Negi, *Some Indological Studies,* Volume I (Allahabad: Kalia Nand Printing Press, 1966), 32-49.

Thakur, V. K., 'Decline or diffusion: constructing the urban tradition of north India during the Gupta period', *Indian Historical Review*, 24 (1998), 20–69.

Thaplyal, K. K., 'Scions of the hitherto unknown royal house of Kausambi vis-à-vis their Gupta overlords: an historical reconstruct', *Indian Historical Review*, 1–2 (1994–1995), 1–8.

Thaplyal, K. K., 'Situating Govindagupta in history', *Indian Historical Review*, 27 (2000), 41–60.

Muslim Wars of Conquest: Arab and Mongol Wars in the Seventh to Fourteenth Centuries

Abd Dixon, A., *The Umayyad Caliphate 65–86/684–705 (A Political Study)* (London: Luzac and Company, 1971).

al-Tabari, M. J., *The History of al-Tabari: The Waning of the Umayyad Caliphate* (trans. Carole Hillenbrand) (New York: State University of New York Press and SUNY Press, 1989).

Amitai-Preiss, R., *Mongols and Mamluks: The Mamluk–Ilkhanid war, 1260–1281* (Cambridge: Cambridge University Press, 1995).

Başan, A., *The Great Seljuqs: A History* (Abingdon: Routledge, 2010).

Bonner, M., *Jihad in Islamic History: Doctrines and Practice* (Princeton and Oxford: Princeton University Press, 2006).

Collins, R., *The Arab Conquest of Spain 710–797* (Oxford: Blackwell, 1989).

Donner, F. M. (ed.), *The Articulation of Early Islamic State Structures* (Ashgate: Variorum, 2012).

Donner, F. M., *The Early Islamic Conquests* (Princeton: Princeton University Press, 1981).

Favereau, M., *The Horde: How the Mongols Changed the World* (Cambridge, MA: Harvard University Press, 2021).

Hashmi, S. (ed.), *Just Wars, Holy Wars, and Jihads: Christian, Jewish, and Muslim Encounters and Exchanges* (Oxford: Oxford University Press, 2012).

Hawting, G. R., *The First Dynasty of Islam: The Umayyad Caliphate 661–750*, 2nd ed. (London and New York: Routledge, 2000).

Hoyland, R. G., *In God's Path: The Arab Conquests and the Creation of an Islamic Empire* (Oxford: Oxford University Press, 2015).

Humphrey, S. R., *Mu'awiya ibn Abi Sufyan: From Arabia to Empire* (Oxford: Oneworld Publications, 2006).

Judd, S. C., *Religious Scholars and the Umayyads: Piety-Minded Supporters of the Marwanid Caliphate* (New York: Routledge, 2014).

Kaegi, W. E., *Byzantium and the Early Islamic Conquests* (Cambridge: Cambridge University Press, 1992).

Kelsay, J., and J. T. Johnson (eds), *Just War and Jihad: Historical and Theoretical Perspectives on War and Peace in Western and Islamic Tradition* (New York: Greenwood, 1991).

Kennedy, H., *The Early Abbasid Caliphate: A Political History* (London and New York: Routledge, 1981).

May, T., 'Military integration in Mongol warfare: the development of combined arms warfare in the Mongol Empire', *Acta Mongolica*, 18 (2019), 41–52.

Noth, A., *The Early Arabic Historical Tradition: A Source-Critical Study* (trans. Michael Bonner), 2nd ed. (Princeton: The Darwin Press, Inc., 1994).

Partner, P., *God of Battles: Holy Wars of Christianity and Islam* (Princeton: Princeton University Press, 1998).

Sarris, P., *Empires of Faith: The Fall of Rome to the Rise of Islam, 500–700* (Oxford: Oxford University Press, 2011).

Shaban, M. A., *Islamic History* A.D. *750–1055* (A.H. *132–448*) (Cambridge: Cambridge University Press, 1976).

Sharon, M., *Black Banners from the East: The Establishment of the Abbasid State: Incubation of a Revolt* (Jerusalem: The Magnes Press, 1983).

Sharon, M., *Black Banners from the East II: The Social and Military Aspects of the Abbasid Revolution* (Jerusalem: The Magnes Press, 1990).

Wakeley, J. M., *The Two Falls of Rome in Late Antiquity: The Arabian Conquests in Comparative Perspective* (Basingstoke: Palgrave Macmillan, 2018).

Byzantine Strategy (AD 630–1204)

Beihammer, D., *Alexander: Byzantium and the Emergence of Muslim Turkish Anatolia, ca. 1040–1130* (New York: Routledge, 2017).

Chatzelis, G., *Byzantine Military Manuals as Literary Works and Practical Handbooks: The Case of the Tenth-Century Sylloge Tacticorum* (London: Routledge, 2019).

Haldon, J., *The Empire That Would not Die: The Paradox of Eastern Roman Survival, 640–740* (Cambridge, MA: Harvard University Press, 2016).

Harris, J., *Byzantium and the Crusades*, 2nd ed. (London: Bloomsbury, 2014).

Holmes, C. 'Byzantium's eastern frontier in the tenth and eleventh centuries', in D. Abulafia and N. Berend (eds.), *Medieval Frontiers: Concepts and Practices* (Aldershot: Ashgate, 2002), 83–104.

Hoyland, R., *In God's Path: The Arab Conquests and the Creation of an Islamic Empire* (Oxford: Oxford University Press, 2015).

Hupchick, P. D., *The Bulgarian–Byzantine Wars for Early Medieval Balkan Hegemony* (Basingstoke: Palgrave Macmillan, 2017).

Kaegi, E. W., *Byzantium and the Early Islamic Conquests* (Cambridge: Cambridge University Press, 1992).

Kaldellis, A., *Streams of Gold, Rivers of Blood: The Rise and Fall of Byzantium, 955 A.D. to the First Crusade* (New York: Oxford University Press, 2018).

Lebeniotis, A. G., *Η πολιτική κατάρρευση του Βυζαντίου στην ανατολή: το ανατολικό σύνορο και η κεντρική Μικρά Ασία κατά το β΄ήμισυ του 11ου αι.*, Volumes I–II (Thessaloniki: Byzantine Research Centre, 2007).

Luttwak, E., *The Grand Strategy of the Byzantine Empire* (Cambridge, MA: Harvard University Press, 2009).

Madgearu, A., *Byzantine Military Organization on the Danube, 10th–12th Centuries* (Leiden: Brill, 2013).

Magdalino, P., *The Empire of Manuel I Komnenos, 1143–1180* (Cambridge: Cambridge University Press, 1993).

Papageorgiou, Aggeliki, *Ο Ιωάννης Β΄ Κομνηνός και η εποχή του (1118–1143)* (Athens: Herodotus, 2017).

Papasotiriou, Charalampos, *Βυζαντινή υψηλή σδρατηγική, 6ος–11ος αιώνας* [Μελέτες Διπλωματίας και Στρατηγικής 4] (Athens: Piotita, 2000).

Shepard, J., 'Constantine VII, Caucasian openings and the road to Aleppo', in A. Eastmond (ed.), *Eastern Approaches to Byzantium* (Aldershot: Ashgate, 2001), 19–40.

Sophoulis, P., *Byzantium and Bulgaria 775–831* (Leiden: Brill, 2012).

Stephenson, P., *Byzantium's Balkan Frontier: A Political Study of the Northern Balkans, 900–1204* (Cambridge: Cambridge University Press, 2000).

Stouraitis, Y. (ed.), *A Companion to the Byzantine Culture of War, ca. 300–1204* (Leiden: Brill, 2018).

Takirtakoglou, K., *Η Αρμενία μετρξύ Βυζαντίου και Χαλιφάτου (885–929)* (Athens: Herodotus, 2018).

Theotokis, G., *Byzantine Military Tactics in Syria and Mesopotamia in the Tenth Century: A Comparative Study* (Edinburgh: Edinburgh University Press, 2018).

Wassiliou-Seibt, K., 'Das byzantinische Verteidigungssystem an der Balkangrenze (Ende 10.–Ende 11. Jh.)', *Byzantinoslavica*, 75 (2017), 164–90.

European Strategies in the Early Middle Ages

Bachrach, B. S., 'Charles Martel, shock combat, the stirrup and feudalism', *Studies in Medieval and Renaissance History*, 7 (1970), 47–75.

Collins, R., *Early Medieval Europe 300–1000* (London: Palgrave, 2010).

Contamine, P., *War in the Middle Ages* (trans. Michael Jones) (Oxford: Blackwell 1984).

Devries, K., *Medieval Military Technology* (Ontario: Broadview, 1992).

Fouracre, P., and R. A. Gerberding, *Late Merovingian France: History and Hagiography 640–720* (Manchester: Manchester University Press, 1996).

France, J., 'The composition and raising of the armies of Charlemagne', *Journal of Medieval Military History*, 1 (2002), 61–82.

France, J., and K. DeVries (eds), *Warfare in the Dark Ages* (Aldershot: Ashgate, 2008).

Halsall, G., *Warfare and Society in the Barbarian West, 450–900* (London: Routledge, 2003).

McKitterick, R., *Charlemagne: The Formation of a European Identity* (Cambridge: Cambridge University Press, 2008).

Strickland, M. (ed.), *Anglo-Saxon Warfare: Studies in Late Anglo-Saxon and Anglo-Norman Military Organisation and Warfare* (Woodbridge: Boydell Press, 1992).

Verbruggen, J. F., *Art of Warfare in Western Europe in the Middle Ages* (trans. S. Willard and R. Southern), 2nd ed. (Woodbridge: Boydell, 1997).

European Strategies in the Later Middle Ages

Ayton, A., 'The military careerist in fourteenth-century England', *Journal of Medieval History*, 43 (2017), 4–23.

Bartlett, R., *The Making of Europe: Conquest, Colonization and Cultural Change, 950–1350* (London: Penguin, 1994).

Curry, A. (ed.), *The Hundred Years War Revisited* (London: Red Globe Press, 2019).

Curry, A., and M. Hughes (eds), *Arms, Armies and Fortifications in the Hundred Years War* (Woodbridge: Boydell and Brewer, 1994).

Fudge, T. A., *The Crusade against the Heretics in Bohemia, 1418–1437* (Aldershot: Ashgate, 2002).

Gillingham, J., *Conquest, Catastrophe and Recovery: Britain and Ireland 1066–1485* (London: Vintage Books, 2014).

Honig, J. W., 'Reappraising late medieval strategy: the example of the 1415 Agincourt campaign', *War in History*, 19:2 (2012), 123–151.

Housley, N., *Religious Warfare in Europe, 1400–1536* (Oxford: Oxford University Press, 2003).

John, S., 'The papacy and the establishment of the kingdoms of Jerusalem, Sicily and Portugal: twelfth-century papal political thought on incipient kingship', *Journal of Ecclesiastical History*, 68 (2017), 223–59.

Jordan, W. C., *Louis IX and the Challenge of the Crusade: A Study in Rulership* (Princeton, Princeton University Press, 1979).

Lambert, C., 'Henry V and the crossing to France: reconstructing naval operations for the Agincourt campaign, 1415', *Journal of Medieval History*, 43 (2017), 24–39.

Morton, N., *The Crusader States and Their Neighbours: A Military History* (Oxford: Oxford University Press, 2020).

Murray, A. V., 'The place of Egypt in the military strategy of the crusades, 1099–1221', in E. J. Mylod, G. Perry, T. W. Smith and J. Vandeburie (eds), *The Fifth Crusade in Context: The Crusading Movement in the Early Thirteenth Century* (London and New York: Routledge, 2016), 117–34.

Rogers, C., 'The Vegetian "science of warfare" in the Middle Ages', *Journal of Medieval Military History*, 1 (2002), 1–19.

Rogers, C., *War Cruel and Sharp: English Strategy under Edward III, 1327–1360*. (Woodbridge: Boydell Press, 2000).

Strickland, M., *War and Chivalry: The Conduct and Perception of War in England and Normandy* (Cambridge: Cambridge University Press, 1996).

Whelan, B., *The Two Powers: The Papacy, the Empire and the Struggle for Sovereignty in the Thirteenth Century* (Philadelphia: University of Pennsylvania Press, 2019).

Hindu and Buddhist Polities of Premodern and Early Modern Mainland South East Asia

Charney, M. W., and K. Wellen (eds), *Warring Societies of Pre-colonial Southeast Asia: Local Cultures of Conflict within a Regional Context* (Copenhagen: NIAS Press, 2017).

Lieberman, V., *Burmese Administrative Cycles: Anarchy and Conquest, c. 1580–1760* (Princeton: Princeton University Press, 1984).

Pre-Columbian Native American Wars

Ames, K. M., and H. D. G. Maschner, *Peoples of the Northwest Coast: Their Archaeology and Prehistory* (London: Thames and Hudson, 1999).

Arkush, E. N., and M. W. Allen (eds), *The Archaeology of Warfare: Prehistories of Raiding and Conquest* (Gainesville: University Press of Florida, 2006).

Chacon, R. J., and R. Mendoza (eds), *North American Indigenous Warfare and Ritual Violence* (Tucson: University of Arizona Press, 2007).

Clark, A. J., and D. B. Bamforth (eds), *Archaeological Perspectives on Warfare on the Great Plains* (Boulder: University of Colorado Press, 2018).

Keeley, L., *War before Civilization* (New York: Oxford University Press, 1996).

Lambert, P. M., 'Indigenous warfare in North America', in B. Meissner, K. Raaflaub, O. Schmitt and R. Yates (eds), *The Cambridge History of War*, Volume I: *War and the Ancient World* (Cambridge: Cambridge University Press, in press).

LeBlanc, S., *Prehistoric Warfare in the American Southwest* (Salt Lake City: University of Utah Press, 1999).

Strategies of the Ottoman Empire 1300–1823

Ágoston, G., *Guns for the Sultan: Military Power and the Weapons Industry in the Ottoman Empire* (Cambridge: Cambridge University Press, 2005).

Aksan, V. H., *Ottoman Wars 1700–1870: An Empire Besieged* (Harlow: Pearson, Longman, 2007).

Davies, B., *Empire and Military Revolution in Eastern Europe: Russia's Turkish Wars in the Eighteenth Century* (London: Continuum, 2011).

Imber, C., *The Ottoman Empire 1300–1650: The Structure of Power* (New York: Palgrave Macmillan, 2002).

Murphey, R., 'Ottoman expansion 1451–1566 I', in Geoff Mortimer (ed.), *Early Modern Military History, 1450–1815* (Basingstoke: Palgrave Macmillan, 2004), 43–59.

Murphey, R., 'Ottoman expansion 1451–1566 II', in Geoff Mortimer (ed.), *Early Modern Military History, 1450–1815* (Basingstoke: Palgrave Macmillan, 2004), 60–80.

Murphey, R., *Ottoman Warfare, 1500–1700* (New Brunswick: Rutgers University Press, 1999).

Shaw, S. J., *Between Old and New: The Ottoman Empire under Sultan Selim III 1789–1807* (Cambridge, MA: Harvard University Press, 1971).

Uyar, M., and E. J. Erickson, *A Military History of the Ottomans: From Osman to Ataturk* (Santa Barbara and Oxford: Praeger, 2009).

Strategies of the Mughal Empire

Aquil, R., *Sufism, Culture and Politics: Afghans and Islam in Medieval North India* (New Delhi: Oxford University Press, 2012).

Bhattacharya, S. N., *A History of Mughal North-East Frontier Policy* ([1929] Guwahati and Delhi: Spectrum Publications, 1998).

Faruqui, M. D., *The Princes of the Mughal Empire, 1504–1719* (Cambridge: Cambridge University Press, 2012).

Flores, J., *Unwanted Neighbours: The Mughals, the Portuguese, and Their Frontier Zones* (New Delhi: Oxford University Press, 2018).

Gordon, S., *The New Cambridge History of India*, Volume II.4: *The Marathas, 1600–1818* ([1993] Cambridge: Cambridge University Press, 2006).

Haidar, M., *Central Asia in the Sixteenth Century* (New Delhi: Manohar, 2002).

Hasan, M., *Kashmir under the Sultans* (Delhi: Aakar Books, 2005).

Islam, R., *Indo-Persian Relations: A Study of the Political and Diplomatic Relations between the Mughul Empire and Iran* (Tehran: Iranian Culture Foundation, 1970).

Kothiyal, T., *Nomadic Narratives: A History of Mobility and Identity in the Great Indian Desert* (Delhi: Cambridge University Press, 2016).

Sheikh, S., *Forging a Region: Sultans, Traders, and Pilgrims in Gujarat, 1200–1500* ([2010] New Delhi: Oxford University Press, 2014).

Subrahmanyam, S., *Explorations in Connected Histories: Mughals and Franks* (New Delhi: Oxford University Press, 2005).

Strategies of China 1368–1911

Dai, Yingcong, *The Sichuan Frontier and Tibet: Imperial Strategy in the Early Qing* (Seattle: University of Washington Press, 2009).

Dardess, J. W., *More than the Great Wall: The Northern Frontier and Ming National Security* (Lanham: Rowman and Littlefield, 2020).

Johnston, A. I., *Cultural Realism: Strategic Culture and Grand Strategy in Chinese History* (Princeton: Princeton University Press, 1995).

Swope, K. M., *A Dragon's Head and a Serpent's Tail: Ming China and the First Great East Asian War, 1592–1598* (Norman: University of Oklahoma Press, 2009).

Swope, K. M. (ed.), *The Ming World* (London: Routledge, 2020).

Waley-Cohen, J., *The Culture of War in China: Empire and the Military under the Qing Dynasty* (London: I. B. Tauris, 2014).

European Strategies 1500–1648

Asch, R., *The Thirty Years War: The Holy Roman Empire and Europe, 1618–1648* (Basingstoke : Macmillan, 1997).

Bayley, C. C., *War and Society in Renaissance Florence* (Toronto: University of Toronto Press, 1961).

Black, J., *Beyond the Military Revolution: War in the Seventeenth-Century World* (Basingstoke: Palgrave Macmillan, 2011).

Blockmans, W., *Emperor Charles V, 1500–1558* (London: Arnold, 2002).

Elliott, J., *The Count-Duke of Olivares: The Statesman in an Age of Decline* (New Haven and London: Yale University Press, 1986).

Hale, J. R., *War and Society in Renaissance Europe, 1450–1620* (Leicester: Leicester University Press and Fontana, 1985).

Holt, M. P., *The French Wars of Religion 1562–1629* (Cambridge: Cambridge University Press, 1995).

Housley, N., *Religious Warfare in Europe, 1400–1536* (Oxford: Oxford University Press, 2003).

Lockhart, P., *Sweden in the Seventeenth Century* (Basingstoke: Palgrave Macmillan, 2004).

Parker, G. (ed.), *The Thirty Years' War* (London: Routledge, 1984).

Parrott, D., *Richelieu's Army: War, Government, and Society in France, 1624–1642* (Cambridge: Cambridge University Press, 2001).

Potter, D., *Renaissance France at War. Armies, Culture and Society, c. 1480–1560* (Woodbridge: Boydell Press, 2008).

Roberts, M., *Essays in Swedish History* (Minneapolis: University of Minnesota Press, 1967).

Stradling, R., *Europe and the Decline of Spain: A Study of the Spanish System, 1580–1720* (London: Allen and Unwin, 1981).

Wilson, P. H., *Europe's Tragedy: A History of the Thirty Years War* (London: Allen Lane, 2009).

Wood, J. B., *The King's Army: Warfare, Soldiers, and Society during the Wars of Religion in France, 1562–76* (Cambridge: Cambridge University Press, 1996).

Early Modern Naval Strategies

Blakemore, R. J., and P. Brandon, 'The Dutch and English fiscal–naval states: a comparative overview', in D. Ormrod and G. Rommelse, *War, Trade and the State: Anglo-Dutch Conflict 1652–1689* (Woodbridge: Boydell Press, 2020), 117–36.

Bruijn, J. R., *The Dutch Navy of the Seventeenth and Eighteenth Centuries* (St. John's, NF: International Maritime Economic History Association, 2011).

Davids, K., and M. 't Hart, 'The navy and the rise of the state: the case of the Netherlands, *c.* 1570–1810', in J. G. Backhaus (ed.), *Navies and State Formation: The Schumpeter Hypothesis Revisited and Reflected* (Zurich: Lit Verlag, 2012).

Glete, J., *War and the State in Early Modern Europe: Spain, the Dutch Republic and Sweden as Fiscal–Military States, 1500–1600* (London and New York: Routledge, 2002).

Groen, P., O. van Nimwegen, R. P. van Reine, L. Sicking and A. van Vliet, *The Eighty Years War: From Revolt to Regular War, 1568–1648* (Leiden: Leiden University Press, 2019).

Hattendorf, J. B., 'Competing navies: Anglo-Dutch rivalry, 1652–1688', in D. Ormrod and G. Rommelse, *War, Trade and the State: Anglo-Dutch Conflict 1652–1689* (Woodbridge: Boydell Press, 2020), 108–16.

Hattendorf, J. B., 'Navies, strategy, and tactics in the age of De Ruyter', in J. R. Bruijn, R. P. van Reine and R. van Hövell tot Westerflier (eds), *De Ruyter: Dutch Admiral* (Rotterdam: Karwansaray Publishers, 2011), 8–19.

Jones, J. R., *The Anglo-Dutch Wars of the Seventeenth Century* (London and New York: Longman, 1996).

Rodger, N. A. M., *The Command of the Ocean: A Naval History of Britain, 1649–1815* (London: Penguin, 2005).

Rodger, N. A. M., *The Safeguard of the Sea: A Naval History of Britain, 660–1649* ([1997] London: Penguin, 2004).

Rommelse, G., *The Second Anglo-Dutch War (1665–1667)* (Hilversum: Verloren, 2006).

Stradling, R. A., *The Armada of Flanders: Spanish Maritime Policy and European War, 1568–1668* (Cambridge: Cambridge University Press, 1992).

Vliet, A. P. van, 'Foundation, organization and effects of the Dutch navy (1568–1648)', in M. van der Hoeven (ed.), *Exercise of Arms: Warfare in the Netherlands (1568–1648)* (Leiden: Brill, 1997), 153–72.

Western Strategies 1648–1789

Ágoston, G., *The Last Muslim Conquest: The Ottoman Empire and Its Wars in Europe* (Princeton: Princeton University Press, 2021).

Baugh, D. A., *The Global Seven Years War, 1754–1763: Britain and France in a Great Power Contest* (London: Pearson, 2011).

Blanning, T., *Frederick the Great King of Prussia* (London: Allen Lane, 2015).

Buckner, P., and J. G. Reid (eds), *Revisiting 1759: The Conquest of Canada in Historical Perspective* (Toronto: University of Toronto Press, 2012).

Cénat, J.-Ph., *Le roi stratège: Louis XIV et la direction de la guerre 1661–1715* (Rennes: Presses universitaires de Rennes, 2010).

Chaline, O., *Les armées du Roi: Le grand chantier* XVIIe–XVIIIe *siècle* (Paris: Armand Colin, 2016).

Clark, C., *Iron Kingdom: The Rise and Downfall of Prussia, 1600–1947* (London: Penguin, 2006).

Cornette, J., *Le roi de guerre: Essai sur la souveraineté dans la France du grand siècle* (Paris: Payot, 1993).

Corvisier, A., *Armies and Societies in Europe, 1494–1789* (trans. A. T. Siddall) (Bloomington: Indiana University Press, 1979).

Dickinson, H. T. (ed.)., *Britain and the American Revolution* (Harlow: Longman, 1998).

Duffy, C., *Frederick the Great: A Military Life* (London: Routledge and Kegan Paul, 1985).

Fonck, B., *Le Maréchal de Luxembourg et le commandement des armées sous Louis XIV* (Seyssel : Editions Champ Vallon, 2014).

Hall, R., *Atlantic Politics, Military Strategy, and the French and Indian War* (Basingstoke: Palgrave Macmillan, 2016).

Hochedlinger, M., *Austria's Wars of Emergence: War, State and Society in the Habsburg Monarchy 1683–1797* (London: Longman, 2003).

Jennings, F., *Empire of Fortune: Crowns, Colonies, and Tribes in the Seven Years War in America* (New York: W. W. Norton, 1988).

Lockhart, P., *Sweden in the Seventeenth Century* (Basingstoke: Palgrave Macmillan, 2004).

Lynn, J., *Giant of the Grand Siècle: The French Army, 1610–1715* (Cambridge: Cambridge University Press, 1997).

Lynn, J., *The Wars of Louis XIV* (London: Longman's, 1999).

McCullough, R., *Coercion, Conversion and Counterinsurgency in Louis xiv's France* (Leiden: Brill, 2007).

Middleton, R., *The Bells of Victory: The Pitt–Newcastle Ministry and the Conduct of the Seven Years War, 1757–1762* (Oxford: Clarendon Press, 1985).

Mortimer, G. (ed.), *Early Modern Military History, 1450–1815* (Basingstoke: Palgrave Macmillan, 2004).

Oury, C., *La guerre de succession d'Espagne: La fin tragique du grand siècle 1701–1714* (Paris: Tallandier, 2020).

Roosen, W., *The Age of Louis XIV: The Rise of Modern Diplomacy* (New Brunswick: Transaction Publishers, 1976).

Rousset, C. F. M., *Histoire de Louvois et de son administration politique et militaire* (Paris: Didier et cie, 1862).

Scott, H. M., *The Emergence of the Eastern Powers, 1756–1775* (Cambridge: Cambridge University Press, 2001).

Showalter, D. E., *The Wars of Frederick the Great* (London and New York: Longman, 1996).

Sonnino, P., *Louis XIV and the Origins of the Dutch War* (Cambridge: Cambridge University Press, 2002).

Stocker, D., K. J. Hagan and M. T. McMaster (eds), *Strategy in the American War of Independence: A Global Perspective* (Abingdon: Routledge, 2010).

Storring, A. L., '"Our Age": Frederick the Great, classical warfare, and the uses and abuses of military history', *International Journal of Military History and Historiography*, 42 (2022), 323–55.

Storring, A. L., '"The age of Louis XIV": Frederick the Great and French ways of war', *German History*, 38 (2020), 24–46.

Stradling, R., *Europe and the Decline of Spain: A Study of the Spanish System, 1580–1720* (London: Allen and Unwin, 1981).

Szabo, F. A. J., *The Seven Years War in Europe, 1756–1763* (Edinburgh: Pearson Longman, 2008).

Szechi, D., *The Jacobites: Britain and Europe, 1688–1788* (Manchester: Manchester University Press, 1994).

Taylor, F. L., *War and Society in Early-Modern Europe, 1495–1715* (London: Routledge, 1992).

Wilson, P. H., 'Prussia's relations with the Holy Roman Empire, 1740 – 1786', *Historical Journal*, 51 (2008), 337–71.

Wilson, P. H., *German Armies: War and German Politics, 1648–1806* (London: UCL Press, 1998).

Winkel, C., *Im Netz des Königs: Netzwerke und Patronage in der preußischen Armee 1713–1786* (Krieg in der Geschichte 79) (Paderborn, Munich, Vienna and Zurich: Ferdinand Schöningh, 2013).

Wolf, J. B., *Louis XIV* (New York: W. W. Norton and Company, 1974).

Strategy in the Wars of Pre-colonial Sub-Saharan Africa

Eldredge, E. A., *The Creation of the Zulu Kingdom, 1815–1828: War, Shaka, and the Consolidation of Power* (Cambridge: Cambridge University Press, 2014).

Etherington, N., *The Great Treks: The Transformation of Southern Africa, 1815–1854* (Harlow: Longman, 2001).

Law, R., *Ouidah: The Social History of a West African Slaving 'Port', 1727–1892* (Oxford: James Currey, 2004).

Macola, G., *The Gun in Central Africa: A History of Technology and Politics* (Athens: Ohio University Press, 2016).

Reid, R. J., *War in Pre-colonial Eastern Africa* (London: James Curry, 2007).

Reid, R. J., *Warfare in African History* (Cambridge: Cambridge University Press, 2012).

Smith, R. S., *Warfare and Diplomacy in Pre-colonial West Africa*, 2nd ed. (Madison: University of Wisconsin Press, 2005).

Thornton, J. K., *A History of West Central Africa to 1850* (Cambridge: Cambridge University Press, 2020).

Thornton, J. K., *Warfare in Atlantic Africa 1500–1800* (London: UCL Press, 2003).

Index

Abar Wizārišn ī Čatrang ud Nihišn ī
  Nēw-Ardaxšīr (On the Explanation
  of Chess and Backgammon), 191
Abbasids, 218–19, 222
  adversaries, 214–15
  dependence on the military, and jihad, 213
  Khorasan troops, 211
  military commanders (*quwwad*), 212
  revolution (750), 224
'Abd al-Malik, 214, 217
Abu Bakr, 205, 212, 215–16, 223
Achaemenid dynasty, 40, 44, 45
Acre, 284, 285
Adamsky, Dima, 16
admiral generals, Dutch Republic.
  See stadholders
admiralty, Amsterdam, 451–2, 461
Aeneas Tacticus, 54, 67
Afghans/Afghanistan, 79, 175, 386–7, 397, 399
Africa, 119
  central, age of warlords, 377–9
  Muslim expansion, 216
  north, 218
  and Ottomans, 365
  provincial organisation, 119
  and Rome, 120, 121, 156
  See also Berbers; sub-Saharan Africa; west
  Africans
Agathias (historian), 149–50
agency, individual and collective, 8
Agincourt, battle of, 276
Agricola, 160–1
agriculture/agricultural regions, 133,
  152, 184, 380
  See also farmland/farmers
Ahmad I al-Mansur Sa'did, 382
Ahom kingdom, 389–90, 399
Akbar (r. 1556–1605), 387, 396–7
  economic factors in campaigns, 391

empire building, 397
fortifications, 395–6
and Gujarat, 398
ministerial offices and war councils, 385
al-Qaeda, 10, 16
Alamanni, 153
Alaungpaya, king of Burma, 314, 325–6
Alba, Duke of, 453
Aleppo, 243
Alexander III of Scotland, 289
Alexander III of Macedon (the Great), 45,
  75–6, 79, 91
  and Asia Minor, 81, 91
  and Bessus, 95
  campaign in Egypt, 93–4
  campaigns in India, 96
  and Darius, 92, 93–4
  death of, 82, 96
  diplomacy, 95
  independence in planning, 74
  and League of Corinth, 91
  loss of strategic vision, 95
  marriage alliances, 96
  and Panhellenism, 81, 91
  and Parmenion, 74
  and Persia, 51, 73, 75, 91, 93–5, 96
  pothos, 93, 96
  sources, 73–4
  tactical genius, 96
  at Troy, 81
  at Tyre, 93
Alexios I, 245, 246, 249
Alfred, king of Wessex, 254, 263–4
Algeria, and Ottomans, 350
Algiers, 433
Algonquians, 339
'Ali ibn Abu Talib, 205–8
Allahabad Pillar Inscription
  of Samudragupta, 173–4

alliances, 5
  common values, 5
  Roman system, 114, 122, 157
  Sassanian, 199–200
  symmachia, 5
  See also coalition warfare; marriage
    alliances
Allsen, Thomas, 310
Americas. *See* Native American wars, pre-
    Columbian; North America
Amherst, Jeffrey, 510
Ammianus Marcellinus, 144
amphibious operations, Dutch Revolt/Eighty
    Years War, 453
Amphictyonic League, 58
Amphipolis, 83–4
An Lushan rebellion, 129, 133, 134, 137, 138–9
Anatolia, 216, 240, 242, 244, 245, 363
Andronikos I, 250
Andronikos II (Byzantine emperor), 357
Angkor, 319, 320, 323
Angkor Wat, 314, 333
Anglo-Burmese War, First, 329
Anglo-Dutch Wars, 451, 455–63
  first, 458
  second, 458
  third, 457, 463
Anglo-Saxon Chronicle, 254
Anouvong Rebellion, 321
Antiochus III (Seleucid king), 111
Antiochus IV, 104
Antoninus Pius (138–61), 161
appeasement, 222, 237, 241
  See also truces
Arabia and Persian Gulf, 198
Arabic (classical), historians, 192
Arabic sources, Mongol strategy, 294
Arabs/Arab tribes, 200
  and Abu Bakr, 213
  and Byzantine Empire, 230, 233, 237, 240,
    241–2
  deep defence, 237–8
  in Khorasan, 225
  and Umayyad collapse, 225
  See also Muslim armed forces; Sassanian
    Iran
Arbroath, Declaration of, 286–7
Arcadians, 59
Arcadius (395–408), 165
archaeological records
  Native American wars, pre-Columbian,
    334, 336–7
  Roman, 100, 146

sub-Saharan Africa, 371
Tlingit of Kuiu Island, 343
archers, 65, 150, 151, 175, 176, 289, 360
Ardashir, Ardaxšīr, Iranian ruler, 153, 198, 200
Argaeus, 80, 83
Argos, 60, 61, 65
aristocracy
  Byzantine Empire, 232–3, 250
  and chivalry, 268
  East Frankish, 268
  faction and ambition, 264
  Gallo-Roman armies, 256
  Marathas, 388–9
  and Mongols, 304, 308–9
  Mughal Empire, 397
  Ottoman Empire, 348–9, 355
  Roman, 100
  Sassanian, 195, 202
  western Europe, 'Dark Ages', 264, 265
  See also nobility/aristocracy
Aristotle, 75
  Politics, 54
Armagnac factions, 276–7
armed force, 18, 138
  Alexander, 79, 95–6
  Austria/Habsburg, 499
  Britain, 515
    American War of Independence, 522
  Byzantine Empire, 234–6
  caliphates, 208, 219.
  See also Muslim armed forces
  Charlemagne, 256, 262
  China, 134–5, 138
    improvements in technology/
      administration, 134
  colonial Americans, and British, 510
  Dahomey kingdom (Africa), 376
  English, 286
  Europe, late Middle Ages, 289
  Franks/Germanic peoples, 260–1
  Frederick II of Prussia, 497
  Frederick William I of Prussia, 498
  Greece, 75
  Habsburgs, 429–30, 434
  Japan, 416
  Jin Empire, 298–9
  Justinian, 149–50
  Konbaung Burma, 319
  Louis XIV of France, 477–8
  Ming and Qing dynasties of China, 418
  Mongols, 295, 306–7. *See also tamma* army
  Mughal Empire, 392–4
  Muslim. *See* Muslim armed forces

armed force (cont.)
  Nguni/Ngoni age sets, 377–8
  Ottoman Empire, 349, 354, 356–7, 366, 367
  Persia, 49, 75
  Philip II, 76–9
  Prussia, 499, 500, 506
  Roman.
    See also legions/legionaries, Roman; naval
      power, Roman
    auxiliary units, 154
    mobile troops and local troops, 163
    Notitia Dignitatum, 146
    recruitment, 150, 154
    superiority of, 150
    taxation, 151
  Siamese kingdoms, 316
  south-east Asian polities (premodern/early
    modern), 319–22
  sub-Saharan Africa, 375–6
  volunteers, 76
  western Europe, early Middle Ages, 256
  See also cavalry; crusades; Gupta army;
    mercenaries; military elite; militias;
    naval power; professional armies;
    Sassanian army; Thirty Years War;
    weaponry; *specific names of wars*
Armenia, 195
  and Arabs, 242
  and Byzantine Empire, 240–1, 243
  conquered by Sassanians, 200
  end of Arsacid rule, 201–2
  and Mongols, 299, 302, 305
  Muslim conquest, 216
  partition, 201
  Torus II, 246
  and Turkish raids, 244
armour, 77, 78
Arnot, Frederick S., 381
Arrian
  Alexander histories, 41, 73, 74
  Anabasis, 73
Arsacids, 195
  See also Parthian Empire
Artaxerxes I, 43
Artaxerxes II, 43, 50, 51
Artaxerxes III (Bessus), 44, 95
Arthur, King (legends), 286
artillery, 66, 499
Ashoka, 182
Asia, south-east
  Indic polities (twelfth–nineteenth
    centuries), 312–33
    actors, 317–19

adversaries, 322–4
application of strategy, 330–2
causes and purposes of war, 324–7
historiographical debates, 332–3
means, 319–22
prioritisation, 329–30
sources, 314–17
strategic decisions, premises underlying,
  327–9
and Mongols, 300
Asia Minor, 76, 221
  Alexander's conquest of, 81, 91
  and Byzantine Empire, 230, 231–2, 243
    resettlement policy for new
      populations, 234
    Turks, 238
  Persia and, 57
  Philip's campaign, 90
  Turcoman tribes, 346
asthapradhan (a council of eight ministers),
  173–4
asvamedha ritual, 182
Athens/Athenians, 43
  alliance with Sparta, 58
  armed force, 76
  financial resources, 66
  hegemonic wars, 60
  military policies, sources on, 54
  military training, 65
  objectives, 61
  orators, 54, 56, 66
  and Peloponnesian War, 59, 61, 70, 72
  prioritisation, 68–9
  and Sicily, 68
  and Sparta, 56–7, 59
  subsidised troops, 65
  support for democracies, 64
Attalids, 117
Attila (leader of Huns), 153, 165, 166
attrition, war of
  Byzantine Empire, 238–9
  Frederick II of Prussia, 505
  Habsburg opponents and, 446
  Louis XIV of France, 481, 483
  Mughal Empire, 400
  Ottoman Empire, and Habsburgs,
    351–2
Augsburg
  League of, 474
  Peace of, 437, 446
Augustus, Emperor, 146, 149, 153–4, 159–60
Aurangzeb (r. 1658–1707), Mughal ruler, 385–6,
  396, 400, 401

Austria
  armed force, 499
  Habsburgs, 436, 437, 471, 488
  Styria, 439
  War of the Austrian Succession, 488
  See also Ferdinand II of Styria, Holy Roman
    Emperor; Habsburgs
Avars, 153, 167, 231–2, 265–6
Ayutthaya (1350–1767), 312, 319, 321
  Cambodian and Tai polities, 328
  and defection of the Khmers, 323
  downfall of, 314, 324, 328, 330, 331
  expansion, 314
  fortifications, 330
  Konbaung Burma siege on, 325–6, 333
  and Lanna, 324, 326
  princes governing *Mueng Lukelaung*, 318
  and Satha I of Cambodia, 323
Ayyubids, 278, 285
azabs, 356–7

Babur, 386–7, 396
Babylonia/Babylonian, 40–1, 43, 49
Bactria/Bactrians, 75–6, 95, 198
Baghdad, 222, 353, 366
Bahadur Shah, 387–8
Balkans, 159, 164, 230
  alliances, 237
  auxiliary corps to Ottomans, 355
  and Byzantine Empire, 230, 238, 239,
    249, 250
  Latin Church targets, 278
  Ottoman vassals, 352, 363
  and Ottomans, 351, 361, 363,
    364
  See also Slavs
Balkh, 390, 392, 399
Ban Gu, *History of the Han Dynasty*, 25
Bana, *Puranas*, 173
Banjara, and Mughal supplies, 394
Bannockburn, battle of, 286
Banu Hashim, 205–8
Barbarossa, Ottoman admiral.
  See Hayreddin Barbarossa
Basil II, Byzantine emperor, 230, 231, 243,
  247, 248
Bavaria, 443, 488, 492, 501, 502
Bayezid I, Ottoman sultan, 363
Bede, 253
Bedouins, 208
benevolence. *See* morality and benevolence
Bengal, 390, 396, 398
Benin Gap, 374–5

Berbers, 210–11, 219, 220
Bessus. *See* Artaxerxes III (Bessus)
Bijapur, 388, 400
Black, Jeremy, xxi, 2, 15
Black Prince. *See* Edward Prince of Wales
Black Sea, 48, 57, 83 f., 88–91, 111, 198, 207, 230,
  234, 239 f., 246, 352 f.
blockades, Dutch Republic, 457, 460, 461
Bohemia, 440, 498, 504
  as Habsburg possession, 442–3, 446–7
  revolt, 440, 442–3
Booth, Ken, 11–12, 15
booty, collection of, 119, 265, 362
  See also raids
borderlands
  and strategic prioritisation, 68, 69
  See also frontier relations/maintenance
Boris I, 247
Bourbon dynasty, 470
bow and arrow, 342–3
  See also archers
Bradley, Guy, 123
Brahmin Hinduism, 312
Brandenburg–Prussia, 492, 495, 497–8, 499
Breslau, Treaty of, 504
bribery, 76, 83, 138
Britain
  American War of Independence, 512–13,
    522, 523–4
  Anglo-Saxon, 255
  Anglo-Saxon Chronicle, 254
  and Canada, 515, 516
  colonists in North America.
    See North America
  declares war on Dutch, 519
  First Anglo-Burmese War, 325, 329
  and Frederick II, 495
  and French, North America, 513
  Hadrian's Wall, 161
  and Hanover, 492
  and Native Americans, 517–18
  and naval-mindedness, 13–14
  and Ottomans, 365
  peacetime army in North America, 515
  and Rome, 156, 160, 167
  and Russia, 494–5
  Seven Years War, 511, 514, 516, 520–1,
    525
  and slave trade, 375, 376
  taxation, 151
  Treaty of Paris, 495
  United Kingdom National Archives, 510
  War of the Austrian Succession, 495

Britain (cont.)
  Westminster Convention (1756), 494, 495, 504
  See also England; Scotland; Wales
Buddhagupta, inscriptions, 173
Buddhism, 182, 312, 324, 325
Buffalo Calf Road, 339
Bulgars/Bulgaria
  and Arabs, 242
  Bulgar–Vlach polity, 250
  and Byzantine Empire, 231, 233, 237, 238, 247, 248
  coalition of nomads, 298
  and Mongols, 307–8
Burghal Hidage, 254, 263–4
Burgundy, 431
Burma/Burmese kingdoms
  challenges from small tribes/kingdoms, 323
  compulsory recruitment (*ahmudan*) to armies, 320
  expansion, 312, 329
  royal chronicles, 315
  and subjugation of tribes, 323
  wars with Siamese kingdoms, 312
  See also Konbaung Dynasty (1752–1885); Toungoo Empire (1510–1752)
Burmese viceroys, 319
Burmese–Siamese Wars, 315–16, 319
Burton, Paul, 123
Byzantine chronicles, on Ottomans, 347
Byzantine Empire, 128
  actors, 227–30
  adversaries, 230–2
  armies, 234–6
  caliphates, 213
  causes and objectives of war, 236–9
  decline, 226, 233, 250, 255
  deep defence, 237–8
  dominant international political/military role, 226
  and emirate raids, 362
  execution/application, 241–50
  means, 232–6
  and the Muslims, 215, 216
  and Ottoman mercenaries, 362–3
  and Ottomans, 350–1
  priorities, 239–41
  and the Rashidun, 213–14, 219
  sources, 226–7
  trade routes, 212
  and the Umayyads, 210, 217, 219–20
  use of term *strategia*, 4
  See also Constantinople

Caddoan-speaking peoples, migration, 342
Caernarfon, 286
Caesar, Gaius Julius
  and Gaul, 100, 102, 112, 119, 121
  and the Helvetii, 120
  invasion of Britain, 105
  mass enslavement, 121
  navy fleets, 105–6
Caffa, siege of, 14
cakravati ideology, 312, 322–3, 324, 325, 328, 332–3
California, southern, Chumash communities, 340
Caligula, 149, 160
caliphates (Rashidun, Umayyad and Abbasid)
  actors, 205–8
  adversaries, 213–15
  causes of war, 212–13
  execution/application, 219–22
  historiographical debates, 222–5
  means, 208–12
  prioritisation, 215–19
  sources, 204–5
  See also Arabs/Arab tribes
Calvinism, 437, 442–3
Cambodia, Siam annexation, 323, 328, 329
Cambyses II, Iranian ruler, 40, 43
Canada
  and Britain, 515, 516, 523
  French in, 511, 514, 515, 516–17
  Seven Years War, 524–5
  See also New France
cannon, 322, 330, 360, 419, 458
Cao Cao (Han warlord), 124
Capetians, 257, 260
capital cities, as military objective, 136
capital gazettes, 407
Capitularies, 254
Caracalla, 149, 162
Carlos II, 474
Carolingians, 253, 264
  and the aristocracy, 267
  breakdown of, 268
  cavalry strategy, 269
  regnum Francorum, 257
  West Frankish kingdom, 260
Carpini, Jon de Plano, 294–5
Carthage, 107, 113
  legacy of conflict with Rome, 117
  and Punic wars, 109–10, 115, 116, 119
  Romans and, 106, 111, 114, 119, 120
carts, ban on, 78
Cassius Dio, 144, 155–6, 162

Castle Rock Pueblo, 341
castles, 268, 286
Catholicism, 273
  and Bohemia, 440
  Charles V, 433
  Counter-Reformation, 437
  Holy Roman Empire, 442
    Electoral College, 443
  Philip II of Spain, 442
  See also papacy
Caucasus, and Ottomans, 352, 362
cavalry, 70
  Alexander, 79
  Benin Gap, 374–5
  Carolingians, 269
  China, 135
  English, 286
  Europe, 262
  Franks/Germanic peoples, 261
  Greece, 64, 65
  Gupta army, 175–6
  Mongols, 311
  Mughal Empire, 393, 394
  Ottoman Empire, 356, 361
  Oyo Empire, 375, 376
  Persian, 75
  Philip II, 76, 77
  Prussian, 498
  Roman, 150
  Sassanian, 199
  Songhay, 373
  south-east Asian polities (premodern/early
    modern), 321
  Uighurs, 131
Celts, 57
central Africa
  age of warlords, 377–9
  source scarcity, 379
Chakirma'ut, battle of (1204), 295–6
Chakri dynasty, Siamese, 318
Chamillart, Secretary, 480
Chamlay, Marquis de, 470
Champa kingdom, 312
Chams, 317
  and Khmer Empire, 323, 327–8
Chandragupta I (r. 319–34), 171, 177
Chandragupta II/Vikramaditya, 177–8
  fighting emperor, 173, 180, 187–8
  and Gujarat, 182–3
  inscriptions, 172
  marries brother's widow, 185
Changduan jing (*Classic of Advantages and
  Disadvantages*), 126

Changping, Battle of, 36
Charidemus (Greek general), 78
Charlemagne
  and the aristocracy, 266
  armed force, 256, 262
  and the Avars, 265–6
  Capitularies, 253–4
  consultation with advisers, 256
  empire, 257–8
  failure to centralise, 264
  organisation and logistics, 270
Charles II of England, 457, 458, 459
Charles II (aka 'the Bald') of West Francia, 251,
  258, 263
Charles V, Holy Roman Emperor, 425, 434–6
  See also Habsburgs, Charles V
Charles VI of France, 500, 501
Charles VII, Holy Roman Emperor, 492
Charles VII of France, 277
Charles Martel, 262, 269
charters, and knights, 271, 282
Chen dynasty (southern), 130, 140–1
Chen Shou, *San guo zhi* (*Record of the Three
  Kingdoms*), 127
Chen Zhongying, 406
Chengpu, Battle of (632 BC), 35–6
Cherson, Crimea, 230, 239
Cheyenne oral histories, 339
Chia, Robert, 17
Chiangmai, Ayutthaya and, 324
chiefdoms, Native American, 338–9
China
  AD 180–1127, 123
    actors, 132–3
    allies, 131–2
    civil wars, 133
    ends of strategy, 133–4
    enemies, 130–1
    means of strategy, 134–9
    outcomes, 139–43
    strategic environment, 129–30
    texts and sources, 125–8
  1368–1911, 403–23 *passim*
    actors, 408–9
    causes of war, 411–14
    enemies of the state, 409–10
    execution and outcomes, 422–3
    historiographical debates, 423
    means, 415–21
    objectives, 414–15
    prioritisation, 421–2
    sources, 405–7
  Eastern Zhou dynasty, 21

China (cont.)
  Mongols and, 298
  Second World War, casualties, 18–19
  See also Han dynasty; Huns; Jin empire;
      Qin dynasty; Spring and Autumn
      period, China; Warring States period,
      China
Chinese military classics, and
    awesomeness, 404
Chinese sources, Mongol strategy, 292–4
Chinggis Khan, and Mongol Empire, 292–311
  actors, 295–7
  adversaries, 297–300
  causes of war, 300–3
  execution/application, 308–10
  family of (*altan urugh*), 304
  historical debates, 310–11
  means, 306–7
  objectives, 303–5
  prioritisation, 307–8
  sources, 292–5
chivalry, 265, 268, 283
Christianity/Christians
  and the Balkans, 278
  caliphates, 214
  and Charlemagne, 265–6
  Charles V, 433
  and Constantine, 164
  conversion to Islam, 355
  and Iberian peninsula, 272
  liturgy, crusading cause and, 282–3
  and Mongols, 278–9
  nomadic people, 249
  orthodox, 247
  Reconquista, 279
  and Rome, 156, 158
  in Scandinavia and the Baltic, 273
  See also Catholicism; Huguenots;
      Protestantism
Chumash communities, California,
    southern, 340
Cicero, 80, 100
Cilicia, 246
cities
  Europe, western (Dark Ages), 261
  See also fortifications
citizen assemblies, Roman, 101–2
citizen soldiers, Roman.
  See legions/legionaries, Roman
citizenship, Roman, 148–9, 150
city states, Greek, 54
  and Alexander, 75
  aspects of strategy and, 53–4

betrayals, 67–8
civic model, 55–6
militias, 64–5
non-Greek adversaries, 57–8
size and demography, 55
wars with Greek neighbours, 57
  See also Athens/Athenians; Greece; *indi-
      vidual city states by name*
civil wars
  Byzantine Empire, 244
  caliphates, 205, 218, 224
  Mongols, 297, 302–3, 308
  Ottoman Empire, 363–4
  See also specific names of countries/empires
Clanchy, Michael, 271–2
classical Greece. *See* Greece
classical warfare, 6
Claudius, 147, 154, 156, 160
Clausewitz, Carl von, 7, 10, 14–15
Cleitarchus, 74
clerics, chroniclers of post-Roman period, 253
clibanarii (boilermen), 150
client kingdoms, Roman, 119, 157
climatic conditions
  and Mongol expansion, 311
  Native American wars, pre-Columbian,
      340, 341, 342, 343–4
Clovis, king of the Francs, 255, 256, 257, 266
coalition warfare, 70, 72
Cock, George, 457
coins/coinage, 160, 173, 175, 227
Colbert, Jean-Baptiste, 468, 475, 476, 478
Colbert family, 468
Cold War, 12
combined-arms warfare, 77
comitia centuriata (citizen assemblies), 101–2
comitia tributa, 118
commanders (military), 102–3
  See also consuls/consulships (Roman);
      military elite
commoners, armed force, 319, 380
communication, routes of
  and Charles V, 432–3
  Mughal Empire, 395–6
concessionary tactics. *See* bribery; diplomacy;
      tribute
Confucians, 124
  See also Ruists (Confucians)
conscription, 64–5, 137
Constantine I (aka 'the Great'), Roman
    emperor, 147, 163–4, 194
Constantine V, East Roman emperor, 234, 235
Constantine VII, East Roman emperor, 239

De Administrando Imperio, 227
self-promotion, 241
Constantinople, 239
  and Arabs, 242
  crusaders' sack of, 285
  land communications, 239–40
  Latins capture, 226, 250
  natural barriers, 240
  Ottomans conquer, 346–7, 348, 350–1, 364
  and sultans, new system, 349
  Umayyads and, 217, 220, 221
  and Valentinian III, 165
Constantius, Roman emperor, 158
consuls/consulships (Roman), 101, 102, 103,
    104, 113–14, 117
  See also legions/legionaries, Roman
consultative decision making
  Europe, late Middle Ages, 273–5
  Mongols, 295
continuity, as strategic theme, China, 134
convoying, 453, 457, 460, 485
Corbulo (Roman general), 147, 156
Corinth, 58
Corinthian War, 43
correspondence
  Charles V, 425
  Europe, late Middle Ages, 272
  George Washington, 510
  Louis XIV of France, 464–7
corvée, 319
cosmology, China, 128
councils of war
  Byzantine Empire, 230
  south-east Asian polities (premodern/early
    modern), 317–18
Cowboy Wash attacks, 340–1
Crimea, 230
Cromwell, Oliver, 455–6
Crone, Patricia, 224
crossbowmen, 322
Crow Creek, massacre, 337, 342
crusades
  Barons' Crusade, 283
  costs, 282
  and Egypt, 284, 285
  end of, 278
  fall of crusader states, 285–6
  Fifth, 285, 290
  First, 245, 278, 279, 284
    and expedition narratives, 271
  Fourth, 250, 284–5, 288
  mortalities, 282
  and popes' legal means, 290

  religious motivation, 280–3
  Second, and Byzantine Empire, 287–8
  Seventh, 275, 278, 285
  size of, 287–8
  Third, 276, 278, 284, 288
  See also knights
cultural patronage, 502
  See also patronage
cultural traits, Roman, and soft power, 123
culture
  and rationality, 12
  uncertainty in war, 15–16
Cunaxa, Battle of (401 BC), 44
Curtius, Alexander histories, 41
Cyprus, 245–6, 278, 284, 365
Cyrus Cylinder, 41, 44
Cyrus II, ruler of Iran (r. 559–530), 40–1, 43
Cyrus the Great, ruler of Iran, 95
Cyrus the Younger, 44

Dacia, 161, 163
Dahomey kingdom (Africa), 375–7
Dali, 305, 308
Dalmatia/Dalmatians, 117, 239, 250
Damrong Rajanubhab, Prince (1862–1943),
    315–16, 332
Danube, 152, 154, 158, 159, 240
Dara, Roman fortress of, 168
Darius I, ruler of Iran, 92, 93–4
  Achaemenid dynasty, 40
  Bisotun monument (DB), 40, 41
  campaigns against rebel leaders,
    50
  consultation with advisers, 42
  delegation of military authority, 42
  on rebellion/victory, and divine
    order, 44–5
  strategic polygamy, 41
  suppression of separatists, 43
Darius III, ruler of Iran, 44
de Ruyter, Michiel, 449, 451, 458
De Velitatione Bellica, 227
Deccan
  Marathas, 388–9, 400, 401
  Muslim sultanates, 388, 400
  rulers of, 386
  and the Safavids, 389
deception, 23
defensive strategies, 69–70
  Greece, 67–8
  Native Americans, pre-Columbian, 336
  Rome. *See* pericentric factors, Rome
Delbrück, Hans, 72

Delhi, 397
Demosthenes, 69, 73
Denmark, 264
Dictionary of Ming Biography, 406
Diocletian, Roman emperor (284–305), 148, 149, 163, 167
Diodorus Siculus, 41, 54, 76, 82
  Bibliotheca, 73
Dionysius I of Syracuse, 61, 66
diplomacy
  Alexander, 95
  bribery and, 66
  Dahomey kingdom (Africa), 376
  Diplomatic Revolution, 512
  Greece, 64
  Khmer Empire, 327–8
  Louis XIV of France, 469, 475, 478–9
  Mongols, 301, 306
  Mughal Empire, 396
  Persia, 40, 45, 50, 51
  Philip II, 76, 82–3, 90
  and political manoeuvring, 24–5, 35–6
  Rome, 112–13, 123, 166
  Sassanian, 202
  See also alliances; marriage alliances; patronage
Discourses on Salt and Iron (Yantielun), 25, 28–9, 32
displacement/resettlement, 382–3
divide-and-rule approach, China, 131
divine right, 224
Domitian, Roman emperor (81–96), 147, 149, 161
Donner, Fred, 223
Dorylaion/Dorylaeum, Battle of (1097), 245, 246
Dresden, 504
Du You, 126
dukes and counts
  of Antioch, 230, 243–4
  of Dalmatia, 230
  doux (dukes), 235
  western Europe, 'Dark Ages', 266
  See also aristocracy; nobility/aristocracy
Dunkirk Privateers, 454
Dutch East India Company (GWC), 451, 458, 461
Dutch Republic
  American War of Independence, 527
  Britain declares war on, 519, 520
  Caribbean colonies, 523
  and Louis XIV, Franco-Dutch War, 472, 474, 475, 481
  naval power, 448–63
    actors, 450–2

Anglo-Dutch Wars, 455–63
Eighty Years War, 452–5
  sources, 449–50
  See also William III of Orange
dynastic histories (*shi*), Ming and Qing, 406
dynasticism, 473

Eckstein, Arthur, 122
ecological thesis, 223
economy/economic factors, 183
  Gupta Empire, 182–3
  Louis XIV of France, 475–6
  Mughal Empire, 391
  North America, 521
  Ottoman Empire, 368
  Persia, 40
  Roman, 151–2
  sub-Saharan Africa, 382
  US economic relationship with Britain, 526
  warfare, 268
  See also financial resources; taxation
Edessa, 247
Edict of Restitution, 445–6
Edward I of England, 286–7, 291
Edward III of England, 276, 289, 291
Edward Prince of Wales, aka the 'Black Prince', 276
Egypt
  Alexander's campaign in, 93–4
  Arab conquest, 242
  crusaders' attempts on, 284, 285
  defensive advantages, 51
  Fatimids, 218, 284
  and the Muslims, 209, 216
  and Ottomans, 350, 353
  and Persia, 43, 44, 45, 49, 51
  and Rome, 119, 151
  and Saladin, 278, 284
  and the Sassanians, 202
  trade embargo on, 290
  Xerxes' campaign, 51
  See also Mamluks
Eighty Years War (1568–1648), 452–5
  causes, 452
  Dutch expenditure on armed forces, 460
  Dutch objectives, 453
  and Philip II of Spain, 452
Eleanor of Aquitaine, 276
Eleanor of Provence, 289
elephants, 79, 175, 176–7, 183, 321–2, 389–90, 394
elites
  Chinese, 35
  Greek, alliances and networks, 64

Roman, 113–14, 152
Roman, land distribution to, 114
Sui, China, 129
emergent strategies, 17
Eminent Chinese of the Qing Period, 406
engines of war and catapults, 78
England/the English
  Anglo-Dutch Wars. *See* Anglo-Dutch Wars
  coronation of William and Mary, 463
  and Denmark, 264
  and France, 432
  Glorious Revolution (1688), 463, 472
  growth in bureaucracy, 271–2
  and Habsburgs, 432
  and the Hanse, 277
  power of *thegns*, 265
  Powhatan's siege warfare, 344
  and Spain, Dutch Revolt/Eighty Years
    War, 454, 455
  supports Dutch rebels, Dutch Revolt/
    Eighty Years War, 455
  Viking raids, 263
  Wales and Scotland, 286–7
  wars with France, Europe, late Middle
    Ages, 275–7
  See also Britain
environmental conditions. *See* climatic
    conditions
Epameinondas (Theban general), 76
epiteichismos, 70
Etruscans, 107, 108
Euripides, 69
Eurocentrism, 1, 2
Europe (western)
  early Middle Ages (aka 'Dark Ages'), 251–70
    actors, 254–8
    adversaries, 261–4
    causes of war, 264–5
    execution/application, 268–9
    historiographical debates, 269–70
    means, 258–61
    prioritisation, 267
    sources, 251–4
    strategic decisions, premises underlying,
      265–7
  later Middle Ages
    actors, 273–5
    adversaries, 275–9
    historiographical debates, 279–83
    means, 287–91
    objectives and prioritisation, 283–7
    sources, 271–2
  See also western Europe

European travellers and diplomats, accounts
    of south-east Asian polities
    (premodern/early modern), 316
European tribes, and Rome, 152, 153

farmland/farmers, 67, 105, 120
Fasti and *Fasti Triumphales* (Consular
    inscriptions), 100
Fatimids, 230, 237, 243, 284
Felipe IV, 474
Ferdinand I, Holy Roman Emperor, 430
Ferdinand II of Aragon, 279
Ferdinand II of Styria, Holy Roman
    Emperor, 439
  Catholicism, 442
  character, 440
  decision making, 438
  Edict of Restitution, 445–6
  imperial courts, 440
Ferdinand III, Holy Roman Emperor, 438,
    446–7
Ferdowsī, *Šāh-nāma*, 192
feudalism, 289, 299
feudatories, Gupta Empire, 185–6, 188
field manual, Siamese, 316
financial resources/expenditure
  Charles V, 434
  cost of crusades, 282
  Dutch Revolt/Eighty Years War, 459,
    460, 461
  England's kings, 286
  Frederick II of Prussia, 505
  Greece, 65–7
  Gupta Empire, 174
  and Habsburgs, 431
  Mughal Empire, 394
  Ottoman Empire, 368
  Prussia, 498–9
  Roman, 166
  See also economy/economic factors
firearms
  Ming and Qing dynasties of China, 404
  Ming dynasty, 418–19
  Morocco, 373, 374
  Ottoman Empire, 360, 364
  See also cannon
fishing rights, England, and the Dutch
    Republic, 456
Fitna, 217, 224
flagships, 457
Flamininus, 103, 104
Flanders, 483
Flavian dynasty, 160

Flemish Navy, and Dutch Republic, 454
Florence, archives, on Ottomans, 348
Florida, Spanish colony, 515, 520, 522
foederati, 164
food supply/shortages, 67–8, 69
Forest People (Hoyin Irgen), 297–8, 308
fortifications
  administration of, Louis XIV of France,
    468–9
  Alfred's 'burh' system, 263–4
  Armenia and Georgia, 299
  Byzantine Empire, 243, 244, 245
  China, 136
  Greece, 66
  Habsburgs, 351–2
  Louis XIV of France, 477–8, 482
  North America, pre-Columbian, 341
  Ottoman Empire, 352
  riverine, south-east Asian polities
    (premodern/early modern), 332
  Roman cities, 151, 163
  and routes of communication, 395–6
  Sassanian, 199
  Song empire, 299
  south-east Asian polities (premodern/early
    modern), 330
  temporary or permanent garrisons, 70
  See also sieges/siegecraft
Four Corners region, 340–1
France/French
  ally with Sweden against Habsburgs, 444
  American War of Independence, 511, 512,
    519, 524
    outcomes, 527
  Archives nationales, 510
  aristocratic disputes over throne, 265
  and British, North America, 513
  in Canada, 511
  civil wars (the Frondes), 467
  colonies, 523
  Diplomatic Revolution, and Austria, 494
  Dutch Revolt/Eighty Years War, 455
  and England, 432
  Franco-Spanish war, 447, 467
  and Habsburgs, 430–1, 444
  and Henry III of England, 289
  ideology, role of in mobilising, 10
  and Italy, 433
  Native American alliances, 339
  Ottoman–French navy defeat of
    Habsburgs, 364, 435
  religious and aristocratic factionalism,
    443–4

Seven Years War, 494, 511, 514, 516–17,
    520, 523
    outcomes, 524–5
  Sino-French War, 414
  and slave trade, 376
  southern, Roman conquest of, 119
  Treaty of Paris, with Britain, 495
  Treaty of Verdun (843), 258
  Vikings' siege of Paris, 263
  War of the Austrian Succession, 493–4, 504
  War of the Polish Succession, 503–4
  wars, 1792–1815, 14
    classical warfare, 6
  wars with England, Europe, late Middle
    Ages, 275–7
  See also Canada; Gaul/Gauls; Louis XIV
    of France
Francis I, king of France, 430–1, 434–5
Franciscan friars, 294–5
Franco-Spanish War (1635–1659). *See* France/
  French
Franks, 153, 157, 255
  and the Carolingians, 253
  East, centralised monarchic patronage,
    267
  in Europe, 257
  fusion of church and state, 258
  Merovingians, 257
  paganism, 255
  regnum Francorum, 257
  West, power of higher aristocracy, 267
  See also Carolingians; Charlemagne;
    Germany
Frederick I, king of Prussia, 499–500
Frederick II, king of Prussia, 277
  actors, 491
  adversaries, 492–5
  application of strategy, 502–6
  and Britain, 512
  causes of war, 495–6
  conflict with papacy, 279
  expansion, 496
  Hohenzollern strategy, 488–507
  means, 497–9
  objectives, 496–7
  prioritisation, 499–502
  sources, 490
Frederick III, elector of Brandenburg, 492
Frederick V of the Palatinate, 439, 442, 443
Frederick William I, king of Prussia, 491, 493,
    496, 498
Frederick William of Brandenburg, Great
    Elector, 497–8, 499, 500

freedom of the seas, principle of, 455
freemen, and East Frankish aristocracy, 268
frontier relations / maintenance
    Ottoman Empire, 361–2
    Rome / Romans, 122, 158, 160, 167, 169
    south-east Asian polities (premodern / early
        modern), 327
fur trade, 298, 513, 514, 517
Futuh literature, 224

Gage, General Thomas, 510
Gallia Transalpina, 119
Gangetic basin, 398
Garenganze, 380–1
Gaul / Gauls, 107, 108–9
    Caesar's campaign, 100, 102, 112, 121
    as Gallia (Roman province), 119
    and Rome, 116, 118, 149
Gedrosian debacle, 82
generals (military)
    American War of Independence, 510,
        525, 526
    Burmese, 318
    France. *See* marshals
    Habsburg, 348, 351–2
    Han dynasty, 39
    Hungarian, 351
    Ming dynasty, 410, 420
    Mughal Empire, 385
    Ottoman Empire, 348
    Rome, 146
    Siamese, and Vietnamese, 330
Genoa, 277, 288, 290, 348
George III of Great Britain, Ireland and
    Hanover, 515, 517, 518
Georgia, 240, 244, 299
Germain, George, 511, 519
German princes, 437, 439, 506
Germanic tribes, 111, 151
Germanicus, 147, 154
Germany, 516
    East Franks form empire, 260
    Frankish settlement, 258
    and Habsburgs / Holy Roman Empire, 424,
        431–2, 435, 490
    the Hanse, 277
    and Lutheranism, 431–2, 435
    and Magyars, 262
    and Rome, 159, 160
    See also Hohenzollerns; Rhine river
Gesta Francorum, 271, 282, 284
Gibraltar, 526
Glorious Revolution (1688), 463, 472

Golconda, 388, 400
Goths, 153, 164, 165, 168, 253, 261
Granada, 279
grand pensionary (*raadpensionaris*), 451–2
grand strategy, 32
    ancient Hindu term, 183
    definition, 448–9
    Ming and Qing dynasties of China, 403, 408
    Rome, 168–9
Gray, Colin, 15
Greece
    causes of war, 58–60
    lack of institutional continuity, 55–6
    means, 64–7
    objectives, 61–4
    and Persia, 40, 51
    Persian–Greek Wars, early fifth cent., 51–2
    prioritisation, 67–9
    sources, 54–5
    See also city states, Greek; Macedonia;
        Persia
Greek historiography, on Persian campaigns
    and strategy, 41
Gregory of Tours, 253, 266
guerrilla tactics, 237–8, 243, 244, 453
Guibert, Count, 6
Gujarat, 175, 182–3, 185, 387–8, 397, 398
gunpowder, 134, 373, 374, 418
Gupta army, 173, 174–7, 187–8
Guptas / Gupta Empire, 171–90
    actors, 173–4
    adversaries, 179–81
    causes of war, 181–3
    civil wars, 184, 185
    collapse of central government and
        division, 188
    execution / application, 186–9
    historiographical debates, 189–90
    means, 174–8
    prioritisation, 184–6
    religion, 172
    sources, 171–3
    strategic decisions, premises underlying,
        183–4
    See also Huns
Gustavus II Adolphus, king of Sweden, 444

Haags Verbond, 459
Habsburg emperors, 425–8
    See also specific names of individual emperors
Habsburgs, 424–38, 492
    Charles V
        actors, 425–8

Habsburgs (cont.)
  adversaries, 430–2
  elected Holy Roman Emperor, 424–25
  execution/application, 434–6
  means, 429–30
  objectives, 432–3
  prioritisation, 433–4
  resources, 428–9
  sources, 425
 fortifications, 351–2
 and Frederick II, 490, 493, 501–2, 504
 generals, on Ottomans, 348
 Ottoman–French navy defeat of, 364
 and Ottomans, 350, 351–2, 361, 367, 501
 War of the Austrian Succession, 500–1
 See also Prussia; Thirty Years War
Hadrian, Roman emperor, 158, 161
Hague, The, 449
Haiti, revolution, 376
Han dynasty, 21, 38–9
 emperors varied foreign policies, 27
 expansion, 28–9, 30, 31
 Ruists attitude to military books, 26
 steppe groups, incursions, 28–9
 tally system for military orders, 137
 Western Han, 124
Han Wudi, 30, 31–2
Handel, Michael, 14
Hannibal, 105, 109, 110, 111, 112, 120
Hanover, 492, 494–5
Hanse, maritime war against England, 277
Harris, William, 122
Hayreddin Barbarossa, 364
Heaven's Will (concept), 300, 302, 303, 307
hegemonic wars, 71, 72
Hellenica Oxyrhynchia, 50
Hellenism, 81
Henri II, king of France, 431, 435
Henri IV, king of France, 443–4
Henry II, king of England, 275–6
Henry III, king of England, 276, 277
 civil wars, 289–90
 marriage alliances, 289–90
Henry V, king of England, 276–7
 1415 campaign, 289
Henry VIII of England, 432
Henry, Duke of Saxony, 262–3, 264–5
Hephthalites, 193, 200
Heraclius/Herakleios I, East Roman
       emperor, 148, 167–8, 230, 234, 242
Hermocrates of Syracuse, 56
Herodotus, 49
 Histories, 41, 45, 54, 60

Hetoemaridas, 56
Hideyoshi, 418, 420
Hindu epics, *Ramayana* and *Mahabharata*,
       181–2
Hindus/Hinduism, 181, 182, 312
Hindustan, 387
Ḥira, Naṣrids of, 199–200
Hisham ibn Abd al-Malik (d. 743), 221
History of the Han Dynasty, 25
Hitler, Adolf, 19
Hiuen Tsang, 176, 184
Hohenstaufen dynasty, 277
Hohenzollerns, 490, 492, 493, 497, 498–9,
       500–1
Holt, Robin, 17
Holy Roman Empire, 428, 492, 505, 506
 See also Habsburgs, Charles V
Hongwu, Ming Emperor, 403, 408
honour, 59–60, 67
hoplites (heavy spearmen), 64, 65, 75, 76, 77
horse archers, 150, 151
horses, 175, 261, 374–5, 394
 See also cavalry
hospitality, rules of, 60
Hospitallers and Templars, 274–5, 278,
       284, 288
Howe, General, 525, 526
Hoyin Irgen, 297–8, 308
Huguenots, 455, 467, 475, 481
Humayun, 387
Hundred Years War (1337–1453), 276–7, 285–6
Hungary/Hungarians, 239
 and Byzantine Empire, 250
 invasion of Saxony, 262
 and Mongols, 279, 299, 305, 311
 and Ottomans, 351, 363, 430
Huns, 153, 165, 166, 201
 Attila (leader). *See* Attila (leader of Huns)
 and Bactria, 198
 and the Guptas, 173, 180–1, 185, 187–8
 and Indian elephants, 183
 inscriptions, 173
 and the Sassanians, 193, 200
Hunyadi Janos, General, 351
hypaspists, 78

Iberia, Caucasian, 202
Iberian peninsula, 272, 276, 279, 285, 481
 See also Spain
Ibn al-Athīr, 294
Ibn Khaldun, 223
ideology, Clausewitz on, 10
Illyria/Illyrians, 75, 83, 90, 239

Imperial Household Department (*neiwu fu*), 409
imperium, holders of (Rome), 102, 123
India / Indians
  Alexander's campaigns, 75, 79, 96
  Dakshinapatha, 179
  and Gupta Empire, 171, 189
  north, Indo-Gangetic system, 179–80
  population and demographic resources, 174–5
  Rajasthan, 397–8
  trade routes, 353
  west, and central Asia, Oxus–Indus system, 179
  See also Guptas / Gupta Empire; Mughal Empire
Indian Ocean, Ottoman Empire, 364
Indo-Gangetic system, 179–80
Indus basin, 398
Industrial Revolution, western Europe, 368
infantry
  Alexander, 79
  China, 134–5
  Franks / Germanic peoples, 261
  Gupta army, 175
  Mughal Empire, 393
  Ottoman Empire, 356–7
  Persian, 75
  Philip II, 76, 77–8
  Roman, 105, 150
  Thracians and Illyrians, 75
inherited culture, 181
Innocent III, pope, 272, 285
inscriptions
  and Gupta strategy, 171–3
  Khmer Empire, 314
  and Mongol strategy, 292
intelligence gathering, 125, 147
interest groups (Roman), 101
international relations
  liberalism and constructivism, 11
  and realism, 11
Ionian Greeks, 43, 45
Ionian Revolt, 60
Iran, 153, 362
  See also Safavids
Iraq, 209, 216, 217, 299–300, 350
Ireland, 475, 485
Iron Mountain, Battle of, 142, 143
Iroquois, 339
Isabella I of Castile, 279
Isidore of Seville, 253
Islam, 10, 255, 302, 352, 355

on the caliphates, 204
  See also crusades
Islamic State, 10, 16
Isocrates, 73
Italy, 483
  barbarians in, 254–5
  fractured polities, 265
  and Greece, 57
  and Habsburgs, 424, 433
  Hannibal ascendant in, 120
  Lombard conquests, 261
  maritime republics, 277
  Nine Years War, 482
  northern pacification, 117
  and Rome, 106–7, 115–16, 117, 119–20
  shifting alliances, 431
  See also Gaul / Gauls; Rome / Romans
ivory, 379, 380

Jābiya-Yarmūk, battle of, 242
Jacobites, 485–6
Jamaica, 526
James I, king of Aragon, 273–4
James II and VII, king of England and Scotland, 472, 485
Jamestown colony, 344
Janissaries, 356, 361
Japan / Japanese
  defeat at Pyongyang, 419
  invades Korea, 413, 416
  mercenaries, 321
  and Mongols, 300, 303
  and naval-mindedness, 14
  Second World War, 14
  Sino-Japanese War, 414
Jayavarman VII, 317, 327–8, 329
Jerusalem, 274–5, 278, 284
Jewish Revolt, 157
Jihad, 212, 213, 223
Jin empire
  and conquest of Xi Xia, 310
  and Mongols, 298–9, 300, 301, 304, 307, 309
  and Ögödei, 309
  steppe groups, 297
Joan of Arc, 277
Jochids, 303, 307–8
John, king of England, 276, 290
John II, 246
Jordanes, 253
Joseph I, Holy Roman Emperor, 492
Joseph II, Holy Roman Emperor, 502
Josephus, 144
Jovian, 158, 201

Julian, Roman emperor, 155, 164, 168
Jurchen, 132, 298, 413, 420
just war, ideology of, 112, 122
justice (*'adl*), Mughal Empire, 391
Justin II, Roman emperor, 154, 168
Justinian (527–65), Roman emperor, 149–50, 154, 157, 158–9, 166, 167, 255
Justinian II, Roman emperor, 220
Juvenal, 144
Juwaynī, 294

Kabul, 392, 396, 399
Kagan, Kimberly, 146, 169, 170
  strategy, definition of, 7
kaisar, 229
Kalidasa, 173, 175
Kamandaka, *Nitisara*, 173, 183
kamikaze bombers, 14
Kandahar, 389, 391–2, 399–400
Kangxi, emperor of China, 404
Karlowitz, peace of (1699), 485
Kashmir, 388, 399
Katanga, 379
Kautilya, *Arthashastra*, 173, 176, 183, 322, 327
Kawād I, ruler of Iran
  Hephthalites assist, 193
  in Mesopotamia, 202
Kennedy, Hugh, 223, 224
Kennewick Man, 338
Khazars, 219, 231–2
Khmer Empire (802–1431), 312
  Angkor rulers and succession, 320
  and the Chams, 314, 323, 327–8, 329
  crossbowmen, 322
  decline of, 314
  expansion, and tribute, 312
Khorasan, 216, 218, 225
Khusro I, ruler of Iran, 194, 198
Khusro II, ruler of Iran, 145, 157, 168, 202
Khwārazmian Empire, 299, 301, 305, 307, 309
kingship, models of
  Europe, late Middle Ages, 273–4
  India (early), 182
  Louis XIV of France, 467
  south-east Asian polities (premodern/early modern), 315, 317, 318
  western Europe, 'Dark Ages', 256, 264, 266
Kitan Liao state, 130, 133
knights, 260–1, 268, 269, 288, 299
  ancestors as exemplars, 283
  charters, 271, 282
  and chivalric culture, 283
  culture of conquest, 279

  and feudal obligation, 289
  Syrian and French, 284
  and the theology of holy war, 282
  See also Templars and Hospitallers
Koguryŏ, 133, 135
Komnenoi dynasty, 236
Konbaung dynasty (1752–1885), 312, 328
  armed force, 319
  and Ayutthaya, 328, 330, 333
  invasion of Siam, 318
  population displacement, 330
  Qing China and Mughal Empire, 329
Kong (Confucius)
  Analects, 22
  on warfare, 22
Korean peninsula, 130, 132
  and Japan, 413, 416, 419
  Koguryŏ, 133, 135
Koryŏ, 299, 306
Kshatriyas, 181
Kulab, K. S. R., 316
kuls (military–administrative slaves), 348–9
Kumaragupta, 173, 177, 180, 182
Kushana Empire, 171, 175, 178, 179, 180

Lan Xang kingdom, 312, 327
lancers, Gupta Army, 175–6
land/landownership, 67
  castle building, western Europe, 'Dark Ages', 268
  Ottoman Empire, 355
  See also agriculture/agricultural regions; farmland/farmers
language and ideology, Roman, concepts of *provincia* and *imperium*, 123
Lanna kingdom, 312
  and Ayutthaya, 314, 324, 326, 328
Latins (493 BC), and Rome, 106, 107–8
Lattimore, Owen, 310
law codes, 253
Le Tellier family, 467–8
League of Corinth, 89, 90, 91
Legalism, 24, 28, 124
legions/legionaries, Roman, 104–5, 116
  citizen versus auxiliaries, 148–9
  expansion, 149
  Italian, 106–7
  non-Roman allies, 106
Leo VI, Byzantine emperor
  strategía, 6
  Taktika, 227
Lepanto, battle of (1571), 365–6, 436
Lewis, Mark Edward, 29

Li Quan, 126
Li Shimin, second emperor of Tang dynasty, 128
Li Su (Tang general), 128
Li Yuan and Li family, 141–3
Libya, 350
Licinius, 164
Liddell Hart, B. H., 8
Linwu, Lord, 23
Lithuania, 278
Little Bighorn, Battle of, 339
liturgy, Christian, crusaders and, 282–3
Liu Bang (256–195 BC), 27, 31, 38
Liu tao, 124
Livy (59 BC–AD 17), 98
Llywelyn ap Gruffudd, 286
Lombards, 253, 255, 257, 261, 264
Lothar, 258
Louis the Pious, emperor (814–40), 258
Louis (843–876), 258
Louis II of Bourbon-Condé, 469
Louis IX, king of France, 275, 276, 282, 288
Louis XIII, king of France, 444, 467
Louis XIV, king of France, 464–87
    actors, 467–70
    adversaries, 470–2
    causes and objectives of war, 473–6
    dynasticism, 473
    execution/application, 481–6
    and *gloire*, 473–4
    historiographical debates, 486–7
    means, 476–9
    Nine Years War, 481, 482
    prioritisation, 479–81
    sources, 464–7
    War of Devolution (1667–1668), 474
    wars of succession, 473
Low Countries, 482, 483
Luba kingdom, 380
Lunda kingdom, 379, 380
Lutheranism, 431–2, 435
Luttwak, Edward, 168–70

Macedonia, 73
    and Epirus, 119
    insecurity of kingdoms, 111
    invasion of Persia, 45
    other opponents, 75–6
    Panhellenism, 75
    and Persia, 44
    Philip II, armed force, 76–9

Roman conflict with, 117–18
    See also Alexander III (the Great); Greece; Philip II of Macedon
Macedonian Wars (218–197 BC), 103, 114
Magadha, 177, 179–80
magic and cosmological approaches, 128
magistrates, Roman, 100, 101, 102
Magyars (Hungarians), 231, 237
Mahabharata, 183
Mahan, Alfred Thayer, 13
Malchus, 144
Malta, 365
Mamluks, 278, 285
    Egyptian, 352
    and Mongols, 300
    and Ottomans, 352, 353
    and Portuguese, 353
Manchu imperial clan, 408–9, 410, 412–13
Manchuria
    Jurchen of. *See* Jurchen
mandala influence, 322, 324–5, 328, 329, 330
'manifesting awe', 404–5
Mansurah, Battle of (1250), 275
Mantinea, second battle of (362 BC), 54
Manuel I, Byzantine emperor, 238, 250
    attempts to secure Hungarian ruler to throne, 239
    and the Bulgars, 231
    crisis following succession, 231
    death of, 233, 250
    self-promotion, 241
    and Turks, 246
Manusmriti/Manusamhita, 183
map collections, Louis XIV of France, 466
Marathas, 388–9, 400, 401
Marcellinus, Ammianus, *Res Gestae*, 192
march lords, 348, 350
Marcomanni, 152
Marcus Aurelius, Roman emperor, 144–5, 148, 152, 161
Mardaites, 220
marriage alliances, 76, 276, 327, 492
    Alexander III, 79, 96
    Byzantine Empire, 232
    Charles V, 435
    China, 143
    Gupta Empire, 177
    Henry III of England, 289–90
    Louis XIV of France, 470
    Ming and Qing dynasties of China, 420
    Mughal Empire, 396–7
    Philip, 83
marshals, of Louis XIV of France, 469–70

Marwan I, 214, 217
Mary II, 463
Massinissa (Numidian chieftain), 121
Maurice, East Roman emperor, 145, 155, 156, 157, 159, 192, 202
Maurya Empire, 175
mawali (non-Arab Muslims), 225
Mazarin, Cardinal, 467
Mecca, 352
Medieval Climatic Anomaly, 344
Mehmed II *Fatih* ('the Conqueror'), Ottoman sultan, 346–7, 348–9, 364
Mehmed Pasha, grand vizier, 349, 365
mercenaries, 71
  Byzantine Empire, 235, 244, 361
  Europe, late Middle Ages, 276, 289
  Greece, 65
  Habsburgs, 429–30, 434
  hoplites (heavy spearmen), 75
  Norman, 232
  objectives, 49
  Ottoman Empire, 354, 360, 361, 362–3
    azabs, 356–7
  south-east Asian polities (premodern/early modern), 314, 320–1
meritocracy, 74
Merkit, 300, 308
Merovingians, 257, 261, 267
Mesopotamia, 195, 202
  Arab conquest, 242
  northern
    and Byzantine Empire, 230
    and the Sassanians, 198, 201, 202
Messenia, 61
Methods of the Sima, The, 404
metrocentric factors, Rome, 122
Miao, 410, 418
military elite
  Habsburgs, 440
  Mughal Empire, 386, 395
  Ottoman Empire, 355, 356, 361
  Roman, 102–3
  See also consuls/consulships (Roman); generals; knights
'military Enlightenment', 6
military manuals/treatises, 54, 227, 466
militias, 64–5, 66, 75
Ming dynasty
  decision making, 408
  expansion, 410, 415, 423
  Korea, as vassal state, 413
  martial spectacles, 420
  and Mongols, 411

in Vietnam, 413, 414–15
  war against Japan in Korea, 413, 416, 418, 419
  war with Qing, 415, 419
  wealth of, 423
Ming emperors, 403, 413
minorities
  China (late imperial), uprisings, 410, 412
  Ottoman Empire, 355
missionaries, European, 369–70
Mithridates VI, 113
Mohács, Battle of (1526), 430
Mohave, on Pima Butte battle, 343
monasteries, 234, 286
Möngke Qa'an (Khan), ruler of Mongol Empire, 302, 308
Mongolia, unification of, 297, 298
Mongols, 130–1, 222, 278–9, 403, 411
  See also Chinggis Khan, and Mongol Empire
Mons, 323
monumental royal reliefs, 191
morality and benevolence
  China/Chinese, 23, 24, 26
  as grand strategy, 34–5
Morgan, David, 292
Morocco, 360, 372–4
mountain ranges, as defence barriers, 240
Msiri, 381
Mu'awiya ibn Abu Sufyan, 208, 209–10, 216, 220
Mughal emperors, 385
  and justice ('*adl*), 391
  mobility of, 396
Mughal Empire, 1526–1707
  actors, 385–6
  adversaries, 386–90
  application of strategy, 397–401
  causes and objectives, 390–2
  and Kandahar, 391–2
  means, 392–4
  prioritisation, 395–7
  sources, 384–5
Muhammad, prophet of Islam, 205, 212
multiple tools, strategy, 8
Münster, 459
muqatila, 210
Muslim armed forces, 209, 210, 212, 219, 261–2
Muslim rebellions, and China (late imperial), 418
Mustafa II, Ottoman sultan, 367–8
mutinies, 137
Mzilikazi, 378

Nabis II, king of Sparta, 103
Nabonidus Chronicle, 40
Naiman, 300, 301, 308
Nantes, Edict of, 475
Naples, 114
Napoleon I (Bonaparte), 6
narrative histories, Europe, late Middle
    Ages, 271
Narses (293–302), 200
Nasawī, Muhammad al-, 294
Nasr ibn Musharraf, 243
nationalist narratives, 332
Native American wars, pre-Columbian,
    334–45
  adversaries, 339–41
  causes of war, 343–4
  strategic alliances, 339
Native Americans, and War of Independence,
    517–18, 522, 527
naval power
  Arab, 242
  China, 135–6
  crusades, 288
  English campaigns, 289
  France, American War of
      Independence, 522
  Greece, 65, 66
  Louis XIV of France, 468, 478, 481, 486
  Mongols, 307
  Muslim, 209
  Netherlands, 438
  Ottoman Empire, 354, 357, 364, 365–6, 430
  Persia, 49–50
  Rashidun and Umayyad eras, 216–17, 221
  Roman, 105–6, 107, 116, 149
  south-east Asian polities (premodern/early
      modern), 331–2
  See also Dutch Republic, naval power;
      Royal Navy, England; ships of war
Navigation Act, 1651, 455–6, 458
Nazi Germany, 19
Nepal, Lichchavi clan, 177
Nero, Roman emperor, 160
Netherlands, 436
  and Habsburgs, 443, 447
  Louis XIV of France, 475
  maritime capacity, 438
  and Ottomans, 365
  and Philip III, 438
  and slave trade, 375
  Spanish, 484
    and Louis XIV, 483–4
  See also Dutch Republic

New England, 518, 520–1
New France, 513, 514, 521
Nguni/Ngoni peoples
  amabutho (age sets), 377
  aversion to slavery, 379
Nian Rebellion, 412, 418
Nijmegen, treaty of, 474
Nikephoros I, 237, 238
Nikephoros II Phokas, 227, 247
Nine Chief Ministers (*da jiu qing*), 408
Nine Years War. *See* Louis XIV of France
Nisibis, 198, 201, 202
niti texts, 173, 181
Nizari Ismailis, 302, 308
nobility/aristocracy
  England, system for contracting armies, 289
  Iran/Sassanian Empire, 192–3
  Louis XIV of France, 467–8
  Macedonian, 77
  See also aristocracy
nomadic people, 129, 130, 212, 230, 248–9, 311
  and Bulgars, 298
  Ottomans, 354
  See also Forest People (Hoyin Irgen);
      steppe groups
Nördlingen, Austro-Spanish victory, 446
Normans, 232, 240, 241, 249, 279
North, John, 122
North, Lord, British prime minister, 518
north Africa, 352, 360
North America
  indigenous warfare. *See* Native American
      wars, pre-Columbian
  War of Independence
    adversaries, 511–13
    causes, 513–16
    colonial manpower, 521
    decision makers, 510–11
    means, 520–3
    objectives, 516–20
    outcomes, 524–7
    prioritisation, 523–4
    sources, 508–10
  See also United States of America
Northern Song, 129, 132, 133
Northern Wei (386–534), 126
Northern Zhou (557–581), 126, 133
Notitia Dignitatum, 146, 149
Nova Scotia, 513
noyans (Mongol commanders), 296
nuclear weapons/war, 12
Nur Jahan (wife of Jahangir), 385
Nyiginya kingdom (later Rwanda), 371–2

Octavia, 119
Odo, count of Paris, 257
Odoacer (barbarian general), 254
Odysseus, 82
Œuvres de Frédéric le Grand, 490
Ögödei, 307, 309
Ohio valley, 514, 516, 521
Oldenbarnevelt, Johan van, 451
Olivares, Count-Duke of, 438, 440–1, 445
opportunism, 71, 90, 112–13, 162, 255–6
oral histories, 339, 371, 379
Order of Command at Sea, Dutch
     Republic, 454
Osman I *Gazi* ('the Fighter the Faith'),
     Ottoman sultan, 346
osteological evidence, Native American wars,
     pre-Columbian, 337, 338
Otto I, Holy Roman Emperor, 263, 266
Otto II, Holy Roman Emperor, 266
Otto III, Holy Roman Emperor, 266–7
Ottoman chronicles, 347
Ottoman Empire, 4, 288, 346–68
     actors, 348–50
     adversaries, 350–2
     causes and objectives of war, 352–4
     decline of, 367–8
     execution/application, 362–6
     and Habsburgs, 430, 445
     interregnum period (1402–1413), 363–4
     key debates, 366–7
     Louis XIV of France, 475
     means, 354–61
     prioritisation, 361–2
     sources, 347–8
     See also France/French; Habsburgs
Oxford Handbook of Grand Strategy, 8
Oyo Empire, 375, 376

Paekche, 135
Paeonia, 83
paganism, 278
Palatinate, 484
Palestine, 209, 242
Panhellenism, 75, 80, 81, 91
papacy
     and Charles V, 428
     correspondence, 272
     Declaration of Arbroath, 286–7
     goal of, 283–4
     and Hohenstaufen dynasty, 277
     legal authority, 290
     and Ottomans, 367
     pre-eminent role of, 273

spiritual means/benefits, 290–1
     and treaties, 290
     use of excommunication, 290
     See also specific names of popes
Papal Comtat Venaissin, 472
paper, 272
Paris, Vikings siege of, 263, 268–9
Parma, Alexander Farnese, Duke of, 454
Parmenion (general), 74, 93, 95
Parthian Empire, 111, 152–3, 154, 162,
     193
     aristocracy, 192–3
     Arsacids, 195
     and the Huns, 180
     rule in Iran, 195
patronage, 232–3, 264, 420, 502
     See also tribute
Paul the Deacon, 253
Pavia, battle of, 431, 434–5
Peace of Callias, 52
peace treaties
     Byzantine Empire, 237
     See also appeasement
peace/stability, cultural ideal of, 161
peasant uprisings, 129, 410, 421
Pechenegs, 248–9
Peloponnesian War, 43, 50, 70, 72
     causes of, 59, 61
     defensive strategies, 67
     Periclean strategy, 72
People (Roman), 104
     See also citizen assemblies, Roman
Perdiccas III, 80
pericentric factors, Rome, 121–2
Pericles, 56, 67, 72
Persepolis Fortification Archive, 41, 49
Persia, 167
     Alexander's campaign in, 51, 75, 91, 93–5,
          96
     and Asia Minor, 57
     financial resources, 67
     and Heraclius, 167–8
     ideology, sources on, 41
     kings, and heroic leadership, 44
     later Aegean policies, 45
     Maurice's alliance with, 157
     Muslim conquest, 216
     Philip's campaign, 89 f.
     siegecraft, 151
     See also Greece; Sassanian Iran; Teispid and
          Achaemenid Persia; Xerxes
Persian Gulf, 198, 353, 365
Persian sources, Mongol strategy, 294

Philip II, king of France, 276, 278, 288
Philip II, king of Macedon, 44 f., 73–96 *passim*
  campaign in Persia, 89–90
  causes and objectives, 79–81
  characteristics, 82, 83, 97
  defeats Athens and Thebes, 89
  diplomacy, 82–3, 90
  grand strategy, 80–1
  Greek city states become allies, 89
  League of Corinth, 89
  and Macedonia, 73
  means, 76–9
  opportunism, 90
  and Panhellenism, 80
  sources, 73
  at Thebes, 76
Philip II, king of Spain, 353, 436–7, 442, 452, 453
Philip III, king of Spain, 437, 438
Philip IV, king of Spain, 439, 440, 445
Philip V, king of Macedon, 103, 104, 111
Philip VI, king of France, 276
Phitsunulok, 327
Phra Ratchapongsawadan, 315
pillaging and ravaging, 69, 71, 268
Pima Butte, battle at, 343
Pinto, Mendes, 320–1
piracy/pirates, 332, 364, 390, 412, 421, 453–4
Pisa, 277, 290
Pitt, William (British prime minister), 510, 516
Placentia (Piacenza), 118
placitum, 256
Plato, *Laws*, 54
plundering expeditions, 303
  See also booty, collection of
Plutarch, 41, 98
  Alexander histories, 74, 81
  on Caesar, 121
poetry
  Ming dynasty, 420
  Nyiginya kingdom (later Rwanda), 371–2
  south-east Asian polities (premodern/early modern), 315, 322
Poland–Lithuania, 495
Poland/Poles, 299, 367
  partitioning of, 488, 491, 495
political alliances, 339
  See also alliances; marriage alliances
political rights, and Rome, 112
politics, Western idea of, 10
Politische Correspondenz Friedrichs des Großen, 490
Pollock, Sheldon, 178

Polybius, 80, 98, 100, 115–16, 117
polygamy, 41, 76, 318
Pomerania, 499
Pompey, 102, 103, 112, 119
Popilius Laenas (Roman consul), 104
Portugal/Portuguese
  and Louis XIV, 482–3
  and Mamluks, 353
  and Morocco, 360
  and Mughal Empire, 390
  and Ottomans, 353–4, 365
  and Philip II of Spain, 437
  and slave trade, 375
  and Spain, 439
Porus, 75, 79
positional warfare
  Louis XIV of France, 485
  See also fortifications; sieges/siegecraft
postal system, Habsburgs, 425
pothos, 93, 95, 96
Powhatan (chief), 338, 339, 344
Prabhavatigupta (Gupta queen regent), 177
Prague, Peace of, 446
prasastis (historical eulogies), 171
princes, Ottoman Empire, succession crises, 349
princes of the House of Orange. *See* stadholders
Priscus, Roman histories, 144
private–public military partnerships, Thirty Years War, 441
Procopius, 144, 192, 253, 258
professional armies
  Byzantine, 235–6
  caliphates, 209
  China, 137
  England, 289
  Europe, late Middle Ages, 289
  Macedonian, 78–9
  Sassanian, 198–9, 203
propaganda, 44, 139
Protestantism, 437, 452
  Lutheranism, 431–2, 435
  See also Huguenots
provincia, 123
proxy wars, 70
Prussia, 488, 490, 494, 498, 501–2
  See also Frederick II of Prussia
Prussian Secret State Archive, 490
Psellos, Michael, 232
psychological tactics, China, 125, 139
Ptaliputra (Gupta capital), 171

Ptolemies, 73, 118
Puebloan groups, warfare, 340–1
Punic Wars
First, 109–10, 116
Second, 103, 105, 109, 119
Third, 115
Punjab, 175, 397
Pyongyang, 419
Pyrrhus, 114, 115

Qa'ans, Mongol, 295, 296
qi (unexpected approaches in warfare), 126
Qin dynasty, 21, 24, 27, 28, 29–30, 36
Qin Xiangye, 406
Qing dynasty
annexation of Xinjiang, 422
corruption, 421
decision making, 408–9
defeat of Zunghars, 413
expansion, 410, 415, 423
government office for military
heritage, 407
imperial tours of countryside, 420
and Manchu invasion, 412–13
Ming–Qing War, 415, 419
and Mongols, 411
religious and cultural rebellions, 412
Sino-French and Sino-Japanese wars, 414
Taiping Rebellion, 415
and Tibet, 414
wealth of, 423
Qing emperors, 404
Qipchaq nomads, 305, 307
Qubilai, 303, 308
queens, Mongol, 296
Quintus Curtius, Alexander histories, 73–4, 95

Rahe, Paul, 72
raids
Burma, 323
Jochids, 303
Native American wars, pre-Columbian, 342
Ngoni, 379
Ottomans and other emirates, 362
south-east Asian polities (premodern/early
modern), 326
sub-Saharan Africa, 372
Zulu kingdom, 378
Rajasthan, 397–8
Rajput kings, western India, 387, 397–8
Rama I, king of Siam, 318
Rama III, king of Siam, 321, 328, 330
Ramagupta, 187

ransom/ransoming culture, 214, 282, 342, 431
Rashid al-Din, 294
Rashidun era
decentralising of military control, 210
expansion, 223
modern scholarship, 223
naval power, 216–17
piety, 224
security maximisation and border control,
215–16
standard of leadership akin to
Muhammad, 208
success of armed forces, 209
rationality/rational actor model, 12, 14–15
Rattanakosin (Bangkok), 312
ravaging and pillaging, 69, 71, 268
realism, international relations, 11, 122
Records of the Historian, 21–2, 38–9
Red Sea, 353, 365
religion
China (late imperial), 412
Europe, late Middle Ages, 290–1
Greece, 60
Gupta Empire, 172, 177
Louis XIV, 475
Nyiginya kingdom (later Rwanda), 371–2
Persia, 44–5
Roman, 157–8
Zoroastrianism, 194–5
See also Christianity; Protestantism
religious motivation, 279, 283
See also crusades; Jihad
Republic of the Seven United Provinces.
See Dutch Republic
rerum repetere, 112
res repetere, 122
Rhine river, 152, 154, 158, 473, 482
Rich, John, 122
Richard I (aka 'the Lionheart'), king of
England, 274–5, 276, 278, 284
consults council, 284
Richardson, John, 123
Richelieu, Cardinal, 444, 467
Ridda wars (632–33), 205, 215, 223
Riley-Smith, Jonathan, 282
river frontiers, 152
See also Danube; Rhine river
roads. *See* communication, routes of
Robert I, king of Scotland, 286–7
Romanos I, Byzantine emperor, 239
Romanos II, Byzantine emperor, 235
Romanos III, Byzantine emperor, 241
Romanos IV, Byzantine emperor, 238, 245

Rome/Romans, 118
  actors, 100–4, 146–8
  ad hoc nature of Roman territorial
    strategy, 119
  adversaries, 107–12, 152
  and Carthage, 110
  causes of war, 112–15, 153–5
  Christianity and, 156
  civil wars, 100, 105–6, 156
  decline to status of regional power, 168
  demographics/population, 151
  dominant power in Mediterranean, 111–12
  elite, and military campaigning, 113–14
  establishment of Republic, 101
  execution/application, 118–21, 159–68
  expansion, 102, 109–10, 114, 153–4
  extreme violence towards resistant
    communities, 121
  and Greece, 110–11
  historiographical debates, 121–3, 168–70
  and Iran, 193, 194, 198
  mass enslavement, 121
  means, 104–7, 148–52
  monarchic period (traditionally 753–509
    BC), 98–100
  multiple theatres of war, 105
  See also legions/legionaries, Roman
  non-Roman allies, 106, 114
  Persian–Roman clashes, Caucasus
    region, 202
  prioritisation, 157–9
  and Punic wars, 109–10
  Republic, 100–4
  sources, 98–100, 144–6
  Sassanian Iran, 192
  and Spain, 110
  strategic decisions, premises underlying,
    155–7
  strategic priorities, 115–18
  third-century crisis, 162, 167
  war profits, 106
  See also Caesar, Gaius Julius
Royal Frankish Annals, 253–4, 265–6
Royal Navy, 457, 478, 511, 520, 522
Ruists (Confucians), 22, 24, 26
Rus', 231, 237, 247, 299, 308
Russia
  alliance with Frederick II, 494, 505
  expansionist aspirations, 352
  and Frederick II, 504
  and Ottomans, 352, 362, 368
  Qing border conflicts with, 413
  Seven Years War, 494

War of the Austrian Succession, 494
War of the Polish Succession, 494

Šābuhr I. *See* Shapur I,
  Res Gestae divi Saporis, 195
Šābuhr II, ruler of Iran. *See* Shapur II
'Sacred Wars', Greece, 60, 65
Sa'did dynasty, Morocco, 372–4
Safavids
  and the Deccan frontier, 388, 389
  and Kandahar, 391–2
  and Mughal Empire, 389, 399–400
  and Ottomans, 350, 352, 361, 365
Saffarids, Persia, 218
šāhān šāh, 192, 193
Sahel, Songhay, invasion of, 372
Sakas, 179, 180, 187–8
Salah al-Din Yusuf ibn Ayyub, aka Saladin,
    sultan of Egypt and Syria, 278, 284, 291
Samnites, 103, 108, 112, 114, 119–20
Samudragupta, 171, 177
  economic motivations, 182
  expansionist war, 184–5
  fighting emperor, 173
  inscriptions, 171–2
  offensive strategy, 180, 186–7
  Vedic ritual, 182
Samuel (997–1014), 247–8
Sand Canyon Pueblo, 341
Sandwich, Earl of, 511
Sanskrit, 173, 178, 312
Saratoga, battle of, 526
sarissa (spear), 77, 78
Sassanian army, 176, 192–3, 198–9, 203
Sassanian Iran, 153, 191–203
  actors, 192–3
  adversaries, 193–4
  and Byzantine Empire, 241–2
  causes of war, 194–5
  execution/application, 200–3
  historiographical debates, 203
  means, 198–200
  objectives, 195
  and Rome, 154–5
  sources, 191–2
  See also Arabs/Arab tribes
Satha I of Cambodia, 323
Saxony, 492–3, 497, 501
  communication routes, 505
  dynastic ambition and security, 266
  Hungarians invade, 262–3
  Prussian invasion, 504–5
Scheldt estuary, 449

Schwerin, Count Kurt Christoph von, 491, 503
Scipio Africanus, 121
Scotland, 286–7, 289–90, 485–6
Scott, Hamish, 504, 505
Scythians, 75–6
'Sea Beggars', 453–4
Second World War, 14, 18
Secret History of the Mongols, 292, 295–6
sehzades (Ottoman princes), 348
Seleucids / Seleucid empire, 106, 111, 117–18
Selim I, Ottoman sultan, 348, 349
Selim II, Ottoman sultan, 349
Seljuks, 231–2, 278
Senate / senators, Roman, 100, 101, 145, 146
Service historique de la défense (SHD), 464
Servius Tullius, 101
Seven Military Classics (Song collection), 124
Seven Years War, 491, 494, 498, 516–17, 520–1
   archives, 510
   artillery, 499
   legacy, 514
   in North America, 511
   outcomes, 524–5
   treaty of settlement, 1763, 516
Severus, 155–6, 162, 163, 167, 193
Shaban, M. A., 225
Shah Jahan (r. 1628–57), 386, 390, 392, 399
Shaka, 377–8
Shapur I, ruler of Iran, 153, 163, 191
Shapur II, ruler of Iran, 154, 195, 200 f.
Sher Shah (ruler of Hindustan), 387
ships of war. *See* naval power; triremes
Shīrāzī, 294
Shivaji Bhonsla, 388–9, 400
Siamese kingdoms
   armed force, 316
   and Cambodia, 323, 328, 329
   Chao Anouvong's insurrection, 318
   expansion, 312, 324
   and First Anglo-Burmese War, 325
   Maha Thiha Thura's invasion of, 318
   Pongsawadan and *Tamnan* chronicles,
      315
   royal chronicles, 315, 321
   Thai sources on warfare, 317–18
   vassal system, 319–20
   viceroy, 319
   war with Vietnam, 331
   wars with Burmese kingdoms, 312
   See also Ayutthaya (1350–1767)
Siberian groups, 298
Sicily, 57, 68, 116, 250, 277
sieges / siegecraft, 65, 151

China, 134
   Huns and Avars, 151
   Louis XIV of France, 485
   Mongols, 307
   Mughal Empire, 393
   Normans, 250
   Ottoman Empire, 360–1, 364, 430
   and pitched battles, 331
   Romans, 120
   Sassanian, 199
   south-east Asian polities (premodern / early
      modern), 330
   Vikings, 268–9
Silesia, 488, 495, 497, 500, 503, 504
   communication routes, 505
silk, 143, 198
Silla, 131–2
Sima Guang, *Zizhi tongjian*, 127
Sima Qian
   narrative of the Qin founding, 28
   Records of the Historian, 21–2, 27
   Shi ji (Historical Records), 127
Simpson, Emile, 16
Sino-French War, 414
Siouan peoples, 342
Skandragupta, 172–3, 180, 185
Slave Coast (present-day Benin), 375
slavery, 59, 146
   Abyssinian military, 388
   American War of Independence, 513
   caliphates, 214
   expansion of, 375, 376
   Islamic military slave system.
      See Janissaries
   Native American wars, pre-Columbian, 342
   objectives, 61–2
   and Rome, 118, 121
   sub-Saharan Africa, 372
   uprisings, 112
   Yeke military, 381–2
   See also kuls (military–administrative
      slaves)
Slavs, 153, 231, 241, 246
   See also Balkans
Smith, Robert, 383
Smith, Vincent, 189
Social War (91–87 BC), 106, 108, 112, 114
socio-economic factors, Rashidun and
      Umayyad expansions, 212
soft power
   Habsburgs, 429
   Ming and Qing dynasties of China, 420–1
   Prussia, 502

Roman, 123
Song empire, 298, 299, 302, 303, 308
Songhay (Mali), invasion of, 372
sources, Greece, 54–5
south Asia, chieftains (*zamīndārs*), 387
south-east Asian polities (premodern / early modern). *See* Asia, south-east
Soviet Union, military, strategic culture (1970s), 11
Spain, the Spanish, 448
  American War of Independence, 512, 520, 524, 527
  Austria, and Bohemian revolt, 440
  and Carthage, 110
  colonies, 515, 520, 522
  Dutch Revolt, 451
  Flemish Navy, 454
  Franco-Spanish war, 447, 467
  and Louis XIV, 470–1, 482
    War of Devolution (1667–1668), 474
  and the Muslim Caliphate, 219
  Muslim conquest, 261–2
  Muslim rule, 279
  New World empire, 437
  peace with Dutch, 447
  pro-Umayyad movement, 218
  and Rome, 110, 117, 119
  and Sea Beggars, 454
  Seven Years War, 511, 514
  Visigoths, 257
  See also Iberian peninsula
Spanish armadas, 454–5
Sparta
  alliances and coalitions, 70
  and Athens, 43, 58, 59
  campaigns against Athenian insurgents, 58
  causes of war, 60
  fortifications, temporary or permanent, 70
  kings, 'generals for life', 55
  and Macedonia, 75
  military policies, sources on, 54
  objectives, 61
  and oligarchies, 64
  and Peloponnesian War, 59, 61, 70, 72
  and Persia, 51
  ravaging and pillaging, 69
  revolt of the helots, 56
  subsidised troops, 65
  and Thebes, 76
spear bearers, elite, 49
speed, 90
spiritual means / benefits, Europe, late Middle Ages, 290–1

Spring and Autumn Annals, 21
Spring and Autumn Period, China, 21, 22, 30, 38, 127
stadholders, 451
state-centric approach, 9–10
States General, Dutch Republic, 450–1
  de Ruyter at, 452
  highest authority in maritime affairs, 460–1
  maritime strategy, 451
  naval budget, 460
  and Philip II of Spain, 453
  standing navy, 458
steel production, China, 134
steppe groups, 27, 28–9, 30, 130, 131, 237, 297, 304
  See also nomadic people; Türks; Uighurs; Xiongnu
Strasbourg, 474
strategic culture, 1970s research, 11–12
strategic practice, 4
strategic studies, Realist approach to International Relations, 11
strategic thought, evolution of, 2–3
Strategies of the Warring States, 21, 24–5, 37–8
strategy
  as concept, 4–8, 53–4
  Kagan's definition, 7
  multiple tools and 'grand strategy', 8–9
  Thai translation of, 316
sub-Saharan Africa, 369–83
  actors, 371–2
  causes and objectives of war, 382–3
  central African warfare, 379–82
  Dahomey, and slavery, 374–7
  Sahel, early modern warfare, 372–4
  sources, 369–72
  Zulus and Ngoni warfare, 377–9
Sufi Muslims, and Qing dynasty, 414
Sui dynasty, 129, 130, 133
  disintegration of authority, 131
  and Koguryŏ, 135
  propaganda, 139
  Yang Jian, and the Chen, 140–1
Suleyman I, Ottoman emperor, 220, 243, 245, 349
sultans, Ottoman Empire, 348, 349, 356
Sun Bin, 21, 22
Sunzi (Master Sun; Sun Tzu), 14, 21, 124, 127, 132
  Art of War, 22, 24, 29, 32, 36, 124
  European translations, 3
  'militarist' category, 22
  on Philip II, 83
  on strategic outcomes, 139–40

Surakiat, Pamaree, 332–3
surprise attacks, 70, 151
  Alexander, 94
  Byzantine Empire, 249
  cavalry, 321
  Frederick II of Prussia, 503–4
  Li Jing, 142
  Native American wars, pre-Columbian,
    342, 345
  Philip II of Macedon, 83
Sweden, 444, 446, 495, 500
Syracusans, 61, 66, 116
Syria, 103, 119, 156
  Arab conquest, 242
  armed force
    Abbasids, 211
    Umayyads, 211
  and Byzantine Empire, 230
  destruction by Aurelian, 198
  and Mongols, 299–300
  Muslim conquest, 209, 216
  and Ottomans, 353

Tacitus, 144, 147
tagmata, 235
Taibai yinjing (military text), 126
Taigong's Six Secret Teachings, 404
Taiping Rebellion, 412, 415
tamma army, 306–7, 310
Tang dynasty, 129, 134, 138
  and alliance with Silla, 131
  collapse of, 129, 130
  early, hegemony, 134
  gender demographics, 132–3
  and Koguryŏ, 131–2
  Li family, and the Eastern Türks, 141–3
  and the Muslim Caliphate, 219
  part-time farmer-soldiers, 137
  rebellion of northern frontier armies, 129
  subjugation of Inner Asia, 131
  tally system for military orders, 137
  and Uighurs, 131
Tang Taizong Li Weigong wendui (*Questions and
  Replies between Tang Taizong and Li,
  Duke of Wei*), 126
Tarentum (282–272 BC), 110–11, 114
Tatars, 300
Taungoo Empire (1510–1752), 312, 314
taxation
  Byzantine Empire, 233–4
  caliphates, 214
  Dutch Republic, 453
    Anglo-Dutch Wars, 461

Gupta Empire, 184
Hohenzollerns, 498–9
Holy Roman Empire/Habsburgs, 428
  and minorities, China (late imperial), 412
  Qing dynasty, 411–12
  Roman, 106, 151–2
  Sassanian Iran, 195, 198
  south-east Asian polities (premodern/early
    modern), 332
  and Thirty Years War, 441
Tây Sơn dynasty (1778–1802), 318
technological innovations, 14, 236
Teispid and Achaemenid Persia, 40–52
  actors, 41–2
  adversaries, 43–4
  available means, 49–50
  objectives, 45–8
  prioritisation of resources, 50–1
  sources, 40–1
  war, causes of, 44–5
  See also Persia
Templars and Hospitallers, 274–5, 278, 284, 288
Temüjin (Chinggis Khan). *See* Chinggis Khan,
  and Mongol Empire
Tetrarchs, 163
Thebes, 60, 62, 65, 70, 75, 76, 90
thegns, 265
themata (Byzantine military and
  administrative units), 234, 236, 247
Themistocles, 56
Theodosius I, East Roman emperor, 164–5
Thessaly, 83
Theuderic of Burgundy, 261
Thirty Years War, 484
  Habsburg strategy, 438–47
    actors, 439–40
    adversaries, 443–5
    objectives, 441–3
    prioritisation and execution, 445–7
    resources and means, 440–1
    sources, 438–9
Thonburi (1767–1782), 312
Thonburi and Rattanakosin period
  (1768–1851), 328
Thrace, 45, 76, 78 f, 85, 88–91, 150, 155, 231,
  236, 241
Thracians, 75
Three Kingdoms, China, 129, 133
Thucydides, 54, 59
Tianshun, Emperor, 411
Tiberius, 146, 149, 160
  and Germanicus, 147, 154
  and Persian war, 159

Tibet/Tibetans, 127, 130, 131, 414
Timur (Tamerlane), 363, 392
Tlingit, 342, 343
tombstones, Roman, *elogia*, 100
Tong dian (*Comprehensive Canons*), 126
Toynbee, Arnold, 2
trade/trade routes
 Byzantine Empire, 234
 caliphates, 212
 Cromwell's Navigation Act against the
  Dutch, 455–6
 and Dutch Republic, 448, 450, 453
 Egypt, 284
 European, sub-Saharan Africa, 369
 Indo-Roman, 185
 ivory, 380
 Ottoman Empire, 352–3, 365
 Sassanian Iran, 198
 Siamese and Burmese polities, 322
 south-east Asian polities (premodern/early
  modern), 325
 and Spain, 448
 and Tang dynasty, 131
 See also slavery; taxation
Trajan, 156, 161, 167
travel sources
 ethnographic accounts of south-east
  Asia, 314
 Mongol strategy, 294–5
 south-east Asian polities (premodern/early
  modern), 316
treaties
 Europe, late Middle Ages, 290
 laws and decrees (Roman), 100
 See also specific names of treaties
tribal assembly, Roman, 118
tribute
 Byzantine Empire, 237, 246, 247
 Dahomey kingdom (Africa), 376
 Khmer, Siamese and Burmese
  kingdoms, 312
 Ming and Qing dynasties of China, 410, 419
 Mongols, 301
 and Msiri, 381
 Sassanian, 200, 202
 south-east Asian polities (premodern/early
  modern), 326, 329
trickery and deception, 23, 141, 143
triremes (warships), 66
Trogus, Pompeius, 80, 96–7
 Historia Philippica, 73, 82
Trojan War, 60
Tromp, Cornelis, 458

Tromp, Maerten, Admiral, 458
Troy, 81
truces, 159, 217, 220, 237
tsetse fly, 374–5
tsunami strategy, 310
Tunis, 350, 433
Turcoman chieftains, Ottoman Empire, 348
Turcoman tribes, 346
 See also Ottoman Empire
Turenne, the marshal, 469
Türks (steppe peoples), 131, 141–3,
  198
Turks/Turkish tribes, 231–2
 and Byzantine Empire, 231–2, 238, 244–5
 defeat at Dorylaion, 245
 See also Ottoman Empire
Tyre, 93, 230
Tyrtaeus (poet), 61

Uighurs, 131, 309
'Umar b. Khattab (d. 644), 205, 213
 armed forces, salaries to, 209
 expansion, 216
 resettlement policy for new populations,
  209, 216
 targeting of religious communities, 213
'Umar II (d. 720), 218
Umarī, al-, 294
Umayyads
 and the Berbers, 210–11
 and the Byzantines, 217, 219–20
 collapse, and Arab tribes, 225
 decentralised military control, 210
 dependence on booty, 211
 'divine right', 224
 expansion, 213, 219, 220
 historiographical debates, 223
 jihad, 214
 military reforms, 209–10
 under Mu'awiya, 208
 naval power, 217, 221
 political disintegration, 222
 state expenditure, 211
Union of Utrecht (1579), 450
United States of America
 economic relationship with Britain, 526
 'grand strategy', 9
 independence of, 526
 See also North America
universalism, 14–15, 17
Urban II, pope, 271, 284
urbanisation, 195
 See also cities

'Uthman b. 'Affan, 205, 209, 216
Uzbeks, 360, 389, 390, 392, 399

Vakatakas, 177, 180, 187
Valens, 145, 164
Valentinian, East Roman emperor, 164
Vandals, 165, 166, 255
  in north Africa, 255, 264
  populations, 258
Varus (provincial governor), 148
vassal system, 319–20, 322, 324, 326, 351, 352,
  363
Vegetius, *De Re Militari* [DRM], 251
Venice, 277, 284–5, 288, 290, 348
Vergennes, Comte de, 511, 519
Veritable Records (*shilu*), 405–6
Versailles, Treaty of, 494
Vespasian, Roman emperor, 160
viceroys, 319
Vienna, 367, 431, 433
Vietnam War, 3, 19
Vietnam/Vietnamese, 130, 328, 330, 331, 413
Vikings, 13, 261, 263, 268–9
Viriathus (147–139 BC), 110
Visigoths, 254, 255, 257, 261, 264
viziers, decision making, 348, 349
Vlachs, 250

Wales, 286
War of Devolution (1667–1668), 464, 474
War of the Austrian Succession, 488, 493–4,
  495, 500–1, 504
War of the Bavarian Succession, 488
War of the Polish Succession, 503–4
War of the Spanish Succession, 464–6, 480–1
Warring States period, China
  Chinese philosophy, golden age, 22
  mass conscript armies, 137
  and military strategy texts, 124
  military texts, 127–8
  Qin dynasty. *See* Qin dynasty
  sanctioned violence as political tool, 29
  Strategies, 37–8
  success of Qin, 27
warships. *See* naval power
Washington, George, 510, 511
Watt, Montgomery, 223
weaponry, 337, 340, 357–60
  See also archers; bow and arrow; firearms;
    gunpowder
Wei dynasty, 129
Weiliaozi, 124
Wellhausen, Julius, 224–5

Wessex, 265
west Africans, American War of
  Independence, 513
West Indies, 516, 518–19, 523, 524
western Europe, 12, 366, 368
  See also Europe
Western Jin dynasty, 129–30
Westminster Convention (1756), 494, 495, 504
Westphalia
  peace congresses, 438, 445, 446–7
  Treaties of, 473, 495
Wettin dynasty, 497, 501
Whydah, expansion of slave trade, 375
William III of Orange, 459
  king of England and Scotland, 463, 472
William of Normandy (later William I), 275
William of Rubruck, 298
Witt, Johan de, 451, 457
  Grand Pensionary, 451–2, 458, 461–2
  murder of, 459
women
  Mughal Empire, 385
  Roman, 146
  warriors, Native American, 339
Worthies and Literati, China, 32
Wu dynasty, 129
Wu Qi (Warring States general), 128
Wuzi, 21, 22
Wuzi, 124, 128

Xenophon, 54, 61–2
  Anabasis and *Hellenika*, 41
  The Cavalry Commander, 54
Xerxes I, ruler of Iran, 42
  defeat of, 56
  Egyptian campaign, 51
  Greek expedition (480–479), 43, 49, 51,
    60, 70
  on Persian ideology, 41
  on rebellion/victory, and divine
    order, 44–5
Xi Xia, 304, 309
  Mongols and, 301, 304, 305, 306, 309,
    310
  Senggüm of the Kereit, 297–8
Xiang Yu (*c.* 232–202 BC), 27, 38–9
Xinjiang, 414, 422
Xiongnu, 27, 28, 31, 39, 139
Xun, 23
  morality and benevolence, 24

Yang Jian, 140–1
Yasodharman (r. 530–40), 186

Yasodharman, inscriptions, 173
Yazawin chronicles, Burma, 315
Yazid I, Umayyad caliph, 208
Yeke military, and slave trade, 381–2
Yemen, 353
Yongli, Ming emperor, 410, 411
Yorktown, British surrender, 526, 527
Yuan Pai poem, 322
Yubi, siege of, 128

Zama, Battle of (202 BC), 121
Zeeland, 453
Zhao Rui, 126
zheng (straightforward approaches in
    warfare), 126

Zhengtong Emperor (later Tianshun), 411
Zhenzong (Song emperor), 138
Zhou Daguan, 319
Zhou dynasty, China, 21, 140
    See also Warring States period, China
Zhuge Liang, 126
Zizhi tongjian, 127
Zongli Yamen, 409
Zoroastrianism, 194–5
Zulu kingdom, 377–8
Zunghar Empire, Mongol, 411, 413
Zuo zhuan, 127
Zuo Zongtang, 422
Zuozhuan, 21, 24, 34–7
Zwangendaba Jere, 378